Children With Multiple Mental Health Challenges

Sarah Landy, PhD, CPsych, is a developmental–clinical psychologist who has worked for more than 35 years in children's mental health. She has a PhD from the University of Regina, Saskatchewan, Canada, and completed training at the Child Development Unit, Harvard University, and at the University of Washington, with Dr. Stanley Greenspan. Dr. Landy has worked as a clinician, home visitor, program developer, clinical and program director, researcher, and teacher. She developed the Merici Center, a program that provided services for Canadian First Nations parents whose children had been removed from their care. While on the staff of the Hincks-Dellcrest Child Treatment Centre in Toronto, Dr. Landy founded the "Growing Together" program, an early-intervention program for high-risk children and their families who came from many cultures and countries throughout the world. The program earned a Peter Drucker Award for program excellence for Canada. Dr. Landy has also received the YWCA award for professional women in Ontario, and the Canadian Psychological Association award for contributions to the community. The program in Western Australia that she works with won the Best Outcome award for the state in 2010.

Dr. Landy has published three books on early-childhood development and intervention: *Pathways to Competence: Enhancing the Emotional and Social Development of Young Children* (2nd ed.) published in 2009; *Early Intervention With Multi-Risk Families: An Integrative Approach* published in 2006. *Pathways to Competence: A Parenting Program* was published in 2007 and has been used in Latvia; parts of Norway; Ireland; and Jamaica; parts of California, where it has been endorsed by the American Academy of Pediatrics; in Florida, where it has been certified as evidence based; in Ontario, British Columbia, and Nova Scotia, Canada; and has been translated into Spanish and Latvian.

Recently, Dr. Landy has been working as a specialist senior clinical psychologist with the Child and Adolescent Health Service, Perth, Western Australia, where the model of practice described in this book is being used. She is an adjunct professor at York University in Ontario. Dr. Landy has recently joined the Circle for Children Foundation in Ontario, Canada, as a consultant, a role to which she brings her understanding of the complex needs of children who have suffered trauma and loss. She is also a consultant to the Mindwerxs4kids Early Learning Centre and Prep School in Toronto, Ontario, Canada.

Susan Bradley, MD, FRCP(C), is a professor emerita in the Department of Psychiatry, University of Toronto; her previous positions include head of the division of child psychiatry at University of Toronto, and chief of psychiatry at the Hospital for Sick Children, Toronto. She was a consultant psychiatrist to the Child and Adolescent Gender Identity Clinic at the new Centre for Addiction and Mental Health–Clarke Division (formerly the Clarke Institute), a clinic that Dr. Bradley founded in the late 1970s. In collaboration with Dr. K. J. Zucker, current director of the clinic, she has seen over 1,000 cases of children and adolescents with Gender Identity Disorder (GID) and related difficulties. Their 1995 book, *Gender Identity Disorder and Psychosexual Problems in Children and Adolescents,* is considered the basic reference in this area.

Dr. Bradley's other research interests include evaluation of parenting problems, especially as they relate to parents of young children. Theoretical interests include models that explain the development of psychopathology integrating findings from the developmental literature. Her book *Affect Regulation and the Development of Psychopathology* (2000) provides a model that integrates biological and psychosocial thinking in psychiatry.

Her interest in prevention has led to the development of the Infant Mental Health Project, a community-based coalition aimed at facilitating the work of front-line care providers with parents of young children. Lastly, Dr. Bradley has played a leadership role in the restructuring of services for children's mental health in Toronto and, as Early Years Champion, led the process of selecting 22 Early Years Centres in Toronto.

Dr. Bradley has had a longstanding interest in teaching and mentoring child psychiatry residents and fellows.

Children With Multiple Mental Health Challenges

An Integrated Approach to Intervention

Sarah Landy, PhD, CPsych

Susan Bradley, MD, FRCP(C)

SPRINGER PUBLISHING COMPANY

NEW YORK

Springer Publishing Company, LLC
11 West 42nd Street
New York, NY 10036
www.springerpub.com

Acquisitions Editor: Nancy S. Hale
Composition: Exeter Premedia Services Private Ltd.

ISBN: 978-0-8261-9959-1
E-book ISBN: 978-0-8261-9961-4

13 14 15 16 17 / 5 4 3 2 1

Library of Congress Cataloging-in-Publication Data
Landy, Sarah, author.
Children with multiple mental health challenges : an integrated approach to intervention / Sarah Landy, Susan Bradley.
p. ; cm.
Includes bibliographical references.
ISBN 978-0-8261-9959-1 — ISBN 978-0-8261-9961-4 (e-book)
I. Bradley, Susan J., author. II. Title.
[DNLM: 1. Child. 2. Mental Disorders. 3. Child Development. WS 350]
RJ499.3
618.92'89–dc23

2013020126

Printed in the United States of America by Bradford and Bigelow.

To Tony Fotias (Manager) and the wonderful staff of Family Pathways, Specialized Child and Adolescent Health Service, Western Australia, who exemplify all the principles of treatment outlined in this book and from whom I have learnt so much.

Sarah Landy

Contents

Contributors

Claudia Koshinsky Clipsham, PhD, CPsych Psychologist, Peel Children's Centre, Ontario, Canada

Rochelle Moukina BSc (Speech and Hearing) Speech pathology coordinator, Specialized Child and Adolescent Mental Health Services of Western Australia, Subiaco, Western Australia

Evelyn Sim, BSc (Occupational Therapy), BEd (Early Childhood Education) Senior occupational therapist, Specialized Child and Adolescent Mental Health Services of Western Australia, Subiaco, Western Australia

Foreword

Many children with early difficulties go on to have avoidable lifelong problems in behavior, emotions, and thinking that could have been alleviated or prevented by appropriate childhood interventions. There are two reasons for this, lack of resources and lack of knowledge. The lack of resources is a policy and political problem that cannot be addressed in a book such as this. However, the lack of knowledge can certainly be overcome and this is the central purpose of this volume, written by Sarah Landy and Susan Bradley.

In chapter after chapter these authors lay out what is known about children's development; how to assess children to determine their problems; and how to treat difficulties in sensorimotor, cognitive, and emotional domains. But of great importance is that these different aspects of the child are presented in an integrative framework that captures not only the advances in our scientific knowledge but also the advances in scientific thinking. This is captured in the author's emphasis on "multiple pathways and processes."

We used to think that every problem had a direct answer. Motor problems had motor answers, cognitive problems had cognitive answers, and emotional problems had emotional answers. What we have learned is that multiple answers are the rule for most problems. Motor problems can be exacerbated by lack of cognitive awareness, cognitive problems can be exacerbated by motor difficulties, and both can lead to or be caused by emotional problems. The lesson for assessment is that multiple domains have to be evaluated to understand the pathway to any single problem and multiple treatments have to be considered to facilitate progress in these pathways. We have also learned that most problems are best considered as multilevel problems. A problem in behavior may be connected to an underlying biological problem or an overarching parenting problem or both. As a consequence, the answer to the problem may involve all three.

This shift in knowledge has been accompanied by a shift from an emphasis on continuity in development to one on discontinuity. Understanding discontinuity is the basis of contemporary science, in general, and developmental science, in particular. Why is it that a biological gene or human trait doesn't always lead to the same outcome? More complex, why is it that some children who are doing well end up as adults with many problems, and, more hopeful, why is it that some children with many problems end up doing very well as adults? The answer lies in the series of development steps in which context amplifies or reduces the effects of prior steps. Multidisciplinary efforts in the biological and social sciences continue to demonstrate that successful developmental predictions from prior genetic or psychological measures are highly dependent on what happens next. Moreover, what happens next can change what came before. It is not only that biology explains the brain, and the brain explains behavior. It is also that behavior can change the brain and the brain can change biology. Changing perceptual, cognitive, or emotional experience can actually change the organization of the brain and the expression of genes.

Discontinuity is a message of hope for parents of children with developmental challenges. It means that things do not stay the same. More important, it means that with good interventions, many challenges can be overcome. It doesn't necessarily mean that a blind child will see or that a deaf child will hear, but it does mean that sensory and motor problems need not prevent a fulfilling life of educational and occupational success. Such interventions are no longer restricted to simply providing a hearing aid or a wheelchair, for examples, but include a wide range of family, social, and educational supports to move the child toward mature successes. For those concerned with improving developmental outcomes, explaining discontinuity has a high priority. Understanding such discontinuities requires integrating analyses of individual behavior with constructs from the full range of biological and social science. The theories, assessments, and interventions described in what follows provide a major service in moving professionals and families toward this goal.

Arnold Sameroff, PhD
Professor Emeritus of Psychology
University of Michigan

Preface

My first therapy job was working with parents who had abused or neglected their children, to enable them, whenever possible, to have their children returned to their care. At that time, we were not aware of the significance of the effects of trauma or of early-attachment experiences across the lifetime. All we knew was that the parents we worked with had almost always experienced horrific events growing up: domestic violence; witnessing murders; extreme deprivation, both physically and emotionally, by parents who abused alcohol and/or drugs; and the suicide of a close family member. One memory is especially fresh from when I was coleading a parenting group for teenage mothers and one of the young women began to talk about the sexual abuse by an older cousin that she had suffered. After a few moments of silence and many tears, one of the girls talked about her personal experience of sexual abuse and this was followed by every one of the girls talking about similar experiences!! Although this was astonishing, it was the passionate commitment of the young mothers to turn things around and to keep their own children safe from this kind of terrible experience that was inspiring. However, for many reasons these mothers had failed to keep their children safe or in an environment that could meet their physical or emotional needs. In other words these mothers had repeated the same kind of parenting they had experienced and seemed unable to reverse this trend. It was also clear that overcoming the tendency to repeat the past was challenging; for some parents we seemed to lack the knowledge and strategies to support them in order to enable them to make gains that allowed them to have their children back and to provide "good enough" parenting to their children.

After this experience, I chose to work with children with extreme and complex difficulties, and again was met with many challenges and a barrage of literature that advocated from different theoretical positions for various approaches to treatment. Different theories about complex children and methods of intervening seemed to proliferate and typically brought highly useful understanding and ideas of how to work with these challenging children. However, one of the problems seemed to be that these theories came in waves: behavioral approaches in schools; attachment theory, family system theory; mindfulness-based strategies, trauma-informed approaches; and more psychodynamic approaches sometimes with an emphasis on being insight oriented or on improving mentalizing or reflective functioning of the child and parent. One of the problems has been that these ideas often go through waves of popularity and some of the valuable knowledge that has been gained by each new approach has often been lost because the approach is not popular anymore and the knowledge it brought has lost its appeal. As well, the new knowledge has not been used appropriately because it has not been integrated and there remains a great divide among the different approaches.

Moreover, the child we are supposed to be treating is often misunderstood or is given a diagnosis that is supposed to determine the best way to work with the child. Unfortunately, children who receive the same diagnosis are often different in multiple ways that could inform treatment planning. Teachers, parents, and others who work with the child often see behavior as being "naughty," "difficult," "attention seeking," "manipulative," or "unmotivated" without any understanding of the difficulties the child may be facing. However, adequate assessment will typically reveal a host of problems that the child is struggling with, such as auditory-processing problems, sensory-integration difficulties, problems with pragmatic language, responding to trauma triggers, executive dysfunction, and problems with social skills. Once we can help parents, teachers, and others in the community better understand a child's challenges and developmental profile, attitudes toward the child can change and new approaches to treating him or her can be found.

As pointed out by Dr. Sameroff in his Foreword, "discontinuity is a message of hope for parents of children with developmental challenges. It means that things do not stay the same. More important, it means that with good interventions, this many challenges can be overcome." It is with this hope in mind that the chapters in this book that include many approaches to both the assessment and treatment of children with multiple mental health problems are offered.

Sarah Landy, PhD, CPsych

Acknowledgments

The effort and endurance of the twists and turns of progress toward completing this book could not have been sustained without the assistance of a number of wonderful people. These people include those who gave significant professional and practical help, and friends and colleagues who were always there to ask me how the book was progressing and to offer a visit or words of encouragement when the progress was slow. These people include Dallas Harrison, Harrison Editorial Services, who did a brilliant job of shortening and tightening the manuscript in order for it to meet the required length for publication. My dear friend, Jacquelin Montgomery, also offered help and friendship without which this book would never have been published. Also I would like to thank the authors who contributed chapters to the book: Rochelle Moukina, Evelyn Sim, and Claudia Koshinsky Clipsham. The effort they put into the chapters in both researching and writing them was amazing, especially at the end of a day working with children with complex needs! The practical approaches from their own practice that they included in the chapters have significantly enriched the book. We are also grateful to Dr. Arnold Sameroff for writing the Foreword to this book, bringing the same wisdom to it with which he has inspired students and practitioners for many years. Many dear friends who were always there with some encouraging words of support or shared some time together include Elizabeth Pederson, Jacqueline Smith, Helen Sugar, Millie Greenfield, Michelle Weiss, Sharon Rapoport, Nilofar Liakat, and Denise Martyn. Also we would like to thank our families who put up with the struggles involved in doing this book. We would also like to thank Nancy S. Hale, Editorial Director for Social Sciences; and Kathryn Corasaniti, Associate Editor at Springer Publishing Company for their support of the book and their efforts in bringing it to publication. Also Michael O'Connor, Senior Production Editor at Springer Publishing Company, and Production Team at Exeter Premedia Services Private Ltd., who patiently and efficiently brought the book through final production to publication. They made a long and difficult process possible. Last but not least, we would like to thank the children and families with whom we have been privileged to work over many years of clinical practice and whose courage, often in the face of significant trauma and challenges, is inspirational.

Introduction

There is increasing concern that the prevalence of mental health problems is high and that their onset is often manifested at a younger age than other health disorders. The World Health Organization (WHO) estimates that about 10% to 20% of children and adolescents worldwide have one or more mental health disorders (Friedli, 2009). Other studies in the United Kingdom and United States have found the same prevalence, and there is evidence that the rate is rising. There are also concerns about the serious consequences of early problems on later learning and social and emotional functioning. Research studies have shown that experiences during the developmental period of infancy and childhood shape health status and functioning in adulthood. Adversity during childhood increases the risk of problems and can have enduring effects on the body and brain development (Gunnar, 2007; Hertzman & Power, 2003). It is now clear that genetic, biological, and environmental factors interact to determine a child's outcome, and children and adolescents can develop serious emotional problems that are comparable in severity to those seen in adults. Left untreated, problems will persist, and half of children will develop mental health disorders that will carry over into adulthood (National Scientific Council on the Developing Child, 2008). Also, the complexity, number, and magnitude of problems experienced by many children and their families require intensive efforts to understand and address their unique challenges. However, not all interventions are equally successful, and the types of treatments that can be successful are seldom available (Juffer, Bakersmans-Kranenburg, & van IJzendoorn, 2005). In this book, ways to assess and successfully treat complex problems of infancy and childhood are provided.

Many children who present challenges to parents, daycares, schools, and the children's mental health centers to which they are often referred have clusters of symptoms that suggest a variety of disorders. The children might have been seen by various disciplines in private practice or various government agencies, including pediatricians, psychiatrists, speech and language pathologists, occupational therapists, physiotherapists, and clinical and neuropsychologists. Although the reports or opinions given are helpful, many parents and teachers might be confused by the diversity of views and suggestions offered. Each professional tends to have a circumscribed view of a child's difficulties, and treatment recommendations are not typically integrated. As well, the developmental pathway that the child has followed and the multiple levels of influence that contribute to the child's presentation are seldom considered.

Case Study: What Can Be Done About Michael?

Ten-year-old Michael was referred to a children's mental health treatment center by a pediatrician because his parents were desperate to find ways to deal with his lack of responsiveness to discipline and his aggressive outbursts, particularly toward his younger sister and peers at school. They reported that the suggestions given at a parenting group that they attended did not work for Michael even though they had found them helpful for dealing with his younger sister. His grandmother admitted that she could no longer look after him. He had hurt her physically a number of times and had run away on one occasion, putting his own safety at risk. Michael was often sent home or suspended from school because of extreme noncompliance with the teacher's instructions or because he had lashed out at other children and hurt them. Following complaints by parents of the other children in the class, the principal believed that he had no choice but to suspend Michael for periods of time. Michael's parents admitted that their relationship was in trouble due to disagreements about what to do about their son. Their jobs were also in jeopardy because, when Michael was expelled from school, one of them had to stay home to supervise him.

Michael had been seen by a clinical psychologist at the local children's mental health center, a developmental pediatrician from a developmental service, a psychiatrist, and an occupational therapist, but no coherent treatment plan had been suggested. Michael was not believed to meet the full criteria for autism spectrum disorder (ASD), attention deficit/hyperactivity disorder (ADHD), central auditory processing disorder (CAPD), or sensory integration disorder (SID), though he had some symptoms of them all. Common to all of the reports were concerns about his apparent total lack of perspective taking and empathy. On his admission to a specialized therapeutic classroom, similar concerns were quickly raised about his callous, uncaring, and seemingly unemotional and derisive presentation toward teachers and other children. Due to these extreme symptoms, it was suggested that, unless Michael could be "reached" and helped in an appropriate way, he could well develop conduct disorder with sociopathic tendencies of aggression toward people and serious violation of rules or the law as he became older.

With an assessment of Michael conducted by several professionals from various disciplines using a variety of tests, ongoing observation in the classroom, and in-home observation and support, it was determined that a number of factors contributed to his presentation that suggested various strategies to help him. They included a diagnosis of ADHD and an understanding that his uninhibited, impulsive temperament did not respond to the usual types of behavior management. It was believed that he needed a more attachment-based approach using rewards and conscious attention directed toward any attempt to be helpful to or show concern for others. Also, though he presented as bright, Michael was found to have a number of learning challenges, including difficulties with reading comprehension, handwriting, pragmatic language, and balance and coordination.

In the specialized classroom that Michael attended, he could receive the right kind of attachment-based discipline, and he developed a significant attachment to a male teacher and the female occupational therapist. With her support, he designed and constructed a spaceship. It was also noticed that he had difficulty communicating and seeing the points of view of others, so he was helped with this in a group setting and became better able to communicate with peers and at home with his parents. Other strategies were put in place to help Michael understand the perspectives of others, such as helping him to realize that how he felt when he was criticized or rejected by his peers was how others felt when he was verbally or physically abusive toward them. Medication for his ADHD also helped to reduce his impulsive behavior and improved his ability to focus at school. The occupational therapist taught him ways to calm himself down if he felt himself becoming emotionally hyperaroused and anxious or angry. He also enjoyed playing the drums and being part of a music group.

With weekly support, Michael's parents were able to learn to respond consistently to their son at home, using strategies similar to those used in the school. They were amazed to find that, gradually, Michael was able to contain his aggressive outbursts and respond when they talked to him about how upsetting his verbal and physical outbursts were for them, his sister, and his grandmother. They came to realize that normal consequences did not affect Michael physiologically or emotionally in the same way that they did his sister, but they found that, as they were able to talk to him about his feelings and make connections with him in a new way, slowly things began to change. After 9 months of receiving treatment in the therapeutic classroom, including focused interventions from various professionals, and from his parents at home, Michael was able to return to his home school successfully, and follow-up has shown that he continues to do well. He now has some friends with whom he can relate in a reciprocal way.

THE USE OF DIAGNOSTIC CRITERIA

There are two major systems for diagnosing mental health disorders in children and adults, the *Diagnostic and Statistical Manual of Mental Disorders,* 5th edition (*DSM-5*) and *The ICD-10 Classification of Mental and Behavioural Disorders* (American Psychiatric Association, 2013; World Health Organization, 1992). Other diagnostic systems have been developed for children of a certain age group or from a particular theoretical position, for example, the *Zero to Three Diagnostic Classification of Mental Health and Developmental Disorders of Infancy and Early Childhood, Revised* (Zero to Three, 2005) and the *Psychodynamic Diagnostic Manual* (*PDM;* PDM Task Force, 2006). The most commonly used diagnostic systems are purely descriptive and based on a symptom level of analysis. In recent years, there has been growing criticism of this categorical approach to diagnosis in which individuals are found either to have or not to have a certain diagnosis (Angold & Costello, 2009; Beutler & Malik, 2002; Helzer, Kraemer, & Krueger, 2006; Widiger & Samuel, 2005). As pointed out by Hudziak, Achenbach, Althoff, and Pine (2008), using only categorical systems with children and adolescents creates a particular problem because of numerous changes that occur over various developmental stages and because decisions are often based on information from multiple informants with modest agreement among them. Other criticisms have identified the following issues.

- The use of diagnostic systems has resulted in children with different symptoms and different etiologies being classified as having the same disorder. An example is conduct disorder, which in *DSM-5* provides a list of 15 symptoms with any three sufficient to receive a diagnosis. As a consequence, children with five totally different sets of symptoms and types of behavior can be given the same diagnosis. In other words, five children could qualify for having conduct disorder without sharing any symptoms (Hudziak et al., 2008). Even more concerning, they could be given the same recommendations for medication and other treatment in spite of having very different difficulties and reasons underlying their problems. Diagnostic systems, therefore, contribute to group heterogeneity and obscure the individuality and uniqueness of a child's difficulties within each diagnosis.
- Many writers have argued that the use of categorical diagnoses obscures clinical experience in which children are seen to lie along a continuum from those who are most compromised to those who have relatively mild difficulties. For example, children diagnosed with an ASD can vary from those children who are relatively high functioning and have few severe symptoms to those children who have profound developmental delays and engage in extreme self-stimulating, aggressive, and self-injurious behavior. Kraemer (2008, p. 15) has argued for adding "dimensional adjuncts" to the current categorical diagnoses that "would reflect the most important sources of heterogeneity."
- Comorbidity also poses problems. Many of the more challenging children are diagnosed with two or more disorders, raising issues about which is most salient as well asquestions about the actual validity of the diagnoses. It can also reduce the possibility

of identifying meaningful subtypes of a disorder, such as the consideration of different types of conduct disorder (Krueger, 2002). Moreover, some individuals meet diagnostic criteria for one disorder at one time and for another disorder at another time during the course of their illness.

- There has been a dramatic increase in the number of disorders from *DSM-II* (2nd ed.; APA, 1968) to *DSM-5*. Similarly, there has been a proliferation in the number of mixed, atypical, and Not Otherwise Specified (NOS) categories within many of the disorders, suggesting that current diagnoses do not fully capture the range and intensity of children's symptoms and behaviors.
- There is also the danger that children who do not meet full criteria for a diagnosis might not be treated, yet have similar issues to children who do receive a diagnosis and are therefore eligible for treatment. This could result in failure to identify children with difficulties early enough for timely treatment of their problems.
- Focusing on various symptoms as part of a categorical diagnosis can ignore the risk factors that contribute to them. For example, a child who is abused is better seen as adjusting to a threatening environment than as having a mental disorder.

Many of the symptoms and challenges in various developmental areas are common to different disorders. Table I.1 shows how functional problems such as emotion regulation and lack of concentration are common to a number of prevalent disorders. This also suggests that strategies or treatments developed for a particular disorder might be useful across a number of disorders. For example, strategies to improve socialization and peer relationships for autistic children can be helpful for children with other disorders, such as aggression.

Table I.1 *Difficulties in Development and Various Disorders*

	Developmental Areas						
Disorders	Sensory–Motor	Speech and Language/ Symbolization	Emotion Regulation	Behavior Regulation	Attention and Concentration	Attachment and Socialization	Effects of Trauma
Autism	✓	✓	✓	✓	✓	✓	
Fetal alcohol syndrome	✓	✓	✓	✓	✓	✓	
Attachment disorders			✓	✓	✓	✓	✓
Behavior disorders	✓	✓	✓	✓	✓	✓	✓
Regulatory disorders	✓	✓	✓	✓	✓	✓	✓
PTSD	✓	✓	✓	✓	✓	✓	✓
ADHD		✓	✓	✓	✓		✓
Learning disabilities	✓	✓			✓		

INTEGRATING CATEGORICAL AND DIMENSIONAL APPROACHES

Although diagnostic or categorical linear systems provide a common language to use across various mental health disciplines, support research on the etiology and treatment of various disorders, and allow children to access services, there is a need for more complex explanatory models and a transdiagnostic approach to understanding psychopathology (Helzer, Wittchen, Krueger, & Kraemer, 2008; Kraemer, 2008). This approach focuses on underlying mechanisms that cut across diagnoses, such as executive functioning and behavior and emotion regulation. As well, Sameroff (2009) has described a transactional model that describes how the child's presentation is a result of multiple influences on development "including individuals, groups, and cultures." These models can help the clinician to understand the various factors that underlie a child's difficulties within the domains discussed in this book. This information is crucial in planning interventions focused on specific areas of concern for each child. Cicchetti and Toth (2009) have argued for the importance of a functional, developmental, and dimensional approach that integrates the conceptualization of psychopathology with the theory of developmental psychopathology and defines impairment in terms of age-salient developmental tasks. Kraemer (2008, p. 15) has suggested that adding a dimensional component to categorical diagnosis to quantify the degree to which an individual meets diagnostic criteria might "revolutionize psychiatric research and decision making and bring progress in dealing with mental disorders in line with progress in dealing with other medical conditions." There are already a number of dimensional measures that could be used for this purpose, such as the Child Behavior Checklist (CBCL; Achenbach, Bernstein, & Dumenci, 2005) and the Generalized Anxiety Disorder Severity Scale (GADSS; Shear, Belnap, Mazumdar, Houck, & Rollman, 2006).

Such an approach considers the child's level of development in various areas that are critical to consider in understanding numerous symptoms. This book uses a functional and dimensional system that examines underlying causal processes or mechanisms and the context in which the child is developing that contribute to symptoms. This allows the most appropriate treatment to be defined. A functional approach to many complex medical diseases, such as heart disease, that have multiple causes and physiological pathways is already being used. When key causal pathophysiological mechanisms are identified, they become the focus of treatment. This can also be the case for children, such as Michael, with symptoms of various social, emotional, and behavioral disorders.

Understanding brain function is critical to a developmental, dimensional, and functional approach. It also includes an examination of various genetic and other biological factors known to contribute to development and brain function. Factors such as temperament, pregnancy or birth complications, learning disabilities, and various illnesses such as diabetes can significantly affect a child's psychological presentation and need to be considered. Increasingly, research shows how parenting and the quality of attachment to caregivers, particularly in the early years, can impact brain development, symptom presentation, and a child's view of the world (Sameroff, 2009; Schore, 2001, 2003). In recent years, trauma has been shown to affect brain development and function, suggesting new approaches for children who experience early trauma (Center on the Developing Child at Harvard University, 2007).

The environment in which a child lives can be a major contributor to functioning. There may be issues such as poor housing, low socioeconomic level, culture, belief systems of the parents, and family systems. How these various factors interact and the extent and nature of linkages or interrelationships among them are also important considerations (Rutter, 2009). This model of development can also be applied to the parents or primary caregivers of the child and can be useful both in understanding their presentation and in deciding how to work with them.

IMPLICATIONS OF THE COMPLEXITY OF CAUSATION

Single causes of various disorders are unlikely. Furthermore, there is much support for the notion of transactional processes (Sameroff, 2009; Sameroff & Mackenzie, 2003), in which child factors influence parent response and vice versa. This complex interaction across time and among factors creates a situation of multifinality and equifinality in which the same factors can lead to different outcomes and similar outcomes can arise from different factors (Cicchetti & Rogosch, 1996). Thus, nonlinearity of development over time is to be expected, making the assessment and formulation of each child's presentation extremely complex (Wachs, 2000). In the model of causality presented in this book (see Figure I.1), two levels of influence are proposed, with Level 1 consisting of multiple risk and protective factors and Level 2 consisting of the child's mind and brain structure and neurobiology, which include various types of representation such as defenses, self-esteem, and view of the world and self. The influence of the brain and mind is bidirectional, with each side being able to impact the other (Bradley, 2000). However, understanding how both the mind and the brain contribute uniquely to influence the child's development and psychopathology is critical to treatment planning. Pennington (2002, 2009) has also recommended a "bidirectional model of causation" and includes a level of analysis of neuropsychology that he believes "bridges the chasm separating brain and behavior, mind and body" (Pennington, 2009, p. 9). The model also elucidates how treatment can focus on providing direct interventions to remediate identified deficits such as auditory processing or language delays that can enhance the structure and neurobiology of the brain or focus on various psychological constructs of the mind, such as the child's sense of self and the world and feelings of self-efficacy (March, 2009). Change in one domain affecting change in another domain is common to a number of approaches. For example, cognitive biases become the focus of intervention in disorders such as anxiety and posttraumatic stress disorder (PTSD), resulting in a reduction in symptoms and overreactive neuroendocrine responses. Although much more needs to be known about the interplay between cognition and neurophysiology, early results are promising (Huppert, Foa, McNally, & Cahill, 2009). Treatment might focus initially on one of these areas of influence followed by the other or, more likely, work at different levels of influence simultaneously. This occurred with Michael. As he was taught new academic skills, strategies to calm himself down, and ways to relate to others, he began to improve some of his academic skills and ability to concentrate and began to feel better about himself and more competent. Concomitantly, his aggression declined, and he began to relate to adults and peers in a different way. As mentioned previously, this model can also be applied to the child's parents in terms of understanding the causes of their problems, designing interventions to improve their sense of self and reduce negative attributions of the child, and initiating psychotherapies focused on attunement and sensitivity to enhance their brain structures and functioning more directly (Cozolino, 2002, 2006; Siegel, 2007; Stern, 2004).

Currently, the focus in children's mental health is on identifying symptoms or surface behaviors of certain disorders and on treating all children with a disorder in the same way, thus ignoring the child's individuality and the context surrounding him. This book discusses the need to address children's mental health issues with comprehensive assessment and formulation that can provide an understanding of the complex and unique challenges and strengths of a particular child.

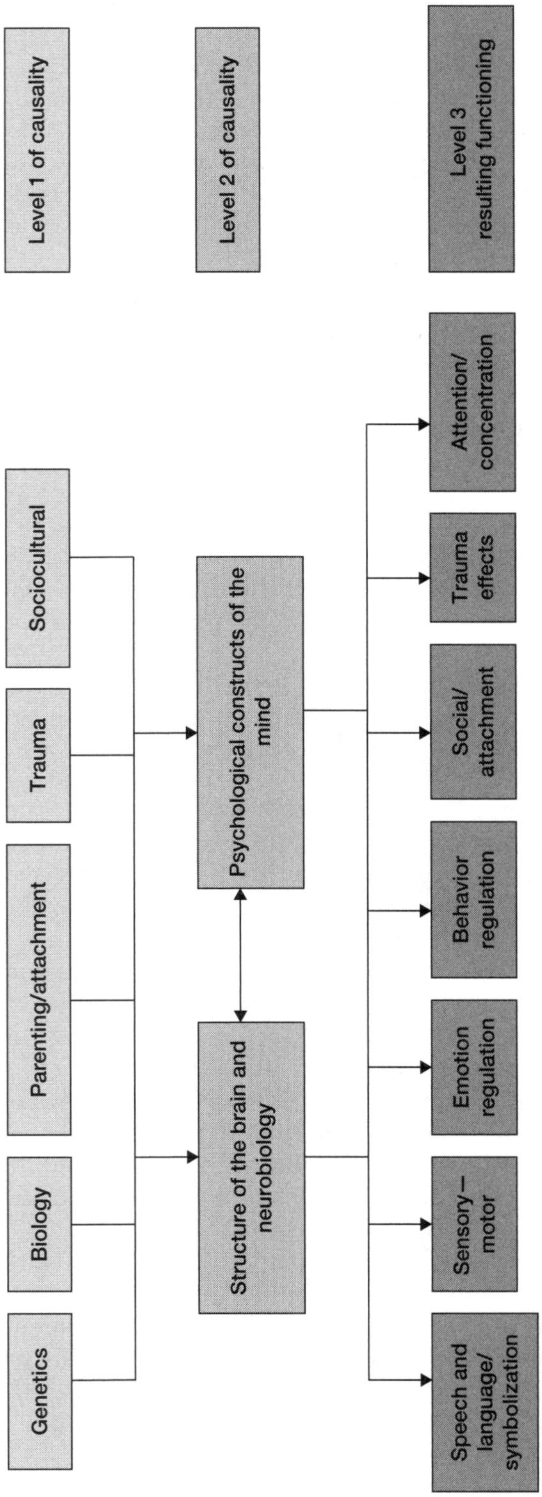

Figure I.1 *A model of complex causality.*

With increasing research on the potential of appropriately focused interventions with children to enhance brain pathways and change developmental outcomes, this kind of approach is essential (Doidge, 2010). Sensitive, emotionally attuned interactions that respond to the child's cues can help to enhance neural connections and the child's functioning in various areas of development (Shonkoff, Boyce, & McEwen, 2009; Siegel, 2007). This book provides information to enable clinicians to identify and assess areas of functional developmental deficits that underlie symptoms and disorders. It also identifies proven strategies to overcome some of these deficits or provide ways in which the child can compensate for areas of concern that cannot be changed. These strategies can change behaviors and in some cases develop new and alternative neural pathways. These approaches identify ways to:

1. Screen the child for difficulties to develop an understanding of the child's unique pattern of functional capacities and information processing that might underlie given diagnoses
2. Focus on the child's developmental problems; this work should be intense and repetitive enough to change behavioral patterns, and in a few cases it might enhance brain structure and create new neural pathways in areas identified as being compromised (Doidge, 2007)
3. Intervene in daycares and schools to encourage them to use these more focused approaches as well as attuned and affectively based interactions particularly with the child who has been identified as having compromised functional capacities (Siegel, 2007)
4. Teach parents new ways to respond to their child to remediate deficits and provide more attuned and attachment-based interactions to enhance security of attachment; disciplinary approaches appropriate to the child's temperament are also suggested

There are few examples of this kind of developmental, functional, and dimensional assessment; formulation; and intervention; and most programs work on isolated skills or with approaches evaluated specifically for certain disorders. There is little consideration given to their suitability for a particular child or the developmental and environmental issues underlying the child's difficulties. For children with problems in more than one domain, parenting classes that focus on teaching parents behavior-management strategies without paying attention to the parents' need to understand their child's individuality and learn other approaches to managing their challenging child are not likely to be effective. This was central to the dilemma faced by Michael's parents. Similarly, classrooms largely focused on behavior-management plans and completing worksheets without consideration of the underlying academic, social, and emotional challenges faced by the child will not provide proper support to that child. Lastly, medication used as the only approach without working with the child, family, or school is often not successful.

At other times, referrals are suggested for parents without giving them any assistance in finding, for example, a speech therapist or physiotherapist who could provide suitable intervention for their child. Michael and his parents struggled with all of these challenges and lacked an integrated assessment of his problems. They found the new integrated assessment meaningful because it was based on an adequate understanding of the individuality of their child and gave them practical strategies to use at home.

WHOM THE BOOK IS FOR

Children With Multiple Mental Health Challenges: An Integrated Approach to Intervention is designed for professionals of various disciplines who work with children up to the age of 13 with complex and challenging difficulties and disorders. It can also be used as a primary or secondary text for advanced undergraduate and/or graduate clinical training programs on child psychopathology and its treatment. Sections can be used for in-service training, workshops on the various areas of difficulty addressed in Section 2, and courses on child psychopathology. The approaches discussed in this book can be used in the home, clinic, and school to treat the child individually or within the family or school setting. This approach is particularly relevant for treating children with multiple and complex needs who are challenging for the most experienced clinicians and teachers. It provides a new way of approaching their assessment and integrating findings to decide on goals for treatment and prioritize them to provide the most successful outcomes. A number of useful websites are listed in Table I.2.

Table I.2 *Websites*

Website	Information on Website
http://www.promisingpractices.net/ default asp.promising practices network	Lists a number of "best practices" or "model programs" for working with children with psychopathology.
www.developingchild.harvard.edu	Provides a number of articles that "translate science into policy."
www.mentalhealth.org.uk/help-information/ mental-health-statistics/children-youngpeople	Provides information on statistics of mental health disorders of children and young people.
www.who.int/mental_health/en/	Provides information on the incidence of mental and behavioral disorders throughout the world. A number of publications on the prevention of mental health disorders, promoting mental health, and emerging evidence on best practice are also available.
www.nimh.nih.gov/statistics/index.shtm/	Website of the National Institute of Mental Health; information on statistics and research on mental health are provided.
www.nami.org	Website of the National Alliance on Mental Illness, the largest grassroots mental health organization dedicated to supporting Americans affected by mental illness; it has a Child and Adolescent Action Center.
www.health.nih.gov	Website of the US Department of Health and Human Services provides public access to a number of articles and reports on mental and physical health.
www.interscience.com	Publishes a number of online articles on children's mental health.
www.aboutourkids.org	Website of the New York University Child Study Center that includes information on disorders and treatments, seeking professional help, and participating in research.
www.ncbi.nlm.nih.gov/pubmed	PubMed has more than 21 million citations for biomedical literature from MEDLINE, life science journals, and online books; citations may include links to full-text content.

OVERVIEW OF CONTENT

Section 1 provides the theory and research that support the proposed developmental, dimensional, and functional approach to assessing and treating children with complex mental health problems. The transactional model for determining the causal mechanisms underlying a particular child's presentation is also provided. Chapter 2 also describes ways to screen children and makes suggestions for further assessment to determine the most appropriate treatments.

Section 2 provides information on understanding and treating complex problems across various areas of development and functioning crucial for optimal performance in typically developing children. These domains are often compromised in children with mental health issues and psychopathologies. These domains are speech and language and symbolization; motor development and sensory integration; emotion and behavior regulation; attachment and socialization; effects of trauma; and attention, concentration, and executive functions. The section also discusses children who are compromised across multiple domains of development. In each chapter, a number of treatment approaches to working with these children and their families in the home and school are provided.

Section 3 discusses work with parents and schools with children with complex difficulties. The last chapter explores issues of importance on an individual level for children, that of neuroplasticity. It also addresses societal and system-level approaches to prevention and early intervention for children who show early problems in various developmental domains, with suggestions for community-based programs.

1

An Individualized Approach to Preventing and Treating Various Disorders of Childhood

The model for understanding multiple levels of influence that affect developmental impairments, symptoms, and psychopathology was briefly described in the Introduction. In this chapter, the model is expanded, and research on the various contributors to both typical and abnormal development is described. Although many theories have informed the model, the main explanatory theories used throughout the book are that of developmental psychopathology and the transactional model. Originally proposed in the 1980s (Cicchetti, 1984; Rutter, 1987; Sameroff, 1983; Sroufe, 1983), the developmental psychopathology theory continues to be expanded as new research findings become available (Cicchetti & Toth, 2009; Sroufe, 2007). Developmental psychopathology is concerned with typical development or adaptation as well as the development of psychopathology. Researchers remain interested in the different pathways that children can take to the same outcome as well as those that can be taken to vastly different outcomes, the etiology of these different pathways, and the psychological processes or underlying mechanisms that contribute to various patterns of child development (Rutter, Kim-Cohen, & Maughan, 2006). The transactional model examines the multiple proximal and distal influences that impact on child development (Sameroff, 2009; Sameroff & Fiese, 2000).

Following is a vignette illustrating different pathways following seemingly similar births.

> *Mary, born at 28 weeks to a single, teenage mother, is developing well and seems to have overcome her difficult beginning. Johanna, on the other hand, was born at 29 weeks into a relatively affluent, two-parent family but at 12 months is quite delayed and has required ongoing medical interventions.*

The question is whether the apparent difference in outcomes is related to Mary's and Johanna's early medical history in the Neonatal Intensive Care Unit (NICU), different genetic vulnerabilities related to the management of stress, or the level of containment and responsive interactions provided by each parent. Of further interest is whether these early trajectories will continue or be reversed with time and development as the children's capacity for language, pretend play, attention, and concentration becomes greater. The children's early attachment to their mothers and how their mothers respond to the new stage of development of separation–individuation might also impact their outcomes.

Fortunately, most children adapt to the changing demands and expectations of their environments as they grow and do not develop symptoms of disorder or psychopathology. For those who move away from a typical developmental pathway, identifying challenges and strengths in their development early allows for interventions that can help to return them to a typical developmental trajectory. Alternatively, treatments can help them to learn ways to adapt to challenges and their environments so that they can find success in the future. Because this book considers problems, difficulties, and disorders of children from a developmental psychopathology framework, it is important to understand typical development.

A DEVELOPMENTAL FRAMEWORK

Described in this section is the typical development in the first 13 years of life: infancy (birth to 14 months), toddlerhood (14–24 months), preschool (2–4 years), early childhood (4–6 years), and middle childhood (7–13 years). What is required from caregivers to optimize a particular developmental capacity is also noted. These stages are arbitrary but as far as possible follow other developmental models (Davies, 2004; Landy, 2009). Although this book focuses on school-aged children, early developmental stages are described since some multichallenged children can have characteristics of very early stages, particularly in areas such as emotional and social development. Children can get off track in some or all of these important developmental areas, and if a delay is identified, by observation or assessment, it provides an opportunity for focused and intense interventions to improve functioning and, as much as possible, return the child to a more typical trajectory. Table 1.1 provides an overview of development from birth to 13 years.

CONTRIBUTORS TO CHILD DEVELOPMENT AND OUTCOMES

Nature or Nurture?

For many years, debate raged about whether nature or nurture alone contributes to developmental outcomes. At times, the pendulum has swung from one side to the other in devastating ways (McEwen & Schmeck, 1994). One of the most disturbing results of the belief that nature works independently from nurture was the development of laws in the 1930s that condemned people with various illnesses, such as schizophrenia, epilepsy, and mental retardation, to compulsory sterilization to avoid contaminating the gene pool. On the nurture side, in the 1960s, mothers of autistic children were labeled "refrigerator mothers" and blamed for their children's disorder, which was seen as a failure of nurture, leading to a suggestion by some professionals that the children should be placed out of the home if they were to improve (Betteheim, 1974). Although less dramatic, in recent years, perspectives focused on one theoretical approach, such as attachment, psychodynamic, or family systems, have been common. They have also strongly influenced the types of treatment offered to children and their families, often ignoring other strategies. Fortunately, there is a growing consensus that developmental outcomes, including various symptoms and disorders, are the result of a "symphony of causation" or a complex interplay between nature (genetics and biology) and nurture (parent–child interactions, home

Table 1.1 *Typical Emotional and Social Development and Important Parenting Strategies*

Age Range	Development	Parenting
Birth to 14 months	■ Attachment relationship is established and child is not indiscriminately friendly ■ Child can interpret and communicate emotions and has more control over their display ■ Explores the world with curiosity and excitement ■ Likes to be around other children ■ Parallel play possible and capable of turn taking ■ Joint attention with an object and uses gestures to point out objects to other people ■ More goal directed and can complete simple tasks	■ Provides experiences that can soothe and calm the child, such as feeding, carrying, rocking, and talking ■ Provides plenty of experiences of touch and physical contact ■ Face-to-face time is provided ■ Supports development of a predictable sleep–wake cycle ■ Provides interactive toys and use of self in games such as peek-a-boo ■ Safety-proof home and allows exploration with movement ■ Comforts and calms child when she is hurt, ill, or upset ■ Remains available to the child when he wants to explore
12 to 24 months	■ Tends to be more negative, and temper tantrums are common ■ Can play some interactive games with other children ■ Uses personal pronouns such as "I" and "me" ■ Might comfort another child who is upset ■ Shows self-conscious emotions such as shame, pride, and embarrassment ■ Only complies with parents' requests about 45% of the time ■ "No" saying is common, and some children might refuse to do things and be quite oppositional ■ Some children may be somewhat aggressive ■ Can only concentrate for relatively short periods of time	■ Provides opportunities for socializing with peers and monitors this if necessary to make sure things go well ■ Provides pretend-play toys that reflect everyday activities such as a cooking stove ■ Avoids setting up battle grounds over eating, sleeping, and toileting but does provide clear routines and structures ■ Provides monitoring in order to keep the child safe ■ Clear rules and structures are put in place, and the child is not allowed to win all the battles or to lose them ■ Encourages child to "use his words" instead of being aggressive ■ Engages in fun activities with the child and activities that use her expanding fine and gross motor abilities ■ Supports the child to concentrate on tasks
24 to 48 months	■ Gains in self-esteem and confidence ■ Generally optimistic and cheerful ■ Play is much more cooperative with other children ■ Degree of compliance now about 65% of the time ■ Expresses thoughts and feelings in words and shows less physical aggression ■ Can empathize with others ■ Begins to integrate good and bad parts of self and others ■ Theory-of-mind and perspective taking in place and can understand the thoughts and feelings of others	■ Encourages gross motor skills and muscle development by supporting climbing, running, throwing, and catching ■ Engages in games with the child that require imitation ■ Demonstrates examples of resolving conflict in the family ■ When discipline is used, the child is not shamed but coached and encouraged to do better the next time ■ Gives the child lots of opportunities to be around other children ■ Continues to comfort the child when she is upset, shows empathy while helping her gain control of her emotions, and encourages her to try out some solutions

(continued)

Table 1.1 *Typical Emotional and Social Development and Important Parenting Strategies (continued)*

Age Range	Development	Parenting
4 to 6 years	■ Shows pride in work and interest in doing new activities and tasks ■ Can solve problems in difficult situations ■ Develops a conscience and knows the difference between right and wrong ■ Might develop fear of the dark or of certain animals and so forth ■ Might have a best friend and enjoys play dates ■ Enjoys complex interactive social games ■ Uses private speech to help concentrate on a difficult task ■ Might be anxious about death and losing body parts and is interested in sexual differences	■ Scaffolds the child when she is attempting a task and encourages her to keep trying and uses self-talk to get through the activity; praises the child's efforts ■ Helps the child to create narratives about things that happen, especially if it was somewhat upsetting for the child ■ When siblings fight, uses the occasion to teach them to solve the conflict and talk them through to finding a solution ■ Encourages the child to be able to sort objects into various categories and talks about what is the same about them ■ Encourages the child to tolerate mixed emotions by talking about them so that he does not have to split them ■ Practices some skills, such as forming letters and numbers and following the words in a book
7 to 10 years	■ Gains increasing independence from parents ■ Develops individuality ■ Works hard to perfect tasks, and willpower to do things is strong ■ Realistic sense of self and what he is good at and has more difficulty with ■ Plans tasks and classifies things in series and categories ■ Although emotions might be up and down, children are more able to regulate their emotions and behavior, and problem solve in more difficult situations ■ Friends are very important, and prosocial behavior is common	■ Supports the child with doing more homework and makes sure that it is done ■ Supports the positive peer relationships that the child has and arranges play dates ■ Supports the child's hobbies and shows interest in her achievements ■ Rules and routines are still important, particularly for children who are getting into trouble in school or are becoming more oppositional ■ Visual perceptual games such as spot the differences, copying, and construction using a model such as with Lego can help the child with a number of skills ■ Watches for any bullying that the child might be experiencing and discusses it with him and the school if necessary
11 to 13 years	■ Withdrawal from the family takes place ■ Worries about her looks and personality ■ Becomes focused on self and who she wants to be ■ Special friend is the most important person in the child's life ■ Usually engaged in a number of activities ■ Much more organized about her school work ■ Can be hypersensitive to criticism, real or perceived, particularly if it comes from peers and the child is bullied ■ Usually less fearful and anxious than at earlier ages	■ It is important for parents to still provide a secure base for the child in the home ■ Parents need to monitor children and know where they are and what activities they are engaged in; this helps the child to stay out of trouble and feel loved and valued ■ Supports the child to be able to problem solve ■ Continues to explore extracurricular activities that develop the child's skills and are of interest to the child ■ Needs to be aware of any dramatic changes in the child's behavior and personality, and get the child professional help if necessary ■ Supports the child if he is struggling academically or socially

environment, and social context) (Boyce, 2006; Burgess, Marshall, Rubin, & Fox, 2003; Rutter, Giller, & Hagell, 1998; Sameroff, 2009; Wachs, 2000). This approach has sometimes been described as behavioral genetics (Hettema, Neale, & Kendler, 2001). Risk factors and mechanisms of influence, described next, are referred to as level 1 of causality in the model described in the Introduction (see also Figure I.1, p. xxiii) and are expanded in this chapter.

LEVEL 1 OF CAUSALITY

Influences Within the Child

Biological and Genetic Influences on the Child

Biological factors and genetic influences can be strengths, creating resilience, or they can compromise the child's development, contributing to the appearance of symptoms or disorders. Even influences during pregnancy can have significant effects on the fetus that continue to affect development (Bennett, Bendersky, & Lewis, 2002; Stratton, Howe, & Battaglia, 2005). The use of alcohol during pregnancy can negatively affect the child's brain development over time. Evidence of structural, neurological, and/or functional damage to the central nervous system (CNS) includes seizures, microcephaly, and abnormal neuroimaging (Bertrand, Floyd, & Weber, 2004). The developmental disabilities that can occur as a result of prenatal exposure to alcohol are now included under the overall term of "fetal alcohol spectrum disorders" (FASD; National Organization on Fetal Alcohol Syndrome, 2004). Most children exposed to alcohol during pregnancy do not meet the three criteria required for fetal alcohol syndrome (FAS). Those who have confirmed prenatal alcohol exposure and meet the criteria for facial dysmorphology and have neurodevelopmental deficits but normal growth have been referred to as partial FAS (pFAS). Children who have confirmed prenatal alcohol exposure and neurodevelopmental deficits but do not meet the other physical requirements for FAS are described as having alcohol-related neurodevelopmental disorder (ARND) (Stratton, Howe, & Battaglia, 1996). The prevalence rate of the full range of FASD is believed to be 2 to 6 per 1,000 and is much higher in foster children (Centers for Disease Control and Prevention, 2007; Chudley et al., 2005) and approaches the estimated prevalence of autism spectrum disorders. Alcohol and the ethanol contained in it, a neurobehavioral teratogen, interfere with normal fetal growth and development, with effects dependent on the amount, timing, and pattern of alcohol exposure. More exposure means more severe neurobehavioral deficits. Episodic or binge drinking is associated with greater fetal damage because it creates peak blood alcohol concentrations. However, any amount of drinking during pregnancy can cause harm to the fetus, and alcohol use at any time during gestation is associated with a higher risk of central nervous system (CNS) dysfunction (Stratton et al., 2005; U.S. Surgeon General's Advisory on Alcohol Use in Pregnancy, 2005). When these defects or disorders occur, the effects on intelligence, academic functioning, and social, emotional, and behavioral development can be devastating (Kodituwakku, 2007).

In the United States, approximately 5% of neonates have been exposed to drugs and alcohol in utero (Substance Abuse and Mental Health Services Administration, 2008). Prenatal exposure to heroin, methadone, or marijuana has shown inconsistent evidence of long-term deficits, clearly attributable to drug exposure (Bennett et al., 2002). However, exposure to drugs might contribute to intrauterine growth retardation and decreased responsiveness, jitteriness, irritability, and the same attention and regulation problems identified for children exposed to alcohol (Hoffer, 2007; Plessinger & Woods, 1993). Exposure to smoking in utero has also been found to be linked to altered newborn behavior (Law et al., 2003) as well as lower scores on cognitive measures persisting to 12 years (Fried & Watkinson, 2000) and behavioral difficulties (Wakschlag, Lahey, Loeber, Green, & Loventhal, 1997; Wakschlag, Pickett, Kasza, & Loeber, 2006).

As well, preterm and low-birth-weight infants, particularly those with extremely low birth weights, can be compromised at birth by immature organs that can result in life-threatening disorders (Rais-Bahrain & Short, 2006). Risk of permanent injury is higher if there has been a brain hemorrhage, hydrocephalus, or asphyxia. These infants are more likely to have later difficulties with cognition, language impairments, attention problems, and memory difficulties. With progressively lower birth weights, the deficits increase, and as many as 30% have behavioral problems and meet criteria for attention deficit/hyperactivity disorder (ADHD; Breslau, Chilcoat, Johnson, Andreski, & Lucia, 2000).

Maternal anxiety and depression during pregnancy have been linked to preterm birth and developmental and behavioral problems in children (Dole, Savitz, Hertz-Picciotto, & Siega-Riz, 2003; Huizink, Robles de Medina, Mulder, Visser, & Buitelaar, 2003; O'Conner, Heron, Golding, Glover, & ALSPAC Study Team, 2003). Although the mechanism by which the fetus is affected is unclear, it is likely due to the effects of increased glucocorticoids or stress hormones crossing the placenta and entering the fetal circulation (Ruiz & Avant, 2005).

Clearly, a number of syndromes and other chronic medical conditions can significantly affect mental health in children. As well, repeated illnesses, hospitalizations, and frequent medical procedures have been found to be related to later psychosocial difficulties (Stuber & Sherrash, 2006).

Physiological Reactivity of the Child

The child's stress reactivity has been seen as a mediator of the relationship between exposure to stress and the development of certain disorders. More stress-reactive children appear to be more vulnerable. Studies have shown increased generalized frontal lobe activation in some infants (Davidson, 2002) and greater activation of the right cerebral hemisphere compared to the left hemisphere in others. Reactions in the right cerebral hemisphere are related to avoidance, withdrawal, and negative emotions, such as sadness and anxiety, and with social reticence and more inhibited behavior later (Baving, Laucht, & Schmidt, 2002; Henderson, Marshall, Fox, & Rubin, 2004). The patterning and balance between the two branches of the autonomic nervous system (ANS), the sympathetic and para-sympathetic, have also been studied and show that children with a more rapid heartbeat and lower vagal tone or respiratory sinus arrhythmia (RSA) are more reactive to normal stressors and more inhibited (Lonigan, Vasey, Phillips, & Hazan, 2004; Raine, 2002). Examining the activity of the hypothalamic–pituitary–adrenal (HPA) axis, some children show a lower threshold of stress activation and higher levels of cortisol throughout the day (Gunnar & Donzella, 2002; Whittle, Allen, Lubman, & Mucat, 2006). If children are exposed to high levels of cortisol over time, changes in brain activity and structure may occur, producing memory and learning problems and lowering the level at which negative emotions are experienced (Perry, 2000).

A number of studies thus suggest that certain individuals show "patterns of increased physiologic arousal and exaggerated reactivity to stressful events or environments which may be observed in several systems simultaneously" (Jemerin & Boyce, 1990, p. 150). Furthermore, the more frequently stress pathways are activated, a process termed "kindling" can occur, producing a stress response at increasingly lower levels of stimulation or stress (Post, Weiss, & Smith, 1995). These patterns of stress/reactivity are also believed to contribute to various configurations of temperament and emotional and behavioral reactions, discussed next.

Temperament of the Child

Since the 1990s, there has been a dramatic increase in research on temperament and individual differences in how infants and children react to similar events and situations (Hirshfeld-Becker et al., 2003). Moreover, these different reactions are believed to reflect underlying physiological and biological differences. Claims for a biological or genetic basis for temperament have found support in a number of twin studies in which children adopted at birth were compared with their biological parents. The research found genetic influences for some, but not all, temperament characteristics, such as expression of negative affect and behavior inhibition (Roisman & Fraley, 2006). The influence of genes on these characteristics and development was less obvious in infancy but increased over time. However, continuity of temperament characteristics has been difficult to prove because the behavioral display of the traits changes at different developmental stages.

A number of traits, such as inhibition and lack of inhibition, difficultness, and capacity for effortful control, have shown the most continuity over time and are believed to have a biological basis. At their extremes, they have also been found to relate to psychopathology. Inhibition has been shown, at the extremes of the distribution, to make children more vulnerable than children in the middle range (Kagan & Snidman, 2004). Those with higher levels of inhibition have been found to have lower levels of social competence and higher levels of social anxiety (Schmidt, Fox, & Schulkin, 1999). Inhibition is also related to parenting, with children receiving controlling and/or oversolicitous parenting more likely to continue with their inhibited styles.

Uninhibited children, on the other hand, are more likely to initiate their behavioral response systems and approach novel situations, appearing to be fearless and impulsive. Fox and colleagues refer to children at the extreme end of this characteristic as "temperamentally exuberant" and describe them as having little fear of novelty and being high in approach behavior. Some uninhibited children are more likely to show frustration and anger about restrictions and rules and want control over events (Donzella, Gunnar, Krueger, & Alwin, 2000; Posner & Rothbart, 2001). They also have more problems internalizing rules and standards and developing a conscience (Kochanska, Murray, & Coy, 1997). Some data suggest that low autonomic arousal or lower heart rate might contribute to this kind of uninhibited temperament. Not surprisingly, this kind of temperament has been linked to behavioral problems in older children (Frick & Morris, 2004). This is more likely to occur when the child receives more harsh, controlling, and punitive parenting (Kochanska, 1997a, 1997b; Kochanska & Aksan, 2006).

Thomas and colleagues described what they called the "difficult child" in 1968, with 10% of children in the New York Longitudinal Study (NYLS) meeting the criteria (Thomas, Chess, & Birch, 1968). They also introduced the idea of an easy–difficult continuum that is still accepted as valid. Nine dimensions of temperament were identified at that time as contributing to temperament, though not all have been validated over time. The difficult child was described as irregular, low in approach, high in withdrawal from novel situations, slow to adapt, having intense relationships, and having negative mood or irritability. Those at extreme risk of difficultness are more likely to have challenging behaviors such as extreme crying during infancy, impulsivity that can result in accidents, and negative reactions to the birth of a sibling. They are also more likely to be difficult to soothe and calm and to settle into a routine in infancy and early childhood. Infants who have difficulty with sensory processing might share many characteristics with the "difficult" temperament infants, and this might explain some of the components of the syndrome. Some have suggested that these children can create stress in their parents, who then tend to react with frustration and intrusiveness in their interactions with their children (Calkins, 2002; Coplan, Bowker, & Cooper, 2003; Dixon & Smith, 2003; Rubin, Burgess, Dwyer, & Hastings, 2003).

The concept of the capacity for effortful control was introduced by Rothbart and Bates (1998, p. 137), who describe it as the capacity to "inhibit a dominant response and initiate a subdominant response." Dixon, Sally, and Clements (2006) added that effortful control also includes the ability to focus and concentrate and inhibit behavior that is not appropriate to the situation. They added that effortful control enables the child to concentrate in situations when the child does not want to do so. Good effortful control allows the child to deal with stress better. It can help children to regulate both emotions and behavior and shift attention from threatening stimuli to more soothing stimuli (Nigg, Goldsmith, & Sachek, 2004; Wolfe & Bell, 2004). Poor effortful control, especially if it includes impulsive behavior, has been linked to behavioral problems (Gartstein & Fagot, 2003; Olson, Sameroff, Kerr, Lopez, & Wellman, 2005) and can place children at risk for ADHD, disruptive behavior disorder, oppositional defiant disorder, and, in an extreme form, aggression and conduct disorders (Frick & Morris, 2004; Hirshfeld-Becker et al., 2003; Raine, 2002).

Genetic Vulnerability of the Child

Although genetics are believed to explain about half of the variance of psychopathology or disorders, environmental sources account for the other half. The goal is no longer to try to find one gene that can account for a disorder. Instead, several genes and many environmental factors provide a better account of complex personality traits and disorders (Plomin & Crabbe, 2000). Furthermore, there is now intense interest in genetic vulnerability to disorders, specifically genes that modify outcomes for children who experience adverse situations in early life (Bradley, 2005).

Recent research on genes for the serotonin transporter and the monoamine oxidase A (MAOA) has found that they have significant effects on children's developmental outcomes that are particularly important for the topics discussed in this book. The serotonin transporter gene is related to the development of anxiety and depression, whereas the MAOA gene is related to the development of impulsive and aggressive behavior and conduct problems. These genes are called alleles and come in a short (S) and a long (L) version. Individuals with two long alleles (LL) are least at risk, those with two short alleles (SS) are most at risk, and those with one of each (LS) have a risk level between the two. In the Dunedin Temperament Study, which followed individuals from birth into adulthood, of those with two short alleles for the serotonin transporter, 43% had a major depression when they were exposed to four or more adverse experiences, whereas those with two long alleles were more resistant to the negative effects of adverse early experiences (Caspi et al., 2003). The same trends were found for children with the genes for MAOA, with those with two short alleles more at risk for externalizing behavioral disorders, antisocial behavior, and even violence (Caspi et al., 2002). More recently, these differences have been found to be related to differential responses to early-intervention programs (Bakermans-Kranenburg, van IJzendoorn, Pijlman, Mesman, & Juffer, 2008).

Although making some individuals more vulnerable, these genes and some traits such as "difficultness" can also make children more able to benefit from positive environments. The area of epigenetics is helping us to understand how genes can be turned on and off and how children appear to be "differentially susceptible" to their environments (Bakermans-Kranenburg & van IJzendoorn, 2011; Pluess & Belsky, 2009). A meta-analysis of gene-environment studies of children up to 10 years of age, concluded that children with less efficient dopamine-related genes did worse in negative environments than the comparison children without the "genetic risk," but they also profited most from positive environments. Pluess and Belsky (2009), in the National Institute of Child Health and Human Development (NICHD) Study of Early Child Care and Youth Development, found that infant difficult temperament interacted with child-care quality to predict teacher-rated socioemotional adjustment at ages 4 and 5. Children with difficult temperaments as infants were highest on behavioral problem scales when exposed to poor-quality care but lowest when exposed to high-quality care. Similarly, Cassidy, Woodhouse, Sherman, Stupia, and Lejuez (2011), examining the efficacy of a brief intervention on the development of secure attachment, found that there were intervention effects only for the highly irritable infants but with differential effects depending on the attachment classification. Although with more secure mothers positive intervention effects were apparent for irritable infants, for dismissive mothers highly irritable infants, as opposed to moderately irritable infants, were more likely to be secure in the control group. Essex, Armstrong, Burk, Goldsmith, and Boyce (2011) examined the impact of physiological and behavioral stress reactivity on the association between Grade 1 child–teacher relationship and adolescent mental health in Grade 7. They found that both physiological and behavioral reactivity moderated the associations of both adverse and supportive aspects of the teacher–parent relationship with Grade 7 symptom severity. These are just a few of the many studies that support the theory of differential susceptibility to the environment.

Parental History and Current Functioning

Research has confirmed that a number of parental characteristics can place a child's development at risk. This can be a direct effect such as observing spousal abuse or occur more indirectly through parents' interactions with their children. For example, when parents have limited intellectual capacity, it can impact on their understanding of the complexity of parenting and the ability of parents to provide for the everyday needs of their children, such as feeding, bathing, and providing adequate stimulation for their developmental needs. A significant amount of support is therefore needed for these parents to meet the needs of their children from infancy to adolescence (Case & Gang, 1999; McGaha, 2002).

When either parent is engaged in criminal activity, it can affect the environments that the children are exposed to, including child abuse and neglect (Brennan, Grekin, Mortensen, & Mednick, 2002). The child's development can also be compromised when one or both parents have a psychiatric condition. The behavior of parents suffering from poorly controlled schizophrenia, personality disorder, or bipolar disorder can be frightening and dangerous (Dunn, 1993; Riorden, Appleby, & Faragher, 1999; Seifer & Dickstein, 2000; Zahn-Waxler, Duggal, & Gruber, 2002). The outcome depends, however, on factors such as severity of the illness, whether the parent is frequently hospitalized, and whether there are other caregivers who can provide consistent and adequate care for the child.

The effects of maternal depression on a child's development have been well documented (Center on the Developing Child at Harvard University, 2009). Some mothers can experience multiple episodes of depression; for others, depression can be more chronic (Horowitz, Briggs-Gowan, Storfer-Isser, & Carter, 2007). Because maternal depression can be a recurring disorder for women in their child-bearing years, it is estimated that 1 in 11 infants will be parented by women experiencing depression (Horowitz et al. 2007). Unfortunately, a number of depressed mothers do not get treatment, and the effects on children can be devastating (Halligan, Herbert, Goodyear, & Murray, 2007; Vesga-Lopez et al., 2008). Exposure to maternal depression has been shown to increase a child's likelihood of developing anxiety, depression, and/or a behavioral disorder (Field, Hernandez-Reif, & Diego, 2006; Goodman & Gotlib, 2002; Gump et al., 2009; Jones, Field, & Davalos, 2000; Radke-Yarrow & Klimes-Dougan, 2002). Also, it has been consistently found that infants of depressed mothers are more likely to have prefrontal asymmetry, with more activation in the right rather than the left prefrontal cortex (PFC). This pattern has been found to be associated with withdrawal behavior and emotions such as sadness and fear (Coan, 2008).

Less obvious or latent variables such as parents' own experiences of being parented can dramatically affect their interactions with their children. Particularly when parents were abused or neglected as children, and if the issues remain unresolved, many will repeat the abuse, whereas others will provide marginal parenting (Lyons-Ruth, Melnick, Bronfman, Sherry, & Llanas, 2004; Schechter, 2004). Other characteristics, such as the parent's ability to "keep their child in mind," show empathy, or have self-reflectivity are critical for their child's development (Fonagy, Gergely, Jurist, & Target, 2002).

Interactional and Parenting Variables

The interaction between parent and child is seen as one of the most important influences on child development. Two theories and bodies of research have dominated the literature: attachment theory and the social learning approach.

Attachment has been defined as the emotional connection between children and their carers, particularly parents. It is rare for children to be unattached to their caregivers, but the quality of attachment varies. Attachment researchers have called the different attachment classifications found in children: secure, insecure–ambivalent/resistant, insecure–avoidant, or disorganized–disoriented. The child's quality of attachment to parents is believed to develop from the parent–child interactions experienced in early childhood and particularly parents' sensitivity and responsiveness to their child's cues. Particularly important is how consistently responsive the parent is to the child when he is hurt, upset, frustrated, ill, or afraid and how well she can help him manage his emotions and behavior. Mothers of securely attached children have been shown to respond consistently to their children's emotional needs. The child is then believed to have a "secure base" of containment to which she can return as needed. Mothers of children with insecure or disorganized–disoriented attachment have more difficulty regulating their child's emotions and meeting his emotional needs. Mothers of avoidant children often ignore a child's negative emotions, particularly sadness or neediness, and consistently fail to respond when the child is upset and crying. Mothers of ambivalent/resistant children only respond when the child shows intense displays of anger or unhappiness and increases these emotions to get attention. The disorganized–disoriented child has generally experienced unpredictable responses from the parent, sometimes presenting as frightened while at other times interacting with extreme hostility and anger. This means that the child has no "secure base" to go to and is placed in an unresolvable conflict when the attachment system is activated. The child might simultaneously want to go to the parent for comfort but also be afraid to do so (Main & Solomon, 1990).

The quality of attachment for many children remains the same over time. However, in more high-risk, disadvantaged populations, changes are often found across time because the family environment is less consistent (Grossman, Grossman, & Waters, 2005; Main, Hesse, & Kaplan, 2005; Sroufe, Egeland, Carlson, & Collins, 2005). Attachment theorists believe that children develop working models of the parent–child relationship, other relationships, and themselves. These schemas are often generalized to relationships with others and activated during interactions with them. Researchers have also found that the quality of the child's attachment to her primary caregiver and her experience of being calmed when stressed affect the activity of the HPA axis and consequently the amount of cortisol secreted in stressful situations (van Bakel & Riksen-Walraven, 2004). Because cortisol levels can be measured in a noninvasive way, measures have been taken in child care.

Securely attached children show decreasing cortisol levels throughout the day, whereas children with insecure and disorganized attachments show rising levels throughout the day (Gunnar, 2006). Children with secure attachments can reach a level of "harmonious equilibrium or homeostasis" in response to the stimulation of child care, whereas children with insecure or disorganized attachments become increasingly stressed and unable to reduce the release of various neurochemicals into the bloodstream (Schore, 2001).

Secure attachment has been found to be correlated with outcomes such as social maturity, social competence, ego-resilience, positive affect, problem-solving skills, and positive peer engagement. Children whose attachment is insecure and disorganized tend to be more anxious, aggressive, and less competent; have poor peer relationships and lower self-esteem; and are often rejected by peers (Booth-LaForce, Rubin, Rose-Krasnor, & Burgess, 2005; Steele & Steele, 2005b; Verschueren & Marcoen, 2005).

Main (1995) and Lyons-Ruth and Spielman (2004) have emphasized that children in the disorganized/disoriented group are the most vulnerable to the development of psychopathology. Physical and mental disorders have been found to be most common with children who have disorganized attachments (van IJzendoorn & Bakermans-Kranenburg, 2003). Similarly, increased rates of insecure attachment have been found in children in a number of clinical groups, including children adopted from Romanian orphanages, medically diagnosed children, children with gender identity disorder, and children of mothers with an anxiety disorder. These clinical groups typically have a predominance of disorganized attachment, and their behavior is often dominated by being extremely controlling in interactions with their parents (Bradley, 2000). However, the relationship between attachment and child psychopathology is not necessarily direct or inescapable. Certain children develop ways of handling the situation by finding alternative relationships or being relatively assertive and not remaining hopeless or dependent on their relationship with the caregiver.

Social learning theories also focus on early parent–child interactions as important contributors to child outcomes. Unlike attachment theorists, researchers from this perspective have measured the behavioral components of the parent–child interaction and how the behavior of the parent and child can reinforce each other. For example, in situations in which parents' interactions are negative, intensely emotional, and punitive, children typically respond with negative behaviors, which in turn can increase parents' negativity. Patterson has described these interactions as "coercive cycles" of parent–child interactions; with multiple repetitions, they result in the child becoming increasingly reactive, demanding, oppositional, and even violent and escaping the parent's demands. The parent's response is often to become more harsh and punitive and critical of the child and can include giving in at times, thus reinforcing the coercive cycles. In the short term, the child gets what he wants, but the parent–child relationship becomes increasingly negative, which limits the child's opportunities for learning appropriate strategies for emotion regulation (Patterson & Fisher, 2002; Scaramella & Leve, 2004).

Bugental also proposed a model that explains how dysfunctional parenting can be developed and reinforced. She talked about "threat-oriented family systems" and described how some parents perceive their child as difficult and having control over his behavior while perceiving themselves as powerless or having little control. The child becomes unable to problem solve and instead acts at an automatic or unconscious level. The parent might then act with frustration and anger and a sense of helplessness. Increasingly, the parent sees herself as the victim and the child as in control and believes that she will lose the battle. As these patterns of behavior escalate, the likelihood of emotional and physical abuse directed at the child increases (Bugental et al., 2002; Bugental & Johnston, 2000).

Although not a focus of the above models, some researchers and theorists have talked about attribution biases from which the child has a negative sense of self and others

(Dodge, 1993). Such schemas can contribute to externalizing and internalizing disorders such as anxiety, depression, and aggression. Dodge and Frame (1982) and Dodge and Rabiner (2004) showed how these "attributional biases" can result in a child misinterpreting the words and actions of peers and adults such as teachers. A child might view and remember ambiguous situations or events as threatening or an intentional attack and react in an aggressive and confrontational manner, eliciting negative reactions in turn.

These theories highlight the importance of consistent and containing interactions for children's positive development and the negative impacts on development when interactions are nonresponsive or helpless or, in the extreme, harsh and punitive. These interactions can be even more detrimental when they alternate between being helpless and harsh and punitive, increasing the child's experience of inconsistency and being out of control.

Although much of the early research on parenting focused on mothers, research now is increasingly acknowledging the important role that fathers play in the development of their children. Fathers' support of mothers in their parenting is important, but fathers have a significant and direct influence on their children's development as well (Cummings & Cummings, 2002; Mezulis, Hyde, & Clark, 2004; NICHD Early Child Care Research Network, 2005; Tamis-LeMonda, Shannon, Cabrera, & Lamb, 2004). Their influence has been found to be particularly important in the area of social relationships for both boys and girls. Fathers who responded negatively to their children's negativity had children who were more verbally aggressive, played less with other children, and shared less.

The Effects of Abuse, Neglect, and Other Trauma

The National Scientific Council of the Developing Child (2007, 2008) distinguished between normal or positive stress, tolerable stress, and toxic stress and discussed the effects of toxic stress on the brain and its development. Positive stress in children's lives, such as meeting new people, dealing with frustration, and resolving conflict, is necessary for development. Tolerable stress is controllable when the body's stress reaction is not activated for too long and the affected child has dependable relationships for support. An example is a separation and divorce when both parents prioritize support for their children and the children continue to spend time with both parents in a way that is containing and nurturing. Toxic stress, on the other hand, results from chronic and uncontrollable events that cause strong, frequent, or prolonged activation of the body's stress response and when the child does not have support from caring adults (for example, severe and chronic maltreatment).

In countries throughout the world, millions of children each year are exposed to toxic stress by being terrorized, abused, neglected, or otherwise maltreated. Children are growing up in situations of chaos, neglect, violence, or threat, without a consistent caregiver to turn to for protection and nurturance (Davids, Harold, Goeke-Morey, Cummings, Shelton, et al., 2002). The number of children exposed to trauma (involving child maltreatment) in the United States each year exceeds 4 million (Briere & Elliott, 2003; Perry, 2000, 2006; Perry, Pollard, Blakley, Baker, & Vigilante, 1995). In the United States, child maltreatment has been pronounced a public health problem of epidemic proportions, and the World Health Organization (WHO) has identified violence as a major public health issue affecting the mental and physical health of millions (Margolin & Gordis, 2000; World Health Organization, 2002). Large numbers of children also experience the loss of a parent without other caregivers available who can fully meet their needs (Agid et al., 1999).

Also, many traumatized children lack the basic developmental experiences critical to learning to regulate their emotions and behavior, socialize and relate to others, communicate, and learn (Perry, 2000, 2006, 2008). Hundreds of studies have made it clear that these experiences during childhood can alter the size, structure, and organization of the developing brain and cause alterations in various neural systems. Trauma to the brain results in a number of negative functional difficulties frequently seen in children who have experienced maltreatment.

Trauma in early years can have enduring effects on four major stress response systems: (1) hippocampus and the HPA axis that is actively involved in the regulation of cortisol; (2) amygdala, locus coeruleus, adrenal gland, and sympathetic nervous system (CNS); (3) vasopressin–oxytocin peptide prohormone system; and (4) gamma-aminobutyric acid (GABA) system (see Table 1.2 for further exploration). Studies with rats and clinical observations of humans have found that early stress primes the brain to be more fearful and increase the release of stress hormones. These hormones have dramatic and profound effects on the developing brain. For example, excessive secretion of cortisol can reduce brain weight and affect DNA content and interfere with myelination and the number of dendrite connections formed in various brain areas. The secretion of cortisol at a critical time can activate the other stress systems that will have greater impacts than the effects of a single hormone.

Table 1.2 *Stress Response Systems*

1. Involves the hippocampus and HPA axis and feedback regulation of cortisol	This stress hormone mobilizes energy; stimulates the release of adrenaline; increases cardiovascular tone; and inhibits growth, immune, and inflammatory responses
2. Involves the amygdala, locus coeruleus, adrenal gland, and sympathetic nervous system	This is a noradrenergic and adrenaline response to stress, which increases blood flow, increases awareness, and mobilizes a fight-or-flight response; greater concentrations of dopamine have also been found
3. Involves the vasopressin–oxytocin peptide prohormone family	Vasopressin triggers release of the adrenocorticotropin hormone
4. Involves the molecular composition of gamma-aminobutyric acid (GABA)–benzodiazepine supramolecular complex resulting in attenuation of GABA	Receptors in the amygdala and locus coeruleus are also involved, which can lead to enhanced fearfulness and anxiety caused by enhancement in production of corticotropin-releasing factor (CRF) and adrenocorticotropic hormone (ACTH)

The hippocampus plays a critical role in the storage and retrieval of memories. A reduction in volume of the left hippocampus and deficits in synaptic connections in the region have been found in adults who have experienced childhood trauma and have a diagnosis of posttraumatic sress disorder (PTSD) or dissociative identity disorder (Southwick & Charney, 1999; Stein, Loverola, Hanna, Torchia, & McLarty, 1997). The amygdala is also vulnerable to early exposure to excessive levels of stress hormones. It has been implicated in fear conditioning, the formation of emotional hormones, nonverbal motor patterns, and triggering of the fight-or-flight response. It is also implicated in kindling, in which repeated intermittent stimulation produces greater and greater neuronal excitability and can even result in seizures and behaviors consistent with anxiety, hyperarousal, and hypervigilance. Changes can also occur with decreased activation of Broca's area, responsible for speech, and other language areas of the brain (Rauch et al., 1996).

The corpus callosum is also vulnerable to early exposure of excessive levels of stress hormones. It connects the two cerebral hemispheres (left and right), allowing communication and integration of information to take place. Reduced size in the corpus callosum has been associated with diminished communication between the hemispheres (Teicher, Andersen, Polcari, Andersen, & Navalta, 2002). The cerebellar vermis is also sensitive to the effects of trauma, and plays a role in modulating limbic irritability, but also influences attention and affect. Language and emotional difficulties seem to result from vermal lesions. In individuals with histories of abuse, there is often a functional impairment in the activity of the cerebellar vermis as frequently stimulating it results in an increase of circulating glucocorticoid levels and plasma cortical levels.

Trauma can also arrest development of the left hemisphere, responsible for language development and initiating activity (Rauch et al., 1996; Teicher, 2000; Teicher et al., 2002). The prefrontal lobes scarcely begin myelination until adolescence, and the process continues into the third decade. These areas exert important inhibitory effects on all the major monoamine projections to the subcortical region, limiting their responses to stress through inhibitory control of the HPA axis. Early stress and maltreatment can alter neuronal development in prefrontal cortical areas.

Hence, trauma can modify brain structures and lead to a highly reactive stress-response system with limbic irritability, hyperarousal, and chronic sympathetic activation that has far-reaching impacts on physical and mental health (McEwen, 2000a, 2000b; Teicher, 2000). This can include problems with self-regulation, aggression toward self and others, problems with attention and dissociation, physical problems, and difficulties with self-concept and the capacity to negotiate satisfactory relationships. Children who have experienced multiple traumas also tend to experience developmental delays and learning disabilities, including cognition, language, motor planning, and socialization skills. They can also have multiple clinical diagnoses, including anxiety, depression, oppositional defiant disorder, ADHD, and phobic disorder.

The Social Context

A number of societal factors are associated with child development outcomes and psychopathology (Rutter, 2000). They include the child poverty rate that in the United States is now 23% and in Canada is 21.3% (Children's Defense Fund, 2002; Doherty, 2001). Nearly 5 million preschoolers in the United States live in families that suffer from chronic poverty. Children living in poverty often live in substandard housing and violent neighborhoods and can be exposed to daily violence as a result (Self-Brown, LeBlanc, & Kelley, 2004). Parents might find it hard to meet children's basic needs for food and shelter or spend time with children. Positive and stimulating interactions might be difficult for parents to provide since their energy can be depleted and they might experience feelings of hopelessness and depression (Conger, McLoyd, Wallace, Sun, Simons, & Brody, 2002; McLoyd & Wilson, 1991). When young children are living in families in the lowest quartile with regard to income, they are twice as likely to have lower IQ levels and psychopathology (Bradley & Corwyn, 2002; Linver, Brooks-Gunn, & Kohen, 2002; McLoyd, 1998). Researchers have also found that low socioeconomic status has a negative effect on older children's cognitive, social, and emotional development.

Children in homeless families (Schteingart, Molnar, Klein, Lowe, & Hartmann, 1995) and children of adolescent parents (Lounds, Borkowski, Whitman, Maxell, & Weed, 2005; Waldfogel, Han, & Brooks-Gunn, 2002) are at risk of developing emotional and behavioral problems. Another significant risk for the child occurs when there is severe family dysfunction, with spousal abuse or extreme conflict between parents. This can result in anxiety or depression or behavioral problems in children (Barletta & O'Mara, 2006; Sturge-Apple, Davies, & Cummings, 2006). Isolation and lack of social supports can also result from living in impoverished environments and contribute to a family's ongoing social difficulties (Moroney, 1992; Ramos, Guerin, Gottfried, Bathurst, & Oliver, 2005).

The most consistent findings from longitudinal research studies have shown that, when there are only one or two risk factors, unless they are extreme, they seldom have a negative impact on development. However, with four or more risk factors, the risk to the child's development increases substantially. In fact, the negative effect is not just additive but also multiplicative. For example, for a child with four risk factors, there is a 16-fold increase in difficulties. This result has been found in a number of studies (Rutter, 2009; Sameroff & Fiese, 1990, 2000).

More recently, a cumulative risk index or profile that estimates risk in a number of domains (for example, child, family, parenting, and community) has been used in latent class analysis to identify subgroups of children with different risk profiles. Identifying these risk profiles can help to refine and target prevention or treatment interventions to groups of children with the same types of problems (Lanza, Rhoades, Nix, Greenberg, & the Conduct Problems Prevention Research Group, 2010).

Studies have also documented links between childhood adversity and later health and well-being. The Adverse Childhood Experiences (ACE) Study, one of the largest studies ever conducted of this kind, showed that, the more adverse childhood events or risk factors a child was exposed to, the more negative outcomes were found (Felitti et al., 1998; Salmon & Calderbank, 1996). A Swedish longitudinal study found similar results and that the risk of mental health problems in children brought up in adverse circumstances, especially if they included neglect and abuse, was 10 to 1 compared with a group not brought up in adverse circumstances. Similarly, the risks for mortality were 9 to 1 (Lundberg, 1993).

As indicated previously, other researchers have studied vulnerability factors, a subset of risk factors, unique to the individual, for example, genetic factors that predispose a child to stress reactivity (Nader, 2008). They can act as "causal mechanisms" contributing to a disorder (Ingram & Price, 2001; Price & Lento, 2001). So risk factors in the environment and the child's vulnerability can act together to determine that child's outcome.

Protective Factors or Resilience?

Protective factors are sometimes described as the opposite of risk factors. For example, disorganized attachment can be a risk factor, whereas secure attachment can be a protective factor (Cicchetti, 2003a). Protective factors can be organized under the same four headings as risk factors (that is, child characteristics, interactional or parenting variables, parental history and current functioning, and sociodemographic and societal factors). In addition, researchers who have examined child resilience have identified protective conditions that can improve resistance to risk factors and contribute to successful outcomes and adaptation despite significant adversity. Typically, these conditions fall into three main categories: (1) personal characteristics and resilience within the child, such as high intelligence, good social skills, and positive temperament; (2) a secure relationship with a warm, empathetic adult in either the family or the community; and (3) a social environment or community that supports positive efforts and behaviors by the child. Protective mechanisms can be set in place and account for variations in child outcomes. They include reducing the impact of a difficult situation, protecting the child's self-esteem, and providing social support for a child living in a difficult situation (Masten & Powell, 2005; Rutter & Rutter, 1993, 2002).

PREDICTING CHILD OUTCOMES

A number of factors in the child and the environment contribute to the development of the child, but multiple pathways and processes determine the ultimate patterns of adaptation or maladaptation and the development of various kinds of pathology in children. Single characteristics rarely predict vulnerability and are influenced instead by mediating (for example, personal motivation and interpersonal relationships) and moderating (for example, secure attachment and supportive caregivers) variables that influence the relationship between a predictive variable and outcomes (Nader, 2008; Yates, Egeland, & Sroufe, 2003). Consequently, predicting a child's developmental trajectory or assessing his potential for resilience or a poor outcome is extremely challenging.

It is crucial, however, to consider not just the predictive factors but also the outcomes being considered. On the one hand, for children with severe developmental delays or certain mental disorders such as autism or schizophrenia, biological and genetic factors are strongly implicated (Batshaw, Shapira, & Farber, 2007; Noble, Tottenham, & Casey, 2005). On the other hand, for children with mild delays and behavioral and emotional difficulties, factors in the environment and parenting relationship can be the most critical (Rutter, 2002; Sameroff & Fiese, 2000). Also, Michael and Rutter (1993) noted that, in addition to the number of risk factors, the type of risk factor is important in determining the child outcome in longitudinal studies. When the sources of risk were family problems such as the mother's mental illness, the father's criminality, or placement of the child in foster care, cognitive and emotional impairments rose significantly. Also whether a risk factor is proximal or distal can affect how it influences development (Sameroff & Fiese, 2000).

LEVEL 2 OF CAUSALITY

The Brain

During the past several decades, new brain-imaging techniques together with animal research and autopsy results on the brain have significantly contributed to our knowledge of the brain and how it works (Couperus & Nelson, 2006). The brain is an amazingly complex organ with billions of interconnected cells or neurons that control the main functions of humans, including metabolism, respiration, the cardiovascular system, the immune system, emotions, behaviors, learning, response to stress, and other functions (LeDoux, 2002a, 2002b; McEwen, 2002). At birth, an infant has approximately a billion brain cells or neurons. During the first year of life, neuronal connections or synapses are overproduced, and they increase 20-fold, from 50 trillion to 1,000 trillion. Also, brain weight increases threefold as a result of this growth. During this early period, the process of synaptic pruning begins, with more active synapses strengthened and less active synapses weakened or even eliminated. This implies that synapses are "fine-tuned" and optimized, though some flexibility or plasticity of the brain is reduced as a result of this pruning (Sowell, Thompson, Tessner, & Toga, 2001).

Development of the Brain

In this section, the model of brain development proposed by Bruce Perry and used by the Child Trauma Academy is drawn on. There are four main areas of the brain that develop and become functional at different times during early prenatal and postnatal development (see Figure 1.1).

These areas of the brain, starting from the base of the brain, are the (1) brainstem, (2) midbrain or diencephalon, (3) limbic system, and (4) cortical area. The brain develops from the bottom up and inside out. The lower areas that include the brainstem are responsible for the more basic and primitive functions such as maintenance of temperature, breathing, and heart rate, and mediate states of alertness, sleep, and hunger. The brainstem must be functioning at birth, or the newborn will not survive, and its functionality is mature at 6 months. At the top of the brainstem, the area known as the diencephalon, which includes

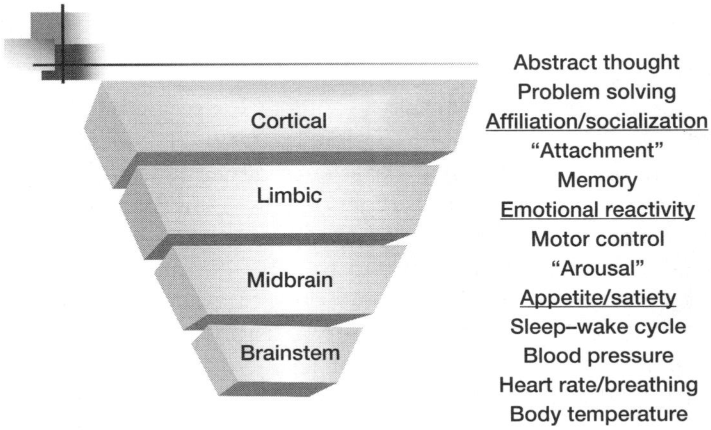

Figure 1.1 *Differential plasticity regions across different areas of the brain.*
From Perry (2005). Reprinted with permission.

the thalamus, has been described as the gateway for incoming sensory information. It also connects to the neocortex and is responsible for motor control and secondary sensory processing. It develops during infancy but reaches functional maturity in early childhood.

The limbic system, responsible for emotion regulation, memory, attachment, and sensory regulation, has its greatest development activity in early childhood and reaches functional maturity in puberty. Some of the most important areas in the limbic system include the hippocampus, which plays a role in storing consciously accessible memories, and the amygdala, responsible for storing unconscious memories. It has extensive input and output pathways to various parts of the brain and can be primarily responsible for integrating brain activity related to social and emotional functioning. The function of behavior and emotion regulation is carried out largely by the limbic regions in conjunction with the frontal areas and plays a central role in coordinating the activity of the higher and lower brain structures. The neocortex is the last area to develop and is responsible for cognitive activities such as reasoning, working memory, problem solving, abstract reasoning, and secondary sensory integration (Casey, Giedd, & Thomas, 2000). It develops during childhood and continues to mature into adulthood. In other words, each of the four brain areas has a different timetable for development and is most sensitive to experiences at times of most rapid growth.

Structure and Functioning of the Brain

Most of the brain is split into the left and right hemispheres, connected with bands of tissue called the corpus callosum and the anterior commissures thought to be responsible for the transmission of information between the two sides. The hemispheres appear to differ in terms of the neurotransmitters that predominate, and the left hemisphere tends to have an "assertive" motivational state governing active engagement with others and approach emotions such as joy and anger, whereas the right hemisphere is seen as more receptive and self-regulatory and connected to withdrawal emotions such as sadness and anxiety. Schore (2001) has also identified the left hemisphere as processing verbal, conscious, and sequential information, whereas the right hemisphere processes unconscious, nonverbal, and emotional material. The billions of neurons that make up the brain are highly interconnected through electrical impulses that are sent down axons and release neurotransmitters at the synapses, which then excite or inhibit the downstream neuron. The transmission of impulses at the synapses is facilitated by neurotransmitters such as dopamine, serotonin, norepinephrine, and endorphins and hormones such as glucocorticoids that are increased during stress (Nelson, 2000; Sapolsky, 1994).

Although the timetable for brain development is determined by genetics, whether it is fully expressed depends on the experiences to which the child is exposed. Plasticity in the brain occurs in two ways: experience dependent and experience expectant (Greenough & Black, 1992). Experience-dependent systems require specific environmental input during a particular window of time for normal development to occur. They include the visual and auditory system and the areas responsible for the development of vocabulary. For example, if babies are born with cataracts, they need early surgery to have the visual input needed to develop normal vision. Experience-expectant plasticity includes the brain's response to unique information in the environment and is highly variable and individualized. Most emotional and social developmental milestones, such as gaining emotion and behavior regulation, are of this type. Interactions with parents and the experience of trauma contribute significantly to this plasticity. Although the age when development is completed in various areas of the brain is unclear, between 8 and 10 years of age, there is a notable decline in recovery-and-saving functions following injury to the brain, traumatic experiences, or failure to receive sufficient stimulation. For example, children adopted into loving homes from orphanages after 2 years of age are far more likely to show chronic impairments in emotional, cognitive, and social development than those adopted in the first year. They are also at more risk for various disorders, such as excessive oppositionality, and internalizing and externalizing behavioral problems (van IJzendoorn & Juffer, 2006; Zeanah, Smyke, & Settles, 2006). Although it is more difficult to affect changes in the brain after the first 5 years, there is increasing evidence of neuroplasticity later, even in adulthood, when the remediation is patterned, intense, repetitive, and focused enough. Such changes have been found in the treatment of dyslexia, learning a new language, and early intervention with children on the autism spectrum (Doidge, 2010; Hyman & Towbin, 2007).

THE MIND

All major theories emphasize certain internal structures that influence how we perceive the world, ourselves, and our relationships with others. These are "hypothesised structures that create expectations based on past experiences about how others will relate to us" (Bradley, 2000, p. 13). Many of these internal structures exist at an unconscious level but can be accessed during therapy and through forms of self-reflection such as mindful awareness (Siegel, 2007). These internal structures have been given different names and definitions, including internal working models, schemata, transference, defenses, attributions, and cognitive structures. Over time, these organizing schemas become entrenched and significantly influence a person's behavior, particularly in emotional and stressful situations and close relationships. These mechanisms become important aspects of personality structure and can remain flexible, changeable, and open to new information or inflexible and rigid, making them difficult to change and resistant to integrating new experiences. Developmentally, these internal structures are not fully functional without the maturation of language, symbolization, and cognition. However, experiences with caregivers before this time, especially in infancy, likely stored in the amygdala as sensorimotor and emotional memories, can be triggered in certain situations and influence the internal structures or representations.

Other critical mechanisms of the mind that can significantly affect behavior and emotional and social development are views of self variously named self-esteem, self-concept, and self-efficacy (Landy, 2009). Other self-system processes are about the self in relation to the outside world and include locus-of-control, threat appraisal, and ability to trust (Hardin, 2001). Generally, a realistic sense of self can enhance a child's resilience and ability to keep striving in challenging situations. In some situations, a strong sense of competence can be drawn on, and such positive cognitions can bring under control physiological arousal in various parts of the brain and prevent the activation of various neurochemical stress systems. However, the child with a negative view of herself or her competence, confronted with challenging tasks in school or expected to manage social situations, can become extremely anxious and stressed. It can be difficult for her to contain the physiological reaction that occurs in her brain, body, and mind, making managing such situations challenging.

INTEGRATING MIND AND BRAIN IN MODELS OF PSYCHOPATHOLOGY

To consider behavior as only a function of brain development and function, or totally determined by the attachment or social system, cannot explain complex behavior or psychopathology, and new models are necessary. A number of writers have mentioned the need to understand the functioning of the mind and the brain to understand both normal and abnormal behavior or psychopathology, and that it is "crucial to solve the brain-behaviour or mind-body problem" (Pennington, 2002, p. 9). Pennington recommends a "bidirectional model of causation" and includes a level of analysis of neuropsychology, which he believes "bridges the chasm separating brain and behaviour, mind and body" (Pennington, 2002, p. 9). See Figure 1.2 for further explanation of this model.

Siegel (2007) draws attention to the need to consider what he terms "the mindful brain." In his discussion, the brain is referred to as an "integrated part of the whole body" and the mind as "mental functions that regulate the flow of energy and information to the brain" (Siegel, 2007, p. 48). He also emphasizes how the mind and brain influence each other in a bidirectional way. He stresses the importance of relationships in influencing both the brain's development and ongoing functioning and the mind or cognitive activity. Davidson and Begley (2012) have provided evidence of how the mind can change the brain and discussed ways that this can occur through improving our basic emotional styles. Bradley (2000) has noted how internal structures influence behavior and provide a way to regulate both relationships and emotional reactions in the brain. In the model discussed in this book, at level 2 of causality, it is proposed that the mind and brain influence each other in a bidirectional way that can influence the child's functioning in a number of areas

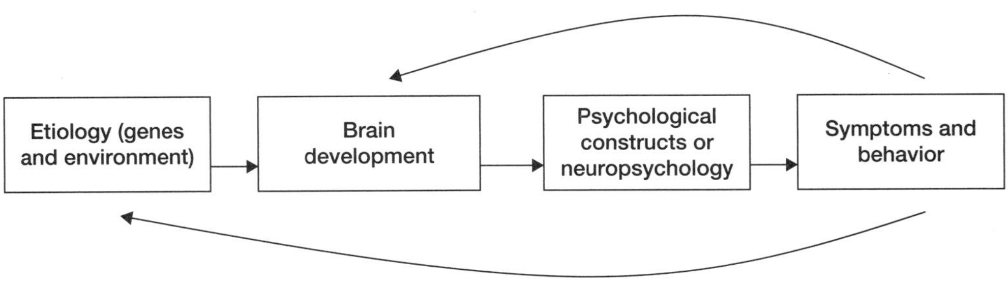

Figure 1.2 *Model of causation of normal development and psychopathology.*
From Pennington (2002). Reprinted with permission.

important for typical development and psychopathology (Pennington, 2002). The focus of interventions of many community programs might largely be on working with parents, with whom efforts are made to enhance parent–child interactions and attachment of the child, reduce ongoing trauma, change negative attributions of the child, and increase social support for the child and parents. Biological interventions include medications that can affect attention, impulsivity, anxiety, and intensity of emotions but can also involve exercise and attention to sleep and diet. Currently, genetic influences are not addressed directly.

FUNCTIONAL AREAS OF THE CHILD

At the last level of the model, children can present with difficulties in one or more of the developmental or functional areas noted in Figure I.1. It is also important to be aware of the child's strengths so that an overall profile of her developmental level and functioning is available (Pennington, 2009). This profile then suggests the areas of influence and the resulting functioning areas where intervention can be targeted. These can be strategies focused on certain aspects of child functioning such as speech and language, sensory processing, hypersensitivity from trauma, or executive functioning, for example. From what is now known about neuroplasticity, some intense, repetitive, focused interventions can change the structure and functioning of the brain. Other approaches might focus on changing the mind (thoughts, attributions, and view of self and others) and, by doing so, more indirectly influence brain development and functioning (Schwartz & Begley, 2002). In Section 2, functioning and intervention in these areas of development will be explored.

For details regarding various websites that offer information and programs on child mental issues, see Table 1.3.

Table 1.3 *Websites*

Website	Information on Website
www.developingchild.harvard.edu	A number of articles that "translate science into policy." Also has a number of articles on issues that may contribute to the development of psychopathology in children such as maternal depression, toxic substances in utero, and other early experiences.
www.mentalhealth.org.uk/help-information	Run by the Mental Health Foundation leading UK charity in mental health and mental disorders and has information on disorders of children and young people.
www.who.int/mental_health/en/	Website provides information on the incidence of mental and behavioral disorders throughout the world. A number of publications on the prevention of mental health disorders, promoting mental health, and emerging evidence on best practice are also available.
www.nimh.nih.gov/statistics/index.shtml/	Website of the National Institute of Mental Health; provides information on statistics and research on mental health as well as a number of useful reports.
www.nami.org	Website of the National Alliance on Mental Illness, the largest grassroots mental health organization dedicated to supporting Americans affected by mental illness. It has a Child and Adolescent Action Center.
www.health.nih.gov	Website of the U.S. Department of Health and Human Services; it provides public access to a number of articles and reports on mental and physical health.
www.aboutourkids.org	Website of the New York University Child Study Center that includes information on child development, disorders and treatments, seeking professional help, and participating in research.
www.ncbi.nlm.nih.gov/pubmed	PubMed website has more than 21 million citations for biomedical literature from MEDLINE, life science journals, and online books, some of which discuss contributors to mental disorders. Citations may include links to full-text content of the citations.
www.aacap.org	Website of the American Academy of Child and Adolescent Psychiatry (AACAP), which addresses concerns about health care and socioeconomic issues affecting children. Has a number of articles on mental health topics by recognized professionals in the field. Also provides practice parameters for children of all ages.
www.nccp.org	Website for the National Center for Children in Poverty (NCCP). It emphasizes preventing or alleviating poverty as well as documenting its effects on development. A number of papers are available on these topics.
www.kimfoundation.org	Website for the Kim Foundation, which has articles on the causes of mental illness.

2

Overview of Screening and Assessment Within Various Areas of Functioning

Many approaches to assessing and treating children with complex mental health issues focus on describing and treating the symptoms, surface behaviors, and disorders. A child might be given a diagnosis used to determine the type of intervention with little or no information on his underlying functioning or the most appropriate individualized treatment strategies to be provided for the specific difficulties identified by the assessment (Greenspan & Wieder, 2000). Such an approach ignores the new information on neuroplasticity of the brain, which indicates that three important facts need to be considered in providing assessment and treatment for children: (1) brain development is not static, and changes are possible well past the first 5 years of life and into adulthood; (2) any interventions that can make changes in the brain need to be focused on the area of the brain that is compromised and be intense and repetitive to be successful; and (3) interventions that focus on changing thoughts or other aspects of the mind can also change brain functioning, including its neurochemistry (Doidge, 2007; Schwartz & Begley, 2002). An example of this kind of focused intervention is enhancing phonological awareness for children with dyslexia, or difficulties learning to read, to change brain repetitive to be successful; and (3) interventions (Merzenich et al., 1996). Similarly, for depression, using a mindfulness-based approach or focusing on changing thoughts, combined with medication, has been found to change activation of various brain areas, change regional brain metabolism, and to be more successful in preventing relapse following treatment than using medication alone (Farb et al., 2010; S. H. Kennedy et al., 2007; Siegel, 2007).

In this book, the emphasis is on understanding and describing both the factors contributing to the child's presentation outlined in Chapter 1 and the problems in the underlying functional developmental capacities in the areas discussed in Section 2. A critical first step in achieving this understanding is conducting screening and preliminary assessment to identify problem areas of functioning. Further comprehensive assessment of deficits and strengths in various recognized areas can inform the implementation of targeted intervention strategies. To reflect the complexities of the presentations of many children, a comprehensive and multidisciplinary approach to assessment is necessary. Only in this way can strategies be individualized to focus on the child's deficits in a way most likely to be successful in changing the underlying brain structure and behavior. In this chapter, the process of screening and assessment is described using a number of case vignettes.

Although many agencies will not have ready access to a neuropsychologist, a neuropsychological "approach" to assessment is recommended (Baron, 2004). Since the advent of noninvasive neuroimaging techniques, neuropsychological assessments have shifted from localizing lesions to "identifying functional profiles of an individual's strengths and weaknesses" (Miller, 2007, p. 23). Such an assessment provides an understanding of the child's behavior and psychological functioning in terms of brain–behavior relationships and the underlying functioning of the nervous system (Bernstein & Waber, 2003). The findings can inform an understanding of when to make appropriate referrals for further assessment when issues with brain functioning are suspected.

Rather than using only one or two psychometric measures such as an intelligence test or a parent questionnaire, a neuropsychological approach to assessment uses a number of ways to assess a broad range of functions such as language, attention, and concentration, fine and gross motor skills, as well as emotional and personality functioning. This type of assessment is based on an understanding of the developing brain and the neural substrates responsible for various behaviors and functions. As well, this type of assessment uses an approach referred to as cross-battery assessment (XBA), in which various standardized and normed tests are augmented with subtests from other measures to obtain important information about circumscribed aspects of the child's functioning (Flanagan & Ortiz, 2007).

PRINCIPLES OF SCREENING AND ASSESSMENT

General

1. Early screening and assessment are critical as changes in the brain are more easily achieved in the early years, so a "wait and see" approach is not recommended.

Sources of Information

2. Information needs to be obtained from several sources (e.g., developmental history, observations, parent and teacher questionnaires, and test performance).
3. Whenever possible, it is helpful to see the child in her group setting (daycare or school), her home, and other community settings. Often these observations can dramatically increase understanding of the issues that she is facing and the type of interventions that will be useful.

Case Study: Elijah

Elijah had been referred for assessment by his parents prompted by staff at the nursery school that he attended. Issues included difficulties with fine and gross motor control and expressive language. Staff were concerned that Elijah was being neglected by his parents, both busy professionals. The father's job involved frequent travel. Staff were concerned that Elijah often came to nursery school looking disheveled and thought that his mother rushed off too quickly when she dropped him off in the morning, leaving him upset and disoriented.

To explore these possible family issues, a home visit was scheduled, and the intervener was invited to attend the family evening meal. Elijah's father was at home as well, giving her a great opportunity to get to know the family. The intervener arrived as dinner was being prepared, and Elijah proudly announced that he was helping his mother cook and showed the intervener how he was mixing the salad and stirring a sauce while his mother stood close by to help him. He also helped his younger sister set the table. The family chatted together until the meal was ready. It was Elijah's turn to say grace, and everyone held hands while Elijah said his favorite prayer. After dinner, the intervener was invited to join the children in their bedroom as their father read them some favorite stories.

Tucked into bed, Elijah was soon asleep. A few days later the intervener spotted Elijah and his father in a store and watched while Elijah laughed hilariously as he hid in one of the shelves until his father found him, a game that they both seemed to enjoy immensely. These observations provided a very different understanding of the family and enabled the examiner to explore other issues by screening Elijah's fine and gross motor skills and referring Elijah for an occupational therapy assessment. It soon became clear that he had significant issues with motor planning, fine motor control, and dyspraxia that contributed to his difficulties in dressing and other self-care activities and significantly affected his expressive language and enunciation.

Elijah arrived at nursery school looking somewhat disheveled because he insisted on dressing himself in the morning even though he struggled to do up buttons and tuck in his shirt. His mother, a lawyer, often had to drop him off and leave quickly because she had to be in court by 9 a.m. and could not stay long at the nursery school.

Approaches to Assessment

4. The purpose of the assessment is not specifically to make a diagnosis but to understand the child's functioning in a number of developmental areas.
5. A multidisciplinary approach to assessment is crucial to understanding the complexity of presentation of children referred for treatment. Ideally, the disciplines involved will include pediatrics, psychiatry, psychology, social work, physiotherapy, speech and language pathology, occupational therapy, and others.
6. A flexible battery, rather than fixed battery, approach (using a strictly controlled series of tests) allows for a more individualized and eclectic use of tests to respond to the referral question and the child's needs.
7. As described in this chapter, a process approach to assessment is recommended in which a set of screening measures is used first, allowing hypotheses to be developed about the nature of the child's difficulties. In a decision-tree fashion, these initial screening measures then guide the rest of the assessment process, particularly the selection of instruments to test the areas of functioning suspected of being compromised in a particular child (see Figure 2.1).
8. The length and style of the assessment must be adapted to the age of the child and his difficulties with, for example, changes in routine or attention and concentration. In some instances, short testing sessions with several rewards and incentives might be necessary to get an optimal performance.
9. Although it is important to maintain a standardized administration of tests to ensure validity whenever possible, observing how a child solves a problem or answers a question can be as important as the scores achieved. Such a process approach can determine what is impacting the child's performance. This can also include "testing the limits" by, for example, extending the time limit or crediting items passed beyond the official ceiling cutoff. The scores can then be reported as potential scores that show what a child is capable of if accommodations can be made in the classroom to compensate for her problems.

Case Study: Molly

Six-year-old Molly was referred because of concerns about her intellectual capacity, schoolwork, and possible attention deficit/hyperactivity disorder (ADHD) (attentional type). The school was

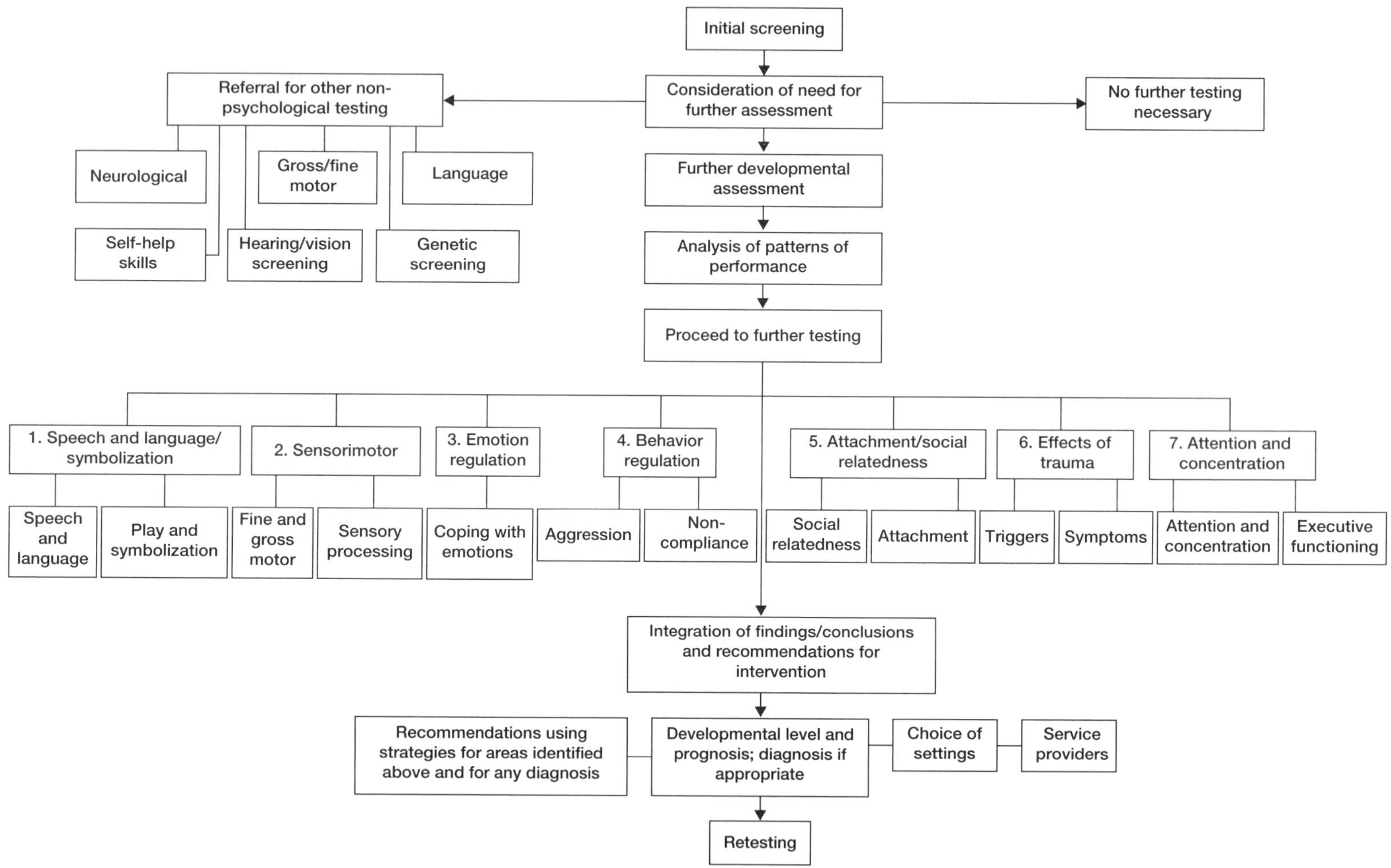

Figure 2.1 *Decision-tree model.*

also concerned about her "stubbornness" and refusal to accept the help that she needed with her academic work.

Molly had a history of severe abuse and neglect until she went to live with her grandparents at 3.5 years of age. She had also been found at 4 years of age to have a severe conductive hearing loss in one ear and intermittent hearing loss in the other ear due to frequent ear infections. At the time of her assessment, Molly was wearing a hearing aid in one ear and had grommets inserted into the other ear so that her hearing was much better than it had been in the past. However, her speech was still affected, and the audiologist indicated that background noise in the classroom could still make it hard for her to understand when multiple instructions were given to the class. Also, she needed people to speak loudly for her to understand them.

Molly was happy to come for testing, and her grandmother accompanied her to the first session and this helped her feel safe. Molly was found to have low average ability for verbal and nonverbal subtests but did better on nonverbal tests. She refused any help, such as moving her chair closer to the table or supporting the page to get her started with writing, even when the task was difficult. It was only possible for Molly to complete two subtests at once before she became exhausted, but she willingly returned to the testing after a snack and playing with some soft toys in the room. During formal testing, by extending the cut-off time limit, she could do much better and get higher than average scores in some nonverbal subtests. Her grandmother reported that the "stubbornness" with her and her husband was significantly reduced at home, as she put it, "as Molly and her twin brother begin to feel much safer with us." Discussion with the audiologist suggested that Molly was still finding concentrating on verbal stimulation very difficult and could become tired quickly with the type of effort required for her to do her work.

From the assessment and further observation of Molly in the classroom, it was found that, with visual cues and an aide to support her with her academic work, she could keep up with her classmates in completing her work. It was also concluded that Molly did not have ADHD and that her concentration and oppositional issues were caused by her hearing loss and the past abuse and neglect, contributing to a need to feel in control of things. Recommendations for enhancing her schoolwork and behavior were then made.

Recommendations for Intervening With the Child and Family

10. Conclusions from the assessment are discussed separately for each functional area but need to be integrated in a way that can make sense of the data for parents, teachers, and other professionals.

11. Assessments are useless unless interventions can be provided in the home and school/daycare and are accessible in the community. These interventions can help the child to generalize skills across various settings.

Case Study: Luke

Luke, age 8 years, was referred for assessment because he was acting out at home and school and because his mother was sure that he must have "some kind of brain problem or autism." He had been assessed for many types of disorder and, though he met criteria for ADHD, had not been diagnosed with any other problem. History included harsh and punitive punishment from early on and a father who could not tolerate spending any time with him. The couple's relationship was significantly impacted by Luke's behavior, believed to have started at 18 months, when his sister was born. Testing did not find that Luke was on the autism spectrum but did show that his intellectual capacity was limited, especially with respect to complex reasoning and working memory. When presented with tasks requiring these skills, Luke became very upset and disorganized. When he came to a specialized classroom for assessment, he was found to have severe difficulty with speech and language and with reading and mathematics. He also became very upset when he was touched and dissociated when this happened.

His complex presentation was discussed with his parents, who were able to have more empathy for his struggles but needed clear instructions on how to show Luke empathy and interact with him. His father began to spend some individual time with him going fishing, an activity that both enjoyed. Teachers were given a number of strategies to help Luke with his schoolwork and were able to support his efforts to play with others on the playground. Knowing how much he struggled intellectually, his parents made sure that they noticed his small achievements and in school he was given some responsibility helping teachers in the classroom, which he did consistently and enjoyed very much.

---

12. In recommending intervention strategies, it is important to be aware that approaches used to enhance development in children with a particular diagnosis might also be appropriate for children who do not meet those diagnostic criteria or have other diagnoses. For example, approaches such as the use of social stories that were developed for autistic children to enhance social abilities might also be helpful for children diagnosed with oppositional defiant disorder (ODD) who lack social skills and have no friends.

THE PROCESS OF ASSESSMENT

As expressed by Lidz (2003, p. 3), "one word that will guide assessment is *multiple.* … [W]e will need multiple samples of data from multiple sources in multiple contexts." She points out that the child needs to be seen in a number of settings using a variety of measures that collect data from many different functional domains. Consequently, for children with multiple complex needs, assessment takes time, several hours over a number of days. The process of assessment is described next.

Referral and First-Interview Sessions

When a child is referred for treatment, vital information is collected, including her name, date of birth, and the names of parent(s) or guardian(s). Names and relationships of other people in the home, including siblings and other children and adults, and the address and phone number of the family, are noted. Reasons for the referral and a full description of any symptoms and diagnoses are also collected. Information on any past assessments and treatments is also gathered. The name of the daycare or school that the child attends, names of the daycare or classroom teacher, and principal, as well as names of her family physician and pediatrician should be included.

The main purpose of the first two interviews with the parent(s) or guardian(s) is to gather information about the child and family and provide information to the family about the program and how it might help the child and family. These sessions can serve to develop rapport and begin a collaborative partnership with the parents and provide an opportunity to obtain information on level 1 of causality (see Figure I.1).

There are differing opinions about how best to conduct these initial sessions, particularly whether the child should be included in the first session. Some argue that it is important to see the whole family first to understand its dynamics and issues with parenting and the parents' relationship. They argue that this understanding is fundamental to decisions about the kind of treatment to be offered. Those who argue for this approach believe that negative comments about the child in the interview are often said to the child in the home anyway. Others argue that the parent(s) should be seen without the child in the first session so that they can speak freely about the child's difficulties and any challenges that they have with the child. That is the position adopted in this book (if it is possible to have more than one session). This can promote trust since the parents feel understood and heard about how difficult it is to manage their child.

In the two interviews, the parents are asked about the following topics:

- They are asked about their child's problems, when they started, how they seemed to begin, and what symptoms the child has and what areas of development are affected. The intervener might want to ask further questions about various areas of development identified as problematic. It is important to get both parents to talk about the child's problems, what they believe is contributing to them, and what they see as being helpful and to record whether there is any disagreement, particularly regarding the best ways to deal with the child's issues.
- Parents are asked about whether the pregnancy was planned and/or wanted and how they both adjusted to it. The mother's pregnancy, any complications, how the mother felt physically and psychologically, and things that went on during the 9 months are discussed. The mother is also asked about anxiety and depression, use of medication, including alcohol, drugs, and cigarettes, and illnesses during the pregnancy.
- Events that occurred before, during, and after the pregnancy are discussed. They could include the death of a close relative that caused feelings of grief and loss. If parents are immigrants, issues of adjustment to their new country and culture can be important.
- Details about length of the pregnancy and birth history are obtained. For example, was the birth long and protracted or short, and were there any complications? The baby's birth weight, Apgar scores, if they are available, and the child's condition at birth are enquired about. How both mother and father felt about having a baby is examined.
- A detailed developmental history is obtained, including length of stay in the hospital and what the baby was like during the stay as well as her condition in the first few weeks at home. This information should include how responsive she was as a baby, whether she looked at adults and liked to be held or seemed to push away and find being touched difficult. It is also important to get information about early temperament, irritability, or colic, whether the baby was breast-or bottle-fed, and how soon she settled into a predictable eating and sleeping routine. Some caregivers find it hard to remember this information, particularly to pinpoint when it occurred, whereas others can get sidetracked as they try to recall details of how things were. In this case, it is important to bring them back to the questions to fill in any gaps in the information requested. Information on how the child was as a toddler and preschooler is also requested on issues such as eating and sleeping, activity level, interest in toys, concentration and attention, tantrums, and ability to play with other children.
- Information about when the child first did the following is collected:

  - rolled over
  - sat up alone
  - crawled
  - slept through the night
  - walked
  - said first words
  - used sentences
  - climbed
  - ran
  - rode a bike
  - skipped

Any comments about delays and unusual behavior, such as extreme tantrums, aggression, hurting animals, and lighting fires, are also requested. For older children, information on their behavior in school is very important. Other important questions include whether the child would come to the parents when hurt and if he showed separation anxiety and how he dealt with transitions. When he first began to have problems and how he dealt with them are also important. Asking the parents to describe their child and their hopes and dreams for him and anything that they worry about concerning his future can also be revealing.

It is important also to ask the parents about possible trauma and age of exposure. Explaining that this could be an accident, abuse, domestic violence, a natural disaster such as a flood or hurricane, or seeing something scary is important. If something like this happened, how did the child behave after it, and what did the parents do to help her recover from it.

Information about illnesses (acute or chronic), medical interventions, hospitalizations, vision and hearing problems, and medications taken previously and currently might be important. Also asking about the child's current functioning in the following areas is essential:

- gross and fine motor development
- balance and coordination
- ability to concentrate and do tasks
- managing emotions
- responses to various sensory experiences
- language and communication
- playing symbolic games, games with rules, and social games
- social ability, friends, and capacity for empathy
- behavioral difficulties in the home and/or school
- sleeping and eating
- self-help skills such as dressing, feeding, toileting, and bathing

In the second interview, it is also important to ask the caregivers about their own histories, relationships with their families of origin and peers, experiences in school, and traumas experienced while growing up. A history of autism, psychosis, depression or anxiety, seizures, or medical diseases in the family is specifically asked about.

It is important to listen to how the parents describe their child and observe how they interact with him, whether he is seen as damaged, powerful, and in control of them. Having each parent play with the child and allowing the clinician to interact with him for about 10 to 15 minutes each can show how relationship differences might be affecting his behavior. The parents' body language, gestures, tone of voice, and conversation together and in interaction with the child can be helpful in understanding his presentation.

Observation of the child for dysmorphic or unusual facial features (e.g., lowered ears, unusual spacing of the eyes, size of the head, and hairline), unusual mannerisms, signs of seizure, or memories of trauma triggered in the interview is important.

Seeing the older child alone talking about her experiences at home and school (particularly being bullied, not understanding schoolwork, or feeling "dumb") can also be helpful. Questions can include the following. What do you worry about? What makes you sad, afraid, or angry? If you could have three wishes, what would they be? Whom would you take to a desert island if you were going to be there for a while? What would you like to be different in your life?

During this session, the parents are informed that, after the child has been assessed, the multidisciplinary team will meet to make decisions about whether to proceed with further assessment, and following that the development of appropriate interventions to help the child and family will occur.

A checklist for the initial interviews is provided in Table 2.1. A number of prompts might be needed to obtain missing information. Sometimes parents have maintained a written record of their child's development that can be useful.

SCREENING OF THE CHILD

Figure 2.1 is a diagram of the decision-tree model used in this book. Screening is the first step to a further comprehensive assessment of functional areas in which possible difficulties have been identified. With information from the initial interviews, observations, and screening process, a decision can be made about the need for further testing. Screening instruments will vary according to the concerns raised. Apart from direct administration of an intelligence test, behavioral scales or questionnaires completed by the parents and teacher are recommended for use in screening as they are excellent tools for generating hypotheses about the potential causes of the child's current difficulties and can be useful for guiding the comprehensive testing.

Developmental and Intellectual Level

The first step of screening might consist of administering a developmental test or an intelligence test if there has been no test of this kind given in the past 2 or 3 years. Intelligence tests have advantages and some disadvantages. Advantages include communication across a variety of related disciplines familiar with such tests, comparison with children of similar chronological age and specific scores on subtests, and domain index scores (e.g., verbal, nonverbal, working memory, and processing speed) that can give important clues about potential strengths and weaknesses in various functioning areas and offer hypotheses to guide further testing. This informs the assessment team about the child's capacity to function, how the child processes data, and how well she can concentrate. Disadvantages include limited predictive reliability and validity for young children. Furthermore, the results are meaningful only if integrated with the child's history, observations, and information from further testing. The scores alone are never enough to understand how the child perceives, processes, expresses, and integrates information.

A number of standardized measures that can be used for this part of the screening process are described next, beginning with intellectual assessments.

The Bayley Scales of Infant and Toddler Development (3rd ed.) (*Bayley-III;* Bayley, 2006) assesses developmental functioning of infants and young children from 1 month to 42 months of age. They are used to identify children with developmental delays so that intervention strategies can be planned. There are three scales: Cognitive Scale, Language Scale (receptive and expressive communication subtests), and Motor Scale (fine and gross motor subtests). The Social Emotional Scale and Adaptive Behavior Scale are completed by the parent or primary caregiver. The *Bayley-III* normative sample was based on 1,700 children divided into 17 age groups from 1 month to 42 months, stratified according to the U.S. census by parent age, gender, parent education, race/ethnicity, and geographical region. The scales' reliability was established by the split-half method, with the average reliability coefficients ranging from 0.86 to 0.91. Test–retest reliability showed high stability coefficients, as did inter-rater reliability correlation coefficients. Validity studies comparing Bayley-III with other tests, including the *Wechsler Preschool and Primary Scale of Intelligence* (3rd ed.) (*WPPSI-III;* Wechsler, 2002), *Preschool Language Scale-4* (Zimmerman, Violettte, Steiner, & Pond, 2007), *Peabody Developmental Motor Scales* (Folio, & Fewell, 2000), and *Peabody Picture Vocabulary Test*, 4th edition *(PPVT-4)* (Dunn & Dunn, 2007). The scales were also found to be sensitive to performance differences in a number of special groups.

Ages and Stages Questionnaires: A Parent Completed, Child Monitoring System (3rd ed.) (*ASQ;* Bricker & Squires, 1999) is a broad screening tool for overall child development from 4 to 60 months that monitors five key areas: communication, gross motor, fine motor, problem solving, and personal–social skills. The questionnaires are photocopiable and culturally sensitive, field tested, and research validated. Cut-off points indicate low and high risk and the need for referral to further testing. There are also Social Emotional Questionnaires that monitor the child's social and emotional development. Although the system has not been normed, internal consistency is relatively high, particularly at younger ages. Test–retest stability has been found after 2 weeks. Concurrent validity has found high agreement with other tests, particularly when children have developmental delays.

Vineland Adaptive Behavior Scales (2nd ed.) (*VABS*; Sparrow, Cicchetti, & Balla, 2005) measures adaptive behavior from birth to 18 years, 11 months in four domains: Communication, Daily Living, Socialization, and Motor Skills. The test can be administered as a semistructured interview or in survey form by a respondent who is familiar with the child. Standard scores, percentiles, and age equivalents are determined for each area as well as a total Adaptive Behavior Composite Score (ABCS) obtained. It has been nationally standardized, stratified by gender, age, race, geographical region, size of community, and parental education. The second edition norms include representation from special populations such as autism spectrum disorders and developmental disabilities. Test–retest reliability coefficients, for an average of 17 days between tests, were high at younger ages and for the ABCS. Correlations between the *VABS* and the *Adaptive Behavior Inventory for Children, Kaufman Assessment Battery for Children*, and *Peabody Picture Vocabulary Test–Revised* ranged from low to moderate, supporting the assumption that adaptive behavior and intelligence and achievement scales measure different areas of functioning. Higher coefficients were obtained when comparisons were made on subjects with handicapping conditions.

Wechsler Preschool and Primary Scale of Intelligence (3rd ed.) (*WPPSI-III*; Wechsler, 2002) assesses the intellectual ability of children from 2.5 to 7.3 years and provides an overall intellectual ability and Full Scale IQ. It is the downward extension of the *Wechsler Intelligence Scale for Children* (4th ed.) (*WISC-IV*). Normative information was based on 1,700 children in nine age groups stratified by educational level, race/ethnicity, and geographical region. Reliability using the split-half method compared with the *Wechsler Preschool and Primary Scale of Intelligence-Revised* (*WPPSI-R*; Wechsler, 1989) ranged from 0.83 to 0.95 for various subtests. For the composite scales, they ranged from 0.89 to 0.95. Test–retest stability from 14 to 50 days ranged from 0.70 to 0.89. Validity studies found internal consistency of factor scores across subsamples of children. Relationships to other measures found high correlations with a number of other tests, including the *Children's Memory Scale, Wechsler Individual Achievement Test–II*, and *Bayley Scales of Infant Development–II*. Special group studies in a number of educational settings (e.g., intellectually gifted, mentally retarded, motor impaired, and ADHD) found strong support for the validity and clinical utility of the *WPPSI-III* to distinguish between normal populations and special groups.

Wechsler Intelligence Scale of Children (4th ed.) (*WISC-IV*; Wechsler, 2004) is an individually administered test for assessing cognitive ability in children from 6 years to 16 years, 11 months. It provides four composite indexes: Verbal Comprehension, Perceptual Reasoning, Working Memory, and Processing Speed as well as a Full Scale IQ. The U.S. standardization edition of the *WISC-IV* was obtained from a stratified sample of 2,200 children who reflected key demographic variables in the U.S. national population. Test–retest stability showed adequate stability across time for all age groups. Validity was assessed by comparing *WISC-IV* scores with scores on other cognitive and achievement tests, with low to moderate correlations found between them. *WISC-IV* results were also able to distinguish between a number of clinical groups.

Other Screening Tests

The various tests suggested next can be used for screening in the functioning areas at Level 3. A number of other tests are available, so these are suggestions only. On the basis of these results, further testing will occur in the areas of development found to be compromised.

Table 2.1 *Checklist for the Initial Interviews About the Child*

Questions (check whether the information was asked for and given)	Yes	No
The child		
Pregnancy, birth, and perinatal information		
Was the baby planned/wanted?		
Events that occurred close to the pregnancy		
Any use of alcohol or other substances, smoking, medications?		
Mother's level of anxiety and depression during the pregnancy		
Any illnesses during the pregnancy?		
Any complications?		
Gestation period (length of pregnancy)		
Birth, length of labor, complications, vaginal delivery or cesarian		
Anything that was traumatic about the birth?		
Baby's condition at birth, Apgar scores, any concerns		
Birth weight and length		
Parents' feelings about the child when they first saw him or her		
Other		
Child's developmental history		
Baby's condition in the hospital, any interventions necessary?		
When did mother and baby go home from the hospital?		
How responsive was the baby immediately after birth and in the first few days?		
Did the baby cry a lot, have colic?		
Feeding, how easily was it established?		
Breast-feeding, for how long? Bottle-feeding?		
Establishing an eating and sleeping routine: How easy, when?		
Age when the child		
Rolled over		
Walked upstairs		
Sat alone		
Dressed self		
Crawled		
Was toilet-trained		
Stood alone		
Walked		
Said first word		
Used sentences		
Ate solids		
Did the child have any developmental problems?		
Any eating and/or sleeping problems?		
Other		

(*continued*)

Table 2.1 *Checklist for the Initial Interviews About the Child* (*continued*)

Questions (check whether the information was asked for and given)	Yes	No
Attachment history		
When did mother feel bonded or attached to her child?		
When did the child show signs of being attached (cried at strangers, cried when left)?		
Did the child show separation anxiety when first left?		
Do parents feel that their child is attached to them now?		
How do the parents feel this child is compared to the other children in the family with being attached?		
Does the child come to them if hurt, ill, or upset?		
Quality of attachment		
Other		
History of child difficulties and trauma		
When did the child first have difficulties, and what were they?		
Any idea as to why they began?		
Did anything different happen around that time?		
How would the parents describe their child's temperament, and when did they first notice the characteristics?		
Shy and inhibited		
Uninhibited and impulsive		
Irritability		
Mood (e.g., generally negative or positive)		
Adjusts to new things or finds change difficult		
Activity level		
Regular routine and rhythm easily established or hard to set up		
Sensitivity to stimulation in the environment (e.g., sights, sounds, touch, textures in food)		
Intensity of reactions		
Distractibility		
Persistence and attention span		
When did parent notice delays or emotional or social difficulties?		
Time and date of any trauma or loss (e.g., accident, violence, abuse, natural disasters)		
Other		
Child's medical history, mental health conditions		
Any chronic illnesses		
Any other acute illnesses		
Hospitalizations, surgeries, and/or injuries		
Vision problems		
Hearing and auditory processing difficulties		
Syndrome?		
Seizures or convulsions?		
Biological and/or developmental issues (e.g., fetal alcohol syndrome)		
Mental health diagnoses and comorbidities		
Other		

Table 2.1 *Checklist for the Initial Interviews About the Child* (*continued*)

Questions (check whether the information was asked for and given)	Yes	No
Current functioning of the child		
Gross and fine motor skills		
Balance and coordination		
Sensory processing		
Speech and language		
Quality of attachment		
Ability to concentrate and do tasks		
Can the child label feelings? How does he manage emotions?		
Managing behavior		
Level of play and play themes		
Cognitive functioning and any learning disabilities		
Academic progress		
Social ability, perspective taking, and capacity for empathy		
Any allergies		
Sleeping and eating		
Self-help skills (e.g., feeding, dressing, bathing, toileting)		
Sense of self and level of self-esteem		
Peer group and friends		
Bully or victim		
Other		
Previous assessments and interventions		
Mental and physical assessments		
Treatments		
Other		
Parents and family		
Parents' history, including genetic history		
Parents' history growing up (e.g., relationship with parents, trauma, rejection, abuse, or neglect)		
Mental or physical illnesses on mother's and father's side of the family		
Other		
Style of parenting and marital relationship		
Style of discipline (authoritarian, permissive, authoritative)		
Attributions of the child		
Nurturing and response to the child's emotions		
Coercive patterns of parent—child interactions		
Marital relationship, level of conflict, or violence		
Single parent		
Teenage parent		
Things they have tried to overcome the child's challenges		
Other		

(*continued*)

Table 2.1 *Checklist for the Initial Interviews About the Child* (*continued*)

Questions (check whether the information was asked for and given)	**Yes**	**No**
Parent support and sources of stress		
Level of support from family and friends		
Sources of stress (e.g., unemployment, lack of suitable housing, poverty)		
Single and/or teenage parent		
Low socioeconomic circumstances or poverty		
Other		
Parents' mental and physical health (current and past)		
Physical illnesses of either parent		
Mental illness, including depression, substance abuse, or criminality, or antisocial behavior of either parent		
Cognitive problems		
Disorganized and chaotic lifestyle		
Unresolved loss and trauma		
Other		
Neighborhood		
High level of violence in the community		
Poor schools and other facilities		
School's understanding of the child		
Presence of gangs		
Peer group and friends		
Other		

Interview With the Child

The interviewer can use open-ended questions and "how" and "why" questions to elicit information. Questions about what the child enjoys doing and finds rewarding can be helpful to start the interview. Asking her about why she believes the referral was made can provide valuable information. Questions about the family, worries, frustrations, and the situation at school and home can also be asked. Projective questions about her three wishes, whom she would take to a desert island, and the things she does with her family can yield useful information. Asking children about how well they sleep, what they become anxious about, and what they do when they are upset and anxious can also be useful, though some children will refuse to answer or be unable to express their opinions or feelings. With younger children, it might be easiest to let them play out their experiences with suitable toys.

Speech, Language, and Symbolization

In this functional area, the level of capacity for pretend or symbolic play will be assessed for children up to about 5 years of age by observations in the play sessions with each parent and the examiner. This will include the child's capacity to create a play theme and develop it into a story with characters that has some beginning, middle, and ending or is in sequence. The sessions will also provide the opportunity to observe the child's ability to interact in the play with others. A list for guiding this observation is provided in Table 2.2, and further information is provided in Chapter 4.

Table 2.2 *Observing Play Interactions*

- Which themes predominate play (e.g., destruction, nurturing, anxiety about certain situations, fights between good and bad, pride in achievement, oral themes about eating)?
- How long can the child remain absorbed in play?
- Which emotions are shown (e.g., joy and happiness, anxiety, apathy, anger, and frustration)?
- Is the play creative and varied or repetitive, rigid, or obsessive?
- Is the play organized, or does it seem fragmented and disorganized?
- How complex or elaborate is the play, and which objects and toys are chosen?
- Does the child show the capacity for symbolic play and imagination?
- Are there any real-life stresses or developmental issues that the child appears to be struggling with?
- Can the child deal with difficult themes and emotions without the play becoming chaotic?
- Any evidence of self-talk or private speech used to direct an activity or calm the child down?

The following tests are recommended for screening speech and language. For younger children, the *Early Language Milestone Scale,* 2nd ed. (*ELM Scale–2*; Coplan, 1990) is recommended. The Scale is useful for routine developmental screening of young children. It can be used from birth to 4 years of age, has 43 items, and takes 5 to 10 minutes to administer. It was developed as an early-identification tool to recognize language delays in children at an early stage. It assesses language development from birth to 36 months and intelligibility of speech from 18 to 48 months. The Scale is divided into three skill categories: Auditory Expressive, Auditory Receptive, and Visual. Information on each item can be collected by parents, by the parent providing a history of language development, and by direct testing or observation. It was normed on 191 children, mostly Caucasian and English speaking. The Scale has moderate concurrent validity with the *Peabody Picture Vocabulary Test–Revised* (*PPVT–R*). In one study, the *ELM* was found to have good agreement with the *Sequenced Inventory of Communication Development* (*SICD*) and correctly classified language level in 79% of 13- to 24-month-old infants and 89% of 25- to 36-month-old toddlers (Walker, Gugenheim, Downs, & Northern, 1989).

For older children, the *Children's Communication Checklist* (2nd ed.) (*CCC-2*; Bishop, 2003) is recommended. It can be used from 4 to 16 years of age and has 70 items. It is completed by the parent or other adult who has regular contact with the child and provides a description of how the child communicates in everyday settings such as home and school. It assesses language with scales for speech, syntax, semantics, coherence, inappropriate initiation, stereotyped language, use of context, nonverbal communication, social relations, and interests. The test can be used to screen for children likely to have language impairment and identify pragmatic problems in children with communication problems. The Social Interaction Deviance Composite (SIDC) can identify children with a communicative profile of autism. The CCC-2 was standardized on 542 parent-completed checklists of children from the general population in the United Kingdom. It was found to have a mean of 10 and *SD* of 3, converted to percentiles. Reliability showed Cronbach's alphas ranging from 0.66 to 0.80 for normal children. Validity among clinical groups diagnosed with specific language impairment, pragmatic language difficulties without autism, high-functioning autism, compared with normal controls, found that all subscale scores of the clinical groups were significantly lower. The test was also sensitive in separating communication disorders from autistic spectrum disorders.

Fine and Gross Motor and Sensory Integration

A screen for parents to complete about their child's development and any problems in these areas is provided in Chapter 3. The areas addressed include gross and fine motor development, vision, activities of daily living, behavior, and sensory areas. Parents are asked to identify the areas in which their children have problems.

Emotion and Behavior Regulation

Some excellent measures can be completed by parents and teachers that give information about the child's functioning in a number of areas, including difficulties with managing emotions and behavior. The questionnaires recommended are the *Child Behavior Checklist* (*CBCL*; Achenbach, 2000), *Behavior Assessment System for Children*, 2nd ed. (*BASC-2*) (Reynolds & Kamphaus, 2004), and *Diagnostic Interview Schedule of Children* (*DISC-4*; (Robins, Marcus, Reich, Cunningham, & Gallagher, 1996).

The *CBCL* is a widely standardized measure that can identify children who display clinically elevated levels of behavior problems and aggression. There are two different sets of questionnaires for children from 1.5 to 5 years of age and from 6 to 18 years of age. There are teacher and parent questionnaires for each age group and a self-report version for 6- to 18-year olds. Each has over 100 items. It yields *T* scores and the percentile on which the results fall for externalizing scores (e.g., social problems, attention problems, and rule-breaking behavior), internalizing scores (e.g., anxious/depressed, withdrawn/depressed, and somatic complaints), and a total problem score. There are scores for the individual behavioral syndromes. All the scales of the *CBCL* have been shown to discriminate between referred and nonreferred samples. It is highly correlated with other parent checklists such as the Conners, Quay–Peterson, and Richman instruments. Test–retest reliability is 0.88 for the version for 6- to 18-year olds.

The *Behavior Assessment System for Children*, 2nd ed. (*BASC-2*; Reynolds & Kamphaus, 2005) is a set of rating scales and forms, including the Teacher Rating Scales (TRS), Parent Rating Scales (PRS), Self-Report of Personality (SRP), Student Observation System (SOS), and Structured Developmental History (SDH). The questionnaires are used to rate the behaviors and emotions of children and adolescents from 2 to 21 years, 11 months of age at three age levels: preschool (2–5), child (6–11), and adolescent (12–21). The scales that are scored include anger control, bullying, developmental social skills, emotional self-control, executive functioning, negative emotionality, and resiliency. The system can be used to identify children with difficulties with emotional and behavioral control and determine behaviors for intervention. Norms are based on the U.S. census population characteristics. Three types of reliability were used: internal consistency, test–retest, and inter-rater reliability. Internal consistency ranged from 0.67 to 0.90 for boys and from 0.64 to 0.98 for girls, test–retest reliability ranged from 0.84 to 0.95, and inter-rater reliability was reasonably high but somewhat lower. Three types of validity were also assessed: factor structure of the scales, correlations with other behavioral measures, and profiles of groups of children with certain clinical diagnoses. It was concluded that the factor models proposed for the measure are appropriate. Scores on the *BASC-2* have been found to correlate highly with scores on other measures of problem behaviors. Used with children with depression, ADHD, conduct disorder, and emotional and behavioral disturbances, high scores and low scores on the expected scales have been found.

Attachment and Social Skills

Scales on the *BASC-2* (e.g., Developmental Social Disorder) and *CBCL* (e.g., Social Problems Scale) can be used to provide information on the child's capacity to make friends and play with peers. Of course, this capacity will be somewhat related to her emotion and behavior regulation, for the child who is emotionally overaroused and/or aggressive with other children will have difficulty with this area of functioning. Information or screening for attachment can come from the mother's description of her relationship with her child, play observations of parent and child, and discussions about the child.

Attention, Concentration, and Executive Functioning

The Behavior Rating Inventory of Executive Function (*BRIEF*; Gioia, Isquith, Guy, & Kenworthy, 2000) is a questionnaire for parents and teachers of children aged 5 to 18 years. The Parent and Teacher Forms consist of 86 items and provide information on eight clinical scales that measure different aspects of executive functioning: Inhibit, Shift, Emotional Control, Initiate, Working Memory, Plan/Organize, Organization of Materials, and Monitor. There are also two validity scales, and the other scales form two broader indexes of Behavioral Regulation and Metacognition and a Global Executive Composite. Reliability was assessed for internal consistency, inter-rater reliability, and test–retest reliability. Internal consistency was high for both Parent and Teacher Forms, but correlations between parent and teacher ratings were moderate overall, with Initiate and Organization of Materials being lower. It is suggested that the demands of school are different from what is expected at home, accounting for the differences. Test–retest correlations showed stability across repeated administration. To test validity, content and construct validity were measured. Content validity was achieved by retaining items with high inter-rater agreement ratings. For construct validity, scores on the *BRIEF* were compared with results obtained on a number of other tests, including the Conners' Rating Scale, and the *BASC*, with generally moderate correlations found for the comparisons.

The *Conners* (3rd ed.) (*Conners-3*; Conners, 2008) is a focused assessment of ADHD and other comorbid problems and disorders in children from 6 to 18 years. There are short and long forms available for parent report, teacher report, and self-report that take into account functioning in home, social, and school settings. It can be used for screening purposes and intervention planning. The test assesses level of aggression, learning problems, inattention, hyperactivity/impulsivity, executive functioning, and peer relationships. The *Conners-3* was normed on a normative sample of 3,400 children stratified by age, gender, and race/ethnicity. Test–retest reliability and internal consistency are very good. Convergent validity (relationship of *Conners-3* to other related measures) and divergent validity (distinguishing children and youth with ADHD from youth in the general population) were high as well.

Academic tests can also be used if the child is reported to have learning problems in school. It is useful to use tests that are acceptable and used in the relevant school district.

Effects of Trauma

The developmental history and relevant family history interview asks parents about any trauma that their child experienced and when it occurred. Unfortunately, parents often do not understand that a number of small events or failures to respond to their infant and young child can be traumatizing for young children. It can be assumed, however, that if the mother suffered from severe postnatal depression, if there was family violence, or if one or both parents were using drugs and/or alcohol or were incarcerated, the child experienced some level of trauma. Under these circumstances, the parents likely did not provide the consistent containment and responsiveness needed for adequate brain development and to avoid hypersensitization (and sometimes hyposensitization) of the HPA axis and chronic secretion of stress hormones and other neurotransmitters.

Children 7 years of age or older can complete the *Trauma Symptom Checklist for Children* (*TSCC*; Briere, 1996), which asks the child about symptoms commonly found in posttraumatic stress disorder (PTSD). It can be used for children from 7 to 18 years of age. The clinical scales of the *TSCC* measure the extent to which the child endorses six scales (anxiety, depression, anger, posttraumatic stress, dissociation, and sexual concerns). There is another version (*TSCCA*) that makes no reference to sexual issues or asks about sexual behavior. It can be used if it is believed that a child or parents would be upset by being asked about sexual behaviors. Normative data are available on 3,008 nonclinical children, 2,399 children who were exposed to community violence, and smaller samples from a study of the effects of stressful life events and children at the Mayo Clinic whose relatives were medical patients there. Reliability and validity were acceptable.

If it is considered unsuitable to have the child complete the *TSCC*, parents of children 3 to 12 years of age can complete the *Trauma Symptom Checklist for Young Children* (*TSCYC*; Briere, 2007) which assesses eight clinical scales related to posttraumatic stress.

Generally, the symptoms reported in the two tests described above are unlikely to be present prior to the trauma. Instead, the child likely will have shown some of these behaviors following the trauma:

- repetitive aggressive play such as banging together cars, miniature people, or action figures, or replay of the traumatic event;
- regression of behavior and loss of capacity acquired at an earlier stage of development, such as no longer being toilet trained;
- dramatic shifts in emotions not previously seen (e.g., fearful and anxious, sad, or frustrated, and/or angry);
- onset of atypical behaviors such as masturbation to an extreme degree, sexual acting out, smearing of feces, destruction of objects, and hurting of animals and people at school or in the family;
- disruption of eating and sleeping and other routines;
- avoidance of children and adults with whom the child was previously friendly;
- academic regression and refusal to go to school.

Another technique developed over many years and supported by research by Mary Sue Moore (personal communication) that can be used with typically developing children involves having the child draw a person and then scoring the drawing for developmental age using the Goodenough–Harris Drawing Test (Harris, 1968) norms. Her experience leads her to believe that the child's response gives the age of the trauma within a 2-year range. For example, if the child has a developmental age of 10 years and draws a human figure at a developmental age of 5 years, then early trauma likely occurred between 4 and 6 years of age. The parents can then be asked about anything that happened to their child in this age range that could have been difficult for him. Sometimes narrowing the age down like this can help the parents to remember a trauma that happened to him at that time.

Another way to verify the occurrence of trauma is to watch for possible triggers when the child gets really upset or dissociates. They can include a loud voice, moving close to her without warning, touching her, and coming up to her from behind. It can also be something more subtle, such as moving away from her to help another child in the classroom or a change in facial expression or body language by someone close to her. Sometimes it is hard to know what has triggered the response, but the child's brain has been activated at a more primitive level such as the brainstem or limbic system area. See Table 2.3 for a list of various screening tests that can be used.

Table 2.3 *Screening Tests*

Type of Test	Name of Test and Type of Administration	Age Range
Developmental and intellectual level	*Bayley Scales of Infant and Toddler Development* (3rd ed.), administered to child	1 to 42 months
	Ages and Stages Questionnaires: A Parent Completed Child Monitoring System (2nd ed.), parent completed	4 to 60 months
	Vineland Adaptive Behavior Scales (2nd ed.), parent or teacher interview or parent or teacher completed	Birth to 18.11 years
	Wechsler Preschool and Primary Scale of Intelligence (3rd ed.), administered to child	Birth to 7 years
	Wechsler Intelligence Scale for Children (4th ed.), administered to child	6 to 16.11 years
Speech, language, and symbolization	*Early Language Milestone Scale* (2nd ed.), completed by parent or other caregiver who knows the child	Birth to 4 years
	Children's Communication Checklist (2nd ed.), parent completed	4 to 16 years
Fine and gross motor and sensory integration	*Occupational Therapy Screen*, parent completed	4 to 16 years
Emotion regulation	*Child Behavior Checklist* (internalizing and externalizing scales), parent and teacher completed	1.5 to 5 years
	Behavior Assessment System for Children (2nd ed.) (anger control, emotional self-control, and negative emotionality scales), parent, teacher, and self-report	2 to 21.11 years
Behavior regulation	*Child Behavior Checklist* (rule-breaking scale), parent and teacher completed	1.5 to 5 years
	Behavior Assessment System for Children (2nd ed.) (bullying, rule-breaking, behavior scales), parent, teacher, and self-report	2 to 21.11 years
Attachment and social skills	*Behavior Assessment System for Children* (2nd ed.) (social problem scale), parent, teacher, and self-report	2 to 21.11 years
Effects of trauma	*Trauma Symptom Checklist for Children*, completed by the child	3 to 12 years
	Trauma Symptom Checklist for Young Children, completed by the parent	3 to 12 years
Attention, concentration, and executive functioning	*Behavior Rating Inventory of Executive Functioning,* parent and teacher forms	5 to 18 years
	Conners (3rd ed.), parent and teacher forms	

The Testing Session

Testing sessions with the child can be extremely important in terms of the quantitative data that they provide about his intellectual capacity and other areas of functioning.

However, sessions can also be relevant in terms of *qualitative* aspects of his performance such as how he manages requirements of the testing, how long he can concentrate, what triggers any upset, and using "testing of the limits." These are informal techniques that go beyond standardized procedures, while maintaining sufficient rigor to score standardized tests validly, that provide additional information on potential and prognosis. A number of things about testing or assessment can be very difficult for young children, especially those with concentration difficulties and emotion and behavior regulation problems. It is therefore important to employ strategies to improve the child's performance. Some suggestions follow:

- Prepare everything ahead of time, including getting the stopwatch, relevant test materials and booklets, pencils, and other equipment needed.
- Clear the room of toys and other materials if possible. A sign should be placed on the door that testing is in progress to help avoid interruptions.
- Move as quickly through the subtests as possible without compromising testing. This is to get as much testing done while the child is able to concentrate well.
- Remember to keep sessions short. Some children who become overwhelmed are able to continue after a break and snack.
- Prepare the child by telling him that the test is for children of his age as well as older children, so there will be some questions that he cannot answer. Remind him of this if he begins to get discouraged about not being able to complete certain test items.
- Sometimes a parent might be invited into the initial testing session to help settle the child. However, the parent must be instructed not to repeat any of the questions since the test requires that set procedures are followed. How the parent behaves during the assessment can also provide valuable information.
- For children who find testing difficult, setting up a reward system can be very helpful; for example, the child could receive a star or sticker for concentrating and trying to do the questions or get a prize from a "treasure chest" at the end of the session.
- Let the child talk a little about her feelings about the testing and show empathy, but let her know that it is still important to complete the test.
- Take sequential notes about the child's behavior and range of responses to maintain a record that can be integrated into the assessment report and an explanation of the child's test behavior. Include the child's motivation to try hard and whether the child became discouraged or refused items. Also note any behavior outside the responses to the actual questions.

The Assessment Report

Although the results will be discussed with parents and teachers, it is critical to have a written report documenting the data for relevant people to view later. The assessment report will not be completed until the in-depth assessments have been conducted by the multidisciplinary team. Speech and language, occupational therapy, and academic reports will also be prepared separately. However, it is important that the main report, typically the Psychological Assessment Report, brings all the results together in a way that makes sense of the data. The importance of assessing children with complex needs is to report findings that will be useful to those involved with the child, including parents and other caregivers, teachers, physicians, and other professionals. Despite the need for detailed findings from the tests used in various areas of functioning, conclusions and recommendations need to be relatively brief, jargon free where possible, and not limited to one theoretical opinion or way of looking at the data and child. Recommendations need to be concrete and specific, with a focus on enhancing instruction in the classroom for the child, reducing difficult behaviors, and supporting caregivers and providers to meet the child's needs. Although parents are often satisfied with having a better understanding of their child, teachers and other service providers need concrete and useful suggestions to use while working with the child in the home or classroom. If these recommendations can be made in collaboration with teachers, then they are more likely to be useful and integrated into the classroom. Although recommendations should not be given in a recipe like fashion, developing a library of useful and up-to-date interventions for commonly occurring referral questions can be helpful. See Table 2.4 for an outline of an assessment report.

Table 2.5 provides an overview of the test findings. Column 1 summarizes any diagnoses that the child might have, column 2 provides a summary of other difficulties that the child has in various functional areas, and column 3 summarizes other issues in the family and the wider context, and notes strengths. It has been found to be very helpful in addition to the report to support understanding of the child's overall functioning.

Table 2.4 *Outline of the Assessment Report*

1. Identify the child's name, date of birth, and age at time of assessment, parents or guardians, date of assessment report, and examiner's name.
2. State the reason for referral as expressed by the referral source, and clearly explain the referral questions.
3. Note developmental, relevant family, and educational histories.
4. Indicate medical history and any biological and genetic issues.
5. Provide previous assessment results and treatments, and professionals still involved with the child.
6. Describe the child's testing behavior, including how well the child concentrated, processed data, what seemed to cause him the most difficulty, etc.
7. Tests used and testing procedures need to be listed to aid in understanding the current results and for any later re-evaluation.
8. Provide current results of screening tests and in-depth assessment in each of the developmental and functioning domains, including charts or figures where appropriate.
9. Detail information on the child's strengths and difficulties in each area assessed. Include diagnoses if appropriate and answer the referral questions.
10. Recommend practical strategies that can be used in the home and at school. Arrange recommendations from the most to the least important. Also emphasize any treatment that might enhance brain development in the areas of impairment (e.g., phonological awareness for children with dyslexia). Suggest how to use the child's strengths in the interventions. Also make suggestions for school placement and other referrals.
11. Summarize test scores in charts that include standard scores, error-of-measurement ranges, and percentile ranks. Additional charts can be provided, such as those in Table 4.5 and suggested interventions.

Table 2.5. *An Overview of the Test Findings*

Genetic/Biological/Neurological Intrinsic Disorders →	Clusters of Symptoms ↔	Other Contributing Factors
Pervasive developmental disorder (NOS) Difficulty socializing and developing peer relationships ■ Lack of social and emotional reciprocity ■ Problems with communication or sharing a conversation with other children ■ Some stereotyped and repetitive use of language ■ Inflexible adherence to routines and rituals ■ Lack of varied and spontaneous pretend play ***Executive dysfunction disorder/ADHD*** ■ Difficulty with inhibiting a response and shifting perspective ■ Difficulty with working memory or holding events in mind and working on them ■ Difficulty with getting started on an activity even when he knows what to do ■ Difficulty with self-regulation of affect and behavior ■ Difficulty with flexible responses and gets "stuck" with a particular idea and cannot be moved beyond it ***Anxiety and depression*** ■ Sometimes talks about wanting to kill himself ■ Very flat and sad much of the time ■ Worries because he has no friends but no energy to seek friends ***Epilepsy*** ■ Believed to have been brain damaged at birth ■ Has had mild seizures from early childhood, usually controlled by medication ■ Causes his parents much anxiety even though seizures are infrequent	***Social and peer relationship difficulties*** ■ Social awkwardness in language and adapting to novel social situations ■ Rejection and teasing by peers ■ Makes no attempt to connect with other children, though likes to talk to adults ■ Would rather play games on the computer than play with friends ■ Has been bullied due to his inappropriate behavior, such as trying to lick other children ***Impulsivity/lack of planning and problem solving*** ■ Flits from one subject to another in talking and learning ■ Lacks cause-and-effect thinking and understanding ■ Extremely distractible and can go off on tangents ■ Finds it hard to organize himself ■ Blurts out comments that have no real meaning to others ***Lacks any interests or hobbies*** ■ Topics often include things in the family that he is anxious about (e.g., finances, school he will attend) ■ Struggles with trying to understand why peers do not like him despite being given information ■ Wants to spend most of his time on the computer and does not want to spend his time on activities with others in spite of parents enrolling him in various activities ***Academic problems*** ■ Difficulties with reading and spelling in spite of an average IQ ■ Significant difficulties with copying material from the board ■ Problems with time management ■ Difficulties with abstract reasoning, making it hard for him to understand complex material ■ Significant difficulties with focusing and following through with his schoolwork ■ Suggestion that he might have dyslexia and is not making progress largely because of these difficulties	***Other challenges*** ■ Medical problems that began in infancy and have persisted (i.e., epilepsy) ■ Difficult parental separation with it being unclear where child will live ■ Maternal anxiety and depression ■ Frequent changes of schools ■ Learning problems result in child hating to attend school ■ Trauma from mother having left family on a number of occasions and his father finding it hard to care for him due to work commitments ■ Eating problems from infancy ■ Insecure attachments resulting from the many issues outlined above ■ Poor self-esteem and at risk for depression about isolation from peers ***Positives/strengths*** ■ Friendly, tries hard to connect with adults and wants to be accepted ■ Average intelligence and good at math ■ Has good relationship with father and paternal grandmother ■ Can acquire new skills if they are taught and well practiced and enjoys surfing with his father ■ Can persist with tasks when scaffolded and when it is something he enjoys

NOS: not otherwise specified.

CONCLUSION

This chapter describes the most important first step in providing services to children with multiple mental health challenges and their families: screening to identify problem areas of functioning of the child followed by further comprehensive multidisciplinary assessment. The second stage of assessment is completed by a team of various professionals, including a speech and language pathologist, occupational therapist, psychiatrist, psychologist, teacher, and pediatrician in order to provide an integrated view of the current functioning of the child. Referral to other specialists may also be necessary if deemed important. The assessment report also makes recommendations for treatment of the child in any of the identified areas of difficulty. The approach described, referred to as XBA, uses various standardized and normed tests augmented with subtests from other measures. The chapter also describes the whole process of assessment, including tests, interviews, and observations that can be used to carry out the screening and assessment. This is often the first time that such an integrated formulation and view of the child's issues has been available. The resulting report can therefore give parents and service providers involved with the child a critical understanding of any challenges that the child struggles with and can often change their negative attributions of the child to a more empathic understanding. In turn, this can enhance the choice of strategies adopted for dealing with his symptoms and any difficult and challenging externalizing or internalizing behaviors. In fact, the strategies for assessment described in this chapter provide an essential part of the process of meeting the needs of children with multiple mental health challenges.

Table 2.6 *Websites*

Website	Information on Website
www.nectac.org/~pdfs/pubs/screening.pdf	Website of the National Early Childhood Technical Assistance Center (NECTAC). Has a bibliography of developmental and screening instruments compiled by Ringwalt in 2008.
www.dbpeds.org	Website of the American Academy of Pediatrics has a web page on recommendations for preventive health care and specifies having a regular screening and assessment for children.
www.icjia.state.il.us	Website of the Illinois Juvenile Justice Commission Mental health screening and assessment, used in the Illinois juvenile system.
www.childrensdefense.org	The website of the Children's Defense Fund: Leave No Child Behind has a Children's Mental Health Resource Kit on mental health screens and assessment.
www.thereachinstitute.org	Resource for Advancing Children's Mental Health (REACH) institute has a tool kit to help parents, educators, and health professionals identify children at behavioral and emotional risk.
http://clas.uiuc.edu/review/childassessment.pdf	Website offers guidelines for selecting instruments on child assessment.
www.Vanderbilt.edu.csefel	The Center on the Social and Emotional Foundation for Early Learning at Vanderbilt University has a research synthesis on screening and assessing social—emotional competence.

(*continued*)

Table 2.6 *Websites (continued)*

Website	Information on Website
www.jgcp.ku.edu/grants/ecrimgd.htm	Website provides information about the reliability, validity, and practical utility of assessment instruments.
www.zerotothree.org	The Zero to Three website has a number of articles on assessment from birth to 3 years of age.
www.edc.gov/ncipc/pub-res/measures.htm	National Center for Injury Prevention and Control lists over 170 assessment instruments.
Websites of Commercial Publishers	
www.parinc.com	Website of PAR publishes psychological assessment materials and discusses assessment needs. Also publishes information on assessment and can provide training in the use of the tests.
www.wpspublish.com	Website of the Western Psychological Services (WPS). Publishes and distributes information on assessment tools, books, software, and therapy tools.
www.proedinc.com	Website of Pro-Ed publisher of standardized tests, books, curricular resources, and therapy materials.
www.Pearsonassess.com	Website of Pearson Assessment that distributes clinical and educational assessment tools.
www.psychcorp.com	Website of Psychological Corporation that distributes assessments.

3

Difficulties and Disorders of Motor Development and Sensory Processing

EVELYN SIM

As a child develops, one of the most obvious changes is his acquisition of motor skills. From his first grasp, playing with his toys, rolling, sitting, crawling, and walking, to riding his first bike, his continual development provides adults with benchmarks of motor progression. With increasing motor skills comes the capacity for exploration and interaction. The child learns concepts such as cause and effect, attributes of different objects, depth and distance, and relationships among objects, people, and their environment. The child typically integrates new sensations with past schemas and develops responses in return. Everything and everyone become the teacher and classroom for the developing child. The skills used to carry out these motor tasks are referred to as sensorimotor skills. They are the sensory and motor components of carrying out an action, including sensory processing, body awareness, planning and controlling a movement, strength, and balance. These skills are required for everyday tasks such as getting ready for school, handwriting, playing, eating, and toileting.

Sensorimotor difficulties can often be symptoms of other disorders, such as cerebral palsy, spina bifida, mental retardation (MR), developmental coordination disorder (DCD), autism, or physical disability. These difficulties can also lead to emotional and behavioral difficulties such as low self-esteem, anxiety, depression, and oppositional problems.

Case Study: Kalaiha

Kalaiha was referred to a mental health service at 10 years of age due to ongoing difficulties with academic learning, speech, acting out (including physical and verbal aggression toward family members), controlling and manipulative interactions with peers, and poor personal boundaries and social skills. Her treating pediatrician suggested that Kalaiha was on a path to developing conduct disorder (CD). Her foster carers, Shelley and Mike, sought services due to her ongoing difficult behaviors.

Kalaiha came to stay with Shelley and Mike at 3 years of age, following her apprehension from her biological mother due to significant neglect and emotional, psychological, and physical abuse. It was reported that her mother heavily abused drugs and alcohol during pregnancy and continued postbirth. Information regarding Kalaiha's developmental history was incomplete, but reports indicated that Kalaiha was born at 26 weeks prematurely and had a birth weight of 2,100 grams. She had multiple complications at birth, including respiratory difficulties that became ongoing. Significant fine and gross motor delays were noted, with Kalaiha crawling at 17 months, walking at 3 years, and talking at 4 years of age. Her biological mother reported that Kalaiha was difficult to soothe, frequently pulling away, arching her back, and turning her head away when picked up.

Shelley reported that she had difficulty bonding with Kalaiha, who was dismissive of her. She reported that Kalaiha appeared hypervigilant in the home environment and often "flinched" when others walked past. She reacted negatively to loud sounds or being touched. When she felt that she was in trouble, she would often hide in small spaces. Shelley reported that, though Kalaiha was often eager to please adults, she could also be obstinate and aggressive if she did not want to do something. Mike reported that she would not admit if she had done something wrong and would often lie despite evidence contradicting her story. Mike and Shelley also reported that Kalaiha never talked about her worries or anything that upset her.

HISTORY OF AND RECENT RESEARCH ON SENSORY INTEGRATION AND PROCESSING

Adequate processing and integration of sensory information are an important foundation for adaptive behaviors such as play and activities of daily living. Deficits in the ability to successfully process information can result in behavioral and learning difficulties (Lane & Schaaf, 2010). The following sections outline some of the ideas and research that have shaped sensory processing and integration theory.

Sensory integration (SI) theory and research were conceived in 1963 by Jean Ayres, educational psychologist and occupational therapist, who went on to produce prolific amounts of research and literature to develop and support her theory (Ayres, 1963, 1972a, 1972b, 1977, 1989). She was later influenced by comparative research showing that a stimulating environment can increase the dendrite branching, synaptic efficiency, and size of the brain (Rosenzweig, 1966; Rosenzweig, Krech, Bennett, & Diamond, 1962). Other research findings at the time also suggested that, though the most dramatic changes in the brain occur in the early years, brain sculpting continues throughout the lifespan (Bach-y-Rita, 1981). These findings led Ayres (1972a) to assume that a child's brain "has considerable potential for change" and that the disorganized child experiencing difficulties with SI has the potential to "'reset' his neural pathways" (p. 17).

Another important aspect of Ayres's theory was developed on the basis of the neurosequential developmental theory current with child developmentalists and psychologists at the time. Ayres (1972a) believed that "each developmental step in some way is dependent upon a certain degree of maturation of the previous step" (p. 4). The hierarchical model on which she based her theory assumed that lower parts of the brain developed first, or the spinal cord, brainstem, and hypothalamus were the first to develop, followed by the cerebellum. Ayres believed that the critical aspects of SI occurred in the lower levels of the central nervous system (CNS); if they were not functioning well, then it impacted on higher-order functioning in the brain. On this basis, she theorized that, by targeting the primitive proximal senses (touch, proprioception, and vestibular), the higher-order functioning skills such as concentration, reading, writing, and problem solving could be improved.

Sensory deprivation studies in the 1950s and 1960s led Ayres (1972a) to make assumptions about the importance of sensory stimulation for optimal brain functioning. Children placed in institutional care were found to have difficulties with organization, structuring, and relating to themselves, others, and objects. Ayres hypothesized that, when appropriate sensory stimulation is provided, processed, and integrated correctly, it promotes healthy brain functioning and growth. However, if the person is having difficulty processing and integrating this information, the results can be similar to those of sensory deprivation and include disorganized responses and poor awareness of self and others. Ayres also suggested that children experiencing difficulty with SI lack "inner drive" or motivation and do not actively engage with or explore their environment, which in turn can impact their motor development. Much of her work was with children with learning disorders. She suggested that any disturbance with sensory processing interferes with the child's ability to "synthesize sensory data and to interact effectively with the environment" (Ayres, 1972a, p. 1).

Further Occupational Therapy Influences

Much research has been conducted on Ayres's SI theory and treatment. After the death of Ayres in 1989, Fisher, Murray, and Bundy (1991) and Bundy, Lane, and Murray (2002) conducted research and collated findings to shape the current clinical practices of SI. Research has led to new interventions, models, and programs in areas such as parent–child bonding (Dunn, 2004; Greenspan & Weider, 2006), sensory defensiveness and modulation (Miller-Kuhanek, Henry, Glennon, & Mu, 2007; Wilbarger, 1994, 1995; Wilbarger & Wilbarger, 2007), and self-regulation (Williams & Shellenberger, 1996).

Extrapolations of the SI theory have been used to describe, assess, and treat children and adults (Kinnealey & Fruiek, 1999; Pfeiffer & Kinnealey, 2003; Urwin & Ballinger, 2005). The theory has been used to describe children with pervasive developmental disorders, including autism and Asperger's syndrome (Baranek, 2002; Watling, Dietz, & White, 2001), anxiety (Hoffmann & Bitran, 2007; Pfeiffer, Koenig, Kinnealey, Sheppare, & Henderson, 2011), schizophrenia (Baranek, 1998, 1999, 2002), attention deficit/hyperactivity disorder (ADHD; Arnold, 2001; Dunn & Bennett, 2002), and cerebral palsy (Blanche & Burke, 1991a, 1991b). Studies continue to be conducted measuring and treating sensory processing/integration among various populations.

Sensory Defensiveness

Influenced by the work of Ayres, Patricia Wilbarger (1995) further explored the issue of sensory defensiveness and developed the concept of "sensory diets" (SDs). She used the term as a metaphor to explain to parents and other clinicians the need for balanced or "nutritious" regular sensory input to promote optimal functioning. She went on to develop the Wilbarger protocol (WP), based on the need for intensive, repetitive, proprioceptive, and tactile feedback to foster change within the CNS to elicit changes in behavior and functioning.

Sensory Thresholds

Dunn (2001), also influenced by Ayres's work, focused on sensory modulation. Dunn introduced the concept of sensory thresholds and created a model to represent her theory. The main characteristics of her model included consideration of one's neurological thresholds (i.e., reactivity), consideration of one's responding or self-regulation strategies, and consideration of the interaction among thresholds and responding strategies (see Table 3.1). Her model suggests that all people have thresholds for sensory information and create behavioral responses that can be passive or active. When a pattern of performance begins to interfere with daily activities, support might be required. For example, children who have a high threshold for sensory information but are passive tend to appear flat and unresponsive to stimuli. They might not notice their environment and require information to be presented in an "obvious" manner. In contrast, a child who has a high threshold but responds actively tends to seek more sensory stimulation constantly to meet her needs. Children who have low thresholds and passive responses become overwhelmed by their environment and can become distressed and easily dysregulated. However, the child who has a low threshold and is active tends to control her environment by engaging in more ritualistic behaviors to reduce the impact of new stimuli.

Table 3.1 *Self-Regulation Strategy Continuum*

Neurological threshold continuum	Passive Act in accordance with thresholds	Active Act to counter thresholds
High neurobiological thresholds (habituation)	Low registration	Sensation seeking
Low neurobiological thresholds (sensitization)	Sensory sensitivity	Sensation avoiding

Source: Dunn's (2001) conceptual model of sensory processing. Adapted with permission.

Influences From Outside Occupational Therapy

Working With Children With Multisystem Developmental Disorders

The model of Greenspan and Wieder (1993) incorporated sensory processing theory. They linked work with emotional development and SI to address difficulties with regulatory and/or multisystem developmental disorders and addressed primarily the autism spectrum. Their model also emphasized the importance of assessing the child's sensory processing, modulation, motor skills, planning sequencing, and tone. They pointed out how deficits in these areas can impact his ability to interact and therefore develop. Their model also fostered positive interaction between the parent and the child and developed "floortime" as an intervention to work with children and their caregivers.

Sensory Integration and Trauma

Perry (2006) and his colleagues at the Child Trauma Academy base their treatment of traumatized children on a neurosequential model of therapeutics. Perry (2006) suggests that lower parts of the brain, such as the brainstem and dicephalon, in traumatized children are poorly regulated and dysfunctional and that "they will disrupt and dysregulate the higher parts of the brain" (p. 39). Perry and colleagues believe that, as Ayres suggested, for intervention to be successful, it needs to reflect the process of normal development or go "from the base up." They believe that, without a regulated and organized brainstem and midbrain, cognitive-based interventions will not be effective. They suggest that rhythmic, repetitive, auditory, tactile, and motor activities that target the brainstem and midbrain areas are regulating.

SI and Attachment

DeGangi with Greenspan and Wieder has made contributions to the understanding of emotional regulation difficulties and attachment disorders. For example, DeGangi, Breinbauer, Roosevelt, Porges, and Greenspan (2000) describe how infants with regulatory disorders have underlying deficits in self-regulation. This impacts their ability to self-soothe and be soothed by caregivers. Children who are particularly sensory defensive have difficulty with feeding and avoid touch. They can even become distressed at their mother's efforts to comfort or soothe them. This can severely interrupt the parent–child attachment process, resulting in an insecure and/or disorganized attachment in the child.

DEFINITIONS

In a recent comprehensive review of the literature, Schaaf and Davies (2010) reflected on the evolution of the SI frame of reference. They, among others, have noted a paradigm shift from

Ayres's original work and the confusion about terminology, definitions, and intervention approaches. The move toward consistent terminology is progressing; however, disagreement among researchers continues to exist (Hanft, Miller, & Lane, 2000; Lane, Miller, & Hanft, 2000; Miller & Lane, 2000). Below we attempt to clarify some of the terminology related to SI and establish a uniform language that will be used throughout this chapter.

SI Terminology

The term "sensory integration" was first described by Ayres in 1963 as "the ability to organize sensory information for use" (Ayres, 1972a, p. 1). In 1989, Ayres expanded this description:

> Sensory integration is the neurological process that organizes sensations from one's own body and from the environment and makes it possible to use the body effectively within the environment. The spatial and temporal aspects of inputs from different sensory modalities are interpreted, associated and unified. Sensory integration is information processing. ... The brain must select, enhance, inhibit, compare and associate the sensory information in a flexible, constantly changing pattern; in other words the brain must integrate it. (p. 11)

More recently, the term "sensory processing" has emerged, but confusion remains regarding its use and how it relates to SI. The terms have been used interchangeably with the latter becoming the preferred term when describing sensory-based processing difficulties that impact daily living (Miller, Anazalone, Lane, Cermak, & Osten, 2007). It has been suggested by Miller et al. (2007) that the term "sensory integration" should be used to describe the theory and specific interventions proposed by Ayres. For the purpose of this chapter, and to avoid confusion, when referring to the theory, the term "sensory integration theory" will be used; however, when referring to the specific treatment strategy developed by Ayres, the term "Ayres sensory integration" will be used. With regard to diagnosis, the term "sensory processing disorder" (SPD) will be used rather than the term "sensory integration dysfunction" (SID).

Performance Component Definitions of Sensorimotor Skills

Regardless of the nosology, certain terms are used consistently among researchers. These terms refer to the performance components of the sensory and motor systems required for effective interaction, interpretation, and understanding of ourselves and the world around us.

Visual Processing/Visual Perception

Visual processing involves the ability to detect and interpret visual information. It entails visual perception, a "highly complex integrative activity involving the understanding of what is seen" (Koppitz, 1970); as cited in Martin, 2006, "It requires the ability to recognise, recall, discriminate and make meaning of what we see" (Levine, 1994, p. 333). This skill is necessary for letter and symbol recognition, reading, spelling, playing sports, and eye–hand coordination. Visual perception can be broken down into several categories (see Table 3.2).

In Tables 3.3 and 3.4, various sensory processing abilities and sensorimotor skills are defined.

Table 3.2 *Visual Perceptual Subcategories and Descriptions*

Visual Perceptual Skill	Description
Eye–hand coordination	Ability to coordinate a hand–motor response to visual information
Position in space	Discrimination of reversals and rotations of figures
Copying	Ability to replicate an image using paper and pencil
Figure–ground	Ability to recognize figures embedded within a general sensory background
Spatial relations	Ability to sense the relationships of objects from each other and oneself (i.e., depth length, direction, etc.)
Visual closure	Ability to recognize an object that is incomplete
Visual memory	Ability to recognize a form after a brief interval
Visual–sequential memory	Ability to recognize a series of forms after a brief interval
Form constancy	Ability to recognize the dominant features in forms and objects as the same in any position, size, or environment

Source: Definitions from Hammill, Pearson, and Voress (1993, p. 2); Martin (2006, p. 12).

Table 3.3 *Definitions of Sensory Processing Abilities*

Terms	Definitions
Touch processing	The tactile system has two parts, protective and discriminative. The protective system is an automatic response alerting the body to withdraw from or defend against stimuli interpreted as harmful. The discriminatory touch system provides the brain with information regarding size, temperature, texture, and shape of objects within the environment (Bissell, Fisher, Owens, & Polycn, 1998).
Proprioception	Proprioception is the awareness of body position in space. Sensations are experienced in the muscles and joints and sent to the brain to provide information about where the joints and limbs are positioned and what they are doing without using vision. It is the sense that indicates where the various parts of the body are located in relation to each other (Godwin-Emmons & McKendry-Anderson, 2005; Yack, Aquilla, & Sutton, 2006).
Auditory processing	Auditory processing describes what happens when the brain recognizes and interprets the sounds around it (National Institute on Deafness and Other Communication Disorders [NIDCD], 2010). Skills include sound localization, auditory discrimination, auditory pattern recognition, and auditory performance in competing acoustic signals (including dichotic listening) and auditory performance with degraded acoustic signals (American Speech–Language–Hearing Association, 1996, 2005).
Vestibular/movement	The receptors in the inner ear perceive information about the force of gravity and movement. The vestibular system aids in maintaining joint stability, posture, balance, motor control, and spatial awareness. It also plays a part in behavior regulation and attention (Bissell et al., 1998).
Olfactory processing	Olfactory processing relates to the detection, interpretation, and recognition of odors. It is an important sense for evoking memories and detecting danger, and it is closely linked to taste (Ayres, 2005)
Oral sensory processing	Oral sensory processing refers to the detection and interpretation of taste, temperature, and texture of oral stimuli. This sense is responsible for food preferences and aversions (Ayres, 2005).

Table 3.4 *Definitions of Sensorimotor Skills*

Terms	Definitions
Postural control	Postural control is the "ability to maintain and change position of the trunk and neck. It is important as it provides a stable base for the limbs" (Levine, 1994, p. 85). When it is well developed, a child can sit in an upright posture with his hands free to manipulate objects.
Muscle tone	Muscle tone is the "ability of a muscle to resist a force for a period of time without changing length. It is also defined as the amount of resistance to passive stretch that is inherent in the muscle or the muscle's potential action" (Levine, 1994, p. 47).
Motor planning/ praxis	"Motor planning or praxis refers to the ability to conceive an idea and to organize and carry out a motor sequence of unfamiliar actions. Motor planning is the first step in learning new skills and requires integration of all the sensory systems. Information from each of these systems is needed to plan, organize, time and sequence an unfamiliar task" (Bissell et al., 1998, p. 12).
Bilateral coordination	Bilateral coordination is the ability to coordinate both right and left sides and to cross the midline. It is an important skill for many fine and gross motor activities, such as developing hand dominance, scissor skills, dressing, and many self-care tasks such as showering and hair washing (Bissell et al., 1998).
Fine motor skills	"Fine motor skills involve the ability to use one's hands and fingers precisely in a skilled activity. Good fine motor skills come from solid motor and sensory foundations" (Bissell et al., 1998, p. 8). It requires trunk, shoulder, wrist, hand, and joint stability, eye–hand coordination, hand manipulation and strength, proprioception, discrimination, motor planning, and bilateral coordination (Bissell et al., 1998).
Ocular control	Ocular control refers to the smooth and coordinated movements of the eyes to attend to and follow movements (Bissell et al., 1998, p. 14). Skills such as tracking, saccades, convergence, and divergence are required for focusing on objects, reading, following a ball for sporting activities, and copying from a whiteboard (Bissell et al., 1998).
Oral motor skills	Oral motor skills are operated by the muscles in and around the mouth, cheeks, lips, and tongue. These skills are necessary for eating, talking, swallowing, and making facial expressions (Bissell et al., 1998, p. 15).

TYPICAL SENSORY AND MOTOR DEVELOPMENT

Understanding typical sensorimotor development of a child is important for any adult involved with children. It is the most observable area of growth that a child will exhibit over his lifetime, and a better understanding of the key developmental stages and behaviors will help the adult to provide age-appropriate responses and activities. It also provides an indicator of problems or delays that might be contributing to behavioral, emotional, and social problems and the need for intervention if the child is not following the typical developmental patterns. Table 3.5 provides a summary of sensorimotor developmental milestones and early warning signs that might indicate that further investigation and assessment, and possible intervention are necessary. The signs might form a pattern such as autism spectrum disorder (ASD) or indicate multiple affected areas. Difficulty within a single area (e.g., sensory sensitivities), especially if it is manageable, might simply indicate a sensitive child.

Table 3.5 *Development of Fine Motor, Gross Motor, Sensory, and Visual Perceptual Skills, and Warning Signs of Problems in These Areas of Development*

Age	Gross Motor	Fine Motor	Sensory	Visual Perceptual	Warning Signs
Prenatal			Primitive response to touch or startle reflexes at about 9 weeks postconception Displays rudimentary reflexes to vestibular input such as the Moro reflex, rooting, sucking, Babkinski reflex, grasp flex, or withdrawal and neck righting (Case-Smith, 2001)		
0 to 3 months	Head—slack control, no more than 45° Trunk—slack, no muscle tone Limbs—remains in fetal position with arms/legs tucked in Mostly involuntary movements By 2 to 3 months, becomes stronger and can lift head 45° and upper chest Might start using hands for support while on tummy	Primitive grasp reflex Hand to mouth Makes a fist Moves hand when excited Brings hand to midline Grasps objects with entire hand	Reflexive responses Startle, Morrow reflex, grasp Cries when hungry or uncomfortable Vestibular system is fully developed but not integrated Babies respond to touch and movement to soothe By 2 to 3 months, orients toward auditory, visual, and tactile stimuli Exhibits habituation or the ability to ignore incoming sensory information	Rudimentary fixation and reflexive tracking (birth) Preference for black and white and contrast colors (birth to 1 month) Follow objects up to 90° during first month and 180° at second month Able to fix on and track an object Starting to distinguish between colors (2 to 3 months)	Difficulty with feeding and settling for sleep Under- or overresponsive to touch, sound, and parent's face Resists being held No visual tracking
4 to 6 months	Head—can hold head upright in sitting position; on abdomen can hold head upright 45° to 90° Trunk—firm back; weak lumbar region requires support Upper/lower limbs are extended; on back, baby can roll from side to side; on abdomen, baby can support himself on forearms Head and trunk are very firm; can raise head and trunk and play with toes in this position	Voluntary use of hands Development of palm grasp imprecise Tactile visual response Grasping objects on contact Opens and closes hands and holds object for a while Tactile motor reaction	Developing vestibular–proprioceptive–visual connections leading to the development of postural and head control Integration of touch and visual senses as child grasps and plays with objects Primitive reflexes less dominant, goal-directed movements result in motor planning	Sight—follows moving objects, bright-colored objects, and can observe them longer Accommodation (ability for eye shape to fix blurred vision), convergence, and oculomotor subsystems are established Depth perception Refining object tracking and location	Asymmetry with grasp and reaching Only turns head in one direction Hard to soothe Does not track with her eyes, which cannot hold still Eyes are crossed most of the time

	Limbs—can be held in standing position, holds most of his weight; can roll from front to back; pedals with feet	Transfers object from one hand to the other Bangs objects		Object permanence Subtle color differentiation	
7 to 9 months	Turns head toward movement Rolls from stomach to back and vice versa Developing crawling skills Learning to sit with support	Reaches out for objects Uses fingertips to hold/play with and explore objects Pincer grip developing Starts learning to drink from a cup Basic pincer grip	Refinement of tactile skills leads to the development of hand skills Auditory, tactile, and proprioceptive skills working together for the child		Only rolls to one side Asymmetric hand function Reduction in engagement and joint attention and withdraws into own world Not settling when upset and can't self-soothe to settle to sleep Not responsive to name
9 to 12 months	Can sit unsupported Pulls self up by furniture Side-step walking with support Might stand/walk alone	Pincer grip more refined Bangs objects together Claps hands Stacks objects Pokes fingers at new objects	Likes to explore the environment by mouthing objects, touching various textures, and moving	Depth perception and acuity almost fully developed but focused on closer objects Learning about her body and where it begins and ends; sense of proprioception more developed	Child not crawling or pulling to standing Does not interact with environment or engage with people Distress in noisy environments Repetitive and non-experimental or imaginative play Difficulty reaching for and grasping objects

(continued)

Table 3.5 *Development of Fine Motor, Gross Motor, Sensory, and Visual Perceptual Skills, and Warning Signs of Problems in These Areas of Development* (*continued*)

Age	Gross Motor	Fine Motor	Sensory	Visual Perceptual	Warning Signs
13 to 24 months	Walks alone Climbs Sits unsupported Sits down from standing Throws a ball Runs Stands on one foot Walks up and down stairs with hand held	Grasps objects in a controlled way Releases objects Scribbles on paper Stacks two to four blocks Imitates vertical and circular strokes Helps feed himself with a spoon Feeds himself with finger food	More capable of self-soothing More anxious about separation and clingy		Fixated on only a few areas of interest and plays with same things repeatedly Does not play with other children and might be aggressive or distressed if other children are "in his space" Distress with haircuts, certain clothes, and significant food aversions
2 to 4 years	Runs with ease Kicks ball Rides tricycle Throws and catches a ball Hops on one foot Balances on beam momentarily Imitates movements momentarily	Strings beads Holds pencil between thumb and fingers Cuts with scissors Imitates drawing a cross and circle Puts simple puzzle together Unbuttons large buttons		Figure–ground ability improving Eyes are mature enough to have acuity tested	Reduced ability to attend to one task Engages in destructive play Unable to hold a pencil or draw vertical and horizontal lines Has not developed a pincer grasp

					Struggles with coordination and motor planning and gross motor activities Appears clumsy and might fall often
4 to 6 years	Climbs up stairs alone, alternating feet Runs well on flat surfaces, turning sharp corners Climbs up playground ladders and other equipment easily Catches, bounces, throws, and kicks a ball Rides tricycle and pedals easily Walks easily on a narrow line Skips on alternate feet Stands on one foot for 8 to 10 seconds (right and left)	Pencil grip developing Cuts curved line with scissors Copies a square Draws a stick person with four distinguishable parts Ties shoelaces Hand dominance established Writes own name		Maximum accommodation achieved Smooth visual tracking and acuity established Can focus on object as distance changes	Avoids writing and other fine motor tasks Complains about a number of sensations, such as sensitivity to certain fabrics, messy play, or noise Overly clumsy Tires easily Difficulty with writing letters and name Has not developed a dominant hand Complains of sore and tired eyes Difficulty staying still during seated tasks

(*continued*)

Table 3.5 *Development of Fine Motor, Gross Motor, Sensory, and Visual Perceptual Skills, and Warning Signs of Problems in These Areas of Development* (continued)

Age	Gross Motor	Fine Motor	Sensory	Visual Perceptual	Warning Signs
6 to 10	Can ride a bicycle (without training wheels by 7 years of age) Skilled with hopscotch, rope skipping, and catching and throwing a ball Runs up and down stairs Gradually becomes aware of own body, movements, sense of space, comparisons to peers Increasingly skilled at sports Enjoys and participates in team games Able to swim Shows increased body awareness and perception Awareness of own physical skills and how they appear to others	Writes independently Draws increasingly complex pictures Manipulates construction toys with increasing complexity Able to cut out various shapes	Can use simple words to convey feelings and use strategies to solve problems Can independently respond to sensory stimuli (e.g., finds a jumper when cold) Able to tolerate delayed gratification	Figure–ground ability stabilized; can perceive and understand more complex designs Prior to this, prefers kinesthetic, tactile, visual, and then auditory senses Form constancy and spatial relationships developed	Poor pencil grasp Letter and number reversals Avoids fine motor tasks Extreme and intense reactions to situations Difficulties with gross motor tasks Struggling academically in many subjects
10 to 13	Motor skills fully developed Able to successfully adjust force and speed and complete complex movements Specialization of particular skills relevant to hobbies, sports, dance, and music	Able to complete complex artwork, craft, and construction tasks Growth in computer skills Self-help skills expanding and can prepare meals, choose outfits, and use money to purchase items		Visual perceptual skills fully developed	Over- or underweight Difficulties with managing school assignments Very clingy or dismissive of other people

ASSESSMENT OF SENSORIMOTOR SKILLS AND SENSORY PROCESSING OF CHILDREN

Early detection and treatment of sensorimotor dysfunction is important for promoting the healthy physical, social, and emotional development of a child. As mentioned earlier, a child learns and develops through using his sensorimotor skills to interact with his environment, so early detection of dysfunction and difficulty is important to provide appropriate intervention to aid development. Sensorimotor difficulties are commonly picked up in a child's early school years, when teachers might notice delays in children's functional skills, such as their play skills, fine motor skills, or gross motor skills, or parents become aware of differences between their child's functioning compared with that of other children of a similar age.

Less recognized are sensory processing difficulties such as sensory modulation disorder (SMD), sensory discrimination and perception disorder, and vestibular processing disorders. The signs and symptoms of these disorders are often interpreted as the child being "naughty, temperamental, or disobedient," or they are confused with more familiar diagnoses such as ADHD, CD, and oppositional defiant disorder (ODD). Research has shown that many comorbid diagnoses occur with SPDs, such as those outlined above. These comorbidities will be discussed later.

PRINCIPLES OF ASSESSMENT

Holistic Multidisciplinary Assessment

Because children with multiple mental health issues, by definition, present with deficits in several areas, it is important that assessment is conducted in a multidisciplinary and multifactorial manner that considers the child, the environment, and her activities within her roles (occupations). When assessing a child, an occupational therapist gathers as much information about her as possible, establishing possible contributing/maintaining factors, which parts of her daily living are impacted, how she is compromised, and her strengths. This invaluable information provides the basis for deciding which intervention is most appropriate and how it can best be delivered. Table 3.5 and Figure 3.1 demonstrate the various areas that an occupational therapist considers when assessing a child.

Case Histories

Case histories are vital when working with any child, especially a child with a complex presentation. Information such as referral reasons; developmental, educational, familial, and medical histories; and environmental contexts can provide clear indicators for further assessment. For example, a student who has a history of difficult behavior in school settings, especially around seated tasks, can indicate difficulty with handwriting, which could be indicative of visual perceptual, fine motor dexterity, and motor control difficulties. Another example is a child who shuts down or has a "melt down" during music class or at the shopping center. A hypothesis might be that the child has SMD and easily becomes overwhelmed by his environment. In both cases, further investigation of these and other hypotheses would be judicious before making any decision about diagnosis or intervention.

Assessing the Child

Occupational therapists often assess a child from a functional viewpoint. They are interested in the parts of the child's everyday life that are affected due to her difficulties. From this viewpoint, the occupational therapist assesses the performance components that might be contributing to the child's presentation. For example, a child who is having difficulty with handwriting, and often exhibits disruptive behavior during it, could have difficulties in postural tone, proprioception, and/or visual perception that are contributing to her presentation. Figure 3.2 provides a framework for the hierarchy of performance components required for functional outcomes. This framework demonstrates the performance components required in a hierarchical manner for higher-order tasks such as writing, abstract reasoning, social skills, and so on. Generally, if the lower components (e.g., sensory processing, balance, and bilateral coordination) are not functioning correctly, then they impact higher-order components.

Assessing the Resistant Child

Often children with multiple mental health challenges are resistant to "testing" situations. They frequently perceive assessments as threatening, challenging, and potentially exposing their vulnerabilities. Other children can have difficulties with attention and concentration, which make it difficult for them to complete testing. These children have often been part of several services and historically considered "untestable" by clinicians. It is often useful prior to assessment to meet with the child and her family in a nonthreatening context (e.g., family home and at school). During this time, the clinician can develop rapport and get an understanding of her interests, strengths, modes of interacting, and difficulties. Investigating what is important to the child, whether there are things that she finds "tricky," and what bothers her is useful in supporting compliance. At times, externalizing the difficulty can help the child to be open to investigating the contributing factors. During the preassessment visit, the clinician can prepare the child by informing her that the next time they meet they will engage in some activities for which there will be rewards for participation (e.g., playtime with clinic toys and equipment). When structuring the assessment sessions, it might be necessary to split them into smaller and more frequent sessions to ensure optimal engagement and attention. Use of movement and activity breaks that are clearly defined can help to maintain compliance. Establishing a clear, motivating system of rewards can help to keep the child on task.

Observation and Screening Tools

Screening Checklists

Screening checklists help to identify areas in which a child might be experiencing difficulty. They are generally age specific and indicate developmental milestones. Deviation from the "norm" might indicate further assessment and possible intervention. Checklists are often developed by a service (e.g., school) and are specific to its frame of reference. For example, the School Age Occupational Therapy Checklist (see the Appendix) directs the therapist to areas of functioning in school and home settings. A number of commercial screening tools are described in Table 3.6.

Observation in Everyday Environments

Observing a child in his usual environments can provide useful information that cannot be extracted from standardized testing and screening alone. Observations of a child performing functional tasks such as feeding, dressing, academic work, and playing can provide clues about how he approaches, plans, and sequences tasks. They can also give

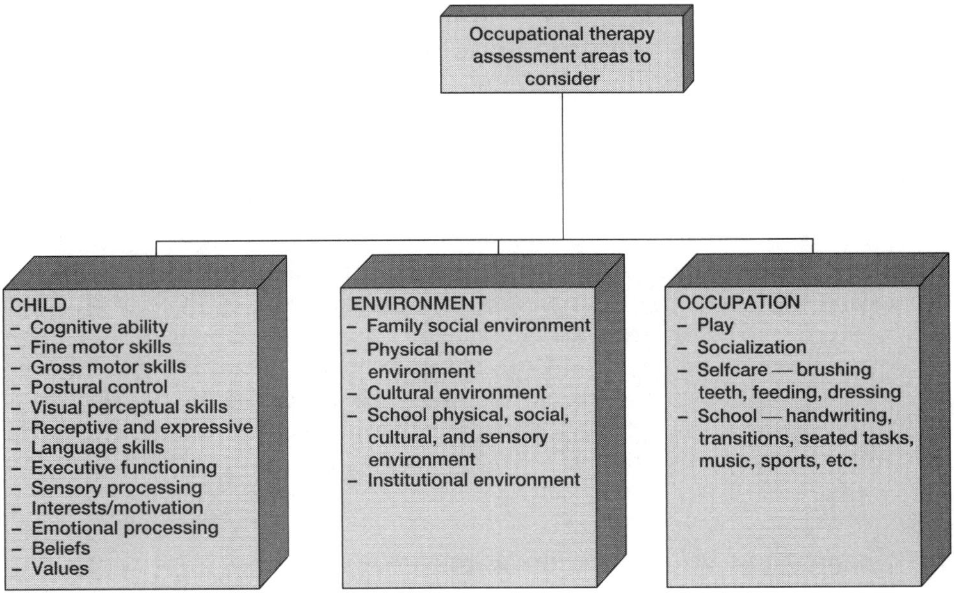

Figure 3.1 *Occupational therapy assessment areas.*

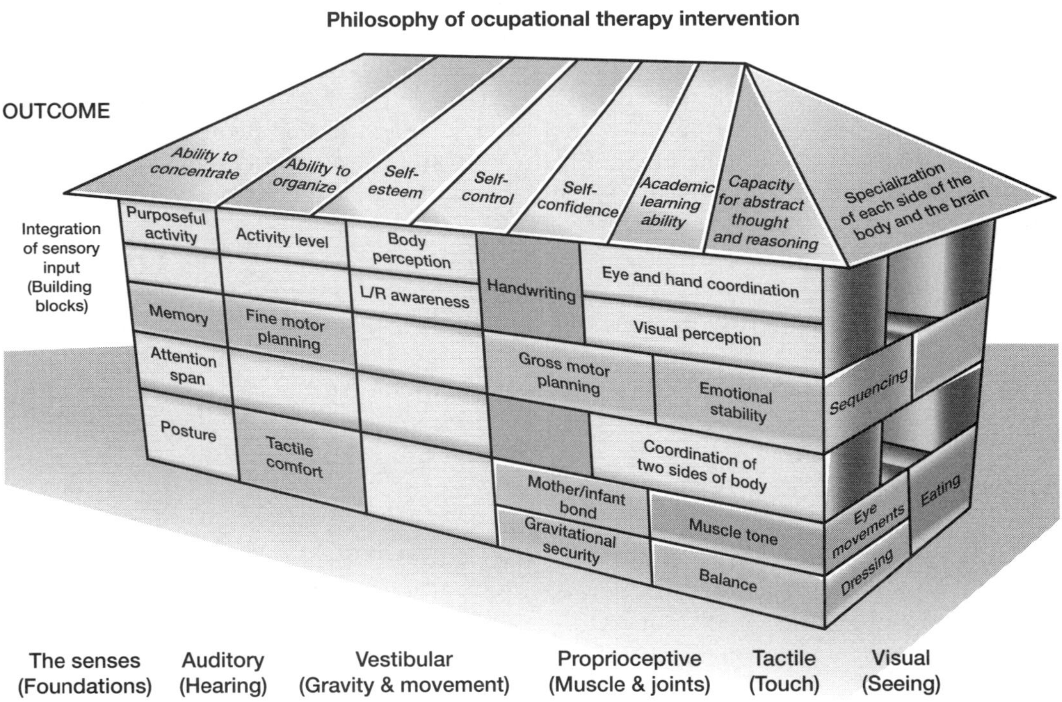

Figure 3.2 *Hierarchy of performance components required for functional outcomes.*
Adapted from Ayres (2005). Reprinted with permission.

clues about his gross and fine motor, proprioceptive, perceptual, cognitive, social, and problem-solving skills. Observations of how he copes in an unstructured activity and/or transitions can be equally important and give clues about sensory processing, confidence, initiation, and problem solving. How the child responds to verbal, visual, and physical cues can indicate strengths and weaknesses. It is also necessary to assess his physical, social, and sensory environments to ascertain which factors might be contributing to his behavior.

One method of contextual observation was originally compiled by Carol Walker and Susan Bonney and then modified by the School of Occupational Therapy, Curtin University of Western Australia, in 1997. Influenced by the Ayres Sensory Integration and Praxis Test (SIPT; Ayres, 1989), this assessment uses neither scores nor standardization to provide a quantitative measure. Rather, it provides valuable qualitative information about motor planning, proprioception, and motor development. The assessment is a collection of sensorimotor activities in 18 areas of performance, including joint laxity, muscle tone, righting reaction, reflex pattern, visual motor skills, and proprioception.

Visual Perceptual and Visual Motor Integration Assessments

These types of assessment have come under scrutiny over the past few years (Brown, Rodger, & Davis, 2003; Burtner et al., 1997). Their ability to provide a direct relationship to functional visual perception has been questioned because two-dimensional assessments do not replicate the three-dimensional environment that people must negotiate (Chapparo, 2009). However, these assessments can indicate two-dimensional visual perceptual skills related to symbol recognition, reading, writing, encoding, and decoding skills. They can also provide evidence for a differential diagnosis regarding the reasons for work-avoidant behaviors. This is especially useful for children who demonstrate good visual perceptual skills but significantly poorer visual motor integration skills. Often this can be seen in children who are relatively good readers but "act up" when writing tasks are presented. The difficulty arises because these children can quickly recognize that their handwriting performance is less competent than that of their peers and often do not want to expose their weakness. Commonly used visual perceptual and visual motor integration assessments are described in Table 3.6.

Sensorimotor, Sensory Processing, and Handwriting Assessments

Information on these assessment tools is provided in Table 3.6.

THE SENSORIMOTOR BRAIN

The functions of the main areas of the brain (see Figure 3.3) involved in sensorimotor functioning and processing are discussed in the text that follows. We will also discuss recent research on and theories of SPDs and DCDs.

Brainstem

The brainstem consists of the medulla oblongata and pons. It also incorporates the reticular formation. The medulla oblongata is located on the superior end of the spinal cord. Its main

Table 3.6 *Standardized Tests to Identify Children With Sensorimotor Difficulties*

Tool/Instrument	Age Range	Items/Administration Time	General Description
Visual perceptual and visual motor integration assessments			
The Beery-Buktenica Developmental Test of Visual Motor Integration—6th ed. (*WMI*; Beery & Buktenica, 2010)	2 to 100 years (long form) 2 to 8 years (short form)	Generally takes 10 to 15 minutes Can be administered to a group or individual	Consists of drawings of geometric forms arranged in order of increasing difficulty that the individual is asked to copy. Supplementary tests are also available to assess visual and motor performance. The test has been standardized on 1,737 individuals aged 2 to 18 years and 1,021 adults from 19 to100 years and has proven reliability and validity.
Test of Visual Perceptual Skills (Non-Motor)—3rd ed. (*TVPS-3*; Martin, 2006)	4 years to 18 years 11 months	Generally takes minutes Responses are made vocally or by pointing	This test assesses various components of visual perceptual skills such as form constancy, visual discrimination, visual memory, visual–spatial relationships, visual–sequential memory, visual figure–ground, and visual closure. It has nationally stratified norms based on data from over 2,000 children. It has high reliability and construct validity.
Developmental Test of Visual Perception—2nd ed. (*DTVP-2*; Hammill et al., 1993)	4 to 10 years	Generally takes 35 minutes	It is a battery of eight subtests that provide scores for visual perception and visual motor difficulties. Norms are based on representative 1990 U.S. census data. Scores are reliable at 0.8 or 0.9 levels. It is used to identify children for special programs.
Sensorimotor assessments			
Bayley Scales of Infant and Toddler Development—3rd ed. (*Bayley-III*; Bayley, 2006)	1 month to 42 months	30 to 90 minutes depending on age of child	There are five scales: cognitive, motor, language, social–emotional, and adaptive behavior. There is also a Behavior Rating Scale to rate behavior during assessment. Fine and gross motor and adaptive behavior are most relevant for an occupational therapist.
Miller Function and Participation Scales (*M-FUN-PS*; Miller, 2006)	2.6 to 7.11 years	Variable according to issues of child	There are three observation checklists for home, classroom, and testing. It includes the areas of visual motor and fine and gross motor skills. It is for children with mild to moderate delays in functional motor areas. It has been standardized on 414 children and has moderate test–retest reliability, good internal and inter-rater reliability, and strong content validity and internal structure.

(continued)

Table 3.6 *Standardized Tests to Identify Children With Sensorimotor Difficulties (continued)*

Tool/Instrument	Age Range	Items/Administration Time	General Description
Movement Assessment Battery Checklist—2 (*MABC-2*; Henderson, Sugden, & Barnett, 2007, 2009)	3–16 years	Depends since it is an observation tool	It is used to identify children who are significantly delayed in motor development. It has checklists of eight tasks of manual dexterity, ball skills, and static and dynamic balance. Currently, reliability and validity studies are minimal.
Perceive, Recall, Plan, and Perform System of Task Analysis (*PRPP*; Chapparo & Ranka, 2004)	Used for infants, children, and adults	Depends on individual's needs	It is a client-centered, occupation-focused, criterion-reference method that uses a behavioral task analysis to identify problems during task performance.
Sensory processing assessments			
DeGangi Berk Test of Sensory Function in Infants and Children (*TSF*) (DeGangi and Greenspan, 1989)	Infants to 5 years	36 items, 30 minutes	It assesses sensory processing and reactivity to identify infants and young children with SI dysfunction, regulatory disorders, or those at risk of developing learning disorders. Psychometric properties suggest good reliability and validity, and interobserver reliability of 81%–96%.
Sensory Profiles (Dunn, 1997, 1999, 2002, 2006)	Profiles for infant/toddler, elementary school-aged children, adolescents, and adults	Profiles from birth to adults based on Dunn's Sensory Processing Model	There are teacher, parent, and self-report questionnaires. Response patterns identify whether individual is sensory sensitive, sensory avoiding, sensory seeking, or has low registration of sensory input. It identifies sensory behaviors common in individuals with regulatory disorders.

Sensory Profile Measure (*SPM*; Parnum, Echer, Miller-Kuhaneck, Enry, & Glennon, 2007)	5 to 12 years	Rating scale system of three forms for home, classroom, and school environment	It assesses sensory processing, praxis, and social participation in elementary school-aged children. Home and school forms were standardized on 1,051 typically developing children.
Handwriting assessments			
Handwriting Speed Test (Wallen, Bonney, & Lennox, 1996)	Primary and high school students	Assesses the child's speed of writing and considers other components of performance	It provides a scaled score of the individual's speed of writing, and the assessor can observe a number of aspects of handwriting. The test has excellent inter-rater reliability, very good test–retest reliability, and some preliminary data for its construct reliability.
McMaster Handwriting Assessment Protocol—2nd ed. (Pollack et al., 2009)	Senior Kindergarten to Grade 6	Comprehensive assessment of handwriting, including speed and child's handwriting on a task done from memory and dictation	It is based on research that has documented standardized norms and current practice.
Detailed Assessment of Speed of Handwriting (*DASH*; Barnett, Henderson, Scheib, & Schutz, 2007)	9 to 16 years	30 minutes to complete, can be used with a group or individual	It measures handwriting speed and includes a copying task, an alphabet-writing task, a fast-copy task, a graphic speed task, and a free-writing task.

function is to relay motor and sensory impulses between the spinal cord and other parts of the brain. It contains nuclei that receive sensory input from or provide motor output to 5 of the 12 cranial nerves. The inferior olivary nucleus within the medulla relays information from the proprioceptors to the cerebellum. The nucleus gracillus and nucleus cuneatus are associated with the somatic sensations such as touch, vibration, and proprioception.

The pons is above the medulla and anterior to the cerebellum. The pons acts as a bridge between the different parts of the brain, relaying impulses from one side of the cerebellum to the other and between the medulla and midbrain. The pneumotaxic and apneustic areas together with the medullary rhythmicity areas control breathing.

The midbrain extends from the pons to the dicephalon. Similarly, this area contains tracts and nuclei. The cerebral peduncles conduct nerve impulses from the cerebrum to the spinal cord, medulla, and pons. The superior colliculi is the reflex center for the eyes, head, and neck in response to visual stimuli, and the inferior colliculi is the reflex center for the head and trunk in response to auditory stimuli. The substantia nigra is responsible for subconscious muscle activity. The medial lemniscus conveys touch proprioception, pressure, and vibration.

The reticular formation area is responsible for alerting the cerebral cortex to incoming sensory signals. The reticular activating system is involved in the sleep–wake cycle and is responsive to incoming stimuli through the eyes, ears, and skin. It also helps to regulate muscle tone.

Located at the posterior of the cranial cavity, the cerebellum is the "quality control center" for motor movements. It evaluates how well movements are made and makes adjustments for smooth, coordinated, complex sequences. The cerebellum plays a major role in posture and balance. Neuropathology of this area has been linked to DCD. Children with DCD have demonstrated soft neurological signs such as difficulties with smooth finger-to-nose touching, rapid hand alternating, and poor postural control, which are linked to cerebellum functioning (Zwicker, Missiuna, & Boyd, 2009). Abnormalities in the cerebellum have also been linked to dyslexia, with postmortem and imaging studies identifying neuroanatomical, morphological, functional, and biochemical differences among individuals with dyslexia and comparison subjects (Francks et al., 2003). Nicholson, Fawcett, and Deals (2001) found that children with dyslexia scored approximately one standard deviation below comparison subjects in posture, muscle tone, and voluntary movement (Francks et al., 2003), indicating association among learning, reading, and motor skills.

The dicephalon consists of the epithalamus, thalamus, subthalamus, and hypothalamus. Of interest are the latter three.

The thalamus relays all sensory input to the cerebral cortex. It also provides crude perceptions of touch, pressure, pain, and temperature. The thalamus includes nuclei for voluntary motor actions and arousal and functions in cognition and awareness. In a small study of thalamic functioning of autistic children (ASD) compared with typically developing (TD) children, Hardon et al. (2008) suggested that the thalamus might play a role in the pathophysiology of autism, especially sensory abnormalities seen in this disorder. It was found that thalamic metabolites (N-Acetylasparate, phosphocreatine, and choline-containing metabolites) were lower on the left side of the thalamus in the ASD population compared with the TD children.

The subthalamus contains the subthalamic nuclei and portions of the nucleus and substantia nigra, positioned mostly laterally to the midline. These regions communicate with the basal ganglia to help control body movements.

The hypothalamus controls and integrates activities of the autonomic nervous system and pituitary gland. It regulates emotional and behavioral patterns and circadian rhythms. It also controls body temperature, regulates eating and drinking behavior, helps to maintain the waking state, and establishes patterns of sleep. The hypothalamus is also at the head of the hypothalamic–pituitary–adrenal axis (HPA), releasing hormones when activated.

Cerebrum

The cerebrum consists of two cerebral hemispheres. The right cerebral hemisphere is involved with spatial awareness and pattern perception is related to recognition of faces, and integrates sensory and emotional stimuli. The right hemisphere is often colloquially referred to as the "artistic" side. The left hemisphere is more analytical and involved with spoken and sign language, numerical and scientific language, and reasoning.

Connecting and transferring information between the two hemispheres is the corpus callosum. Difficulties with laterality have been linked to dysfunction with transferring information across the corpus callosum. DCD has also been linked to dysfunction within the corpus callosum (Kirby & Drew, 2003; Sigmundson, 2003). In general, females have larger corpora callosa than males, and it has been suggested that the difference in size can be related to the higher prevalence of DCD among males, found four times more often in males than females (Kirby & Drew, 2003).

The basal ganglia receive input and provide output to the cerebral cortex, thalamus, and hypothalamus. The caudate nucleus and putamen control automatic movements of the skeletal muscles. The basal ganglia also coordinate gross, automatic muscle movements, regulate muscle tone, and are involved in motor control and motor learning.

Limbic System

Of particular importance in the limbic system is the amygdala, linked to the survival response to perceived danger or the fight, flight, freeze response. The limbic system controls the emotional aspects of behavioral regulation. It modulates, dampens, and regulates fluctuations in attention responses through coordination of the autonomic, somatic, and behavioral systems. It also discriminates objects in time and space and processes novel stimuli, changes, and inconsistencies in stimulus features.

Cerebral Cortex

Each cerebral hemisphere contains four lobes: frontal, parietal, temporal, and occipital. These lobes can be further broken down into specific sensory, motor, and associational areas (see Figure 3.3).

The hippocampus is situated between the cortex and limbic system. The parietal lobes are superior to the occipital lobes and posterior to the central sulcus (fissure) and frontal lobes. Together the two specialize in the organization of spatial, sequential, and emotional learning and memory (Cozolino, 2006c). Dysfunction of the parietal lobe has been linked to DCD. Children with DCD typically have significantly poorer visual–spatial processing than typical controls, regardless of their visual acuity or motor task involvement (Zwicker et al., 2009).

Located in the anterior portion of the parietal lobe, the somatosensory area receives nerve impulses from the sensory receptors for touch, proprioception, pain, and temperature. Unlike the hypothalamus, it provides precise detection and location of sensory stimulation on the body. It also plays a role in regulating emotions and social behavior.

The temporal cortex is where sensory information from the cortical, limbic, and orbital frontal areas is integrated, organized, and combined.

The primary motor cortex is located anterior to the somatosensory area. As its name suggests, it controls voluntary contractions of specific skeletal muscles and muscle groups.

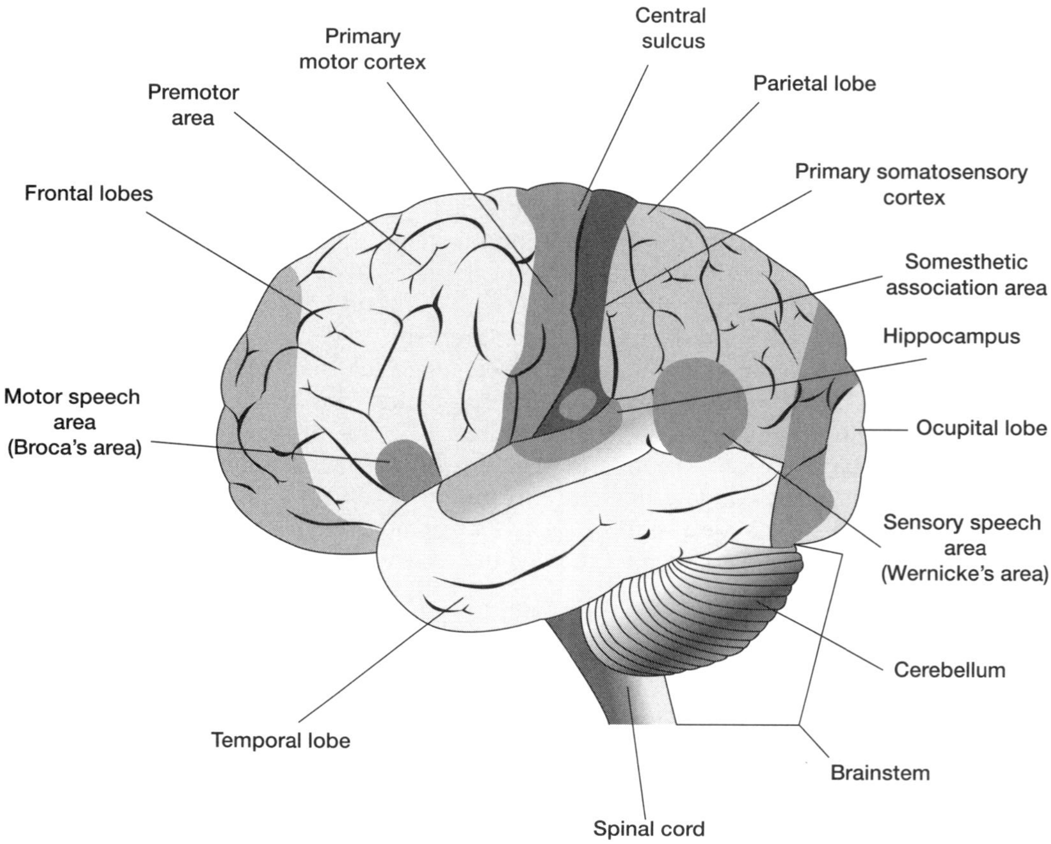

Figure 3.3 *Major areas of the brain involved in sensorimotor functioning and processing.*

CURRENT RESEARCH ON SENSORY PROCESSING AND INTEGRATION

Electrodermal Responses

Miller et al. (1999) compared electrodermal responses of 19 children identified with SPD with a control group of children without the disorder. Children with SPD had higher-magnitude electrodermal responses and less evident habituation over repeated exposure to sensory stimuli.

Mangeot et al. (2001) conducted an electrodermal study of children with ADHD. They found that these children demonstrated a larger initial reaction to stimuli. However, they demonstrated subsequent habituation to levels similar to those of children who were TD.

Electrophysiological Studies

Russo et al. (2010) conducted high-density electrophysiological mapping of 17 children with autism (ASD) (aged 6–16 years) compared with a typical group of children (TD).

Somatosensory stimulation was presented to the child's hand for 30 milliseconds using vibro-tactile stimulation while children were watching a silent movie. Auditory stimulation consisted of a 1,000-Hz tone presented through a speaker placed on the child's right ear. The two stimuli could be presented alone or together. The findings of this study suggest that there were significant differences between the two groups. Differences in auditory and somatosensory information appeared between the populations, where multisensory integration (MSI) was detected in the TD group but not the ASD group. It has been suggested that children with ASD do not automatically combine sensory inputs early in the processing hierarchy to the same degree as TD individuals.

Electroencephalography Studies

Davies and Gavin (2007) conducted a study of children aged 5–12 years with and without SPD. The findings indicated that children with SPD exhibited less sensory gating than TD children. Also, the correlation between sensory gating and age was not seen in children with SPD, as it is in TD children. Sensory gating is the brain's ability to filter out repeated or unnecessary stimuli. Thus, a child with SPD shows less ability to do this. The study also found that the electroencephalographic (EEG) brain activity results correctly identified 86% of children with SPD. In a much earlier study, McIntosh, Miller, Shyu, and Hagerman (1999) also found that children with SPD had higher electrodermal responses and less evidence of habituation over repeated sensory stimulation compared with TD children.

MRI Studies

DeLange, Haggart, and Toni (2005) measured neurovascular activity with fast event-related MRI, distinguishing responses parametrically related to motor images from responses evoked by visual imagery and other task-related phenomena. Posterior parietal and precentral cortex increased their activity as a function of mental rotation only during motor imagery tasks. During the intended action, the posterior parietal cortex combines somatosensory and visual motor information, whereas the dorsal premotor cortex generates the actual motor plan, and the primary cortex deals with movement execution.

PET Striatal Dopamine Measures

In a study of the timing of prenatal alcohol exposure on rhesus monkeys, Schneider et al. (2009) described dopamine (DA) as an important neurotransmitter, modulating activity in many brain regions, promoting both excitatory and inhibitory signals. Their study found that, if dopamine D_2 receptors (DAD_2R) levels in the infant monkeys were too high, sensitivity to novel stimuli was considered to be heightened; conversely, low density can result in reduced sensitivity. The levels of DAD_2R were also linked to the timing of alcohol exposure in utero.

NEUROBIOLOGICAL AND GENETIC CONTRIBUTORS TO SENSORIMOTOR DISORDERS

Genetics and Heritability

Relatively recent research on rhesus monkeys has linked the presence of the serotonin transporter gene polymorphic region (rh5-HTTLPR) short allele in the infant to sensory processing difficulties when the mother is under prenatal stress (Schneider et al., 2005; Schneider et al., 2009). This might tie in with other research linking the short allele to increased risk of psychopathology (Caspi et al., 2003).

No study has yet investigated the underlying heritability and/or brain basis of developmental coordination disorder (DCD). Deborah Dewey of the Alberta Children's Hospital is currently investigating the heritability of developmental motor disorders in children diagnosed with DCD only, ADHD only, reading disability (RD) only, and DCD and co-occurring ADHD and/or RD.

Alcohol

Several researchers have found that children with fetal alcohol syndrome (FAS), fetal alcohol effects (FAE), and fetal alcohol spectrum disorder (FASD) have greater sensory processing problems than those not exposed to alcohol (Carr, Agnihorti, & Keightley, 2010; Franklin, Dietz, Jirikowic, & Astley, 2008). Morse, Miller, and Cermak (1995) found that children with FAS and FAE displayed sensory processing deficits two to six times greater than regular populations. Jirikowic, Carmichael, and Kartin (2008) studied 25 children with FASD and 26 children of typical development. Sensory processing profile and *Bruiniks–Oseretsky Test of Motor Proficincy* (2nd ed.; *BOT*-2, Bruininks & Bruininks, 2005) assessments were conducted, among other tests. The results indicated that FASD children performed significantly lower than their TD peers. They demonstrated more problems with sensory modulation and poorer sensorimotor performance. Indeed, 88% of children with FASD had results that were different (significant clinical range) from those of the comparison group. FASD children also presented with tactile sensitivity, reduced responsiveness, sensory seeking, reduced auditory filtering, and visual/auditory sensitivity. These children also demonstrated subtle sensorimotor performance deficits. They were generally found to be low average to below average in fine motor skills and displayed visual motor impairments under timed conditions (Adnams et al., 2001).

Riley and McGee (2005) discussed the impact of FAS on the brain, noting reduced size in areas of the brain in general, namely, the cerebellum, corpus callosum, and basal ganglia. These reductions were believed to exert an impact on overall intellectual functioning, language, attention, visual–spatial abilities, executive functioning, adaptive social skills, and fine and gross motor skills. Interestingly, balance was particularly affected in children with FASD. Such children rely heavily on somatosensory input. However, when their performance is atypical in this area, they cannot compensate using visual and vestibular information, likely due to cerebellar anomalies associated with FASD.

In an interesting series of studies, Schneider and colleagues (Schneider et al., 2005; Schneider et al., 2008; Schneider et al., 2009) found that prenatal stress and exposure to alcohol and lead resulted in sensory processing and regulatory problems in rhesus monkeys that possess the rh5-HTTLPR short allele. In their latest study, Schneider et al. (2009) found that monkeys with the rh5-HTTLPR short allele exposed to alcohol in the early stages were underresponsive to stimuli in contrast to monkeys exposed late in gestation, which were found to be overresponsive.

Prenatal Drug Use

Although no research is currently available that specifically links illicit drug use with sensory processing issues, there is work that implicates maternal drug use with poorer developmental outcomes and behavioral and regulatory difficulties (Lester et al., 2009; Nguyen et al., 2010; Schuetze, Lawton, & Eiden, 2006).

Birth Weight/Prematurity

There is a great deal of literature on the impact of prematurity on motor development. For example, Kilbride, Thorstadt, and Daily (2004) performed a study comparing preschool outcomes of 23 pairs of full-term siblings with their extremely low birth weight (ELBW; less than 801 g) siblings. Their findings suggested that ELBW children's motor skills were significantly related to preterm status but not socioeconomic status. Salt and Redshaw (2005) conducted research on the motor development of children born prematurely and found that they were 40% to 60% more likely to have neurological and sensorimotor development below the normal range. In another study, 44% of children born before 33 weeks of gestation performed below the 15 percentile rank in their overall performance in the movement ABC assessment and below the 17 percentile in the visual motor integration assessment (Jongmans, Mecurin, De Vries, Dubowitz, & Henderson, et al., 1997).

Preterm children have been found to have more difficulties than full-term children with fine motor, visual motor, visual perceptual, and visual–spatial tasks. These tasks include drawing, cutting with scissors, dressing, writing, copying figures, perceptual mapping, spatial processing, finger tapping, and pegboard performance (Goyen, Lui, & Woods, 1998). In a study of 5-year-old children with birth weights of less than 1,500 g, 23% had impaired fine motor skills, and 71% scored one standard deviation or more below average on tests of fine motor function (Goyen et al., 1998). Below-average performances in visual motor skills and visual perceptual tasks were noted for 17% and 11% of the children, respectively. These problems were most common in children born at less than 28 weeks of gestation. However, more mature preterm children remain at risk for these problems; a third of school-age children born at 32 to 36 weeks of gestation were found to have poor fine motor and writing skills (Huddy, Johnson, & Hope, 2001).

Premature children were also found to have sensory processing difficulties. Wiener, Long, DeGangi, and Battaile (1996) found that children born prematurely scored lower on tests of sensory functioning and had a different sensory profile than typically developed children. They reflected on the work of Porges (1988), which showed that premature infants had less neonatal vagal tone than full-term infants. This finding suggested that premature babies have limited ability in the parasympathetic nervous system to regulate behavioral states.

Institutionalization/Sensory Deprivation

The negative impact of institutionalized care has been documented for many years (Cermak, 2009; Haradon, Bascom, Dragomir, & Scripcaru, 1994; Pollak et al., 2010). Many studies of children in institutionalized care demonstrate that children deprived of a nurturing environment, including lack of stimulation and interaction, have ongoing behavioral, cognitive, developmental, emotional, and sensory issues (Cermak, 2009).

Pollak et al. (2010) found that children adopted after 12 months of age had poorer visual development than children adopted earlier. They proposed that, because the visual system is not mature at birth, it relies on early exposure to develop the neural architecture for more complex visual processing. Studies have demonstrated that, if visual input is delayed by as little as 2 months, permanent visual processing deficits result (Le Grand, Mondloch, Mauer, & Brent, 2003; Lewis & Maurer, 2009). Cermak (2009) summarized the current research on institutionalized care and its impact on sensory processing. Her findings indicated that children adopted from orphanages "frequently had behaviours suggestive of sensory modulation difficulties in areas such as touch, movement and vision." Also, children who spent more time in institutions displayed more difficulties on the Sensory Integration and Praxis Test (SIPT) than those who had shorter durations of stay. Wilbarger, Gunnar, Schneider, and Pollak (2010) also found that children adopted later had more sensory processing difficulties than early adopted and nonadopted children. This included sensory sensitivity and sensory-seeking behaviors.

Trauma

A child with SPD might have a heightened or lowered sensory threshold such that her tolerance for sensory stimuli is more or less than the typical child's. It is common for a child who has experienced trauma to exhibit a low threshold for stimuli such as noise, touch, smell, and visual information. A child who has difficulty modulating sensory information might act out as the stimuli are perceived as a threat or become dysregulated to combat the "discomfort" or avoid what she is experiencing. Another child might "shut down" to attempt to drown out information or engage in repetitive behaviors to control and self-soothe. Henry, Sloane, and Black-Pond (2007) found that children exposed to prenatal alcohol and postnatal trauma had lower intelligence scores, more severe motor developmental deficits, and delays in language, memory, visual processing, motor skills, and attention than traumatized children without prenatal alcohol exposure.

Attachment and Regulation

When a child's primary regulation needs are not met and the child is not attended to, he is likely to display ongoing dysregulation and become disorganized in his arousal. He cannot experience a calm state and becomes unable to differentiate between pleasant and unpleasant experiences. Children diagnosed with disordered attachment styles have been known to display dysregulated behavior and sensory modulation difficulties. Positive attachment not only enhances the regulation of the infant's psychobiological state but also triggers the synthesis of neurons, protein synthesis and neural growth, and positive SI. Furthermore, positive attachment can act as a protective factor for children who possess the rh5-HTTLPR short allele, who are more likely to display dysregulation and sensory processing difficulties.

DISORDERS OF MOTOR DEVELOPMENT AND SENSORY PROCESSING

Although many neurological disabilities come under this heading (e.g., cerebral palsy and spina bifida), the disorders discussed here are limited to those frequently seen in child and adolescent mental health settings. Disorders associated with motor and sensory skills are DCD and SID/SPD.

DCD

DCD as described by the American Psychiatric Association (2000), in the *Diagnostic and Statistical Manual of Mental Disorders* (*DSM-IV*) is the "marked impairment in the development of motor coordination … that significantly interferes with activities of daily living … and is not due to any other medical condition." Various terms, such as clumsy child syndrome, sensory integrative dysfunction, and developmental dyspraxia, have been used to describe DCD and are often used interchangeably and inconsistently (Magalhaes, Missiuna, & Wong, 2006). In 1994 and then 1998, a consensus was reached by a group in London to clarify the terminology. They recommended that DCD be considered an umbrella term with subtypes (Magalhaes et al., 2006). Children with DCD demonstrate impaired motor coordination, which results in delays in meeting motor milestones. These children often have difficulties with fine and gross motor skills, impacting self-care, educational performance, and physical activities (Dunford, Missiuna, Street, & Sibert, 2005; Wang, Tseng, Wilson, & Hu, 2009; Zwicker et al., 2009). New activities can be difficult for these children because they have problems planning and organizing their bodies in efficient ways.

For some children, DCD can lead to secondary mental health and educational issues, including poor social competence, poor academic performance, low self-esteem, anxiety, and depression (Cocks, Barton, & Donelly, 2009; Cummins, Piek, & Dyck, 2005; Zwicker et al., 2009). Behaviorally challenged children might avoid particular activities by engaging in disruptive or passive behaviors. Some children might display their frustration through aggression, destruction of their work, and negative self-talk. In terms of socialization, these children might avoid social situations that require motor skills and seek younger friends who have similar play skills (Missiuna, 2003; Zwicker et al., 2009).

DCD has a high comorbidity with other developmental disorders such as ADHD, ASD, SPD, and language impairment (Cocks et al., 2009; Howard, 1997). Research has also linked DCD with physiological disorders such as obesity and coronary vascular disease (Cairney, Hay, Faught, & Hawes, 2005; Faught, Hay, Cairney, & Flouris, 2005). It is estimated that 6% of children aged 5 to 11 years have DCD (*DSM-IV*, 2000), and it is reported to affect males four times as frequently as females. Children born prematurely and with ELBWs are at a significant risk of demonstrating DCD.

SPDs

There remains debate over the terminology of sensory processing/integration disorders. Ayres (1972a) originally identified six categories of sensory integration dysfunction (SID). Bundy et al. (2002) suggested two areas: dyspraxia and poor modulation. Dunn (2000) described the four areas of SMDs. Miller et al. (2007) proposed a uniform nosology (see Figure 3.4) and a paradigm shift to rename SID to SPD. However, no consensus exists, and debate continues (Schaaf & Davies, 2010). Here I use the model suggested by Miller et al. (2007).

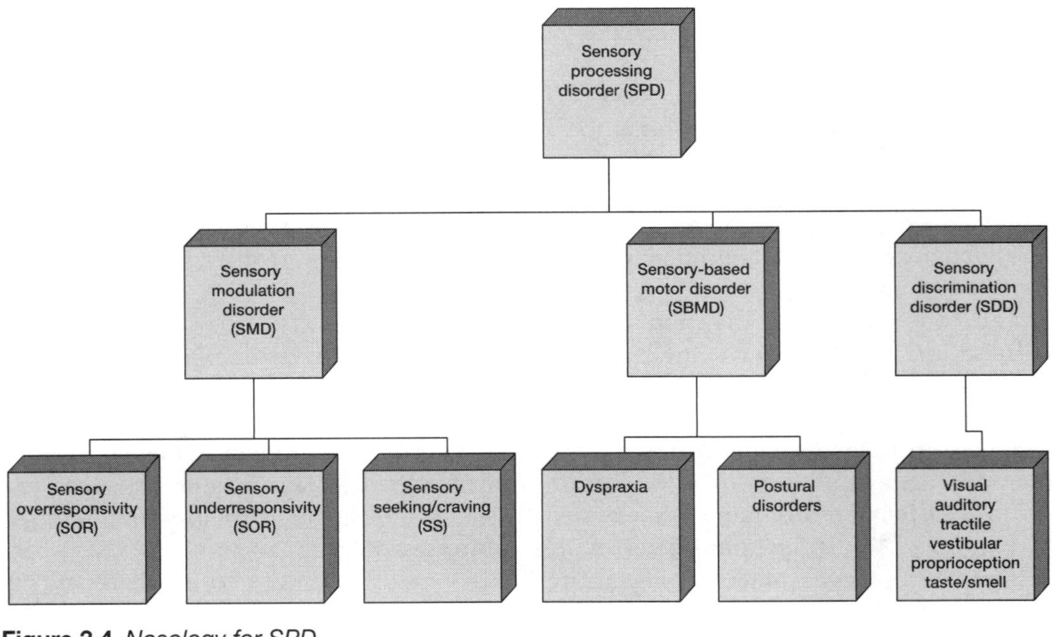

Figure 3.4 *Nosology for SPD.*
Source: Miller et al. (2007, p. 137). Reprinted by permission.

Although the presence of SPD does not necessarily suggest psychopathology, it can indicate increased risk of learning disorders, autism, and schizophrenia. Deficits in the processing of vestibular and tactile information are common among children with learning disorders and motor coordination problems (Ayres, 1972a; Chu, 1996).

Despite the confusion regarding terminology, there is agreement that sensory processing/integration "does not refer to one particular type of problem but to a heterogeneous group of disorders that are thought to reflect subtle, primarily subcortical, neural dysfunction involving multisensory systems" (Parham & Mailloux, 2005, p. 349).

SMDs

Sensory modulation is the ability to respond appropriately to sensations. With SMD, the brain does not filter and interpret sensory information correctly. Thus, the person experiences difficulties interpreting sensation at the appropriate intensity. Cermak (1988a) and Royeen (1989) hypothesized that there is a continuum, with hyporesponsivity at one end and hyperresponsivity at the other end. The optimal level of arousal and orientation lies in the center (see Figure 3.5).

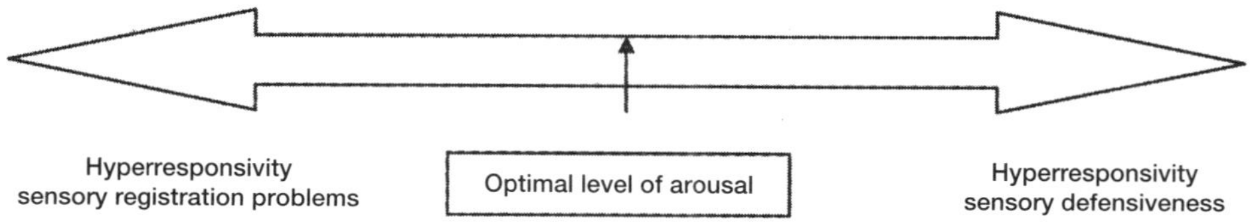

Figure 3.5 *Arousal spectrum.*
Sources: Cermak (1988); Royeen (1989).

Dunn (2000) further expanded this in her conceptual model to describe the behavioral response of the child to sensory thresholds. She hypothesized that "all people have thresholds for sensory information, [and] in response to these thresholds people create behavioural responses which can be passive or active" (Dunn, 1997, p. 2). This conceptual model is represented in Table 3.1.

Children who are "sensory seekers" have a high threshold for sensory information. They do not register sensory information as well as others and tend to need "more" than the usual amounts of sensory stimulation. These children appear restless, fidgety, often engaging in rough play, stomping, bumping, and falling. Often they might not register their body parts or positioning and require intense proprioceptive feedback to do so. The behaviors that these children engage in to meet their needs are often inappropriate or disruptive.

Before sensory information can be used functionally, it needs to be registered within the CNS. However, some children have difficulty registering relevant stimuli to create an appropriate response. As a result, children with low registration tend not to interact with their environment as well as other children. The child might not respond to touch, pain, taste, smell, or movement, and she might be underresponsive in more than one area or all areas. Children with autism often display little or no interest in exploring their environment. Consequently, a child with this difficulty can lack the "inner drive" to explore and learn from his environment. This can significantly impact his long-term development and learning. Safety is of particular concern regarding these children. Their ability to detect danger is altered, and they might not seek help when injured.

A child who is hyperresponsive registers sensory information quickly and intensely. She might have difficulty in one area (tactile defensiveness) or several sensory areas (sensory defensiveness). Often her responses seem unexpected, disruptive, or aggressive. However, she often does not have control over her physiological responses. It is thought that children who exhibit this disorder are responding in a fight/flight manner. Their behaviors are often worse in unstructured environments, where stimulation is generated outside their control. These children are often seen as willful, controlling, and rigid.

Sensory Discrimination Problems

Sensory discrimination can occur in all senses. Children can have difficulty in one or more areas yet be good in others. The difficulty lies in the organization and interpretation of stimuli. However, children with this problem can have difficulty with modulation and with discriminating one stimulus from another. A possible example is auditory discrimination, in which a child might have difficulty differentiating "d" and "b," whereas a child with tactile discrimination difficulties might be unable to identify objects by touch alone.

Vestibular Processing Disorders

These disorders refer to motor functions related to vestibular processing. Ayres originally described it in 1972 as "postural and bilateral integration dysfunction" due to a cluster of symptoms that occurs between children's postural ocular performance and integration of the two sides (Ayres, 1972a). Fisher et al. (1991) suggested the name "vestibular–proprioceptive disorder" because the two systems are so linked to each other in terms of postural control and motor performance. Regardless of the name, the signs and symptoms remain the same, and children who have vestibular processing disorders exhibit poor equilibrium reactions that impact their ability to engage in activities such as bike riding, hopping, and skating. Low muscle tone, especially in their extensors, results in the child slouching or leaning on furniture. On the postnystagmus subtest in the SIPT, these children display a delayed eye reaction to movement, suggesting postural ocular deficits, which can impact their ability to dribble a basketball or track a ball while moving. Bilateral coordination is also impacted, reflected in poor hand dominance and discrimination difficulty with tasks that use two hands, such as using scissors and dressing.

Neurological connections between the reticular activating system and the limbic system also put children with vestibular processing disorders at risk for problems with attention, communication, and modulation of arousal.

Somatodyspraxia

Praxis is the ability to conceptualize, plan, and execute a nonhabitual motor act (Ayres, 1978). Dyspraxia refers to difficulty with praxis that cannot be explained by a medical diagnosis or developmental disability and occurs during ordinary environmental opportunities for motor experiences. Somatodyspraxia is a result of somatosensory dysfunction (e.g., impaired tactile and proprioceptive processing). Cermak (1988a) suggests that not all children who have dyspraxia have difficulty with SID. It is hypothesized that, through correct tactile proprioceptive processing, a person can gain correct understanding of his body schema and then the ability to conceptualize motor planning. Children with this difficulty have problems with kinesthesia, finger identification, localization for tactile stimuli, and proprioception.

COMORBIDITY

ADHD

There is a significant correlation with ADHD and DCD and motor coordination difficulties (Cocks et al., 2009; Piek, Pitcher, & Hay, 1999). Barkley (1990) suggests that up to 50% of boys with ADHD have DCD. Other findings indicate that children with ADHD (predominantly inattentive) have poorer fine motor and kinesthetic abilities, whereas children with ADHD (combined type) primarily have difficulty with gross motor skills (Piek et al., 1999). Numerous studies have investigated the link between sensory processing problems such as modulation disorder and ADHD (Cermack, 1988b; Dunn & Bennett, 2002; Yochman, Parush, & Ornoy, 2004). These studies have found a strong correlation with SMDs in children with ADHD.

Mental Retardation

MR is the most common of the developmental disabilities, affecting between 0.8% and 3% of the population (Rogers, Gordon, Schenzenbacher, & Case-Smith, 2001). MR encompasses three main factors: significantly impaired intellectual ability, onset before 18 years old, and impairment of the adaptive abilities necessary for independent living. Children diagnosed with MR can be characterized by delays in motor and speech milestones, feeding difficulties; nonresponsiveness with physical contact; decreased alertness and spontaneous play; and signs of neurological difficulty affecting balance, motor symmetry, perceptual motor skills, and fine motor skills.

Autism and Pervasive Developmental Disorders

The prevalence of sensory processing difficulties in autism ranges from 42% to 88% (Baranek, 2002; Watling et al., 2001). The greatest difficulties are found in the underresponsive/sensation seeking, auditory filtering, and tactile sensitivity areas. Children with autism can fluctuate between being hyperresponsive and hyporesponsive to the same and different stimuli (e.g., be hypersensitive to touch one day and not notice it another day or be hypersensitive to noise and hyposensitive to movement). Behaviors commonly observed are tactile sensitivities resulting in difficulty with hygiene and grooming (Baranek, Foster, & Berkson, 1997). Children with autism also use peripheral vision to inspect objects (Lord, Rutter, & Le Couteur, 1994). However, their "visual spatial skills are often more advanced" (Baranek, 2002, p. 398). Adrien and colleagues (1993) found that children with ASD exhibited nine behaviors that discriminated them from other children, such as finger flicking and body rocking. Many children with autism also have difficulties with motor skills. Asperger's syndrome is on the autism continuum. It is commonly associated with motor clumsiness, motor planning, coordination, and fine motor difficulties. Some studies have noted that up to 80% of children with Asperger's syndrome have deficits in motor coordination, though not part of the diagnostic criteria (Ghaziuddin, Tsai, & Ghaziuddin, 1994; Miyahara et al., 1997).

Regulatory Disorders

DeGangi (2000) reports that infants with regulatory disorders also have underlying deficits in self-regulation and sensory processing. Moderate regulatory disorders can also lead to developmental delays and parent–child relationship difficulties. Greenspan and Wieder (2006) report that infants who do not use their senses to form emotional bonds are at risk of early attachment difficulties. Avoidance of human sounds, touch, and even scents can produce flat affect, recoiling, arching of the back, difficulty feeding, and averted gaze, which can be interpreted by the caregiver as rejection. Studies of infant dysregulation indicate that mothers with infants who are difficult to soothe have higher levels of ambivalence toward their infants and psychological distress. DeGangi (2000) reported that infants with regulatory disorders have difficulty organizing reciprocal interactions and can become distressed by everyday sensory experiences, impacting their ability to organize social exchanges.

OTHER DIFFICULTIES AND DISORDERS

Green, Baird, and Sugden (2006) provided parents of 47 children with DCD with the Strengths and Difficulties Questionnaire (SDQ), a brief measure of prosocial behavior and psychopathology. Results indicated that 62% of the children had significant behavioral problems, whereas 13% had results in the borderline range.

Several research studies have linked DCD with academic and mental health issues, such as poor social competence, poor academic performance, low self-esteem, anxiety and depression, and emotional and behavioral disorders (Cocks et al., 2009; Cummins et al., 2005; Zwicker et al., 2009).

Hoffmann and Birtan (2007) investigated the relationship between social anxiety disorders and sensory processing sensitivity. Their results indicated that sensory processing sensitivity is highly correlated to harm avoidance and agoraphobia behaviors and generalized anxiety disorders.

Rieke and Anderson (2009) conducted a preliminary study comparing the adolescent/adult sensory processing profiles of 51 adults with obsessive-compulsive disorder (OCD) with a "typical" group. Their findings indicated that the OCD group scored higher in areas of sensory sensitivity and sensory avoidance and low registration. However, they also scored lower in sensation seeking. The researchers hypothesized that many sensory processing traits are represented in the symptomology of people with OCD. For example, their need to impose structure and stability might be a construct of sensory avoidance; by providing predictability, they limit their exposure to unexpected stimuli. Similarly, the inability to inhibit behavioral responses to stimuli might be an extension of sensory sensitivity. Research in this area is still in its infancy, and further studies are needed to provide conclusively the link between OCD and sensory processing difficulties.

IMPLICATIONS OF SENSORIMOTOR COMPONENT DISTURBANCES

Joint Laxity/Hypermobility

Joint laxity is often found in childhood and decreases with age (Silman, Haskard, & Day, 1986). This condition for many people does not affect their lives, though for others it can mean an increased chance of dislocations, sprains, and secondary osteoarthritis. In occupational therapy practices, it is commonly seen in children with handwriting difficulties (Summers, 2000). Joint laxity is described as any joint that extends beyond 30°. Laxity in the thumb and index finger is thought to impact a child's ability to use a pencil properly. Summers (2000) conducted a study of joint laxity in the index finger and thumb and its relationship to pencil grasp. Although the results were not statistically significant, there was an effect of thumb interphalangeal laxity on pencil grasp. Occasionally, joint hypermobility is a sign of a rare, serious disorder, such as Ehlers–Danlos syndrome or Marfan syndrome. For this reason, joint hypermobility accompanied by joint pain should be evaluated by a doctor.

TREATMENTS AND STRATEGIES FOR CHILDREN WITH SENSORIMOTOR AND SPDS

Interventions for children with complex presentations require a multidisciplinary approach; no one discipline can address all the needs of the complex child. It is important to determine the possible contributors to a child's presentation and then determine which interventions are required and their priority. The principles of intervention follow:

- Understanding the child's capabilities and difficulties in a multimodal manner is important before commencing intervention. Understanding her cognitive, language, academic, emotional, and psychological profile provides clues about which treatment strategies will be the most successful.
- Any intervention should be goal oriented. Goals ideally are developed in conjunction with the child, her caregivers, and other relevant parties and need to be measurable and realistic. The therapy must be relevant and motivating to the receivers, especially the child.
- Activities should be fun and not a chore, given in the context of the child's interests and hobbies and her attention span and capabilities.
- Consistent and clear boundaries and expectations are required when working with children. However, playfulness, attunement, reciprocity, and external rewards can be used to increase engagement and compliance (see Figure 3.2).

Impairment-Oriented and Performance-Oriented Approaches

Polatajko and Cantin (2010) describe two different perspectives on approaching therapy with children with sensory processing difficulties. They can be extended to working with children with sensorimotor issues. The impairment-oriented approach is "based on the assumption that competent occupational performance depends on properly functioning nervous and musculoskeletal systems and that damage or abnormal development of one or more of these systems results in dysfunction" (Polatajko & Cantin, 2010, p. 417). Thus, intervention aims to reduce impairment and restore function. It tries to address the foundational skills (those at the base of the house in Figure 3.2) to improve the skills in the upper walls and roof.

Performance-oriented treatment is focused on functional performance and not the underlying impairment. This type of treatment focuses on a specific activity (e.g., writing, riding a bike, and using a computer). It generally uses "top-down" or "cognitive" approaches and targets the top level of the wall of the house.

Depending on their perspective, the therapist might use one or the other approach or both approaches together. The approach chosen should depend on the child's presentation and the goals that the child and his parents have chosen for treatment.

Ayres's Sensory Integration

Ayres's SI treatment was designed to provide the child with appropriate sensory stimulation to promote motor adaptation and higher cortical learning. Ayres (2005) thought that good SI is required for development and learning and that successful acquisition of skills leads to organization of the nervous system's SI (adaptive responses). Through positive adaptive responses to simple skills, children can develop more complex skills.

"Therapy is grounded in play, where the child's interest and choices guide the therapist in arranging and selecting therapeutic activities" (Ayres, 2005, p. 143). Intervention involves controlled sensory input to create just the "right challenge" to meet the needs of the child; this is done by adapting the environment and activity. Intervention is child directed and requires active participation of the child. That is, she helps with the selection of an activity while the therapist creates choices that meet her goals, and the setup and process of the activity (i.e., promoting planning, sequencing, and motor planning). The more a child is motivated to participate in activities, the greater the chance that she will persist if challenged, likely leading to improved functioning.

The goals of Ayres' SI therapy are to improve sensory modulation related to behavior and attention and to increase abilities for social interactions, academic skills, and independence. The activities are meant to help the nervous system modulate, organize, and integrate information from the environment, resulting in future adaptive responses.

Many studies have investigated the effectiveness of this treatment, but most of these studies have been flawed in their methodology or used small sample sizes, impacting statistical validity. In a recent systematic review, May-Benson and Koomar (2010) found a trend toward positive results for the SI approach in contrast to no intervention. In an effort to provide clinically sound research, Miller et al. (2007) conducted a randomized control pilot study. They found that, using a manualized SI treatment protocol, children with SMDs made significant gains in goal attainment, attention, cognition, and social competence. Electrodermal tests in the same study indicated that there was an improvement in tactile hypersensitivity.

Wilbarger's Protocol (WP)

The WP of brushing was designed by Patricia Wilbarger to help with the treatment of infants, children, and adults who exhibit sensory defensiveness and related social–emotional disorders. The theory behind the protocol is that brushing provides deep proprioceptive feedback, which influences the peripheral nervous system and the CNS, which are central to developing and maintaining automatic self-regulation functions (Wilbarger & Wilbarger, 2007). Similar to massage, the intervention is thought to increase the release of serotonin, dopamine, and endorphins and reduce the level of cortisol in the bloodstream.

WP involves the application of deep tactile pressure over arms, legs, and back through firm strokes with a special soft-bristled brush. This is followed by a series of joint compressions to the large joints of the trunk and extremities. The protocol is repeated every 1.5 to 2 hours during the child's waking hours; it is believed that the dampening input lasts only this long. The brushing program is generally administered for at least 2 weeks and can be reviewed and used longer or restarted when required. The program is especially useful for children who are sensory defensive. The protocol is intended to be used in conjunction with information provided to caregivers, schools, and the client and a specially developed SD.

WP has been reported to result in better organization, modulation, attention, sleep, feeding, and behavior (Foss, Swinth, McGruder, & Tomlin, 2003; Kimball et al., 2007). Some children also improve in fine and gross motor skills, removing the barrier that was interfering with their ability to use underlying motor skills. Kimball et al. (2007) conducted a study with four 3- to 5-year-old boys and tested their salivary cortisol levels pre- and posttreatment. Results indicated that the cortisol levels of three of the four boys decreased, whereas that of the other boy, who had the lowest level, increased. Evidence of the effectiveness of the protocol has been obtained only with small samples and case studies, so definitive conclusions about its effectiveness cannot be made.

Sensory Diet (SD)

"Sensory diet" is a term coined by Patricia Wilbarger and involves an activity plan throughout the day to meet the sensory needs of a particular child. The term is a metaphor for nutritional diet and describes the need for balanced, "nutritious," regular sensory input to promote optimal functioning (Wilbarger, 1995). The "diet" is often created with the family in consultation with an occupational therapist. Various activities are scheduled throughout the day that can affect the child's alertness/arousal. They typically involve sensory activities or "meals" that engage the deep tactile, proprioceptive, and vestibular systems, believed to have stronger and longer-lasting effects, and sensory "snacks" that engage tactile, oral, gustatory, and auditory senses. Examples of sensory activities are listed in Table 3.8. Activities that engage the proprioceptive systems can be used for hypo- and hyperresponsive children since these activities are thought to be organizing for the child. An SD needs to be client centered, functional, and realistic (or able to be carried out). An example of an SD is given in Table 3.7.

Alert Program

First published in 1994 and revised in 1996, the Alert program, based on SI principles and arousal theory, was designed by Williams and Shellenberger (1996). They created an analogy program to describe children's arousal levels. The primary focus is to "help children learn to monitor, maintain and change the level of alertness so that it is appropriate to a situation or task" (Williams & Shellenberger, 1996, p. 1). Using the analogy of engine speed, they use top-down approaches to recognize physiological cues regarding how children's engines (or arousal states) are running. In response, they embark on individual strategies, namely, somatosensory approaches (touch, proprioception, and movement), to help children regulate their arousal states to "just the right engine speed." The Alert program has been used successfully with children with language difficulties because it uses analogies and visual cues.

Several articles have been published regarding the effectiveness of the Alert program (Barnes, Vogel, Beck, Schoenfeld, & Owens, 2008; Bertrand, 2009; Cahill, 2006). Although studies are anecdotal or have small sample sizes, current research indicates that the program has positive outcomes for improving attention and behavior.

Weighted Vests

Weighted vests are widely used by occupational therapists to provide proprioceptive feedback to enhance organization, attention, and regulation, thought to occur by promoting the production of neurotransmitters such as serotonin and dopamine via the CNS (Honacker & Rossi, 2005; Vandenberg, 2001). Fertel-Daly, Bedell, and Hinojosa (2001) and Vandenberg (2001) explored the effectiveness of weighted vests. Their findings indicated that wearing the vests increased time spent on task behaviors and reduced self-stimulating behaviors. These studies, however, were conducted on a small sample and should only be taken as preliminary findings. In both studies, the weight of the vest was calculated at 5% of the child's body weight. The length of use was inconsistent, however. Generally, it is suggested that weighted vests should be used for 15- to 20-minute sessions.

Table 3.7 *An Example of an SD*

Name: Ben **Age:** 6 years, 2 months

Time	Key Events in the Day	DPPT*	OTT**	Other SD Activities	Comments
0700	Wake up	x	x	Pull ups on top bunk Crawl downstairs to breakfast	
0800	Breakfast			Have breakfast on therapy ball Crunchy and chewy cereal Drink through a straw	
0830	Before school starts	x	x	Carry own backpack 5 minutes on climbing equipment Quiet corner with tactile "feely box"	
0845	School starts			Line up with fiddle toy Regular movement breaks every 20 minutes	
1015	Recess	x	x	Crunchy, chewy food Sipper cup	
1200	Lunch	x	x	Crunchy, chewy food Sipper cup Gross motor play	
0315	Home	x	x	Jump on trampoline for 10 minutes Sensory snack of apples Watch TV in bean bag for 10 minutes	
0600	Dinner	x	x	Use of wobble cushion and weighted vest while at dinner	
0815	Bedtime	x	x	Game of hotdog or earthquake in bed Bedtime story in bed with cushions	

*Deep pressure and proprioceptive technique; **oral tactile technique.
Adapted from Wilbarger and Wilbarger (2007).

Sensorimotor Approaches

Sensorimotor interventions provide a variety of motor activities with various stimuli. They are based on the assumption that motor systems cannot operate optimally without processing and integrating sensory information (Dunn, 1997). Fisher et al. (1991) advise that SI is a form of sensorimotor treatment.Examples of sensorimotor activities and the performance components required are listed in Table 3.8.

Table 3.9 lists various activities that can be used with the hyperresponsive child to calm him down or with the hyporesponsive child to alert him.

Sensorimotor Art Research Team (SMART)

This new treatment model combines SI, art therapy, sensorimotor, and child trauma principles for therapy for children who have experienced trauma (Koomar, 2009). The use of Ayres's sensory activities and equipment creates a playful and regulating atmosphere. By engaging in rhythmical, safe play, children's organization is fostered, promoting self-reflection and regulation.

Table 3.8 *Sensorimotor Activities and the Performance Components Required*

	Auditory Processing	Body Awareness	Coordinating Both Sides of Body	Fine Motor	Motor Planning	Ocular Control	Oral Motor Skills	Perception of Movement	Visual–Spatial Awareness
Balloon volleyball	x				x	x			
Hopscotch					x			x	x
Catching and throwing		x	x		x	x			
Blowing bubbles					x		x		
Copying postures		x			x	x			
Jump rope	x		x		x				x
Blowing cotton wool					x	x	x		
Tracing			x	x	x	x			
Mazes			x	x	x	x			x

Developmental, Individual Difference, Relationship-Based Model

Floortime is the cornerstone of intervention for the Developmental, Individual Difference, Relationship-Based Model (DIR) approach. The intervention focuses on engaging the infant/child in interactions that mobilize her six core developmental capacities (Greenspan & Wieder, 2006):

1. shared attention and regulation;
2. engagement and relating;
3. two-way intentional affective signaling and communication;
4. long chains of co-regulation, emotional signaling, and shared social problem solving;
5. creating representations;
6. building bridges between ideas and logical thinking.

The goal of floortime is to build a warm, trusting relationship with the child in which shared attention, interaction, and communication occur on her terms. Floortime is unstructured, spontaneous, imaginative play with the therapist, following her lead, interests, and rhythms. The adult engages with the child in a suitable environment, opening and closing the child's circles of communication, extending interaction, and initiating exploration. Floortime is introduced to parents by a therapist, and the parent is guided through the sessions using the DIR principles. Parents are encouraged to set aside 20 to 30 minutes to spend with the child in floortime. It should occur daily, and if possible, several times throughout the day.

Performance-Oriented Treatment

Cognitive Orientation to Daily Occupational Performance Approach

A growing body of evidence is building on the effectiveness of the cognitive-oriented approach (Mandich, Polatajko, Macnab, & Miller, 2001; Missiuna, 2001; Ward & Rodger, 2004). Developed

Table 3.9 *Activities and Strategies for Children Hyper- or Hyporesponsive to Sensory Stimulation*

	Calming Strategies for the Hyperresponsive Child	**Alerting Strategies for the Hyporesponsive Child**
Movement	■ Slow, small movements ■ Linear movement ■ Movement with some repetitive, predictable quality (e.g., rocking chair)	■ Fast, big movements ■ Rotational movements ■ Movement that is unpredictable ■ Movement activities before the child sits down to complete desk work
Auditory	■ Quiet, soothing voices ■ Slow, rhythmical music and sounds ■ Decrease of environmental noise ■ Use of ear plugs and headphones with calming music	■ Loud noises or voices ■ Fast-paced, unpredictable music ■ Headphones with alerting music ■ Get the child's attention before giving instructions
Touch	■ Deep pressure and touch (e.g., hugs) ■ Slow, repetitive strokes used on skin ■ Warm temperatures (e.g., warm drinks and warm bath)	■ Light touch ■ Fast, quick touch ■ Colder temperatures (e.g., ice drink, cold bath, and cold water on face)
Visual	■ Decreased lighting (e.g., curtains, hat and sunglasses) ■ Reduced visual distractions in the environment (e.g., only have needed items on desk) ■ Less information on the page ■ Use of light blue or light green paper for worksheets	■ Bright lights ■ Lots of color, bold writing, high contrast ■ Brightly colored books or mobiles
Proprioception	■ Engaging in heavy work activities (e.g., pushing, pulling, carrying, and hanging) ■ Using bean bags or soft cushions for child to sit in ■ Heavy clothes, fitted clothes ■ Crashing and jumping into soft cushions and pillows	■ Engaging in heavy work activities (e.g., pushing, pulling, carrying, and hanging) ■ Using bean bags or soft cushions for child to sit in
Oral	■ Gradually introducing food ■ Crunchy, chewy food ■ Straws for drinks ■ Warm food and drink ■ Bland food	■ Crunchy, chewy food ■ Straws for drinks ■ Cold food and drink ■ Strong flavors (e.g., sour and spicy food)
Multisensory	■ Reducing the amount of stimulation ■ Simple worksheets, plain text ■ Consistent prompts ■ Repetitive structure ■ Providing deep touch and pressure	■ Bright, bold colors and text ■ Physical, verbal, and auditory prompts ■ Deep pressure ■ Vestibular work (i.e., those in movement section)

by Polatajko and Mandich (2004), the model is a child-focused approach to helping a child with DCD achieve functional goals. The Cognitive Orientation to Daily Occupational Performance (CO-OP) approach is based on the premise that cognition plays an important role in the acquisition of functional skills. Children are taught a global problem-solving strategy and encouraged to use self-talk to get through new challenges (see Figure 3.6).

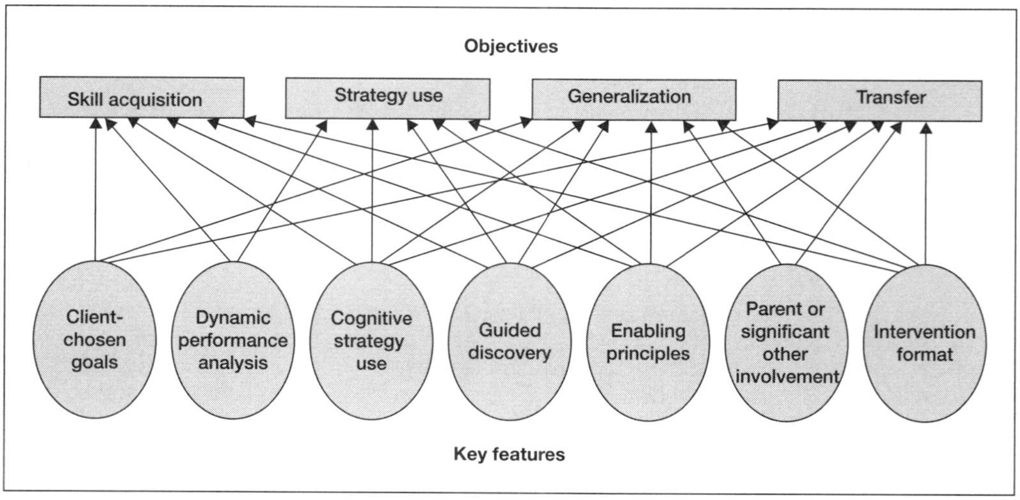

Figure 3.6 *Key features of the CO-OP approach.*
Source: Polatajko and Mandich (2004) (p. 53). Reprinted by permission.

The three major objectives of the CO-OP approach are skill acquisition, building cognitive strategies, and generalization and transfer. For the intervention to be effective, the child must have sufficient cognitive and language ability, have the potential to identify and accomplish goals, be motivated, and be able to attend and respond. However, children with complex presentations might not be able to meet the above criteria, so adaptation of the approach might be required. Rodger and Brandenburg (2009) found preliminary positive results using the CO-OP model with children with Asperger's syndrome.

Handwriting Programs

There are many handwriting programs available from commercial publishers. Programs such as Peggy Leggo, Scribble to Script, Pointing in the Right Direction, Handwriting without Tears, and Callirobics use a variety of sensorimotor and visual motor cues as well as verbal cues and rhymes to promote handwriting skills. The consolidation of prewriting skills, such as top-down, left to right, vertical, horizontal, and diagonal strokes, seated posture, and pencil grasp, are often emphasized in the programs. Letter formation is taught via tracing, practice worksheets, and body movements that represent the shapes of the letters in an attempt to consolidate the motor movement required for writing. Certain programs, such as Peggy Leggo or the Barchowsky fluent method, group letters that have similar shapes to teach correct letter formation.

Adaptive Equipment/Assistive Technology

Often, when tasks are too difficult for the child and a quick resolution is required so that he can "get on" with his activities, adaptive technology is recommended or used in conjunction with therapy. Simple equipment such as pencil grips, larger pens and pencils, and larger lined paper can assist a child who has handwriting difficulties. Bowls with lips, nonslip placemats, water bottles with straws or sippers, and larger-grip cutlery can assist a child who has difficulty self-feeding. Laptops and computers are often recommended for children who have significant difficulty with handwriting, especially in the older years when the workload is more demanding. Visual schedules can be used for children with anxiety or auditory processing or organizational difficulties.

Environmental Changes

Education of the adults involved with the child, particularly parents and teachers, can provide an understanding of sensory processing and the child's particular difficulties with it. Through education about interaction styles, communication techniques, and SDs, changes can be made in the child's social, physical, and sensory environment to support the child to achieve optimal functioning.

For example, a child with auditory processing difficulties can become dysregulated in a noisy environment and find it difficult to focus on what the teacher is asking him to do. In this situation, seating within the classroom, quiet spaces, headphones, and ear plugs can assist the child by eliminating unwanted sounds. Combined with visual cues, these strategies can assist the child in understanding instructions and what is expected of him.

Activities of Daily Living

Children who have difficulty with sensorimotor skills and sensory processing often have problems with tasks such as feeding, brushing teeth, getting a haircut, toileting, and sleeping. Strategies to teach these skills are varied. One method is starting with a simplified task and gradually increasing the complexity of the task. Another tool is backward chaining, in which the child is taught the task in reverse, usually completing the last few steps and slowly increasing the number of steps until she is able to complete the entire task. Adaptations or assistive technology, visual schedules, prompts, and/or modifications of the task are also strategies that can be used.

Community Integration and Functional Skills

Children with complex needs, especially those with regulatory disorders, might have difficulty engaging and accessing community groups and services. They might miss social cues, be impulsive, or withdraw. As a result, they can miss out on important activities and have difficulty negotiating the outside world. Community integration training can be effective for children who have difficulty generalizing skills and require explicit teaching of splinter skills. For example, the therapist might teach a child with anxiety and poor visual perceptual skills to catch public transportation. Skills taught can include negotiating the timetable and money to successfully catch the train to and from home and school. Occupational therapists can use CO-OP strategies, as outlined, or create visual cues and prompts. They can suggest certain equipment to make it easier for the child, such as a preloaded bus-ticket card, a watch with an alarm, or a mobile phone to check timetables.

Assistance with transitioning these children into extracurricular activities such as gymnastics, taekwondo, or swimming lessons might be required because instructors might need information regarding the child's needs. The child might also require an SD or regulation activities to aid attention and organization prior to commencing the activity.

Sensorimotor Play

The use of play should not be confused with the term "play therapy." Many occupational therapists have undergone postgraduate training in play therapy and provide such services. However, play is also used as a therapeutic tool to engage the child. Because play is generally the most enjoyable activity for a child, its lure in a therapeutic setting is often appealing. Depending on the therapist and with input from the child, the sessions can be directive, partly directive, or nondirective. However, in all sessions, the therapist must provide (1) clear boundaries and rules to ensure safety; (2) choice; (3) an "out" if the child feels unsafe; (4) praise, support, and scaffolding, (4) a measure of success; and (5) an air of playfulness and reciprocity.

The use of play is particularly successful with children with executive dysfunction, behavior and emotion regulation difficulties, low self-esteem, selective mutism, or traumatic experiences. Perry (2006) suggests that traumatic experiences can shut down language areas and the prefrontal cortex when the brain is flooded with stress hormones accompanying threat; thus, language-based psychotherapies might not be effective initially (Koomar, 2009). Also, children with auditory processing difficulties might find the instructions hard to follow. Sensorimotor play sessions facilitated by an occupational therapist using SI principles can provide nonthreatening, enjoyable, child-directed sessions while providing organization and regulation. From these sessions, the child can increase his capacity to self-reflect, discuss, and engage in psychotherapy.

Service Provision

How the intervention is provided depends on the child, parents, resources, goals, and systems. Below we discuss the variety of ways that intervention can be provided and the clinical reasoning behind them.

Individual Work

Individual work is often selected when the goals that have been identified are unique to the child and require individualized adjustments. Often children with complex presentations can feel exposed and threatened in group situations and thus are not able to perform at their potential. At times, individual work is required before group work can be introduced. Certain strategies such as Ayres's SI dictate that the intervention be individualized to be responsive to the child and make any required adjustments.

At times, when a child has several difficulties, working cooperatively with another therapist such as a speech therapist or psychologist in an integrative approach can be useful. The benefits can be fewer intervention sessions and a consistent approach to intervention for language, sensory, emotional, and behavioral difficulties. Several sources of information can be pooled together for parents to understand, and as a result they can be more usable. Disadvantages of this approach are that too many adults can be overwhelming for the child. However, this problem can be overcome if therapists have a clear understanding of roles and rapport building with the child. Another disadvantage is that appointment times can be limited when negotiating among different clinicians.

Group Work

Group work can be used for a variety of reasons. It is cost-effective when working with a group of individuals with similar presentations. The group process itself can be a therapeutic tool to encourage social skills, build rapport, and establish confidence through sharing of experiences and information. It can also be used as an assessment tool to observe interactions and problem solving to improve social behaviors and sensorimotor skills. Many types of groups can be conducted in the context of improving sensorimotor and sensory processing skills. There are sensorimotor and handwriting groups, calming, and Alert program groups. Other programs that can aid in regulating and enhancing coordination are brain gym, drumbeat, and body awareness groups.

Education/Consultation

Education for parents and other caregivers is a crucial part of any intervention. Feedback regarding assessment results and findings can often lead to a better understanding of a child and a change of perspective. Children with complex presentations often have several assessments and recommendations. The provision of information in an integrated, concise, user-friendly, and compassionate manner is imperative for parental understanding and compliance.

Because the child spends most of her week in an educational setting, it is important to provide the school with information about her needs and proposed interventions. This is often provided by a multidisciplinary team to ensure consistent and manageable strategies. Education about and strategies for specific disorders are often helpful to the school and can be used for many other children in the classroom.

Home/School Programs

Home and school programs are generally developed for each child to ensure consistent language and strategies to help him perform to his maximum potential. SDs and environmental changes are often coupled with other strategies provided by teachers, psychologists, and speech pathologists.

INTEGRATION OF TREATMENT MODALITIES

Integration of treatment modalities is an important practice among therapists from various disciplines. An integrated approach occurs when a therapist uses her knowledge of various practices and theories to gain a clearer picture of the child's problems and to plan and implement the most effective intervention program (Fisher et al., 1991).

Impairment-oriented and performance-oriented strategies are often integrated, especially when the goal is skill development (e.g., self-feeding, buttoning shirts, and handwriting). In these instances, performance-based strategies are often faster and more functional. Therapies such as Ayres's SI and sensorimotor integration aim to improve foundational senses such as auditory processing, proprioception, tactile, visual, and vestibular to improve higher-order functioning (Ayres, 1972a, 1972b, 2005).

To promote the integration of these senses (middle of the house in Figure 3.2), sensorimotor and Ayres's SI strategies can be useful. These skills all impact the child's ability to perform higher-order skills because they help with the development of perception, organization, planning, and performing tasks.

However, specific skills such as handwriting, feeding, and dressing (top level of bricks of the house) in Figure 3.2 might need to be explicitly taught through performance-oriented strategies such as handwriting programs, CO-OP, and skills training.

The following example illustrates how the integrated approach was used with a child with a number of different sensorimotor and sensory processing problems.

Case Study: Kalaiha

Assessment

Kalaiha, described at the beginning of the chapter, had significant difficulties with self-regulation, poor body awareness, and significant sensory sensitivities to noise and touch. She also had difficulties with fine and gross motor skills, related to motor planning. Kalaiha also had receptive and expressive speech difficulties and very low self-esteem and self-worth. Her cognitive functioning was in the low-average range.

Upon discussion with Kalaiha, it was discovered that she wanted to make friends and do well at school. However, she thought that she was "stupid" and "ugly" and that kids did not like her. As a result, she was hypersensitive and would often react when she thought she was being criticized or attacked. Kalaiha also did not like to take risks that might expose her difficulties to others.

Intervention

A team intervention plan was developed for Kalaiha. Her case manager's role was to work with her parents to address parenting and attachment issues, and speech therapy was provided to address expressive and receptive language difficulties. Educational support was given to adapt and educate her school system regarding her difficulties, capabilities, and needs. Joint nursing and occupational therapy were provided to address her various issues.

Priorities were to (a) develop Kalaiha's awareness of her body, (b) increase her tolerance to stimuli, (c) introduce and teach self-regulation techniques, (d) develop a means for Kalaiha to communicate her worries and thoughts, and (e) address handwriting issues.

Kalaiha was seen once a week by the occupational therapist and once a week by the nurse specialist. The aim was to provide a supportive environment for her to express her concerns while using sensorimotor activities. Kalaiha did not respond well to traditional talking therapy but did engage in conversation when involved in movement activities. The occupational therapist believed that the linear vestibular movement had a calming, nonthreatening, and organizing effect on Kalaiha, which allowed her to discuss her concerns. Because she had been in the clinic classroom setting, she had previous knowledge of the Alert engine speed program. Sessions with the occupational therapist primarily began with linear movement activities such as jumping on the trampoline and catching balls, lying prone on a therapy ball and sorting items, and pulling herself on a scooter board. During this time, the therapist would discuss how Kalaiha had been and times during the week when her engine speed had gone off the chart. They would discuss the event leading up to the problem, focusing on what had happened, why it had happened, how it had made her body and mind feel, and which strategies she had used to help bring her speed down. Following this, a body awareness activity was conducted, such as pulling faces in front of a mirror, creating emotion clay figurines, coloring, drawing characters, drumming, and facial expression guessing games. These tasks were initially difficult for Kalaiha, but the therapist graded the activities with simple tasks such as drawing and using different mediums to explore textures. Kalaiha's favorite activity was drumming, which became the main activity of most sessions. Following this activity, the therapist would describe the findings of the session and discuss with Kalaiha whether they were a correct reflection of what had happened. This information was then passed on to the nurse, who would see her in the next session. The nurse used a similar formula, consolidating information in worksheets that she helped to fill out about Kalaiha and her world while incorporating drumming and other motor activities. Kalaiha's handwriting issues were discussed with her teachers, pencil grips were given to Kalaiha, and the use of computers to conduct schoolwork was discussed.

In conjunction with the school room, speech pathologist, and school nurse, the occupational therapist designed a system for the classroom using an emotion wheel and a red/green dot for Kalaiha to indicate whether she was having difficulty and what she was feeling.

After two terms in the school system and receiving individual therapy, Kalaiha could indicate to adults what she was feeling and choose strategies to help her regulate. She also had a better understanding of her body and could identify early warning signs when her engine speed was "revving." She responded well to adults' observations of her engine speed and adjusted her speed accordingly by using several strategies. Within the school system, she made several good friends, and when one of her friends was leaving the program she did a drumming performance in front of the class, teachers, and parents for her friend. Upon discharge, the team provided feedback to the follow-up services, and ongoing therapy was offered by a clinical psychologist who would use the strategies implemented by the team.

CONCLUSION

SPD symptoms can be similar to those of other difficulties or disorders and often be overlooked for more common diagnoses. It is important that sensory processing and sensorimotor difficulties are considered when developing a formulation of the case and deciding on treatment. This is important when working with infants and toddlers, for effective sensory processing results in positive brain organization and regulation of the child. Also with older children it can bring a different perspective and understanding about the child's difficulties and provide parents and teachers with successful ways of improving the child's development and functioning.

Effective sensory processing and sensorimotor skills play an essential role in the development of a child. Without correct processing of information, children are at risk of misinterpreting their environment, resulting in incorrect and/or inappropriate responses. This in turn has serious implications for their ability to effectively learn and respond to their physical, social, and emotional environments, impacting their self-esteem and socialization. Difficulties in sensory modulation in early life can result in poor attachment to and bonding with caregivers. Research has shown that children with difficulties with their motor skills and/or sensory processing are at increased risk of social, attentional, behavioral, and emotional problems and of developing a negative sense of self and the world (Cocks et al., 2009; Cummins et al., 2005; Green et al., 2006; Hoffman and Birtan, 2007; Zwicker et al., 2009). Thus, early detection and intervention are important for the prevention of poor mental health outcomes.

For information on various websites that offer related programs, see Table 3.10.

Table 3.10 *Websites*

Website	Information on Website
www.spdfoundation.net	Website of SPD. Foundation that provides online education on multiple topics.
www.ot.utoronto.ca	Website of CO-OP Academy. "It is a therapeutic treatment approach for people having difficulty performing motor-based skills." Includes children with DCD and adults recovering from stroke. Has information for parents, provides workshops, and a number of publications.
www.sensorysmarts.com	Website of Sensory Smarts that provides information on occupational therapy and sensory processing.
www.alertprogram.com	Website of Therapy Works, Albuquerque, New Mexico. The Alert Program is described.
www.out-of-synch-child.com	Contains articles, and interviews with Carol Kranowitz, author of the *Out-of-Synch Child* or children with SI issues.
www.wfot.org	Website of the World Federation of Occupational Therapists (WFOT). It has approved educational programs and a resource center. Also publishes the *International Journal of Therapy and Rehabilitation.*
www.aota.org	Website of the American Occupational Therapy Association. inc. Has information and publishes *OT Practice Magazine.*
www.icoll.com/dirfloortime/overview/index.shtml	DIR and Floortime model used to conduct comprehensive assessments and to develop an intervention plan.

APPENDIX

Occupational Therapy Screening Measure
School Age
Parent Questionnaire

Child's DOB:______________

Please write down any concerns you have about your child's development:____

____

____

Has your child received occupational therapy at another service?
If so, when and with whom?

____

____

____

	Right	Left	Either
Which hand does your child prefer to use?	☐	☐	☐

Gross motor

Does your child

	Yes	No	Comment
Run, skip, and hop effortlessly?			
Play on outdoor equipment confidently?			
Catch and throw a small ball?			
Catch and throw a large ball?			
Often slouch at the table?			
Appear clumsy, fall over, and knock herself often?			
Avoid sporting activities?			

Fine motor

Does your child

	Yes	No	Comment
Hold his pencil correctly?			
Produce legible handwriting—size, shape, spacing, structure?			
Cut along a line with scissors?			
Manipulate construction toys easily—Lego, craft work, model toys?			

(continued)

Vision

Does your child

	Yes	No	Comment
Use a finger as a pointer when reading?			
Skip words when reading?			
Copy work from the whiteboard?			
Complain of tired and/or sore eyes?			

Activities of daily living

Does your child

	Yes	No	Comment
Dress independently?			
Tie shoelaces?			
Do/undo zippers and buttons?			
Use a spoon, fork, knife correctly?			
Pour himself a drink?			
Make a simple snack such as a sandwich?			

Behavior

Does your child

	Yes	No	Comment
Become anxious when separating from you?			
Follow routines easily?			
Make and keep friends easily?			
Complete her schoolwork efficiently?			
Follow instructions?			
Ask questions in an appropriate manner?			
Start activities independently?			

Sensory

Does your child present as

	Yes	No	Comment
Sensory sensitive? Overreacts to sensory stimulation, seen as negative or defiant behavior, might be fearful and anxious, distractible, and/or hyperactive			
Sensory avoiding? Resistant to change, relies on rigid rituals			
Sensory seeking? Very active, continuously engaged in her environment, fidgety, and excitable			
Poor registration? Does not interact with environment much, tends to be passive, fatigues easily, and appears lethargic			

4

Language and Communication Impairment and Emotional and Behavioral Disorders in Children

ROCHELLE MOUKINA

This chapter explores complex emotional and behavioral disorders of childhood and the contribution of language and communication problems to those disorders. The relationship between these problems and such disorders in children has been the focus of research in recent years (Hill & Coufel, 2005). Children with language impairment are at significant risk of developing later psychosocial problems compared with children with no language impairment. Law, Rush, Schoon, and Parsons (2009) conducted a birth cohort study in the United Kingdom of 17,196 children. They found a strong relationship between early language and learning difficulties and the later development of poor literacy, mental health, and employment outcomes.

However, in clinical settings, impaired language and communication skills are often overlooked as contributors to the child's emotional and behavioral presentation. To provide appropriate differential diagnoses and interventions for multichallenged children, it is important for clinicians and researchers to seriously consider the relationship between language and communication impairment and a child's emotional and behavioral functioning. The correlation between language deficits and psychopathology is complex and interactional. Language deficits impact psychopathology; conversely, psychopathology impacts a child's language and communicative development and functioning. Furthermore, longitudinal studies robustly identify that the rate of comorbidity between language impairment and emotional and behavioral disorders increases and strengthens over time (Baltaxe, 2001).

In this chapter, the nature and contribution of language impairments associated with particular psychopathological presentations, along with assessments and interventions, are considered. Two case studies are introduced and discussed later in light of functional intervention approaches.

Case Study 1: Andrew

Andrew was an 8-year-old only child referred to a mental health outpatient clinic following a presentation at the local children's hospital emergency department with thoughts of suicide and reported auditory hallucinations. An assessment by the interdisciplinary team showed that he experienced difficulties with emotion regulation, generalized anxiety disorder, suicidal ideation, sleep problems, and significant difficulties with interpersonal relationships with peers. Andrew had a complex social and medical history. He was born addicted to opiates since his mother was on the methadone program during pregnancy to stabilize her heroin use at the time. Andrew was weaned off opiates in a special care nursery as a newborn. During this time, he experienced feeding difficulties, and it was discovered that he had a cleft palate. During this early postnatal period, his mother resumed her recreational drug use. When Andrew was 5 months of age, his mother resumed full-time work, and he was cared for by his father, who was an active drug user and emotionally absent. Andrew's home life was described as chaotic, with periods of domestic violence and homelessness. Andrew did not attend day care or play groups during his early years, and attendance in Kindergarten was his first experience of formal schooling and socialization. He had a series of painful medical procedures and surgeries to correct his cleft palate, dentition problems, and chronic otitis media. Once attending school, he presented with a severe expressive and receptive language delay and speech disorder related to his cleft palate. Andrew continued to present with chronic otitis media, had multiple sets of grommets inserted, and was fitted with bone conduction hearing aids.

Case Study 2: Sarah

Six-year-old Sarah was in a long-term foster care placement after being apprehended at 4 years of age. She was a twin and had experienced a traumatic birth, requiring resuscitation, and had very low birth weight. All of her developmental milestones were delayed. Her early childhood was marked by extreme neglect and abuse. Sarah was diagnosed with posttraumatic stress disorder and reactive attachment disorder, and attention deficit/hyperactivity disorder (ADHD) was queried. Cognitive assessments showed that she had a borderline IQ but would not meet criteria for special educational support. Her expressive language and comprehension skills appeared to be very delayed. In the school environment, Sarah was described as noncompliant, work avoidant, and oppositional in the classroom around educational tasks. On the playground, she easily became overwhelmed and could become aggressive, resulting in her absconding from school and having a number of suspensions. Sarah was diagnosed with a severe expressive and receptive language disorder (LD) and auditory processing disorder (APD) with extreme auditory sensitivities.

HISTORICAL RESEARCH

Research on communication and language difficulties and disorders has emerged from four clinical perspectives. Although the body of research is deepening, a few studies have systematically characterized patterns of comorbidity in language and behavior or investigated the processes linking language difficulties and psychopathology (Nelson, Benner, & Rogers-Adkinson, 2003). This research is described next.

Research From Language-Impaired Populations

Baker and Cantwell (1987) conducted a study investigating the prevalence of emotional and behavioral problems in children identified as having a speech and language problem. This research included 600 children from a speech and language clinic who were administered a standardized language assessment and psychiatric evaluation. Children were subsequently categorized based on the *Diagnostic and Statistical Manual of Mental Disorders*, 3rd edition (*DSM-III*; American Psychiatric Association [APA], 1980) as being psychiatrically well or psychiatrically ill; 50% of participants were identified as psychiatrically ill. It is important to note that, the most significant difference between the groups was in linguistic functioning compared to either socioeconomic status, psychosocial ability, or developmental milestones. The researchers identified that speech and language factors were significantly associated with psychiatric illness. Interestingly, girls with a specific language impairment

(SLI) were at the greatest risk of emotional disorders, as indicated by internalized negative representations of self. Research by Leonard (1991) with a sample of 156 children with an SLI referred to a specialist clinic supports these findings.

Although the relationship between language impairment and emotional and behavioral problems has been established, qualitative research investigating types of language impairment and specific behavioral problems has had less development. Daal, Verhoeven, and van Balkom (2007) investigated such a relationship. They extensively assessed the language abilities and behavioral profiles of 71 5-year-old children. Forty percent of children had significant behavioral problems as assessed by the Child Behavior Checklist (CBCL; Achenbach, 2001). The most frequent problems were withdrawn behavior, somatic complaints, thought problems, and aggressive behavior. These behavioral problems were associated with difficulties in three of the four language areas: syntax, semantics, and phonology, with semantic problems particularly related to internalizing behaviors. A conclusion that Daal et al. (2007) made was that different mental health problems might be associated with different language impairments from a young age.

Psychosocial outcomes for children with language deficits are sobering. Longitudinal studies have demonstrated an increased prevalence of mental health problems in children identified with significant speech and language impairments (Beitchman et al., 2001; Clegg, Hollis, Mawhood, & Rutter, 2005) and increased risk of poor academic and vocational outcomes. Longitudinal studies have identified socialization problems associated with language impairments and that the language, social, and behavioral problems of school-aged children increased with age (Conti-Ramsden & Botting, 2004).

Research From Psychiatric-Impaired Populations

Benner et al. (2002) conducted a literature review of 26 studies investigating the relationship between language deficits and antisocial behaviors. They identified four principal findings based on this review and previous research reviews.

- Children with an SLI affecting comprehension skills were at a significantly higher risk of antisocial behavior and have higher rates of behavioral problems than children with other speech and language deficits.
- Comprehension problems were frequently unidentified compared with expressive difficulties. Children with comprehension difficulties were also at an increased risk of reading impairments.
- Researchers estimated that the concomitant prevalence of language deficits in children with antisocial behaviors was 10 times higher than in the general population.
- Language deficits have a serious adverse effect on developing and maintaining important life relationships. In fact, difficulties in social relationships have been indicated as a mediating variable in the association between language deficits and antisocial behavior.

Cohen, Davine, Horodezky, Lipsett, and Isaacson (1993) examined the prevalence of unsuspected language impairments in 4- to 12-year-olds in a mental health outpatient clinic. In their study, 399 children were routinely screened with standardized language tests and parent and teacher behavioral checklists. The results showed that, of the sample of 288 children referred for psychiatric or internalizing disorders, 34.4% (N = 99) had a language impairment that had not been previously identified, and 111 had a previously identified language impairment. So approximately one third of the child psychiatric outpatients had an unidentified language impairment detected only through routine screening, and one third had an identified language impairment. Cohen (2001) reported that children with externalizing behavior presentations who were rated as more aggressive were likely to have an unidentified LD, whereas children with internalized behavioral presentations, such as being withdrawn and anxious, were likely to have their language impairment identified prior to referral. The nature of language impairment differed between the previously identified language-impaired group and the unidentified language-impaired group. A summary of the findings of Cohen et al. (1993) follows:

- Children with unsuspected language impairment had the most serious externalizing behaviors compared with children with normally developing language.
- Children with previously identified language impairment had more internalizing problems compared with children with normally developing language.
- A higher proportion of children with previously identified language impairment were diagnosed with severe language impairment as opposed to moderate or mild impairment.
- Most children in both the identified and the unidentified language-impaired groups presented with mixed receptive and expressive language impairment.
- Expressive syntax (grammar and sentence formulation) was the greatest area of impairment in the previously identified language-impaired group.
- Impaired receptive language skills (comprehension) were identified as significantly problematic in the group.

Relationship of Shared Etiology

Early language development is interrelated with cognitive, emotional, and social domains of development. A combination of genetic, biological, and environmental factors can contribute to significant language and communication problems and complex emotional and behavioral disorders of childhood. Evidence of an early link between language and emotional/behavioral disorders has been investigated. Researchers investigating early risk factors that predict both LD and emotional and behavioral disorders have identified shared risk factors in early childhood, including biological factors such as preterm birth (Cohen, Parmelee, Beckwith, & Sigman, 1992; Siegel, 1982); exposure during the prenatal stage of development to alcohol and drugs (Soby, 2006); early childhood trauma (Simpson, Colpe, & Greenspan, 2003); and genetic factors such as heritability of ADHD and language impairment or pervasive developmental disorders.

LANGUAGE, SPEECH, AND COMMUNICATION DISORDERS

Communication is a complex cognitive and social behavior that involves conveying a message from one person to another via a number of mediums. Language can be defined as a set of symbols organized by convention to communicate ideas. These conventions or rules are shared by individuals to allow them to engage in the exchange. Language is the key tool that we use to shape our understanding of the world, form social relationships, problem solve, and educate (Crystal, 2002; Gascoigne, 2006; Tarshis, Rodriguez, & Seijo, 2007). For children who experience language acquisition difficulties, despite adequate exposure, these difficulties affect most aspects of their lives, with deficits impacting their relationships, education, and capacity to interact with their world (Gascoigne, 2006). See Table 4.1 for definitions of these disorders.

Language Components

Language is often described in terms of expressive language and comprehension skills. Linguists, however, define language based on unitary components, considered the building

Table 4.1 *Definitions of Language, Speech, and Communication Disorders*

Disorder	Definitions of Disorders
Communication disorders	Impairment in the ability to receive, send, process, and comprehend concepts or verbal, nonverbal, and graphic symbol systems. A communication disorder may range in severity from mild to profound and be either developmental or acquired (ASHA, 1993).
Speech disorders	An impairment of the articulation of sounds, fluency, or voice. This definition includes articulation disorder, fluency disorder (stuttering) and/or voice disorder (ASHA, 1993).
SSD	Also known as a phonological or articulation disorder and is the result of a child experiencing difficulties in producing, sequencing, and organizing the sounds in language resulting in poor speech intelligibility.
CAS	Childhood Apraxia of Speech (CAS) results in difficulties in producing sounds, syllables, and words due to the brain's difficulty in coordinating oral–facial muscle movements (ASHA, 2007).
Dysarthria	Dysarthria occurs when the muscles of the mouth, face, and respiratory system have become weak, low in tone, or move slowly. As a result, the child may present with slurred speech, a slow rate of speech, or alternatively a fast rate of speech with a mumbled quality; limited lip, tongue, and jaw movement; and poor voice and prosody modulation (ASHA, 2007).
Stuttering	Stuttering is a disorder affecting the fluency of speech. It is characterized by repetitions of sounds, syllables, part or whole words or phrases; prolongation of sounds; or blocking of sounds.
Language disorder	Language disorder involves impaired comprehension and/or use of spoken, written, and/or other symbol systems. The disorder may involve: (a) the form of language (phonology, morphology, and syntax), (b) the content of language (semantics), and/or (c) the function of language in communication (pragmatics) in any combination (ASHA, 1993).
SLI	SLI is diagnosed when normal language does not develop and cannot be explained in terms of physical or intellectual disability, hearing loss or environmental deprivation (Bishop, 1992).
Auditory processing disorder	This is a disorder in the function of the central auditory structures, which results in impaired ability to process (manipulate/use) acoustic signals (Stach, 2003).
Social (pragmatic) communication disorder	Pragmatic language refers to the appropriate use of language or the rules governing appropriate language use for the purpose of communicating (Paul, 2006). A SCD is when there is a persistent difficulty in the social use of verbal and nonverbal communication (*DSM-5*; APA, 2013)

blocks of language. They are morphology, semantics, syntax, pragmatics, phonology, and prosody (see Table 4.2). However, in a communicative act, language components "typically bind together in a seamless manner to form what seems to be a single unitary skill" (Tommerdahl, 2009, p. 23). This is reflected well in Bloom and Lahey's (1978) taxonomy of language model (see Figure 4.1), which demonstrates how the different elements of language are interrelated. The model describes language as comprising three areas: form, content, and

Table 4.2 *Speech, Language, and Communication Terminology*

Language Term	Definition
Communication	A complex cognitive and social behavior that involves conveying a message or information from one person to another via a number of mediums, such as language, gesture, and written language.
Language	Language is a set of symbols that are organized in a convention to communicate ideas. The conventions or rules are shared by the individuals who are communicating, allowing for an exchange.
Morphology	This refers to the smallest unit of meaning in language. A morpheme is a linguistic unit. A word is one morpheme (e.g., garden) but a plural is two morphemes (e.g., gardens).
Semantics	Semantics refers to the meaning carried by words and the relationship that exists between words in one's lexical system.
Syntax	Syntax refers to the rules that underlie word order, sentence construction, and word combinations.
Phonology	Phonology refers to the sounds of a language system.
Prosody	Prosody refers to the intonation and rhythm of speech.
Narrative	Narrative is the recounting of a temporal sequence of events. A narrative may be procedural, personal, or a retell.
Pragmatics	Pragmatics refers to the rules governing appropriate use of language or the social conventions of how we interact.
Conversational discourse	Conversational discourse refers to the understanding and use of language embedded in conversation.

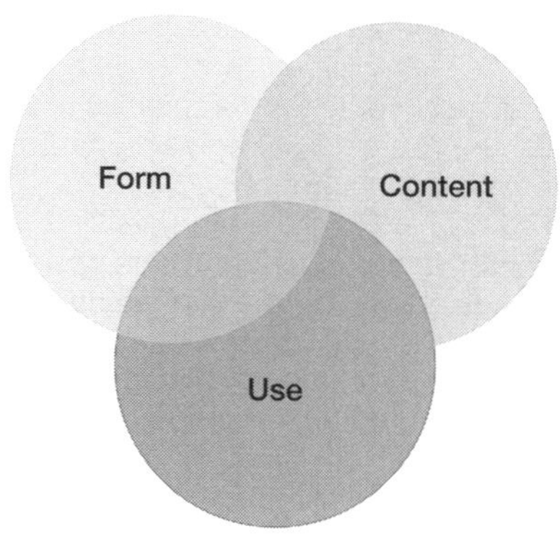

Figure 4.1 *Bloom and Lahey's (1978) taxonomy of language.*

use. *Form* refers to syntax, morphology, and phonology; *content* refers to semantics and the meaning of the message conveyed; and *use* refers to pragmatics and the appropriateness of language use in a particular context. Effective communication requires development in all modalities.

Communication and Written Language Disorder (LD)

Communication disorders encompass speech, language, and processing disorders. Communication disorders are classified as a group of neurodevelopmental disorders that onset during the early developmental period (*DSM-5*; APA, 2013). An LD is impairment in comprehension and/or use of spoken, written, and/or other symbol systems (American Speech-Language-Hearing Association [ASHA], 1993). Difficulties can be with language form, content, and use. Leonard (1998, p. 177) defined children as having language problems "whenever their language abilities are below those expected for their age and their level of functioning."

Primary and Secondary LDs

The literature often differentiates between a primary and secondary LD. In the literature the former was often referred to as a specific language impairment (SLI) and the child does not have another disorder related to the delay. The latter is identified when a child has communication impairment as a result of a hearing impairment, cognitive impairment, developmental delays, autism spectrum disorder (ASD), neurological impairment (for example, epilepsy or brain injuries), and/or environmental deprivation. When a child presents with a secondary LD, the level of communication impairment often reflects the broader cognitive profile of the primary disorder (Rice & Warren, 2004).

Language Disorder (LD)

LD is diagnosed when normal language does not develop and cannot be explained in terms of physical or intellectual disability, hearing loss, or environmental deprivation (Bishop, 1992; APA, 2013). Previously LD's were referred to in the literature as a specific language impairment (SLI). It is important to note that LD is evident while nonverbal developmental domains are within an age-expected range. Epidemiology research suggests that 7% of 5- to 6-year-olds have an LD (Tomlin et al., 1997). Historically, LD subtypes have been defined as expressive LD and mixed expressive and receptive (comprehension) LD (APA, 2000). An expressive LD is identified when production difficulties with semantics, syntax, and phonology occur. Even though this disorder has been considered a distinct disorder, evidence suggests that these children also have limitations in language knowledge and/or processing (Leonard, 2009). Comprehension impairment refers to difficulties in constructing the meaning of a message or text (Skarakis-Doyle & Dempsey, 2008). Therefore, a child's comprehension deficit can be experienced as difficulties in understanding semantic or syntactic information (see Table 4.2). *DSM-5* (APA, 2013) describes LD deficits in comprehension and production as reduced vocabulary, limited sentence structure, and impairments in discourse.

Children with LD are often perceived as incorporating a heterogeneous group of disorders. Under the umbrella of LD is a diversity of presentations and profiles of strengths and weaknesses that can be evident in a clinical setting (Bishop, 1992). Hence, two children given the same diagnosis, such as expressive language delay, can present very differently depending on the qualitative nature and severity of their individual deficits. Researchers have postulated a number of hypotheses to explain LD etiology; however, "given the diverse range of linguistic manifestations that are encompassed under this diagnostic label (SLI), it may be unrealistic to look for a single underlying factor that can explain all cases of SLI" (Bishop, 1992, p. 53). It is therefore important for clinicians to be mindful of a variety of complex influences such as cognitive, linguistic, and sensory processes that can be impacting LD presentation.

Late Language Emergence

Late talkers present with a delay in the onset of language in the first 24 months of life with no other developmental difficulties. Epidemiological research has shown that 13% to 19% of children present as late talkers (Zubrick, Taylor, Rice, & Slegers, 2007). Risk factors identified for late talkers were being male (boys were three times more likely to be late talkers), being born at less than 85% of optimal birth weight, and having a family history of late talking (Zubrick et al., 2007). In a follow-up study, children with late language emergence were twice as likely to be identified as having language performance below normative levels (Rice, Taylor, & Zubrick, 2008). However, not all late talkers persisted with a later language delay. Dale, Price, Bishop, and Plomin (2003) found similar results. This research has two significant outcomes. First, it identifies late language emergence as a risk factor for ongoing language impairment. Second, it confirms the need for early identification of late talkers for the purpose of intervention (Dale et al., 2003; Rescorla, 2005; Rice et al., 2008).

Speech Sound Disorders

Speech sound disorders (SSDs) were previously known as phonological or articulation disorders and may result when a child experiences difficulties in producing, sequencing, and organizing the sounds in language. An SSD can be a problem with making sounds (articulation) or with phonological processes (sound patterns such as substitutions and omissions of groups of sounds) (ASHA, 1993).

Motor speech disorders include childhood apraxia of speech (CAS) and dysarthria. CAS results in difficulties in producing sounds, syllables, and words due to the brain's difficulty in coordinating oral–facial muscle movements (ASHA, 2007). Feldman (2005) characterized CAS as an SSD that results in difficulties in planning, programming, and producing speech sounds. Dysarthria involves the muscles of the mouth, face, and respiratory system. These muscles have become weak, low in tone, or move slowly (ASHA, 2007). As a result, the child can present with slurred speech, a slow rate of speech, or a fast rate of speech with a mumbled quality; limited lip, tongue, and jaw movement; and poor voice and prosody modulation (ASHA, 2007).

Childhood-Onset Fluency Disorder (Stuttering)

Stuttering is a disorder that affects the normal fluency and time patterning of speech (*DSM-5*, 2013). Secondary characteristics can include unusual facial expressions, uncontrolled motor behaviors, and tics. Emotional and social factors associated with stuttering include embarrassment, social avoidance, high levels of anxiety, and even social or phobic anxiety (Craig & Tran, 2006b). The anxiety caused by stuttering may limit and impact social, academic and or occupational performance (*DSM-5*, 2013).

Social (Pragmatic) Communication Disorder

Social communication disorder (SCD) refers to a primary disorder in the pragmatic use of language but is also influenced by a child's discourse skill and narrative ability. Children experience significant difficulties in using verbal and nonverbal communication to socially engage and form relationships (*DSM-5;* APA, 2013). The *DSM-5* identifies manifestations of Social Communication Disorder as including: deficits in the social functions of language; difficulties in following conversational rules; difficulties in modifying ones language to match the context or listener; and difficulties with non-literal or ambiguous language, such as making inferences and humor. Successful social communication incorporates elements of pragmatic language, conversational discourse, and narrative skill.

Pragmatic Language Impairment

Pragmatics refers to the appropriate use of language or the rules governing appropriate language use for the purpose of communicating (Paul, 2006). Pragmatics was described by Prutting and Kirchner (1987) as including verbal utterances, paralinguistic utterances, and nonverbal behavior. Verbal utterances include topic initiation and maintenance, turn taking, use of context, interruptions, and amount of talk; paralinguistic utterances include intensity, intelligibility, tone, and rhythm of speech; and nonverbal behaviors include eye contact, facial expression, physical proximity, and gestures. Based on this definition, a pragmatic deficit is not limited to spoken language and can include deficits in understanding gestures and facial expressions. Characteristics of pragmatic language impairment also include difficulties in reciprocity; turn taking; appropriate use and integration of body language, facial expression, and eye contact; and difficulties in repairing the conversation when there is a breakdown.

Conversational Discourse Impairment

Conversational discourse refers to the understanding and use of language embedded in conversation. Essentially, it is the ability to converse effectively. It is a complex, dynamic, interactional process (Crystal, 2002; Ford & Milosky, 2008). It requires the child to integrate both linguistic and cognitive abilities to communicate thoughts in an organized style (Nippold, Hesketh, Duthie, & Mansfield, 2005). It also requires the child to comprehend, monitor, integrate, and infer meaning during an interaction. The organization of discourse typically includes five components: initiation of conversation, turn taking, maintenance of conversation, conversational repair, and topic or conversational termination. Disorders in the development of discourse skills impact the child's capacity to engage in social interactions that lead to the formation of friendships and have implications for academic functioning.

Narrative Impairment

Narrative is the recounting of a sequence of events. A complete narrative includes appropriate macrostructural elements (beginning, middle, and end); microstructural elements (syntactic and linguistic features); and flow (making it cohesive). Interruptions in the development of narrative skills have significant implications. A narrative is the construct by which people share and engage. It is considered a higher-level language skill, and difficulties with narrative lead to social difficulties, such as peer rejection and bullying (Conti-Ramsden & Botting, 2004), and academic difficulties (Crais & Lorch, 1994). Language-impaired children's oral narratives are typically characterized as being more simplistic, with fewer words, shorter and less complex sentences, grammatical errors, limited cohesive strategies, and generally poorer quality (Fey, Catts, Proctor-Williams, Tomblin, & Zhang, 2004). *DSM-5* (APA, 2013) identifies that difficulties in the ability to explain or describe topics or a series of events is evidence of an LD.

Auditory Processing Disorder (APD)

APD, also known as central auditory processing disorder (CAPD), was defined by Stach (2003, p. 51) as a "disorder in the function of the central auditory structures which results in impaired ability to process (manipulate/use) acoustic signals." ASHA (2005, p. 2) defines APD as "difficulties in the perceptual processing of auditory information in the central nervous system as demonstrated by poor performance in one or more skills." These skills include sound localization, auditory discrimination, auditory pattern recognition, auditory performance in competing acoustic signals (including dichotic listening), and auditory performance in degraded acoustic signals (American Speech and Hearing Association, 1996, 2005). APD is not a deficit of neural processing of auditory stimuli, nor is it due to problems with higher-order language or cognitive factors, but it can lead to higher-order language, learning, and communication difficulties. It can coexist with other disorders, such as ADHD, SLI, and ASD, but is not caused by these disorders (American Speech and Hearing Association, 2005).

Learning Disorder and Literacy Problems

Research has established the strong relationship between persistent speech and language difficulties and later literacy problems in children. Literacy risks are greater for children with SSDs, with idiosyncratic or unusual speech productions, compared to a speech delay that has more typical substitutions (Nelson, 2011). Children with language impairment are also at great risk of later reading and literacy difficulties (Catts, Fey, Zhang, & Tomblin, 1999). Furthermore, children with both SSDs and language impairment are at the highest risk of literacy difficulties and later learning problems (Peterson, Pennington, Shriberg, & Boada, 2009).

Prevalence of Communication and LDs

Epidemiology studies frequently address the prevalence of language impairment in certain age groups. Language impairment is considered a lifespan disability (Nippold & Schwartz, 2002), with speech disorder and LD disproportionately affecting boys more than girls (twice the prevalence). It is estimated that approximately 6% to 8% of children between 0 and 11 years of age have speech, language, and communication problems (Tomblin, Records, Buckwalter, Zhang, & Smith, 1997). The prevalence for children with severe and complex functioning difficulties and disorders might be even higher (Gascoigne, 2006). Given the lifespan trajectory of language deficits, the prevalence of language-learning disability in children and adolescents increases and is estimated to be between 10% and 15% (Conti-Ramsden & Botting, 2004). Throughout the lifespan, the modalities of language impairment might change, but the persistence of language impairment is maintained. For example, language impairment can present in terms of literacy difficulties and learning problems in later childhood and adolescence (Catts, Hogan, & Adolf, 2005).

SSDs are highly prevalent in preschool children, with approximately 16% of 3-year-olds having a speech delay. Approximately 3.8% of these children will continue to have a phonological delay at 6 years of age (Shriberg, Tomblin, & McSweeny, 1999). Ongoing academic difficulties in language- and literacy-based tasks such as reading, writing, and spelling will continue for more than half of these children (Lewis, Freebairn, & Taylor, 2003). Diagnosis of a learning disability is not uncommon for this group, and remedial services might be required for 50% to 70% of these children who presented with persistent phonological disorders at 6 years of age.

LANGUAGE AND THE BRAIN

Understanding the location of language in the brain is exceptionally complex. Language lateralization, referring to hemispheric dominance for the function of language, has been of great interest to researchers. Left-hemispheric dominance for language processing is typical for 95% of right-handed people and 70% of left-handed people (Lurito & Dzemidzic, 2001). Left-lateralization bias for language was confirmed when researchers identified a slight anatomical asymmetry of the planum termporale lobe in right-handed adults, which is also evident in 70% of newborns (Witelson & Pallie, 1973). Although most language processing occurs in the left hemisphere, processing of prosodic features of speech involves the right hemisphere (Baum & Dwivedi, 2003; Meyer, Alter, Friederici, Lohmann, & von Cramon, 2002

Research into neurodevelopmental correlates of reading and language disability is developing. A study by Leonard, Eckert, Given, Virginia, and Berninger (2006), using functional magnetic resonance imaging (fMRI), identified anatomical risk factors for SLI and developmental dyslexia. This study indicated that children with relatively smaller and symmetrical brain structures presented with the severe comprehension impairments typical of an LD profile. These children had severe deficits in reading and language function, in particular comprehension. Children with larger, more asymmetrical brains had fewer deficits, with relatively intact comprehension but a reading disability. Finally, the best performances were found in children with normal neuroanatomy. The area of the brain believed to be associated with dyslexia has had considerable neuroimaging investigations compared with other LDs. An important finding in adults with dyslexia has been termed "disorganization of the language network" despite the absence of lesions (Démonet, Thierry, & Cardebat, 2005, p. 80). This possibly reflects the high level of organization and complexity required for typical language processes, such as reading.

Preliminary research investigating electroencephalographic (EEG) results of infants at risk of LD has shown possible indicators in the first months of life. Friederici (2004) identified that 2-month-old infants at risk of LD had significantly delayed brain reactions when discriminating between vowels of different lengths. Weber, Hahne, Friedrich, and Friederici (2004) showed that 4- to 5-month-olds at risk of LD had reduced brain wave responses when discriminating between prosodic stress patterns of two-word syllables. These studies indicate auditory processing differences between children at risk of LD and controls during infancy.

Brain Organization and Language Functions

The classic model of understanding where language processing occurs in the brain was based on a neuroanatomical model derived from lesion studies (Démonet, Thierry, & Cardebat, 2005). In this model, language processing consisted of a frontal expressive area of the brain, known as Broca's area, and a posterior receptive center, known as Wernicke's area (see Figure 4.2). Broca's and Wernicke's areas were believed to be connected via a white-fiber tract known as the arcuate fascicular. This classic model is now considered overly simplistic, particularly since the advent of neuroimaging techniques such as fMRI and position emission tomography (PET). A cognitive model of language processing has now been developed to reflect different levels of organization of language representation and the interconnectedness of language processing (Smits et al., 2006). Based on the cognitive model, language processing is grouped by modalities of language, including orthography, phonology, syntax, and lexical–semantics (Smits et al., 2006). New neuroanatomical models are more complex and based on this cognitive model.

Recent research using PET and volumetric analysis on individuals with an identified severe speech disorder has shown involvement of the caudate nucleus (Tallal, Jernigan, & Trauner, 1994; Watkins et al., 2002). The cerebellum, noted as important for motor development and complex motor sequences, has also been indicated in some articulatory difficulties, such as dysarthria (Ackerman, Vogel, Peterson, & Poremba, 1992). More recent studies have indicated that the cerebellum might also contribute to language functions such as word recognition (Watkins et al., 2002). One study by Riva and Giorgi (2000) showed that children with right cerebellar tumors presented with impairment in auditory sequential memory and language processing. Preston, Frost, Mencl, Fullbright, and Landi (2010) identified that the thalamus and putamen are also involved in linguistic processing. They analyzed the neural activation patterns of early, on-time, and late talkers. Their study identified that late talkers had a significantly lower level of activation in the bilateral thalamus and putamen. Structural abnormalities identified in some individuals with dyslexia have been found in the corpus callosum, temporal parietal regions (Robichon, Bouchard, Démonet, & Habib, 2000), and cerebellum (Eckert et al., 2003). (See Figure 4.3 for an approximate schematic guide to the location of these structures in the brain that are involved in various aspects of language functioning.)

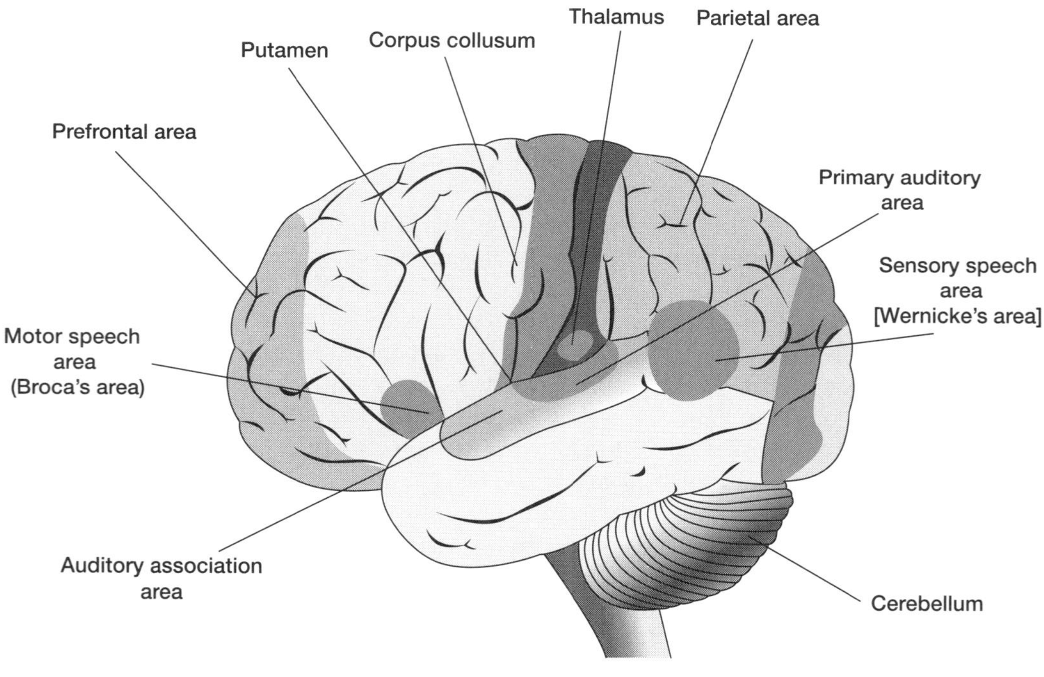

Figure 4.2 *Language functions of the brain.*

Plasticity

The potential for brain plasticity for language functions or brain changes with certain interventions shows promise. The development of language extends into adolescence, suggesting that the potential for neuroplasticity might extend through this developmental period (Démonet et al., 2005). Signs of plasticity have been seen in the success of certain early-intervention programs in high-risk populations; an example is the Verbal Interaction Project (Levenstein, O'Hara, & Levenstein, 1983). This project provided a home-visiting program conducted by paraprofessionals for children 21 to 35 months of age for 2 years, emphasizing enhancement of language. Families were primarily African American living in low-income housing with low levels of educational attainment and employment in semi-skilled jobs. The children were followed up in Grade 7 and had significantly higher IQ scores, better grade retention, and required less special education than those who did not receive the intervention.

Exciting research in the area of pediatric dyslexia showed changes in language performance and brain activity following intensive therapy targeting phonological processing and orthographic training (Kujala et al., 2001; Simos et al., 2002). Research on the treatment of lexical–semantic processing also showed changes in event related brain potentials (ERP) following a 5-week, narrative-based intervention for 6- to 8-year-old children (Popescu, Fey, Lewine, Finestack, & Popescu, 2009).

CONTRIBUTORS TO THE DEVELOPMENT OF LD

Research has demonstrated that the three most significant factors increasing the risk of developing a speech and language impairment are being born a boy; having a family history of speech, language, and reading disorders; and having a history of hearing loss, usually due to middle ear infections (Feldman, 2005). Other significant biological and environmental factors are reviewed next.

Familial and Genetic Factors

Language and literacy impairments have strong genetic contributions (Barry, Yasmin, & Bishop, 2007). Evidence comes from familial aggregation studies, twin studies, and molecular genetic studies. LD clusters are found in families, and familial links are evident for LD and speech and reading disorders. Children with LD and SSD have shown higher prevalence for family members to present with an LD or SSD, particularly siblings (Tomblin, 1989) and fathers. Boys are four times as likely to have an LD or SSD as girls. Genetic factors have also been demonstrated in twin studies, with a higher concordance of LD and SSD in monozygotic rather than dizygotic twins (Bishop, Adams, & Norbury, 2005; Bishop, North, & Donlan, 1995; Lewis, Shriberg, Freebairn, & Hansen, 2006). In fact, research by Barry et al. (2007) indicated that nonword repetition or gestures can even be a behavioral marker of a family at risk for language impairment. Familial aggregation research in the field of autism has shown pragmatic problems in first-degree relatives, providing further support for a genetic predisposition to such language problems (Piven, Palmer, Jacobi, Childress, & Arndt, 1997).

Research on genetic factors that increase an individual's susceptibility has identified variants in four genes relating to spoken LDs (Newbury, Fisher, & Monaco, 2010). The genes identified so far are FOXP2 gene on chromosome 7q, correlated to difficulties with articulation; CNTNAP2 gene on chromosome 7q, associated with genetically complex forms of SLI; and genes ATP2C2 and CMIP on chromosome 16q (Newbury et al., 2010). In the future, the clinical implication of identifying genetic risk might allow for improved diagnosis and early identification and intervention programs for at-risk children (Fisher & DeFries, 2002; Lewis et al., 2006).

Hearing Impairment

Hearing impairment is a significant risk factor that can predispose a child to language delay. A child might have a conductive, sensory neural, or mixed hearing loss. Both conductive and sensory neural hearing loss can be congenital or acquired. A conductive hearing loss is caused by an obstruction or damage to the outer or middle ear affecting transmission of the acoustic signal. A sensory neural hearing loss is caused by dysfunction or damage in the neural processing of the acoustic signal either in the cochlear (sensory part) or auditory nerve (neural part).

Otitis media (OM) is the most common form of conductive hearing loss and is responsible for the highest rates of antibiotic prescription for children in the United States. Acute otitis media (AOM) has been termed "serous otitis media" or "glue ear." Otitis media effusion (OME) describes the presence of middle ear effusion without signs or symptoms of infection, also referred to as "silent ear infection" (Gould & Matz, 2010). Recurrent silent ear infections, resulting in intermittent hearing loss, are difficult to detect, being asymptomatic. Recurrent intermittent bouts of otitis media limit the child's exposure to sounds and language, impacting the development of her speech and language system, which can increase her vulnerability to developing a language or speech disorder.

Outcomes for children with congenital hearing loss are far more successful if interventions begin prior to 6 months of age (Tierney, Brown, & Serwint, 2008). The auditory system requires reasonable levels of sound exposure to develop normally. Through repeated exposure to sounds, an infant's auditory system and language centers develop well-formed and organized synaptic pathways. Without such exposure, there appears to be a size reduction in the cells of the auditory pathways, affecting ongoing language development. However, if interventions are started early, then language can develop normally (Tierney et al., 2008).

Prematurity

Follow-up studies of preterm and low-birth-weight infants report that receptive language and vocabulary are within normal limits. However, syntactic development, specifically the mean length of utterance (MLU), and more complex language skills, including abstract reasoning and comprehension of syntactic forms, are weaker compared with those of full-term, normal-birth-weight controls (Salt & Redshaw, 2005). Deficits in later language skills, such as deficits in articulation and prereading skills for 6-year olds, were identified as being three to five times more likely in very preterm infants compared with age-matched peers (Le Normand & Cohen, 1999). Preterm and low-birth-weight babies need to be considered a vulnerable group who require monitoring of language developmental milestones.

Prenatal Exposure to Alcohol

Prenatal exposure to alcohol is known to affect a child's cognitive and behavioral functioning. O'Leary, Zubrick, Taylor, Dixon, and Bower (2009) conducted a large population-based (N = 1,739) study of the association between dose and timing of prenatal alcohol exposure and its relationship to language acquisition. The results showed that 13% of children in the population-based study at 2 years had delayed language based on the Ages and Stages Questionnaire (O'Leary, Zubrick, Taylor, Dixon, and Bower, 2009). The percentage of children with language delay was highest for mothers who had patterns of binge drinking in the second and third trimesters (29.4% and 33.3%) and for mothers who consumed moderate to heavy amounts during the third trimester (16.5%). Prenatal exposure to alcohol increases the child's risk of other developmental problems, such as executive functioning disorder and FASD, which (if comorbid with an LD) could significantly compromise a child's functioning. Furthermore, the impact of a child's neurocognitive compromise, which can impact skills such as memorizing, planning, and organizing, has implications for language development in the early years and in school.

Parenting and Attachment

Language and social communication develop in the context of relationships with significant attachment figures in the child's life (Rosenkoetter & Walness, 2006). However, the association between secure attachment and language competence has not always been confirmed in the literature (van IJzendoorn, Dijkstva, & Bus, 1995). Researchers suggest that lack of identification of the relationship between language and attachment might be due to studies not considering the complexity of other processes in parent–child interactions that can relate to language development and the multitude of factors that can contribute to secure attachment (van IJzendoorn et al., 1995). A study by Belsky and Fearon (2002) showed that early attachment can predict language skills, but the effect on expressive language varied depending on the level of social-contextual risk.

Trauma

Studies show that 23% to 65% of maltreated children show cognitive delays and that 14% to 64% of maltreated children demonstrate speech and language delays (English et al., 2005). Among foster children, the estimated prevalence of language delays ranges from 35% to 73% (Stock & Fisher, 2006).

Studies investigating maltreatment identified significant language difficulties in 2- to 7-year olds, such as reduced sentence length (syntactic development), poor expressive vocabulary, and a lower rate of decontextualized language (Stock & Fisher, 2006). Studies suggest that children who have experienced physical abuse or neglect have higher rates of language delay compared with other types of abuse. However, a recent study by Nol et al. (2010) of the relationship between sexual abuse and language development has shown that girls who experienced childhood sexual abuse have significant and long-term receptive language difficulties and poorer educational outcomes.

Language and communication impairments might be a risk factor for maltreatment. A British review of children on the Child Protection Register showed that young people with communication disorders were three times more likely to be registered than their normally developing peers (Spencer et al., 2005). Research by Sullivan and Knutson (2000) reviewed the prevalence of child abuse and neglect for children with an identified speech and language problem. This population was five times more at risk of neglect and physical abuse, three times more at risk of sexual abuse, and seven times more at risk of emotional maltreatment. Clearly, children who have experienced trauma should be considered an at-risk group. Physical abuse, sexual abuse, and neglect are identified as significant risk factors for the development of language deficits, which would further compound long-term psychosocial outcomes for this vulnerable group.

Language Difficulties and Other Cognitive Functions

Language and cognition are interconnected. Language deficits do not occur in isolation and impact cognitive and academic functioning. Although children with LD have primary deficits in receptive and/or expressive language and apparent age-appropriate measures of nonverbal intelligence, research has demonstrated limitations in other cognitive realms. Cohen et al. (1998) demonstrated that children with LD can also experience deficits on cognitive measures, including short-term memory, working memory, and executive function. Research by Wolfe and Bell (2004) investigated the contribution of language in the prediction of working memory capacity and impulse control. Their research demonstrated that language (specifically receptive vocabulary) can be a significant predictor of working memory and impulse control. Bishop (1992) reported that children with LD not only have linguistic deficits but also frequently demonstrate deficits in processing speed and memory. Because the literature has established that a child's deficits in neurocognitive functions can impact language capacities, it is important to consider the child's intellectual levels and executive functioning levels in planning assessment, diagnosis, and intervention.

Typical Development of Language and Communication

As Menkes, Sarnat, and Maria (2006, p. 1097) report, "postnatal neurological maturation underwrites the gradual acquisition of an extensive repertoire of cognitive skills," including language. The communication process begins at birth and develops over an extended period of time. Increasing evidence supports the concept of a "critical or sensitive period" for language learning, in the first 3 years of life (Perry, 2006). It should be noted that during this period of vast synaptic, neural, and cognitive development, the language system develops at a rate unlike that of any other period. However, there is evidence of neural plasticity for children beyond this age, who can still make tremendous gains in language development. Also, language development continues throughout the school years and into adolescence, including the acquisition of reading, writing, and higher-level social and pragmatic skills.

Language development occurs from the first months of life, with the building blocks of language being well established prior to the formal use of words and sentences (Wetherby, Warren, & Reichle, 1988; Wetherby, Goldstein, Cleary, Allen, & Kublin, 2003). In fact, children's prelinguistic language development is closely linked to later language development (Camaioni, Aureli, Bellagamba, & Fogel, 2003). Children are typically immersed in language and learn it in a social context in interactions with caregivers (Yoder and Warren, 1998). An optimal language-learning environment provides children with opportunities to learn language, motivations to interact, and feedback on their communicative attempts (Gascoigne, 2006). Figure 4.3 highlights the development of language, Table 4.4 outlines language development from birth to 13 years of age, and Table 4.3 outlines the development of play and symbolization from 9 months to 2.5 years.

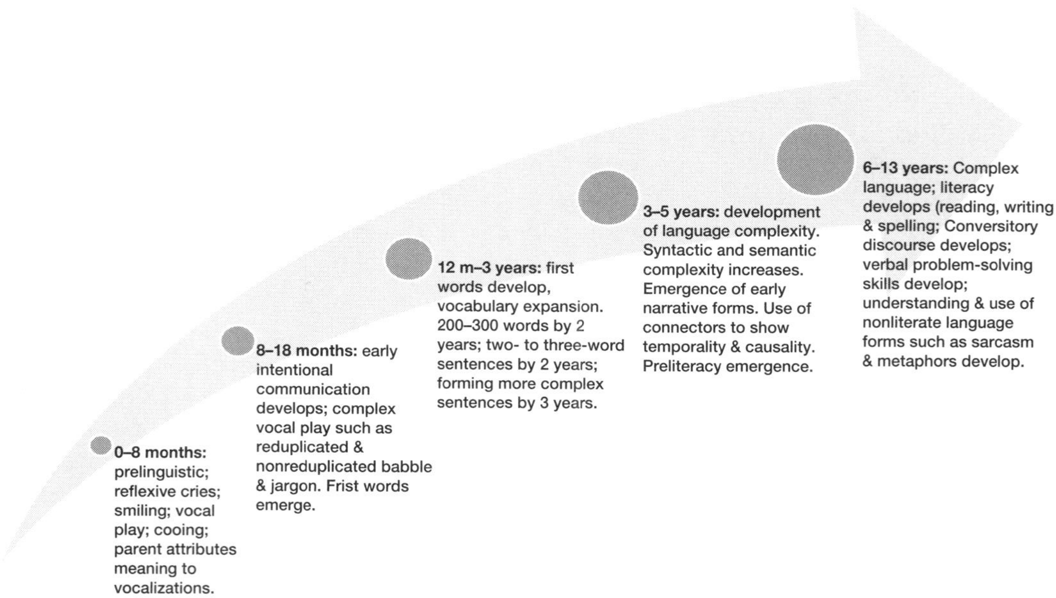

Figure 4.3 *Prelinguistic to complex language development.*

SYMBOLIZATION AND PLAY DEVELOPMENT

Symbolization refers to the use of certain symbols such as language and pretend play to represent objects, thoughts, and events. It is related to the use of language and includes the growth of symbolic play, which has been described as "an often-overlooked important scaffold to emerging literacy" (Zigler, Singer, & Bishop-Josef, 2004). Both language and symbolic play signal the development of representational thought. The development of symbolic play peaks during the preschool and early primary years (3–5 years) and declines during the middle childhood years, usually by 7 years. The development of symbolic or pretend play, in which the child is using objects in the environment in a way that is different from the actual purpose of the object, has a strong relationship with the development of language. Note that during pretend play, language is used continuously with children often taking on roles of adults and emulating their more sophisticated language (Singer & Singer, 2004). Table 4.3 describes the development of symbolic play.

Table 4.3 *Development of Symbolic Play*

4–8 months	■ Child explores toys with hands and mouth ■ Makes noise with toys by banging them together, shaking them, or squeezing them ■ May roll a car back and forth and make noises while doing so
9–12 months	■ Imitates actions of caregivers ■ May play a hiding game
13–24 months	■ Now engages in simple pretend play ■ Pretends to drink from an empty cup ■ Pretends a banana is a telephone ■ May pretend to use a spoon to stir things in a bowl ■ Pretends to feed a baby doll
2–4 years	■ May use the same object for different substitutions such as using a stick for a gun and for a fishing rod ■ Uses play figures as if they have thoughts, feelings, and beliefs ■ Pretends to be someone else such as a parent or a super-hero ■ Often uses play themes related to the family or daycare ■ May act out aggression or anxiety through the characters in the play who may be "good," "bad," or frightened
4–6 years	■ Increasingly uses play to act out difficult things going on in his or her life ■ Much more complex play themes are not possible ■ May be integrated with games with rules ■ Increasingly play is with others who share the roles in the play ■ May see more segregation of boys and girls in the play

Atypical Development

Children are biologically wired to acquire language, yet acquisition is affected by genetic, developmental, and environmental factors (Tommerdahl, 2009). Despite natural variations in the rates of development of typical children, there are milestones for typical speech and language development. Usually, the first clinical indicator of possible language delay is the child's failure to acquire first words by 12 months, a core vocabulary of at least 50 words by 2 years, and/or two-word combinations by 2 years. A child with these clinical indicators would be considered a late talker. Other signs that a child might be experiencing speech and language acquisition difficulties and thus need a referral for assessment are described in Table 4.5.

Table 4.4 *Development of Language and Communication and Caregiver Responses*

Age Period	Development	Caregiving
Birth to 12 months	■ Communicates by crying and on a reflective level ■ Can engage in turn taking during face-to-face interactions ■ Turns toward sounds and when someone is talking ■ Can distinguish between certain sounds such as "pa" and "ba" ■ Babbles and uses sounds that sound like speaking ■ Shows joint attention with caregivers ■ Uses "dada" and "mama" ■ May use gestures when communicating (e.g., waving)	■ Responds consistently and shows interest in the infant's communication ■ Uses "parentese" or a high-pitched voice ■ Engages in face-to-face interactions setting them up often ■ Reads simple books and names the pictures ■ Lets child know he or she has been heard and responds appropriately ■ Sings songs and recites nursery rhymes with actions to get the infant's attention ■ Labels child's actions and feelings during caregiving throughout the day
12 to 24 months	■ Can name body parts when they are pointed to ■ When an object is named can show it by pointing to it or picking it up ■ Responds to name consistently ■ Follows simple directions such as "throw the ball" ■ Has receptive vocabulary or understands about 500 words ■ Uses an expressive vocabulary of 50–300 words ■ Puts two words together correctly ■ Can engage in two-way conversations if well supported ■ Follows simple directions ■ Can listen to a story for increasing periods of time ■ Can understand some prepositions such as "in" and "on"	■ Keeps conversations going by asking simple questions and assists with the answer when necessary ■ Extends child's speech into phrases but does not correct grammar ■ Fills in missing words when needed ■ Models clear speech and repeats words the child says ■ Uses actions and gestures to illustrate the words and to help the child to remember them ■ May encourage pretend play and join the child in it ■ Continues to use songs and rhymes ■ Uses books with increasing numbers of words ■ Gives simple directions that the child can understand to facilitate activities and games
24 to 36 months	■ Can now understand the concept of time and words that refer to past and future events, and later and next ■ Can understand most parts of speech ■ Understands longer and more complex sentences and 1,000 different words ■ Can point to pictures in books that are referred to by caregiver ■ Uses correct grammatical inflection ■ Uses past tense and plurals ■ Carries on a back-and-forth conversation asking questions appropriately like "why" and "who"	■ Encourage the child to learn about time by talking about the sequence of events in the day ■ Repeats phrases with correct grammar ■ Uses open-ended questions so the child is encouraged to elaborate stories or the telling of events ■ Extends phrases and sentences building on what the child has said ■ Reads to the child regularly and uses questions about the story or the pictures in the book to enhance understanding ■ Responds to the child's constant questions and uses them as opportunities for enhancing language ■ Introduces new words, including unusual words such as in the Dr. Seuss books

3 to 6 years	■ Talks about things not in sight ■ Now can pronounce almost all sounds correctly ■ Uses adult sentence structure and has all the basics of grammar ■ Has about 50% of language development ■ Takes turns in conversation and uses words to express feelings ■ Sustains longer conversations with peers ■ Can say 2,000 words and understands even more ■ Uses verbal descriptions of events ■ May begin to recognize letters and the sounds that they make	■ Caregivers facilitate conversations by keeping them going and speaking for the child at times ■ Provides scaffolding to introduce and extend conversations ■ May introduce the perspective of others in conversations to encourage the capacity for empathy ■ Continues to read to the child and to ask questions about what is going on in the story ■ Uses gestures to enhance meaning of conversation ■ Talks about events with the child and encourages the child to do so ■ Corrects grammatical mistakes that the child makes often ■ Helps child resolve conflicts and express difficult feelings with words ■ Teaches the child the sounds of certain letters
7 to 10 years	■ Develops literacy skills such as reading and writing ■ Transitions to phonetic reading ■ Demonstrates a receptive vocabulary of 40,000 words by 10 years of age ■ Can tell a coherent narrative from the beginning, middle, and end ■ Enjoys word plays and jokes ■ Understands figures of speech more easily ■ Understands metaphors, similes, and imagery	■ Supports reading and writing and encourages the child's efforts whenever possible ■ Encourages the child to put feelings into words instead of acting them out ■ Supports engagement with peers who become a major source of language stimulation ■ Responds to the child's jokes and word plays with interest ■ Encourages the child to recall events and to describe what happened ■ Reminisces about past events ■ Reminds child during conversations about the perspective of others ■ Provides richer more advanced reading materials and continues to read to the child ■ Includes poetry in choice of reading materials
10 to 13 years	■ Uses humor, irony, and metaphors ■ Repairs communication breakdowns and problem solves with language ■ Deduces the meaning of unfamiliar words and phrases by looking at other components of the sentence or paragraph ■ Negotiates with others in a more complex way ■ Understands the point of view of others and expresses his or her own perspective	■ Encourages verbal expression and conveys to the child the idea that words are an important way to understand what is going on in the world and to communicate with others ■ Encourages child to put private thoughts into words and to use private speech while doing activities ■ Has extended discussions with teenagers at appropriate times ■ Discusses subjects of interest to teenagers whenever possible and corrects misconceptions during the discussions

Table 4.5 *Indicators of Language and Play Difficulties by Age*

Birth to 8 months

- Not responding to noise/s in the environment
- Not turning to mother's voice
- Not showing eye contact
- Not vocalizing or cooing
- Significant feeding issues
- Lack of babbling

9 to 12 months

- Limited vocalizations and lack of babbling
- Poor eye contact
- Limited use of pointing
- No single words emerging by 12 months
- Does not appear to seek out or engage with caregiver
- Not responding consistently to noises or speech in the environment
- Not using gestures, such as waving, by 12 months
- Not searching for toys or using sensory exploration such as mouthing toys

12 months to 2 years

- Difficulties feeding, eating, or drinking
- 18 months—not saying 10 to 20 words
- 24 months—not saying 200 to 300 words
- 24 months—not using two-word sentences
- Poor eye contact and lack of gestures
- Not demonstrating a range of communicative functions (e.g., protesting, greeting, requesting, showing, etc.)
- Not interested in joining in play with caregiver
- Difficulty understanding simple instructions or questions
- No pretend play such as rocking a doll and helping a doll drink from a cup

3 to 5 years

- Speech is difficult to understand (should be intelligible 75% to 100% of the time)
- Not following two-step instructions or "what" and "where" questions
- Using only two- and three-word sentence combinations
- Evidence of a stutter
- Evidence of a harsh voice quality
- Does not engage in play with objects or play out familiar events, such as going to the doctor

5 years + Signs of expressive difficulties

- Frequently having trouble finding the right word
- Using the wrong words in sentences
- Not understanding the meanings of words
- Limited vocabulary
- Making grammatical mistakes and using poor sentence structure
- Relying on short, simple sentence construction
- Having difficulty retelling a story or relaying information

5 years + Signs of comprehension difficulties

- Not appearing to listen when spoken to
- Lack of interest when stories are read
- Inability to understand complicated sentences
- Inability to follow verbal instructions
- Reliance on gestures and other nonverbal clues to help understand
- Parroting words and phrases
- Difficulty in problem solving

LD in Children With Mental Health Challenges

For multichallenged children with complex clinical presentations it is difficult to understand the areas of functioning that are contributing to their difficulties. Incorporating a multidimensional model of development allows clinicians to consider the various

Table 4.6 *Speech and Language Qualities Associated With Emotional and Behavioral Diagnosis*

Functional Impairment	Profile of Communication, Language, and Speech Difficulties
Difficulties with emotional regulation (internalizing disorders such as anxiety and depression)	■ Semantic problems have been particularly related to internalizing problems ■ Social communication difficulties such as difficulties with initiating conversations ■ Noted higher prevalence of anxiety associated with fluency disorder ■ May be at increased risk of selective mutism (SM) if the child also has social anxiety ■ May experience difficulties in identifying emotions and describing emotions
Difficulties with behavior regulation (externalizing difficulties)	■ Language deficits are frequently in the areas of comprehension, pragmatics, and narrative ■ Pragmatic difficulties at a discourse level such as topic maintenance ■ Difficulties in interpreting verbal and nonverbal signals such as facial expressions and gesture (particularly evident with oppositional defiant disorder (ODD)) ■ Impaired negotiation skills ■ Reduced emotional language terms
Executive dysfunction and ADHD	Language ■ Demonstrates difficulties in comprehension, expressive language, and pragmatics ■ Difficulties with sentence formulation particularly with complex sentences; dysfluency in expressive language characterized by frequent pauses, stopping, starting, and repetitions ■ Evidence of circumlocution behaviors and use of deictic terms (nonspecific terms, e.g., 'it, that, those' which may indicate lexical access or word finding difficulty) ■ Difficulties being concise in the process of conveying information clearly Speech ■ May speak louder, experiencing difficulties in modulating voice volume ■ May have a faster rate of speech ■ Comprehension/listening ■ May experience difficulty in following instructions ■ May experience difficulty in listening ■ May be slower and less efficient with complex sentence comprehension ■ Difficulties with, attention, listening, and memory may impact comprehension or the ability to follow discourse Pragmatics/social communication ■ Problems in modifying language to the listener ■ May speak for longer while taking his or her turn (monologue style) ■ Frequent short pauses but not substantial enough to allow for planning and organization of thought ■ Disorganized language secondary to the executive functioning difficulty ■ Performs well on language standardized testing but has weaker functional language skills ■ Discourse may be disorganized, incomplete, or tangential ■ Narrative can be tangential

(continued)

Table 4.6 *Speech and Language Qualities Associated With Emotional and Behavioral Diagnosis (continued)*

Functional Impairment	Profile of Communication, Language, and Speech Difficulties
Socialization and relationship difficulties	■ Difficulties with pragmatic skills ■ Difficulties with conversational discourse ■ Difficulties with reading emotions and emotional understanding ■ Difficulty decoding and understanding auditory information ■ Initiates less conversations and has difficulties with responding on conversation ■ Difficulties with conversational repair
Selective mutism	■ Both expressive and receptive language difficulties have been associated with SM ■ Impairment in narrative skills; oral narratives tend to be shorter, more simplistic, and with less detail ■ SSDs have been associated with SM ■ Pragmatic language difficulties such as difficulties with conversation initiation, conversation maintenance, and repair
Fetal alcohol spectrum disorder (FASD)	■ Articulation difficulties associated with craniofacial anomalies such as cleft palate and recurrent middle ear problems ■ Middle ear disease resulting in hearing impairment, which increases the child's risk of speech and language difficulties ■ Hypotonia and dyspraxia ■ Pragmatic and conversational discourse difficulties such as poor topic choice, difficulties with conversational repair, limitations in communicative functions, and poor reading of social cues; may perseverate in conversation
ASD	■ Early difficulties include impairment in structural language, semantic content, and language use ■ Delays in lexical and syntactic knowledge, phonology, and morphology ■ Significant difficulty with pragmatic language, such as poor eye contact, poor nonverbal communication skills, and poor reciprocity ■ Idiosyncratic language such as echolalia, stereotypic language, and perseveration ■ School-age children ■ Pragmatic language most impaired ■ Stereotypic language ■ Perseverative and sometimes pedantic ■ Problems with turn taking, discourse, and poor listener awareness

determinants impacting a child's presentation and identify where the child's functioning is compromised. This then leads to the development of appropriate and effective interventions. Determining the contribution of language or communication impairment to these complex presentations is important to guide interventions. Cohen (2001) explored the association between a number of psychiatric disorders and language impairment. She highlighted that some diagnostic criteria for specific psychiatric disorders can be impacted or even explained by language and communication impairment. Table 4.6 identifies some of the research-based language and communication qualities identified with specific psychiatric disorders.

LANGUAGE IMPAIRMENT AND DIFFICULTIES IN FUNCTIONAL AREAS

Various language impairments have been found to be associated with a number of mental health problems and functional delays. In this section, we will briefly outline some of the language difficulties that have been found in the functional areas detailed in this book.

Emotional Regulation: Difficulties and Disorders

Research has also been conducted on internalizing disorders such as depression and anxiety and has found in both longitudinal and epidemiological studies that these children often have persistent speech and language impairments. There is a developmental relationship between emotion and language development. Emotions come under verbal control in the typical child in the preschool years and language can be used during the school-age years as a mechanism to problem solve, regulate behavior, and reflect (Cohen, 2001; Zadeh et al., 2007). Consequently, when there is an interruption in the developmental relationship between emotion and language, this can lead to emotion-regulation difficulties and externalizing or internalizing behavior problems and emotional and social difficulties.

Anxiety, depression, withdrawn behavior, low self-esteem and limited emotion regulation skills have all been associated with language impairment (Cantwell & Baker, 1987; Fujiki, Brinton & Clarke, 2002; Jerome, Fujiki, Brinton & James, 2002; Lindsay & Dockerall, 2002). Research by Daal et al. (2007) identified that semantic language problems are particularly related to internalizing difficulties. For example, anxiety has often been found to be associated with communication impairments such as stuttering. Research has clearly disputed that anxiety causes stuttering; however, communication fears are significantly higher in children who stutter and these fears increase with age (Hancock et al., 1998). Social anxiety and language impairment are both considered risk factors for the development of SM (McInnes, Fung, Marassis, Fiksenbaum, & Tannock, 2004).

Children with language impairments also have greater deficits in emotional understanding such as processing emotions, which seems to be slower, and difficulty with reading and identifying people's emotions during conflict. Greenberg and Kusche (1994) hypothesized that language may be most important in understanding complex emotions rather than basic emotions, as children with LD are frequently able to label facial expressions but have increased difficulty in identifying emotions in a story. Ford and Milosky (2008) demonstrated that children with LD experienced difficulties in inferring emotions from simple scenarios, and Spackman, Fujiki, and Brinton (2006) showed that children with LD are less sophisticated in their ability to describe emotions. Further research has also demonstrated that children with LD experience difficulties in identifying the emotion conveyed by prosody embedded in short narratives (Fujiki, Spackman, Brinton, & Illig, 2008).

Behavior Regulation: Difficulties and Disorders

As described in Chapter 7, some of the most common disorders of behavior regulation are conduct disorder (CD) and ODD (Zadeh, Im-Bolter, & Cohen, 2001). Research has also demonstrated that youth with verbal deficits are at increased risk of developing antisocial and delinquent behavior (Moffit & Henry, 1991; Munoz, Frick, Kimonis, & Aucoin, 2008). It has been suggested that behavior-regulating problems or externalizing behavior problems and verbal deficits may share a common neurodevelopmental pathway (Moffit & Henry, 1991). Barkley (1998) has emphasized the inability to use private speech or internalized language that may result in some of the difficulties seen in children with executive dysfunction, including ADHD. Private speech is a functional skill that children use to problem solve and facilitates reflection and self-regulation of behavior. Studies have found that children with ADHD have delays in developing internalized speech but go through the same five stages of developing it as typically developing children (Berk & Potts, 1991; Corkum, Humphries, Mullane, & Theirfault, 2008). Research analyzing the internalized speech of children performing problem-solving tasks found that typically developing children had developed internalized speech as a method of problem solving and regulating their behavior often by 10 to 11 years, whereas children with ADHD continued to use task-relevant and guiding comments and external manifestations of inner speech (Berk & Potts, 1991; Corkum et al., 2008). They also produced more task-irrelevant external speech forms (Corkum et al., 2008).

Research has shown that between one third and two thirds of children referred with a diagnosis of CD have comorbid speech and language difficulties (Baltaxe, 2001; Gidden, 1991; Gilmour, Hill, Place, & Skuse, 2004). Language deficits were typically in the areas of comprehension and pragmatic language skills (Cohen, 1993; Gilmour et al., 2004). Pragmatic language difficulties at a discourse level, such as poor topic maintenance, impaired negotiation skills, and difficulties in interpretation of verbal and nonverbal signals have been identified in ODD (Audet & Ripich, 1994). Compounding the problem was that children with externalizing behavior presentations were more likely to have an unidentified LD (Cohen, 2001).

Research by Gilmour et al. (2004) investigated the pragmatic communication deficits in a community sample of antisocial children who were facing school exclusion. A significant proportion of children with CD, in both clinically referred and community-based samples, presented with pragmatic skill deficits equivalent in severity to pragmatic deficits observed in ASD. Gilmour et al. (2004) suggested that there may be a common neurocognitive impairment underlying the pragmatic difficulties experienced by these two clinical populations. It further reinforced the severity of pragmatic deficit experienced by children with CD. Other research investigating the origins of persistent and severe antisocial behavior considered verbal neurodevelopmental deficits as a risk factor (Moffitt, Caspi, Rutter, & Silver, 2001). Recent research by Zadeh et al. (2007) demonstrated that language functions as a mediating role between social cognition and externalizing behaviors. Subsequently children with poor language skills experience greater difficulty in solving social problems verbally and may result in physical strategies or inefficient verbal strategies (Zadeh et al., 2007).

Executive Functioning Difficulties and Disorders

Neurocognitive deficits associated with executive dysfunction, such as memory, planning, attention, and organization, may impact more complex language tasks, such as narrative, discourse, and problem solving, as these tasks require an integration of planning and organization in order to execute them.

Language and communication profiles of children with executive functioning difficulties may be considered disorganized language, secondary to the primary cognitive impairment resulting in language difficulties (Barkley, 1998). Neurocognitive deficits of attention and memory impact language processing and comprehension, which has subsequent effects on children's ability to respond and express themselves appropriately. For example, the child with executive functioning difficulties may experience weaknesses in listening and poor attention that may impact comprehension and memory. Children with executive functioning difficulties typically present with adequate core language skills on standardized testing measures but have weaker performance in functional skills (Richard & Fahy, 2005). Particular difficulties have been observed in the area of pragmatic language and discourse skills. Discourse deficits have been characterized as being disorganized, incomplete, verbose, and with a tangential narration style (Richard & Fahy, 2005). Pragmatic language difficulties include problems with perspective taking and poor integration of verbal and nonverbal cues (Richard & Fahy, 2005).

A significant amount of research examining the language impairments of children with ADHD has been conducted. It has been found that these children have difficulties in expressive, receptive, and pragmatic language areas. Although receptive language skills are typically stronger than expressive language, these children generally experience difficulties with listening, processing, or understanding spoken instructions (Baker & Cantwell, 1992; Barkley, 1998; Beitchman, Hood, Racton, & Peterson, 1989).

Expressive language deficits may be characterized by difficulties in sentence formulation, particularly with complex sentences; patterns of dysfluency in expressing oneself, such as frequent pauses, stopping and starting; and repetitions that may indicate either planning difficulties or semantic/word-finding difficulties; and difficulties with the specificity of their language, such as the overuse of deixis or nonspecific words. Children may talk more excessively but the quality of their language in terms of semantic and syntactic skills may be comparatively weak or convoluted (Barkley, 1998). Children with ADHD and LD have qualitative impairments in their narrative such as typically providing less information and having less organized narrative in terms of macrostructure (Zentalli, 1988). Pragmatic language deficits that may be demonstrated include difficulties with monitoring and attending to the listener in conversation and turn-taking difficulties demonstrated by initiating and interrupting inappropriately, and speaking for longer than their turn (Tannock & Brown, 2009). Bishop and Baird (2001) further characterized pragmatic deficits in children with ADHD as having more stereotyped conversations, difficulties with rapport, and poorer social relationships.

Social Development: Difficulties and Disorders

The most significant impairment in longitudinal and epidemiological studies of LD individuals is poor social functioning and impairments in relationships (Clegg et al., 2005; Rutter, Kim-Cohen, & Maughan, 2006). This core deficit in social function has serious implications for the continuity of mental health disorders (Rutter et al., 2006). By taking a developmental perspective on the trajectory of mental health disorders, it is useful to consider what we know about the early emergence of socialization difficulties in children with LD and communication impairments.

Children with language disorders experience greater difficulties in social interactions, demonstrating less prosocial behaviors and are at greater risk of social withdrawal problems such as reticence and solitary play (Fujiki, Brinton, Morgan, & Hart, 1999; Fujiki, Brinton, & Todd, 1996). During interactions, children with language impairment appear to experience difficulties in formulating and expressing their thoughts quickly and concisely resulting in the overuse of fillers and pauses in conversation (Vallance, Im, & Cohen 1999). Comprehension, processing speed, and memory deficit can also impact interactions, affecting the child's efficiency of decoding and understanding auditory information, and as a result limits the child's ability to respond quickly and appropriately. Encoding and integrating verbal and nonverbal information during discourse requires an intact and efficient language system.

LD children are more likely to be excluded and ignored by peers and more likely to be victims of relational aggression, and subsequently have fewer opportunities to practice and develop peer interaction skills, and may experience greater difficulties in forming meaningful relationships (Fujiki et al, 1996; Ostrov & Godleski, 2007). Children with LD initiate less during conversations and are less astute at conversational repair strategies. Despite difficulties with initiations, these children do respond to peers; however, their responses tend to be inappropriate or unrelated (Brinton & Fujiki, 1993) and they require greater discourse support and experience increased difficulties in meeting conversational demands (Craig & Gallagher, 1982; Gallagher, 1996). It is apparent that the child with an LD potentially experiences a "vicious cycle"socially in that he or she lacks skills to process and respond to the fast-paced discourse of conversation. As a result, the child may be ignored or excluded from peers or social exchanges, which subsequently results in less opportunities to participate in conversations, which is essential to developing social skills.

Children who present with comorbid LD and social difficulties frequently experience difficulties in pragmatic skills, conversational discourse, and social cognitive processes (Westby & Cutler, 1994). Social cognition is defined as the thought processes involved in understanding people in social situations. Proficient social communication is a complex and dynamic process that relies on adequate linguistic structures and social cognitive processes. Research regarding the relationship between social cognition and language impairment is still developing. Cohen (1993) showed that language-impaired children demonstrated greater deficits in emotional understanding and problem solving, which are important for social cognition. Difficulties in emotional understanding included limitations in emotional decoding, misperception, and slow processing of emotions and limitations in identifying peoples' feelings during conflict (Cohen, 2001). Problem-solving difficulties included limitations in generating solutions to problems and evaluating strategies in solving problems (Cohen et al., 1998).

Theory of Mind

Theory of mind is an aspect of social cognition that children typically develop between 2 to 4 years of age (Landy, 2009) and it increases with age (Wellman, Cross, & Watson, 2001). By 4 years, a child should understand that other people have different thoughts, beliefs, and feelings to themselves (Astington & Jenkins, 1999; Astington & Olson, 1995; Wellman et al., 2001). When developed, it is critically important for social functioning and for the development of relationships with others.

There is emerging longitudinal evidence to support a developmental relationship between language and theory of mind (Farrar & Maag, 2002; Watson, Painter, & Bornstein, 2001). Astington and Jenkins (1999) found that 3-year-old language ability (semantic and syntactic skills) significantly predicted their theory of mind 7 months later. Training-study results by Lohmann and Tomasello (2003) support the conclusion that language plays a causal role in the development of theory of mind. Further research has also demonstrated that children with LD present with delayed development or impaired theory of mind (Farrant, Fletcher, & Mayberry, 2006; Homes, 2002). Research investigating whether a child's exposure to talk about mental states predicts development of theory of mind has demonstrated such a relationship (Ruffman, Slade, & Crowe, 2002) and that understanding of theory of mind was correlated with participation in family talk about feelings and causality (Dunn, Brown, & Beardsall, 1991).

SM

Selective Mutism (SM) is considered a rare disorder with prevalence in population studies ranging from 0.2% to 0.7% (Bergman, Piacentini, & McCracken, 2002; Kopp & Gillberg, 1997; Kumpulainen, Rasanen, Raaska, & Somppi, 1998). The prevalence rates in girls is greater than boys, with a ratio of up to 2:1 (Black & Uhde, 1995; Kristensen, 2000). *DSM-5* (APA, 2000) defines SM as being characterized by a child's consistent failure to speak in specific social situations such as outside the home, despite speaking in other situations, such as inside the home, to a degree that interferes with educational or occupational achievement or with social communication. It has persisted for more than one month (APA, 2000).

The etiology of SM is not well understood although two factors are associated with the disorder, those of anxiety (particularly social anxiety) and communication impairments. Between 30% to 50% of children with SM have an identified speech disorder and LD or a delay in speech and language development (Kristensen, 2000; Steinhausen & Juzi, 1996).

Speech and language deficits identified in the literature include articulation and phonological disorders; and receptive and expressive language delays. Deficits in narrative skills, including shorter, linguistically simpler and less detailed narratives have also been found (McInnes et al., 2004). Clinical questions regarding the language and social communication deficits of the child with SM need to be explored further, particularly given the level of comorbidity of SM with a language impairment. Certainly the trajectory for a child with persistent SM (lasting longer than 6 months) and in children over 5 years as opposed to transient SM (affecting younger children with symptoms resolving in the first year at school) is concerning. One follow-up study investigating outcomes showed that 60% of young adults, previously diagnosed with SM, had persistent social communication problems (Remschmidt, Poller, Herpertz-Dahlman, Hennighausen, & Gutenbruner, 2001), demonstrating the long-term implications for children with SM and LD and communication problems.

FASD

Children with a diagnosis of FASD are vulnerable to a number of feeding, speech, and language difficulties (Malbin, 2002). A newborn child with FASD is at risk of having feeding difficulties as a result of cleft palate, craniofacial abnormalities, and velopharyngeal weakness (Richard & Fahy, 2005). Articulation difficulties that are secondary to palatal and craniofacial structural problems are also prevalent, including hypernasality. Hypotonia and dyspraxia have also been less frequently observed (Richard & Fahy, 2005). Children with FASD are prone to middle ear disease, which increases their risk for speech and language delays (Sparks, 1993). Middle ear disease includes otitis media, and scarring of the tympanic membrane causing a conductive hearing loss. Sensory neural hearing loss and APD also have higher prevalence rates in the FASD population (Richard & Fahy, 2005). Language delays also identified with this diagnosis include difficulties in the area of syntax, semantics, and pragmatics.

Research has demonstrated that children with FASD are vulnerable to social skill deficits that are probably related to their level of executive dysfunction and capacity to regulate their emotions and behavior (Schonfeld, Mattson, Lang, Delsi, & Riley, 2001). Characteristics of social skill deficits include difficulties understanding social cues and communicating in a social context (Schonfeld et al., 2006). Social communication difficulties include problems with poor topic choice and the overuse of questions as a conversational strategy (Richard & Fahy, 2005). These children may also perseverate in conversation and demonstrate echolalia behaviors (Richard & Fahy, 2005). Neurocognitive deficits associated with FASD, such as difficulties with attention and memory, may have implications for the child's language profile.

ASDs

One of the most disabling disorders that significantly impacts social interactions and the development of relationships is autism spectrum disorder, which is reviewed in Chapter 9. In this chapter, the language deficits of ASD are discussed.

Differential diagnosis between an ASD and LD is a frequent clinical question. ASD and SLI are distinct disorders, but share common features (Tomblin, Hareman, & O'Brien, 2003). The diagnostic criteria of language delay, structural language difficulties, and social communication impairments are present in both LD and ASD (*DSM-5*, 2013). Researchers have identified that the profile of language impairment changes for both ASD and LD groups throughout development (Lord & Paul, 1997; Ozonoff, Heung, Byrd, Hansen, & Hertz-Picciotto, 2008). In early childhood, preschoolers with ASD present with impairments in structural language, semantic content, and language use. Difficulties are characterized by delays in lexical and syntactic knowledge, phonology, morphology, and most significant, pragmatics (Lord & Paul, 1997). However, as the child transitions into older school age and into adolescence, pragmatic deficits are the most pronounced (Rapin & Dunn, 2003). Children with LD also present with impairments in structural language, content, and use; however, their most pronounced area of difficulty is typically structural language and semantic–lexical deficits. However, as these children transition into older school age and adolescence, they too experience increased deficits in pragmatic language skills.

Characteristics of early language presentation in ASD include language delay and idiosyncratic language features, such as echolalia, stereotypic speech (either words or phrases), and perseverated speech (Ozonoff et al., 2008; Paul, 2006). Linguistically the child may experience difficulties with pronouns beyond the age of 3, particularly when referring to self (Paul, 2006). Children with ASD also tend to have a limited range of language functions, such as difficulties with intentionally requesting, socializing, responding, sharing, and attention seeking. Please refer to Table 4.7, which highlights possible indicators of ASD in early childhood (Osterling & Dawson, 1994; Wetherby, Woods, Allen, Cleary, Dickinson et al., 2004).

Table 4.7 *General Developmental Warning Signs of Possible ASD in Preschool Children*

- Delay or absence of spoken language
- Looks through people; not aware of others
- Not responsive to other people's facial expression/feelings
- Lack of pretend play; little or no imagination
- Does not show typical interest in or play near peers purposefully
- Lack of turn taking
- Unable to share pleasure
- Qualitative impairment in nonverbal communication
- Does not point at an object to direct another person to look at it
- Lack of gaze monitoring
- Lack of initiation of activity or social play
- Unusual or repetitive hand and finger movements
- Unusual reactions, or lack of reactions, to sensory stimuli
- Repetitive play and extreme interests in parts of objects (e.g., wheels) and repetitive actions such as lining things up

Source: This table is reproduced from SIGN 98, *Assessment, diagnosis and clinical interventions for children and young people with autism spectrum disorders*, by kind permission of the Scottish Intercollegiate Network.

School-Age Language Communication and ASD

Some children are not diagnosed with an ASD until entering school (Williams, Thomas, & Sidebotham, 2008). The school context, where the pressures to socially engage and to form and maintain peer relationships in addition to conforming to the structural demands of the classroom, may highlight a child's difficulties (O'Hare, 2009). These children may be diagnosed with Asperger syndrome (AS) when their early developmental history indicates intact cognitive development and no delays in early language milestones. *DSM-5* describes AS as a form of ASD that is characterized by significant impairment in social interaction and restricted, repetitive, and stereotyped patterns of interests and behaviors (APA, 2000). Although early language milestones are reported as normal in children with AS, they typically have significant pragmatic language deficits and difficulties with nonliteral language forms (Toth & King, 2008).

Abnormalities in language development of school-age children with ASD include poor integration of verbal and nonverbal communication. This refers to the ability to naturally coordinate eye contact, with gesture, facial expression, and verbal language to communicate a congruent message. Prosodic features observed in ASD include odd or inappropriate prosody, such as a monotone voice or the presence of an unusual foreign accent caused by vowel distortions. Additionally the child may have a tendency to monopolize conversation, particularly around his or her topics of interest. The child may present with convoluted speech that may be characterized by semantic errors, dysfluency, and repetitions. Sometimes it has been referred to as "empty speech" in which the child is engaged verbally but the point of the conversation is unclear. The child may also have an unusual vocabulary, which may sound pedantic or "pseudo mature." However, despite his or her use of technical language, the child may take things literally and/or fails to understand nonliteral language such as humor, sarcasm, or metaphors.

ASSESSMENT OF SPEECH, LANGUAGE, AND COMMUNICATION DIFFICULTIES

Children with complex clinical presentations are diagnostically challenging as is identifying the developmental and functional areas that are contributing to these complex presentations. Coggins, Timler, and Olswang (2007) investigated the compounding effect of prenatal exposure to alcohol and an ongoing adverse home environment on children's communication skills. They referred to this situation as "a state of double jeopardy." Coggins et al. (2007) formulated some interesting observations regarding our clinical formulations of complex presentations.

There is a need for clinicians to understand complex clinical profiles and the notion that "multiple risks contribute to multiple deficits" (Coggins et al., 2007, p. 125). This deliberation of multiple risks and deficits needs to be considered for children with complex presentations. Hummel and Prizant (1993, p. 219) recommended that "clinicians ... view language, communication and social development as inseparable." Whether a child's communication difficulties are due to an emotional–behavioral disturbance, a language or developmental impairment, environmental factors, or some combination requires meticulous attention. This becomes increasingly complex as language complexity and abstract language use develop in later childhood and into adolescence. See the previous section on contributors to the development of LDs.

Purpose of Assessment

Due to the complexity of multichallenged children, assessment should be undertaken by an interdisciplinary team. Assessment needs to diagnose between a speech disorder and

LD and other developmental disorders and syndromes of childhood, such as ASD and intellectual disability. Because language interacts with cognitive and behavioral factors, influencing a child's presentation, it is unrealistic to think that it can be viewed in isolation. An interdisciplinary team can work to identify factors influencing a child's presentation, such as attentional difficulties, executive dysfunction, emotional regulation difficulties, or behavior problems.

The speech and language specialist must also consider the possibility of comorbid presentations or the differential diagnosis between a speech disorder and LD, a developmental disorder, and other emotional and behavioral presentations. The American Psychiatric Association (2000) and the World Health Organization's *The ICD-10 Classification of Mental and Behavioural Disorders* (1992), have identified diagnostic categories that include communication impairment (see Table 4.8).

Table 4.8 *Diagnostic Categories That May Include Communication Impairment*

- ADHD and ADD
- ASD
- SM
- Learning disorders
- Developmental LD
- Developmental speech disorder
- Behavioral disorders
- Schizophrenia and psychosis
- Infant/child abuse and/or maltreatment/neglect
- Anxiety disorders (separation anxiety disorders and reactive attachment disorders)
- Intellectual disability
- Feeding and eating disorders

An assessment should attempt to identify whether a child has a primary LD or a secondary LD caused by either congenital or biological factors. Ozonoff, Heung, Byrd, Hansen, and Hertz-Picciotto (2008) recommend that the team consider the following factors when determining comorbidity and differential diagnosis: the child's developmental history, age of onset of symptoms, changes in functioning from the child's typical baseline, onset of new symptoms, and worsening of symptoms.

Family-Centered Practice

The need for greater family participation in early intervention is well established, and family-centered practice (FCP) is the primary theoretical approach recommended for assessment of and intervention in early language problems. FCP recognizes a parent's knowledge and expertise about her own child and her ongoing role in management and specific interventions. FCP enhances the parent's ability to become an informed decision maker and advocate for her child compared with a traditional role in which the parent would simply describe her child's behavior (Crais, Roy, & Free, 2006).

Principles of FCP encourage parents not only to describe their child's ability (Crais, Douglas & Campbell, 2004) but also to observe and rate their child's behavior as a mechanism to discuss and synthesize the perspectives of clinician and parent. Subsequently, the clinician and the parent can collaboratively pinpoint the child's strengths and needs. With this consensus, the parent is more likely to follow through on recommendations. Crais et al. (2006) investigated the most valued speech and language assessment practices from both parent and clinician perspectives (see Table 4.9).

The FCP approach also allows the clinician to understand the child in the context of his family system. This includes a clearer understanding of the family system's inherent strengths and limitations. This is particularly important if the clinician wants to proceed with parent training or parent-directed intervention approaches.

Table 4.9 *Most Valued Speech and Language Assessment Practices Identified by Parents*

- Identifying the family's most important concerns
- Making positive comments about the child
- Asking the family what the child does well
- Explaining and summarizing assessment results
- Asking whether observed behaviors are typical
- Identifying next steps for both family and clinician

Hearing Assessment

Normal hearing is essential for the development of language. If the child has a history of recurrent middle ear infections, demonstrates difficulties with listening and/or hearing, or presents with a delay in speech and language, a hearing impairment should be considered as a contributing factor. Recurrent or chronic otitis media can also contribute to APD since the child has fewer opportunities to develop important neural auditory connections due to deprivation of the acoustic signal (Gravel & Wallace, 1992). Further research has shown that APD has been associated with LD, dyslexia, and ADHD (Sharma, Purdy, & Kelly, 2009). Some children might also require an auditory processing assessment (see Table 4.10).

ASSESSMENT PROCESS

A range of approaches can be implemented to identify and assess a child's level of linguistic and communicative functioning. Approaches include obtaining a developmental and family history, administering screening questionnaires and standardized language measures, obtaining informal language samples, conducting natural observations in the home and school, and using dynamic assessment. An adequate assessment requires a combination of these measures to formulate a robust understanding of a child's linguistic and communication system.

Table 4.10 *Indicators That a Child Might Need an Auditory Processing Assessment*

- Difficulty with listening, especially in noisy environments
- Difficulty with following complex verbal instructions
- Spelling and reading difficulties
- Poor phonological awareness
- Difficulty with maintaining auditory attention; appearing distractible
- Short-term auditory memory (STAM) difficulties
- Difficulty with participating in groups or classroom discussions
- History of recurrent middle ear infections
- Appearing frustrated

Screening Tools

Language screening tools and parent report measures are important components of the speech and language assessment. Tools frequently used include the MacArthur–Bates Communicative Development Inventories (CDIs; Fenson et al., 2006) and the Rossetti Infant–Toddler Scale (Rossetti, 1990). As Law and Roy (2008, p. 198) noted, parent report measures can be "versatile, efficient and valid," but they also highlighted the limitations of early language measures in predicting persistent language delay. The primary issue in using a developmental screen is the high level of variability in the trajectory of early language development. As a result, it is difficult to make predictions about long-term outcomes or develop intervention goals based purely on parent report measures. Screening tools can also be used to evaluate a child's social communication functioning where natural observations are not possible.

Developmental and Family History

Parental reporting is an important part of a language assessment as a mechanism to acquire information, determine parents' concerns, and establish rapport. Due to high rates of speech and language delays in the general population, it is useful to understand a child's "risk" of developing a delay in terms of the risk factors discussed previously. Because speech, language, and learning problems can cluster in families, it is important to identify whether a child has a family history of such difficulties to determine her level of risk. By identifying her attainment of developmental milestones, a clinician can determine the nature of any language delay. In certain circumstances, parent reporting might be the most accurate in determining a child's level of functioning, particularly if the child is shy or intimidated by the testing process.

Standardized Assessment

Speech–language pathologists rely heavily on standardized and formal testing procedures to "accurately pinpoint the area of greatest difficulty for a child with language impairment" (Hassen & Botting, 2010, p. 249). Standardized language assessments provide useful information regarding a child's performance compared with the same-aged peers. However, normative data are not valid if the strict parameters of the testing process are not followed. For children considered difficult to test, particularly due to emotional or behavioral difficulties, reliance on standardized tests alone is not always possible due to their lack of flexibility and invalidity of normative data if not administered as required. If a clinician is unable to adhere to the testing parameters, then the child's scores can be either invalid or an underestimation of her true ability. Furthermore, the formal testing context might trigger anxiety or work avoidance in the child.

Dynamic Assessment

Dynamic assessment uses a range of clinical techniques to assess a child's potential for learning as opposed to his independent achievement or a formal test. Dynamic assessment investigates his level of functioning when provided with support, reflecting his developmental potential compared with a pure analysis of performance. Dockrell (2001) questioned the limitations of standardized testing, referring to the complex nature of language being evaluated using single measures. One approach to dynamic assessment is to provide incremental levels of prompting in a task to identify the child's performance in a supportive context, thus providing the clinician with useful information regarding intervention targets and strategies. Hassen and Joffe (2007) reported that dynamic assessment encourages observation and identification of important qualities in a child's learning behaviors, such as learning styles, problem-solving abilities, and strengths and weaknesses. Furthermore, dynamic assessment is considered particularly appropriate for children who are difficult to test and those whose scores on standardized testing are not valid.

Natural Observation

Observing behavior and obtaining a language sample are important in ascertaining a child's functional communication and social interaction with primary caregivers, teachers, and peers. An observation assessment allows the clinician to identify the range of communicative functions, strategies used to communicate (verbal, nonverbal, and behavioral), social communication skills, and qualities of the parent–child interaction, including strategies used by caregivers to support the child. In the school context, natural observation of a child in her peer group allows the clinician to observe social communication skills. A functional observation of a child's capacities, strengths, and deficits enables a clinician to plan appropriate interventions.

Play-based assessment is a useful part of language assessment for younger children because both play and language represent forms of symbolic development. As Paul (1995, p. 236) reported, play analysis allows the clinician to identify whether the child has achieved other levels of nonlinguistic symbolic development while yielding "insights into the child's conceptual and imaginative abilities." See Table 4.3 for an outline of the development of symbolic development.

Early Language Assessment

A speech disorder and LD are not typically diagnosed before a child is identified as being a late talker or having a language delay. Although a degree of developmental variation is typical, most children achieve certain language developmental milestones in the first 2 years of life, such as first words emerging by 12 months, two-word combinations by 24 months, and core vocabulary of at least 50 words by 24 months; failure to attain these milestones can indicate a language delay and would qualify the child as being a late talker. Research indicates that communication behaviors observed before 12 months can be markers of later difficulties (Paul, 2006). These early indicators include the following:

- *eye gaze*: limitations in eye gaze to express emotion, attention, or interest; delays in following another person with eye gaze;
- *gesture*: limitations in the range and use of gestures such as waving goodbye, or child might rely on gestures instead of vocalizations;
- *communication*: infrequent vocalizations or gestures to communicate, limited range of communicative functions, limited number of consonants and syllables when babbling; and
- *feeding difficulties*: history of problems with sucking, lip seal, tongue movement, and swallowing, might indicate later speech difficulties.

Children who present with a language delay are usually identified between 2 and 3 years of age. An early language assessment of a child between birth and 3 years would comprise a developmental screening tool, developmental and family history interview, natural observations, informal play assessments, and standardized testing if possible using a test such as the *Communication and Symbolic Behavior Scales* (*CSBS*; Wetherby & Prizant, 1993), *Pre-School Language Scales*, 4th ed. (*PLS-4*; Zimmerman, Steiner, & Pond, 2005), and *Reynell Developmental Language Scale* (Gruber & Reynell, 1990). Within a play-based assessment, the clinician can use environmental manipulation to optimize the use of target language behaviors.

School-Age Language Assessment

A school-age child might be referred for a language assessment for a number of reasons. The purpose of the assessment might be to screen for language difficulties, diagnose an LD, determine a profile of language strengths and weaknesses, differentially diagnose and/or identify comorbidities, and determine goals and strategies for intervention. Frequently, in pediatric mental health settings, the referred child has presented with a significant level of impairment in functioning across home and school settings. With the adoption of a developmental and multidimensional model of practice, it is important that the language assessment facilitates an understanding of the possible contributions of language problems to the child's emotional and behavioral presentation; this understanding will help in developing appropriate strategies to improve emotional and behavioral functioning.

Typically, a school-age language assessment should include an investigation of core language skills and narrative, literacy, pragmatic, and discourse skills. Children with core deficits in oral language that persist after 5 years of age are at increased risk of literacy problems and learning disabilities. Hence, it is common for children with language and learning difficulties to present with work avoidance and off-task behaviors as the cognitive demands of the classroom and curriculum increase. See Appendix 4.1 for a summary of standardized tests frequently used for the assessment of language, literacy skills, and pragmatic language–social communication skills.

INTERVENTION

Models of Intervention in Pediatric Mental Health Settings

Perry (2006) commented that the benefit of intervention depends on the nature, timing, pattern, and duration of therapy. Because the relationship between psychopathology and language impairments has been recognized, best practices for management and intervention approaches are being considered. For example, when working with a child who has experienced complex trauma, the speech and language specialist might need to consider interventions that look quite different from traditional approaches. Traditionally, the speech–language pathologist focuses on linguistic and communicative deficits, with strategies implemented to modify the delay. Due to the complexity of this clinical group, a traditional model of clinical practice might be ineffective. Geller and Folley (2009) propose that clinicians planning language and communication interventions should consider adopting a "relational and reflective" model. Such a model incorporates both mental health constructs and the clinician's discipline-specific knowledge of speech, language, and communication.

Stern (1995) coined the term "ports of entry" to refer to the "best intervention approach in which to gain access into the client's psychological and linguistic system in order to target particular goals" (cited in Geller & Folley, 2009, p. 5). Traditional speech and language intervention practice leads the clinician to work in isolation with a child or parent and focus on changing observable patterns of behavior. Geller and Folley (2009) characterize this as "working from the outside in." This model can target isolated skills and is less likely to consider emotional and behavioral states that might be impacting the presentation. An alternative "port of entry" is to work from a more relationally oriented perspective or "working from the inside out." By working from the inside out, the clinician attempts to understand the feeling states of the child (and parents) and their impacts on intervention and development (Geller & Folley, 2009). This is a dynamic process whereby the clinician continuously monitors and integrates emotional, behavioral, and linguistic states, adjusting management accordingly.

Medically At-Risk Infants and Speech and Language Interventions

At-risk infants might be preterm, seriously unwell, or have low birth weights, and they are highly vulnerable to developmental, cognitive, and language difficulties. These infants are vulnerable to a paucity of interaction-based stimulation due to their fragility, the invasiveness of their medical needs, and the disruption in the natural progression of the parent–child relationship (Paul, 2006).

Interventions for At-Risk Infants With Feeding Difficulties

Children with congenital or developmental difficulties at birth can present with feeding difficulties. For example, children with FASD are vulnerable to a number of feeding difficulties as a result of cleft palate, craniofacial abnormalities, and velopharyngeal weakness (Richard & Fahy, 2005). Specialist expertise in the assessment and management of such difficulties can contribute to interventions to reduce both infant and maternal distress and facilitate attunement between mother and infant. Causes of failure to thrive in the first 6 months include oral–muscular/mechanical feeding difficulties (for example, poor sucking and swallowing), trauma from early intensive feeding interventions, and psychological factors (for example, maternal depression and poor attachment) (Gahagan, 2006). The speech–language pathologist (SLP) has an important role, in collaboration with the interdisciplinary team, in differentially diagnosing between mechanical feeding difficulties and emotionally related feeding difficulties. Intervention strategies to manage infant feeding difficulties can significantly reduce maternal and infant distress and have a positive impact on the mother–baby bond.

Early-Language-Intervention Principles

Some contemporary early-language intervention programs have incorporated mental health constructs such as relationship-based learning, attachment theory, reflective functioning, and "use of self." Programs targeting early-language development, such as the Hanen Centre programs, the Developmental, Individual Difference, Relationship-based (DIR) Model, and Milieu Teaching (MT), incorporate components of these mental health constructs into their models. Such programs consider the family as critical for the child's language development, and the intervention is focused on the parent–child relationship (Kalmanson & Seligman, 2006). In relationship-based work, key elements for developmental change are the "strengths and capacities of the child and the parent" (Geller & Foley, 2009, p. 7). The clinician's role is to empower parents so that they can understand their capabilities. Similarly, the DIR Model views parents as the primary agents of change and encourages clinicians to work primarily with parents (Geller & Foley, 2009). The MT approach has strong empirical evidence to support its effectiveness for preschool children who present with significant cognitive and language delays, have an ASD, and/or belong to a high-risk family (Hancock & Kaiser, 2006). MT is a model of early-language intervention that incorporates a natural conversational-based strategy for teaching language and communication skills (see Table 4.11).

Table 4.11 *Milieu Natural Teaching Approaches*

Approach	Description	Key components
Milieu teaching (MT)	▪ The parent teaches functional language in the context of natural conversations. ▪ Prompts are used in conjunction with functional consequences.	▪ Environmental arrangement ▪ Modeling ▪ Time delay ▪ Incidental teaching
Responsive interaction (RI)	▪ Parents model developmentally appropriate language in conversational interactions. ▪ Models, meaning recasts, and expansions are contingent on child communication.	▪ Following the child's lead ▪ Semantically responsive feedback ▪ Modeling talk at target level ▪ Expansion of phrases ▪ Balanced turn taking
Enhanced Milieu Teaching (EMT)	▪ The parent's MT prompts are embedded in responsive conversational interactions with the child.	▪ Environmental arrangement ▪ RI ▪ MT
Blended EMT and behavioral interaction	▪ The parent uses the EMT approach and positively supports the child's behavior.	▪ Environmental arrangement ▪ RI ▪ MT ▪ Behavioral support techniques

Source: Hancock and Kaiser (2006). Reprinted with permission of Paul Brooks Publishing.

Early-Intervention Strategies

Research has supported the adoption of a few primary principles for effective early-intervention programming. The strongest body of evidence supporting the efficacy of these techniques is for children with an identified expressive language delay, specifically vocabulary delay, morphological delay (word endings), and syntactic delay (word order and sentence construction) (Baxendale & Hasketh, 2003; Fey, Cleare, Long, & Hughes, 1993). Strategies supported in the research are summarized in Table 4.12.

Preschool Language Intervention Strategies

Once children enter the preschool period (3–5 years), interventions typically target vocabulary, syntax, speech sounds, and comprehension. Interventions during this developmental period are critical, for research has shown that children who present with an LD at 5 years of age are likely to persist with ongoing difficulties. Knowledge of research-based interventions and strategies is pivotal to management and outcomes. A meta-analysis of interventions for children with a primary speech disorder and LD was conducted by Law, Garrett, and Nye (2004). Treatment efficacy was shown for expressive vocabulary and phonological difficulties, and a differential treatment effect was found for expressive syntax.

Typically, preschoolers with an LD demonstrate trends in their deficits. Children with language impairment frequently have poor expressive and receptive word-learning skills. These problems tend to be with fast linguistic mapping, which includes recognizing that a lexical label is represented by a phonological sequence (that is, the word). Another frequent difficulty that children experience is recognizing the concepts associated with a word (for example, an orange is a round, orange-colored fruit). Children with semantic difficulties

Table 4.12 *Early Language Intervention Strategies Identified in Research*

Child-entered strategies	■ These strategies include getting down to the child's level, following her lead, and catering to her interests compared with parent-directed topics. The parent responds verbally or nonverbally to all child-initiated attempts.
Parent training Psychoeducation	■ Research supports the adoption of parent-administered/indirect treatment models. Through psychoeducation, parents learn how to be more sensitive to their child's communication cues (verbal and nonverbal) and optimal methods of responding to his communication attempts. ■ Parents learn to "follow their child's lead" and engage in the child's focus of attention.
Natural interventions	■ Research suggests that natural approaches are more successful than formal teaching in stimulating language development. Language is mapped onto the environment and the child's focus of attention.
Building social routines	■ Socially repetitive games within the routine are invaluable in terms of exposure and the ability to target reciprocity and anticipatory events in play (e.g., games such as peek-a-boo).
Interaction promotion strategies	■ Respond to all child-initiated attempts; encourage the child to take turns through circles of communication; ask questions or make comments and wait expectantly for a response. ■ Respond to the presumed meaning of a child's communication, such as her communicative intent compared with the actual linguistic utterance. ■ RIs aim to facilitate the child's transition from prelinguistic to linguistic communication. The adult models the target word and encourages the child to produce it.
Environmental modification arrangement	■ Environmental changes can promote language development by increasing opportunities to communicate. ■ Increase the opportunities to use language purposefully, or for functional communication, and increase the frequency of "teachable moments." ■ Adopt incidental teaching strategies.
Language modeling strategies	■ These include labeling, linguistic mapping, imitative responses, expanding utterances, and extending topics. ■ Linguistic mapping is when the adult states or labels what the child is attempting to communicate; for example, if the child walks to the fridge and says "mo," the parent can respond, "Oh, you want some milk," subsequently mapping the language onto the context and mapping the meaning for the child. ■ Imitative responses occur when the adult imitates the child's verbal or nonverbal communication.

require increased exposure to new words compared with typically developing children. They experience difficulty with verb acquisition and use of verb particles (for example, "sit up" and "get down") and identifying semantic features in word classes (Paul, 2006). Children with syntactic and morphological difficulties tend to have poor acquisition of bound morphemes, auxiliary verbs, articles, and pronouns, and poor production of complex or elaborate sentences (Paul, 2006). A summary of early-language and preschool language interventions is provided in Table 4.13.

Table 4.13 *Preschool Intervention Strategies Identified in Research*

Strategy	Description
Environmental modification/ arrangement	■ Environmental changes can promote language development by increasing opportunities to communicate. ■ Increase opportunities to use language purposefully, or for functional communication, or increase frequency of "teachable moments." ■ Incidental teaching strategies can be used.
Language modeling strategies	■ These include labeling, language mapping, imitative responses, expanding utterances, and extending topics. ■ Linguistic mapping is when the adult states or labels what the child is attempting to communicate; for example, if the child walks to the fridge and says "mo," the parent can respond, "Oh, you want some milk," subsequently mapping the language onto the context and mapping the meaning for the child. ■ Imitative responses occur when the adult imitates the child's verbal or nonverbal communication.
Aided language stimulation (ALS)	■ ALS refers to pointing to picture symbols in conjunction with language stimulation. Research has supported the use of ALS in early vocabulary interventions when the child has little or no functional speech (Dada & Alant, 2009).
Focused stimulation	■ Focused stimulation is when a limited number of target words are presented repeatedly to a child (Wolfe & Heilmann, 2010). There are two types of focused stimulation: focused stimulation with simplified input (target words are presented in one- or two-word phrases), and focused stimulation with expanded input (target words are presented in natural speech). ■ Research supports both methods, with slightly different expressive language outcomes. Both methods can result in increased production of target vocabulary, but focused stimulation with simplified input resulted in increased target vocabulary, and focused stimulation with expanded input resulted in more overall expressive language (Wolfe & Heilmann, 2010).
Conversational recasting	■ Research has demonstrated that language input has a significant role in shaping grammatical development. Adult input has been found to be particularly effective if the adult utterance builds on the child's spoken utterance. By doing this, the adult provides new grammatical models. ■ Typical children exposed to a high frequency of complex sentences demonstrate a greater use and understanding of complex sentences (Hassink & Leonard, 2010). ■ Conversational recasting is particularly useful for verb development.

Experiential learning & introducing new topics and information	■ Adding syntactic or semantic information to a child's spontaneous utterance has been addressed through conversational recasting. Furthermore, an adult can introduce new information and concepts to the child. Through this process, the adult extends the child's knowledge and understanding of a concept or deepens her experience of a concept. ■ Using experiential tasks that incorporate a multisensory component (e.g., seeing, hearing, touching, and moving) can increase the child's level of interest, and active involvement can facilitate her understanding or memory.
Zone of proximal development	■ It is important to work in the child's "zone of proximal development"—the level between a child's current ability and his performance with guidance (potential ability) (Estes, 2010).
Theme-based targets	■ Working in themes can support semantic development.
Movement and rhythm activities	■ Movement can be particularly useful for some children to facilitate concentration. Being involved in an activity can increase the child's interest and participation, allowing for increased repetition and exposure. ■ Some research has shown that movement and rhythm can facilitate the frontal lobe of the brain and enrich language development (Campbell & Brewer, 1991). ■ Using appropriate music and rhyming activities can develop listening skills.
Visual support strategies	■ Children who experience difficulties in processing auditory information due to problems with comprehension, auditory processing, and phonological working memory limitations might require visual support strategies to reduce the auditory and cognitive load and facilitate learning.

Comprehension

Law et al. (2004), in their meta-analysis of treatment studies for comprehension, showed that there is a significant gap in quality research targeting interventions for children with severe receptive language difficulties. Of the studies reviewed, the treatment effect size was not significant when comparing intervention and nonintervention groups. Comprehension problems are the most serious form of LD, with a high frequency of comorbidity with other disorders, and they are a consistent indicator of poor long-term outcomes (Law, Campbell, Roulstone, Adams, & Boyle, 2008). Part of the difficulty is a lack of understanding of deficits that can impact a child's comprehension, such as memory, processing speed, and linguistic understanding, which may require intervention strategies as well.

Recent studies by Cohen et al. (2005) and Bishop, Adams, and Rosen (2006) hypothesized that the difficulties with teaching comprehension skills might be due to the context-specific nature of comprehension. It cannot be generalized from one context to another, for the context itself is extremely important to comprehension (Law et al., 2008). Possible causes of comprehension difficulties include processing limitations, such as impairments in verbal working memory or processing speed, and representational difficulties, which include difficulties in phonological processing of auditory stimuli (Tallal et al., 1996).

Strategies that can support comprehension and have been used frequently in clinical and educational settings include repeating questions or instructions, emphasizing keywords, and using rehearsal to develop understanding of grammatical meaning in context and visualization strategies (Gill, Klecan-Aker, Roberts, & Fredenburg, 2003). See Table 4.14 for a summary of strategies that can be used to enhance children's comprehension.

Table 4.14 *Strategies to Support Children's Comprehension*

Repetition

- Repetition can support children whose comprehension difficulties are related to difficulties with working memory, processing speed, auditory processing difficulties, or inattention.

Chunking information

- This strategy can also support children who have problems with working memory, processing speed, and auditory processing because it reduces the demands on memory and processing.

Visual support strategies

- To reduce the demands on auditory memory and processing speed, the use of visual supports, such as picture cues, keywords, and gestures, can support recall.

Comprehension checks/monitoring

- Interactional adjustments between the child and adult, such as monitoring whether the child has understood the instruction or question, can allow for clarification and lead the adult to adjust the linguistic input and subsequently support the child's understanding (Cabrera & Martinez, 2001).

Routine cues

- Children can have improved comprehension within a routine as they understand what is expected and use their knowledge of the routine to facilitate their understanding of an instruction.

Rehearsal and visualization strategies

- Evidence supports the systematic training of rehearsal and visualization strategies to increase the child's ability to follow verbal directions (Gill et al., 2003).

Narrative

Narrative interventions can focus on both macrostructure and microstructure elements. Macrostructure refers to the overall content and organization of the narrative, such as initiating events, character responses, planning, consequences, character development, and internal states. Microstructure refers to specific language components of a story, such as the use of referencing and cohesive devices and conjunctions to establish temporal and causal relationships in stories. Preliminary research on the effectiveness of narrative interventions has shown promise. Research on the treatment of lexical–semantic processing has also shown changes in ERP following a 5-week narrative-based intervention for 6- to 8-year-old children (Popescu et al., 2009). See Table 4.15 for a summary of strategies to facilitate narrative language.

Table 4.15 *Strategies Identified as Facilitating Narrative Production*

- Integrating oral and written narrative targets
- "Stickwriting," whereby students plan and record stories using pictures, each stage in the story being sketched quickly and simply (Ukrainetz, 1998)
- Story maps and story webs used to break up the story into its macrostructural elements (beginning, middle, and end)
- Story webs used to visually brainstorm characters' qualities, development, and thoughts and feelings
- Modifying highly familiar stories using visual story plans
- Verbal story prompts
- Specific conjunctions targeted separately, and temporal and causal conjunctions targeted at a sentence level, demonstrating the connection between two concepts

BEYOND LINGUISTIC INTERVENTIONS

Historically, a linguistic perspective has driven language assessment and intervention approaches. As a result, the field of speech–language pathology (SLP) has developed a solid base of standardized assessment instruments and empirically tested interventions to manage the core language areas of semantics, syntax, morphology, and phonology. Social interaction theories and pragmatic language theory have been pivotal in the development of knowledge of social communication, pragmatic language, and conversational discourse. In the past 20 years, Gallagher (1996, p. 418) highlighted that "pragmatic theories have increased speech language pathologists' awareness of the social role of language by highlighting the interpersonal nature of communication. Language use is viewed as an inherently social phenomen[on] with interpersonal consequences." Gallagher also reported that the impetus to consider social communication was the robust literature base showing a strong relationship between a child's language skills and social competence with peers.

Social Communication Interventions

Pragmatic language is considered a pivotal component of the social communication construct. Social communication can be considered as an episode within an interaction, such as entering a peer group or sustaining a conversation, and pragmatic language skills are required to achieve peer group entry or reciprocal conversation, such as eye contact, topic initiation, and turn taking (Timler, Vogler-Elias, & McGill, 2007). Social communication skills are complicated and involve the seamless integration of social cognitive processes, executive functions, and linguistic and pragmatic language skills (Adams, 2004, 2005; Timler et al., 2007). Successful social communication seems effortless to many, yet remediating it in children with multiple challenges is complex. This is partly due to the interplay of pragmatic, linguistic, social cognitive, and executive functioning components. Possible intervention targets are identified in Tables 4.16 and 4.17.

Table 4.16 *Social Communication Targets for Intervention*

- Entering peer groups
- Initiating interactions/conversations
- Sustaining reciprocal interactions
- Negotiating and resolving conflicts
- Repairing conversational breakdowns or clarifying information
- Terminating conversations/topics

Table 4.17 *Pragmatic Language Targets for Intervention*

- Nonverbal perception and use of eye contact, facial expressions, social distance, and gestures
- Verbal perception and use of voice (including tone and volume), and clarity and rate of speech
- Developing listener awareness and monitoring communication partners' nonverbal skills
- Reciprocity—the "to and fro" of conversations
- Conversational repair

Source: Spence (2003).

Pragmatic interventions have flourished with research on social skills programs. An effective intervention program requires two components. The first is skill-based learning, which includes observation, modeling, performance, rehearsal, and feedback (Michelson, Sugai, Wood, & Kazdin, 1983). The second focuses on generalization of these skills during peer interactions (Timler et al., 2007).

According to Gresham, Sugai, and Horner (2001), there are three types of deficits in the development of social skills, noted below:

1. Acquisition deficits: the child has not acquired the skills. Intervention targets the learning of a new skill using multiple strategies.
2. Performance deficits: the child might have demonstrated the skill but is inconsistent in her use of it and might not perform it in all appropriate contexts.
3. Fluency or frequency deficits: the child might attempt to perform a social skill but experiences difficulties in appropriately executing it.

Depending on the type of deficit, the clinician can use a variety of intervention strategies to teach a new skill, generalize an existing skill to be performed in a variety of contexts, or refine a skill so that it is executed more appropriately. Pragmatic language and social skill interventions can also be mediated by a teacher or peer, depending on the goal of intervention. Effective intervention strategies are listed in Table 4.18.

Generalizing Social Communication Interventions

When evaluating the success of an intervention, Timler et al. (2007, p. 167) stated that two outcomes must be achieved: "enhancement of language and social skills, with a particular focus on pragmatics, and generalization of these skills during authentic interactions with peers." Table 4.19 summarizes intervention strategies that promote generalization.

Table 4.18 *Intervention Strategies for Pragmatic Language and Social Communication Development*

Modeling and direct instruction	■ Children typically learn pragmatic language skills and conversational skills through observation, imitation, and trial and error until they achieve competency. However, children with poor pragmatic language and social skills have experienced a breakdown in this process by not being able to adequately observe, perceive, imitate, or moderate their skills. Subsequently, the process of modeling discrete behaviors, such as good listening or eye contact, is essential for improving pragmatic language skills. ■ Explicit modeling of skills is used in combination with direct verbal instructions, coaching, and an evaluation of performance or a feedback process. ■ Direct instruction is effective in teaching children a specific rule or the steps needed to demonstrate an appropriate pragmatic skill. This can be combined with scripting or a social story as a visual prompt. ■ Direct instruction can target a skill and provide an opportunity for the child individually or in a group setting to practice the skill in a play context (Goldstein, Kaczmarek, & English, 2002).
Role play and rehearsal	■ Opportunities to rehearse either through role play or real experiences are essential for pragmatic skill development. ■ Role play can be used in conjunction with video modeling to review and analyze the skill. ■ The clinician can work as a coach supporting the child as they rehearse appropriate pragmatic and conversational skills. ■ Role play can be used in a number of formats: adult role playing, children role playing, adult and children role playing, or using puppets to role play.
Scripting and fading	■ The concepts of scripting and fading come from ASD research interventions. ■ The premise is that the clinician develops age-appropriate scripts to teach initiating, question asking, and commenting (Krantz & McClannahan, 2005). The scripts typically identify the steps in the interaction/communicative act. For example, (1) walk up to your classmate, (2) look at him, (3) say "Hi," and (4) say "Can I play basketball with you?" ■ The script can be written out and/or picture symbols can be used. ■ Once the child has rehearsed and achieved a level of competency with the script (first with an adult and then with peers), it can gradually be faded (by removing parts of the script/visual prompt), until eventually the script is eliminated but the scripted responses remain intact. ■ The scripts can be as simple as single words or sentences but should be grammatically correct. ■ Students can also develop their own scripts.

(continued)

Table 4.18 *Intervention Strategies for Pragmatic Language and Social Communication Development (continued)*

Social stories	■ Social stories were developed from ASD intervention research (Gray, 2000). However, they have also been demonstrated as an effective tool in changing targeted behaviors in children with emotional and behavioral difficulties. Social stories can be particularly effective for children who have poor social skills and experience difficulties in understanding the perspectives of others. ■ Gray (2000) defines a social story as a personalized story that explains a confusing or socially challenging situation. The social story needs to be visually engaging, using pictures and sometimes photos of the child, and attempts to communicate the perspective of the student, the perspectives of others, and the appropriate or target behavior. ■ Social stories have been used to target social behaviors that are perceived as penalizing or can further isolate a child from her peers (Toplis & Hadwin, 2006). ■ Gray (2000) recommends a framework when writing a social story: (1) descriptive statements, (2) perspective statements, (3) affirmative statements, (4) control sentences, and (5) cooperative sentences.
Comic strip conversations	■ Similar to social stories, comic strip conversations are a useful tool to illustrate what people "think" and "say" during conversations. They can facilitate a child's understanding of conversation content and different perspectives in the conversation (Gray, 2000).
Incidental teaching and environmental arrangement	■ The use of incidental teaching or teachable moments is often associated with late language development in early intervention. However, real opportunities in the classroom, home, or clinic with older children that allow for the development and practice of pragmatic language skills should be used. ■ Environmental arrangements and modifications can also be employed to increase opportunities to teach pragmatic language skills. This involves systematically arranging materials and scenarios for a problem situation to allow children to engage in cooperative play, problem solving, and small-group discussions.
Video modeling	■ Video modeling or videotaping the child with behavioral analysis is an intervention strategy used to develop social skills well established in the ASD literature (Bellini, Akullian, & Hopf, 2007; Nikopoulos & Keenan, 2003). ■ Research on the effect of video modeling on children with an emotional or behavioral disorder has demonstrated that this intervention results in increasing peer interaction and decreasing inappropriate behavior (Baker, Lang, & O'Reilly, 2009). ■ Video modeling has been incorporated into a number of formal social communication programs, such as the Social Use of Language Programme, as a mechanism to both motivate/engage and provide visual feedback to children (Rinaldi, 2001). ■ Students are videotaped as they role play interactions and communication acts, such as greeting, good listening, or resolving a conflict. ■ The intervener can rehearse or have scripts to prompt the students. ■ The video analysis involves discussing students' reactions to the video. ■ The video analysis focuses on one element of the interaction, such as facial expression, eye contact, tone of voice, body distance, body language, or communication style. ■ Finally, students can decide how successful the interaction was.

Event-based learning techniques	■ The aim of this strategy is the repetitive rehearsal of specific interactional routines or problematic social scenarios. Through this explicit process, the child can develop an understanding of conversational structures and rules (Gallagher, 1996). ■ Socially penalizing behaviors are targeted. The aim of this intervention is first to identify the negative behavior; then a functional analysis of that behavior needs to be performed; then the negative behavior is replaced by a more appropriate behavior through direct instruction, modeling, role play, and feedback (Brinton & Fujiki, 1993). ■ Acquiescence training was developed to focus on building the skill of "acquiescence," defined as being flexible with the needs and desires of peers. The premise is that, by teaching a "keystone" skill, it will result in widespread improvements in behavior and socialization. The aim is to build peer interaction skills in children with severe behavioral problems (Ducharme, Folino, & Derosie, 2008).
Teaching communication styles	■ A number of social skill programs discuss and model communication styles, including being angry, timid, and assertive. ■ One aim is to develop skills in identifying nonverbal signs that a person is angry or assertive. Children are encouraged to focus on the different verbal and nonverbal signs of how someone looks when he is angry, timid, or cool. Then the children are encouraged to role play and rehearse positive communication roles.

Table 4.19 *Generalization of Pragmatic Language and Social Communication Skills*

Teacher-mediated strategies

- The aim of teacher-mediated interventions is to facilitate peer interactions (Girolametto & Weitzman, 2007). Timler (2008) identified that this can be achieved by
  - encouraging children to play together;
  - promoting interaction by prompting children to play together;
  - facilitating conversational repair by rephrasing and restating one child's statement to another when communication breakdowns occur;
  - praising children who are playing and working together;
  - adopting a "[r]edirecting strategy whereby the teacher encourages the LI student to redirect their question or request for help to a peer, as a result increasing the number of peer spontaneous interactions" (Timler et al., 2007); and
  - reinforcing rules that govern peer interaction.

Environmental modification strategies can also be implemented to facilitate cooperative play opportunities.

Peer-mediated strategies

- Peer-mediated interventions focus on encouraging and prompting typically developing peers to engage with and respond to peers with social communication impairments (Timler et al., 2007).
- Prosocial peers are selected to participate in the intervention.
- Giving the child with social communication difficulties, opportunities to interact with typical peers, allows her to practice skills and be exposed to positive role models. In addition, it can facilitate tolerance and possibly acceptance of the peer with socialization difficulties by her typical peers, given that such children are at greater risk of being ignored or rejected by their peers (Brown & Conroy, 2002).

Other examples include establishing a peer support network for the child or a buddy system whereby a socially competent child is identified to support the child who is struggling (Haring & Breen, 1992).

Clinician-mediated strategies

- Clinician-mediated strategies typically occur as individual sessions or in the context of small groups.
- The clinician moves through a standard framework of targeting a specific skill and implementing the intervention strategies of direct instruction, modeling, role play, rehearsal, feedback, evaluation, and praise.
- Generalization is supported by using
  - prompts graded within a hierarchy from most intrusive to least intrusive; the aim is for the clinician to gradually use the least intrusive prompts to support the child during peer interactions (Timler et al., 2007);
  - peer practice incorporated early on in the intervention; and self-monitoring, which includes identifying the target skill, practicing the skill, video recording the skill, and evaluating whether the skill was implemented correctly.

Incidental teaching and environmental arrangement

See Table 4.16 for an explanation.

EFFECTIVE INTERVENTION STRATEGIES WITH SPECIFIC DISORDERS

Multichallenged children can present with a range of possible diagnoses. Although children with a specific diagnosis do not present as a homogeneous group, and individual variations in presentation need to be considered, research has identified specific strategies that are effective for certain diagnoses (see Table 4.20).

Table 4.20 *Intervention Strategies for Children With Various Diagnoses and Comorbid LDs*

Executive functioning difficulties & ADHD	■ Due to possible deficits in processing speed and working memory, verbal instructions should be explicit, short, and repeated to facilitate comprehension. ■ Listening skills should be taught specifically. ■ Reduce the cognitive load in complex tasks, and break large amounts of information into smaller amounts for the child to work on. ■ Use visual strategies such as gestures, picture symbols, photos, pictorial prompts, charts, or schedules. ■ Have steps within tasks visually represented and a process for the child to review or complete the steps. ■ Behavioral repetition and rehearsal are effective. ■ Target skills are made concrete and explicit. ■ Explicitly teach social skills.
FASD	■ Visual support strategies are highly effective. ■ Behavioral repetition and rehearsal are critical. ■ When teaching language, attempt a "multisensory instructional" approach in which all forms of language are targeted (e.g., verbal, written, gestural, and nonverbal). ■ Use environmental arrangement to create opportunities for functional language use in concrete situations. Abstract/hypothetical scenarios are less effective. ■ Pragmatic and social communication need to be targeted (see Table 4.13). ■ Consider the behavioral factors that impact language and treat them with behavioral methods. ■ Minimize auditory and visual distractions during interventions.
SM	■ Applied behavioral analysis (ABA) has been effective in addition to the use of reinforcement regimes (Viana, Beidel, & Rabian, 2009). ■ Use positive reinforcement with the fading of prompts (Beare, Togerson, & Creviston, 2008). ■ Build in a system of prompts and cues that can be gradually reduced. ■ Dramatic play and role play can lead to spontaneous speech and other positive outcomes, such as enhancing self-esteem (Oon, 2010). ■ Work directly on specific language difficulties, such as semantics and narrative skills (see Table 4.13).
ASD	■ Picture exchange. ■ Prompt. ■ Social stories.
APD	■ Environmental strategies and modifications that aim to improve quality of the acoustic signal, reduce background noise, and improve environmental acoustics are useful. ■ Develop compensatory strategies; work on higher-order skills such as memory and attention to facilitate improved auditory processing. ■ Auditory training can utilize computer programs.

MODEL OF LANGUAGE INTERVENTION FOR CHILDREN WITH COMPLEX TRAUMA

Cook, Spinazzola, Ford, and Laktree (2005) proposed a model for the treatment of complex trauma based on an attachment, self-regulation, and competency (ARC) framework. It adopts a systematic approach with milieu-based interventions. This model proposes that SLP has a potential role to play. Ball and Khan (2009) used the ARC framework to propose a model highlighting the potential role for SLP during the three therapeutic stages of attachment, self-regulation, and competency, which will now be discussed. Please refer to Figure 4.4 for the ARC model.

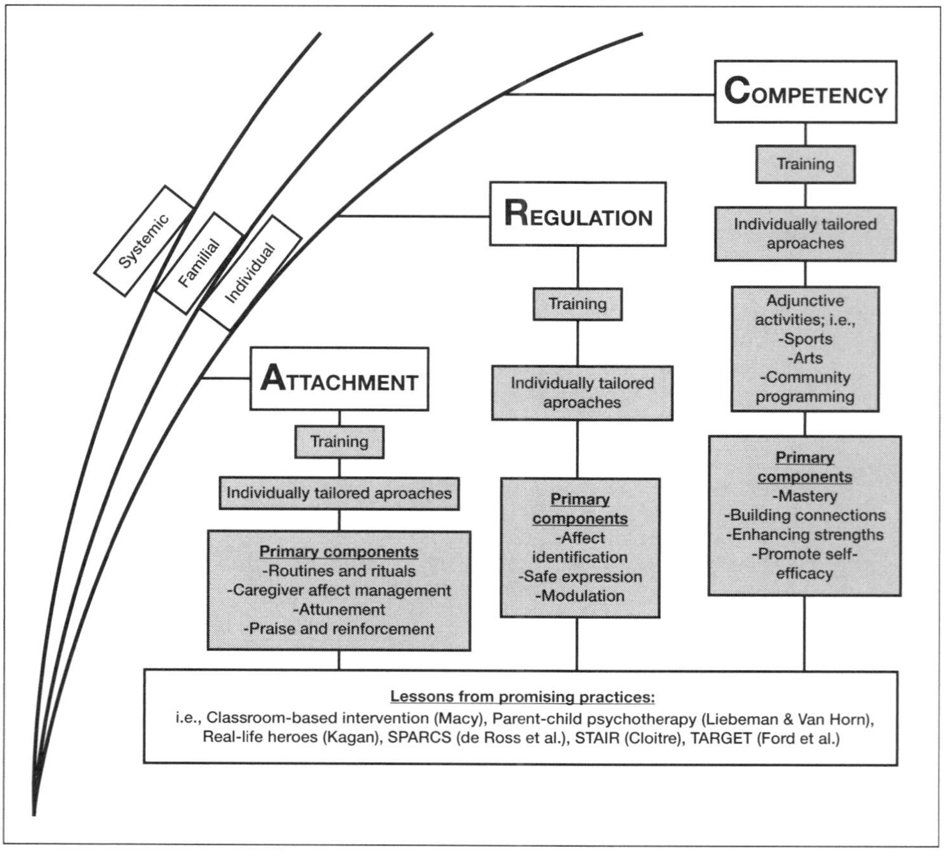

Figure 4.4 *The ARC model.*
Reprinted with permission from Kinniburg, Blaustein, Spinazzola, and van der Kolk (2005).

Attachment Phase

The primary goal of the attachment phase is to establish a feeling of safety and security for the child. Providing intervention to a child who has experienced complex trauma and has comorbid language impairment means that clinicians need to accommodate her communication difficulties. The SLP provides vital information about her level of comprehension, language-processing capacity when calm and dysregulated, and expressive language capability. This information will support the mental health practitioner in providing interventions at an appropriate linguistic level. Many therapeutic interventions, such as cognitive-behavioral therapy (CBT) and psychodynamic therapies rely heavily on the process of interaction and language-based skills such as discussion, self-talk, and reflection. See Table 4.21 for language targets during the attachment phase of the ARC intervention.

Self-Regulation Phase

According to Kinniburg et al. (2005), in the self-regulation phase, the child learns to regulate her emotional states to move from a state of arousal to emotional equilibrium. Children who have experienced complex trauma can have difficulties in managing their overwhelming feelings. The self-regulation process involves both nonverbal and verbal strategies. Nonverbal

Table 4.21 *Attachment Phase of Intervention in ARC Program and Language and Communication Targets*

Purpose of attachment stage: to establish a feeling of safety and security for the child (Kinniburg et al., 2005).

Potential language and communication targets

- ✓ Perform a language assessment to identify core language abilities and participate in differential diagnosis and language contributions to the psychopathological presentation.
- ✓ Visual prompts, such as visual schedules and social stories, can help a child to feel more secure and establish feelings of predictability. These prompts can also facilitate comprehension of events and changes (Ball & Kahn, 2009).
- ✓ Educate caregivers and teachers on the impacts of the language impairment on behavior; for example, perceived disobedience might be a result of poor comprehension of an instruction, or inappropriate responses in conversation might be due to a pragmatic language difficulty as opposed to the child being rude or difficult.
- ✓ Establish a common language for behavior management that can be consistent across all environments (Ball & Kahn, 2009). This includes phrases and processes that the child readily comprehends.
- ✓ Identify language barriers that might inhibit the establishment of attachment, such as extreme noise sensitivity or adverse reactions to loud voice tone or overtalking.

Table 4.22 *Self-Regulation Phase of Intervention in ARC Program and Language and Communication Targets*

Purpose of self-regulation phase: the child develops skills to respond to altered emotional states and regulate them (Kinniburg et al., 2005).

Potential language and communication targets

- ✓ Explore the child's emotional literacy, ability to recognize and label emotions in others and self, and ability to recognize emotional states in a complex task, such as problem solving (Ball & Kahn, 2009).
- ✓ Explore the child's capacity to self-talk during problem-solving tasks. Self-talk supports his ability to reflect and subsequently problem solve himself.
- ✓ Identify the child's capacity to verbally express the relationship between feelings and experiences and identify and verbally express cause-and-effect relationships.
- ✓ Develop his emotional language through the use of therapeutic social stories, problem-solving frameworks, and role plays.
- ✓ Identify the child's ability to formulate a narrative and its temporal and causal relationships (Ball & Kahn, 2009).
- ✓ Providing mental health clinicians with an appropriate narrative framework can help to scaffold the child's expression of events, which can facilitate with "integration of the client's traumatic experiences and with self-reflective information processing" (Ball & Khan, 2009, p. 147).
- ✓ Educate caregivers about modeling emotional language to facilitate the child's emotional literacy.

processes include recognition of warning signs and independent implementation of strategies to regulate the emotional state. However, typical children use language to regulate changes in their emotional states. Strategies typically include self-talk (see Table 4.22 for language targets during the self-regulation phase of the ARC intervention).

Competency Phase

Based on the ARC model, when a child reaches the competency phase, she has the capacity to be involved in developmentally appropriate speech and language interventions (Ball & Khan, 2009). The ARC model refers to competencies developing in four domains: cognitive, emotional, intrapersonal, and interpersonal. Language and communication skills can impact all four domains but are particularly important for interpersonal and cognitive development. Interpersonal competencies include positive peer relationships and socialization skills, and cognitive competencies include language development, academic performance, and executive functioning skills such as problem solving (Kinniburg et al., 2005). See Table 4.23 for language targets during the competency phase of the ARC intervention.

Table 4.23 *Competency Phase of Intervention in ARC Program and Language and Communication Targets*

Purpose of competency phase: skill development stage.

Potential language and communication targets

- ✓ Core language interventions focus on deficits in semantics, syntax, and phonology.
- ✓ Social skill training is provided.
- ✓ Interventions target literacy problems and learning difficulties.

Modified from Ball and Khan (2009). Reprinted with permission.

Case Studies

We can now return to the case studies and outline the intervention strategies implemented to support these children within the framework of the ARC model for complex trauma.

Case Study 1: Andrew

Andrew was a sensitive child who felt quickly shamed around any mention of his cleft palate or speech difficulties. This issue pertained to his poor self-concept and self-esteem and was addressed in a therapeutic context by his case coordinator. Because his articulation was quite good, the primary residual problem related to his cleft palate was "acoustic turbulence" (a low rumbling sound, like snoring at the back of the nasal cavity, evident when talking extensively). The acoustic turbulence improved significantly with increased voice volume and breath support. Subsequent intervention focused on Andrew using a "strong voice" and developing voice projection and breath support to improve his voice quality and overall intelligibility. This was targeted in role-play activities in the context of social skill groups in which good communication skills and assertive behavior were encouraged.

Andrew's continued hearing difficulties and receptive language problems were addressed through the use of strategies used with all children in the class as Andrew was highly resistant to any withdrawal interventions that made him appear different from his peers. This intervention included environmental modification strategies to improve classroom acoustics and transmission of the spoken message to him, and simplification of the length and complexity of instructions and questions through the use of visual cues and chunking.

Attachment Phase

- Reviewed file, attended initial clinical case presentation, and liaised with case coordinator and educational staff. A speech and language assessment was performed. It included a standardized assessment, informal assessments during free-play activities, and classroom-based observations.
- Andrew was identified as having a moderate receptive and expressive LD and an SSD related to his hearing impairment and his cleft palate. This feedback was provided to family and educational staff.
- From assessment and observation, it was apparent that Andrew's hearing levels were not adequate, but it was unclear if this was a result of deterioration of hearing or inadequate functioning of his hearing aids. As a result, his listening and comprehension skills were adversely affected.
- A request was made for an immediate review of hearing and hearing aid suitability.

- A request was made for a specialist medical review of his cleft palate.
- Visual schedules and prompts were recommended for the classroom routine to facilitate hearing and comprehension to reduce outbursts related to misunderstanding or anxiety.
- Barriers to listening were identified, such as classroom noise levels, and strategies such as room modifications and more appropriate seating positions were arranged.

Self-Regulation Phase

- Due to Andrew's difficulties with hearing, attention, and listening, the process of overtalking or debriefing issues verbally was not helpful for Andrew and contributed to his anxiety. This feedback was provided to family and educational staff. An alternative strategy was recommended to allow him to draw a picture of what happened, thereby giving him time to formulate his thoughts. Once this was completed, he was more able to formulate and express his opinions. This process appeared to facilitate self-regulation during difficult situations.
- In addition, problem-solving skills were identified as an area of significant impairment and frequently resulted in Andrew resorting to physical aggression. His ability to self-talk during problem-solving tasks was reviewed, and a visual framework was established to support him to problem solve and reflect on social problems.
- A social story was developed to explain and reflect some of Andrew's social and communication difficulties.

Competency Phase

- Individual treatment focused on oral narratives, semantics, and comprehension. Narrative was targeted through the use of frameworks to develop story macrostructure and character concepts. Semantics was targeted by focusing on language concepts related to the theme of the classroom. The clinician explored vocabulary concepts related to the target curriculum, such as space, to prepare Andrew for the vocabulary content used in the classroom. Processes such as brainstorming and semantic maps with visual supports were incorporated. A smaller laminated copy was placed in his desk, allowing him to refer to it during classroom activities. This facilitated his concept recall and word recognition.
- Attendance in the social skills group was an important component of intervention.
- Comprehension strategies were implemented, such as providing visual supports (picture cues, gestures, and written instructions on the board), chunking information, and repeating instructions.
- Comprehension-monitoring skills were developed to improve independence in recognizing when Andrew did not hear or understand an instruction. He was encouraged to request support independently via a nonverbal system. With this strategy, he had a small laminated circle, red on one side and green on the other. When Andrew struggled to understand, he could turn the circle to the red side to indicate that he needed support. This was further developed to encourage him to put his hand up and explain his difficulty.

Case Study 2: Sarah

Sarah presented with significant expressive and receptive language difficulties. Expressive language intervention was primarily targeted through the development of lexical processing and semantic conceptualization. Strategies included the use of mind maps along with brainstorming processes to familiarize her with language concepts and vocabulary used in the classroom, and to develop her understanding of the links between concepts targeted in the curriculum. Sarah's oral and written narrative skills were also very impaired. Narrative skills were targeted through the use of narrative frameworks and story maps. Visual prompts were also incorporated to support this process. Comprehension-monitoring skills were targeted along with strategies to develop her independence in requesting support from teachers when struggling with classroom demands. Problem-solving skills were also an important target for Sarah. A problem-solving visual framework was used to support her ability to identify social problems, reflect on how she felt, and generate solutions to the problems.

Attachment Phase

- Due to the complexity of the case, a review of all previous assessments was collated and a new assessment conducted. It incorporated parent and teacher interviews, standardized assessment, informal assessments to investigate social communication and discourse skills, and classroom-based observations.
- Sarah presented with multiple and complex risk factors. Given her level of cognitive impairment, developmental delay, birth trauma, and history of abuse and neglect, it was reasonable to suggest that her level of language impairment was reflective of her cognitive functioning and environmental deprivation. As such, she was considered as having a secondary LD (secondary to a primary cognitive impairment).
- Sarah was described as "noncompliant, work avoidant, and oppositional in the classroom and around academic tasks." Academic work, particularly literacy-related tasks, was beyond her ability and triggered strong feelings of anxiety, which had a negative impact on her behavior. In collaboration with educational staff, a modified curriculum was formulated; it made classroom work more accessible and subsequently reduced Sarah's levels of anxiety related to school. Through this process, funding was also provided for an educational assistant to support Sarah with academic work.
- Provide psycho-education to carers and educators regarding her level of LD and its impact on her emotional and behavioral presentation. This included recommendations on how to adapt communication to support Sarah's comprehension and expression.

Self-Regulation Phase

- Given Sarah's significant difficulties with comprehension, a social story was developed to facilitate her understanding of expectations of school behavior and important aspects of daily routines, such as getting ready for school.
- Nonverbal strategies to request assistance were implemented.
- Explored visual strategies to support Sarah's ability to express her thoughts and feelings. Provided fellow mental health clinicians with strategies to support their clinical interventions that were language orientated.

Competency Phase

- An interdisciplinary team approach was used due to the complexity of need. In the area of language impairment, individual treatment focused on oral narratives, semantics, and comprehension.
- Sarah had demonstrated significant difficulties in socialization that frequently led to threatening and aggressive playground behavior. To support her in alternative methods of problem solving, a visual problem-solving framework was developed. It supported her in identifying social problems. It went through stages of reflecting on how she felt about the problem and then generating solutions to the problem. In addition, the social skill group program focused on developing an assertive communication style in social situations and strategies to "keep cool" when Sarah was feeling anxious or angry. These strategies included walking away, telling a safe adult, and so on.

CONCLUSION

The relationship between childhood and adulthood mental disorders has led researchers and clinicians to consider a developmental perspective in psychopathology continuities. Both longitudinal and epidemiological studies have identified neurodevelopmental disorders as a significant causal mechanism that increases the likelihood of long-term mental health diagnoses for individuals. LD and ASDs are considered significant contributors to poor adult mental health outcomes. This was clearly demonstrated in the longitudinal study by Clegg et al. (2005) that investigated long-term outcomes (early childhood to mid-30s) for a group of males with an identified SLI in childhood, compared with their siblings and an IQ-matched control group.

Clegg et al.'s (2005) follow-up study in adulthood showed that the LD group presented with a primary impairment in social functioning and relationships. Other interesting findings were the poor occupational outcomes for the LD group, with significantly lower rates of paid employment. Relationship outcomes were also poor, with the majority of the LD group never living independently, and over half experienced impairments in friendships, and only a quarter had experienced a cohabiting relationship, compared with 100% of their siblings and 90% of the IQ-matched control group. Factors such as an individual's poor social functioning, limitations in the number and quality of healthy relationships, dysfunction in friendships, and poor occupational outcomes place an individual at risk of social isolation and mental health problems.

Speech, language, and communication impairments in isolation have significant impacts on a child's social, academic, and vocational outcomes. Children with comorbid language and emotional and behavioral disorders are particularly at risk. The challenge for clinicians is to integrate knowledge from both developmental pediatrics and pediatric mental health to devise a holistic intervention that leads to long-term meaningful functional gains for this highly at-risk group of children and their families.

Appendix 4.1 *Assessment Tools*

Assessment Tool	Age Range	Main Purpose
Early language		
Ages and Stages Questionnaire (ASQ-3): A Parent-Completed Child-Monitoring System (3rd ed.). Squires and Bricker (2009)	4–60 months	Developmental questionnaires sent to parents of at-risk children. Areas screened include gross and fine motor control, communication, personal–social, and problem solving
Rossetti Infant–Toddler Language Scale. Rossetti (1990)	Birth–3 years	Areas assessed include play, interaction, attachment, gesture, pragmatics, language comprehension, and expression
MacArthur–Bates Communicative Developmental Inventories (CDIs). Fenson et al. (2003)	8–37 months	The *MacArthur–Bates Communicative Developmental Inventories (CDIs)* are parent-completed measures in which the parent documents the child's understanding of words and gestures and those used by the child
Receptive Expressive Emergent Language Test—3rd ed. Bzoch, League, and Brown (1991)	Infants and toddlers	Assists in the identification of infants and toddlers who have language impairments or who have other disabilities that affect language development
Communication and Symbolic Behavior Scales (CSBS). Wetherby and Prizant (2001)	9 months–2 years	The *Communication and Symbolic Behavior Scales (CSBS)* examine the communicative, social, affective, and symbolic abilities of children whose functional communication age is between 9 months and 2 years. The scales are used to identify children with communication problems as early as possible and to devise intervention programs for them
Symbolic Play Test (2nd ed.). Lowe and Costello (1998)	1–3 years	A diagnostic tool that helps identify the early skills required for language development
Early language/preschool language		
Preschool Language Scale-4. Zimmerman, Steiner, and Pond (2005)	3–6.11 years	Format is appropriate for very young children Identifies children who are at risk for an LD and need further evaluation Screens a variety of skills, including language, articulation, connected speech, voice, fluency, and pragmatics
Preschool Language Assessment Instrument-2 (PLAI-2). Blank, Rose, and Berlin (2003)	3–5.11 years	Assesses children's abilities to meet the demand of classroom discourse

The Early Language Milestone Scale (2nd ed.) *(ELM Scale-2)*. Coplan (1993)	Birth–4 years	The *Early Language Milestone Scale*, 2nd ed. (*ELM Scale-2)* was developed as an early identification tool to identify language delays in young children
Reynell Developmental Language Scales—2nd Revision (RDLS). Reynell and Huntley (1985)	1–6 years	The *Reynell Developmental Language Scales-2 (RDLS)* consist of two scales: the Verbal Comprehension and the Expressive Language
Preschool/school-age language		
Renfrew Language Scales: The Bus Story; Renfrew Action Picture Test; Word Finding Vocabulary Test. Renfrew (1998)	3–8 years	***Action Picture Test*** This test assesses responses produced from a simple question about a corresponding picture card; it assesses the information content and grammatical usage of each response and provides the age level the individual is functioning at for both these areas
	3–9 years 3–8 years	***Word Finding Vocabulary Test*** It assesses the child's ability to name 50 line drawings of objects which are arranged in order of difficulty ***Bus Story Test*** This test assesses the child's information content, sentence length, and grammatical usage in consecutive speech by retelling the bus story
Clinical Evaluation of Language Fundamentals—Preschool, 2nd ed. *(CELF–P-2).* Semel, Wiig, and Secord (2006)	3–6.11 yrs	Assesses a broad range of language functions in pre-primary children
Clinical Evaluation of Language Fundamentals, 4th ed. (CELF-4). Semel, Wiig, and Secord (2006)	Elementary school-aged children	Assesses a broad range of language functions in elementary school-aged children
Expressive One Word Picture Vocabulary Test—4th ed. *(EOWPVT-4).* Martin and Brownell (2000)	2–12 years	The *Expressive One-Word Picture Vocabulary Test—Revised (EOWPVT-R)* asks children to name items, usually with one word, illustrated in 100 pictures. This test assesses a child's speaking Kindergarten readiness
Receptive One Word Picture Vocabulary Test—4th ed. *(ROWPVT-4).* Martin and Brownell (2000)	2–18 years	*The Receptive One-Word Picture Vocabulary Tests—Revised (ROWPVT-R)*
Peabody Picture Vocabulary Test—4th ed. (*PPVT-4*). Dunn and Dunn (2007)	2.6 years–adult	Assesses receptive vocabulary

(*continued*)

Appendix 4.1 *Assessment Tools (continued)*

Assessment Tool	Age Range	Main Purpose
School-age language		
Clinical Evaluation of Language Fundamentals, 4th ed. (*CELF-4*). Semel, Wiig, and Secord (2004)	5–21 years	Assesses receptive, expressive, grammatical, and semantic skills
Test of Auditory Comprehension of Language—3rd ed. (*TACL-3*). Carrow-Woolfolk (1999a)	3–9.11 years	The test is an individually administered measure of receptive spoken vocabulary, grammar, and syntax
Test of Early Language Development—Primary (4th ed.) (*TELD-P-4*). Hammill and Newcomer (2008)	2–8 years	
Test of Language Development—Intermediate (4th ed.) (*TOLD-I-4*). Hammill and Newcomer (2008)	8–8 years	
Test of Language Competence—Expanded Edition. (*TLC-E*) Wiig and Secord (1989)	5–18.11 years	The *TLC-E* provides a consistent format to assess emerging metalinguistic abilities and linguistic strategy acquisition; emphasis is placed on assessing a student's ability to perceive, interpret, and respond to the contextual and situational demands of conversation
Test for the Reception of Grammar (2nd ed.) (*TROG-2*). Bishop (2003)	4 years and above	Assesses grammatical comprehension by measuring understanding of 20 constructions four times each using different test stimuli
Evaluating Communicative Competence: A Functional Pragmatic Procedure. C. S. Simon (1986)	10–18 years	Language processing, metalinguistics skills, and functional uses of language
Comprehensive Assessment of Spoken Language (CASL). Carrow-Woolfolk (1999b)	7–21 years	Lexical, syntactic, pragmatic awareness of appropriate forms, and complex comprehension; it provides a precise picture of language-processing skills and structural knowledge, allowing the tester to document development from preschool through the postsecondary years

Oral and Written Language Scales (OWLS). Carrow-Woolfolk (1996)	5–21 years	Measures use of conventions, linguistic forms, and the ability to communicate meaningfully in writing
Assessment of Literacy and Language (ALL). Lombardino, Lieberman, and Brown (2005)	Preschool to year 1	Assesses spoken language and written language skills
Articulation		
Goldman–Fristoe Test of Articulation, 2nd ed. (*G–F-TA-2*). Goldman and Fristoe (2000)	2–21.11 years	Provides information about a child's articulation ability by sampling both spontaneous and imitative sounds. Measures articulation of consonant sounds and determines types of misarticulation. The Sounds-in-Words section is norm referenced. The Sounds-in-Sentences and Stimulability sections are not norm referenced.
Literacy		
Neale Analysis of Reading Ability—3rd ed. Neale (2011)	6–12.11 years of age and special needs students through to adult level	To measure the accuracy, comprehension, and rate of reading, monitor reading progress and obtain diagnostic observations of reading behavior
The *Sutherland Phonological Awareness Test—Revised (SPAT-R)*. Neilson (2003a)	Grades 1–4	A comprehensive standardized test that provides an overview of the phonological awareness skills required for early literacy development
Astronaut Invented Spelling Tests (AIST). Neilson (2003b)	Grades 1–3	The *AIST* is a test where children are asked to "have a go" at spelling the names of a set of four humorous astronaut figures. Each first and last name contains one or two syllables, involving simple consonants, a range of vowels, and consonants that are more difficult to segment.
Phonological Abilities Test—PAT. Hulme, Muter, and Snowling (1997)	4–7 years	A diagnostic test to assess the nature and extent of phonological difficulties in children with literacy difficulties or as a screening tool to identify younger children at risk for literacy difficulties

(continued)

Appendix 4.1 *Assessment Tools (continued)*

Preschool and Primary Inventory of Phonological Awareness (PIPA). Crosbie, Teitzel, Ozanne, McIntosh, and Dodd (2000)	3–6.11 years	Identifies difficulties in the knowledge and manipulation of sound structures in young children.
Pragmatics		
Children's Communication Checklist—Revised (CCC—2). Bishop (2003)	4–16.11 years	Rates a child's communication skills to determine if further testing is required.
Problem Solving		
Test of Problem Solving—Elementary-3 (TOPS-3 Elementary). Bowers, Huisingh, Barrett, Orman, and LoGiudice (1994)	6.11–11 years	Addresses critical thinking abilities based on students' language strategies in the following areas: making inferences, sequencing, predicting, determining causes, problem solving, and negative questions.
Token Test for Children, 2nd ed. *(TTFC-2).* McGhee, Ehrier, and DiSimi (1978)	3–12.11 years	A screening measure for assessing receptive language in children.
Narrative		
Peter and the Cat (2nd ed.). Leitao, Allan, and Phillips (2004)	5–9 years	Provides a descriptive profile of the child's development of key narrative competencies.
The Expressive, Receptive and Recall Narrative Instrument (ERRNI). Bishop (2004)	4–15 years	Assesses the ability to relate, comprehend, and recall a story after a delay. The parallel forms allow for retesting while minimizing practice effect.

5

Difficulties and Disorders of the Effects of Trauma

Children can be referred for treatment with a number of disturbing symptoms and several diagnoses, often without any consideration of the possible effects of trauma on their presentations. We use the case of George and Emily in this chapter as we explore the effects of trauma and their treatment.

Case Studies: George and Emily

Ten-year-old George was referred for treatment by his grandmother, Jeannie, prompted by his school. As the principal explained, they were finding George's oppositional behavior and aggression toward his peers unmanageable. He also struggled in the classroom with a number of subjects and with concentration. The situation had escalated when George had run away from the classroom and could not be found for 2 hours eventually being discovered in an enormous hole he had dug so he "could disappear." All of this raised concerns about his safety and those of other children in his school. Jeannie, George's paternal grandmother, had taken in George and his two siblings after they had suffered neglect, abuse, and rejection by their biological father and his various partners. Holding back tears Jeannie explained she "had tried everything, I tell him I care for him every day and then something happens and he's out-of-control or hiding in the cupboard ... the other two are doing well but he pushes me away all the time ... I don't know how much more I can take." Her pain was palpable as she contemplated what would happen to him if he didn't "come around."

Emily's mother, Mary, and her partner laughed almost hysterically as they described how 5-year-old Emily kept their household in a state of constant anxiety and confusion. They wanted desperately to understand what was causing her oppositional behavior and why she always created a disturbance wherever they were. They wanted to know how to help her. Her older brother hated to be around her, and her baby sister looked at her in amazement and fear as Emily raced around the house causing "destruction in her wake." She had been removed from two daycares, and her Kindergarten teacher was exhausted and threatened to leave unless something was done about Emily. Mary had become pregnant with Emily soon after she was married. Although Mary was excited about the baby, she became increasingly concerned about her husband's drug use and erratic behavior. Consequently, she was depressed and anxious throughout the pregnancy and in the postpartum period. However, up to 15 months of age, Emily was a happy and responsive baby. When she was about 16 months old, her father had a drug-induced psychotic breakdown and nearly killed her and her mother with a metal bar. After this terrifying ordeal, Emily awoke frequently from dreams of the event and during the day often cried. Sometimes during this time, Mary shut herself in her bedroom and slept for hours to avoid her husband and Emily's screaming. As things worsened, Mary left her husband and went to a shelter with Emily. Later she moved in with her new partner, John, who had a boy about 2 years older than Emily, and the couple had a new baby. Although Mary felt very supported by her new partner, she still experienced depression and felt concerned that he would leave if Emily "couldn't be straightened out."

BACKGROUND ON TRAUMA

Trauma in many forms, such as famine, plague, murder, and rape, has been an unavoidable part of the experience of people across the world since the beginning of time (Perry, 2008). Yet not until recently, following recognition of the adverse reactions of combat troops returning from Vietnam and the September 11, 2001, terrorist attacks, have its effects been more widely recognized. However, long before these events, a few writers—such as Freud (1919/1954), Grinker and Spiegel (1945), Janet (1889), Kardiner (1941), and Pavlov (1926)—recognized how overwhelming the effects of trauma can be and that traumatic events can change a person's neurobiology (Herron, van der Kolk, & Hostetler, 1994).

Since the work of these early writers and researchers, there has been a growing literature on the effects of trauma that has moved beyond an emphasis on the effects of war to consider the dramatic effects on victims of all ages of different types of trauma. However, posttraumatic stress disorder (PTSD) was not introduced into descriptions of mental health disorders until the 1980s, when the diagnosis was first included in the 1980 edition of the *Diagnostic and Statistical Manual of Mental Disorders,* 3rd edition (*DSM-III*; American Psychiatric Association [APA], 1980). Seven years later, in 1987, the revised edition, *DSM-III-R,* recognized that children are affected and that, instead of having flashbacks and nightmares, they can reenact past traumatic experiences in play and artwork. It was also realized that children can regress developmentally, losing skills that they had gained previously. Many clinicians did not think that the inclusion was broad enough to define the complex presentations of individuals who had experienced chronic, early, and interpersonal types of trauma or a catastrophic event such as a brutal gang rape or massive disaster. Findings from a multisite field trial supported the construct validity of a complex PTSD diagnosis for this kind of trauma and the clinical relevance of the symptoms described (van der Kolk, Roth, Pelcovitz, & Mandel, 1992). However, the new diagnosis was not included in *DSM-IV* (4th ed.; APA, 1994) but had been recommended again for inclusion in *DSM-5* (5th ed.; APA, 2013).

DEFINITIONS OF TRAUMA

Before discussing the effects of trauma, it is important to define the meaning of the term. "Trauma" refers not to the stress or reaction that often occurs as a result of trauma but to the event itself. Events considered traumatic include military combat; sexual, physical, and emotional abuse and neglect; violent attacks such as rape and physical or sexual assault; man-made disasters (wars, torture, and terrorist attacks); natural disasters (hurricanes, earthquakes, fires, volcanoes, and floods); life-threatening illnesses and painful medical procedures; serious motor vehicle accidents; extreme bullying; and partner violence.

Characteristics believed to influence the degree of the effects of trauma are predisposing factors (neurobiology of the child and earlier experiences with attachment figures);

the trauma itself (type, number, timing or age when it occurred, within or outside the family, chronic, or catastrophic); and post-trauma variables (support available in the family and community) (Herman, 1992; Nijenhuis, van der Hart, & Steele, 2002).

Variables found to result in higher levels of PTSD and more internalizing problems and externalizing problems include being exposed to ongoing trauma and several events rather than one event (Fletcher, 2003). The death of a significant individual during a traumatic event has also been associated with increased PTSD symptoms in children (Nader, 1997; Pfefferbaum et al., 1999). This can lead to a more complex set of symptoms than normal bereavement (Gray, Prigerson, & Litz, 2004). When the trauma is a single event, it is referred to as a Type I trauma; if the trauma is chronic or if there are multiple events, it is called a Type II trauma. Whether it is Type I or Type II, trauma can influence how the individual is affected and the kind of treatment needed (Schuder & Lyons-Ruth, 2004).

Some trauma can be "hidden" and be characterized as small "t" trauma because it might not be realized either that it occurred or how significant it was for the developing child. Infants and preschool children are totally dependent on caregivers for the containment of fearful arousal and psychobiological regulation. Consequently, their experience of stressful events is significantly affected by how available and effective caregivers are in calming them. Hidden traumas occur when caregivers are unavailable, extremely inconsistent in their care, or dysregulated themselves, as can occur with mentally ill or substance-abusing parents. As well, parents who consistently convey negative parental attributions of their child can contribute to the child being traumatized and internalizing a negative sense of self and feelings of incompetence (Lieberman, Silverman, & Pawl, 2000).

PREVALENCE OF TRAUMA

According to 1998 estimates by the U.S. Department of Health and Human Services, each year more than 1 million children are abused and neglected in the United States, with 80% of the maltreatment being inflicted by the children's parents and another 10% by other relatives (U.S. Department of Health and Human Services, 2008; van der Kolk, 2005). Thousands more children undergo traumatic medical and surgical procedures and suffer from life-threatening illnesses, experience natural and man-made disasters, or are exposed to family or community violence. In inner city areas in the United States, 80% of adolescents have witnessed an assault, 40% a shooting or stabbing, and 25% a homicide (Bell & Jenkins, 1993; Schubin, Scott, & Tzelepis, 1993). These numbers are staggering since very few of these traumatized children receive adequate treatment, and in any year there are millions of children who have been traumatized, have not been treated, and continue to suffer from the effects of trauma, sometimes for their lifetimes. Of course, across the world, millions of children are traumatized every year, and childhood trauma has been described as one of the most important public health challenges facing society (Demyltenaere, Briffaerts, & Posada-Villa, 2004; World Health Organization, 2001, 2006).

One of the most important studies that highlighted the extent and effect of trauma was the Adverse Childhood Experience Study (ACE; Fellitti et al., 1995). Of 17,000 patients interviewed while attending a routine medical appointment at health maintenance organizations (HMOs) in the United States, 52.5% reported a high-magnitude stressor during childhood. Most frequently reported were physical abuse (28%), sexual abuse (20%), neglect (15%), domestic violence (27%), substance abuse of parents (20%), and the mental illness of a parent (23%). Many other stressors were reported, such as illness, death of a loved one, and man-made and natural disasters. Of course, these numbers do not include small "t" or hidden traumas or low-magnitude stressors that might have occurred, particularly in early childhood. They would not have been reported because the person would have had no understanding of their importance and possible effects. A graded relationship was found between the number of adverse childhood events and adult physical and mental health and risk-taking behaviors 50 years later. With four or more events compared with no events, there was a 4- to 12-fold increase in depression and suicide attempts; there was also a 2- to 4-fold increase in health risk behavior such as smoking, substance abuse, multiple sex partners, family violence, and history of sexually transmitted diseases. Early trauma was also related to an increased risk of diabetes, cancer, stroke, ischemic heart disease, hypertension, liver disease, and immune disorders. Other diseases, such as chronic fatigue syndrome, chronic pain, and fibromyalgia, were also common. Obviously, increased risk of the development and persistence of mental and physical health problems contributes to increased use of medical, correctional, social, and mental health services (Kessler, 2000; Kessler, Berglund, Demler, Jin, Koretz, et al., 2003; Perry, 2008; van der Kolk, 2006). Other surveys of the general population in the United States have also found that a significant percentage of adults, at least 50%, have experienced at least one major traumatic stressor (Kessler, Sonnega, Bromet, Hughes, & Nelson, 1995).

EFFECTS OF TRAUMA

DSM-5 Diagnoses

In the *DSM-5* (5th ed.; APA, 2013) four disorders related to the effects of trauma or trauma- and stressor-related disorders are described: Posttraumatic Stress Disorder; Acute Stress Disorder; Adjustment Disorders; Other Specified Trauma- and Stressor-Related Disorder; and Unspecified Trauma- and Stressor-Related Disorder. Unlike *DSM-IV-TR* (4th ed., text rev.; APA, 2000) there is a Posttraumatic Stress Disorder for children 6 years and younger that includes different symptoms to those experienced by older children, adolescents, and adults. Trauma is described as "exposure to actual and threatened death, serious injury, or sexual violence" that may occur by the direct experience of the event, witnessing it, by learning about events that were violent or accidental that occurred to a family member or friend, or "experiencing repeated or extreme exposure to aversive details of the traumatic events" such as can occur for first responders such as police officers or ambulance personnel. Acute Stress Disorder includes as well intrusion symptoms, negative mood, and/or dissociative, avoidance, or arousal symptoms.

Other Diagnostic Suggestions

It is important that the effects of trauma are studied as dimensional and continuous rather than categorical disorders, and there have been suggestions that the effects of trauma should be considered as a spectrum disorder to reflect the continuum of presentation from most severe to less intense (Andrews, Charney, Sirovatka, & Regier, 2009; Fletcher, 2003; Scheeringa, Peebles, Cook, & Zeanah, 2001). Beyond this suggestion, various experts have pointed out that the listed symptoms do not include many that are clearly evident in children or take into account that, as children develop, their symptoms can change. Also, neither diagnosis covers the severe, chronic, and pervasive difficulties that can develop, particularly when the trauma is not a single event, occurs in the early years, and is inflicted by parents and other family members (van der Kolk, McFarlane, & Weisaeth, 1996).

When there has been loss of a significant relationship symptoms that can include trouble with accepting the death, inability to trust others, excessive bitterness, difficulty with moving on, numbness or detachment, feeling that life is empty and meaningless, feeling that the future is bleak or holds no meaning, and dysfunction in social, occupational, and other important domains. Brown and Goodman (2005) confirmed this set of symptoms for youth aged 8 to 18 years as criteria for complicated grief.

Another way of conceptualizing PTSD has been to view the common symptoms of internalizing disorders such as anxiety and depression as "stress related fear circuitry disorders" (Andrews et al., 2009). The authors suggest that posttraumatic stress syndromes need to be understood as dimensional disorders and that identifying the fear circuitry or neurocircuitry activated during processing of threatening or frightening events is critical. Although this paradigm is helpful, it does not account for other frequently found extreme symptoms, such as externalizing and aggressive behaviors and those of attention deficit/hyperactivity disorder (ADHD), often found in traumatized children and adults (Orr, Metzger, & Muller, 2004).

CHILDREN AND TRAUMA

In *DSM-5,* a number of symptoms are listed that are likely to be found in children 6 years and younger with posttraumatic stress disorder. The predominant effect of trauma can best be described as a severe dysregulation of behavior and emotion (Ford, Albert, & Hawke, 2009). As a consequence, children severely affected by trauma are often diagnosed with a variety of disorders or comorbidities, such as oppositional defiant disorder (ODD), conduct disorder (CD), generalized anxiety disorder (GAD); depression, ADHD, adjustment disorder, separation anxiety disorder (SAD), and phobic disorder (van der Kolk, 2005). In children affected by trauma, as in adults with PTSD, at least one comorbid disorder is present at least 90% of the time, with ODD (75%), SAD (63%), and ADHD (38%) being the most frequent (Scheeringa, Zeanah, Myers, & Putnam, 2003). Often children are diagnosed with disorders with externalizing symptoms such as ODD, CD, or ADHD without the understanding of what might underlie their most obvious presentations. As a consequence, the treatments suggested for traumatized children might be inappropriate.

The typical symptoms found in traumatized children in various age groups and the areas of functioning commonly affected are described in the text that follows. The symptoms can also be found in children with other disorders not associated with trauma. In fact, for a particular child, often it is not possible to distinguish among the possible causes of a symptom or group of symptoms, so care must be taken in ascribing them either to trauma or to a particular genetic or biological cause. For children with more complex presentations, their symptoms are most often the result of interactions among biology, genetics, trauma, and parenting. In addition, children who have experienced early, chronic, interpersonal (Type II) trauma such as maltreatment and family violence frequently have more intense and pervasive sets of symptoms that overwhelm their capacities to function adequately in the home, school, and community (D'Andrea, Spinazzola, & van der Kolk, 2009). These include extreme difficulties in the following areas of functioning.

Infants (Birth to 12 Months)

- Severe feeding disorders such as failure to thrive.
- Regression, with loss of skills previously gained (sitting).
- Signs of depression (flat affect and withdrawal).

- Constant crying with no apparent cause.
- Sleeping problems and difficulty with settling and being soothed.
- Fear reactions (significant startle reaction).
- Severe separation anxiety.

Toddlers (1 to 3 Years)

- Severe feeding disorder such as failure to thrive.
- Regression, with loss of skills previously gained (running and climbing).
- Signs of depression (flat affect and withdrawal).
- Constant crying with no apparent cause.
- Sleeping problems and difficulty with settling and being soothed if upset.
- Sudden fear reactions and separation anxiety.
- Dissociation, staring into space, or psychic numbing.
- Social withdrawal.
- Extreme night terrors.
- Extreme uncontrollable tantrums.
- Oppositionality and disobedience.
- Repetitive play re-enacting the trauma situation.
- Extreme aggressive outbursts toward other children.
- Generalized anxiety and hypervigilance.
- Sexual acting out.
- Extreme recklessness and placing self at risk.

School-Aged Children (4 to 13 Years)

- Somatic symptoms.
- Reactions to trauma triggers (loud noise, being touched, and feeling rejected).
- Aggressive outbursts.
- Dissociative reactions or psychic numbing.
- Avoidance of certain places and people associated with the trauma.
- Night terrors and difficulty falling asleep and staying asleep.
- Difficulties with peer interactions.
- Difficulties with concentrating.
- Irritability, hyperreactivity, and exaggerated startle response.
- Intensification of normal fears and hypervigilance.
- Decline in academic performance.
- Sexual acting out.

Changes in Memory

Children who were traumatized very early do not have a conscious memory of the trauma, and the unconscious memories can be triggered in a way that can lead to acting-out behaviors or dissociative symptoms. Even for events that occur later, the cognitive or conscious memories and the emotional or sensorimotor memories may become separated, and the latter are not typically available to conscious control (Brown, Cohen, Johnson, & Salzinger, 1998). Dissociation in traumatized children can affect their day-to-day levels of consciousness. Withdrawing into their own worlds, avoiding human contact, or dissociating gives them a way to avoid painful memories (Silva, 2004). They can also become split off from their bodies and not be aware of bodily sensations or experiences. The dissociation can also lead to difficulties with remembering things that they have learned (Perry, Pollard, Blakley, Baker, & Vigilante, 1995).

Difficulties With Emotion Regulation and Arousal

Problems with emotion regulation can be a core dysfunction in traumatized children (Ford et al., 2009). They tend to overreact to what appear to be neutral situations, such as a child not throwing a ball to them or being asked to do some schoolwork. They have difficulty staying calm and once aroused find it very difficult to calm down. They have problems with identifying their emotions and talking about them. This can result in difficulties with anger and aggression, anxiety, and depression, and they can engage in heightened levels of risk-taking behaviors. Some children can change rapidly between being overaroused and withdrawn and numb or dissociated. Others can become anxious if they are having fun or if something positive happens, presumably because it triggers feelings of being overaroused, as occurs during traumatic events (Schore, 2003; van der Kolk, 2003). Perhaps the most challenging aspect of this difficulty with regulating emotion and behavior is that the child can become triggered by something in the environment into aggressive acting out that can quickly escalate. Once aroused, he has no capacity to engage in rational or logical discussion about what happened.

Damage to Self-Concept and Self-Perception

Maltreatment typically leads to the child feeling helpless, ineffectual, bad, and unworthy. Children also feel totally out of control but are desperate to feel some control over their worlds and particularly the people in them. Many believe that they caused the abuse and neglect since these traumatic events happened when they saw themselves as "the center of the universe" and therefore caused everything. Perhaps most powerful is their sense of shame and self-loathing, so at a deep level they might believe that they deserved the abuse (Hughes, 2006). If they are "bad," then their parents are "good," a belief that gives them hope that they can make things better by behaving well. They also have difficulty with eliciting and responding to social support from others outside the family (Herman, 1997).

Problems With Cognitive Functioning

Traumatized children often have significantly lower IQ scores than control groups of nontraumatized children, with verbal IQ showing the greatest difference. Delays in expressive and receptive language, visual-spatial functioning, executive functioning, abstract reasoning, and problem solving are also common (Saigh, Mrouch, & Bremner, 1997). These delays might result partly from the effects of trauma on the structure and functioning of the brain. Also, a child who is constantly hypervigilant will have problems with concentrating and learning in school. Trauma also results in many children having rigidity in their thinking that can inhibit their ability to make plans, try different ways of doing things, and learn new things. They also have attributions of themselves and others that are extremely distorted and negative and can affect their behavior dramatically. These internal working models of themselves, other people, and the world, because they are unconscious, are extremely difficult to talk about or change. As summed up by van der Kolk (1987, p. 101), referring to a study of 6- to 11-year-olds with or without a history of abuse, "our strongest finding in these abused children was an inflexibility of organized schemas and structures in all domains [of intelligence]."

Problems With Concentration and Hyperactivity

Because traumatized children are hypervigilant and continuously scan the environment for signs that something will happen to them, they are often inattentive to schoolwork. Some children can also withdraw or dissociate and become unable to concentrate. Others can become excessively restless and active as they become triggered or overwhelmed by what is going on around them in the classroom. It is estimated that up to 45% of severely maltreated children have ADHD symptoms compared with the normal population, which has about 3% to 5% with these symptoms (Barkley, 1998).

Problems With Relationships

Children with histories of trauma almost always have difficulties socializing with other children and having friends. They can shift between being clingy, particularly with parents, and being oppositional when asked to do something. Others are distrustful of people, and some can be overcompliant and trusting in an effort to get attention. As with all children, their early experiences and interactions with parents and other caregivers become their models for relationships with others. They often have an obsessive desire to be in control, fight against authority, and have difficulty with reciprocal relationships with other children. They feel rejected and shame is readily triggered if they are not in charge. Some can be bullies, others victims, whereas others are both bullies and victims (James, 1994; Shields & Cicchetti, 2001).

Alterations in Belief Systems and Sense of Hope

Traumatized children often feel hopeless about the future. They no longer believe that life can make sense or have a purpose. There is often a profound sense of helplessness and lack of competence and a belief that nothing they can do will change anything for the better (Yates, Egeland, & Sroufe, 2003). These belief systems can result in views full of anger toward the world, and the children might have a desire to retaliate against the people in it or withdraw from participating in anything, feeling that things will never work out.

Somatization

Failure to translate somatic states into words and symbols can cause traumatized children to experience emotions as physical problems. However, trauma can also impact at a biological level and lead to overactive stress reactions. Traumatized children are more at risk of a range of physical illnesses, and when they become adults they have a 10% to 15% increased risk of developing digestive problems, cancer, heart disease, and diabetes. They often have unusual physical symptoms, for which no diagnosis is made, that might represent an unconscious way of communicating their emotional pain (Briere & Scott, 2006).

In adults, if the trauma remains unresolved, these extreme difficulties are often diagnosed as personality disorders and can lead to intergenerational repetition of problems with parenting unless appropriate treatment is provided for the parent or for the parent–child relationship.

NEUROBIOLOGICAL CONTRIBUTORS TO COMMON SYMPTOMS

Various neurobiological reactions and their effects on brain development and organization underlie the emotional, behavioral, cognitive, and social difficulties frequently found in traumatized children. However, it is a complex task to describe the common neurobiological contributors to trauma effects and even more difficult to identify them in a particular child. This difficulty is due to a number of issues.

- Because different types of trauma are likely to affect neurobiology differently, no clear pattern has been found for all abused or neglected children or for other kinds of trauma.
- Children can have different neurobiological reactions to the same trauma according to factors such as their age, gender, the presence or lack of support systems, individual differences in temperament, and other biological and genetic contributors.
- A number of neurochemicals can be involved, and studies have often found mixed results and contradictory findings about their influences, especially in unique combinations. In other words, much is yet to be learned about how the neurochemicals act, combine, and vary under different conditions.
- Different models have been developed to explain how stress can damage the brain, though it is unclear how much stress is necessary to cause damage. Obviously, it will vary according to individual biology and genetics and the supports and nurturance available from caregivers.

The Stress Response to Trauma

When a person is faced with threat (perceived or real), physiological and mental reactions occur known as the "fight, flight, or freeze" continuum. During a threatening event, the amygdala in the limbic system sends a message to the hypothalamus (see Figure 5.1), which stores memories, which in turn activates the sympathetic nervous system (SNS) arm of the autonomic nervous system (ANS) that prepares the body for action, either to fight or to run away (Davis & Whalen, 2001). These reactions include increased heart rate, blood pressure, and respiration; the release of stored sugar and an increase in muscle tone as blood is sent to the skeletal muscles; dilated pupils; and hypervigilance. Epinephrine is also secreted as part of this SNS reaction. When a response to threat happens, the hypothalamic–pituitary–adrenal (HPA) axis is activated, and various hormones are released into the bloodstream and sent to virtually all major brain areas. The hypothalamus releases the corticotropin-releasing factor (CRF), which in turn causes the pituitary gland to release the adrenal–corticotropic hormone (ACTH). This flows through the bloodstream to the adrenal glands, which secrete the steroid hormone cortisol. Cortisol is the antistress hormone believed to suppress the immune response, calm things down in the brain, and help the mind and body to return to and maintain a calm state. Endorphins and opiates are also secreted that help to quiet the reaction and restore the body to its natural state. See Figure 5.1 for an approximate schematic guide to the location of the brain structures involved in the trauma response.

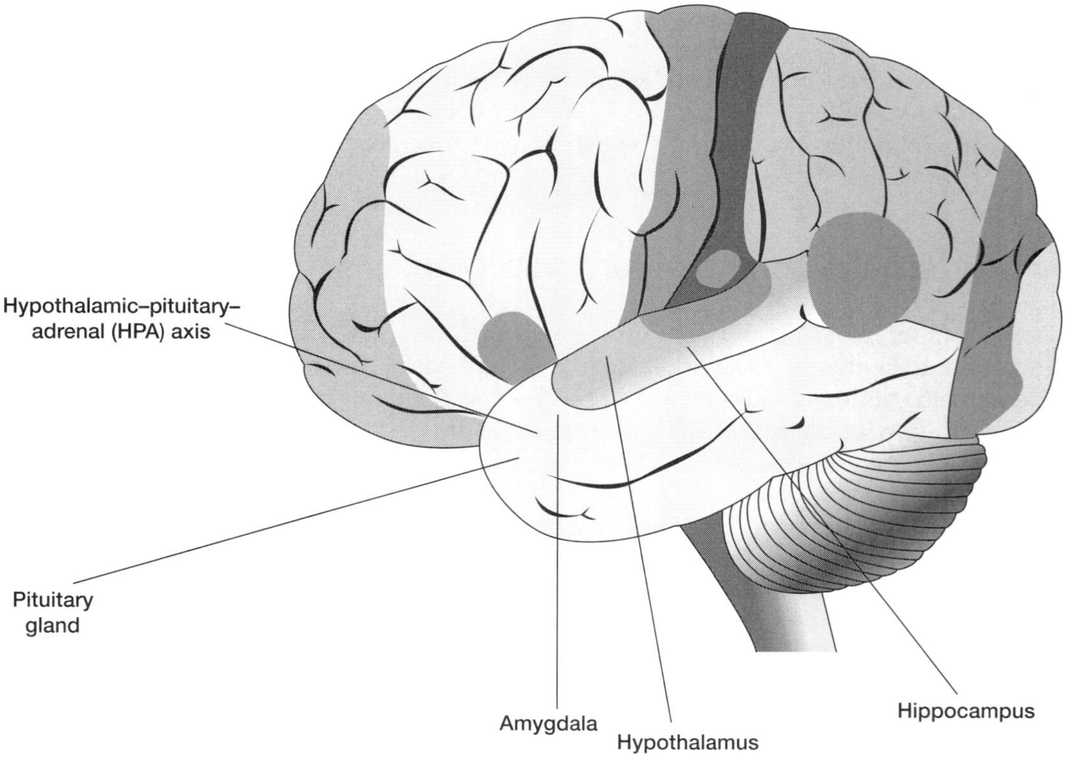

Figure 5.1 *Areas of the brain involved in stress response to trauma.*

Although this stress reaction is crucial in a traumatic situation, it can put processes such as digestion, growth, socialization, and reproduction on hold. In PTSD, the normal restraining role of the medial prefrontal cortex, especially the anterior cingulate gyrus and orbitofrontal cortex, is disrupted, resulting in recurrent fear conditioning or kindling as increasing numbers of ambiguous stimuli activate the stress response, lowering the threshold for fearful reactivity (Post, Weiss, Smith, He Li, & McCann, 1997). In this model, two pathways to reactivity can result partly from adrenergic hyperreactivity and HPA dysregulation (Friedman & McEwen, 2004). If the fear response becomes sensitized, it can result in persistent hyperreactivity, anxiety, behavioral impulsivity, sleep problems, tachycardia, hypertension, and a variety of neuroendocrine abnormalities. Pavlovian fear conditioning has also been proposed as a model for PTSD.

The arousal or fight/flight reactions have been the most talked about responses to trauma but are usually seen in adult males. However, a freeze response is the most common first reaction. Following this, when the person can neither fight nor flee, as is common with women and children, they are most likely to have a more dissociative response of freeze or surrender. This type of response is also common if physical injury, pain, and torture are involved. Freezing allows for visual observation of the environment for threat, trying to hear and see what is out there, increased anxiety, and decreased cognitive processing. If the threat to the child continues, she will feel more anxious and out of control and might start feeling threatened and then terrorized, and the freezing might escalate into complete dissociation if the threat persists. This implies disengaging from the external world and engaging in the internal world. It also involves different neurobiology than the hyperarousal response (van der Kolk & Fisler, 1995). In this dissociative response, while vagal tone is increased, blood pressure and heart rate are decreased. The dopaminergic systems (mesolimbic and mesocortical) are activated, as is the endogenous opioid system that induces euphoria. Other brainstem, midbrain, and limbic system neurotransmitters are also involved in the response. The neurochemistry of this dissociative response after chronic stress can lead to the child feeling immobile, helpless, and powerless. It can also result in frequent daydreaming, going to a fantasy world, depersonalization, derealization, or a fugue state (Mackie, Cicchetti, & Toth, 2001). Some children keep going to a "different place" in their heads or assume the character of a hero or animal. The child might seem numb, robotic, or nonreactive and unavailable for normal interaction. Although it is used as a coping strategy, it can be seen as oppositional defiant behavior by caregivers (Perry et al., 1995; see Figure 5.2).

One major traumatic event or ongoing trauma, especially when it occurs in childhood, can alter the structure, organization, and chemistry of the brain and result in the symptoms and personality characteristics found in traumatized children (DeBellis, 2001). Researchers using brain imaging have found cortical atrophy in children who have experienced global neglect (Perry, 1997) and smaller intracranial volume in children referred for chronic PTSD (De Bellis et al., 1999). As mentioned, prolonged stress can make the stress response become triggered much more easily and by less and less intense stimulation or minor stressors, and kindling takes place. Various kinds of sensory input that are reminders of the trauma can then automatically activate the stress response in areas such as the amygdala in ways that seem irrational in the situation. These responses can include emotional or physical outbursts or freezing and becoming helpless (van der Kolk, 2006). At the same time, areas such as Broca's area, responsible for speech, and the prefrontal cortex, responsible for bringing emotional outbursts under control, are deactivated. This can cause problems with being fully engaged in the present and able to talk about what happened.

Many studies have measured cortisol as a way to assess the effects of trauma because it is the only noninvasive means for measuring stress. For example, Cicchetti and Rogosch (2001), in a series of studies of neuroendocrine functioning in maltreated children, found diverse patterns of cortisol regulation, with some maltreated children having higher cortisol

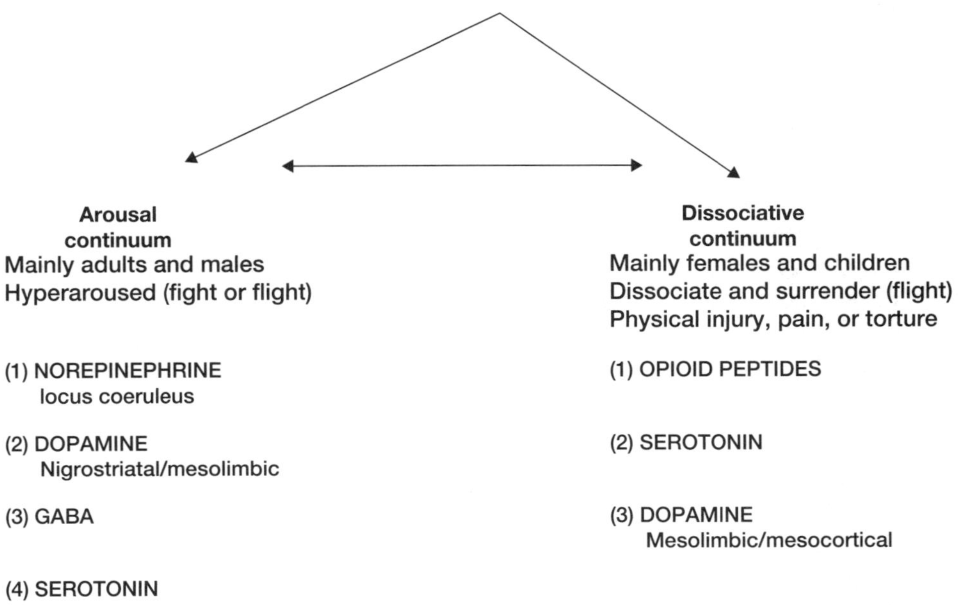

Figure 5.2 *Threat (real or perceived).*
Adapted from Perry et al. (1995). Reprinted with permission.

levels and others lower levels. They concluded that the brains of maltreated children are not "uniformly affected by the experience of maltreatment" (Cicchetti, 2003, p. 352).

Besides the main stress responses and the secretion of cortisol, other neurochemical and brain systems are affected by trauma. Some of them are the serotonin, dopaminergic, and gamma-aminobutyric acid (GABA) systems. These systems affect various functions, such as arousal, attention, response to stress, vigilance, emotional responses such as anxiety, oversensitivity and being in a state of fear, behavioral impulsivity, motor hyperactivity, sleep disturbances, tachycardia (rapid heartbeat), hypertension, and a variety of other neuroendocrine abnormalities. In addition, various aspects of brain organization are affected.

Other Neurotransmitter or Neuromodulator Systems Affected by Trauma

Serotonin is a modulatory neurotransmitter that plays an important role in modulating sleep, appetite, memory and cognition, sexual behavior, motor and movement function, and limbic/affective responsiveness. It is well known for its use in antidepressant medications known as the selective serotonin reuptake inhibitors (SSRIs). Its function is very complex, and it has been implicated in depression, anxiety, aggression, eating disorders, and chronic pain. It inhibits activation of the HPA axis and mediates fear, anxiety, and mood. It also has a significant role in neurological development and is involved in cell division and differentiation and synaptogenesis. The serotonin function is also regulated at the level of serotonin synthesis, reuptake, and degradation. Disruption at any of these levels can have longstanding effects on emotionality, and both excessive extracellular serotonin and reduced levels of serotonin can be problematic and affect the emotional system at the circuit level. An excess of serotonin can cause relaxation and sedation, and deficiency is associated with low mood and increased anxiety, lack of willpower, and dysregulation of aggression. Children in the first 3 years of life can be particularly affected when brain circuits important to anxiety are developing. Although the role of serotonin in PTSD has not been systematically studied in humans, shocked animals have been shown to have decreased serotonin (van der Kolk, 1994).

Dopamine plays a role in the brain related to motor behavior and action, and the rate of its release rapidly increases under stress. Schore (1994) has suggested that dopamine system development is dependent on an early responsive and containing relationship between the caregiver and the infant. It also regulates several brain areas, such as the frontal cortex, striatum, and nucleus accumbens. A dysregulated dopamine system is implicated in personality disorders, antisocial behavior, and some neuropsychiatric conditions. It is also a key finding in studies of ADHD (Ernst & Zametkin, 1995).

Gamma-aminobutyric acid is the principal inhibitory neurotransmitter system in the brain. It decreases the excitability of individual neurons and limits excessive neuronal activity. It has projections to various brain areas involved in the stress response. It is assumed that dysfunction of the GABA-ergic systems can contribute to enhanced stress responsiveness after early life stress (Siegel, 2003).

Left and Right Brain Development

The right (ventral) and the left (dorsal) brain are distinct areas of representational functioning. The right brain processes nonverbal signals, such as voice tone, gestures, and facial expression, in a holistic, parallel, visual–spatial way, and reads emotions and body states. Experiences generated in the right hemisphere cannot be explained in words, placed in context, and assigned meaning. On the other hand, the left hemisphere, which develops later, is responsible for language-based narratives and processes in a linear and logical way. It is responsible for cause-and-effect reasoning. The two hemispheres are connected by the corpus callosum. Alan Schore has written extensively about the right and left brain and how negative experiences in the early years can affect integration between the two hemispheres and consequently affect behavior and emotion regulation (Schore, 1994, 1997, 1998, 2001, 2003). The right brain is dominant in terms of growth during the first 3 years of life, and nurturing regulation of the infant's limbic system at this time by caregivers and the resulting secure attachment can help to develop an efficient right brain that becomes a factor in enhancing resilience. Yet it is believed that sensorimotor and emotional memories of trauma or a lack of containing regulation are processed in the right side of the brain. It is thought that, without adequate integration of memory within the two hemispheres, memories of the trauma will be stored separately, so the person might be able to give a factual account but one removed from the emotional and sensorimotor memories of the event, which are outside conscious memory and control and can continue to be triggered.

Trauma (particularly maltreatment) impedes the development of the left hemisphere. A number of studies have found that left-hemisphere deficits are six times more common in abused children (Teicher, 2000). The same group of researchers studied electroencephalographic (EEG) coherence tests and administered psychological tests and found better visual–spatial ability than verbal performance in maltreated children and that the cortex of the left hemisphere was not as well developed. The researchers speculated that interference in the myelination of nerve fibers can contribute to this lack of development of the left hemisphere. Underdevelopment of the left hemisphere can impede development of language and reasoning, and interfere with development of metacognition (or the capacity to think about thinking) and ability to regulate negative emotions.

Memories need to connect across the two hemispheres so that the left brain can tell a logical story drawing on information from the right brain. In one study of abused children, they were less able than nonabused children to use both brain hemispheres to process experience (Teicher, 2000). The reason is believed to be abnormalities in the corpus callosum (Bremner, 2001a, 2001b). In children exposed to trauma, in contrast to a control group of nontraumatized children, hemispheric activation has been found during discussion of a neutral memory and right activation during an unpleasant or traumatized memory (Schiffer, 2000; Schiffer, Teicher, & Pananicolau, 1995). Also, Teicher et al. (1997) found that children who had suffered emotional, physical, and sexual abuse or neglect all had abnormalities in the corpus callosum in terms of size, whereas regional differences occurred by gender and type of abuse (Teicher, 2000). Physical abuse and neglect had the greatest effects, possibly because they tended to occur earlier. De Bellis et al. (2002) also found abnormalities in the corpus callosum of abused children.

Because positive emotions are processed in the left hemisphere and negative emotions in the right, if the two hemispheres are not operating in concert, these emotions cannot be experienced or understood at one time. Consequently, abused children can experience people, including themselves, as negative or "all bad" or as positive or "all good" or have a tendency toward splitting. This can lead them to present as "Jekyll and Hyde" at various times and in certain situations, suddenly switching their presentation between being happy to being angry and aggressive rather than maintaining a more balanced view of a situation and of themselves or others.

Memory Systems

The conscious memory system (also known as explicit or declarative memory) is mediated by the hippocampus and medial temporal lobe, which store experiences that can be retrieved and talked about. There are two major forms: semantic (factual) and episodic (autobiographical), and by the preschool period, the ability to understand the self in the past, present, and future is usually developed and integrated in the orbitofrontal cortex. Yet implicit memory systems function outside recall. They include procedural memory, which involves the motor areas of the brain used for learning and remembering skills such as riding a bike or playing a musical instrument. Implicit memories consist of emotional and sensory experiences in the here and now (for example, sights, sounds, smells, tastes, and touches). These memories are stored in the amygdala and other areas of the limbic system and the motor cortex and sensory cortex. Fear responses, the amygdala's automatic response to traumatic events, are this kind of memory. These conscious and unconscious memory systems are independent and interdependent of each other as most stimuli and experiences activate both systems.

Traumatic memories can become disconnected from explicit memories and stored in the right hemisphere as images, sounds, smells, bodily sensations such as running, and emotions such as fear. As noted by van der Kolk, Hopper, and Osterman (2001, p. 9), "trauma memories are characterised by fragmentary and intense sensations and affects, often with little or no verbal narrative content." These traumatic memories do not go away, and their triggering is not under conscious or voluntary control. They can intrude on awareness when the person is exposed to a reminder of the event. Reasons for the failure to integrate traumatic memories are believed by some to relate to the high levels of stress-related chemicals that can impair the functioning of critical brain structures, especially the hippocampus and amygdala. Highly negative and traumatic events that are repetitive and prolonged can disrupt memory functioning to varying degrees (Joseph, 2003). This can result in a lengthier period of childhood amnesia or the person having her first recallable memories at a later age than typical. When this occurs, the hippocampus becomes unable to integrate the trauma memories with the autobiographical memories. There are also problems in functioning of the prefrontal cortex (especially the medial and orbitofrontal cortex) and anterior cingulate. In a number of studies, smaller left hippocampal volumes, 12% less than those of control groups, were found in war veterans and abuse victims, which in turn can lead to the distortion and fragmentation of trauma memories (Bremner, 2001a, 2001b). However, it can be unclear whether this pre-existed the trauma (Marko & Merchbach, 2004).

CONTRIBUTORS TO THE EFFECTS OF TRAUMA

There are a number of contributors to how trauma affects child development and the degrees and types of symptoms that occur. As noted above, the predominant effects of trauma are severe dysregulation of behavior and emotion, so factors that contribute to these symptoms are particularly relevant.

Genetic Contributors

Some research has considered the possible contribution of genetics to the likelihood that an individual exposed to trauma will develop PTSD. For example, data from the Vietnam Era Twin Registry showed a heritable difference in the likelihood that an individual exposed to a traumatic event would develop PTSD. There was also a familial vulnerability that contributed to the comorbidity of PTSD and major depression and the comorbidity of PTSD and dysthymia (Koenen, Harley, & Lyons, 2002; Koenen, Lyons, & Goldberg, 2003). Another study using structural magnetic resonance imaging studied hippocampal volume in monozygotic twins who experienced combat with and without PTSD compared with their twin brothers who did not see military action in Vietnam. Veterans with PTSD had smaller hippocampal volumes than veterans without PTSD; however, noncombat–exposed twin brothers of the PTSD combat veterans also had smaller hippocampal volumes (Gilbertson, Shenton, & Ciszewski, 2002). The results suggested that smaller hippocampal volume can be a risk factor for developing PTSD rather than a consequence of it.

In the Dunedin temperament study, which followed children from infancy to adulthood, it was found that the effect of trauma on long-term development was mediated by genetic variability. These differences included the serotonin transporter gene (SERT) with respect to depressive symptoms, and persons homozygous for the short allele or heterozygous (one short and one long allele) tended to be the most vulnerable and had a markedly increased risk of depression when exposed to abuse, whereas those with two long alleles seemed unaffected by the abuse that they experienced growing up (Caspi et al., 2003). A similar pattern was found for the monoamine oxidase A gene (MAO-A), with short or heterozygous alleles increasing the risk of adolescent and adult antisocial behavior if there was childhood abuse (Caspi et al., 2002). The catechol-O-methyltransferase (COMT) gene has a variant (MET) known to affect fear extinction, anxiety, and vulnerability to negative affect and recently has been shown to increase the risk of developing PTSD in contrast to the more typical form (VAL). This enzyme breaks down catecholamines, such as dopamine and norepinephrine, and the MET variant reduces efficacy of the enzyme (Kolassa, Kolassa, Ertl, Papassotiropoulis, & De Quervain, 2010).

Because intelligence is the most heritable characteristic of children, intellectual capacity can contribute to resilience or vulnerability to developing effects from trauma, with children with lower intelligence being more susceptible to fear conditioning, more aroused by threatening stimuli, and more resistant to extinction of fear after danger has passed. In one study of a sample of 1,285 children between 9 and 17 years of age who had experienced trauma, higher IQ contributed to better adjustment. In another study of inner-city children, higher verbal IQ was found to be the strongest measure of resiliency that protected against developing PTSD (Silva, 2004).

Ongoing research led by George Meaney in Montreal, Canada, has shown that poor parenting of rat pups can not only affect brain structure but also alter function of the gene, called the neuron-specific glucocorticoid receptor or NR3C1 promoter, that controls the brain's response to stress. The offspring of rat mothers that showed reduced pup licking or grooming showed more HPA response to stress compared with the offspring of high-licking mothers that had increased glucocorticoid receptor levels, which inhibit CRF activity and dampen stress responses. More recent, these researchers found clear differences in the brains of suicide victims who had been abused and those of people who had died by suicide or traffic accidents but had not been abused. The same differences in the NR3C1 gene found in the rat research were found with suicide victims who had been abused: that is, lowered activity of the gene. These findings might explain how vulnerability to depression and the personalities of later offspring can be passed on biologically (Meaney & Szyf, 2005; Weaver et al., 2007). The studies also found that environmental adversity affects parenting behavior and that pharmacological treatment with rats can reverse the phenotype, suggesting that drugs might help humans in a similar way in the future.

Biological Contributors

A number of aspects of a child's biology have been linked to changes in brain chemistry and particularly the stress system, which can create vulnerability in the child and increase the likelihood of more significant reactions to trauma occurring. They include temperament or characteristics of emotional style and sociability that affect a person's style of approach–withdrawal reactions to events in the environment (reactivity). It has been identified as a factor that can increase children's vulnerability to traumatization (Strelau, 1995), their traumatic and stress reactions, behavioral problems, and psychiatric symptoms (Ruchkins, Schwab-Stone, Koposov, Vermeiren, & Steiner, 2002), and their memory of traumatic events (Howe, 1997). In other words, children's temperament traits can serve as risk or protective factors.

Temperament studies have explored a number of physiological systems as possible contributors to individual differences in behavior. They have included differential patterns of activation between left and right hemispheres; patterning of the ANS and balance between the sympathetic and parasympathetic systems; and activity of the HPA system, which plays a major role in emotional response, stress resistance, and learning and memory. If a child has a greater tendency toward negative affect reactivity and is more socially reticent and inhibited, his development can be more affected by trauma. Hence, many studies suggest that certain individuals show a pattern of increased physiological arousal and "exaggerated reactivity to stressful and environmental events which may be observed in several systems simultaneously" (Jemerin & Boyce, 1990, p. 150). These patterns can contribute to a vulnerability to experience more intense reactions to and chronic symptoms of various kinds of trauma.

In another study, U.S. forces were exposed to an extremely stressful training experience during which neurohormone samples were obtained. Troops who had the greatest capacity to mobilize neuropeptide Y and sustain elevated levels throughout training coped with severe stress and performed better than troops who could not do this (Morgan, Wang, & Southwick, 2000). In a prospective study in Australia of fire fighters, it was found that those with an elevated auditory startle response (measured by eye blink electromyograms and skin conductance responses) were more vulnerable to posttraumatic stress responses (Guthrie & Bryant, 2005).

Other Contributors

Other factors that can increase the likelihood that a child will be dysregulated as a result of trauma include the following:

- anxiety and depression during pregnancy
- exposure to alcohol and other toxins during pregnancy
- premature birth and birth complications
- maternal depression in the postpartum period

Contributions of Parenting

Obviously, in many cases of complex trauma, maltreatment and family violence are the main contributors to the symptoms that result. In cases in which the child is not maltreated but shows symptoms of trauma, parenting can be frightening or frightened, and in neither case is the child provided with a sense of safety or attuned containment (Lyons-Ruth, Zoll, Connell, & Grunebaum, 1989). The parent can be frightening by being menacing, threatening, yelling at the child, saying that he is bad or worthless, and in extreme cases abusing him. The frightened parent, on the other hand, can seem scared of the child, anxious in his presence, and withdraw from him, in extreme cases dissociating in a way that can frighten him. Some parents can alternate between the two styles, making it even more confusing and chaotic for the child (Lyons-Ruth, Yellin, Melnick, & Atwood, 2005). With these interactions, he does not receive either the stimulation or the nurturing containment that he needs to feel secure and comfortable in exploring his world. As a result, he can miss essential components of child rearing. Parents often repeat the parenting that they experienced, and unresolved trauma can be passed intergenerationally from parent to child.

Parental mental illness can place a child's development at risk, either directly through its effects on parent–child interactions or by affecting the life circumstances in which the child is raised. The most prevalent disorders are depression, schizophrenia, bipolar disorder, drug addiction, and various personality disorders. All can cause significant difficulties with caring for infants and children, making it hard for parents to provide consistency and regularity of care. Children can consequently have difficulties in school, perform lower on cognitive tests, and be more at risk of later mental health problems themselves (Goodman & Gottlieb, 2002; Lovejoy, Graczyk, O'Hare, & Neuman, 2000). The parent with mental health issues can become a source of the child's trauma. Also, if the child is traumatized by other events or situations, such as domestic violence or a natural or man-made disaster, the parent can find it extremely difficult to support the child in a way that can resolve the trauma.

Parental Response to a Child's Experience of Trauma

Following a traumatic event, a child will manage much better if the parent can do the following:

- contain the child's hyperarousal, fear, and anxiety
- provide as much safety, stability in routines, and environmental "sameness" as possible
- let her talk about what happened, answer any questions as far as possible; show empathy for her anxiety, and talk about survival and the future
- validate the child's feelings of fear, sadness, and anger
- nurture and hold her as much as possible, providing warm drinks and nurturing food
- stay close to her as much as possible and let her know that she will be kept safe
- provide opportunities for play, such as water play, that are soothing
- ask her what her biggest worry is since the trauma; let her know that her thoughts and feelings are normal and will pass in time
- seek professional help if the child is not doing well, or if her behavior regresses, she becomes aggressive or withdrawn, or her sleeping or eating is seriously impacted

Sometimes a parent is hurt, traumatized by the event, and cannot be available to provide this kind of support. If so, then it is important to have someone else who can support the child in these ways (Cohen, 2009; Keren & Tyano, 2009).

Case Studies

Contributors to George's Presentation

George's symptoms and difficulties were mainly related to extreme physical and emotional neglect that occurred both as a baby with his mentally ill mother and with his father's girlfriend as a toddler. When George was a baby, his mother was frequently gone for hours leaving the children unattended and there was often no food in the house. It is almost certain that he was physically abused by his mother and her many boyfriends and as a toddler was physically restrained in a stroller by his father's girlfriend because she wanted to keep him like a baby. The older children had reported to the teachers at the school that they had all been sexually abused by one of their mother's boyfriends.

There were many physical arguments between his father and his partners and George talked later about hiding in his bedroom under the bed with his dog when this happened. Throughout his time with his father, George was accused by him of being the cause of everything that happened. In other words, he had caused his mother's breakdown, made his new girlfriend leave because he cried when he was put in the stroller, and his "bad" behavior made it impossible to take care of him. Perhaps most damaging, when his father remarried and had another baby, the children were told that he never wanted to see any of them again, especially George, who caused all the problems. After they went to live with their grandmother he refused to phone them, acknowledge their birthdays, or to have them visit his new home. As with any child, it was extremely difficult to be certain about what experience had contributed to George's presentation. It is hard to be certain about the significance of other contributors to his presentation. They are likely to be as follows:

- His mother's use of substances during pregnancy that may have affected his temperament and caused issues with concentration.
- There may also have been a genetic contribution with his mother's mental illness and two cousins with autism.
- It is likely that failure on the part of his early caregivers to provide nurturing containment and adequate stimulation as well as the maltreatment are the most important contributors.

Contributors to Emily's Presentation

Emily's symptoms were extremely severe for a 5-year-old, and her Kindergarten teacher thought that Emily had the most puzzling presentation that she had seen in her many years of teaching. Mary, Emily's mother, was obviously caring and nurturing and wanted nothing more than to help her daughter. She explained that she had suffered from severe depression and anxiety since she was 16 and still took medication, though she did not find that it helped much anymore. Mary described being depressed and anxious throughout her pregnancy because of the drug use and violent behavior of her husband. However, the birth was easy, and Emily was in good condition and breastfed easily. However, she and her mother were in the hospital for 10 days while Mary was treated for postpartum depression and to "help them with bonding."

Up to 15 months, Emily was a very easy baby, but at that time Mary's husband became increasingly violent and verbally abusive, and there were fights daily, requiring the police to come to the house to settle things down on a number of occasions. After the savage attack by her father, Emily's behavior changed as Mary struggled to recover, deal with her depression, and set some limits on her daughter's behavior. She also had to return to work and put Emily in daycare. From then on, there were multiple changes in daycare, and Mary often went out in the evening in an attempt to get over her depression. Emily was taken care of by her grandmother, who had strict limits on her behavior and a very different way of dealing with her than her mother. Soon after meeting her new partner, John, Mary moved in with him and his son, and Emily's behavior seemed to escalate again. After the birth of the couple's baby, Mary found her daughter's behavior more and more difficult, and she was concerned that John might leave her because of rising tensions between them about Emily. Emily had been diagnosed with ADHD, executive dysfunction, suspected autism spectrum disorder, and auditory processing disorder. Because of her age, ODD was not diagnosed, though her mother, after reading about it on the Internet, thought that she should be diagnosed with it and often used the term when she talked about Emily. It was hard to know how much of Emily's presentation was genetic and biological. Emily might well have been affected by her mother's depression during pregnancy and postpartum. Also, there was a strong genetic loading for a number of disorders, including intergenerational depression on the mother's side. Mary's brother had ADHD and a substance-abuse problem. Her maternal aunt had severe epilepsy. Her father had significant mental health problems that required hospitalization, and several relatives on the father's side had severe depression. However, Emily was a content and easy baby before the marriage deteriorated into violence, so it can be assumed that at least some of her symptoms were related to the experience of family violence.

EFFECTS OF TRAUMA ON DEVELOPMENT

Development can be significantly compromised by trauma in a number of important areas. They include difficulties with emotion and behavior regulation, the ability to attend and concentrate, and the capacity to develop empathy and socialize with peers. Children's sense of self and memory of previous experiences can be severely compromised. Sensory processing and integration can be affected due to the effects of trauma on the nervous system. There can be delays in a number of other areas, such as language and communication and motor development.

ASSESSMENT OF EFFECTS OF TRAUMA ON CHILDREN

Evaluating the Type of Trauma

The first step in assessing a child for trauma is to determine whether she has experienced trauma and if so what type. When the child has been exposed to a particular, easily identified event such as a traffic accident or natural disaster, caregivers can usually identify it and describe what happened. Also, chronic illness or painful medical procedures are relatively easy for parents to report. What is less clear, even with these kinds of events, is how much the child was protected from their effects and how much and what kind of support were available after the trauma. Knowing the details of a traumatic event will assist in understanding the nature and depth of the child's reaction, how it might have affected development, and which reminders of the trauma are likely to occur. A single traumatic incident can be reported more easily than more chronic and interpersonal traumas (usually related to the quality of caregiving). Assessing the impact of trauma can also be complicated in situations of chronic maltreatment in which the child's relationship with caregivers is inevitably compromised. Where there has been severe maltreatment involving pain, intrusive behavior, and threats that caused the child to fear death, she will likely display complex and significant symptoms affecting multiple areas of development (Haugaard, 2004).

It is extremely difficult in many situations to determine both the amount and the severity of any small "t" trauma that a child might have experienced in infancy and the preschool period. Parents might not realize how compromised their parent–child interactions were in the early years and not appreciate the impacts of their interactions psychologically and on brain development. Sometimes, because that time of their lives was very difficult and possibly chaotic, parents might not remember how their child was and how they reacted to or parented her.

As pointed out by Scheeringa and Zeanah (2001), the current stressor criteria used for adults are particularly problematic for infants and young children. Also, experiences that are not traumatic for older children and adults can be very traumatic for infants and preschoolers (Scheeringa, Zeanah, Myers, & Putnam, 2005).

Collecting Information

Information on the infancy and preschool period is best collected through exploration with parents about their child's developmental history and other things that might have been going on in the family at that time. Areas that need to be explored and questions that need to be asked if they are not spontaneously raised include the following:

- Was the mother depressed or anxious during the pregnancy? To what degree?
- Were there any previous miscarriages or loss of a baby before this pregnancy? If so, how close to the pregnancy?

- Did the mother experience postnatal depression, anxiety, postpartum psychosis, or intrusive thoughts of harming her baby? Did she get support? How?
- Was there family violence or excessive verbal abuse? Were there disagreements and arguments between the parents?
- Did the mother and father feel that they bonded with their baby? If not, did this change? How would they describe their relationship with their child now?
- Were any extreme behaviors noticed for the infant in the first year, such as excessive crying and difficulty calming and settling, turning away, and rejecting holding and interacting? What about as a toddler and preschooler?
- Was there loss of anyone significant during the pregnancy or the first few years of the child's life?
- Was there any other trauma, such as a traffic accident, natural disaster, or loss of job by the wage earner?
- Was there any alcohol or drug use, smoking, or medication used by the parents during this early period?
- Was there homelessness? If so, for how long?
- Was there recent immigration? Loss of extended family?
- How do the parents describe their child currently and their relationship with him? Whom does the child remind them of?
- Were there any hospitalizations, painful medical procedures, or acute or chronic illnesses experienced by the child?

Other information volunteered is also recorded.

A number of questionnaires can be used with adults/parents and children to determine the type and extent of the trauma that the child might have been exposed to. A few examples are discussed below.

Exposure Questionnaires

The *Traumatic Events Screening Inventory—Parent Report Revised* (*TESI-PRR;* Ghosh Ippen et al., 2002) can be used for children from 6 to 18 years of age and is completed from information provided by the parent. It is based on the *TESI-C* completed by the child but has additional items for young children and uses more simple language than the previous measure. It screens for a child's exposure to traumatic experiences. Using it as an interview schedule is recommended. When used in this way, there are two stages: Stage 1, when the parent is asked about events that have happened to the child in the home, school, or community, and Stage 2, which follows up if the parent mentions an event that the child was exposed to and collects further information about what occurred. It has good test–retest reliability.

The Dimensions of Stressful Events (*DOSE*; Fletcher, 1992) can be used with children from birth to 17 years of age and was developed to assess the degree to which a certain event was traumatizing. There are 25 items that ask about the number of traumas experienced, relationship with the abuser, and exposure to single-incident events. Proximity, duration, frequency, and degree of exposure to child abuse are also asked about. The questionnaire is scored by the rater with information from both the parent and the child.

Assessing the Child's Reaction to Trauma

It is important to assess the child's reaction to the trauma and the symptoms that the child experienced after being exposed to the trauma. Obviously children may experience symptoms and behavioral and emotional difficulties that are not fully described in *DSM-5* under the Disinhibited Social Engagement Disorder, Posttraumatic Stress Disorder (PTSD), and Acute Stress Disorder. Some may be described under the new Adjustment Disorders; however, it is useful to identify other symptoms that may be present as a result of past or present trauma, such as those described on pages 157 to 158 in this chapter. Measures used to collect this information can be completed by the child or are used to interview children about their psychological reactions. They have been well researched and found to be effective. Many have been frequently revised as new and more effective ways to elicit information and make the process easier for the child and family are found (Yule et al., 2000). Some children can minimize their symptoms, thinking that they should not be feeling upset and should have "got over" them because it was some time ago and other children who experienced the same thing seem to have recovered. In a number of studies, children have been found to report more symptoms about their reactions to the trauma than their parents reported for them. Children have also been more able to report about their anxieties and feeling depressed than parents can when asked about what they think their children are feeling and thinking (Handford et al., 1986). However, most of the research has been conducted following traumatic events, and questionnaires used to collect data on reactions to these events might not be helpful to identify symptoms when children were abused or neglected, especially in the early years. The child might be completely unaware that her anxiety or hypersensitivity is unusual or in any way related to her early history.

Children who have been traumatized might have a significant range of symptoms and patterns of behavior not defined or included in *DSM-IV-TR*. It can be difficult to ask about these symptoms and patterns, and it can be very difficult for children to retrieve information about the past. This is especially true when trying to access unconscious memories. Also, it is necessary to take into account how children at different ages are affected by trauma and how the effects can change over time. Reactions to intense, ongoing, or multiple traumas also need to be considered.

The *Pediatric Emotional Distress Scale* (*PEDS*; Saylor & Swenson, 1999) was developed to fill a need for a measure of the effects of trauma on young children from 2 years of age. It relies on parent reporting, asks 17 questions about the child's general behavior, and has four trauma-specific items. Subscales are anxious or withdrawn, fearful, and acting out. It has good internal consistency and satisfactory inter-rater reliability.

The Child Report of PostTraumatic Symptoms (*CROPS*; Greenwald, 1997) is a 26-item scale and asks about symptoms in addition to those defined for the PTSD criteria in *DSM-IV-TR*. It can be used from 5 to 17 years of age, and children and youth are asked whether they have experienced the symptoms over the preceding week and to rate them on a 0- to 2 point scale (none—some—lots). Scores are continuous rather than divided into diagnostic categories. It has good test–retest reliability.

The Trauma Symptom Checklist for Young Children (*TSCYC*; Briere, 2005) is a 90-item parent report scale for use with children from 3 to 12 years of age who have experienced abuse and neglect, victimization by peers, violence, major losses, and natural disasters. It is recommended as appropriate for initial screening for a history of trauma.

Projective Tests

Projective tests are based on the principle of projection or the assumption that people project their feelings, thoughts, needs, and motivations into a particular ambiguous or nonspecific stimulus. The responses evoked from the subject are believed to be an expression of his private world and personality. Responses are a combination of perception, imagination or fantasy, and the unconscious. The original studies with projective methods involved primarily adults, but many have been adapted for use with children by developing age norms. They have been very useful in work with children who often have difficulty remembering the traumatic events or verbalizing their thoughts and feelings, particularly if the approach used causes anxiety or discomfort. Projective tests have been criticized by many in the scientific community because they are subjective measures and sometimes result in faulty interpretations. To overcome these difficulties, some researchers have developed quantitative methods for assessing responses. Usually, however, projective tests are used to generate hypotheses to be explored further, including whether the child might have experienced trauma of various types. Some methods that have been used to elicit interpretations are described next. As is true for the use of all methods of assessment, proper training and supervision in use of the tests are essential. It is also critical that variables such as language skills, drawing abilities, and cultural differences are taken into account in interpreting the tests.

The Rorschach Psychodiagnostic Test has been used as a diagnostic tool as well as to form hypotheses on thought processes and personality structures. A number of studies of traumatized children have been conducted, including burn victims and sexually abused children, and found significantly different responses from normative groups, particularly in terms of animal and human content and sexual content (Clinton & Jenkins-Monroe, 1994; Nader, 2008).

Use of drawings with traumatized children aids both assessment and treatment. They are used as assessment tools to gain insights into a child's emotional state and to understand how the child views himself and his world. Size, placement, and other characteristics of the drawings can be analyzed as indicative of emotional conflicts and attitudes. However, no single diagnostic sign should be used. Observations of the child's behavior during the assessment, such as motor dexterity, tenseness, and insecurity, are also important. Some of the more popular drawing tests are listed below:

- *Goodenough–Harris Drawing Test* (Harris, 1963) asks the child to draw a person. It has been used to estimate the intelligence of school-aged children and suggest the developmental age of the child when the trauma occurred.
- *Draw a Person* (Machover, 1952) asks the child to draw a person and then a person of the opposite sex. The drawing of the first person is believed to reflect the child's sense of self, especially body self, emotional state, and reality testing. Also, some important clinical signs have been found useful in differentiating various populations or disorders.
- *House–Tree–Person* (Hammer, 1967) asks children to draw a house, tree, and person. These were chosen due to their acceptance and familiarity to children and their ability to stimulate a number of associations. The test gathers data regarding the child's degree of personality integration, maturity, and efficiency. The house can express feelings about interpersonal dynamics within the home. The tree is believed to be associated with the person's life experience and personal characteristics.
- *Kinetic Family Drawing* (Peterson & Hardin, 1997) asks the child to draw his family doing something. This often elicits rich and dramatic information about family interactions, his situation and place in the family, and any support that he receives.

Interpretations of Pictures

Picture tests provide a series of pictures shown to the child, who is asked to tell a story about them. The responses are assessed for coping style, feelings, needs, and themes. Some of the most commonly used tests are *The Children's Apperception Test* (*CAT-A* and

CAT-H; Bellak & Bellak, 1980) and the *Thematic Apperception Test* (*TAT*), typically used with adolescents and adults. Other picture tests are *Robert's Apperception Test* (2nd ed.) (Roberts-2; Roberts & Gruber, 2005) and *The Plenk Storytelling Test* (*PST*; Plenk, Hinchey, & Davies, 1985).

Sentence Completion Techniques

Sentence completion tests consist of a number of sentence stems, and the child is asked to complete the sentences. He is asked to do this and include his real feelings. Among the most used are *Rotter Incomplete Sentence Blank* (Rotter & Rafferty, 1950) and *Sentence Completion Series* (Brown & Unger, 1992). The former test has 40 sentence stems that are brief and nonspecific.

Projective Pretend Play

Toys are chosen for the play session that are believed to be able to gain access to the child's inner and outer worlds. They usually include a doll family, animals, planes, action figures, aggressive animals, Play-Doh, and puppets. Some play therapists use a sand tray with miniature toys.

Assessing Parents' Exposure to Trauma

Given the wide-ranging effects of trauma, a parent with unresolved trauma can find parenting extremely difficult. The birth of an infant can trigger difficult emotional and physiological reactions, particularly if the parent's trauma happened during early childhood (Schechter, 2004). This can contribute to poor reflective functioning, difficulties with attuning to the child, and negative attributions of the child. Parents with unresolved loss and trauma, particularly of childhood abuse and neglect, can show what has been called atypical disruptive communications or interactions with their infant. As pointed out by Crittenden, Lang, Claussen, and Partridge (2000), parents tend to react without thinking during parenting interactions and rely on procedural memory. As a consequence, under stress they might perpetuate the interactions that they experienced growing up.

Some signs of unresolved trauma in parents include the following:

- There is incoherence in providing a narrative about their past and discussing their background and particularly any traumatic events.
- The parent does not accept that the past has an effect on her current functioning and particularly her parenting.
- The adjectives that the parent uses to describe her relationship with her own parents are not supported by examples of how her parents behaved toward her as a young child. For example, if a parent describes her own parent as "loving," can she relate some experiences that match the description? For example, "My father, although he worked hard, always read me a story when he came home or tried to call me if he was away." Or do the examples given not fit with the description of "loving"? For example, "My mother always made sure our clothes were clean."
- There are signs of dissociation or "going away in her head" or staring into space when certain situations are described.

- There are signs that thoughts or intense feelings from the past are being triggered, perhaps by the parent becoming distressed and flushed. The parent might talk about such experiences as if they are happening in the present.
- The parent might talk about difficult early experiences of being parented and appear to have come to some acceptance or resolution of them. However, if she is excessively preoccupied with the past, or totally denies the influence of the difficulties, they are likely to not be resolved.

Because parents with unresolved loss and trauma are likely to repeat the parenting that they received, it is important to include measures to identify parents' earlier traumas. This is especially important in assessing a child with small "t" trauma, for parenting difficulties can help to explain some of the child's symptoms. Some of these measures are described below.

Parent–Child Interactions

Many parent–child interaction measures are for young children, whereas those for older children tend to emphasize discipline rather than reciprocity in interactions. The *Atypical Behavior Instrument of Assessment and Classification* (*AMBIANCE*; Bronfman, Parsons, & Lyons-Ruth, 2000) assesses disrupted communication in the mother with her infant or young child. From 10 to 20 minutes of parent–child interaction are filmed and scored for disrupted communication and "FR" (frightening or frightened) behaviors. Two types of disrupted communication are identified: intrusive/self-referential (frightening) and helpless/fearful (frightened). In addition, the *AMBIANCE* provides a summary score of five dimensions of parenting that indicate disruption in the ability to respond to the infant in a manner that allows the child to effectively elicit care. FR behaviors are correlated to infant disorganization, which is related to psychopathology in the child in longitudinal studies.

TREATMENT OF TRAUMA

Although treating traumatized children is complex, challenging, and often lengthy, there is a growing belief that in many instances it can be successful (Ford et al., 2009; Perry, 2006). However, service systems often provide little or no access to appropriate therapeutic services, and instead of creating safety, consistency, new healing relationships, and interventions that can remediate brain functioning they often "recreate the chaos, fragmentation, trauma and neglect these children have experienced in their home" (Perry, 2006, p. 29). In other words, treatment is often too little too late and inadequate to heal a child who has experienced years of maltreatment, humiliation, and terror.

The Goal of Treatment

The goal of treating traumatized children is to encourage a return to normal development that includes increasing the child's capacity to deal with stress and helping the child to maintain normal levels of arousal rather than resort to impulsive acting out, withdrawal, or dissociation. Treatment will enable the child to establish more reciprocal and fulfilling relationships with others in the home, daycare or school, and community.

Principles of Treatment

Before commencing treatment, it is important to complete a thorough multidisciplinary assessment to find out about the child's unique challenges and strengths. This assessment attempts to determine the child's developmental age in a number of functioning areas. Other crucial information includes nature and timing of the trauma, symptoms that the child displays, and any comorbid diagnoses such as ODD, depression, ADHD, and GAD. Information will be obtained from the child's parents and teachers, an interview with the child, and observations at home and school and must be integrated. The assessment must result in recommendations for practical strategies that can improve the child's functioning in various settings.

Treatment might need to be very different for a child with a Type I or simple trauma (one sudden trauma) and a Type II or complex trauma (a series of traumas, particularly maltreatment over a period of time). In general, shorter-term intervention is suitable for uncomplicated forms of trauma, whereas intensive, longer-term, multimodal intervention is needed for children with more complex histories of multiple traumas beginning early. In other words, Type II trauma is more likely to require a range of therapies over 1 to 3 years, whereas Type I trauma can be successfully treated if treatment is provided shortly following the trauma, in 2 to 16 sessions.

As far as possible, Type II trauma treatment should be a phased or staged intervention. Although it might be difficult to specify stages of intervention that can apply to all children, staging interventions should be considered and implemented where possible. The following three stages have been recommended for adults and need to be considered in choosing treatments for children (Chu, 1992, 2012; Courtois, 2004; Ford et al., 2009; Herman, 1992). At times, the treatment might move back and forth between the stages. When only short-term interventions can be provided, only Stage 1 strategies are typically appropriate.

- *Stage 1:* Assessment, stabilization, and symptom reduction by teaching the child self-soothing techniques that can be used if he is becoming hyperaroused or dissociated. Assure as far as possible that he is in a safe and nurturing environment both at home and at school.
- *Stage 2:* When the child feels safe enough and has strategies to calm himself down, retrieving trauma memories and integrating and resolving them comprise the next step. Research suggests that structured, focused treatment approaches to doing this work are better than other approaches (Cohen, Berliner, & Mannanno, 2000). For young children, this process can include play therapy approaches provided in a directive, structured, and focused way. Exposure (or telling the trauma story over and over) and eye movement desensitization and reprocessing (EMDR) have been found to be effective for children in middle childhood (Greenwald, 2006).
- *Stage 3:* The third stage involves moving forward and reintegrating into the world in a way that is fulfilling for the child, such as by making new friends, enjoying activities in the community, or pursuing interests such as sports, drama, dancing, or music. Increasingly, learning to trust others, knowing who they are, and having dreams for the future are also goals at this stage.

As far as possible, ensure safety and predictability while treatment is happening for traumatized children. This implies the absence of physical danger, psychological maltreatment, and rejection. This is important so that the child can begin a process of relaxing hypervigilance toward expected danger and beginning to heal. Assurance of stability of living arrangements, food, and absence of chaos is critical.

Providing the child with relational opportunities that can give him a sense of warmth, reliability, respect, and acceptance is crucial. This includes working on the parent–child relationship and helping her to find other people whom she can rely on in school or the extended family. For young children completely dependent on parents, enhancing the parent–child relationship is a priority.

Use of medication can be an essential component of treatment for many children with extreme problems of behavior or concentration and hyperarousal to help the child calm down sufficiently to manage better at home and school. This does not imply that medication should be used instead of other kinds of treatment, only that it can be a useful adjunct to psychosocial treatment.

There is constant pressure to use evidence-based approaches to treatment. This means that the treatment has been demonstrated to be better than no treatment or equal to an established treatment. Best practices, on the other hand, refer to methods that show promise and have demonstrated reliable outcomes. However, there are not enough empirically supported studies to date to determine which treatment is best for a particular child with a unique trauma history, set of symptoms, and current situation. This can mean that approaches showing promise, usually by having demonstrated some success with particular groups of children, can be the best available treatments. They include approaches that have a sound rationale (for example, neurosequential model of therapeutics [NMT]; Perry, 2006) and approaches that support reduction of the child's stress response (van der Kolk, 2006). Clearly, manualized treatments do not enable intervention to be tailored to a particular child, and research has not been able to show true efficacy for various treatments by following treated children into adulthood (Spinazzola, Blaustein, & van der Kolk, 2005).

The neurodevelopmental approach of the NMT has a number of theoretical and practical strategies that can be integrated into group settings and the home (see Table 5.2). This approach suggests that treatment needs to be adapted to the developmental stage of the child or the level of the brain first affected when the trauma started. For example, if the child was traumatized during the perinatal and postpartum periods, she will often need intervention that is repetitive and of sufficient duration to remediate the brain from the bottom up. Some approaches include movement, music, dance, or drumming, and those should be chosen that the child finds rewarding and fun and gives her a sense of mastery.

Given the range of developmental issues that severely traumatized children have, and because developmental tasks are usually derailed by trauma, it is crucial to promote a return to normal functioning in the following areas:

- emotion regulation;
- developing a positive sense of self and the world;
- forming attachments and showing empathy;
- identifying triggers, avoiding triggering as much as possible, and giving the child strategies to calm down if already triggered; and
- behavioral difficulties and lack of conscience.

Enhancing them in intervention in group settings and the home through parent interactions can be crucial.

With seriously traumatized children, at first individual treatment is usually better than group methods for two reasons: in group situations, traumatized children can find it too stressful and become hyperaroused by other children; and being close to the acting-out behavior of another group member can trigger aggressive behavior or dissociation. However, for children who are becoming more settled and using coping strategies if they are becoming hyperaroused, group strategies can be useful to enhance social skills and provide opportunities for the positive experience of working with others toward a common purpose, such as making something, creating a drama, or playing music together.

Attention to the child's cultural background is crucial because it can have an important influence on his willingness to be involved in treatment. Consequently, his family's values, beliefs, cultural norms and expectations, and cultural healing practices are important considerations in any treatment plan.

In the next section, we describe interventions that are considered evidence based or best practices (because they have shown promise and demonstrated reliable outcomes in clinical practice) or are endorsed by leading researchers and clinicians in the field.

APPROACHES TO TREATING TRAUMATIZED CHILDREN

Dyadic Approaches to Treating Infants and Young Children

Attuned interactions with caregivers are an essential part of early development. Without caring relationships, babies and young children can develop small "t" traumas and will not learn to calm and regulate their emotions. If they experience abuse and/or neglect, they learn that they cannot trust caregivers and often believe that they must be "bad" or worthless. It is crucial, therefore, to restore safety and healthy interactions for these children either with their biological parents or with adoptive or foster parents. A number of approaches have been developed to enhance parent–child relationships and repair the developmental disruptions resulting from various kinds of trauma in the early years (Van Horn & Lieberman, 2009).

Child–parent psychotherapy (CPP) was originally called infant–parent psychotherapy (Fraiberg, 1980). This approach emerged from a tradition of relationship-based therapies to treat children abused and neglected by parents where it is assumed that parenting interactions are disrupted because of early parental trauma causing secondary traumatization for the child. CPP is based on psychodynamic principles, including attachment theory, and incorporates components of trauma theory. Parents learn about the impact of trauma and are encouraged to become the agents of change. The manual (Lieberman & Van Horn, 2005, 2008), despite the lack of a staged approach, does incorporate ways to help the parent better understand the child's internal world. The treatment modalities are as follows:

- promoting development through play in which the parent is encouraged to observe the child's play and learn to understand it,
- offering developmental guidance,
- modeling appropriate interactions with the child and keeping her safe,
- interpreting feelings and actions that she shows in play,
- providing emotional support, and
- offering concrete support and crisis intervention.

Modified Interactional Guidance is a brief, focused intervention that can be used in situations in which the parent has unresolved loss and trauma and the child either has or is at risk of developing a disorganized attachment (Benoit, Madigan, Lecce, Shea, & Goldberg, 2001). It builds on the use of Interaction Guidance used to enhance positive interactions (McDonough, 2000) and has a similar goal to increase sensitive responsiveness in the parent. However, this modified approach focuses on reducing atypical parent-disrupted communication and behaviors identified on the *AMBIANCE* associated with disorganized attachment. In a pilot project that compared the intervention with the use of behavior modification, the Modified Interactional Guidance, but not the other intervention, was found to significantly reduce the number of atypical behaviors shown in the interactions and decrease the disrupted communication (Madigan, Hawkins, Goldberg, & Benoit, 2006).

The *Watch, Wait, and Wonder* (WWW) approach was introduced by Wesner, Dowling, and Johnson (1982). It was later expanded and researched as a short-term intervention for parents and young children with attachment difficulties (Muir, Lojkasek, & Cohen, 1999). Theoretically, the program is based on attachment theory, and the emphasis is consequently on enhancing the mother–child relationship. The WWW technique has two components: an infant-led interaction and discussion with the therapist of the mother's observations on what occurred in the session and her experience of it. The intervention is carried out in a room with toys suitable to the child's developmental level. During the interaction, the parent is asked to get down on the floor, remain in contact with her child, and follow his lead. It has also been shown to help mothers understand and deal with the intense and difficult emotions that can be elicited by the interactions in the first part of the session. Containing a parent's feelings and helping the parent to reflect on their meaning can also contribute to the development of self-reflectivity, especially as it relates to her experience with her infant. For the evaluation of the effectiveness of the WWW program, it was compared with another intervention used at a children's mental health center, a short-term psychodynamic family approach (Cohen et al., 1999). Both groups improved on all variables, but the infants in the WWW group were more likely to be securely attached, and disorganization was more reduced. At a 6-month follow-up, positive effects were maintained or improved further in both groups, but for WWW an advantage continued with the mother's comfort in dealing with infant behaviors and ratings of parenting stress (Cohen, Lojkasek, Muir, Muir, & Parker, 2002).

Approaches Often Used in Stage 1 of Treatment

Establishing safety in the environment: It is difficult for treatment to be successful if the child is not in a safe environment. If he is being maltreated, efforts to have him removed from the home and placed in foster care are necessary. If the situation does not include maltreatment but there are concerns about his psychological safety, a focus of treatment is often on working in the home and school to improve understanding of the child and the strategies and interactions being used with him.

Strategies for calming the physiology: one of the most disturbing and difficult results of exposure to childhood trauma is dysregulation of the physiology of the stress system. This results in a state of hypervigilance and physiological reactivity that can impair brain structure and function. As noted by a number of theorists and researchers, the first step of trauma treatment (or Stage 1) should include giving children strategies to soothe themselves physiologically before moving to Stage 2 (Perry, 2006; van der Kolk, 2003, 2005). This has also been proposed by Goodyear-Brown (2010) as one of the first steps of her Flexibly Sequenced Play Therapy (FSPT). She recommends a "multiplicity of play-based stress inoculation techniques [that] can help children impact the state of their own arousal" (p. 108). Like Perry (2006) and Lieberman and Van Horn (2008), she believes that "playfulness" can help to counter symptoms of hyperarousal, and because play activities are fun children are more likely to use them in other settings. Also, if they learn to use them themselves, they can gain some sense of control over their own bodies, which can be empowering. Van der Kolk has also emphasized the need for approaches that work with the body before more cognitive approaches are used (van der Kolk, 2006; van der Kolk et al., 2001). Recommended approaches include the following:

- Relaxation exercises, using various props such as balancing a feather (Kagan, 2007), can be used to begin and end a session.

- Breathing exercises, such as breathing in to a count of five and holding breath for a count of five, can be used. Using bubbles can increase engagement and a sense of fun. Other props can also be incorporated into this exercise.
- Progressive muscle relaxation has been used for pain management (McCallie, Blum, & Hood, 2006) and with traumatized adults (Briere & Scott, 2006).
- Creating a safe place for the child to "go to" can also help her relax and feel some sense of control over her feelings. With adults, this is typically done through visualization but can be created concretely by creating a special place in a sand box or playroom and by drawing pictures or making models of special places. Some children might even want to write a story about a place that they visualize as being peaceful, whereas others might like to have a story about a peaceful place read aloud to them.
- Galantino, Galbavy, and Quinn (2008), in a review of the literature, suggest that yoga is a very promising technique for stress reduction for children as well as adults. It can increase heart rate variability, increase brainstem regulatory integrity, and positively affect regulatory mechanisms in the brain.
- Therapeutic or positive touch can be very healing for some children as long as they control where and how they are touched. Of course, adequate protocols and sufficient supervision have to be in place.
- Theraplay activities and approaches that are fun and rhythmic and those that are nurturing can be very helpful if they are modified for a particular child and for parents and caregivers (Jernberg & Booth, 1999; Wood, 2000). See Munns (2000, pp. 364–379) for a description of some theraplay activities.

Approaches Used in Each Stage of Therapy

Overcoming the triggering of trauma memories: Children who have experienced trauma, especially during the first 5 years of life, are easily triggered by seemingly innocuous reminders of the trauma. This can start a stress reaction leading to acting-out behavior, dissociation, or withdrawal. Identifying what triggers these responses and how they can be avoided and dealt with if they do occur is crucial. Some suggestions for doing this follow.

Helping with feeling out of control: All children who have been traumatized have an intense need to feel in control and can become quickly triggered if they are told to do something that they do not want to do.

> *Emily had an intense desire to be in control and found it extremely difficult to be part of a group. Giving her a choice, for example between doing what was asked and getting a reward or spending time inside during recess, often allowed her to feel that she had some control and was listened to, and this could avoid her being triggered. Since she loved drama, if she had a leading role in the acting out of a story or was given some responsibility in the classroom or with the new baby at home, she could settle more easily and feel that she had some control in her life.*

Integrating left- and right-hemisphere functioning: As discussed earlier, traumatized children frequently have significantly higher scores on perceptual reasoning than verbal comprehension. Perhaps even more important, this means that they have difficulty with creating a narrative about their lives that is logical and sequential and integrates emotional experiences. It can also result in problems with being able to integrate two views of self and other, often leading to dramatic shifting between "good" and "bad" personas. This switching is often referred to by teachers and parents as "Jekyll and Hyde" characters and seems to occur without any reason. A number of strategies can be used to help integrate different kinds of information in the left and right hemispheres.

- Visual cues of schedules and activities to be completed can assist a child with right-brain dominance. It is important to acknowledge that many children are unable to remember more than one instruction or, when there are several, only the first or last one. This can be misinterpreted by caregivers as opposition. Having instructions presented visually and using a timer to remind children when to do something or finish an activity can help.
- Speech therapists can improve a child's capacity for telling a story and including information on how the child felt about what happened.
- When the child becomes upset and sees himself or someone else as "bad," it is important to acknowledge his feelings as legitimate while also suggesting alternative or more positive ways of viewing the person or situation. This can help the child to have a more balanced or integrated view of things. This worked well with Emily when she saw herself as "bad and worthless" when her biological father let her down again by not showing up for a visit.

Relationship building: Those involved directly with the child, such as teachers and parents, should notice any positive behavior and comment on something positive about a child on a particular day. This can be achieved by setting up a reward system or using comments such as "You really worked hard today" and "I liked the way you helped Mary." If the child has to be disciplined, repairing the relationship and discussing what happened are important.

Establishing developmental capacities: It is important to establish for a particular child which developmental areas are compromised and to use suggested parenting strategies to help her gain the undeveloped capacity. For example, if she does not have empathy, providing strategies to enhance perspective taking is crucial. If she lacks social skills, teaching them and encouraging her parents to spend time with her will be helpful.

Pharmacotherapy: Because traumatized individuals experience a variety of chronic biological difficulties, pharmacotherapy is a likely option for many cases. Various biological systems can become dysregulated, resulting in changes in neurochemistry. Depression and anxiety often accompany these changes. A number of drugs have been used with children with PTSD, including antidepressants, stimulants, and atypical antipsychotics. None of these drugs has an identification for treating children with trauma, so all use is "off label." However, depending on which domain of the child's functioning is disordered, clinicians can elect to do trials of these medications. When used, it is important that a focus on change is identified and progress monitored using standardized questionnaires. In adults, there is evidence that antidepressants reduce problems with anger and irritability, especially when the trauma has not become chronic. Significant aggression can respond to atypical antipsychotics, as it will for nontraumatized children, but can be problematic in terms of weight gain and induction of diabetes. All pharmacotherapy can only be considered adjunctive because the medication does not address the disordered memories that cause the symptoms. Despite these caveats, it is sometimes difficult to treat some children without the physiological support provided by medication. Referral to a psychiatrist or physician will often be an important aspect of early sessions in Stage 1 of treatment.

NMT (see Table 5.1 at end of chapter): Perry maintains that a key to successful treatment is recognition that the brain develops in a "hierarchical fashion" from the most simple (brainstem) to the most complex (frontal cortex) and that certain interactions and experiences are key to its development and repair (Fosha, 2003; Tronick & Weinberg, 1997). Perry (2006) and Perry and Hambrick (2008) describe work with abused and neglected children "from a neurodevelopmental perspective" that provides understanding of the symptoms that many of the children display. Such a perspective also provides the basis for the NMT treatment approach described here. Perry (2006, p. 29) maintains that "therapeutic experiences [can] change the brain in ways that allow healing, recovery, and restoration of healthy functioning." However, he emphasizes that the higher cortical regions change

Table 5.1 *Difference Between Stagnant and Dynamic Posttraumatic Play*

Stagnant Posttraumatic Play	Dynamic Posttraumatic Play
Affect remains constricted	Affect becomes available
Physical constriction remains	Physical fluidity becomes evident
Interactions with play remain limited	Interactions with play become varied
Interactions with clinician remain limited	Interactions with clinician become varied
Play stays precisely the same	Play changes or new elements are added
Play is conducted at the same spot	Play occurs in different locations
Play is limited to specific objects	Play includes new objects
Themes remain constant	Themes differ or expand
Outcomes remain fixed and nonadaptive	Outcomes differ, and healthier, more adaptive responses emerge
Play remains rigid and repetitive	Rigidity of play loosens over time
After-play behavior indicates constriction/tension	After-play behavior indicates release or fatigue
Out-of-session symptoms are unchanged or increase	Out-of-session symptoms may remain unchanged or peak at first, but then decrease

Source: Gil (2006). Reprinted with permission.

most readily, whereas the more primitive regions are affected in maltreated children and are much harder to remediate, particularly when the abuse and neglect occurred in the early years and were intense and chronic. This knowledge has fuelled development of the NMT and the following principles of therapy.

- To make changes in neural systems and ultimately in the child's emotions and behaviors, new experiences must be provided that are matched to the child's developmental rather than chronological age and repeated so that the brain can be rewired. New relational experiences that provide unconditional acceptance and repetitive nurturing are critical to repair relationships when difficulties have occurred. These experiences need to be frequent, predictable, and consistent. This means that experiences cannot just be provided in weekly therapy sessions but need to be available at home and school.
- Therapeutic experiences must be provided for that area of the brain that was developing when the trauma occurred, and for many children this will be the brainstem. The sequence of therapeutic strategies is crucial; if the child is dysregulated, anxious, hypervigilant, and extremely reactive, brainstem activities are critical (for example, music, movement, dancing, drumming, and massage). They need to be intensive and repetitive and as much fun as possible. Just being kept warm and nurtured with food can be helpful, and once the child is calmer and less readily dysregulated other strategies can be introduced.
- Once the child is more regulated, simple stories or narratives can be introduced. They can be provided in theraplay sessions, which include rituals and acting out nursery rhymes and stories, and nurturing when the child has a scratch or bump (Jernberg & Booth, 1999; Munns, 2000).
- As the child seems more securely attached to parents and other caregivers, movements can be more complex, and play therapy and creative activity can be introduced.
- As the child becomes capable of parallel play, small groups can be introduced, with support provided for the interactions.
- Not until the child is capable of containing emotional outbursts and has a sense of security and safety should traditional therapies such as insight-oriented and cognitive-behavioral therapies (CBT) be introduced.
- Interventions must have an element of reward, whether providing positive reinforcement or making the intervention itself fun and rewarding.

- Intervention needs to be provided in a healthy relational context in which there is consistency and predictability that can create healing and learning.
- Intervention must be intense, repetitive, and of adequate duration, beginning with brainstem activities.

The NMT has been evaluated with a quasi-experimental design in a therapeutic preschool setting (Barfield & Gaskill, 2005) in which a more "behavioral discipline" curriculum was used and compared with NMT. Children who received the NMT approach improved more than the comparison group in social/emotional development, emotion regulation, impulse regulation, cooperation, and empathy. The approach has now been described as "best practice" because it has demonstrated some reliable clinical outcomes.

Approaches Often Used in Stage 2 of Treatment

Creative or expressive therapies include a variety of modalities such as art therapy, dance/movement therapy, music and drama therapy, writing and journaling, poetry, and psychodrama. Originally, creative therapies were seen as alternatives to "talking" therapies (Malchiodi, 2008). They can also be used as adjuncts to CBT techniques. However, creative therapies have been used to overcome a variety of symptoms of PTSD and improve associated conditions, such as depression, hyperarousal, and anxiety. Creative therapies can provide a safe place to explore feelings about trauma and help access nonverbal memories. These therapies often overlap with CBT techniques that use relaxation, desensitization, and changing cognitive distortions. Sometimes a particular aspect of the trauma is worked on, whereas at other times the client engages in drawing, dance, and music/singing, and the clinician deals with issues linked to the trauma as they arise. The treatment is often brief, about 6 to 8 weeks, but can be longer term. In some cities, theater groups have been used with traumatized children and adolescents as they provide an alternative physical experience and can help to overcome a sense of hopelessness. Creative therapies are usually well accepted by children. It is critical, however, that clinicians using them are cautious about accessing trauma memories too quickly or with too much intensity. Also, there are limited research studies that can demonstrate their effectiveness with traumatized children (Malchiodi, 2008).

Life story work with traumatized children: Having a life story or narrative is important for all children but critical for those who have been traumatized and removed from biological parents and placed in a foster or adoptive home. Children from 4 to 17 years of age can profit from making a life story or life book. One way to create a life story is to make an album in which the child's life is described and any important documents, pictures, drawings, clip art, and descriptions are compiled from birth to moving into the new home. There are a number of phases of this activity: gathering information and putting the events in sequence; discussing any thoughts or beliefs of the child about the events; and creating the book. However, though the events are important, the life story is more than just a factual account of the past and will include what the child knows or believes about what happened. This allows any misconceptions to be corrected. The book is physically created by the adult. It is important for the child's caregiver (biological, foster, or adoptive parent) to be involved to enhance the process for the child (Cohen & Duvall, 1996; Engel, 1995; Rose & Philpot, 2005). The book should not romanticize what happened to the child, but it is important to include positive events. As described by Rose and Philpot (2005, p. 129), "life story books are like a manual about the child, this is what they have been through, what they understand about themselves and their experiences and those with whom they interact, and crucially, who they are now." The book can help the child to integrate memories that can be used to explain himself to others in certain circumstances. If skillfully and thoughtfully done, it can help him to understand that he was not to blame for what happened, that his biological mother was unwell, and that he was unprotected and must have been sad and afraid at times. If a child refuses to talk about a certain event or the abuse that he experienced, this needs to be respected. Sometimes a child can get stuck in describing things and might need help to put into words what he feels and remembers.

Case Study: George

George created his life book with his grandmother, home visitor, and play therapist present.

Fortunately, George's grandmother, Jeannie, had been involved in Michael's and his siblings' lives as much as possible. Some of the highlights of creating George's life book are described next. Jeannie was at Michael's birth and had the hospital pictures of him but also several she had taken and one of her holding him. George's aunt had also been at the hospital and had knitted him a little suit that Jeannie still had. Hearing how excited everyone was about his arrival into the world and how cute he was, was obviously exciting news for George and he marveled about how small the knitted suit was and how cute. There was very little information about the time George and his siblings spent with their biological mother, especially when his father was away as a long-distance truck driver. It was explained that his mother was not well at that time and unable to take care of them properly and his father had to make money so they could have food and clothes and a place to stay. During the discussion of what happened, Jeannie said that it was very hard and showed George her empathy for what happened by holding him and wiping his tears. It was explained that his father wanted to make sure they were safe and had given up his job to be with them for a while. Again Jeannie had been involved as much as she could at this time. Discussion of the time the children spent with their father's new girlfriend was also very revealing for Jeannie. For example, George talked about hiding under his bed with his dog when his father and his girlfriend fought and he explained that they hit each other and screamed and yelled. He described covering his ears but that it "still did not go away." He also talked about the children being left alone at times without enough food and how scary this was. Jeannie again showed him great empathy and apologized for not being there for them. Jeannie also explained that one of her roles was to keep the children all safe in a way that they had not been before and that was why she had to discipline them at times. She explained that she thought about him all the time and wondered how he was and this "keeping him in mind" was a new idea for George and one he liked. Perhaps one of the most poignant moments came at the end when George was discussing why his father did not phone or visit them and he summed it up in this way, "it's hard to get a good wife and I guess he doesn't want to lose her" to which Jeannie replied how it was hard to find such wonderful children and she never wanted to lose them either and would always keep them safe.

Play therapy is a "psychotherapeutic method based on psychodynamic and developmental principles, intended to help relieve the emotional stress of young children" (Webb, 1991, p. 27). Different models and approaches have evolved, including sand therapy and art therapy. Some of the most contentious issues include whether the therapy should be short or long term and directive or nondirective. As noted by Gil (2006), as with other treatment approaches for traumatized children, it has to be adapted for a particular child and her trauma history and current situation, and a cookie-cutter, or one-size-fits-all, approach is not helpful. Play therapy is most frequently used in the preschool years but can be used up to 10 to 11 years of age with the inclusion of appropriate toys or games. It allows the traumatized child to symbolically express experiences that are too difficult to talk about. Play can also be useful for diagnostic purposes, to enhance the therapeutic relationship, and to improve the child's ability to play. Toys are made available for a particular child and can include art supplies (for example, Play-Doh, scissors, paper, paint, crayons, dolls and action figures, puppets, and suitable board games). A number of writers have elucidated the main steps of using play therapy within a broader treatment plan (Gil, 2006; Goodyear-Brown, 2010; Lieberman & Van Horn, 2005; Terr, 2008; Van Horn & Lieberman, 2009). The emphasis here is on trauma-focused play therapy (TF-PT; Gil, 2006).

As Gil points out, even within this approach, therapists use different methods, but she and others advocate a combination of directive and nondirective approaches (Shelby & Felix, 2005). The steps are outlined in Gil (2006), in which she discusses how to respond to posttraumatic play that is "literal, repetitive, highly structured, and joyless" (p. 151). This type of play can rework trauma by gradually exposing children to the trauma. However, it has also been described as "dangerous" if it does not move beyond continual repetition. If the play becomes "stagnant," with the child replaying the trauma constantly in a rigid way, it can cause the original fear and terror and feelings in the body to be continually replayed (Terr, 2004; see Table 5.2). If this happens over many sessions, the therapist needs to become more directive and intervene to move therapy forward. This can include narrating what is going on in the play, directing it, or videotaping it to replay it back to the child. If she can use the play to feel more in control of it and find positive solutions in it, she can move toward resolution and acceptance (see Table 5.2).

Case Study: Emily

Play therapy with Emily was believed to be essential to help her integrate the terrifying attack on her mother witnessed when she was 16 months of age. Her mother was able to be nurturing with her children, and up to 15 months of age Emily was described as a happy and responsive baby. Therefore, it was likely that the sensorimotor and emotional memories were stored separately from her cognitions of the event and when triggered were contributing to a number of her symptoms. It was decided that a directive and short-term approach that focused on enabling Emily to integrate these memories into her conscious memories would allow her to have more control over them.

The playroom was set up with the doll's house in the middle of the room with the doll family inside and a street with cars outside the house. Small sticks were placed inside the house to represent the weapons used by Emily's father. Almost as soon as Emily entered the playroom, she started playing with the miniature family in the dollhouse, quietly at first as the "family" had dinner and sat down to watch television. Suddenly, everything changed, both Emily's demeanor, which became more agitated, and her play with the toys became more dramatic. A "man" burst into the house and began to beat the mother with one of the toy sticks. Although Emily was clearly involved in the play, she showed little emotion, and no connection was made with the therapist. The same play scene was repeated time and time again, beginning calmly and quickly escalating into the attack. Cries of "she's bleeding" were also repeated. There was no acting out of other scenes after the attack, and Emily seemed driven to keep repeating it without resolution. Her parents reported no change in her symptoms.

After about 3 weeks of this kind of play, the therapist introduced themes of rescue and overcoming the attack. The therapist knew that the police had come and that Emily and her mother had been taken to the hospital for medical checks before returning home that night. The therapist introduced these "rescuers" into the play using a police car, ambulance, doctor's kit, and a kind policeman, ambulance driver, doctor, and nurse who took care of everything. When Emily next introduced the traumatic scene, the rescuers came and took control of it, showing concern and caring for Emily and her mother and washing the blood off them. Gradually, Emily began to relax and started to interact in the play metaphor having the therapist taking the role of her mother.

Other new toys and characters were introduced, including a neighbor who came to help and her grandmother who went to the hospital. This scene was then expanded during the next 3 or 4 weeks and included time in the shelter and toward the end of the therapy began to include her mother's new partner, whom Emily called Dad, and her siblings. She seemed to understand now that she and her mother and siblings could be kept safe, and her use of the imaginary play to internalize this new reality was an important part of the therapy. Her parents began to report a significant decrease in her more extreme symptoms and a sense that the family was gradually returning to calmness and safety.

Table 5.2 *Treatment Approaches: A Neurosequential Model*

Normal Age of Active Growth	Brain Systems	Activities Involved	Treatment
0 to 9 months	Brain stem	Regulates internal homeostasis; heart rate, blood pressure, level of arousal, some reflexes, first stop for internal and external sensory input, perception is unconscious	Brainstem regulation or process of administering safe, predictable, repetitive sensory experiences that are not time limited
	Cerebellum	Coordination of motor, social, emotional, and several cognitive functions; balance (initially controlled movement)	Patterned, repetitive somatosensory activities that provide patterned neural activity for re-organization of the brainstem
		State regulation in everyday situations	Positive nurturing interactions with trustworthy caregivers
		Early attachment experiences with parents and caregivers	Dance, music, therapeutic massage, yoga (breathing), movement, drumming, and other safe, predictable, repetitive sensory input
6 months to 2 years	Diencephalon	Sensory integration approaches	Movement activities are more complex and require more motor planning
		Motor control approaches by occupational therapist	Simple narratives are used with the children describing recent events that have happened
		Relational experiences with a range of intervenors	Reiki touch and therapeutic massage introduced with care
		Attunement and reciprocity in interactions	

(continued)

Table 5.2 *Treatment Approaches: A Neurosequential Model (continued)*

Normal Age of Active Growth	Brain Systems	Activities Involved	Treatment
1 to 4 years	Limbic system	Maintaining the balance between internal and external reality; urges, appetites, attachment, affect regulation, and aspects of emotion, self-preservation, evaluation experience for its emotional significance, links sensation (pleasure or pain) to context; the hub of memory	Relational related traditional art and play therapies Introducing a pet Approaches so child can identify emotions and calm himself down when he is becoming hyperaroused
	Hypothalamus	Maintaining homeostasis by regulating functions such as temperature, blood pressure, and glucose levels, exchanging information between brain and body	Approaches to calm the child who is easily hyperaroused such as teaching self-talk and positive messages Identifying trauma triggers and what calms the child down (social stories, teaching parents and school personnel this information)
	Amygdala	Conditioned learning, ability to learn by association, storing of fearful memories, monitoring incoming stimuli for threat, instigates fight–flight response when danger is detected	Sensory integration approaches Neutral fun tasks and physical games, so the child can feel sense of mastery
	Hippocampus	Processing of all conscious memories, conditioned learning, learning by association, linking stimuli to context (pain, sustenance, pleasure)	Teaching social skills Approaches to activate the child who is hypoaroused such as theraplay
	Thalamus	Relaying information to other systems; permitting use of senses in combination	Attunement to the child's level of emotionality in a way that the child feels "heard" and understood
	Corpus callosum	Connecting cortical areas of right and left hemispheres, allowing exchange of conscious information between the two	Emotion coaching Relaxation and guided imagery
	Anterior commissure	Carrying unconscious, emotional information between the hemispheres	If dissociating re-engagement in environment is needed Relationship therapy

3 to 6 years continuing into early adulthood	Cortex	Analyzing and interacting with the external world, abstract cognition, complex language, reasoning, planning, judgment, problem solving, working memory	More verbal and insight oriented using a variety of cognitive–behavioral or psychodynamic approaches
			Creating a life book
	Neocortex	Cognition and metacognition (thoughts about thoughts, emotions and behaviors	Teaching problem solving and decision making
	Dorsolateral prefrontal cortex	Mediating language and cognition	Storytelling
			Drama
	Medial prefrontal cortex	Fear responding and emotional dysregulation, the interface between the lower subcortical areas that generate emotional states and the higher cortical areas that regulate these states, receiving multimodal sensory input	Formal education
			Traditional insight-oriented and cognitive behavioral approaches (CBT)
	Orbitofrontal cortex (the right region)	Self-regulation, moral foundations	EMDR

Note: Activities should be developmentally appropriate according to when the trauma occurred but also not age-inappropriate (or at a minimum age-acceptable).
Based on Perry (2006). Reprinted with permission of the author.

Dyadic developmental psychotherapy (DDP): Daniel Hughes has developed an approach to working with infants, children, and adults who have been exposed to trauma, neglect, loss, or extreme failure to provide them with nurturing interactions, particularly in the early years. The child is likely to display symptoms of trauma and have difficulty with accepting and responding appropriately to efforts by caregivers to show affection and commitment to his ongoing welfare. He sees the world as chaotic and unreliable and himself as worthless, bad, and unlovable. During the DDP sessions, an important attachment figure is present to support a sense of greater safety and containment for the child in the session. With a child or adolescent, this attachment figure will be the natural parent, foster or adoptive parent, or staff member from the group home or other institution in which the child is living. The therapist adopts an attitude described by Hughes as PLACE: *p*layfulness, *l*ove, *a*cceptance, *c*uriosity, *e*mpathy.

Within the "holding" environment provided by the therapist and attachment figure, the therapist adopts a directive, client-centered stance to "explore, resolve and integrate a wide range of memories, emotions, and current experiences that are frightening, shameful, avoided or denied" (Hughes, 2006, p. 2). This process can allow previously unconscious or dissociated memories to be integrated into a coherent, personal narrative or new autobiography. This new narrative is co-constructed with the client, therapist, and attachment figure in such a way that the child experiences understanding, empathy, affective matching, empathy, and containment, making the elicited memories tolerable, understandable, and validated. Development of the child's attachment to his parents and integration of his sense of self are the goals of treatment. The therapist uses a number of strategies in the sessions by communicating to the child verbally and nonverbally and with affective matching or attunement to provide "moments of meeting" or true understanding and acceptance. At times, psychodrama, illustrated stories, journaling, and paradoxical interventions are used to facilitate attachment between the client and the attachment figure and reintegration of the traumatic memories. As well, the approach has been used successfully to reduce severe symptoms of aggression, withdrawal, chronic arousal, and/or dissociation.

EMDR is a complex treatment that combines behavioral and client-centered approaches and is used as a Stage 2 trauma approach primarily with adults. It was developed by Shapiro (2001, 2002). There is less research on the efficacy of its use with children, and the method might need to be modified to work with children of different ages and developmental levels. As with many treatment approaches, it is critical that formal training and follow-up supervision are available and integrated into a comprehensive treatment program.

CONCLUSION

Clearly, traumatized children present a challenge to caregivers and often have complex presentations with contributions from genetics, biology, parenting, socioeconomic situation, and of course, the trauma itself. Recent research has delineated the neurophysiological difficulties that underlie and contribute to the behavioral, emotional, social, and developmental issues seen in many traumatized children. New ways of treating these children and supporting their families are being researched, and many show positive outcomes for these children over time. It is a constantly evolving field with an immense literature that changes daily, and has moved beyond seeing traumatized children as permanently damaged with no hope for them in the future to providing strategies that can significantly improve outcomes of the children. However, unless the right kinds of treatment are available, outcomes for these children can be extremely negative and destructive for the child, his family, and society.

See Table 5.3 for details regarding various websites that offer related information.

Table 5.3 *Websites*

Website	Information on Website
www.developingchild.harvard.edu	A number of articles that "translate science into policy." Articles on the effects of trauma.
www.ocsc.vic.gov.au	Website of the Commission for Children and Young People, Government of Victoria, Australia. Has a useful and accessible publication: *Calmer classrooms: A guide to working with traumatized children.*
www.dhs.vic.gov.au/everychildeverychance	Website of the government of Victoria, Australia. Every child, every chance, response approach to child protection.
www.childtrauma.com	Website of the Child Trauma Institute. Provides training on treating trauma in children and adolescents.
www.childtraumaacademy.org	Website of Child Trauma Academy provides a number of articles on the effects of trauma and on treating trauma in children and adolescents.
www.cwti.org	Website of the Child Welfare Training Institute (CWTI), University of Southern Maine, In-Service Training.
www.danielhughes.org	Website of Daniel Hughes that provides information on Dyadic Developmental Psychotherapy and a list of books and upcoming training and consultation.
www.istss.org	Website of the International Society for Traumatic Stress Studies (ISTSS). Promotes advancement and exchange of knowledge about traumatic stress. Publishes *Journal of Traumatic Stress*.
www.ctrp.org	Website of the Center for Trauma Response, Recovery, and Preparedness.
www.sidran.org	Website of the Sidran Institute for Traumatic Stress Institute. Helps people to understand and recover from trauma.
www.traumacenter.org	Website of the Trauma Center, Justice Resource Institute. Provides specialized assessment and treatment services.
www.hhs.gov	U.S. Department of Health and Human Services has information on mental health.
www.nctsn.org	Website of National Child Traumatic Stress Network (NCTSN). Initiative of the U.S. Department of Health and Human Services. Advances a broad range of effective services and interventions for childhood trauma working with established systems of care such as health, mental health, juvenile justice, and education.
www.starrtraining.org/trauma-and-children	Parent Trauma Resource Center (TLC) at National Institute of Trauma and Loss in Children. Provides information on grief and trauma reactions and provides ways that parents can help traumatized children. Also provides training for professionals working with trauma.
www.advancedtrauma.com	Contains *Trauma Affect Regulation Guide to Education and Therapy.*
www.tsicaap.com	Website of the Traumatic Stress Institute/Center for Adult and Adolescent Psychotherapy.

6

Difficulties and Disorders of Emotion Regulation

SUSAN J. BRADLEY

Emotion regulation refers to a broadly understood, but not always well-defined, cluster of developmental skills that appears to assist the individual in managing emotional and social situations. It comprises understanding and labeling feeling states and ways of managing expression. It is generally understood that adaptive management of feelings involves flexible strategies suited to different situations (Bradley, 2000). Effective emotion regulation prior to school entry predicts reduced levels of behavioral problems and better social competence in school (Eisenberg et al., 2001; Eisenberg, Hofer, & Vaughan, 2007). Socioemotional learning skills, defined as the ability to encode, interpret, and reason about social and emotional situations, correlate with the level of social competence in both typically developing and clinically referred children (McKown, Gumbiner, Russo, & Lipton, 2009). Emotion regulation is part of a larger set of cognitive skills, sometimes labeled self-regulation and referred to as effortful control. This includes the capacity to attend, delay gratification, and think of consequences (Feldman, 2009).

There are different conceptual approaches to defining emotions and feelings. We follow Frijda's (1993) approach, which sees a broad concept of arousal leading to a positive or negative affect state. This arousal can be hard for the individual to label with accuracy but is experienced as pleasant or unpleasant. Emotions, in contrast, are triggered by events, memories, or situations and lead to preparedness for action. They involve a perception of the trigger, a physiological response, typically a cognitive assessment of the situation, and a sense of motor preparedness (e.g., fight or flight in a situation of fear). Feeling states or moods represent a more prolonged, less discrete, reaction that can involve different emotions.

Generally, negative affect requires regulation, though with high states of excitement positive affect also requires management (Shields & Cicchetti, 1998). Young children who display good knowledge of emotions and ability to regulate them, according to the demands of the situation, prior to school entry, tend to do better socially because they engage with peers in school and have fewer behavioral problems.

There has been increasing interest in the importance of positive affects in development. Fredrickson (2001) articulated a theory that positive feelings allow a broadening of experience that increases opportunities to learn and contributes to the development of resilience in contrast to negative emotions that narrow one's focus and can permit effective automatic responses such as fight or flight. Isen (2004, p. 275) reviewed the literature on positive emotions and concluded that "positive affect promotes social interaction, helpfulness, generosity, and social responsibility, while not undermining attention to a person's own long-term welfare. Furthermore, positive affect facilitates flexible thinking and problem solving, and at the same time gives rise to careful, thorough thinking." Generally, children who display more positive affects also have better emotion management skills (Denham, Bassett, & Wyatt, 2007).

Emotional intelligence, a term that encompasses emotion regulation, typically used in adult populations, was recently shown to moderate the impact of earlier sexual abuse on suicidality in adolescence. Adolescent girls (all of whom had been sexually abused as children) rated as high in emotional intelligence displayed low levels of suicidality in contrast to similar girls who were low in emotional intelligence and showed high levels of suicidality (Cha & Nock, 2009).

Development of emotion-regulation skills follows a path from regulation by the caregiver and self-soothing infant strategies to language-based approaches as the child matures (see Bradley, 2000). The early development of these skills occurs in mini conversations about feelings and how to manage them, between child and parent, and between child and siblings, and is enhanced by similar conversations with peers in imaginative play (Denham, 1998; Denham et al., 2007; Dunn, 2007; Dunn, Brown, & Beardsall, 1991). Clearly, a child's language and capacity to attend will impact on this development. Temperament also plays a role as some children are more intense in their reactions to emotional situations, and this intensity can interfere with developing regulatory strategies. Fearful children might withdraw from stressful situations and have more difficulty learning adaptive skills to manage their distress (Bates & Petit, 2007; Nigg, 2006).

Brain areas (see Figure 6.1) involved in supporting effective emotion regulation involve the amygdala, a cluster of cells in the temporal lobe that reacts to a variety of affective stimuli and connects with frontal areas that work in interpreting the situation and enhancing or dampening the reaction. The hippocampus, which stores episodic memories, also contributes to interpretation and input to the frontal areas that coordinate the response. This coordinated emotion system regulates a variety of physiological (both sympathetic and parasympathetic systems) and motor responses to the stimulus. Genetic factors also affect emotion regulation.

Clearly, parenting influences a child's success in understanding feelings and their management. Parents less comfortable with their own feelings might be less able to support their child's discussions about feelings. Parents also model ways of handling feelings, and this can be a powerful template that impacts later development not only through showing adaptive and maladaptive ways of emotion management but also through intimidation of the child's expression with high levels of negative affect.

Undercontrolled emotions are likely to lead to later behavioral difficulties and interaction problems with caregivers and other adults and peers. Overcontrolled emotions can also contribute to a variety of internalizing difficulties.

Strategies to support adaptive emotion regulation include using teachable moments when children might be most open to learning and understanding, supporting parents in modeling their own adaptive emotion regulation, cognitive-behavioral therapy (CBT) programs to teach coping strategies, and medications to help children with intense reactions to have more time to use strategies. Some of these strategies (e.g., CBT) have good evidence to support their efficacy, whereas others have not been as well tested but appeal at a common-sense level. See Figure 6.1 for an approximate schematic guide to the location of brain structures involved in emotion regulation.

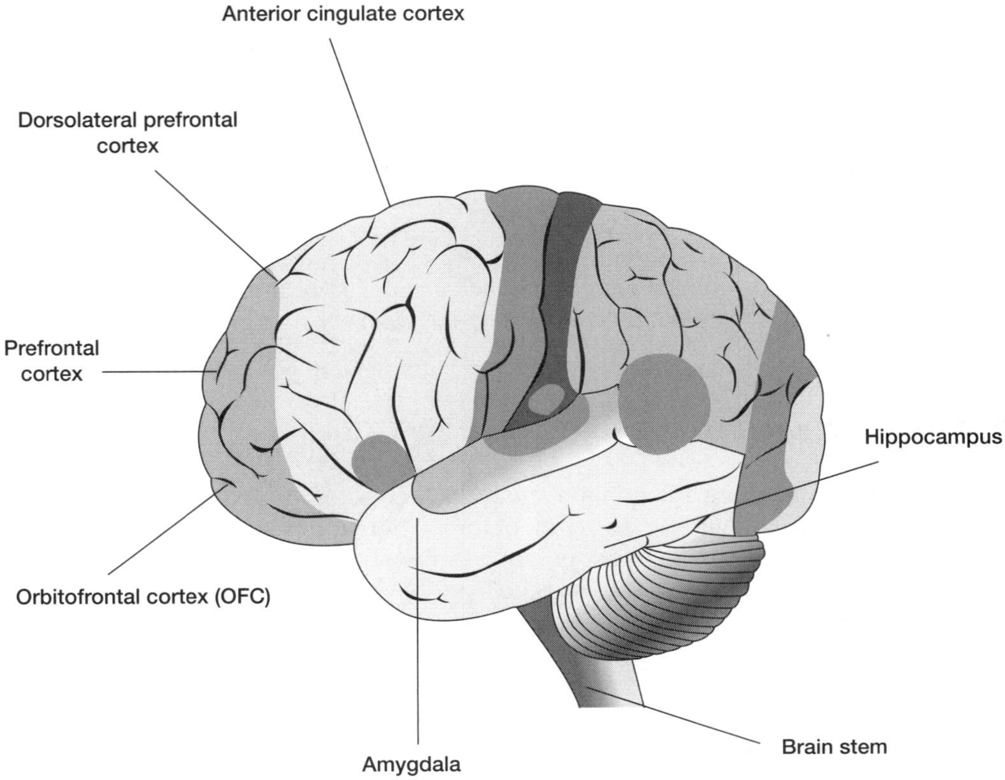

Figure 6.1 *Brain areas supporting effective emotion regulation.*

Case Study: Jay

Jay, the youngest child of a single parent, was challenging from early toddlerhood. He was intense in his reactions and resisted adult control and expectations. His mother sought help early on and found that she had to accommodate him at every step. Efforts to take him shopping required a graduated process of going for one item and then working up to a longer list over weeks. Jay needed advance notice of any change and reacted strongly to not getting his way. His mother learned that she had to stay calm and not engage Jay when he was getting upset. The effort for all involved in his care to stay calm was complicated by the fact that his older siblings and elderly great-aunt often looked after him while his mother worked, and these individuals were less skilled in managing him.

Kindergarten was very difficult for Jay, and he was frequently sent home. His mother sought more professional help, which led to his psychological assessment. He scored in the gifted range, particularly verbally. He demonstrated exceptional skills in areas that interested him but showed marked difficulties in social interaction and anger regulation. Psychiatric assessment found him to meet criteria for being in the autism spectrum, high functioning, with marked oppositional traits. Stimulant medication was suggested to deal with his impulsive responses, and it did help, though it did not completely control the aggression, so risperidone was also prescribed. Despite the medication and after a tumultuous time in Kindergarten, Jay went to a day treatment program for Grades 1 and 2. He did very well in this small program, which focused on helping him manage his anger, noncompliance, and social interaction. His return to the regular school system was problematic as the supports that Jay needed were not available, and he began to revert to his former behaviors of noncompliance and aggression. A variety of medications was tried, with limited success. At age 9, he was admitted to a hospital psychiatric ward for adolescents. He told his mother he wanted to stay there.

Although Jay's story is still unfinished, it illustrates the difficulties faced by children and their caregivers when a child has a severe problem with emotion regulation. Being a bright child, Jay learned when motivated to do so. He responded partially to medications that can support reductions in impulsivity and aggression. Unfortunately, it was difficult to continue the needed level of support in the school when he returned from the highly supportive day treatment program. Medication management became problematic; without the programmatic support, his medications needed to be increased but were not as effective as good programming. After intense advocacy, his mother finally convinced the school board to provide a child and youth worker skilled in working with children in the autism spectrum to support Jay in class. Unfortunately, this was "too little too late," and he had to return to a day treatment program for further individualized support. The inability of the system to properly support Jay led to immense demoralization of both him and his single mother.

BRAIN AREAS KNOWN TO SUPPORT THESE FUNCTIONS

As indicated previously, the amygdala, a small cluster of cells located in the temporal lobe, has long been associated with the appraisal of threat. Numerous studies have documented its role in alerting the organism to danger. In addition, because of its connection to brainstem areas (which control arousal) and higher-order brain areas (cortical areas controlling cognition, attention, and memory), it appears to provide affective valence to experience. Studies have shown that the amygdala responds to fearful stimuli but also to other stimuli, such as angry and happy faces. It has been identified as showing abnormalities in anxiety and depression as well as other forms of psychopathology (Monk, 2008). The amygdala does not act alone in the recognition of feeling but is part of a network that involves the frontal lobes (executive function), other parts of the limbic system, including the striatum (action preparedness), insula (disgust experience and recognition), the hypothalamus and the sympathetic and parasympathetic nervous systems (physiological response), the hippocampus (episodic memory), and the anterior cingulate cortex (ACC; response inhibition and conflict monitoring) (Heberlein & Adolphs, 2007). There is overlap between the brain areas involved in emotional functioning and those recruited for social functioning (Norris & Cacioppo, 2007).

There is no clear description of the neurobiological basis of emotion regulation. There are, however, several interesting theories that appear to have some empirical support.

Ochsner and Gross (2007) proposed a model of cognitive control of emotion comprised of two components. The first consists of the dorsal prefrontal cortex and cingulate regions referred to as a top-down "description-based appraisal system" that *describes* the emotional state of the individual and properties of the emotion-eliciting stimulus. The other is called the top-down "outcome-based appraisal system" that consists of orbitofrontal and ventral prefrontal cortex and cingulate regions. The latter is concerned with *appraising emotional outcomes* associated with various choices. These authors hypothesize that the two top-down systems work in concert with a bottom-up perceptual and affective processing system in posterior cortical and subcortical regions to regulate emotional experience. Their model allows for individual differences related to temperament, experience, and culture in any of these processing regions (e.g., enhanced amygdala reactivity) to affect function and presumably the development of psychopathology.

Tucker and Luu (2007) described the ACC as the crossroads of the dorsal and ventral networks for emotion regulation. Using electroencephalographic (EEG) event-related potential assessment of dorsal and ventral pathways in the ACC, Moadoab, Gilbert, Dishion and Tucker (2010) recently provided evidence for the theory that reduced dorsal control is related to undercontrolled symptoms (externalizing behaviors), whereas internalizing symptoms (overcontrol) were related to increased ventral control or overengagement of ventral limbic systems. This study is embedded in Eisenberg's notion of effortful control as a central part of the individual's capacity to regulate attention as well as emotion, extremes of which can presage internalizing or externalizing psychopathology (Eisenberg et al., 2007). A recent neuroimaging study examining activity in the subgenual portion of the ACC showed that adolescents who showed heightened activity in this region during an online peer-rejection experience were more prone to symptoms of depression 1 year later (Masten et al., 2011). Rothbart and Bates (2006) argued that individual differences in self-regulation (attention, emotion, and motor) are the result of an interaction between temperamental factors and effortful control. Yap et al. (2011) pursued this approach, integrating Eisenberg's notions of effortful control in a study of adolescents in interaction with their mothers. High negative emotionality and low effortful control showed the highest levels of depression. Adaptive and maladaptive responses to negative affect mediated the association between temperament and depressive symptoms.

Other researchers have studied differences in hemispheric frontal activity (Davidson, 2002). The right frontal hemisphere appears more concerned with negative emotion, where activation correlates with withdrawal, in contrast to the left frontal hemisphere, where activation correlates with approach behavior and seems more connected to positive feelings, though anger can also elicit right-hemisphere activation. Depressed and anxious individuals tend to exhibit more right frontal hemisphere activation than left. Children of depressed mothers show greater right than left activation. There is a degree of contralateral inhibition between the hemispheres, such that underactivity or development of one hemisphere releases the other hemisphere to be more dominant (Kinsbourne & Bemporad, 1984). The left prefrontal cortex has been conceptualized by Davidson (2002) to exert control over the amygdala, such that reductions in this control can lead to increases in emotional behavior. There is a history of left hemisphere cognitive deficits in abused populations (Teicher et al., 2003) and more recent evidence indicates that abnormalities in left-hemisphere function mediate the relationship between abuse and later psychopathology (Miskovic, Schmidt, Georgiades, Boyle, & MacMillan, 2010). It has been suggested that these deficits in left-hemisphere connectivity produced by abuse can impair emotion regulation development and thus lead to greater vulnerability to later psychopathology.

Hartley and Phelps (2010) described what is known about brain structures related to different strategies for managing fear. These regulatory strategies are considered basic aspects of developmental coping and therapeutic approaches. They comprise *extinction,* a gradual decrease in fear related to the uncoupling of a conditioned fear reaction from the original fear stimulus. They conclude that connections among the hippocampus, ventromedial prefrontal cortex (vmPFC), and amygdala are important in modulating fear expression during extinction. This pathway has been shown to have reduced functional connectivity in individuals who have reductions in serotonin transporter capacity and might provide an explanation for vulnerability to anxiety disorders. *Cognitive regulation strategies* (the use of thoughts to modify emotions) involve the same connection between the vmPFC and amygdala but also activate the dorsolateral prefrontal cortex (an area thought to be involved in interpretation of the event). *Active coping* involves problem solving (active learning to avoid a fearful event) as a way of reducing fear. In addition to several pathways within the amygdala, a connection between the amygdala and the striatum appears to reinforce the active-avoidance response. A newer area of research focuses on *reconsolidation,* the active disruption of the memory trace that maintains fear. Although initially researched in animals using medication to disrupt memory consolidation (intraamygdala injections), recent behavioral approaches (extinction training) have shown promise in preventing the return of conditioned fear. It is believed that this effect is due to blocking the connections within the amygdala between conditioned stimulus and unconditioned stimulus.

The brain structures related to social cognition (a complex set of abilities relevant to social interaction) and necessarily relevant to emotion regulation are beginning to be understood. A recent review by Pelphrey and Carter (2008) suggests that the superior temporal sulcus (critical to understanding biological movement and therefore human intent) is part of a network comprising the amygdala, fusiform face area (face perception and recognition), extrastriate body area (visual perception of human bodies), and "mirror neuron system" (registration of another's movement and one's own movement) that connects with prefrontal areas to facilitate social development. Abnormalities in various aspects and interconnections within this system are thought to be involved in the social cognition deficits associated with autism.

Neurotransmitters are the chemical messengers that connect various parts of the brain. Dopamine, norepinephrine, and serotonin are the major neurotransmitters related to affectively meaningful activity. These neurotransmitters can be up or down regulated by a variety of events, and these changes can affect both development and function. A recent review by Mead, Beauchaine, and Shannon (2010) describes the ways in which early adversity can impact these various neurotransmitters and account for later behavioral and emotional difficulties.

GENETIC CONTRIBUTIONS

No studies specifically address the genetics of emotion regulation because of the complex nature of such a task. There are studies, however, that do address genetic vulnerability to disorders such as anxiety and depression. They have focused largely on the serotonin transporter gene and its variants (Hariri & Forbes, 2007).

Serotonin (HT) is an important neurotransmitter in the brain areas involved in emotional behavior. The serotonin transporter is responsible, among other things, for uptake of serotonin from the synaptic cleft. The gene regulating the serotonin transporter is referred to as 5-HTT. Genetic variants described as long (L) and short (S) alleles have been shown to have differing effects on the availability of serotonin and serotonin transmitters. Carriers of the short allele show greater reactivity of the amygdala to emotional stimuli. In addition, a longitudinal study of child development has shown greater vulnerability to stress in adolescence and adulthood in carriers of the short allele who suffered adverse events in early childhood (Caspi et al., 2003). Kochanska, Philibert, and Barry (2009) have also shown a gene-by-environment interaction with respect to the development of self-regulation, of which emotion regulation is considered a subcategory. These researchers followed children from late infancy to 36 months, examining the interaction among secure attachment, presence of the short allele (risk status), and self-regulation. They found that insecurely attached children with the short allele showed deficits in self-regulation, whereas securely attached children, regardless of risk status, performed similarly and better than their insecurely attached peers. Similarly, Zimmermann, Mohr, and Spangler (2009), in a study of gene–environment interaction in adolescents, showed more agreeable autonomy in short allele carriers who were securely attached and more hostile autonomy in insecurely attached dyads. These studies have led to theories about greater responsivity (plasticity) in both positive and negative ways connected with genetic variations (Ellis, Boyce, Belsky, Bakermans-Kranenburg, & van IJzendoorn, 2011). More recent, neuroimaging studies have shown that the role of the short allele in amygdala reactivity occurs because of differences in connectivity between limbic and cortical circuits, particularly connections between the anterior cingulate and amygdala. Hariri and Forbes (2007) provided an interesting discussion of the likely complex interaction of this system of emotion regulation with development.

Monoamine oxidase is an enzyme that breaks down catecholamines such as norepinephrine and dopamine. Evidence is accumulating that variations in the genetic control of this enzyme can have an effect on the development of psychopathology. Genetic variants that produce lower levels of the enzyme have been linked to externalizing disorders, whereas variants that increase activity of the enzyme (producing fewer neurotransmitters) are linked to internalizing disorders. Studies examining this association reveal a complicated relationship between early adversity and genotype, such that high levels of the enzyme predispose to major depression and low levels to antisocial personality disorder in the presence of early maltreatment. However, antisocial personality disorder and child maltreatment also predict major depression independently (Beach et al., 2010).

According to the "polyvagal theory" of Porges (2007), the vagal nerve, which controls heart rate, acts as a brake to allow efficient functioning of the organism during nonstressful situations. Removal of the brake when challenges arise allows the organism to respond as needed. This capacity to regulate response according to the situation contributes to greater flexibility and has been shown to relate to better emotion regulation (Propper et al., 2008). In a recent study, Propper et al. (2008) examined a possible dopamine genetic mechanism related to vagal function. The DRD2 gene has a "risk allele" that produces less dopamine and in this study presumably less efficient vagal function. They found an interaction between maternal sensitivity and the risk allele, in that maternal sensitivity appeared to buffer the negative impact of the reduced dopamine function in terms of reactivity of the vagal brake.

BIOLOGICAL CONTRIBUTIONS

Stress reactivity refers to the individual's ability to accommodate stress. It is mediated by the body's stress response system, which includes the hypothalamic–pituitary–adrenal axis (HPA), the sympathetic and parasympathetic nervous systems, and close connections with the limbic and frontal networks. Some individuals appear to be genetically predisposed to be more reactive, that is, to display a stronger and more prolonged response to stress. This propensity appears to be related to the development of anxiety and depression and can lead to withdrawal in new or unfamiliar situations, particularly in younger individuals. Stress reactivity can be up or down regulated by a variety of situations and rearing conditions. Evidence from animal studies shows a positive effect of nurturant caregiving behaviors, such as licking and grooming and skin-to-skin contact in rat pups, in reducing the physiological impacts of stressful events such as separations from the mother. Conversely, harsh, punitive, and neglectful caretaking environments appear to initially increase stress responsivity but with prolongation of the stressors can lead to hyporesponsiveness of the HPA system. Repetti, Taylor, and Saxe (2007) provided an excellent overview of the psychobiology of this system and its perturbations. They articulated a "risky families" model arguing that early adversity can set in motion a series of physiological and neuroendocrine disturbances that affect the development of social and emotional competence and that these early disruptions can have profound effects on later development. In addition to the more studied effects on the HPA axis, they noted changes in neurotransmitter (norepinephrine, serotonin, and dopamine) functioning and reductions in vagal tone. Vagal tone as indicated above (Porges, 2007) is an index of physiological regulatory capacity and appears to be related to emotion regulation, social competence, and temperament. A recent study of a longitudinal sample of children followed from late childhood into adolescence showed that improvements in vagal tone correlate with improved emotion regulation (Vasilev, Crowell, Beauchaine, Mead, & Gatzke-Kopp, 2009). Although more research is needed to confirm the Repetti model, these studies confirm what is often seen in children from "risky families": that is, disruptions of different neurobiological systems appear to interfere with optimal development of regulatory functions in a number of domains.

Feldman (2007b), a researcher of infants, has been studying "synchrony" between mother and child in the first year of life. By this, she refers to affect matching, vocalization, and visual gaze that develop a synchronous quality over time and with repetition, and, she argues, with evidence from her research and that of others, that it becomes a necessary input for development of the social brain. Citing many normative studies as well as studies of infant biological and maternal risk, she provides evidence that synchrony contributes to the development of self-regulation, symbol use, and empathy. There is evidence that synchrony is less than optimal in some preterm infants, especially those with very low birth weights and intrauterine growth retardation, in infants exposed to cocaine, in triplets and siblings of children with autism, in psychologically referred infants with feeding problems and those with withdrawal, and in dyads where the mother is depressed or anxious. She argues that these impairments in synchrony affect the infant's physiology in a way that contributes to difficulties in self-regulation and increased levels of negative affect. In a similar vein, in a longitudinal, 5-year study of high- and low-risk premature births, Feldman (2009) reports that measures of physiological regulation (sleep cyclicity and vagal tone) predict attention and emotion regulation in the second year, and they mediate executive function, self-restraint, and behavioral difficulties at age 5. Furthermore, vagal tone has a direct negative relationship with later behavioral problems. Feldman argues for the importance of a general concept of "regulation" that underlies many important aspects of development.

Prematurity, particularly very early and accompanied by some form of brain damage, has long been recognized as contributing to difficulties with regulation of attention and later increases in both externalizing and internalizing behavioral difficulties (Bhutta, Cleves, Casey, Cradock, & Anand, 2002). The processes by which these later difficulties arise have been less clear. A recent longitudinal study of very premature and extremely premature infants compared with full-term births followed up to age 4 showed delays in self-regulation (encompassing emotion regulation) in the extremely preterm compared with the full-term children from ages 2 to 4. These differences in self-regulation were most marked in infants who at birth had evidence of white matter abnormalities. There was also evidence that mothers of the extremely preterm group showed higher levels of insensitive and intrusive parenting that was also related to less optimal self-regulation (Clark, Woodward, Horwood, & Moor, 2008).

Sleep has long been understood as an important antidote to the stressors of the day. Until recently, however, there was little evidence of just how or why sleep might contribute to emotional well-being. van der Helm and Walker (2007) provided an interesting, albeit complicated, review of the evidence and a theory of how sleep "heals the soul." It appears that sleep reduces emotional reactivity and allows a rebalancing after stressful events. They also discussed the fact that shifts in sleep architecture and duration associated with illness, such as major depression and posttraumatic stress disorder (PTSD), can interfere with this restorative effect and actually increase negative emotionality.

PARENTING AND TRAUMA

Parents model expression of emotions and support the child's understanding and development of regulation strategies. In an optimal situation, parents can accept the child's positive and negative feelings, provide soothing when the child is distressed, and enjoy the child's exuberance. Ideally, they teach labels for feelings, support the child in learning to manage feelings by "using words instead of hands," and problem solve ways of dealing with conflict and frustration. They model positive management of their own feelings and avoid significant negative reactions to the child's behavior. Maternal sensitivity to infant distress has been shown to predict fewer behavioral problems and higher social competence at 36 months and in reactive infants to better emotion regulation (Leerkes, Blankson, & O'Brien, 2009).

Many parents have not developed comfort with expression of their own feelings and thus might have difficulty adequately supporting expression, particularly of negative affects, as their children develop. Bowlby's (1969) original formulation of the role of attachment included emotion regulation in his notion of an internal working model that creates expectancies of caregiver responsiveness in the infant. Bowlby assumed that sensitive caregivers acknowledge both positive and negative affects and support their children in learning how to manage these feelings. In contrast, he believed that less sensitive mothers, prone to avoidance or exaggeration of their own feelings, would convey to their children a biased message about management of feelings. Goldberg, MacKay-Soroka, and Rochester (1994), in a pilot study, tested out Bowlby's hypothesis by observing parents' reactions to children's emotional displays. They were able to support his original theory, showing that mothers in securely attached dyads reacted supportively to both positive and negative affects in their children, whereas mothers in avoidantly attached dyads tended to ignore their children's negative feelings but did respond to their positive feelings. In contrast, mothers in ambivalent/resistantly attached dyads became overfocused on the child's negative displays and seemed otherwise inattentive to the child's positive affects. Although there has been little systematic study of this in disorganized/disoriented dyads, one can presume that the mother's frightened and frightening behaviors would interfere with the child's comfort in expressing affect, most likely creating inner confusion about feelings.

Many parents who perceive their young children as challenging find themselves raising their voices to get their children's attention. This often occurs in the context of their own frustration at the child's noncompliance. This transactional process can interfere with the child's learning about feelings in many ways. With escalation and increased anger on both sides, children can learn that yelling (or sometimes hitting) is a way of managing anger, but they can also learn not to express their anger for fear of inciting more parental anger or being abandoned because of their anger. There is an extensive literature about the negative effects of high levels of expressed emotion (EE) in various forms of psychopathology and in interfering with later adjustment when patients return to environments with high levels of EE (Silk et al., 2009). Some individuals are more vulnerable to distress related to EE or conflict—presumably the anxiety engendered by such an environment makes it difficult to find ways to regulate feelings comfortably (Denham et al., 2007). Moore (2009) recently examined the impact of exposure to anger on an infant's (6 months old) and the mother's vagal reactivity and showed an increase in the mother's reactivity that persisted after the exposure. She suggested that anger can alter the flexibility of the vagal response and interfere with the mother's capacity to adequately support her infant's development of emotion regulation. These interactions and transactions between parent and child can differ according to cultural values related to expression of emotion (Cole & Tan, 2007; Saarni, 2000; Supplee, Skuban, Shaw, & Prout, 2009).

Trauma, both in a caregiver's past and in a present context, can disrupt a child's learning about feelings. Caregivers who experienced trauma as they were growing up but have not been able to address the psychological impacts of that trauma on their own capacity to manage feelings (often referred to as unresolved) can experience dissociative episodes and/or flashbacks, sometimes triggered by their child's behavior or other experiences when the child is present. Disorganized/disoriented attachment relationships are seen as developing in the context of unresolved traumas that cause the parent to vacillate between "frightening" and "frightened" behaviors (sometimes related to dissociative episodes or flashbacks; Liotti, 1997; Main, 1997). These experiences can prevent the caregiver from being able to support the child's understanding and regulation of feelings and leave the child confused about her own and her parent's reaction in an emotional context. The child might react with anger and/or anxiety but not understand what has happened to generate these feelings or what to do in the future. Children in these situations, one can presume, will be more vulnerable to later difficulties with emotion regulation. This might be the reason why children with disorganized/disoriented attachment relationships are more prone to both internalizing and externalizing psychopathology as they mature.

Present *traumas and losses* (domestic violence, separations, and accidents), *adverse social situations*, as well as *maternal mental illness* can affect the caregiver's emotional availability and capacity to support the child's distress. This can cause children to act out feelings to engage a preoccupied parent and/or hide feelings for fear of worrying a distressed parent. In either scenario, the effects can be long-lived. The child can continue to use these strategies to engage the parents, or the acting-out behavior can lead to a negative cascade of transactions between parent and child. Relationship difficulties emerge from such transactional difficulties and increase negative perceptions between parent and child and can further promote maladaptive emotion regulation approaches. *Maternal depression* has long been observed to produce increased levels of negative affect and decreased levels of positive affect in exposed offspring (Seifer & Dickstein, 2000). The underlying mechanism is not clear, but recent research using the still-face paradigm suggests early differences in emotion-regulation strategies in infants of depressed mothers (Manian & Borenstein, 2009).

Children who have been *abused or maltreated* display difficulties with emotion regulation. Shields and Cicchetti (1998) demonstrated higher levels of aggression, particularly reactive aggression, in abused children as well as attention deficits, emotion dysregulation, affective lability/negativity, and socially inappropriate expression of feelings. They showed that the dysregulation of emotions fostered by difficulties with attention provided the mechanism that led to reactive aggression. Shipman and Zeman (2001) examined child and maternal perceptions of dealing with feelings, comparing maltreated and nonmaltreated children aged 6 to 12. Maltreated children reported expecting less support from their mothers around their feelings and were less likely to display their feelings. They also acknowledged less effective strategies for coping with emotions than their nonmaltreated peers. Maltreating mothers reported less understanding of their children's expression of feelings and less effective approaches for helping their children cope with difficult feelings.

TYPICAL DEVELOPMENT

Infants enter the world with varying levels of capacity to deal with situations that make them feel comfortable or uncomfortable (Feldman, 2007b, 2009). Their response to smiling faces is prewired but becomes an important part of early social learning. The parent who understands the language of smiling creates the beginning of social awareness and control as he smiles and coos in response to the infant and stops when the infant turns away. This turning away is an early form of regulatory control of stimulation and allows the infant to rebalance and return, when ready, for more. Infants have a variety of other regulatory strategies, such as sucking and squirming, that allow them to moderate input but also communicate their needs. As infants develop, they move from these more primitive strategies for control of affect to language-based approaches (Kopp, 1989). Emotion regulation, in sensitive dyads, is initially provided by the caregiver who responds to the infant's distress with soothing strategies such as rocking and cooing. Warm, sensitive parents, comfortable with their own feelings, can help the toddler, with the development of language, to understand her feelings and the situations that can evoke such feelings (Gondoli & Braungart-Rieker, 1998). Dunn et al. (1991) showed that these early conversations between parents and child about affectively charged situations are instrumental in her understanding and regulation of emotions. Dunn and coworkers showed that, as the child is able to engage with peers in imaginative play, conversations occur between peers about feelings and how they are managed that predict later social and emotional competence.

As with all the dimensions of development discussed in this book, emotion regulation develops gradually and, as outlined previously, is significantly influenced by the child's biology and the parenting that the child receives. The development of emotion regulation in young children from infancy to age 6 shows that while the infant has little ability to soothe himself and co-regulation by a caregiver is crucial by 4 or 5, preschoolers have fewer fluctuations in emotions and usually have developed a number of strategies to regulate their emotions themselves. Much less is known about the normal development of emotion regulation as children mature although certain characteristics of the child and various events can at least temporarily disrupt this process. This can include the birth of a sibling, a divorce, loss of a caregiver, and the onset of puberty. When disrupting events occur, children may experience regressions and capacities already gained may be disrupted.

In Table 6.1, the typical development of emotion regulation is outlined and the parenting strategies that can promote it are described. As noted, these strategies differ dramatically from birth to early adolescence.

There is an interesting discussion emerging in the literature about the role of attention in learning about and managing emotions. There is evidence that children who can direct their attention toward and away from situations flexibly become better able to manage their feelings flexibly. Because there is also evidence that feeling states can interfere with attention control, there is some theoretical interest in whether adaptive emotion regulation can facilitate development of attention. This becomes important in trying to prepare children for school entry, where good attention predicts better academic performance (and better social skills and behavioral regulation). As indicated earlier, the mediators and moderators of this complicated developmental set of trajectories are not yet clearly defined, and it is likely that there is a facilitation of social/emotional development through attention development and vice versa (Carlson & Wang, 2007; Trentacosta, Izard, Mostow, & Fine, 2006). Furthermore, Feldman's (2009) work on the follow-up of high- and low-risk premature infants provides evidence for the interaction of emotion and attention regulation in development.

Lazarus and Folkman (1984) described two opposing strategies for managing feelings: problem focused and emotion focused. Generally, problem-focused coping attempts to relieve negative affects required to change the situation causing the distress or changing one's perception of the situation so that the affect is more manageable. In contrast, emotion-focused strategies are deployed when resolving a problem seems less feasible or the individual does not attempt to resolve it. Various forms of emotion-focused coping have been defined, such as suppression (active efforts to forget or ignore the feeling) and repression (a subconscious or unconscious process that causes the affects to be less available to conscious processing). Emotion-focused approaches are seen as working less well, especially when the individual experiences significant emotional stress.

Table 6.1 *Typical Development of Emotion Regulation*

Age	Development of Emotion Regulation	Caregiving
Birth to 12 months	▪ Emotional reactions are very global and display generalized distress ▪ Most emotions can be displayed by 12 months, including happiness, disgust, fear, and anger ▪ Can suck on thumb or look at object to self-soothe and calm down ▪ May look away if becomes overaroused in interactions ▪ Fear of heights emerges at 7 months and separation anxiety by 8 to 12 months ▪ Positive emotions more common from 7 months on when infant can laugh	▪ Needs regulation by caregiver using touch, holding, and rocking ▪ Face-to-face interactions are crucial with caregiver attuned and in synchrony with the infant ▪ Caregiver can use voice to help calm infant (e.g., use of parentese) ▪ Calming of the infant when he is upset is crucial so he does not become chronically hyperaroused ▪ Supports child to settle into a predictable eating and sleeping routine ▪ Structures the environment so that infant is not overwhelmed by too much stimulation
12 to 24 months	▪ Increase in emotions that are experienced with jealousy and guilt now included ▪ Self-conscious emotions (e.g., shame, pride, and embarrassment) are possible by 18–24 months ▪ Uses social referencing or looking at parents' facial expression to get clues on how to respond to situations ▪ From about 12 to 18 months child often shows a predominance of elation ▪ From about 18 months on increase in tantrums and other angry responses is common ▪ May also be an increase in jealousy toward siblings ▪ If suffers a loss of someone close may see increase in fear reactions, especially separation anxiety, and depression	▪ As child is looking toward parent's facial expression for guidance, encourages exploration when appropriate ▪ Responds to child's interest in sharing an experience and need for special assistance ▪ Continues to provide attunement and synchrony in interactions ▪ Positive encouragement of the child's efforts ▪ Provides child with transitional object to calm down and helps her fall asleep at night ▪ Responds to tantrums or difficulty separating with calmness while setting limits and without shaming the child

24 to 36 months	■ Tantrums and aggression are often at their height in second year ■ Child learns to talk about emotions and what caused them ■ Able to solicit help from caregivers when comes up against a problem that cannot be solved ■ Pretend play can be used to play out difficult feelings ■ Fears are common and may have difficulty with falling asleep and with nightmares ■ Toward third birthday, tantrums beginning to reduce and to be able to recover from them more quickly ■ Cannot conceive of mixed emotions with "splitting" predominant and sees others as all "good" or "bad"	■ Encourages child's ability for pretend play and joins child in interactive play ■ Talks to child about emotions displayed in imaginative play or in reality ■ When child really gets upset and aggressive, disciplines the child but is sure to "repair the relationship" ■ Is available and provides "teaching on the fly" as needed ■ Makes sure the environment is as free from conflict as possible ■ When conflict does occur models conflict resolution and supports the child to resolve conflict with others ■ Provides some fun and cooperative times so child does not get overwhelmed with negativity
3 to 6 years	■ More aware of situations that elicit pride, worry, jealousy, or shame and can talk about the feelings ■ Can avoid the situations better and not get triggered by them as much ■ Becomes capable of a theory-of-mind by 5–6 years and shows perspective taking and empathy ■ Capable of feeling guilt ■ Understands the rules and follows them most of the time so emotions less intense ■ Starts school as learns to hold back angry feelings in order to fit in the classroom and with peers ■ Can negotiate conflicts with some assistance ■ Can now display an emotion that is not predominant (e.g., smile when receives a gift that is not the one she wanted) ■ Emotion and cognition are well integrated and are expressed in an organized way ■ Increasing capacity to use distraction, focusing attention, self-talk and perspective-taking to self-calm and get through difficult situations	■ As child is now able to feel shame makes sure disciplines without the child feeling inadequate or "bad" about himself ■ Noticing the child's emotions and using "emotion coaching" and acknowledges emotions and does not dismiss them ■ Continues to discuss emotions with the child and how he relates to the world ■ Has discipline in place that child responds to 65% of the time ■ Makes sure no one in the family is put down verbally and explains how hurtful this can be ■ Keeps stimulation to a level that the child can tolerate and is not overaroused by it ■ Begins to teach the child ways to deal with uncomfortable emotions by using deep breathing and self-talk. ■ Talks about mixed emotions so child learns to understand them and distinguish between them ■ Praises child for efforts toward containing emotions ■ May need to scaffold homework so it gets done

(continued)

Table 6.1 *Typical Development of Emotion Regulation (continued)*

Age	Development of Emotion Regulation	Caregiving
7 to 10 years	▪ Child is generally calmer and is more serious about schoolwork ▪ Will think things through and as a consequence is less impulsive ▪ Uses logical thinking and conscious control of arousal to control emotions ▪ Feels guilt if hurts someone's feelings ▪ Can manage interactions with peers for the most part without becoming angry	▪ Continues to support the child when he is upset about something and may help her to problem solve it ▪ Encourages opportunities for the family to come together to share and talk about what is going on in their lives ▪ Talks to child if he loses control with someone and becomes verbally or physically aggressive and explains about the feelings of the other person ▪ Listens to child if he is upset about something and helps him problem solve what to do about it
11 to 13 years	▪ Emotions are very up and down and child may have periods of intense moodiness ▪ Mood swings may be quite extreme due to hormonal changes that are occurring ▪ Most children will now have a number of defenses and can use them to manage emotions such as repression and sublimation into hobbies and new activities ▪ If involved in drugs, emotions may be very intense or the child may be more nonmotivated than previously ▪ Anxiety generally lessens although child may worry about peer relationships and grades ▪ May worry about the future if not doing well or things are uncertain at home ▪ May be angry toward parents a lot of the time because they believe they do not have enough freedom and may argue to have more	▪ Although children are beginning to withdraw from the family, parents still need to monitor the child and enforce rules and limits ▪ Rules need to be adjusted with young person's input ▪ Different parenting is needed at this time as children often reject suggestions in favor of peer group's way of seeing things ▪ Tries to be available to child if he seems upset and offers support ▪ Looks out for any signs the child is feeling out of control with her world and seeks help for her if necessary ▪ Talks to child if he seems to be being bullied or is bullying as both are very prevalent at this age ▪ Monitors use of the Internet to see he is not playing violent games or is at risk for being on dangerous sites ▪ Sensitive attunement to the child's fears and anxieties such as with peer rejection and academic achievement when child is ready to talk ▪ It is important for caregivers to be supportive of and attune to the child's positive emotions and enthusiasm when the child speaks about her interests

THE CONTRIBUTORS TO THE DEVELOPMENT OF EMOTION REGULATION

It has been assumed that language competence is important for the development of more mature emotion-regulation strategies, such as problem solving. Fujiki, Brinton, and Clarke (2002) reported less effective emotion-regulation strategies in a population of children with specific language impairment in contrast to typically developing peers. This difficulty with the development of emotion-regulation approaches can contribute to the increase of psychiatric difficulties in this population. Gumora and Arsenio (2002) reported a significant association between emotion-regulation ability, affective disposition, and academic affect on academic performance in a population of students in Grades 6 to 8. A recent study examining maternal response to positive affect in early adolescents suggested that sensitive attunement to affect still matters. Yap, Allen, and Ladouceur (2008) reported that maternal dampening of adolescent positive affect increases emotional dysregulation, which in turn mediates depressive symptoms. Clearly, as the brain matures, and as pruning occurs in the context of learning, certain patterns are likely to become more fixed. Disruptions in stress reactivity that are part of pubertal changes will impact the intensity of feelings and possibly their expression (see Dahl & Gunnar, 2009; Spear, 2009). Opportunities to experiment with novel ways of managing feelings (substance use, dress, and music) during this period will also impact the adolescent's skills in managing feelings.

ASSESSMENT OF EMOTION REGULATION

Most clinicians rely on interview material and questions directed at the parents and child with respect to their ability to use words to label feelings and whether the child can talk about his feelings. Questions about how comfortable the parents are discussing their feelings and whether they talk about feelings with their child, when affectively salient events are happening, can provide a perspective on the child's knowledge of emotions and capacity to express his feelings. If the child seldom lets the family know how he is feeling, except when it is obvious that he is angry, gentle questions about why he does not tell his parents can be productive. Some children will deny anger in situations that typically elicit anger, and one then supposes that there is a barrier to open expression of anger. Asking whether the child is afraid that her parent might become angry if she reveals that she is upset is logical as many inhibited or internalizing children are fearful of alienating their parents further. This can lead to a discussion with the family about how parents respond when upset or stressed, and it might become obvious that the intensity of their response would intimidate the child's open discussion of feelings.

Narrative approaches such as the *MacArthur Story Stem* test use affectively salient stories that require the child to complete the stem in terms of how the story will end. Although developed by Bretherton, Ridgeway, and Cassidy (1990) for assessment of attachment, such narrative approaches can reveal how a child deals with a trigger that should stir up feelings. They are scored for coherence, thematic content, and child's behavior (Oppenheim, 2006).

A number of questionnaires have been developed to assess the child's emotional knowledge and regulation. They are not widely used clinically but have been tested in research studies looking at the predictive value of emotion awareness, expression, and regulation to later outcomes such as social competence and psychopathology.

The *Emotion Regulation Checklist* (ERC; Shields & Cicchetti, 1998) is a 24-item scale filled out by adults, familiar with the child, about her capacity to label and manage positive and negative emotions. It includes items related to the intensity of her reactions, affective lability, flexibility, and situational appropriateness of emotional expression. Items are rated on a 4-point Likert scale as to how characteristic they are of the child, from 1 (almost always) to 4 (never). In the study previously indicated on reactive aggression, the children ranged in age from 6 to 12 years old.

The *Emotion Awareness Questionnaire* (Rieffe, Oosterveld, Miers, Terwogt, & Ly, 2008) is a 30-item scale, recently revised, with items that monitor feelings, ability to differentiate feelings, and awareness of causes of emotions. In addition, it explores how the individual values emotional expressiveness. This scale was tested on older children and adolescents and showed good psychometric properties, criterion validity with another measure of emotional intelligence for adolescents, and concurrent validity with scales tapping anxiety symptoms.

The *Children's Emotion Management Scale* (CEMS) is a 23-item scale for children 6 to 12 years of age comprised of three factors: suppression or hiding of feelings, dysregulated expression, and coping with feelings. Internal consistency and construct validity appear to be adequate. The same group has developed the *Emotion Management Interview—Child* version (for elementary school-age children), consisting of narrative vignettes used to elicit the child's description of his coping behaviors and expectations about his mother's responses to his feelings. The *Emotion Management Interview—Mother* version uses the same vignettes and seeks to understand the mother's beliefs about the appropriateness of her child's display of feelings and how the mother sees herself as assisting the child in managing feelings. Information on these three instruments is available in Shipman and Zeman (2001).

Fabes, Poulin, Eisenberg, and Madden-Derdich (2002) developed the *Coping with Children's Negative Emotions Scale* (CCNES). Parents are presented with 12 scenarios and asked to respond as they normally would. Their responses are grouped according to whether they are problem focused, emotion focused, encouraging, minimizing, punitive, or distress related. The Scale has been used in research to evaluate change in parent behavior in a program focusing on teaching parents to use positive strategies in supporting their child's development of emotional competence (Havighurst, Harley, & Prior, 2004).

For older children, questionnaires such as the *Dysfunctional Attitudes Test* have been adapted from adult measures. These measures have been developed within a CBT framework and are generally not used for younger children. From this perspective, neurobiological approaches are being developed to assess components of emotion regulation. Specifically, a component of the EEG event-related potential, the late-positive potential, does appear to measure a facet of emotion regulation and reappraisal, in both adults and children, and correlate with internalizing symptoms (Dennis & Hajcak, 2009).

COMMON DIFFICULTIES

Children who are poorly regulated physiologically, emotionally intense, or display high levels of negativity from a young age present their caregivers with more challenges (Bates & Petit, 2007; Feldman, 2007a). Depending on the maturity of the caregiver, past parenting, trauma history, and social support, many caregivers will have difficulty responding to these challenges in an adaptive fashion. This can lead to negative parental reactions such as anger, intrusiveness, lack of responsivity, or neglect and further increase the child's negativity or emotional distress (Denham et al., 2007; Feldman, 2007a). Further attachment insecurity is more likely in very irritable/difficult infants, and this can compound the young child's learning ways to manage her feelings comfortably. Providing support and scaffolding to learn about feelings and how to manage them becomes a more complicated task in these situations, leaving children more likely to overreact or underreact when faced with emotionally laden situations (Bernier, Carlson, & Whipple, 2010). The parent–child relationship is often filled with tension as each anticipates the other's negative response. In this scenario, oppositional defiant behavior is common, as are early anxiety manifestations such as separation anxiety disorders.

Children with significant internalizing behavior (overcontrolled) are often withholding and oppositional with their families but less so in situations such as among peers at school. Such children might be perceived as shy but socially adept with a small group of friends. Depending on the extent of their distress, however, they can develop school refusal and difficulty with social events or anything unfamiliar. They can experience periods of more overt and intense anxiety often related to beginning school or losses or stresses within the family. If the conflict in their relationships becomes exacerbated, then their anxiety, anger, and low self-esteem escalate. Often it is difficult for these children to express how they are feeling, and parents describe them as not talking about their feelings. Parents are sometimes surprised to find how upset they feel as sometimes their behavior is interpreted as manipulative. With little intervention, this pattern of not expressing feelings can also lead to denial of feelings, particularly anger, and vulnerability to depression, obsessive-compulsive disorder (OCD), and panic disorders. Among other factors, maternal negativity and overprotection have been found to predict later anxiety in a follow-up study of preschoolers (Edwards, Rapee, & Kennedy, 2010). This strongly suggests that relationship difficulties contribute to internalizing disorders. A recent study of psychiatrically hospitalized adolescents showed significant difficulties with emotional awareness and acceptance in adolescents who had primarily internalizing difficulties as opposed to externalizing symptoms. Lack of emotional control was related to severity of both internalizing and externalizing symptoms. Perceived relational aggression was related to poorer emotion regulation in both groups (Adrian et al., 2009).

Children with externalizing behaviors, exhibited outside their families (undercontrolled), are typically seen as oppositional and defiant, often with relationship problems with peers and teachers. Many of these children also suffer from low self-esteem related to their sense that people important to them—parents, peers, and teachers—are often angry with them. They are regularly perceived as angry. Some children say that they feel angry but often say they are sad. They might also say that they feel sad and angry when their parents are angry with them. Parents can be confused at the child's "hurt," interpreting his oppositional and defiant stance as "not caring." Without intervention, such children can continue to act out their anger with peers and others, developing an attributional belief that others are always against them and becoming more angry and hurt at the ongoing rejection. This can lead to association with deviant peers who share the same anger and hurt and might encourage more acting out in the community. Depressive feelings are common as this trajectory moves forward. A subpopulation of children within the conduct disorder (CD) spectrum is labeled as "callous/unemotional" (C/U). This trait has been linked to later "psychopathy" but also has some resemblance to individuals within the autism spectrum who are higher functioning. In contrast to the individuals described above who feel some remorse over their aggressive behavior toward others, C/U individuals appear to be devoid of feelings and especially empathy toward others. This lack of empathy might relate to continuing violent behavior as these individuals mature, in contrast to an overall reduction in violent or aggressive behavior over time for most individuals (see Calkins & Keane, 2009; Frick & Viding, 2009).

COMMON DISORDERS

Internalizing symptoms are associated with the spectrum of anxiety and depressive disorders. In children, separation anxiety, social phobia, OCD, and depression are commonly seen. When children qualify for a diagnosis, there is interference in functioning, and this aspect is extremely important as it tends to predict later difficulties even when symptom presentation might be below the threshold for making a diagnosis (Angold, Costello, Farmer, Burns, & Erkanli, 1996).

Undercontrolled expression of feelings, typically referred to as externalizing symptoms, leads to oppositional defiant disorders and eventually CD. Oppositional defiant behavior is not uncommon in young children but tends to lessen as they mature. Children with ADHD, especially the mixed type in which there is significant impulsivity, are more prone to the development of oppositional defiant behavior. Clinics treating children with disruptive behavior problems regularly see comorbid presentations of ADHD with ODD, ADHD with CD, but also ADHD with a variety of anxiety disorders and depression. Tic disorders are also common in children with ADHD and some or all of these comorbid conditions. Increasingly, we are aware that a number of children initially presenting with ADHD, ODD, and some anxiety might be better understood as being in the autism spectrum, high functioning.

INTERVENTIONS

In clinical practice, the focus of the intervention must follow the results of the assessment of the child and family. In these situations, teaching the child about feelings, labels, bodily reactions, contexts for the development of feelings, how individuals can react differently to the same situation depending on their experience or interpretation, how to deal with feelings in adaptive ways, and how to problem solve with others in situations of conflict are now part of routine clinical practice. Similarly, teaching parents about children's feelings and how to support children in terms of regulating and problem solving is a fairly central part of good practice. Many tools, including books and videos, can be used to do this work. Increasingly, these concepts are incorporated into a variety of programs used in early childhood intervention.

As part of the Incredible Years programs, the Dinosaur program was developed specifically to teach young children about feelings and how to problem solve and regulate their feelings when distressed. It has been used in Head Start programs and schools and has demonstrated efficacy in enhancing problem-solving knowledge and reducing negative behaviors. The material can be used to work with children individually and in groups in clinical settings and as a preventive intervention. Generally, in clinical settings, the child program is run alongside the parenting program. Information about this program, including references, is available at www.incredibleyears.com.

The PATH (Promoting Alternative Thinking) program developed by Greenberg, Kusche, Cook, and Quamma (1995) has been well evaluated in elementary school–age children and recently tested in a preschool version in Head Start programs (Domitrovich, Cortes, & Greenberg, 2007). This is a universal program designed to improve children's social competence and reduce problem behaviors. In a randomized, controlled trial of 3- and 4-year-old children in Head Start, the children exposed to the PATH preschool program showed improved emotional knowledge skills and were judged by parents and teachers to be more socially competent than nonexposed peers.

Other programs that have been evaluated include Izard's Emotion Course, designed to be used in Head Start settings. Pilot work has demonstrated improvements in emotional knowledge and reduced negative emotional expression compared with peers not exposed to the program (Izard, Trentacosta, King, & Mostow, 2004).

In contrast to these programs, where the focus is on direct teaching of children, Havighurst and colleagues (2004) developed a six-session program directed at teaching parents how to support their young children's emotional competence. Following the program, parents reported that they were using more positive approaches to supporting their children's learning about feelings and that the children were displaying less problem behavior after the program. Although preliminary, these results are encouraging and suggest that involving parents as well as children in learning about feelings is important.

Interest in a direct focus on supporting emotion regulation in depression has led to the modification of Parent–Child Interaction Therapy (PCIT; Zisser & Eyberg, 2010) with the addition of a module on emotional development, called PCIT-ED, currently being tested on depressed preschoolers. This novel approach, if effective, will add an important intervention component. Similarly, Contextual Emotion Regulation Therapy (CERT), developed by Kovacs et al. (2006), focuses on supporting adaptive emotion regulation strategies in children 7 to 12 years old with dysthymic disorder using parents as coaches. Although only pilot tested, it does appear very promising and acceptable. Child–parent psychotherapy is another intervention that focuses on supporting emotion regulation skills in preschoolers who have witnessed violence. It has shown persistence of initial therapeutic benefit 6 months after completion of a 1-year treatment program (Lieberman, Ghosh Ippen, & van Horn, 2006).

Treatment of anxiety disorders using CBT approaches is well established in adults and now in children and adolescents (Kendall, 2006; Manassis, 2008; see Manassis, 2009, for a guide for practitioners). This approach uses an emotion-regulation framework, emphasizing teaching about feelings and how to manage them adaptively. Kendall's Coping Cat program (Kendall, 2006; see www.workbookpublishing.com) was the initial standard and provided a framework from which others have drawn. Basically, children are taught about feelings, what causes them, where they are felt in the body, how thinking can affect how they feel, how to use more adaptive thoughts or ways of talking to themselves to feel better, how to use breathing and relaxation techniques to calm themselves, and how to remind themselves that they can cope better. Descriptions of specific strategies for children, for example, tummy breathing, are available in all of the above references.

Barish (2009) recently incorporated an emotion-regulation framework into a dynamically oriented perspective that includes CBT, systems theory, and attachment. He emphasized the importance of empathy and the capacity to repair emotional injuries to promote healthy growth and development in working with children. This book provides invaluable ways of integrating different perspectives into therapeutic work with children.

Medication can be used to support better emotion regulation. There are no direct indications for the use of medication, so it is used "off label." Yet there are a number of situations in which marked emotional dyscontrol becomes sufficiently problematic so that the use of medication is justified. Three main classes are used and are reasonably effective. The first class is stimulant medication (various formularies of dexedrine or methamphetamine). Stimulants can be used when there is an element of impulsivity that contributes to the child's outbursts. Often reducing the impulsiveness that can interfere with the child's efforts at emotion regulation is productive. In such cases, medication is used as is for the treatment of ADHD, and issues about monitoring for therapeutic benefit versus side effects are the same.

The second class is second-generation antipsychotics such as risperidone and quetiapine. These medications are usually effective in reducing aggression but have side effects. They cause some sedation and are best used at bedtime if possible. In addition, they can lead to weight gain and a metabolic syndrome, which can predispose one to diabetes and obesity (see Correll & Carlson, 2006). They should be used at the lowest effective dose (usually beginning at 0.25 mg at bedtime) and with a plan to discontinue use when the child's emotional coping strategies have improved.

The third class of drugs is comprised of the antidepressants, mainly selective serotonergic reuptake inhibitors (SSRIs). They can reduce anxiety and are the main medical treatment for depression. However, they can be used in some children when anxiety, anger, or irritability interferes with their progress or learning coping strategies. Caution is needed if there is a family history of bipolar illness as very occasionally a manic episode can be provoked by antidepressants.

Generally, medication should not be considered the main form of treatment for children with problems with emotion regulation but can be a helpful adjunct when it is difficult to get an effective program in place or a child's placement is threatened by her behavior (see Gleason et al., 2007, for guidelines for the use of psychotropic medication in very young children).

In conclusion, effective emotion regulation is essential to healthy psychological growth and development. The path to developing skills in labeling and understanding feelings, being emotionally aware and capable of managing emotions flexibly and effectively, is not an easy one for many children, in some instances related to constitutional/biological factors, in other cases to psychosocial factors, and often to interactions among these factors. We know a great deal more about the brain basis for emotional behavior, and this knowledge will guide us in future studies of how best to support children's development in this important area.

See Table 6.2 for details of various websites that offer related information.

Table 6.2 *Websites*

Website	Information on Website
www.developingchild.harvard.edu	A number of articles that "translate science into policy." Articles on contributors to problems with emotion regulation.
www.gottman.com/parenting/research-on-parenting	Website of Gottman Relationship Institute that includes research on parenting and the five elements of emotion coaching.
www.childtrends.org/?programs=cognitive-behavioral-therapy-for-anxiety-disorders	Describes the success of a cognitive-behavioral therapy (CBT) program conducted by Dr. K. Manassis and other researchers with children diagnosed with anxiety disorder.
www.pathstraining.com/main/curriculum	Website for the Promoting Alternative THinking (PATH) program that teaches children ways to self-regulate their emotions and effective problem-solving strategies.
http://terpconnect.umd.edu/~sporges/polyvag.htm	Access to article by Porges (1995) on theory of his polyvagal theory.
www.ncbi.nlm.nih.gov/pmc/articles/PMC2890316	Articles on the role of sleep in emotional brain processing.
http://incredibleyears.com/programs/parent	Information on the Incredible Years Parenting program developed by Carolyn Webster-Stratton. Includes information on the Dinosaur Program for preschool and primary grade school children.
www.psych.udel.edu/index.php/news/detail/Izard-Leads-team-updating-training-program-to-help-at-risk-kid	Website describing Dr. Carroll Izard's "Emotion Course" used to help at-risk children. It describes the use of puppets and storytelling to help Head Start children learn from emotional experience and gain emotional knowledge. The Teacher's Manual describes the program.
www.tuningintokids.org.au	Website describes a program "Tuning in to Kids," developed to help parents develop emotional intelligence in their children.
www.anxietytreatmentnyc.org/copingcat.html	Website of the Columbia University Clinic for Anxiety and Related Disorders. Describes a cognitive behavioral program called the "Coping Cat Program," a group program to supplement the individual program being provided for children and adolescents.
http://pcit.phhp.ufl.edu	Website for PCIT that describes the program and identifies training opportunities to learn how to use the program.

7

Behavior Regulation and the Development of a Conscience

Problems with behavior regulation in children are among the most common and costly disorders confronting treatment systems and often the most difficult to treat effectively. They extract high personal and social costs, yet many questions about their origins and the best approaches for their prevention and treatment remain. Research on aggression and antisocial behavior in children is not new. The disciplines of psychology, psychiatry, pediatrics, criminal justice, and sociology have examined these problems in childhood over the past 80 years. More recent investigation into theories of neurobiology, developmental psychopathology, and integrated biosocial approaches have considered biological and environmental factors and their interaction in trying to better understand antisocial behavior. A common finding has been that aggression and antisocial behavior are heterogeneous and thus need different treatment approaches.

Case Study: Maggie

Maggie was referred when she was 11 years old for sexual acting out and aggression. Her mother, Maureen, admitted that during her pregnancy she was heavily involved in drugs, smoked, and drank alcohol. The birth was normal, though Maggie showed signs of addiction and was kept in the hospital to recover from the effects of the drugs that her mother had taken during the pregnancy. After the birth, Maureen separated from Maggie's father, and there were many men in and out of the house. Also, Maureen lived a chaotic life and was often under the effects of drugs for days on end and consequently not physically or psychologically available to her daughter. Maggie had significant problems from 4 years of age, when she started school. Some of the problems had to do with schoolwork, whereas others were related to oppositional behavior, sexual acting out, and aggression. She was rejected and bullied by a number of the children in her class since she often came to school dirty, hungry, and poorly clothed. There was also suspicion that Maggie had been sexually abused by one of the men who frequented her mother's house. However, this was not reported and had not been proved. Her behavior escalated, and she started to refuse to go to school or, if sent by her mother, would run away with some other girls. Concern was raised that she had joined a gang and might be living on the street. It was also believed that Maggie was stealing to buy food and possibly drugs, and concern was expressed by her school counselor about her safety. Maggie was diagnosed with conduct disorder (CD), though most of her acting out was indirect and covert, involving behaviors such as stealing and shoplifting. Maureen felt unable to discipline Maggie or stop her acting out, explaining that she had been very similar at the same age and was not worried about it.

RESEARCH ON AGGRESSIVE AND DISRUPTIVE BEHAVIOR

Violence and Crime

There is a growing body of research on the epidemiology of these disorders. Studies show that these problems are not rare, varying according to the sampling time frame used (Connor, 2002). In the United States, aggression and antisocial behavior in community samples have increased in both severity and frequency, making them a major public health concern. In a number of prevalence studies conducted in many countries, rates have varied from 0.9% to 20%. It is believed that criminal justice estimates of "index offences" and arrests for crimes such as homicide, rape, robbery, burglary, aggravated assault, larceny over $50, motor vehicle theft, and arson actually underestimate the true rates for youth under 18 (Connor, 2002). As a result, alternative methods of detecting child and adolescent offences have been developed. One is the "self-report delinquency" method, which asks young people, their parents, and their teachers about the youth's problem behaviors (Loeber, Green, Lahey, & Stouthamer-Loeber, 1991). These self-report studies of crime indicate a high incidence of undetected offences committed by young people, most of which are theft related (Rutter, Giller, & Hagell, 1998). The prevalence of aggression has been as high as 90% of children and adolescents treated in outpatient, inpatient, and residential programs. This population is consequently becoming a major challenge for pediatric mental health practitioners. A recent development in the United States has been the rise in violence and attacks on students in schools. In fact, many adolescents now report that aggression and violence in schools and neighborhoods are major concerns. The percentage of high school seniors who reported worrying "sometimes or often" about crime and violence is high: 79.4% in 1986, 90.1% in 1996, and 84.4% in 1998.

Aggressive and Antisocial Behavior

Over the past two decades, longitudinal and cross-sectional studies have demonstrated the continuity of aggressive and antisocial behavior from early childhood to adolescence (Tremblay, Masse, Perron, LeBlanc, Schwartzman, & Ledingham, 1992). Stability coefficients have varied from 0.33 to 0.53 (Broidy et al., 2003). Similar stabilities have been found for children referred to mental health centers. Other studies have found individual differences in the stability of these behaviors. Children with early-onset aggression, in the preschool years, are more likely to display high rates of aggression across time. On the other hand, for some children, aggressive and antisocial behavior is time limited and most common in adolescence as a result of peer influences.

Historically, research focused on direct forms of aggression, particularly physical aggression. However, in the 1980s and 1990s, a number of researchers began to focus on a wider range of aggressive behaviors, including more indirect or covert or relational aggression. This research has suggested that these different types of aggression can have different trajectories and underlying contributors.

Few studies have examined aggressive, oppositional, and hyperactive behavior from the preschool period into the school-age period. One difficulty has been that diagnosis of disorders in the preschool period can be challenging due to rapid changes in organization of behavior and contact with the social world during this period (Wakschlag, Tolan, & Leventhal,

2010). In a review of studies of the early years, Campbell, Shaw, and Gilliom (2000) noted that continuity was most common in boys with multiple risk factors, including attention deficit/hyperactivity disorder (ADHD), high levels of negative parenting, and family stress.

Comorbidity Studies

Understanding the etiology of various behavior disorders is complex, and the diagnostic criteria in the *Diagnostic and Statistical Manual of Mental Disorders*, 5th edition (*DSM-5;* American Psychiatric Association [APA], 2013) do not adequately account for such complexities. Increasingly, it is understood that children with these disorders often have other mental health conditions or comorbidities. One disorder most likely to co-occur is ADHD, which increases the risk of poor peer relationships, delayed academic achievement, and violent and disruptive behavior (Babinski, Hartsough, & Lambert, 1999). Another common comorbidity is depression, increasingly studied in the past 20 years (Drabick, Gadow, & Sprafkin, 2006). In one study of children referred to a juvenile detention center for various legal offenses, 42% were found to be also suffering from depression (Pliszka, Sherman, Barrow, & Irick, 2000).

Important Contributors to Aggressive and Antisocial Behavior

The most influential theory regarding the role of parenting in the development of CD is the coercion model formulated by Patterson and associates (Patterson, 1982; Patterson, Reid, & Dishion, 1992). They identified a pattern of reciprocal negative parent–child interactions (named "coercive patterns") believed to reinforce and increase the child's negative behavior over time. The parents' behavior is seen as fluctuating between angry responding/withdrawing and giving in, so children learn to get what they want through their demanding (coercive) behaviors that wear parents down (Patterson, Forgatch, Yoerger, & Stoolmiller, 1998). However, the theory does not consider characteristics of the child in these interactions, focusing primarily on reactions of parents (Greene & Ablon, 2006).

Other theories have considered characteristics of the child that increase the likelihood of aggressive behavior. Dodge (1991) and Crick and Dodge (1994) researched children with reactive and proactive aggression and developed the social information theory that examines the social cognitive processing of children with oppositional defiant disorder (ODD). They developed a six-stage model and showed that aggressive children process social information differently than nonaggressive children and typically interpret other children's benign behavior as having "hostile intent." These distortions increase the likelihood that the child will behave aggressively.

Caspi and Moffitt (1995) emphasized a neurobiological approach to understanding aggressive and antisocial behavior. They considered variables such as prenatal development and exposure of the fetus to drugs and alcohol and deficits in language and executive functioning as key contributors. Their model also implied that both biological and environmental factors contribute to cognitive deficits that in turn can lead to CD.

Mitchell and Blair (2000) described the violence inhibition mechanism (VIM), a cognitive mechanism typically activated when a person sees nonverbal communications of distress in another person, causing the person to withdraw from the attack. Blair (1995) believed that, in the individual with psychopathic traits, the VIM is not activated because of a number of neurological and cognitive factors.

Other theorists have used research on causal modeling to describe the origins of an individual's difficulties to better understand the multiple determinants of aggressive and antisocial behavior and develop treatment strategies (Krol, Morton, & De Bruyn, 2004). This framework shows promise because it can result in the design of individualized treatment for children and adolescents with disruptive behavior disorders.

Subtypes of Aggressive and Antisocial Children

Because aggressive and antisocial behavior is so heterogeneous, attempts have been made to describe various subtypes. The purpose is to enhance communication across disciplines and lead to more specific types of treatment. Subtypes include overt and covert aggression, relational aggression, reactive and proactive aggression, and callous/unemotional (C/U) reactions or children with psychopathic traits.

Gender Differences

Much of the early research on antisocial behavior was on males, leaving the development of antisocial behavior in females less well understood. A recent review of 46 studies of antisocial behavior in females found a variety of trajectories similar to those found in males, including those that began early and had life-course persistence, those that were limited to childhood or adolescence, and those that began in adult years. Girls who showed early onset and adolescent antisocial behavior were at risk of adjustment problems in adulthood (Fontaine, Carbonneau, Vitario, Barker, & Tremblay, 2009). The paucity of studies on female aggression has been due to a focus on physical aggression. In the past two decades, there has been more interest in indirect and relational aggression, likely under recognized in early studies. Including these types of aggression shows an increase in aggressive and antisocial behavior in girls. This incidence can be as high as it is in boys as the children reach adolescence. As anticipated, indirect and relational aggression is more common and frequent in girls (Connor, 2002).

School Violence and Cyberbullying

Although bullying in schools and communities is not new, increasingly in the United States children are reporting concerns about violence in schools, and school authorities are having to monitor for weapons brought to school. More recently, cyberbullying (threatening comments over the Internet) has become a source of concern, with reports of suicide in a few targeted children (Hinduja & Patchin, 2009). Cyberbullying can include threats, sexual remarks, false statements, and ganging up on victims. It is believed to affect almost half of American teenagers and can result in stress, low self-esteem, and even suicide (Hinduja & Patchin, 2009; Ybarra, Mitchell, Wolak, & Finkelhor, 2006).

Intervention

There have been three major approaches to reducing antisocial behavior and violence among young people: the "get tough on crime" movement, proactive prevention, and comprehensive intervention.

The "get tough on crime" movement has been given prominence by politicians and law enforcement agencies particularly after public outcry over a serious crime or act of violence. Youth who commit acts of violence are seen as early starter criminals. Consequently, lengthy sentences and incarcerations are given to children who commit crime to deter other children from engaging in similar behaviors. In the United States as a result of this movement, it is becoming easier to transfer these children from juvenile court to adult court, where they are sentenced as adults. This trend is occurring even though there is no evidence of a resulting reduction in crime among children and adolescents (Connor, 2002).

Early-onset aggression places children at risk of a long-term trajectory of aggression, oppositional behavior, and criminal outcomes (Moffitt, Caspi, Harrington, & Milne, 2002; Rose, Rose, & Feldman, 1989). During the past two decades, there has been growing interest in using knowledge from developmental processes with the study of child psychopathology to prevent the child from having a long-term problem. Aggression usually reduces at about

3 years of age, so studying children with persisting tantrums and aggression can point to important determinants of these behaviors. It is important to intervene early with comprehensive programs focused on supporting parents and daycares to enhance children's language, compliance, cooperation, social skills, and positive emotionality to prevent conduct problems from developing (Speltz, 1990).

The third approach has been to focus treatment on the multiple risk factors affecting children with more severe and intransigent problems. Comprehensive intervention programs such as the Multimodal Treatment of ADHD (MTA) have been developed, implemented, and evaluated in an effort to focus on the risks that these children face. The program provided behavioral training sessions for children and families, school-focused interventions regarding child management, and aides in the classroom for 7- to 10-year-old children diagnosed with ADHD, combined type. The children attended an 8-week summer program that included training in social and recreational skills. They also received well-monitored medication supervised by a clinician. The treatment was compared with psychosocial interventions alone and in groups in the community. The combination and medication-alone groups were both more successful than the psychosocial interventions (MTA Cooperative Group, 1999a, 1999b).

DEFINITIONS OF DIFFICULTIES AND DISORDERS OF BEHAVIOR REGULATION

Multiple terms have been used to describe children with behavioral problems, and definitions have varied somewhat by the systems and disciplines that provide services for them, including schools, juvenile justice, and mental health services. Recently, various subtypes of aggression and oppositional behavior have been described and distinctions made between whether the aggression is adaptive or maladaptive.

General Definition

It has been hard to come up with one term that can describe the heterogeneous nature of children with aggressive, antisocial, and oppositional behavior. Bloomquist and Schnell (2002, pp. 3–4) used the term "aggressive conduct problem" (ACP), which "denotes children who manifest some form of early onset aggressive behavior and who also display, or are at risk for displaying, covert antisocial actions." Greene and Ablon (2006, p. 1) described these children as having "severe resistance to imposition of adult will and corresponding explosive outbursts." Another definition is disruptive behavior disorders, which include three separate but overlapping disorders: conduct disorder, oppositional defiant disorder, and attention deficit/hyperactivity disorder, with research verifying that they are independent of other disorders. Aggression can be adaptive when, for example, it is used to escape an abusive home situation, to retaliate to the violent bullying of peers, or to survive when living on the street. When it is more adaptive, it might not require mental health or other services. Aggression is seen as maladaptive when it causes negative consequences for the child carrying it out, other individuals, and the community (Connor, 2002). Also problematic is unregulated aggression that occurs as the result of disordered internal mechanisms such as hyperarousal of the central nervous system (CNS). Such aggression typically occurs across a number of settings; is unusual in terms of intensity, frequency, and duration; and can worsen over time.

Overt and Covert Aggression

Overt hostile behaviors are marked by aggression and include kicking, biting, hitting, getting into fights and bullying other children, and using various kinds of weapons to attack others. Covert or indirect hostile behaviors include stealing, fire setting, lying, vandalism, and shoplifting. Some researchers have used the term "covert" to refer to hostile acts that focus on harming another child's social relationships or not allowing that child to be included in a peer group (Bjorkquist, Osterman, & Kaukialnen, 1992). The relationship between overt and covert aggression has been verified in a number of studies by using factor analysis or multidimensional scaling (Card, Stuckey, Sawalani, & Little, 2008). Children with the highest rates of overt aggression have also been found to have high rates of covert–hostile behaviors. They also have the highest rates of out-of-home placements and greater occurrence of physical abuse in their backgrounds. This distinction can inform the use of different prevention and intervention strategies.

Bullying

Bullying can occur both in and out of school. Because of the devastating effects that it can have, it is identified as a subtype of behavioral problems, though typically it occurs with other types of disruptive behavior. Bullies are usually aggressive to both children and adults. Although many children explore the use of power over others through bullying, few children engage in it frequently and persist with it (Pepler, Jiang, Craig, & Connolly, 2008). A small group of children (about 10%) engaged in a high amount of bullying in elementary school and continued in this pattern in secondary school, suggesting that they were at risk of learning to use power and aggression to cause distress and to hold control over others in their adult relationships. Children who continue with bullying have been found to be impulsive, lack empathy, and have lower anxiety than children who are not bullies (Olweus, 1994). Bullies are most frequently boys who bully both boys and girls, but some girls do bully other girls. Kochenderfer and Ladd (1996) identified two types of victimized children: those who are aggressive and hot tempered, and those who are passive and insecure. The passive children might cry and make no effort to stop the attacks. They are often cautious, sensitive, and quiet children who see themselves as failures or exhibit behaviors that make them appear different or vulnerable to peers (Veenstra et al., 2007). Children who are victimized can develop very negative feelings toward themselves and school and resist going (Salmivalli & Isaacs, 2005). Victimization is also associated with physical complaints and academic problems (Juvonen & Graham, 2001). Some children end up being both bullies and victims. These children tend to have significant psychological problems and very disturbed relationships with their parents (Kumpulainen et al., 1998).

Relational or Social Aggression

In the 1980s and 1990s, a number of researchers began to consider a range of aggressive behaviors, including more indirect and social aggression (Crick & Grotpeter, 1995). Such aggression is aimed at damaging the victim's social relationships and has been called social or relational aggression (Crick, 1995). Behaviors covered by these terms include gossiping, excluding certain children from the group, and spreading rumors. Usually, direct confrontation of the victim is avoided. Conceptual expectations are that girls engage in this type of aggression more than boys. However, the literature is inconclusive, and Archer (2004) found in a meta-analytic review of 78 studies that included children, adolescents, and adults that, when using observations, peer ratings, and teacher ratings, girls did engage in more of this behavior than boys but not when peer nominations and self-reports were used. When the expected gender differences were found in a few studies, they ranged from small to medium.

In a meta-analysis of 148 studies that did not include adults, Card et al. (2008) found little gender difference; though statistically significant, it was trivial in magnitude. The gender difference was the same across age, ethnicity, and country. The most significant finding was that children who engaged in relational aggression had more internalizing and social and emotional problems, tended to be rejected by peers, and were defiant, depressed, and anxious (Crick, 1995; Murray-Close, Ostrov, & Crick, 2007). Some children and peer groups have been found to view relational aggression as acceptable and normal. Card et al. (2008) also found it to be related to higher prosocial behavior in some girls. It was suggested that the children using indirect aggression also had prosocial skills to get the support and assistance of other children. It was hypothesized that relational aggression is used by girls to hurt other girls or interfere with their forming and maintaining intimate friendships (Crick & Grotpeter, 1995).

Reactive and Proactive Aggression

Efforts to distinguish reactive from proactive aggression have a long history. Reactive aggression is a hostile, angry reaction to perceived frustration. The goal is to defend oneself against a threat (real or perceived) and involves intense CNS arousal and an unplanned attack on the source of frustration (Dodge, 1991). Children with reactive aggression are likely to have difficulty with social information processing and interpreting others' cues, especially in situations in which they tend to interpret those cues as having hostile intent (Arsenio, Adams, & Gold, 2009). Proactive aggression is planned with a desired outcome in mind. The child is generally calm, with little CNS arousal, irritability, or fear (Crick & Dodge, 1994, 1996). This type of aggression is tied less to hostile attributional biases than to an expectation that the aggressive act will bring satisfaction (Arsenio et al., 2009). Research on these subtypes has focused on assessing elementary school children in community settings. It has studied the social cognition and information processing of these children. There is a tendency for reactive aggression not to predict disruptive behavior in adolescence (Vitaro, Gendreau, Tremblay, & Oligny, 1998). On the other hand, Pulkkinen (1996) found males assessed as having proactive aggressive behavior at 14 years of age to be more likely to be aggressive and engage in antisocial behavior and criminality during adulthood.

Psychopathic Traits

Children with psychopathic traits have been identified as a subgroup at increased risk of lifelong aggressive and antisocial behavior (Dadds et al., 2009; Frick et al., 2003; Viding, 2004). The definition of psychopathy originally focused on the frequency, severity, and type of antisocial behavior. More recently, the temperamental variables and psychological characteristics that underlie these behaviors have been studied (Dadds et al., 2006; Frick & Morris, 2004). They include lack of empathy, remorse, and guilt; reduced sensitivity to signs of distress in others; manipulation; superficial charm; and grandiose sense of self-worth (Frick, Bodin, & Barry, 2000; Hare, 1996; van Baardewijk, Stegge, Bushman, & Vermeiren, 2009). A number of researchers are studying these interpersonal and affective features of psychopathy as having prognostic value and suggesting certain interventions. Factor analysis has shown that psychopathic features are distinct from the symptoms of CD, ODD, and ADHD (Dadds, Fraser, Frost, & Hawes, 2005; Pardini, Obradovic, & Loeber, 2006). In many of these studies, the affective features of psychopathy have been labeled C/U traits. These affective and interpersonal dimensions of psychopathy are associated with early emerging and persistent forms of antisocial behavior. They have been identified in children as young as 3 years old and found to predict persistent forms of delinquency and antisocial personality disorder (ASPD) in adulthood (Pardini & Loeber, 2008). In these children, deficits in cognitive empathy were found in both sexes in early childhood, and for males severe deficits in affective empathy were found across all ages but not for females (Dadds et al., 2009). Children and adolescents within the autism spectrum who are high functioning display some of these traits (lack of empathy, grandiose feelings, justification of retribution, and little remorse), though this observation has not been subjected to empirical study.

Callous/Unemotional Traits

Callous/unemotional traits are the most important characteristic of children considered at risk of developing ASPD or psychopathy and are comprised of lack of empathy and guilt, shallow emotions, and lack of remorse for antisocial acts, and they represent a subtype of children with CD (Frick & White, 2008). C/U traits have also been linked to proactive aggression or behavior carried out to achieve a certain result (Kimonis et al., 2006). They have also been shown to increase the risk that the child will engage in direct and indirect bullying. These traits show modest stability in childhood and adolescence and can predict more severe and persistent psychopathology later (Rowe et al., 2010). There is also evidence that these traits identify a subtype of antisocial behavior and CD (Frick, 2006; Frick & White, 2008). Children with these characteristics also prefer thrills and adventure-seeking activities, a reward-dominant response style, and deficits in processing emotional stimuli. In a longitudinal study of twins for whom teacher ratings were collected at 7, 9, and 12 years of age, four different trajectories were identified: stable high, increasing, decreasing, and stable low. Genetic and to a lesser extent environmental factors (negative parental discipline, chaos in the home, and negative parental feelings) were identified as the major influences on these trajectories. The stable-high group showed the most heritability (Fontaine, Rijsdijk, McCrary, & Viding, 2010). Similar results were found in a preschool sample, with behaviorally uninhibited temperament, C/U features, and harsh parenting contributing to the development of aggression in preschool children (Kimonis et al., 2006).

DISORDERS OF BEHAVIOR REGULATION AND THEIR PREVALENCE

In the fifth edition of the *DSM*-5 (5th ed.; APA, 2013), under the overall category of "Disruptive, Impulse-Control, and Conduct Disorders" there are seven separate but overlapping diagnoses related to behavior regulation in children up to 13 years of age. These disorders are Oppositional Defiant Disorder, Intermittent Explosive Disorder, Conduct Disorder (Childhood Onset), Antisocial Personality Disorder, Pyromania, Kleptomania, Other Specified Disruptive, Impulse-Control, and Conduct Disorder. The category of "Unspecified Disruptive, Impulse-Control, and Conduct Disorder" is used when there are problems with conduct and impulse control that do not meet full criteria for the other disorders but there is clinically significant impairment.

Comorbidity

Oppositional Defiant Disorder (ODD), Intermittent Explosive Disorder (IED), and Conduct Disorder (CD) have commonly been found to be associated with other disorders, particularly ADHD and anxiety and/or depression. In teenagers, it is more common to find comorbidity than a single disorder. When ODD is comorbid with ADHD, it can predict the early onset of

CD. The strongest association has been found with symptoms of hyperactivity/impulsivity. Co-occurrence with ADHD predicts a poorer outcome with a higher risk of the young person becoming involved in crime (Lahey & Waldman, 2003).

In adolescence, antisocial behavior and ODD and CD are strongly associated with depression and/or anxiety (Rowe, Rijsdijk, Maughan, Hosang, & Eley, 2008; Zoccolillo, 1992). In some studies, up to 42% of youth with CD had depression, and 37% of adolescent boys with depression were comorbid for CD (Hinshaw, 2002; Kazdin, 2002; Pliszka et al., 2000). The combination increased risk and led to increased severity and worse short-term and long-term outcomes. These presentations point to an overall problem with emotion regulation.

Rates of learning disabilities are reported to be high in children with ODD and CD. There is evidence that weaknesses in verbal learning and reading can predict later CD and antisocial outcomes (BMA Board of Science, 2006). When ADHD is also present, the prognosis is particularly poor (Fergusson & Lynskey, 1997; Smart, Sanson, & Prior, 1996).

Posttraumatic stress disorder (PTSD) can increase the risk of aggressive and antisocial behavior. Traumatic events—particularly when experienced in childhood, are chronic, and the result of abuse—can result in re-experiencing of the event and autonomic nervous system (ANS) overarousal (American Psychiatric Association, 2000). This triggering can present as irritability, anger outbursts, and hypervigilance. Physically abused children, both boys and girls, are at particularly high risk of continued physical aggression, violence, and antisocial behavior. In some studies, PTSD has been associated with CD at higher rates than would be expected by chance (McLeer, Callaghan, Henry, & Wallen, 1994; Tisl & Cicchetti, 2008). Also, the risk-taking and antisocial behavior that children with ODD and CD engage in can increase the likelihood that the child or adolescent will be exposed to more traumatic events, keeping the PTSD active.

BEHAVIOR REGULATION AND THE BRAIN

Research on the neurobiology of behavior regulation disorders or disruptive behavior disorders is complicated. Differences in research findings are common due to study design and methodological differences. Findings on related neurobiology can differ according to the subtype of ODD or CD being investigated and any comorbidity involved. A number of different physiological measures and brain-imaging techniques have been used to describe the underlying structures and activities in the brains of children with behavior disorders compared with control-group children without any difficulties.

Brain-Imaging Studies

In a recent review of studies using functional magnetic resonance imaging (fMRI) to understand the neuroanatomy and development of CD and ODD, Crowe and Blair (2008, p. 1145) noted that there are few fMRI studies of children or adolescents with ODD and CD and that they had to "rely on a variety of studies with adult populations and infer results that we can anticipate from child and adolescent samples." In general, studies have focused on regions of the brain responsible for emotion regulation, including the limbic–hypothalamic–pituitary–adrenal (LHPA) axis, the amygdala, and the prefrontal cortex (Blair, 2001; Sterzer, Stadler, Krebs, Kleinschmidt, & Poustka, 2005). In support of this approach are findings that individuals with known brain lesions in the amygdala are likely to be aggressive and show behavioral symptoms similar to individuals with CD (Angrilli et al., 1996; Sterzer et al., 2005). Similarly, lesions in the orbitofrontal cortex (OFC) and anterior cingulated cortex (ACC) can contribute to impairments in social, emotional, and moral behavior (Anderson, Bechara, Damasio, Tranel, & Damasio, 1999; Bechara, Damasio, Damasio, & Anderson, 1994). See Figure 7.1 for an approximate schematic guide to the location of brain structures involved in behavior regulation.

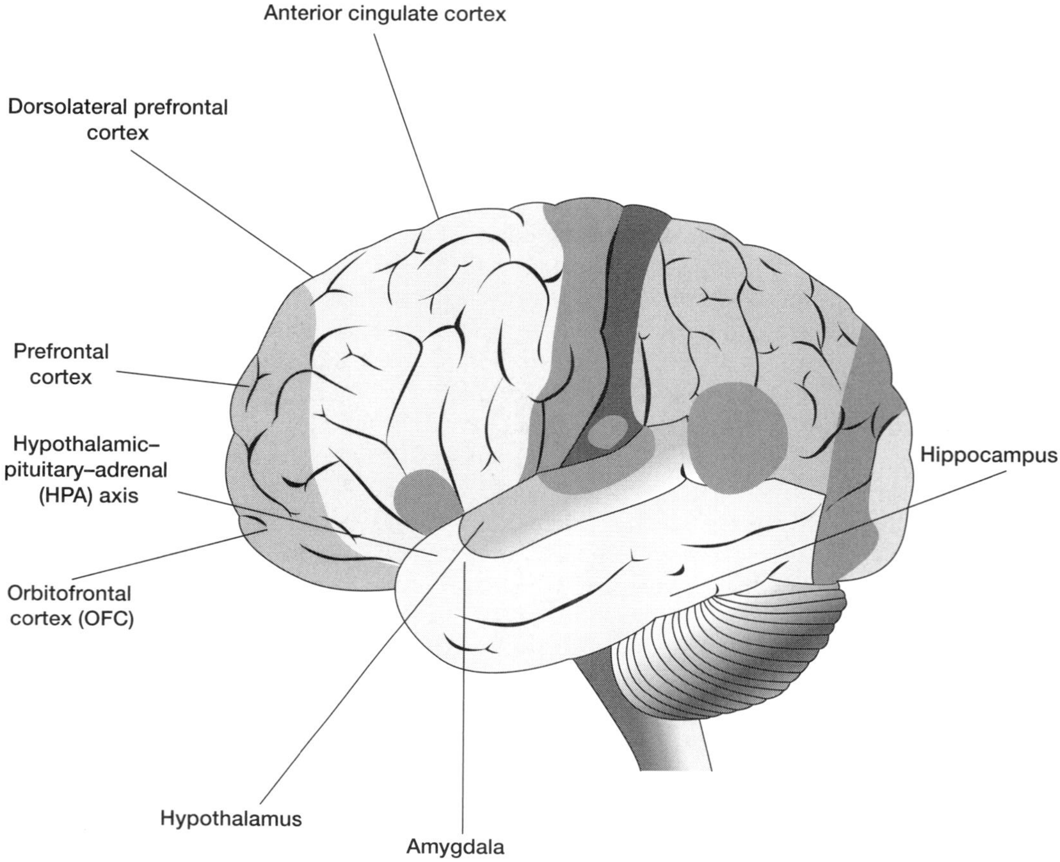

Figure 7.1 *Parts of the brain involved in behavior regulation.*

As mentioned previously, different studies have found different types of reactions in the LHPA axis, the amygdala, and the prefrontal cortex (PFC) in children with ODD and CD, with some reporting increased amygdala responsiveness and others reduced amygdala responsiveness. This can occur because of various comorbidities. Children with comorbid PTSD, for example, will show increased amygdala responsiveness to certain stimuli, whereas children with psychopathic tendencies or traits might show reduced amygdala responsiveness (Herpertz et al., 2008). Crowe and Blair (2008) also distinguished between the responses expected in children and adolescents with reactive and proactive and instrumental aggression and particularly those with psychopathic tendencies. In a study comparing fMRI data for 22 children with childhood-onset CD (16 with comorbid ADHD) with controls with no identified psychopathology, enhanced amygdala activation to negative, positive, and neutral pictures was found in the children with CD (Herpertz et al., 2008). The researchers suggested that comorbid anxiety and emotional problems as well as methodological differences might explain their findings. Also, individuals with PTSD have consistently been found to have increased amygdala responsiveness to trauma-related cues and fearful facial expressions. Etkin and Wagner (2007) conducted a meta-analysis of studies of the processing of various trauma-related stimuli and emotional words. Recent studies with fMRI have shown that individuals with psychopathy show reduced amygdala responses to fearful and sad faces relative to control groups (Birbaumer et al., 2005; Blair, Colledge, Murray, & Mitchell, 2001; Dadds et al., 2006; Mueller et al., 2003; Sterzer et al., 2005). Some studies have also found reductions in response in the ventromedial PFC (Pietrini, Guazzeli, Basso, Jaffe, & Grafman, 2000). These findings are particularly common in children with a comorbidity of ADHD (Crowe & Blair, 2008).

So, though there is a relatively small research literature on structural and functional neuroimaging and ODD and CD, particularly in children and adolescents, results suggest that there are subtle CNS differences compared with healthy controls and that the differences can vary by subtype, such as children with reactive as opposed to proactive aggression, and by comorbidity (Connor, 2002).

Electrodermal Activity

Measures of electrodermal activity (EDA) provide an indirect, short, and inexpensive measure of the brain circuit implicated in emotion regulation and fear conditioning, including the ANS, amygdala, and OFC. It is particularly useful for studies of young children. EDA refers to various indicators of electrical conductance measured across the skin of the person. They can include the level of electrical activity when the skin is at rest, skin conductance, and any spontaneous fluctuations and changes in response to a stimulus. Connor (2002) summarized the results of various studies conducted from 1980 to 2002. Of the eight reviewed studies, five reported significantly lower EDA or underarousal in groups of children and adolescents with aggression and CD. Two studies reported no differences, whereas one study found results in the opposite direction. In another important study, EDA was used as a measure of fear conditioning in 3- to 8-year-old children (Gao, Raine, Venables, Dawson, & Mednick, 2010). EDA was measured annually among these ages, and antisocial behavior and hyperactivity–inattention were measured at 8 years of age using the Children's Behavior Questionnaire. High-aggressive children showed lower EDA responses or deficits in fear conditioning compared with low-aggressive children across all ages and did not manifest the age-related increased conditioning found for nonaggressive children. These results were believed to suggest abnormal amygdala functioning.

Heart Rate

Heart rate level (HRL) and heart rate reactivity (HRR) have been studied extensively in children with aggression, conduct disorder, and oppositional defiant disorder. Although the measures are easy to take, they are difficult to interpret because they can be affected by factors that need to be controlled, and results have been somewhat inconsistent. However, though some studies have found no differences between heart rate in aggressive and nonaggressive samples, the majority of studies, including those with longitudinal and cross-sectional designs, have found a relationship between lower heart rate and aggression and conduct problems. When these differences have not been found, study and methodological differences are suggested (Connor, 2002). In fact, Raine, Venables, and Mednick (1997) indicated that low resting HR is the best and most consistent biological marker of antisocial and aggressive behavior in childhood and adolescent community samples. Connor (2002, p. 182) also concluded that "further investigations of resting HRL and HRR might be fruitful." He also noted that recent advances in spectral analysis of heart beat variability have found reduced heart period variability, suggesting deficient parasympathetic ANS modulation of heart rate variability in boys with stable aggression (Mezzacappa,

Kindlon, Saul, & Earls, 1998). Porges and colleagues studied vagal tone, which measures heart rate activity that occurs during changes in respiration (respiratory sinus arrhythmia or RSA) (Porges, Doussard-Roosevelt, Portales, & Suess, 1994). These and other researchers have found vagal tone to be related to both reactivity and regulation of emotions in infancy, with infants with high vagal tone tending to have better self-regulation of attention than those with low vagal tone. Measures of low vagal tone at 9 months have predicted difficult behavior at 3 years (Porges et al., 1994).

Event-Related Potentials

Event-related potentials (ERPs) are measured from surface electrodes on the scalp to study the efficiency of information processing in the brain. They can be elicited with visual, auditory, and somatosensory stimuli. ERPs have been used to study children and adolescents with aggression problems, delinquency, and other antisocial behavior. The literature on juveniles does not demonstrate that aggressive/antisocial juveniles always have deficient information processing in all settings. It suggests that persons with psychopathic traits might exist in a state of cognitive underarousal and stimulus deprivation and seek stimulating events to increase their level of cognitive arousal (Raine, 1989). The data also support the two-factor theory of Gray (1985) that described a behavioral activation system (BAS) that initiates behavior when needed and a behavioral inhibition system (BIS) that inhibits behavior when useful. Quay (1993) suggested that aggressive antisocial children have an underactive BIS and an overactive BAS. However, the data are not totally supportive of these theories and suggest instead that a number of aggressive and conduct-disordered individuals do not have these patterns, including youth with borderline personality disorders and comorbid externalizing and internalizing disorders.

Electroencephalogram

The electroencephalogram (EEG) measures the electrical activity of the cortex, though some subcortical structures are probably involved in controlling cortical activity. Hundreds of EEG studies of individuals with aggression, criminal activity, delinquency, and psychopathy have found nonspecific abnormalities in habitually violent adults and adolescents in 25% to 50% of cases (Mednick, Volavks, Gabrielli, & Itil, 1982). This compares with the prevalence of EEG abnormalities in the general public of about 12%. However, there has been much criticism of these statistics since early studies were flawed and relied on visual inspection of the EEG instead of quantitative analysis of band frequency. Also, the EEG changes with development and CNS maturation and can be unstable, and the studies did not control for head injuries and substance use, which are prevalent in this population. More recently, cross-sectional and prospective longitudinal studies of nonreferred younger children before diagnoses have been conducted. With these methodologies, three of four longitudinal studies and all prospective studies of community samples found EEG evidence of cortical underarousal, which matches some of the research using other measures of neurophysiology (Mednick, Volavka, Gabrielli, & Intil, 1998; Raine, Venables, & Williams, 1990; Schmidt & Fox, 1998).

Neurobiology

There is evidence that aggressive and antisocial individuals are less sensitive to certain kinds of stress. This is believed to be so because they place themselves in risky, stressful, or dangerous situations more frequently than others and seem to have a relative lack of fear. It is also possible that aggressive children are underaroused and that the experience of too little stress is aversive. It is believed that this is related to certain neurobiological pathways and systems that might be disrupted in individuals with hypofearfulness and underarousal.

One area of consideration has been differences in concentrations of neurohormones (particularly cortisol) and neurotransmitters such as serotonin, dopamine, and norepinephrine (see Connor, 2002, for a review). Cortisol in the bloodstream has been measured by assessing the amount of cortisol in the saliva of children with CD, and in some studies severe antisocial symptoms were associated with low levels of cortisol (McBurnett, Lahey, Rathouz, & Loeber, 2000; Shoal, Giancola, & Kirillova, 2003). In a study of adolescent girls with CD, decreased levels of cortisol were found (Pajer, Gardner, Rubin, Perel, & Neal, 2001). However, in some studies, no such relationship has been found. Similar results have been found in children with CD during exposure to competition, frustration, and provocation (van Goozen et al., 1998; van Goozen, Matthys, Cohen-Kettenis, Buitelaar, & van Engeland, 2000 A number of neurotransmitters have effects on various CNS activities, such as depression, sleeping and eating, memory and learning, and mood. Low serotonin levels, for example, have been linked to a number of mental health issues, such as depression and anxiety, and medication that increases serotonin in the brain can reduce symptoms associated with these disorders (Emslie, Portteus, Kumar, & Hume, 2004). Levels of serotonin in the brain cannot be measured directly or as easily as cortisol can be measured, by using saliva samples. Instead, indirect methods, such as the level of serotonin in cerebrospinal fluid, have been used. Although low levels of serotonin have been found in studies of aggressive adults, they are found less consistently in aggressive youth (Coccaro, Kavoussi, Sheline, Berman, & Csernansky, 1997). Support for this relationship also comes from the success of using antidepressants that make serotonin more available in the brain for children with CD and comorbid depression and anxiety. Studies have shown a reduction in CD symptoms by 85% to 87% (Mpofu & Conyers, 2003). Other neurotransmitters implicated as being under functioning in youth with externalizing disorders are norepinephrine and dopamine, but results have been mixed, particularly for dopamine, with the expected relationship not being found in some studies.

OTHER CONTRIBUTORS

Genetics

Although aggression and antisocial behavior tend to run in families, particularly more overt types of aggression, it is unclear whether this pattern reflects genetic influences, shared environmental factors, or interactions between them (Connor, 2002). To understand this interaction, various methodologies have been used. The first step usually includes family studies in which the rates of CD and ASPD in biological parents and relatives of children with CD and in control children without CD are compared or the children of adults with ASPD are assessed for CD. These studies have shown that CD and persistent problems with aggression tend to run in families (Szatmari, Boyle, & Offord, 1993). The other common types of research are twin and adoption studies. Identical or monozygotic (MZ) twins share 100% of genes, whereas fraternal or dizygotic (DZ) twins share only 50% of genes. In these studies, it is assumed that the environment is roughly the same for the pairs of twins. Different concordance for adult criminality has been found for the MZ twins (between 26% and 51%) and DZ twins (between 13% and 23%) (Rutter et al., 1990). Slutske et al., 1998, in a retrospective study of twin pairs, found an estimate of heritability of 71%. However, it is impossible to know if the shared environment was the same for both twins. In a meta-analysis of twin and adoption studies, Mason and Frick (1994) found that 50% of the difference between measures of antisocial and nonantisocial behavior was attributable to genetic effects. Some studies have focused on the interaction between genetic risks and environmental risks such as parent psychopathology and marital problems. Other studies have compared heritability in different subtypes of aggression, with hyperactive and impulsive behavior having a more heritable influence (Rutter, Silberg, O'Connor, & Simonoff, 1999). Studies have also been conducted with individuals with elevated rates of C/U traits found to be highly heritable (81%), but without C/U traits it is only moderately heritable (30%) (Viding, Blair, Moffitt, & Plomin, 2005).

Underarousal of the ANS found in aggressive children with psychopathic traits might be inherited (Frick, 1998; Lahey, Hart, Pliszka, Applegate, & McBurnett, 1993). No single gene can account for aggression and antisocial behavior, but future studies should more clearly define gene–environment interactions that contribute to the subtypes of aggressive disorders (Connor, 2002).

In a meta-analysis of twin and adoptive studies, Rhee and Waldman (2002) concluded that antisocial behavior is heritable. Currently, there have only been molecular genetic investigations. Later studies might be able to identify the genes associated with decreased emotional and amygdala responsiveness often found in individuals with antisocial behavior and reduced empathy and remorse (Blair, Finger, & Marsh, 2009).

Prenatal and Perinatal Risk Factors

Complications during the prenatal period (conception to the seventh month of pregnancy) and perinatal period (seventh month of pregnancy through 28 days after birth) affect CNS development and are related to increased risk of antisocial behavior (Kandel & Mednick, 1991). It has long been known that prenatal factors affect brain development of the fetus. Such factors include exposure to tobacco, alcohol, cocaine and other drugs, viral and bacterial infections, nutritional deficiencies, and maternal stress. One study found that maternal anxiety during pregnancy caused difficult temperament up to 3 years of age and explained 15% of the variance of externalizing problems. Anxiety at 12 to 22 weeks was a predictor, whereas anxiety at 32 to 40 weeks was not (van den Bergh & Marcoen, 2004). Exposure to alcohol during pregnancy can cause anatomical abnormalities in its most extreme form of fetal alcohol syndrome (FAS). Elevated rates of psychopathology, including impulsive aggression and antisocial behavior, have been found in samples of children, adolescents, and adults exposed to alcohol in utero even after controlling for confounding variables (Olson et al., 1997). Nicotine exposure has also shown significant associations with being arrested, aggression and violence, and CD after controlling for a number of potential confounding variables (Brennan, Grekin, & Mednick, 1999). Studies of the effects of prenatal exposure to cocaine have been mixed, some studies finding few differences, other studies finding effects only immediately after birth, and some longitudinal studies finding a higher incidence of behavioral problems in 3- to 6-year-olds (Connor, 2002). Another study found that children born near term, with lower 5-minute Apgar scores and smaller head circumferences, were more likely to have antisocial behavior (Nomura, Rajendran, Brooks-Gunn, & Newcorn, 2008).

Minor Physical Anomalies

Minor physical anomalies (MPAs) consist of features such as low-set or asymmetrical ears, a furrowed tongue, or a single palmar crease. They are associated with disorders of pregnancy and thought to be markers for neural malformation toward the end of 3 months of pregnancy. They can be caused by anoxia, bleeding, and infections or have a genetic basis. In some studies, MPAs have been found to be related to increased risk of developing behavioral problems in childhood and aggressive acts and criminal activity in adolescence (Arseneault, Tremblay, Boulerice, Seguin, & Saucier, 2000; Ozen, Ece, Oto, Tirasci, & Goren, 2005). It is highly unlikely that MPAs cause these outcomes, but they appear to reflect increased brain vulnerability to later difficulties (Pine, Shaffer, Schonfeld, & Davies, 1997).

Temperament

Some types of temperament associated with conduct problems in childhood and adolescence include the difficult temperament described by Thomas and Chess (1968): overactivity, undercontrol, high intensity of responses, inattention, predominantly negative mood, and low adaptability to new situations. These characteristics were found to be linked to increased risk of psychopathology, including aggression, CD, delinquency, and other antisocial behavior. Other temperamental traits linked to later externalizing behavior include those that Fox and colleagues (2001) labeled "temperamentally exuberant": novelty seeking, exuberance, impulsivity, uninhibited behavior, fearlessness, and sensation seeking. In several studies, these traits have been linked to extreme frustration and anger over restrictions and rules and desire to control events (Donzella, Gunnar, Krueger, & Alwin, 2000; Posner & Rothbart, 2000). These types of temperament have also been linked to higher levels of conduct problems, aggression, and criminal involvement (Stifter, Putnam, & Jahromi, 2008). The other temperament trait linked to disruptive behavior is effortful control (Olson, Sameroff, Kerr, Lopez, & Wellman, 2005; Rothbart & Bates, 2006). It is defined as the child's capacity to inhibit a dominant response in favor of a subdominant response. Individual differences in effortful control develop in preschool years and show levels of continuity during childhood. Poor effortful control has been linked to impulsive–inattentive behavior and negative emotionality in 3-year-olds and externalizing conduct problems in school-aged children (Eisenberg et al., 2009; Olson et al., 2005). Effortful control can also change in either direction during elementary school, and this might represent a period during which approaches to change it can be successful (Zhou et al., 2007).

A temperament trait that has received a great deal of attention in the study of antisocial youth has been C/U, characterized by deficit in the ability to show emotional arousal to fear and distress in others, and lack of response to consequences and danger. These children have also been found to have impairment in recognizing fearful vocal affect in others. These traits are related to a tendency to pursue thrill and novelty and a reduced response to consequences imposed on behavior. These deficits are both emotional and cognitive and might relate to lack of amygdala responsiveness and reactions in related neural circuits. These fearless temperaments have been linked to lower scores on measures of guilt and conscience development (Fowles & Kochanska, 2000; Kimonis et al., 2006).

Cognitive Functioning and Information Processing

Neuropsychological studies have consistently found an 8- to 17-point deficit in global IQ for the antisocial youth (Moffitt, 1990). Children with conduct problems have also been found to have increased rates of reading and spelling and other learning disabilities. Children with aggressive and antisocial behavior often lack cognitive flexibility and have black-and-white thinking. They can take things literally and not pay attention to situational factors that might change their perspectives. This can result in getting "stuck," perseverating, or insisting on sticking to a plan that is not working (Greene & Ablon, 2006).

As well, delinquent youth have been found to have higher performance IQ than verbal IQ due to language-based deficits. In fact, the results of decades of research show that children with disruptive behavior and antisocial behavior often have various language impairments (Cohen, 2001; van Daal, Verhoeven, & van Balkom, 2007). Phonological problems are common, and severe deficits in social communication abilities, including pragmatic skills, have been found (Gilmour, Hill, Place, & Skuse, 2004). These deficits can be as "severe as those of children with diagnoses of an autism spectrum disorder" (Gilmour et al., 2004). In some studies, however, children with C/U or psychopathic traits do not fit this pattern and often show no impairment in their verbal abilities, though their use of language is unusual, including lack of insight and self-centeredness (Munoz, Frick, Kimonis, & Aucoin, 2008). These deficits might reflect less lateralized linguistic functioning and inefficient left hemispheric information processing (Raine, 1993).

Other research has examined ear advantage in children with CD by using dichotic listening tests. Typically, sounds presented to the right ear are processed in the left hemisphere, and sounds presented to the left ear are processed in the right hemisphere. In children with psychopathic traits and disruptive behavior disorders, reduced right ear advantage and reduced lateralization for verbal information processing to the left hemisphere have been found (Pine et al., 1997).

Some research has also examined the processing of emotional signals of other people in children with disruptive behavior disorders, especially in children with psychopathic traits, as a possible contributor to lack of empathy and various externalizing symptoms (de Wied, Goudena, & Malthys, 2005). Some studies have found reduced empathy and responsiveness to sadness and fear in others in children and youth with these difficulties. In other words, there is an inverse relationship between aggression and both cognitive and affective responsiveness to sad and fearful facial expressions (Blair, 1999; Blair et al., 2001) and sad and fearful vocal intonations (Blair, Budhani, Colledge, & Scott, 2005; Stevens, Charman, & Blair, 2001). Although the findings are somewhat mixed, Blair and colleagues (2005) have suggested that this is due to different parts of the neural system being unresponsive to these emotional reactions in others and that they imply amygdala dysfunction.

Children with disruptive behaviors often have very poor social skills and do not seem to be aware of how their behaviors affect others. Another important line of research has arisen from the social information processing model, which has considered how children with conduct problems process social information (Crick & Dodge, 1994; Dodge, 1993; Gifford-Smith & Rabiner, 2004). Aggressive children, particularly those with reactive aggression, attribute hostile intent to the actions of others and see others as intentionally and consistently hostile toward them (Arsenio et al. 2009; Schwartz & Proctor, 2000). In their model, Crick and Dodge (1996) identified a number of steps that children can go through in response to the actions of others:

- encoding social cues and information (i.e., registering what other children are doing)
- interpreting this information
- thinking of a number of possible responses to the situation
- choosing the appropriate response
- carrying out the response and evaluating its success

Aggressive children do not consider the perspective of the other child or group and are likely to respond in an aggressive way. Lemerise and Arsenio (2000) integrated emotional experiences such as frustration and anger that can influence how information is attended to, recalled, and responded to. Other research has examined the information processing of children with reactive or proactive aggression. Reactive aggression was related to hostile attributional biases, whereas proactive aggression was related to an expectation that the aggression would bring material and emotional rewards (Arsenio et al., 2009).

Recent research has also suggested that hostile attributions also increase the incidence of misbehavior at home and school.

Sense of Self

The prevailing view is that children with externalizing problems such as ODD and aggression have low self-esteem. In the Dunedin Multidisciplinary Health Longitudinal Study that followed a birth cohort of 1,037 children from birth to 26 years of age, data on self-esteem and externalizing behavior problems were collected at 11, 13, and 15 years of age. It was found that low self-esteem contributed to a variety of externalizing behaviors during childhood and adolescence, including antisocial and delinquent behavior, and criminal behavior in early adulthood (Trzesniewski et al., 2006). The contribution of self-esteem was independent of relationships to parents and peers, IQ, and socioeconomic status. These results held cross-sectionally and longitudinally after controlling for these variables. In three studies, Donnellan, Trzesniewski, Robins, Moffitt, and Caspi (2000) found a robust relationship between low self-esteem and various externalizing problems, such as aggression, antisocial behavior, and delinquency.

Baumeister, Smart, and Boden (1996) noted that, compared with children who are nonaggressive, those who are aggressive are more likely to overestimate their competence (Hughes, Cavell, & Grossman, 1997). A number of writers have identified a group of individuals with a pattern of grandiose, inflated, egocentric views of self and feelings of omnipotence that might result in high scores on self-esteem measures. When their self-esteem is threatened, they are likely to respond in irrational ways that can lead to destructive and violent behaviors (Baumeister et al., 1996). Some writers have also identified narcissism and the rage that can be activated as a likely cause of these violent outbursts (Bushman & Baumeister, 1998; Martens, 2005; Robins, Tracy, & Shaver, 2001; Stucke & Sporer, 2002). Hare (1993, p. 38) also identified some of the same dynamics in psychopaths, whom he described as having a "narcissistic and grossly inflated view of self-worth and importance," showing a "truly astounding egocentricity and sense of entitlement," and seeing "themselves as the center of the universe, as superior beings."

As pointed out by Baumeister and colleagues (1996), when children and adults with inflated self-esteem based on some of these characteristics are confronted with a threat, or when favorable views of themselves are challenged, contradicted, questioned, or put in jeopardy, they can become aggressive or have uncontrollable rages. Decreases in self-esteem are difficult for everyone, but when self-esteem is inflated and grandiose, to cover feelings of shame, some individuals might perceive threats as catastrophic. In a study that assessed narcissism in young adolescents, those ranked as narcissistic were more aggressive when shamed in an experiment than those without this diagnosis (Thomaes, Bushman, Stegge, & Olthof, 2008).

Obviously, children with aggression have difficulty with emotion regulation. They find frustration and anger hard to manage and are often irritable and impatient. They find it hard to stay calm. They can also have difficulty with anxiety and depression. It is almost as if they became stuck at a developmental stage typically found in children about 2 to 3 years of age, when egocentricity and grandiosity are expected.

Parenting/Attachment/Parents' Attributions of the Child

Many parenting practices have been studied as possible antecedents of aggressive and antisocial behavior. These have included lack of supervision and inconsistent discipline, lack of involvement and warmth, and harsh, punitive discipline (Rothbaum & Weisz, 1994). Corporal punishment, a relatively common practice, has been shown to put children's development at risk, can lead to anger in children, and might compromise the development of conscience (Bender et al., 2007; Gershoff, 2002; Patrick, Snyder, Schrepferman, & Snyder, 2008; Rothbaum & Weisz, 1994). On the other hand, greater maternal sensitivity, support, and warmth at 6 years of age were associated with greater attentional control and less externalizing behavior at 6, 8, and 10 years of age (Belsky, Pasco-Fearon, & Bell, 2007). A high level of power assertion, insisting on obedience without allowing children to express their ideas, has been associated with increased odds for children to become physically aggressive at home and school (Joussetnet et al., 2008). As stated previously, Patterson's "coercive family process" theory has been influential in the field of delinquency studies. Parenting interactions of laxness and then harshness are frequently found in families of children with disruptive behaviors. These patterns are ineffective in improving the child's behavior and likely to escalate it because they result in high conflict and negative affect. The child's negative behavior increases as a result and is increasingly used in interpersonal interactions within and outside the home. Recent research has also suggested that, as the child's behavior escalates, parents develop hostile attributions of the child that also increase the incidence of misbehavior (Snyder, Cramer, Afrank, & Patterson, 2005). However, the model does not take into account the individual characteristics of the child and how they influence the interaction.

Other theories have looked at clusters or styles of parenting behaviors and how they influence child outcomes. They include the theory of Baumrind (1973) and the authoritative, authoritarian, and permissive parenting styles, with authoritarian and permissive styles linked to antisocial behavior and aggression and authoritative (firm but encouraging the child's input) linked to positive outcomes for children.

Parent attributions are causal inferences about how a child develops and behaves (e.g., aggressive or oppositional). A number of theories have described how parents' perceptions of their child influence their interactions with her and her developmental outcomes. Attachment theory has looked at parents' working model of the child and how it can influence her quality of attachment (Lieberman, 1999). A number of attribution theorists have found that attributional biases are linked to parental behaviors and child outcomes. When parents believe that their child's behavior is directed at them or motivated by malicious intent, it can lead to negative affective states and parenting behavior that is extremely punitive or even abusive. Bugental and colleagues (1992) conducted studies of the role of parents' attributions in the etiology of child abuse and called those that attribute high control to the child and low control to themselves "threat-oriented schema," with parents seeing themselves as having a power disadvantage (Bugental, Blue, & Cruzcosa, 1989; Bugental, Lyon, Krantz, & Cortez, 1997). The message given to the child is primarily negative and often confusing, raising in turn anger and anxiety in her. In an attempt to cope with these feelings, she might withdraw and become difficult to control. These patterns can also lead to abuse.

Parents' knowledge of child development and parenting can also be powerful contributors to how parents interact with their children and outcomes for them. Parenting knowledge is influenced by upbringing, cultural values, religious beliefs, level of education, and socioeconomic status. When this knowledge is incorrect (e.g., that children need to be spanked to be obedient), it can have a significant effect on the development of aggressive and antisocial behavior.

Kochanska (1995, 1997a) examined the bidirectional effects of different kinds of parenting on the moral development of fearful and fearless children. This research illustrated how characteristics of the child, such as temperament, impulsivity, oppositional behavior, and aggression, can shape parenting behavior, which in turn negatively influences the child's behavior. In one study, very fearful children showed greater conscience when mothers used gentle guidance rather than harsh control. In contrast, fearless children did not respond to gentle control and responded best to firm, consistent discipline and positive, mutually reciprocal, warm interactions with parents and a secure attachment relationship. Kochanska suggested that in fearless children gentle discipline does not arouse the necessary level of discomfort for development of conscience or internalization of rules because they are not afraid or motivated to avoid anxiety. Instead, they become motivated to behave well by the desire to be like or identify with the emotionally available parent (Kochanska, Aksan, & Joy, 2007).

Attachment theory has also been used to understand the development of behavioral problems. Research has shown that early relationships with caregivers have continuing effects on behavior and social development. Both organized forms of insecure attachment (avoidant and ambivalent/resistant) and disorganized attachment are risk factors for the development of behavioral problems. However, in a meta-analytic study, disorganized attachment was associated with a higher risk of externalizing behavior; either avoidant or ambivalent/resistant attachment was not found to have a significant influence (Fearon, Bakersmans-Kranenberg, van IJzendoorn, Lapsley, & Roisman, 2010).

Associations between insecurity and disorganization and behavioral problems are stronger in higher-risk compared with lower-risk samples. In low-risk samples, the results of these associations have been inconsistent (McCartney, Owen, Booth, Clarke-Stewart, & Vandell, 2004; Moss, Smolta, Cyr, Dubois-Comtois, Mazzarello, & Berthiaume, 2006).

Unresolved states of mind of parents on the *Adult Attachment Interview* (AAI) (George, Kaplan, & Main, 1996) have been studied from infancy to older children and adolescents. There has been a consistent association at 6, 8, 10, and 13 years of age with behavioral problems and unresolved states of mind in parents but only in those with insecure, dismissing, or preoccupied states of mind. This relationship has not been found for parents who are secure/autonomous (Madigan, Moran, Schuengel, Pederson, & Otten, 2007).

A common problem is maternal depression, and its link to later child problems has been the most examined (Beardslee, Versage, & Gladstone, 1998). Higher severity and chronicity of depression have been linked to more behavioral problems in children (Gross, Shaw, Burwell, & Nagin, 2009). Parental psychopathology has been linked to increased risk of both internalizing and externalizing behaviors in adolescence (Connell & Goodman, 2002).

Child Maltreatment

The United States has a high prevalence of child maltreatment, with 905,000 children documented as victims of maltreatment in 2006 (U.S. Department of Health and Human Services, 2008). The highest rate occurred in children under 3 (16 per thousand) and in older children, the rate was somewhat lower (12 per thousand). This rate, of course, does not include abused children who have not been brought to the attention of authorities. A clear link has been found between child maltreatment and psychopathology in childhood and adolescence, with boys more likely to engage in physical aggression and girls in relational aggression (Alink, Cicchetti, Kim, & Rogosch, 2009; Appleyard & Runyan, 2010; Cullerton-Sen et al., 2009). In a 22- to 26-year follow-up study of a community sample of nonreferred children who had suffered early maltreatment, physical abuse, and neglect, maltreatment was found to be significantly associated with arrest for violent crime in adulthood by age 32 relative to controls who had not experienced maltreatment (Widom, 1998). In another study of 51 youth referred to a psychiatric residential setting, a relationship was found between early physical abuse and chronic aggression. It was also related to other comorbidities and a significant predictor of "treatment resistant aggression" (Connor, Melloni, & Harrison, 1998). A number of factors have been found to mediate or moderate this relationship, with low self-esteem contributing to it and social support moderating it. In many children, however, this relationship can be mediated by the development of PTSD and its neurobiological consequences.

Family and Community Violence

Since the mid-1990s, the significance of fighting between couples and family violence on children's emotion regulation has been more fully documented (Maughan & Cicchetti, 2002; Osofsky, 1998). The number of children exposed to violence in the United States each year is staggering (Margolin & Gordis, 2000). Estimates are that as many as 10 million children in the United States witness violence in their homes (Straus & Gelles, 1990), more than 900,000 children are victims of maltreatment, and approximately 70% of youths are victims of or witness community violence. In one study, 40% of urban adolescents had witnessed a shooting or stabbing in the past year, and the whole of the sample had witnessed at least three types of violence in their lifetimes (Gorman-Smith, Henry, & Tolan, 2004).

There is clear evidence that interparental conflict (IPC) and family violence are linked to behavioral problems in children. Statistics show that 40% to 50% of children exposed to severe marital hostility and violence exhibit extreme behavioral problems (Rhodes, 2008). Seeing violence is among the most consistent predictors of aggressive and violent behavior later (Gorman-Smith & Tolan, 1998; Farrell & Bruce, 1997; Schwab-Stone, Jones, Henrich, Lechman, & Ruchkin, 2003). This relationship is believed to arise not only because the child learns that violence can be used to solve interpersonal problems but also because he becomes hypervigilant to threat (Cummings, Schermerhorn, Davies, Goeke-Morey, & Cummings, 2006). There is also evidence that IPC affects childrearing practices, reduces the warmth of parents, and results in withdrawal, less availability, and hostility (Krishnakumar, Buehler, & Barber, 2003). Although less talked about, hostile, aggressive, and coercive interactions among siblings can also contribute to the development of externalizing problems. In one study of hostility among siblings, a modest but significant effect on the development of externalizing problems was found (Natsuaki, Ge, Reiss, & Neiderhiser, 2009).

Hence, exposure to violence is a significant risk factor for the child perpetrating violent acts. In a meta-analysis of 18 studies, Wilson, Stover, and Berkowitz (2009) concluded that, though some studies suggested a direct link from early exposure to violence to aggressive and antisocial behavior, other studies suggested that other factors also affect the outcome.

Peers and Schools

Children with aggressive behavior and other disruptive behavior have lower academic achievements than children who are typically developing. Quality of the teacher–child relationship can also predict changes in the level of aggression from Kindergarten to Grade 5 (Stipek & Miles, 2008). The researchers hypothesized that academic failure and high amounts of conflict can develop negative feelings toward school and academic work in children.

Peer group interactions and peer pressure become increasingly important during late childhood and adolescence. Socialization within the peer group has been shown to influence aggression (Espelage, Holt, & Henkel, 2003) and deviant behavior (Kiesner, Cadinu, Poulin, & Bucci, 2002). The extent of the group influence can be affected by the degree of identification with the peer group (Kiesner et al., 2002), the adolescent's status in the peer group (Crosanoe & Needham, 2004), and the family environment (Dishion, Patterson, Stoolmiller, & Skinner, 1991). Ellis and Zarbatany (2007), in a study of preadolescent and adolescent peer socialization, found that children who engage in deviant behavior and antisocial activity are initially drawn together but then become susceptible to the influence of the group, which can lead them to more serious acts of deviancy. Peer rejection might also have contributed to their initially joining a deviant group. Acceptance of aggression also results, but in some children the aggression tends to become more covert, manipulative, and relational than overt over time. These relationships between peer deviancy and training in aggressive behavior are most common in late childhood and adolescence but have also been found between 5 and 9 years of age (Snyder et al., 2008).

Peer victimization is a severe problem in many countries. As many as 30% of children report that they have been beaten up, threatened, or otherwise humiliated by peers (Brendgen et al., 2008). The incidence is particularly high in elementary school, with a subsequent decline (Monahan, Steinberg, & Cauffman, 2009). Many children who experience peer victimization or rejection develop high rates of aggression that seem related to retaliation against peers (Monahan et al., 2009). Not all children who are victimized develop aggressive behavior, and various factors that might buffer against this happening have been considered, including self-worth and having friends. Other research has suggested that a genetic risk or vulnerability might contribute (Brendgen et al., 2008).

TYPICAL DEVELOPMENT OF BEHAVIOR REGULATION AND A SENSE OF CONSCIENCE

The capacity for behavior regulation and for engaging in moral behavior is obviously not present at birth but changes rapidly between birth and 6 years of age and then continues to improve into early adolescence. Early theories suggested that infants and young children are not capable of understanding moral rules until 4 or 5 years of age. However, it is now understood that even young children by 6 years of age understand the difference between behaviors that go against the rules and those that violate a moral principle. In other words, they have developed a conscience and feel guilty if they break a rule. There is typically also a gradual transition from behavior being controlled by caregivers to behavior being under the control of internal factors in the child. However, for some children this process does not happen adequately. Not only is the development of compliance and a conscience slow but it can seem to stand still or even regress if the child's life is disrupted by various events, especially if they are traumatic. As well as being affected by events the type of discipline children receives also affects the development of behavior regulation and the internalization of the rules and standards of home, school, and society. See Table 7.1 for an outline of the development of behavior regulation and the parenting that supports it.

DEVELOPMENT OF AGGRESSIVE AND ANTISOCIAL BEHAVIOR

If the child's development begins to show signs of aggression or behavioral problems, it is important to intervene as quickly as possible. From birth to 2 years can be a stage when problems with conduct and aggression begin. Children who develop these problems often have high emotional reactivity, poor regulation skills, and irritability, making them hard to soothe when they are upset (Degnan, Calkins, Keane, & Hill-Soderlund, 2008). They also begin to be oppositional, angry, and easily frustrated.

The preschool period from 3 to 5 years of age is when the child's difficult behavior accelerates. Hyperactivity, impulsivity, and poor attention can become more evident. Tantrums, argumentativeness, and defiance might persist and impulsivity escalate (Rose, Rose, & Feldman, 1989). Internalization of moral beliefs and social reasoning or empathy

Table 7.1 *Highlights of the Development of Typical Behavior Regulation and Parenting*

Age Range	Development	Parenting
Birth to 12 months	▪ First stages of behavior regulation include beginning to be able to regulate their frustration for brief periods ▪ Uses sucking and staring at an object to begin to self-regulate ▪ Begins to establish a predictable routine with more predictable routine and schedule of eating and sleeping ▪ May begin by the end of the first year to develop an understanding of what is dangerous and of needing to stay away from these situations ▪ May sometimes show signs of a beginning of empathy or picking up on another's emotion and may cry when someone is upset	▪ Caregiver provides face-to-face interactions that encourage the child's focused attention and reciprocity or mutuality with others and teaches about turn taking and discourse ▪ Parent remains available for child and is responsive and warm ▪ Supports the infant by setting up a predictable routine of eating and sleeping so that the infant feels predictability and organization around them ▪ By 12 months is beginning to enforce some rules in order to keep the infant safe (e.g., not climbing on the stove and not getting too close to the edge of something he could fall from) ▪ Clear body language and facial expressions are used to let the infant know whether something he is doing is unsafe or hurtful (e.g., hitting another child or hurting an animal) ▪ Notices and acknowledges whether the infant is careful around other children or avoids something dangerous
12 to 24 months	▪ Toddler pushes to become more independent and to do things herself ▪ Frequent tantrums and "no" saying are at their height ▪ May take another child's toys and possessions ▪ Child only complies with requests and follows the rules about 45% of the time ▪ Will sometimes be able to stop doing something but this is unreliable ▪ May show pride if she tries to help ▪ Shows genuine concern for another person's distress ▪ Begins to be able to share but will still take another child's toys and possessions. ▪ Increase in joint attention and in responding to the facial expressions of primary caregivers ▪ Recognizes if something is broken, demonstrates an understanding of internalized standards of how things should be ▪ May show some self-control by stopping a behavior he knows he is not supposed to do	▪ Caregiver provides a balance of supportive affection and discipline and containment ▪ Encourages the development of language by imitating words and following the child's lead ▪ Provides authoritative parenting and explains rules and consequences ▪ Encourages and helps child to inhibit a negative action by setting necessary limits and supporting the child in trying a more adaptive behavior ▪ Begins to develop a cooperative and mutually responsive orientation to negotiation around discipline ▪ Limits the number of rules to important routines such as the bedtime routine and those that are essential to keep the child and others safe ▪ Begins to make sure rules are followed through with so that the child understands what is expected and what will happen if she does not do what is requested

2 to 4 years	■ New self-conscious emotions of pride, embarrassment, and shame appear and support behavior regulation ■ Can stop a behavior about 85% of the time. For "do" requests follow through about 30% of the time ■ Begins to use private speech to help with following through with rules ■ Can distinguish between right and wrong in moral stories ■ During pretend or imaginary play may tell dolls or animals what to do ■ May have difficulty with transferring rules across settings such as from home to daycare ■ While usually more compliant by 3 years of age, some 3-year-olds may use words to argue and to try to negotiate everything ■ By 4 years of age negativism reduces and the child is more able to conform to social norms ■ Child may realize she has done wrong and apologize (e.g., if hurts another child)	■ Parent provides a balance between providing support and encouraging child's independence ■ Encourages the child to use private speech to enhance the capacity to follow a rule and to avoid a temptation to misbehave ■ Continues to provide discipline for the child and to support the child in inhibiting immediate responses if appropriate ■ Children may need to be told why a rule is important ■ Parent tries to avoid unnecessary conflicts around rules by warning the child ahead of time about transitions, and changes that are coming up ■ Prepares for outings and activities to avoid confrontation ■ Consequences are made clear and followed through with and good behavior is noticed ■ Modeling of appropriate behavior by the parent is important as well as the use of directives as the language used will be internalized ■ At this stage it is important to provide a balance so that the child neither wins or loses all the "battles" and an atmosphere of mutuality is developed ■ Parent brings the perspective of others so that the child can be motivated by how the other person may feel in certain situations

(continued)

Table 7.1 *Highlights of the Development of Typical Behavior Regulation and Parenting (continued)*

Age Range	Development	Parenting
4 to 6 years	■ With theory of mind or perspective taking, child is not so egocentric in his thinking and has a sense of fairness toward others ■ Can inhibit immediate impulsive responses such as not running in the road or hurting another child ■ By 5 years of age child wants to follow the parents' standards and rules ■ Can perform simple chores and self-help tasks with reminders (e.g., tidying bedroom and clearing dishes from the table) ■ By 5 years of age the child's conscience is in place and he will feel bad if he does something he knows is against the rules of the family, school, and community ■ May be quite strict about the rules and tell children who come over to play to follow the rules of their household ■ Noncompliance and defiance are rare although at times if the child is tired or upset she child may still argue and try to negotiate rules that are non-negotiable ■ Has a well-developed sense of fairness ■ Can present a narrative that shows understanding of moral rules ■ May want to help the poor or other people in need ■ Internalizes the rules of the family, school, and society ■ More able to use thinking, words, and fantasy instead of impulsive action ■ Capacity for empathy continues to develop and the child may want to help the poor or think about doing another cause	■ Induction is very important at this stage to develop conscience (i.e., explaining why the rules are necessary and the effect of the child's behavior on other people) ■ If there are two parents they need to work together and to use the same rules and routines ■ Parent avoids making negative statements to the child about his characteristics (e.g., "You're so bad, you will never amount to anything and you'll end up in jail") ■ Important to use positive reinforcement and notice when child is trying to behave in a positive way ■ Parents understand that they can manage the child's behavior and have strategies to do so ■ Remains consistent and has a reliable program of consequences in place ■ If there are two parents a united front is presented and any differences are identified and discussed ■ Allows the child some flexibility and an opportunity to express her point of view about certain issues ■ Important to understand the child and the reasons he is having problems with regulating his behavior; problems could be due to difficulties the child has with executive functioning, sensory integration, or speech difficulties particularly with receptive vocabulary ■ Uses problem-solving strategies if discipline difficulties occur

7 to 10 years	▪ Increased selfreliance of the child ▪ Takes more responsibility for household chores and looking after his own possessions ▪ Child should have a clear view of right and wrong and be able to reject any suggestions from peers to engage in antisocial or bullying behavior ▪ Child does not show ongoing stubbornness or get into conflict with authority figures such as teachers ▪ Child attends school regularly and understands and follows the rules of school ▪ Completes homework on time and is able to keep up with the requirements of school ▪ Accepts personal responsibility for his behavior ▪ Sees things from the perspective of others ▪ Now motivated by wanting to fit into peer group	▪ Parent still keeps a close eye on the child and monitors her behavior and social activities ▪ Parent makes sure that homework and chores are initiated and completed ▪ Structures and routines are provided in the home sometimes with visual cues so that the child can get herself organized and follows through with the activities of the day ▪ Provides an overall containment and support for the child's activities and responsibilities ▪ Makes sure that any concern around schoolwork or behavior raised at school is attended to ▪ Monitors use of the Internet and warns the child about possible dangers that may be there ▪ Checks that the child is not feeling rejected or bullied and follows up on any sadness or anger that seems out of character for the child ▪ If child is developing negative behaviors that he did not have before, makes sure that they are dealt with immediately and checks for things that are going on that could cause the difficulty
11 to 13 years	▪ Child is increasingly independent and interested in activities outside the home ▪ Relationships with parents and their help are still important but child may push them away temporarily ▪ Helps out with chores and may babysit younger siblings or for pay outside the home ▪ Child is usually less impulsive and can delay gratification enough to work hard to achieve a goal ▪ Manages school schedule with changing teachers and schedules ▪ Begins to have long-term goals such as going to college and pursuing a particular career	▪ Child needs to feel support for his independent activities and monitoring of parent to keep them safe ▪ Parent keeps the child away from negative influences as much as possible such as negative peer influences, and drugs and alcohol ▪ Parent plays a monitoring role at more of a distance to keep the child safe ▪ Explains some of the dangers that the child can be exposed to and continues to support positive activities and school performance ▪ Continues to enforce the rules and knows where the child is and insists on certain curfews and forbids activities that could endanger the child ▪ As much as possible makes sure that the child has a positive peer group ▪ Encourages hobbies and activities so that child is occupied in a positive way

for others does not develop (Tisak & Jankowski, 1996). If aggression escalates in young children it is important to assess the behavior and introduce strategies to improve the child's behavior (Wakschlag & DAnis, 2004). Poor parenting is likely to exacerbate the child's problems, leading to greater disruptive behaviors (Degnan et al., 2008).

The early elementary school years from about 6 to 8 years of age show a stabilization of the problems, with some escalation. Overt aggression and defiance persist, and more covert antisocial behavior, such as stealing or lying, can occur. Teacher interactions with the child can also become coercive, and the teacher might think that the child is unmanageable. The child might experience rejection from well-functioning peers and become involved with antisocial and aggressive peers. Some children might experience early school failure and become alienated from school. Atypical processing of social situations can occur and lead to escalation of the negative behaviors. This is therefore an important time to intervene if possible (Walker, Stiller, Severson, Feil, & Gally, 1998).

The later elementary and middle school years (9 to 13 years of age) can see escalation and elaboration of the earlier antisocial and aggressive behavior. Aggression can become more violent, and covert behaviors might increase, including school skipping, fire setting, and substance use.

By the time children with these problems are referred for treatment, their parents have typically tried for a long time to find answers using a number of services. Many parents have attended parenting groups, conscientiously applied the recommendations, and found that they have not been enough for their child to improve. Often they have felt blamed by service providers and that nobody has really tried to understand their child or situation. Therefore, before any recommendations for treatment are made, it is crucial that a full assessment of the reasons for the child's behavior is made. In each situation, there will not be a single factor that accounts for the symptoms. Rather, there will usually be complex individual, family, and contextual factors that have resulted in the child's presentation.

Screening

It is important to begin assessment by clarifying some of the risk factors that might be contributing to the child's presentation. Screening identifies areas that require further assessment.

Broad-Band Behavioral Rating Scales

Behavioral rating scales collect information from parents, teachers, and children about a child's behavior. They assess a number of domains of behavior. Some of the most commonly used are *Behavior Assessment System for Children,* 2nd ed. (*BASC-2;* Reynolds & Kamphaus, 2004); *Child Behavior Checklist* (*CBCL;* Achenbach, 2001); *Conners-3 Rating Scales* (Conners, 1997); and *Personality Inventory of Children—Revised* (*PIC-R;* Lachar & Gruber, 1991).

Other Behavioral Rating Scales

A number of other rating scales have been developed to assess children with behavior-regulation problems. Only those related to the contributing factors discussed in this chapter are mentioned.

Inventory of Callous–Unemotional Traits (ICU; Essau, Sasagawa, & Frick, 2006). This is a 24-item scale for children, and there are three versions of the scale designed to provide a comprehensive assessment of C/U traits. They ask the person to rate the items about C/U traits on a 4-point Likert scale from 0 (not at all true) to 3 (definitely true). There are parent, teacher, and self-report versions. Three subscales have been identified: callousness, uncaring, and unemotional. However, it has mostly been used with children from 12 years old and above, though the authors suggest that it can be used with slightly younger children. The construct validity of the scale was supported with C/U traits being associated with a measure of the Big Five personality dimensions. The total scale showed predicted associations with aggression, delinquency, personality traits, and psychosocial impairment.

Proactive and Reactive Aggression Parent and Teacher Rating Scales (Brown, Atkins, Osborne, & Milnamow, 1996). There is no manual for the scale, but there are a number of articles about development of the scale and its validity. A study of boys in Grade 3 to 5 classrooms found validity for the two scales of proactive and reactive aggression. The Scale is available in five versions: Youth Self-Report, Youth Parent Report, Youth Teacher Report, Parent Report (Preschool Version), and Teacher Report (Preschool Version).

Why Kids Do Things (Crick, 1995). This is a measure of intent attributions that involves hypothetical stories of socially ambiguous relational and instrumental provocation situations. Children are asked to imagine being in certain situations and then asked to guess the intent of the behavior or whether the person in the story intended to be mean. It can help to understand attributions of the child in ambiguous situations.

Antisocial Process Screening Device (*APSD*; Frick & Hare, 2001). This scale screens for antisocial tendencies in children from 6 to 13 years of age. There are parent, teacher, and combined forms. Each takes about 5 to 10 minutes to complete. The *APSD* was normed on a community sample of 1,120 children. It measures three dimensions of behavior: C/U traits, narcissism, and impulsivity. Test–retest reliability is high for all three scales. Validity has been assessed by comparing scores on the APSD with results on other scales. The scales have shown association with the *Children's Symptom Inventory-4*, with all three scales moderately to strongly correlated.

Observation of the Child at Home and School

Observation of parent–child interactions in the home can involve sensitivity and reciprocity of parents' reactions to the child and the type of discipline that parents tend to use. A number of measures can be used in the home. Observation of the child in different settings can identify remediable aspects of the environment that might contribute to the child's behavior. Standardized observational systems define the behaviors to be observed and the methods for recording them. They can provide valuable data to complement information from other methods. However, they can be time consuming. Three of these measures are discussed below.

Dyadic Parent–Child Interaction Coding System—Revised (*DPCICS-R*; Robinson & Eyberg, 1981). The *DPCICS-R* evaluates the interactions of children from 5 to 8 years of age with their parents in the home environment. The child's behavior and parents' responses are assessed. It has 39 behavioral categories for parents and 8 for children. Behavior is coded during 5-minute episodes of free play, parent-guided interaction, and clean-up interaction. A compliance ratio is assessed indicating how often the child responds to parental requests.

The Disruptive Behavior Diagnostic Observation Schedule (*DB-DOS*; Wakschlag et al., 2007). This schedule is a semi-structured system that can be used with preschool children from 3 to 5 years of age to identify clinically significant disruptive behavior syndromes and disorders. The observation period of 50 minutes includes three tasks during which the child's behavior is recorded. Two main domains of behavior are coded: Behavioral Regulation and Anger Modulation. A companion coding system for assessing parenting behavior is also available. Reliability and validity of the DB-DOS have been reported. Training is required to administer the schedule in a research protocol.

Observation in the school is best done before the clinician has met the child to make sure that she does not act differently. Her behavior in the classroom and on the playground is observed as well as the educational setting. This observation can see how she attends to the curriculum, relates to peers, and displays externalizing behaviors. The success of strategies used to help her can also be estimated.

Interviews

Interviews with parents can be structured or semi-structured and are best conducted on the first occasion without the child present so that the parents can openly describe his developmental and medical histories and current symptoms. Interviews about the child with teachers and other school staff should collect data on the following:

- his level of adjustment to school,
- his academic functioning,
- his ability to concentrate and complete work,
- his behavior in the classroom and on the playground,
- the teacher's understanding of what is contributing to his difficulties,
- his responses to discipline,
- his peer interactions and ability to make friends,
- his type and level of aggression,
- what triggers his outbursts,
- his capacity for empathy and remorse,
- any accommodation in the classroom or specialized teaching, and
- results of any assessments that have been conducted by school personnel.

Interviews with the child can be totally unstructured, and the interviewer can use open-ended questions and "how" and "why" questions to elicit information. Interviews designed for children with behavioral issues are provided next.

Composite International Diagnostic Interview (CIDI; Kessler & Ustun, 2004). This interview was developed by the World Health Organization and can be used for assessment of CD. It is fully structured, needs no training to administer, and provides diagnoses according to the definitions and criteria for CDs of *DSM-IV* (4th ed.; APA, 1994) and *The ICD-10 Classification of Mental and Behavioural Disorders: Diagnostic Criteria for Research* (World Health Organization, 1992).

Diagnostic Interview of Children and Adolescents—4th edition (*DICA-IV*; Reich, 2000). This is a semi-structured interview for use with children and adolescents. It provides an assessment of the symptoms of various *DSM-IV* disorders, including CD. It has adequate reliability and validity.

Diagnostic Interview Schedule for Children, 4th edition (*DISC-4*; Robins, Marcus, Reich, Cunningham, & Gallagher, 1996). The *DISC-4* is a highly structured measure based on the *DSM-IV* diagnostic criteria and probes for problem behaviors or symptoms that have occurred in the past 6 months. It has acceptable levels of reliability and validity, which are increased if both the child and parent reports are used.

Direct Assessment of the Child

Assessment of the child can follow the assessments discussed above or be done at the same time. The tests given will depend to some degree on the tests already completed and the areas identified as needing further assessment. These tests are often critical for a successful intervention because they provide information on cognitive functioning, academic achievement, and neuropsychological functioning. They need to be detailed enough to provide information from which to develop interventions.

TREATMENT OF CHILDREN WITH BEHAVIOR REGULATION AND CONSCIENCE DEVELOPMENT PROBLEMS

Treating children with behavior regulation problems can be extremely demanding, particularly if the child is frequently aggressive, oppositional, and defiant. For children who have been traumatized, the desire to be in control can be overwhelming and reflects a desperate need not to feel overpowered or overwhelmed again. Consequently, they can be quickly triggered and become aggressive when instructed to do something or stop doing something. This need for control can also reflect a primitive and basic need for survival in some children who have constantly felt threatened by situations in their environments. Some of the important principles of treatment of children with behavior regulation problems and difficulty with developing a conscience are listed below:

- In most cases, a number of factors contribute to the child's difficulties, so approaches need to be multimodal and multidimensional.
- Treatment must be individualized to fit the needs of a particular child and family. No one theoretical or treatment approach can meet the needs of all children and families. The difficulties can reinforce one another, so improvements in one can often cause improvements in others.
- Treatment approaches should be evidence-based when possible. However, approaches found to be efficacious with children with similar challenges or with a particular child can be integrated into the overall treatment plan.
- Parent training programs have been the most evaluated interventions for children with disruptive behaviors; although they are successful in a number of families, up to a third do not attend, drop out, or attend but do not improve. Consequently, clinicians need to be flexible in introducing other approaches to behavior management.
- Because generalization across settings is often poor for children with behavior regulation problems, psychosocial interventions might need to be provided in multiple arenas in the child's life, including home, school, and other appropriate community settings. Once-weekly clinical sessions for the child generally are not sufficient or effective. Because the problems are often chronic, treatment needs to be intense at first, followed by ongoing support by community agencies.
- Although children with disruptive behaviors need consistent routines and structures, behavior management alone is not effective. Needed are other treatment approaches that can enhance interactions of the child with parents, teachers, and other caregivers.
- A full assessment of the child's functioning in multiple developmental areas is essential before clear recommendations can be made to parents, teachers, and other caregivers for optimal ways to manage and improve her functioning. Also, the assessment, as far as possible, needs to take into account the neurobiological mechanisms likely to underlie her behavior.
- Regardless of the diagnoses that the child has, it is critical to understand the causal mechanisms contributing to her presentation and focus treatment on improving them both within her and in the systems around her.
- Clinical interventions that focus on a single psychosocial process believed to be contributing to the child's behavior are bound to be ineffective, for multiple interacting processes will contribute to his particular type of conduct problem (e.g., reactive versus proactive aggression) and his particular challenges and strengths.
- The younger the child, the more critical the involvement of his family. However, parents are often exhausted, angry, and burnt out and have felt blamed by service providers. Also, some of the recommendations made might not have been appropriate and thus have not worked. Consequently, it might take a long time for some parents to be open to treatment suggestions. Therefore, it is critical to show respect, empathy, and understanding and work with them to find solutions for their child's difficulties.
- It is also critical to work with the child's school if services are not already in place to accommodate the classroom as much as possible to the child's needs and integrate strategies to overcome some of her most significant issues.

- Where possible, approaches discouraging deviant peer involvement and encouraging socially appropriate peer networks need to be included to help overcome socialization issues.
- Individual treatment of the child needs to be adapted to age, processing style, and capabilities. Various approaches might be needed, such as skill training, cognitive-behavioral approaches, and psychotherapy. It is critical to teach and build up basic capacities that are delayed in children.
- Medication for extreme symptoms and comorbid disorders such as ADHD and depression might be necessary and can often be effective.
- Beliefs about discipline and attributions of the child can affect the success of intervention. The relationship between the parent and the intervenor and how information is provided can be powerful determinants of whether the parent is willing to accept suggestions for working with the child. As well, parents' readiness for change is important in determining whether new information and suggestions will be used (Prochaska, 1999).

Interventions in Parent–Child Interactions

Coercive parent–child interactions are common when children have behavior regulation problems. It is important, therefore, to examine these interactions and provide strategies to improve areas where difficulties are found. Sometimes parents themselves have mental health issues, including ADHD, substance abuse, and depression. These difficulties can interfere with their ability to improve their interactions with their children. When parents resist engaging in intervention, it is important to use a shared problem-solving and empowerment approach (Scott & Dadds, 2009).

Changing Parents' Negative Attributions of Their Child

Parents of children with conduct problems often develop negative attributions of their children and the meanings of their behaviors. Some parents believe that their child's behavior is intentional, under his control, and deliberately designed to upset them (Dadds, Mullins, McAllister, & Atkinson, 2003). Others believe that the behaviors have been inherited from a disliked family member. Sometimes what is needed is to get the attributions out in the open and discuss them several times as treatment progresses. Sometimes gentle questioning about whether they can think of any other explanation for his behavior often provides constructive ideas.

Attributions can change when the results of an assessment indicate that the child is struggling with problems with cognition, receptive and expressive language, gross and fine motor functioning, and/or sensory integration. For example, the child might have significant problems with auditory processing and receptive language that can make it difficult for her to follow instructions, so what might have been seen as oppositional behavior is in fact a functional impairment. This information can help parents to understand their child better and increase their empathy for her. They might also be more willing to follow through with suggestions to help them adapt their interactions to support her particular challenges better. Greene and Ablon (2006), in their highly successful book and approach to intervention, *Treating Explosive Kids*, describe their Collaborative Problem-Solving (CPS) Approach in which parents and other caregivers learn about the deficits that impair the child's ability to contain frustration. The clinician is given ways to both help the child and problem solve with the parent(s) to handle conflict with their children more successfully.

Bugental and colleagues (1997) used their model of "threat-oriented" schema to describe attributions of high-risk parents who attribute high control to their child and low control to themselves. These attributions can result in anger toward the child and even abuse. Bugental used this model to develop an intervention with parents to redefine attributions of their children and to help them find new ways to interact with and discipline their children. The parent is asked to describe a behavior of the child that is particularly difficult to deal with. The intervenor then helps the parent to problem solve, come up with a strategy that she believes will work, and supports her to try it for a week. If successful, another behavior is chosen, and the process is repeated. If unsuccessful, further problem solving takes place, and the parent is helped to find an approach that should work. Once the parent has achieved some success, she can change her attribution of herself as being controlled by the child to believing that she is in charge and her child is manageable.

Enhancing Parents' Discipline of Their Child

Parent Management Training (PMT) is usually provided in groups and has been one of the most popular approaches to treatment for children with aggression and ODD. Many of the programs provide clear guidelines on how to implement the standardized treatment in groups. The training is based on social learning theory, in particular operant behaviorism, and focuses on increasing the child's capacity to regulate his destructive and oppositional behaviors. Coercive family interactions are targeted, and attempts to replace lax and harsh punitive parenting with appropriate consequences such as instituting time-outs and eliminating negative behaviors are used. PMT also promotes positive parenting practices such as skill encouragement, resolving parenting problems, and monitoring children and adolescents. Several randomized control studies have found that, for some children, PMT does decrease their aggression and the coercive behavior of their parents. PMT programs include Parent–Child Interaction Therapy (Brinkmeyer & Eyberg, 2003), Defiant Children (Barkley, 1997), Parent Management Training from Oregon (Forgatch & DeGarmo, 1999), Triple P (Sanders, 2008), Helping the Noncompliant Child (McMahon & Forehand, 2003), and Incredible Years (Webster-Stratton & Reid, 2003). There is enormous variability in their success, and a quarter to a third of families and their children do not benefit either because the parents drop out or because they do not implement the strategies effectively. This can be as high as 50% of parents of children with more severe difficulties (Cavell, 2000; Kazdin, 2005; Martinez & Forgatch, 2001; Prinz & Miller, 1994). As a consequence, some programs have included strategies to intervene with parents' personal, marital, and family issues such as increasing social support and self-care, personal self-control, and family interaction skills. These programs (e.g., BASIC and ADVANCE programs; Webster-Stratton, 2003) improved family functioning and reduced dropout rates. However, PMT is useful only for a limited number of parents with children with severe behavioral problems, and other approaches are essential for treatment to be effective.

It is critical that parents gradually believe that they can manage their child and their own emotional reactions and begin to enjoy their child. Children with behavior regulation problems need consistent reactions from both parents and teachers, using a style of discipline that emphasizes a strong and obedience-oriented approach to setting limits. In other words, the child needs reassurance that the adult is in control and intends to remain so. It is important for both parents to decide on ways to stop aggressive behavior and support each other in enforcing them. It is also critical to have a regular routine in the home, as much as possible, and an outline of it in a place that the child can see. It is useful to let him see how he is progressing through the routine in the morning and at night. This can be done, for example, by using pictures stuck on with Velcro as the steps of the routine are completed.

It is critical not to shame the child when he has to be disciplined for verbally or physically aggressive behavior or when what he is doing places him at risk or is an antisocial behavior such as stealing. Once the child has calmed down, parents can reconnect with him and gradually return him to rational thinking. Because he is likely to have a distorted view of what happened, it is important to correct any misperceptions, as much as possible. Listening to his point of view, being supportive, and letting him know that you understand it is hard for him and will support him to do better next time are crucial. This can be an opportunity to take a close look at what happened and find alternative ways to handle the difficult emotions and stressful situation. This consistent response to aggression and extreme acting-out behavior, along with reliable routines, will give the child a sense that his parents and teachers are in charge and can keep him safe. It is also critical to notice and reinforce any responsible behavior shown by the child and model this behavior in the home as much as possible. In fact, children with behavior management problems need to hear positive comments about efforts and improvements far more often than they hear negative comments when being disciplined. If parents constantly lose their tempers and use harsh and punitive discipline rather than model the behavior that they seek from the child, discipline will be useless. When this approach is repeated each time the child becomes aggressive, he will realize what is unacceptable behavior and begin to understand his responsibility for what happened.

New research shows that, although behavior management and reinforcement are useful, for children who have traits of impulsivity and disinhibition, these strategies are unlikely to be sufficient. The usual consequences used to encourage good behavior and reduce bad behavior do not cause enough physiological arousal in these children for them to learn the consequences of their behavior. Such children need clear boundaries and limits, but discipline also needs to be provided within a warm and responsive relationship while incorporating many other strategies, such as mental state talk and empathy. In other words, a caregiver–child mutually responsive orientation (MRO) that encompasses warmth and nurturance, positive affect, cooperation, and responsiveness to cues is needed (Kochanska, Forman, Aksan, & Dunbar, 2005). This is very difficult to provide for aggressive children who hurt others, but it is important for parents to try to understand their child's vulnerabilities and communicate this understanding to the child.

Increasing Parents' Responsiveness and Sensitivity to Their Child

By the time children are referred for treatment of severe behavioral problems, they are often involved in ways to try to manage their behavior that are ineffective and actually increase that behavior. It is therefore critical to break these patterns and increase both the child's and the parents' capacities for positive engagement. Parents like to be supported in different ways. Parents with a more dismissive and knowledge-based style might want to be given information and have their questions answered. Parents with a preoccupied attachment style might welcome opportunities to talk about their experiences and reflect on what is going on with their child. Suggesting that parents play with their child or take her on an outing can be helpful.

Another useful approach is to ask parents to use a daily diary of when negative and positive behaviors occur, examine the data to determine patterns, and then share the information with them to problem solve ways to avoid any identified triggers and deal with the recognized issues in different ways.

For younger children who show aggression past the age when it is typically reduced, various approaches have been developed to improve the responsiveness of parents and enhance the sensitivity of their interactions with their child. Video feedback was found to reduce externalizing behavior in 1- to 3-year-old children and reduce daily cortisol production in some of them (Juffer, Bakermans-Kranenburg, & van IJzendoorn, 2008). However, the most reduction was found in children with the DRD4 7 repeat allele or who were genetically characterized by a less efficient reuptake of dopamine. Videotape viewing can also be helpful for parents to consider what their older child is thinking and feeling and to talk about how they felt during the interaction and at other times with their child.

Errorless Compliance was developed (Ducharme, Atkinson, & Poulton, 2000) to work with children with severe oppositional behavior from violent and abusive homes and has been effective in reducing parent–child conflict. The treatment is designed to provide both the parent and the child with a sense of success in their daily interactions. The program is focused on enhancing parent–child cooperation and reducing negative behaviors in the child. Parents are initially asked to come up with a list of requests ranging from those that the child will cooperate with readily (e.g., "throw me the ball" and "eat your cookie") to those that she will typically ignore (e.g., "turn off the TV" and "pick up your toys"). The parent begins the intervention by providing requests that almost always lead to cooperation and compliance, giving the parent many opportunities to praise her. After a few weeks, requests that are a little more challenging for the child are gradually introduced by the parent, who is encouraged to continue praising her for following through with the requested tasks. This process is continued for several weeks until the most difficult requests, those that presented serious compliance difficulties before treatment, are introduced. With this gradual and positive approach, parents typically find that their children are considerably more cooperative in demanding requests. Parent participants in the program report high levels of satisfaction with immediate success in getting their child to cooperate and improving their relationship with her. The parents' sense of success is enhanced, and daily conflicts are significantly reduced. These gains are achieved without the use of punishment or coercion. The program has also been successfully used in the classroom.

Strengthening the Parenting Subsystem

When a family has a child with conduct problems, the hierarchical parent structure typically becomes disorganized because parents are split over how to manage the child and cannot work together to support or discipline him. When this happens, the relationship needs to be targeted and the parental subsystem in the family strengthened by holding sessions in which the parents are seen together without their child. One result of frustration over dealing with a challenging child is that parents and the nonproblem child(ren) become increasingly close, whereas the problem child's sense of alienation and rejection increases. The parents in this case need to be helped to apply discipline to both children and reward both when they are not fighting or acting out. This can reinforce a more positive child subsystem.

Enhancing the Child's Functioning in Various Areas

Some intervention strategies need to focus on enhancing the child's capacity in areas identified by the multidisciplinary assessment as delays or deficits. Some areas are most frequently compromised in children with more reactive aggression, whereas others are particularly important when children have proactive and C/U traits. Whenever possible, it is helpful to parallel the strategies at home and school.

Encouraging the Development of Conscience and Empathy

By about 5 years of age, children have usually internalized a conscience or sense of right and wrong, can follow rules, and show remorse and empathy. Impaired early development of a conscience is a risk factor for the development of conduct problems, antisocial behaviors, and psychopathic traits. A number of theorists and researchers have proposed that the early parent–child relationship can encourage the development of conscience and have described responsiveness, sensitivity to the child's needs, and reciprocity as the characteristics needed for this to occur (Belsky, 1999). Kochanska and colleagues have described a

Mutually Responsive Orientation (MRO) that supports the child's desire to be cooperative and follow rules (Kochanska, 1997b, 1998, 2002; Kochanska, Forman, Aksan, & Dunbar, 2005). They describe MRO as having two components: "mutual responsiveness and shared affective positivity." The approach has also been described as attachment-based and encourages identification with a positive attachment figure. Consequently, to enhance the child's capacity for conscience and empathy, enhancing the positivity of the interaction can be a promising approach.

Induction has been shown to contribute to the development of conscience, and using "mental state talk" when communicating with children can be helpful in developing empathy. Social understanding and competence require that children be aware of the mental states of others or develop a theory of mind (TOM). Research has clearly demonstrated that children learn about TOM or understand the perspectives of others from their parents and other caregivers who talk about the thoughts and feelings of other children and adults. When children hear mental state discourse, reasoning about mental states is encouraged and internalized. Mental state language refers to mind- and emotion-related comments as opposed to talking about behavioral or physical characteristics of people. It can be about thoughts, desires, and feelings in the caregiver's mind, the child's mind, or another person's mind. This type of discourse, though simple in some ways, has been linked to secure attachment, perspective taking, prosocial behavior, and social competence.

Mental state talk can take place in play, discipline, and while watching a digital video disk (DVD). It includes attributing meanings to vocalizations such as "You are really interested in that game." When disciplining children, it can be a comment such as "When you disobey the rule, I am very disappointed with you." When watching a DVD, pointing out the feelings of characters is helpful (e.g., "Simon believes his father went away because he was mad at him, but his father really went away because he had to do some work in an office in another city"). In this kind of mental state discourse, the child is asked about how he is feeling and what he is thinking about so that his perspective can be understood and the other person's point of view explained. Included in the dialogue can be a description of why the parent thinks the other child is thinking or feeling a certain way. It can include comments about nonverbal cues such as facial expressions: "He looks mad because he has an angry face and his fists are clenched." Sometimes the comments can be about what the parent thinks the child is thinking, believing, or feeling (e.g., "I think you are sad and don't want grandma to go home"). Such comments can encourage a two-way conversation and provide further opportunities for mental state talk to occur (see Table 7.2).

Table 7.2 *Using Mental State Talk*

Cognitions	Beliefs	Feelings
"John must be thinking about having to learn his sounds for his spelling test."	"John believes that he will manage to do well in the test because his mum often tells him he is a smart kid."	"John still gets anxious about his test and worries he won't do well."
"It looks like Michael is thinking about starting school tomorrow and wonders who will be in his class."	"Michael believes that he will like his first day in school as he knows his friend will be in his class."	"Michael feels a bit jealous as his younger brother and sister will get to spend all day with his mother and he will miss being at home with her."

When parents notice spontaneous helping behavior and let their child know how pleased they are, such prosocial behavior is reinforced. Children can show caring behavior in a number of ways: protecting a sibling, comforting a friend, feeding a pet, or sharing a treat with another child. Any instances of this kind of behavior that happen spontaneously should be noticed and appreciated. The child needs to be told about the pleasure and pride that others feel when he is helpful.

Improving Emotion Regulation

Many children with behavior regulation disorders have problems regulating their negative emotions, and emotion socialization processes within the family can contribute to these difficulties (Chaplin & Cole, 2005; Cicchetti, Ackerman, & Izard, 1995). Negative parental socialization can lead to child deficits in emotion regulation and contribute to externalizing behavior. As well, some children have more disinhibited temperaments or have experienced trauma, so their aggression tends to be more reactive to certain triggers in the environment.

In one study, mothers' emotion coaching was related to better emotion regulation in children in later elementary school, and this in turn was related to less externalizing behavior (Shortt, Stoolmiller, Smith-Shine, Eddy, & Sheeber, 2010). Given these results and the frequent comorbidity of aggression and anxiety/depression, it is important to consider emotion coaching approaches to intervention. Gottman, Katz, and Hooven (1997) outlined an approach to emotion coaching using the following steps. They pointed out that it is important to notice small emotions before the child gets too wound up and explodes if it is anger and frustration or withdraws if it is fear, sadness, or depression. Connection during these moments can enhance the relationship and help the child to feel understood and the parent to feel a better connection with her child. When a small emotion is noticed that the parent believes might escalate, the parent goes through the following steps:

1. Acknowledges that the child is frustrated or upset and that what he is going through is difficult. She asks him why he is so upset if it is not obvious and shows empathy for his frustration or anxiety.
2. Shows understanding and acceptance of his feelings.
3. Sets limits on his behavior if necessary, letting him know what is not acceptable. For example, he must not hurt anyone.
4. Encourages him to problem solve and find a strategy to prevent the problem from happening again (e.g., putting toys where the younger sibling will not be able to get them). The parent can suggest some options.
5. Goes through suggestions until a workable one is found and assists the child to use the strategy the next time a similar situation occurs.

This approach can move an immediate and limbic system emotional response to a more cognitive response using the frontal cortex. As well, it is helpful to get children to express how they are feeling and to talk about it, and then provide guidance on better ways to express feelings.

It is important to help parents notice when a child is experiencing increased anxiety or anger and showing signs of losing control so that they can de-escalate the situation and return the child to a baseline or calm state. Different approaches work for different children, including giving the child assurance of support, removing her for some exercise, listening to him about how he is feeling and thinking, and planning what to do next time she is upset. It is important to understand the function of the behavior or if she has simply become overaroused. Sometimes the child will have difficulty with expressing verbally what she is thinking or feeling, but it might be possible to determine what is happening by taking into account the child's tone of voice and facial expression. Responses that reflect on what the child seems to be thinking and feeling can be helpful.

Many children with conduct problems struggle to understand what other people, especially peers, are trying to communicate to them and often misinterpret what is meant and believe that the other person is intentionally hurting them or is angry with them when this is not necessarily the case. There are a number of individual and group approaches to enable this to happen. Sometimes the approaches begin with helping children read facial expressions, their own and those of others in a mirror, and to notice the tones of voice. Sometimes role playing can be used; children take turns trying to show a certain emotional facial expression while the others try to guess what it is, and then the roles are reversed. Sometimes interactions can be videotaped so that the children can see how they look and how easy or difficult their expressions are to guess.

Some children, particularly those with psychopathic traits, have reduced reactions to facial and vocal cues of distress (e.g., fear and sadness) in others. They are typically more able to recognize other emotions, such as happiness, anger, and surprise (Blair et al., 2005; van Baardewijk et al., 2009). Drawing attention to emotional signals in others can be a useful way to reduce aggression. Also, using the induction methods discussed earlier can be extremely helpful and improve long-term outcomes.

Medication

Because a number of biological mechanisms underlie aggressive/antisocial behavior, medication is often recommended to help reduce aggressive and antisocial behavior and enable the child to use other interventions. There is evidence that medication use with chronic maladaptive aggression is common. However, Connor (2002) recommended that it should not be considered until a thorough psychiatric assessment has been completed and that it should only be prescribed as part of a thorough psychosocial and psychoeducational treatment plan. When the child has early-onset aggression that is chronic, severe, frequent, and accompanied by impulsive, hyperactive, and explosive outbursts, it can respond to pharmacological treatment, which is also likely to improve ODD and reactive aggression. On the other hand, aggression that is premeditated and associated with low levels of ANS arousal does not seem to be responsive to medication (Connor, 2002). Five main classes of medication have been used: (1) neuroleptics and antipsychotics, (2) stimulants, (3) antidepressants, (4) mood stabilizers, and (5) adrenergic agents (see Connor, 2002).

Dealing With Issues of Control

Some children with behavior regulation problems want to be in control at all times often because they were maltreated and felt powerless as infants and young children, because their parents failed to respond to them. It may also be because they have difficulty with schoolwork, simple tasks, or self-care. Sometimes giving the child a choice about doing something that he has to do can make a big difference to it getting done and the child feeling good about it. For example, for the child who typically does not want to go to the mall, he can be given a choice of staying with an aunt whom he is not fond of or going with the family. If he decides to go to the mall, at least he will know that it is his choice.

Enhancing the Child's Capacity for Socialization

Social Competence Training

Social competence training (SCT) focuses on enhancing a child's social and emotional capacities. Various approaches have been used and include trying to reduce negative behaviors, such as hitting and annoying others, and teaching children social skills such as cooperating, sharing, communicating, and listening. Another approach teaches children perspective taking, self-talk, and social problem solving. SCT also focuses on finding solutions to entering groups and maintaining interactions with a partner using skills such as negotiation and cooperation. Children are trained to assess the climate and rules of the group that they want to join and to match their styles of entry correspondingly. The last approach focuses on emotion regulation, particularly for negative emotions such as anger and frustration. Reducing negative behavior does not seem to generalize to other situations. However, the approaches have been successful in certain situations, with the American Psychological Association concluding that problem-solving and anger-coping interventions are the most effective (Lonigan, Elbert, & Johnson, 1998). However, Taylor, Eddy, and Biglan (1999) examined the SCT literature as it applies to children with aggression and conduct problems and found that the interventions were only moderately effective and that there was little evidence that they were clinically significant long term. Another problem was that there has been little attention paid to providing diverse approaches to subtypes of behavior regulation disorders. They recommended that SCT be used only as part of a more comprehensive, evidence-based approach that includes parent, family, and classroom interventions.

Changing the Child's Negative Attributions of Others

In social situations, children with acting-out behaviors frequently misinterpret the behaviors of others and attribute deliberate hostile intent to the interactions of peers. The child then believes that the other child deserves retaliation. Various approaches to changing attributions have been used, the idea being that children can learn to recognize accidental causes of negative social behavior in ambiguous situations. One such program, BrainPower, is a 12-lesson intervention with materials and activities for children in Grades 3 to 6 (Hudley et al., 1998). The program was evaluated in terms of improving social cognition and social behavior among aggressive and nonaggressive children. The program was found to be highly successful for some students but not for others. Those who benefited showed improvements in self-control, which persisted over time. They also made improvements in attributions and showed reductions in attributions of hostile intent, but they were not maintained over time. The results also suggested that changes in attributions contributed to improvements in self-control. The researchers suggested that the program is best used as part of a comprehensive program and for children who show difficulty with ascribing hostile attributions in ambiguous situations.

Cognitive-Behavioral Therapy

Child-focused cognitive-behavioral therapy (CBT) was originally a skill-building intervention and helped the child to overcome some of the deficits described above. It included role playing, modeling, problem solving, and rehearsing skills used in real-life situations. Early studies found significant behavioral improvement, but more recent research has found little improvement from single-component programs (Schneider, 1992). More recently, treatments have focused on children's cognitive processes and distortions. Coping Power is a program used in the school in which children review social situations and discuss social cues and the motivations of others in social encounters. It has been effective in reducing disruptive and aggressive behaviors (Lochman, 1992).

Encouraging Problem Solving in Interpersonal Situations

Problem-solving skill training has also been developed to teach problem-solving skills in interpersonal and academic tasks. Improvement has been found in children with serious aggressive behavior (Kazdin & Weisz, 1998). However, the more the risk factors, the smaller the gains are likely to be (Kazdin, 2005). Another approach has been anger coping, which has also been successful. The combination of CBT and PMT has been effective for children from 5 to 13 years of age (Webster-Stratton & Hammond, 1997). An example of such a program is the Stop Now and Plan (SNAP; Earlscourt and Family Centre, 2001). It is delivered to both parents and children once a week for 14 weeks in group format (Bloomquist & Schnell, 2002). The program has been found to result in decreases in externalizing behaviors compared with children in an attention control group, with treatment gains maintained over 6- and 12-month follow-up periods (Augimeri, Farrington, Koegel, & Day, 2007).

Overcoming Trauma-Related Reactions or Triggering

The TARGET program has been used with high-risk men and women and boys and girls in the juvenile justice system. It provides a 12-session individual therapy version and a 10-session group version. TARGET teaches a practical seven-step sequence of skills for processing and managing trauma-related reactions triggered by current nontraumatic stressors. These skills include emotion regulation, cognitive reappraisal, goal/value clarification, and use of new behaviors in current stressful experiences. The program also includes creative arts exercises to create personal lifelines and emphasizes helping participants to recognize their personal strengths (Ford, Mahoney, St. Juste, & Hennessey, 2009).

Dealing With Violence or Aggressive Outbursts

One of the most difficult behaviors in children with behavior regulation disorders is overt and covert aggression. It can lead to the child being expelled from school, to foster homes breaking down, to becoming involved in the legal system, and to escalating violence in the home. It is therefore crucial that strategies to deal with it are present in both the home and the school. The main contributors to the child's outbursts include the following:

- difficulties with language and communication, particularly social communication and pragmatic language, that can make it difficult for the child to express anger in appropriate ways (see Chapter 4);
- problems with sensory sensitivity and integration, which can lead the child to be overwhelmed by certain things going on in her environment (see Chapter 3);
- trauma, which can lead to certain sounds, sights, smells, and emotions being triggers for a "fight" reaction or to acting out aggressively (see Chapter 5);
- difficulties with executive function and control of the frontal cortex, which can contribute to impulsive outbursts (see Chapter 8); and
- black-and-white thinking, which can mean that the child becomes "stuck" and cannot move beyond a certain idea or position or adapt to a change in routine (see Chapters 8 and 9).

Obviously, these characteristics need to be taken into account and strategies to overcome them developed. As far as possible, triggers for the child should be identified, but sometimes they vary, almost day to day. Noticing that the child is becoming upset and moving in quickly to show concern and empathy and problem solve with the child can be helpful and avoid an outburst. Sometimes making sure that the child has opportunities to run around or go to a calming place can be helpful. There has also been a move toward having sensory rooms to which children can be removed for sensory input that is calming and pleasant. However, due to children's unique sensory profiles, the sounds and sights need to be adaptable for a particular child at a certain time. However, in spite of these efforts, aggressive outbursts can still occur.

Removal to a Safe Place and Physical Restraint

It is crucial to have a plan in place if the child does become violent to separate him from others to avoid injury. Ziegler (2005), the executive director of SCAR in Jasper Mountain, Oregon, a renowned treatment center for children with serious mental health disorders, most of whom have been maltreated, has talked about the need for and therapeutic value of using physical intervention when children become violent. He also acknowledges that extensive training is required to assure that the strategies meet required guidelines and that "holding therapy," which is intrusive and forces the child to be held, is not sanctioned by any legitimate organization. He points out that children must learn that physical touch does not always end in being hurt. A number of programs have been developed on how to avoid aggressive outbursts and deal with them when they do occur. These programs include training in physical restraint. The Therapeutic Crisis Intervention approach has been used successfully in a number of classrooms and residential settings (Day, 2008). See Table 7.3 for a summary of these approaches and other possible strategies.

Approaches That Intervene With Multiple Systems

Multisystemic Therapy

Multisystemic therapy (MST) is a family system approach to treating children and adolescents with conduct problems. It focuses on the multiple systems that impact the child or adolescent, including family, school, neighborhood, and peer group. The program uses various interventions as needed to intervene in the multiple systems affecting a particular child. MST has been effective for the most difficult to treat and impaired populations of antisocial youth, and it has reduced problem behavior and aggression and increased family cohesion (Heneggler, Melton, Smith, Schoenwald, & Hanley, 1993). Treatment effects have been maintained over time.

Other Comprehensive Multicomponent Programs

By developing more comprehensive programs, more risk factors can be addressed. These programs bring together a number of separate interventions in one program usually provided by practitioners from different agencies. The difficulties of the children are seen as chronic, and the interventions are intensive and multiyear. The goal is to reduce risk factors and enhance protective factors. Some examples are set out in Table 7.4.

Community-Wide Interventions

Community-wide programs provide support for children and families, reduce risks, and promote protective factors. They focus on a whole group of children (e.g., in a classroom or school) instead of individual or high-risk groups of children.

Mentoring and after-school programs provide care for children, recreational and sporting activities, and coaching with homework. The trained people who run the programs often serve as identification figures for the children and support them to be involved in positive activities rather than being on the street and becoming involved in gangs and antisocial behavior.

Therapeutic foster care places traumatized children with behavioral problems with specially selected foster parents who receive additional training and ongoing support, which can prevent frequent breakdowns of the foster placement (Dozier & Rutter, 2008).

Table 7.3 *Treating Factors That Contribute to Difficulties With Behavior Regulation*

Main Area of Difficulty	Targeted Area of Difficulty	Treatment Strategies
Parent focused		
Parents' view of their child is negative and might attribute hostile intent to her	▪ Negative attributions (child is deliberately negative, behavior is intentional) ▪ She has inherited behaviors from a disliked family member ▪ She is seen as in control of the parent; the parent is seen as unable to control her or has "threat-oriented schema"	▪ Discussing attributions with parents, correcting misattributions, and talking from the child's point of view ▪ Speaking for the child ▪ Providing feedback on assessment of the child, areas that she finds difficult, and her strengths ▪ Redefining attributions to be less threat based and blaming ▪ Problem solving with parents to find new ways to interact with and discipline their child ▪ Providing parent–child interactional therapy
Parent discipline or management of the child	▪ Parent and child have developed "coercive cycles" of interaction in which parents are inconsistent with discipline and threaten punishment but do not provide consequences, resulting in an increase in aggression	▪ Parents supported to set up consistent routines and responses to negative behavior ▪ Emphasis on stopping aggression in the child and reducing parents' harsh, punitive punishment or lax, permissive approach ▪ Support parents to repair the relationship after the child has been disciplined ▪ Notice positive behaviors and attempts to be responsible
Parents' interactions lack sensitivity and responsiveness	▪ Lack of warmth and responsiveness with the child ▪ Lack of self-reflection or understanding thoughts and feelings of the child ▪ The parent does not respond to the child when he is upset, frightened, frustrated, or otherwise dysregulated	▪ Using a daily diary to identify how and why the negative behaviors happen and discuss how they might be avoided and dealt with in context ▪ Using video feedback to increase understanding of the thoughts and feelings of the child ▪ Using errorless compliance to increase positive responses to the child ▪ Emotion coaching to increase moments of emotional connection ▪ Listening to the child, communicating that her point of view is understood, and showing empathy for her feelings and frustrations
Family subsystems are divided (e.g., between parents and parents and siblings)	▪ Parents are divided about ways to work with the child ▪ Parents and non-problem child(ren) are close and exclude the problem child	▪ Parents seen without the child to discuss how to discipline her and make decisions together ▪ Family system therapy to enhance the total family system

Child focused		
Lack sense of conscience, empathy, and remorse	■ At a very egocentric and grandiose stage of development ■ Does not feel normal reaction if he breaks a rule or hurts another person ■ Does not show empathy or remorse ■ Lacks a TOM or perspective taking	■ Using induction and mental state talk when interacting with the child ■ Developing empathy and caring by reminding the child about how he feels when similar things happen to him ■ Talking about the perspectives of others whenever possible
Poor emotion regulation	■ Becomes angry and frustrated easily and escalates into aggressive outbursts ■ Can be anxious and depressed	■ Emotion coaching ■ Increasing capacity to read emotional and nonverbal cues of others ■ Medication might be essential ■ De-escalating the child before an aggressive outburst occurs
Desire for control	■ Easily triggered if made to do something ■ Has difficulty accepting or listening to suggestions	■ Choices can be helpful whenever possible ■ Listening to the point of view of the child can enable him to feel understood ■ Letting him have a say in problem solving and family decisions when possible
Negative attributions of others/ problems with social cognitive processing	■ Child misinterprets the behavior of others and attributes deliberate hostile intent not there in interactions with peers ■ Lacks capacity for interpersonal problem solving	■ Help child to problem solve what happened when he becomes upset and has inaccurate perceptions of what occurred ■ Help him to come up with a different interpretation of what happened ■ Help him to come up with a different solution to what happened, make suggestions if he struggles with this ■ Reflect on why they might be helpful and how they might work
Trauma-related reactions and triggering	■ Child can be triggered by what is going on in the environment, such as noise, visual stimuli, smells, touch, or too much activity	■ TARGET program ■ Use of sensory rooms or other calming situations that the child can move to and avoid an outburst ■ Chance for some exercise can be helpful for some children to calm down ■ CBT and trauma-related therapy
Excessive exuberance, novelty and thrill seeking, and impulsivity	■ Child places himself at risk by engaging in thrill-seeking behavior ■ Might have a need to be constantly on the move ■ Acts impulsively, without thinking or planning what to do first	■ Make it clear that the child will be protected and kept safe and that impulsive behavior will be stopped ■ Support other fun activities for the child

(continued)

Table 7.3 *Treating Factors That Contribute to Difficulties With Behavior Regulation (continued)*

Main Area of Difficulty	Targeted Area of Difficulty	Treatment Strategies
Social difficulties	▪ Difficulties with processing nonverbal and emotional cues of others ▪ Problems entering a group and keeping interactions going ▪ Finds it difficult to cooperate with others on an activity	▪ Forming a relationship with the child can help her to experience reciprocity and attunement ▪ Teach her about nonverbal cues of others (e.g., facial expression and tone of voice) ▪ Programs such as Coping Power can be used in the classroom ▪ Training of social skills in areas where they can be used most effectively (e.g., park and playground) ▪ Work collaboratively with the child and help her to think of a solution ▪ Identify skills that she needs and teach them to her
Lack of fear	▪ Child is not affected by normal consequences ▪ Can act dangerously without anticipating possible consequences of his behavior	▪ Talk to the child about concern for his safety ▪ Explain possible consequences of his behavior
Rigidity or black-and-white thinking with lack of flexibility in schedule	▪ The child has difficulty with situations that are not predictable ▪ Can be anxious and become aggressive if routines are changed ▪ Lacks flexibility in problem solving and socialization ▪ Can lead to black-and-white thinking and interpretation of herself and others as bad	▪ Listen to the child's concerns and ideas and request her input ▪ Show empathy for her frustration ▪ Let her know why the change or discipline is necessary with as few words as possible ▪ These approaches need to be repeated and practiced
Unrealistic sense of self or self-esteem	▪ Might have very low self-esteem and be sensitive to any perceived negative comment ▪ Might have grandiose, narcissistic, and egocentric sense of self ▪ Has difficulty integrating positive comments or praise into view of self	▪ Important to work with strengths and help the child to realize that practicing skills is important ▪ When the child puts himself down and sees himself as a failure, help him to find a solution ▪ For the child with grandiose self-esteem, provide support when things do not work out and encouragement to try again ▪ Avoid praising him for everything, but notice efforts and managing not to act out all the time ▪ Arrange for him to have experiences of success by scaffolding activities or making sure that an activity is stopped before he becomes overwhelmed or out of control

Table 7.4 *Comprehensive Multicomponent Programs*

Name of Program	Description of Program
Linking the Interests of Families and Teachers (LIFT; Reid, Eddy, Fetrow, & Stoolmiller, 1999)	Intervention is for children identified as being at risk in Grade 1 or 5 and is a 10-week program. It includes classroom-based social competency training: school playground behavior interventions, parent–school communication procedures, and a parent training group. It was successful immediately following the program, and at a 3-year follow-up the original first- and fifth-grade children had lower levels of behavioral difficulties than children in the control group who did not receive the program.
Families and Schools Together (FAST Track; Conduct Problems Prevention Research Group, 1999a, 1999b)	FAST Track is a large, multisite demonstration program for children identified in Kindergarten as being aggressive at home and school and includes social skill training, parent–child interactions, and home visits. Following the program, parents used less aversive discipline, and children were less disruptive in school settings.
Early Risers (August, Realmuto, Bloomquist, and Hektner, 2001)	Early Risers is an intensive, multicomponent, multiyear prevention program for children with ACDs. Children are identified at 6 years of age, and the program continues for 3 years. The children participate in a 6-week summer program that provides parent training/support throughout the academic year. After 3 years, the children showed reduced aggression and improved self-regulation and academic work. Parents improved on a measure of discipline.
Dinosaur School (Webster-Stratton & Hammond, 1997)	Dinosaur School is a combination approach for 3 to 8-year-old children that combines a child and parent training program with group training for children and parent group sessions from the BASIC and ADVANCE parent training curriculums. The combination program was more successful than child and parent training alone in enhancing children's social competence and their behavior at home and improving parent–child interactions.

Case Study: Treating Maggie

Emphasis on Direct Treatment

As outlined at the start of the chapter, Maggie was likely sexually abused, and her home life was chaotic since she was a baby. Her mother, Maureen, had little commitment to being involved in treatment, so Maggie was referred to a counselor to help her more directly with her problems. A number of issues made this a particularly difficult case.

- Maggie's behavior, poor hygiene, unusual and dirty clothes, and habit of stealing money meant that Maggie was excluded by the more popular children at school who could have been a more positive peer group for her.
- Maggie was aggressive and a bully at times but teased and victimized at other times. Children who are both bullies and victims typically have more severe psychopathologies and more negative home situations.
- Maggie joined a gang of girls in which she felt some sense of connection, but the girls did not attend school most of the time and were stealing money to buy food and drugs and often lived on the streets.
- Maggie had difficulties with speech and language and learning to read, and she found school very challenging, having little incentive to do her homework. Hence, "talking therapy" might be a poor option for her.

- Maureen had no concerns about her daughter's behavior because she thought that Maggie was just like her at the same age. She showed no interest in being involved in multisystemic therapy, which is usually well received and effective for multirisk families.
- Maggie's probable sexual abuse had never been reported to the Department of Child Protection or treated, and as a consequence Maggie acted out sexually, putting herself at risk, especially with the group that she was hanging around with.

For children in such situations, often few options are available for treatment. One option was for Maggie to see a counselor who could relate to her vulnerability and show empathy for her situation. Over time, such treatment could allow Maggie to talk about her sexual abuse and give her ways to get support to keep her safe. A referral was made to Child Protective Services and a file opened that allowed treatment agencies to access funding to support Maggie and alert her mother to concerns over possible sexual abuse of her daughter.

Assessment and School Intervention

Since Maggie was still relatively young, she was referred to a specialized classroom with nine other children that allowed her to be fully assessed and her challenges and strengths identified. She was picked up from home by a staff member of the school, assuring that she would attend school regularly. Assessment was done of her academic level, speech and language, gross and fine motor and sensory integration, level of hyperarousal, and ability to concentrate and plan and organize her work. At first, Maggie rejected the classroom and refused to accept praise or positive comments. She frequently became aggressive, often hitting other children and staff. She also used obscene language that distanced her from some of the children in the classroom. During the early weeks of her time in the school, Maggie sometimes had to be restrained and secluded to keep herself and the other children safe. It was made clear to her that this was not a punishment but necessary to keep her from being hurt and from hurting others. It was clear from her immediate reactions that Maggie had never been in a situation with a clear routine and structure that she had to follow and that understood her challenges. She was often reminded by teaching staff and other professionals who worked in the school that they were there to keep her safe and worried about her or had her "in mind." Gradually, after several weeks, Maggie became somewhat calmer, and it was noticed that she really enjoyed art, cooking, dancing, and drumming, which were real strengths for her.

Rules and the consequences and rewards that would follow were made clear to Maggie. At first, she did not want to acknowledge that she had won an award but later was able to accept her success and take pride in it. To let her think that she had some control, she was often given a choice between two positive behaviors. Maggie also attended groups to improve her social skills and enhance her pragmatic language and social communication skills. In these groups, she was helped to recognize facial expressions and what they meant about the thoughts and feelings of others. It was possible to correct any misattributions and give her ideas on how to connect to peers in positive ways. Maggie also attended an art group once a week and painted some colorful pictures showing that she had some talent, and she became enthusiastic about this, and it seemed to give her a way to express some of her sadness and anger. The Department of Child Protection funded her to attend a local art group.

Other areas of concern were also addressed, and because the school was in a high-risk area the whole class was taught self-help skills, including taking a shower, regularly washing their clothes, and styling their hair. It was clear that Maggie had no support in gaining these skills at home. However, she did manage to come to school a little cleaner and with her clothes matching more, and whenever this happened she was noticed for her efforts. A counselor was assigned to Maggie at the program, and she was encouraged to discuss anything worrying her with this person. This usually occurred early in the morning after a brief time on the computer, and Maggie was encouraged to talk about anything that had happened during the weekend or the previous evening. Because she had a longer-term counselor, the discussions were very much about what was happening on a daily basis. Sometimes Maggie opened up to the case coordinator who drove her in, and once in the car she seemed more relaxed and able to talk about things that were bothering her. Her other counselor planned to deal with her past trauma but was waiting until Maggie had developed enough resilience and ability to calm herself down to be able to integrate any memories of trauma.

Contact With Maureen, Maggie's Mother

At the end of the first term, Maureen approached the case coordinator and school staff and acknowledged that she had seen improvements in Maggie's behavior. She indicated that she now had her driver's license back and could drive Maggie to school one day a week. This gave the teachers an opportunity to welcome her and give her positive feedback on her daughter. While Maureen was at the school, she could talk with other professionals who worked with her daughter and hear their positive perspectives on the changes that Maggie was making. Maureen told them that no one had liked her when she was at school or helped her in any way, and this was one of the reasons that she had not pushed Maggie to attend her other school, where she had felt that she and Maggie were being judged. Maureen gradually seemed to realize that it would be different at this school and came to meetings scheduled with other parents and began to learn that she was not the only one who had struggled with her child.

When it was time for Maggie to reintegrate into her home school, both Maureen and Maggie cried. Maggie said she was "attached to the place" and would miss everyone. However, she and her mother were happy that she had made so many gains with her schoolwork and were excited about her art, dancing, cooking, and drumming, with Maureen keen to find more classes for Maggie in the local community. Follow-up sessions were continued for Maureen in the home, and she continued to attend the parenting group.

CONCLUSION

Clearly, a number of factors contribute to children developing behavior regulation difficulties, and once the negative patterns are in place they can be extremely difficult to shift. When these behavioral patterns develop in the early years, children are likely to have severe problems across their lifespans. It is thus important to provide intervention for high-risk children in infancy and early childhood as much as possible (Landry, Smith, Swank, & Guttentag, 2008). However, when intervention has not occurred, it is imperative that children receive it before it is extremely difficult to intervene and parents have given up trying. Research indicates that this is particularly true for children with C/U traits and proactive aggression, who show a more severe, aggressive, and stable pattern of antisocial behavior than those who have more reactive aggression.

The interventions needed are complex, demanding, and expensive, but without them the crime rate will not be reduced, and violence in society will continue to remain at unacceptable levels. Research is desperately needed on children with various behavior regulation problems to determine the causal pathways that contribute to them and find the most successful treatments for them. It is also important that future interventions integrate information on stress neurobiology into the design of new and effective interventions.

See Table 7.5 for details of information sources that are available online.

Table 7.5 *Websites*

Website	Information on Website
www.developingchild.harvard.edu	A number of articles that "translate science into policy." Also has a number of articles on issues that may contribute to the development of psychopathology, including behavior problems in children such as maternal depression, toxic substances in utero, and other early experiences.
http://livesinthebalance.org	A nonprofit organization founded by Dr. Ross Greene, child psychologist, author of the *Explosive Child* and *Lost at School* and originator of the CPS approach. Website has information on how to implement the model and includes a videotape and other articles.
www.surgeongeneral.gov	Report of the surgeon general on causes, prevention, and treatment of youth violence. A number of evidence-based programs are suggested.
www.who.int/violence_injury_prevention/child/injury/world_report/en	Website of the World Health Organization. This report talks about violence throughout the world and discusses prevention (Peden et al., 2008).
www.cdc.gov/violenceprevention/pub/yv_bestpractices.html	Website for the Centers for Disease Control and Prevention, National Center for Injury Prevention and Control. Publication on youth violence (Thornton, Craft, Dahlberg, Lynch, & Baer, 2002).
www.colorado.edu/cspv/blueprints	Website of the Center for the study and prevention of violence, Institute of Behavioral Science, University of Colorado at Boulder.
www.promisingpractices.net/programs.asp	Website of the Promising Practices Network on Children, Families, and Communities funded by the RAND Corporation. Information on proven and promising programs to improve outcomes for children.
http://pathstraining.com	Website for the Promoting Alternative Thinking Strategy (PATHS) that provides information on the curriculum for use in schools and the training services offered as well as research on the program.
www.violencepreventionworks.org/public/olweus_bullying_prevention_program	Website for the Promoting Alternative Thinking Strategy (PATHS) that provides information on the curriculum for use in schools and the training services offered as well as research on the program
www.findyouthinfo.gov	Website of Helping America's Youth, with an overview of 180 intervention programs.
www.thereachinstitute.org	The Resource for Advancing Children's Mental Health (REACH) Institute helps parents, educators, and health professionals identify and treat children with emotional and behavioral challenges with effective therapies. Has information on CD and ODD.

8

Difficulties and Disorders of Executive Functioning

Difficulties and disorders of executive functioning can have profound influences on affected individuals so that they are permanently compromised. Despite research findings and high rates across cultures and countries, there are still a lot of misconceptions about such difficulties and disorders. There is considerable evidence that executive dysfunction is a problem of the prefrontal cortex (PFC), other diverse neural circuits, and inadequate release of specific neurotransmitters in regions of the brain that manage this functioning. There is often a strong genetic basis as well. Children with executive functioning difficulties frequently have learning disabilities and one or more psychiatric disorders (MTA Cooperative Group, 1999b). This complexity, particularly the presence of other disorders, can complicate both assessment and treatment of executive functioning from childhood to adulthood.

Case Study: Peter

Eight-year-old Peter was referred by his single mother because he was "totally out of control." He had nearly burned the house down, attacked his younger sister with scissors, ran impulsively on the road or wandered in the neighborhood, and terrorized his mother, threatening to kill her on a number of occasions. His mother and maternal grandmother were both terrified of him and worried about the safety of his sister. Peter struggled with getting started and finishing his school work and had no friends at school. He was sent home from school frequently for aggression, and this was extremely difficult for his mother, who held a responsible administrative position. The police had been called to the home on two occasions and were helpful in talking to Peter about the consequences of hurting others. His mother admitted to a lot of alcohol use during her pregnancy with him. She and his father were very young at the time of the pregnancy and decided to marry to try to make things work for the sake of the baby. After Peter was born, his mother enjoyed being a mother and loved holding and cuddling him but admitted feeling very challenged by the "terrible 2's" and the temper tantrums that he started to have. The couple separated when Peter was about 4 years of age. His mother also seemed to have difficulty with getting organized at home and was always going to organize the house, type up rules and routines for Peter, and be more consistent with discipline but never did it. Once issues with executive functioning were identified, Peter was prescribed medication, with significant improvements almost immediately at home and school.

RESEARCH ON EXECUTIVE FUNCTIONING

Effects of Frontal Lobe Damage

Research on the frontal lobes and their relationship to executive functions began in 1848 with the case of Phineas Gage, a 25-year-old foreman on a railway construction site. An explosion at the site resulted in an iron bar entering his skull and destroying a large part of his frontal lobes. Gage remained fully conscious during the ordeal, walked away from the accident, and was able to converse rationally. He developed a wound infection that he recovered from and was only left with blurred vision in one eye and some facial palsy. He seemed to retain his intellectual capacity. However, his personality changed drastically, and he became increasingly erratic, swore all the time, did not follow through with plans, and could not hold down a job (Bigelow, 1850; Harlow, 1868).

Since this original case, dozens of reports have been published of individuals who suffered gunshot wounds, accidents, and strokes in which massive damage to the frontal lobes dramatically changed the person's personality while most cognitive capacities remained intact. These case reports showed that a number of characteristics became impaired or markedly disrupted following frontal lobe injury, and though they varied from case to case they usually included disruption of the ability to delay gratification or sustain concentration without perseveration and lack of mental flexibility. During the early 1900s, this research created a debate between those who saw the frontal lobes as the seat of the highest integrative functions of the brain and those who emphasized that only some capacities were affected by such damage (Mesulam, 2000). This controversy was gradually resolved when sophisticated assessment methods, particularly neuropsychological instruments, were developed and began to show quantifiable deficits in areas such as concentration, information retrieval, and inhibition of inappropriate responses in patients with frontal lobe damage. These patients typically continued to do well on tests of perception, language, and spatial attention except when the task demanded a high degree of motivation (Benton, 1968; Milner, 1963, 1982).

Understanding Attention Deficit/Hyperactivity Disorder

As outlined by Barkley (1998), scientific interest in attention deficit/hyperactivity disorder (ADHD) began in the early 1900s with the description of children brought for treatment who had behavioral problems, difficulties with sustaining attention, and delaying gratification (Still, 1902). Still (1902) and Tredgold (1908) conceptualized these difficulties as biological and likely genetic in origin. In the United States, following an epidemic of encephalitis, clinicians found that a number of children who survived the disease were left with many of the characteristics found in children with ADHD, such as hyperactivity, impaired attention, and impulsivity. It was called postencephalitic behavior disorder and considered the result of brain damage (Cantwell, 1981; Kessler, 1980; Stewart, 1970). Researchers began to examine other possible causes of these behavioral problems, including intellectual delays, epilepsy, learning disabilities, and brain damage due to birth trauma or infection (Werner & Strauss, 1941). By the 1950s and 1960s, the term "minimal brain dysfunction" (MBD) was used to describe these children despite little evidence of brain damage. Critical reviews of use of the term to describe children with no evidence of brain damage eventually led to its abandonment. One term that received a great deal of interest was "hyperactive child syndrome," considered to be due to a biological cause (Chess, 1960; Laufer & Denhoff, 1957). This syndrome, now a disorder, was then included in the second edition of the *Diagnostic and Statistical Manual of Mental Disorders*, 2nd edition (*DSM-II*; American Psychiatric Association [APA], 1968). By the 1970s, features of the hyperactive child were expanded to include impulsivity, short attention span, distractibility, and aggression (Marwitt & Stenner, 1972). By this time, stimulant medication had become the most common treatment for children with characteristics of ADHD (Barkley, 1998). Also, the exclusive emphasis on hyperactivity was questioned, and some argued that deficits in sustaining attention and impulse control were more critical in explaining the child's symptoms (Douglas, 1972, 1980; Douglas & Peters, 1979).

During the next two decades, a number of views of the causes of hyperactivity became popular, only to be refuted later because of a paucity of evidence. They included food additives, resulting in the Feingold diet that eliminated such additives (Feingold, 1975), and poor child rearing and management, leading to an emphasis on behavior management (Campbell, 1987). In the *DSM-III*, attention deficit disorder (with or without hyperactivity) was introduced with specific symptom lists and guidelines for age of onset and duration of symptoms (American Psychiatric Association, 1980). In a later revised edition of *DSM-III*, the disorder was renamed attention deficit/hyperactivity disorder (American Psychiatric Association, 1987). Since then, there has been tremendous progress in both assessment and treatment of the disorder as well as significant advances in understanding its etiology. This has included numerous neuropsychological studies of the deficits in performance of these children, neuroimaging studies of brain structure and functioning, and genetic studies of families of the children (Jensen, Martin, & Cantwell, 1997).

In the 1970s and early 1980s, ADHD was seen as a disorder of childhood, and it was believed that the symptoms improved and eventually disappeared in puberty. More recently, follow-up studies have shown that 30% to 70% of children continue to have symptoms in adolescence and adulthood (Barkley, 2002; Weiss & Hechtman, 1993). Furthermore, in a large epidemiological study of adults conducted by Kessler et al. (2005), a prevalence rate of 4.4% for ADHD was found. Some of the difficulties experienced by these adults were severe and included impairments with activities of daily living, underachievement in academic performance, difficulties in the workplace, and problems with relationships. These difficulties were found to be more serious when there were also comorbid disorders, especially conduct disorder, learning disabilities, anxiety, and depression (Hechtman, 2009).

Although medication and parent training continue to be critical aspects of treatment, there has been growing interest in classroom support and computer-based programs focused on enhancing the child's executive functions. They have included computerized training of working memory (WM; Klingberg et al., 2005; McNab et al., 2009), switching behavior (Kuhlman, Little, & Sekuler, 2006), and sustained and focused attention (Shalev, Tsal, & Mevorach, 2007). Results have shown improvement in the executive function targeted by the training but also that other executive functions improved and parent-rated inattentive symptoms of ADHD diminished. These approaches appeal to children and show promise in reducing symptoms and possibly improving brain functioning.

DEFINITIONS OF EXECUTIVE FUNCTIONING

There is no single agreed-upon definition of executive functioning. Some theorists include a large number of functions, whereas others define it more narrowly. There is also no agreement on how the term "executive dysfunction" relates to ADHD. Brown (2009, p. 4) described executive function as a "term that should be used to refer to brain circuits that prioritize, integrate, and regulate other cognitive functions." Goldberg (2001) defined it as the directive capacities of the human brain. The metaphors "chief executive officer" and "orchestra conductor" of the brain have been used to indicate its role of directing all behavior (Brown, 2005). There is some consensus that executive functions help to exert mental control and self-regulation to achieve a goal. Scores from different measures of executive functions do not always correlate highly with each other, suggesting that they are measuring different aspects of executive functioning or that they are differentially affected by another cognitive process, such as processing speed. These executive functions are diverse but related and overlap. It is therefore critical to assess each child in terms of his "executive profile" so that intervention can be provided in the areas in which he has problems (Cooper-Kahn & Dietzel, 2008; Gioia, Isquith, Kenworthy, & Barton, 2002).

Other capacities seen as important aspects of executive functioning are metacognition and the motivation to sustain effort. Metacognition or reflective functioning is often understood as the ability to stand back and think about thinking. This capacity allows a person to be self-reflective about problem solving and actions, particularly useful when one's actions do not seem to be working or are creating problems (Dawson & Guere, 2010).

Having the motivation to sustain effort even when the task is hard and something that the individual does not enjoy doing can be the key for academic achievement and sustaining employment. The idea of attention being a problem has often been confusing for parents. The child might be able to sustain attention while watching television or playing computer games, playing a sport, or engaging in a hobby that she enjoys. Because of this, children are often accused of being lazy or having no willpower, and it is not acknowledged that the capacity to perform tasks that they do not enjoy is not under their conscious control (Brown, 2009).

Table 8.1 outlines executive functions and some of the difficulties that can occur if they are compromised.

TYPICAL DEVELOPMENT OF EXECUTIVE FUNCTIONING AND THE PARENTING THAT ENCOURAGES IT

The full capacity for executive functioning is not present at birth. It shows rapid and substantial changes between birth and 6 years of age and typically continues to improve until adulthood or about 22 years of age. Different executive functions develop at different times with some capacity for problem solving and focusing being present quite early, whereas others, such as planning and organizing develop much later. In typically developing children each of the executive functions, as long as they are practiced, generally shows improvement during the lifespan until a gradually decline later in life. The developmental trajectories of different children for any one executive function and overall executive capacities can vary significantly. Some of the capacities the children develop in various stages from birth to 13 years and the parenting that can support their development are set out in Table 8.2.

DISORDERS OF EXECUTIVE FUNCTIONING AND THEIR PREVALENCE

In the *DSM-5* (5th ed.; APA, 2013), only one diagnostic category is closely related to problems with executive function—attention deficit/hyperactivity disorder (ADHD) with the child being diagnosed as combined presentation, predominantly inattentive presentation, or predominantly hyperactive/impulsive presentation. Current severity is also specified that can be mild, moderate, or severe. It is included as one of a number of neurodevelopmental disorders. ADHD affects from 5% to 12% of the school-aged population worldwide (Faraone, Sergeant, Gillberg, & Biederman, 2003; Polanczyk, de Lima, Horta, Biederman, & Rohde, 2007). It is about three times more common in boys than girls (Biederman, Mick, & Faraone, 2002; Levy, Hay, Bennett, & McStephen, 2005). ADHD also affects about 4% of adults. A significant number of children who meet criteria for ADHD are also diagnosed with another disorder, such as autism spectrum disorder, learning disability of one kind or another, mood disorder, or oppositional defiant disorder (ODD)

Table 8.1 *Executive Functions and Related Difficulties*

Executive Function	Description	Related Difficulties
Activating or initiating	Ability to get started independently on relevant tasks and prioritize certain tasks over others	Difficulty with initiating work on something and tending to procrastinate
Planning	Ability to think ahead to reach a short- or long-term goal or complete a task	Might act out impulsively without thinking things through or completing what was started
Organization	Capacity to put systems in place to keep track of information or possessions, and also to start and prioritize the steps of a task	Struggles with getting things together to start a task and might lose things needed for a task; once started on an activity, might get "lost in the middle" and start to do something else
Time management	Ability to complete a task in the required time frame and monitor how time is passing and adjust input accordingly	Struggles to complete tasks in an adequate time frame
Working memory (WM)	Capacity to hold things in mind to perform complex tasks and to draw on past experience and use it in the present	Has difficulty with more complex tasks and remembering information previously learned
Focusing	Ability to maintain attention on the most important part of a task or situation, ignoring less relevant parts, and shifting focus when necessary	Can get caught up in irrelevant details and find it extremely difficult to ignore what is going on around him
Effort	Motivation to sustain effort and engagement with a task that she has to perform	Can show sustained attention in activities that she enjoys but cannot concentrate on uninteresting tasks
Flexibility and shifting	Ability to change focus and shift emphasis if things change in the environment; capacity to generate ideas or problem solve and correct errors of thought and action	Might perseverate and become "stuck" on an idea or particular way of doing something even when it is not working
Emotion control	Ability to contain frustration and modulate emotions to manage the task at hand	Is easily triggered and can show extreme anxiety, sadness, or anger that interferes with social, emotional, or academic functioning
Inhibition	Ability to inhibit certain behaviors and thoughts and remain focused on relevant parts of a problem or the environment	Ability to cope at home and school is compromised by difficulty with inhibiting or stopping behavior or impulsivity
Self-monitoring	Ability to monitor performance and measure it against some expected standard, such as school grades	Might not check ahead of time what needs to be done and ends up forgetting details; does not check her work to see if it measures up to requirements

(continued)

Table 8.2 *Highlights of Typical Executive Functioning Development and Parenting*

Age Range	Development	Parenting
Birth to 12 months	■ Shows selective and focused attention to certain visual and auditory stimuli ■ Learns about cause and effect (e.g., if cries someone comes; kicks to activate a mobile) ■ Able to persist if something does not work the first time (e.g., persists in reaching for something) ■ Uses trial and error to problem solve (e.g., tries to crawl to reach a toy or cries out to caregiver) ■ Establishes object permanence and knows that an object still exists if it is hidden and may persist in searching for it ■ Engages in joint attention with another person by pointing or drawing attention to an object or situation ■ Uses exploration and trial and error in order to understand the environment	■ Initiates face-to-face interactions that encourage focused attention and mutuality with others ■ Directs infant's attention to certain part of an object and points out how and when the infant's action led to a particular goal ■ Supports the development of a routine of eating and sleeping so that the infant can see the sequence of events in a day and feels predictability and organization around him ■ Provides appropriate toys that can enhance the infant's capacity for problem solving ■ Provides toys and activities that are just beyond what the infant is capable of completing on his own ■ Demonstrates various activities so that infant can learn from seeing someone else do the activity ■ Sets up activities so that the infant can experience some success in completing the task ■ Talks to infant about what is going on in her mind ■ Encourages working memory (WM) by hiding objects for the infant to find
12 to 24 months	■ Toddler pushes to become more independent and to do things himself ■ Focuses attention and persists on tasks beyond capabilities in order to try to complete them and this increases the capacity for attention and concentration ■ Tremendous gains in a number of cognitive areas that affect the child's ability to problem solve ■ Major gains are made in the use of words to get what they want and to reason ■ Engages in pretend play that can help problem solving and planning ■ Begins to think ahead and plan in her head rather than using trial-and-error problem solving ■ Increasingly able to inhibit a response or restrain an immediate motor response ■ Experiments to find different solutions to problems ■ Sets standards for self and works on problems	■ Continues to talk to child about what is going on in her mind ■ Caregiver provides a balance of supportive affection and discipline and containment ■ Continues to set up tasks to encourage the child to solve problems ■ Models tasks that are beyond the child's capability ■ Encourages the development of receptive and expressive language by encouraging the expansion of vocabulary ■ Encourages the development of working memory (WM) by giving instructions and making sure the child can understand them, by repetition if necessary ■ Joins in pretend play with the child and expands play themes ■ Provides authoritative parenting and explains rules and consequences so the child learns about cause and effect ■ Encourages and helps child to inhibit a negative action by setting necessary limits and supporting the child in trying a more adaptive behavior

2 to 4 years	■ Length of attention span increases and child can spend a longer time following through to complete a task ■ Ability to inhibit a nondominant response improves ■ Begins to use private speech to help during problem-solving activities ■ Play and language are increasingly complex and can help make meaning of experience across time and space ■ Child becomes much more able to think ahead and plan an action in order to solve a problem ■ Tries out different solutions to problems and plans and monitors solutions ■ More able to distinguish between appearance and reality ■ Begins to be able to categorize objects into classes such as animals, food, etc. ■ Some understanding of past, present, and future ■ Increases frustration tolerance and increases capacity for impulse control	■ Scaffolding is provided by parents in problem-solving tasks and tasks are chosen at an appropriate level to challenge but not overwhelm the child ■ Parent provides a balance between providing support and encouraging child's independence ■ Provides parent–child narratives about past and future events ■ Discusses events and encourages joint construction of important parts of the events to increase child's memory of the event ■ Encourages the child to use private speech to enhance attention and persistence during problem-solving activities ■ Continues to provide discipline for the child and to support the child in inhibiting immediate responses, if appropriate ■ When gives instructions makes them short and checks that the child understands them
4 to 6 years	■ Has a theory of mind, so is not so egocentric in his thinking ■ Thinking changes from animism to understanding the difference between man-made objects and living objects ■ Children's ability to classify now includes shapes, colors, and size and some concepts of numbers ■ Can hold information in mind to help in planning and problem solving ■ Can inhibit immediate impulsive responses and for longer periods such as not running in the road or hitting another child ■ Can perform simple chores and self-help tasks with reminders (e.g., tidying bedroom and clearing dishes from the table) ■ Understands board games and games with rules	■ Parent shares plans and perspectives with the child and jointly plans with him when possible ■ Continues to scaffold activities and encourages the child's self-talk to get her through a task ■ Structures the environment to encourage attention on tasks for longer periods ■ Makes sure the child stays focused enough in order to have some experiences of success ■ Helps child organize her things for school and her daily routine in the morning and after school ■ Sets up brief "homework" sessions and activities so that the child learns to organize, focus, and concentrate for a short period of time ■ If child gets "stuck" on an idea or a routine, caregiver encourages alternative ideas and gives the child choices

(continued)

Table 8.2 *Highlights of Typical Executive Functioning Development and Parenting (continued)*

Age Range	Development	Parenting
7 to 10 years	▪ Increased self-reliance of the child in completing self-care activities and in getting organized for completing homework ▪ Takes more responsibility for household chores and looking after his own possessions ▪ Can initiate, focus, and complete various tasks with a minimum of scaffolding ▪ Brings papers home from school and completes homework assignments ▪ Plans school projects such as book reports ▪ Keeps track of changing daily schedule at school and for outside activities ▪ May be involved in a number of after-school activities such as music, sports, clubs, etc.	▪ Parent still keeps a close eye on the child and monitors her schedules and activities ▪ Parent makes sure that homework and chores are initiated and completed ▪ Structures and routines are provided in the home sometimes with visual cues so that the child can get herself organized and follow through with the activities of the day ▪ Provides encouragement if the child is finding schedules and school demands overwhelming at times ▪ Provides an overall containment and support for the child's activities and responsibilities
11 to 13 years	▪ Child is increasingly independent and interested in activities outside the home ▪ Relationships with parents and their help is still important but child may push them away temporarily ▪ Helps out with chores and may babysit younger siblings or for pay outside the home ▪ Child is usually less impulsive and can delay gratification enough to work hard to achieve a goal ▪ Manages school schedule with changing teachers and schedules ▪ Begins to have long-term goals such as going to college and pursuing a particular career	▪ Provides support for child's independent activities and monitoring to keep child safe ▪ Parents keep the child away from adverse influences as much as possible such as negative peer influences, and drugs and alcohol ▪ Explains some of the dangers that the child can be exposed to and continues to support positive activities and school performance ▪ Continues to enforce the rules, monitors the child's whereabouts, insists on curfews, and forbids dangerous activities ▪ Parents play a monitoring role at more of a distance to keep the child safe

(Brown, 2009). ADHD is diagnosed if the symptoms were present before 7 years of age; impairment is present in at least two settings; there is clinically significant impairment in social, academic, or occupational functioning; and symptoms are not better accounted for by another mental disorder.

The categorical approach used in *DSM-IV-TR*, in which a child must have six symptoms in one of the areas to have a diagnosis of ADHD, can miss children who, for example, have five symptoms but just miss out on the diagnosis. It also fails to distinguish between a child who has 18 symptoms and one who just meets criteria for one of the types. Because of concerns about the utility of diagnostic categories, some researchers have chosen to examine individual symptom domains of ADHD rather than rely entirely on the categorical approach of *DSM-IV-TR*.

The relationship between difficulties with executive functioning and ADHD has been difficult to determine, and the two are not synonymous (McCloskey, Perkins, & Van Divner, 2009). One way of examining how the two relate has been to administer neuropsychological executive functioning measures to groups of children and adolescents with and without ADHD. In a meta-analysis of 83 studies of this kind, Willcutt, Doyle, Nigg, Faraone, and Pennington (2005) found that the group of children with ADHD showed significant impairment on some measures of executive functioning, such as response inhibition, WM, and planning, but not others, and these differences were not found in all individuals with ADHD. Hervey, Epstein, and Curry (2004) found similar results with adults with ADHD. In fact, the two studies found that only about 30% of those with ADHD had significant executive functioning impairment. Children with ADHD are not the only ones who experience executive functioning problems, and children with other conditions might have executive functioning problems or be extremely disorganized but not meet criteria for having ADHD.

There are two major theories or models of understanding the executive functions underlying ADHD: those of Brown (2009) and Barkley (2006). Both see ADHD as a developmental impairment of executive functions and describe some of the neurobiological underpinnings, unlike other models that do not directly link impairments of executive functions and symptoms of ADHD. These other models include more simplistic views of ADHD as a behavioral disorder that usually remits in adulthood or see it as a lack of willpower because the person can pay attention to specific activities that interest him (Brown, 2009). Also, Brown (2009) points out that *DSM-IV-TR* does not include problems with emotion regulation as a symptom in its description of ADHD, though they are key in most clinical presentations of children with ADHD (American Psychiatric Association, 2000).

Barkley (1998, p. 345) proposed five essential executive functions that gradually evolve from birth to early adulthood: behavioral inhibition, WM (nonverbal), internalization of speech (verbal WM), self-regulation of affect/motivation/arousal, and reconstitution. Behavioral inhibition is seen as the basis of the model and the executive function that begins to emerge between about 8 and 12 months and on which other executive functions depend. Barkley described behavioral inhibition as the ability to delay or stop a response that was previously an immediate response to an event, stop an ongoing response when it has been unsuccessful, and avoid being distracted or interrupted by things that can interfere with other executive functions. If successfully developed, behavioral inhibition precedes the other executive functions and stops them from being interrupted.

Brown (2009), on the other hand, described six executive functions that "work together in various combinations" and saw behavioral inhibition as just one of them and not as controlling other executive functions. The executive functions that Brown described are activation (organizing, prioritizing, and activating work), focus (focusing, sustaining, and shifting attention to tasks), effort (regulating alertness, sustaining effort, and processing speed), emotion (managing frustration and modulating emotions), memory (using WM and accessing recall), and action (monitoring and self-regulating action) (p. 6).

Other important models include those of Mirsky and Duncan (2001), who looked at five elements of attention (focus/execute, sustain, encode, shift, and stabilize [consistency in response time]), and Denckla (1991), who proposed constructs of attention similar to Mirsky and Duncan's and encompassed many of the executive functions, such as attention and impulse control, seen in adults with ADHD.

EXECUTIVE FUNCTIONING AND THE BRAIN

Research using neuroimaging has identified the PFC and associated networks of subcortical brain structures as regions related to executive functioning (Miller & Cummings, 2006; Stuss & Knight, 2002). However, examinations of patients with lesions in these areas have found a number of different patterns or types of behavior related to location of the lesions (Eslinger, Biddle, & Grattan, 1997). Areas of the frontal lobes involved in executive functioning include the dorsolateral PFC, the orbitofrontal cortex, and the anterior cingulate. Loops or connections have also been described between, for example, the dorsolateral PFC and other subcortical areas. When one of the executive functions is operating, only part of the frontal lobes is activated (Lichter & Cummings, 2001; Mesulam, 2002). However, when part of the frontal lobes is activated, additional nonfrontal areas of the brain act in concert with it (Picton, Alain, & Knight, 2002). Although we can talk about self-regulation or inhibiting certain mental processes as an executive function, people can vary in their capacity to regulate different aspects of these mental processes, for example, emotion regulation versus impulse control, and interpersonal situations and academic tasks. It is also likely that different neural circuit activation patterns in the frontal lobes are responsible for these different types of self-regulation.

Different components of executive functioning depend on different parts of the PFC. Some information has been acquired by observing activity of the brain while individuals are completing various tests of executive functioning. The ability to hold information in WM, as in the digit span task, relies on the lateral PFC (Groenewegen & Uylings, 2000; Pabhakaran, Narayanan, Zhao, & Gabrieli, 2000). The ability to inhibit responses, assessed by the Stroop Test, during which subjects must state the color that the word is written in while not reading the work itself, relies heavily on the anterior cingulate and medial and lateral prefrontal cortices (Brown et al., 1999). The ability to switch between tasks and suppress perseveration has been related to mental flexibility and found to be associated with activity in the lateral and medial prefrontal cortices (Funahashi, Chafee, & Goldman-Rakic, 1993; Kruger, Moll, Zahn, Heinecke, & Grafman, 2007). The anterior cingulate has been associated with focused attention and processing of emotional information, with the two subdivisions separately processing the two kinds of information. The cognitive (dorsal) division connects the PFC, parietal cortex, and various motor areas (Lutcke & Frahm, 2008; Peers et al., 2005), whereas the emotional (ventral) subdivision connects with the amygdala, hippocampus, and orbitofrontal cortex. The capacity to initiate/activate has been linked to the orbitofrontal cortex, anterior cingulate, dorsolateral PFC, and superior medial temporal sulcus (Lichter & Cummings, 2001; Stuss & Knight, 2002). The capacity to seek novelty (as opposed to difficulty facing novel situations) allows the individual to seek multiple solutions to similar problems (Mesulam, 2002) and is dependent on functioning of the PFC.

Many neurotransmitters are involved in executive functioning, including dopamine, norepinephrine, and serotonin, and there is a growing literature on them with exciting findings (Biederman & Spencer, 1999; Prince, 2008). See Figure 8.1 for the location of executive functioning in the brain.

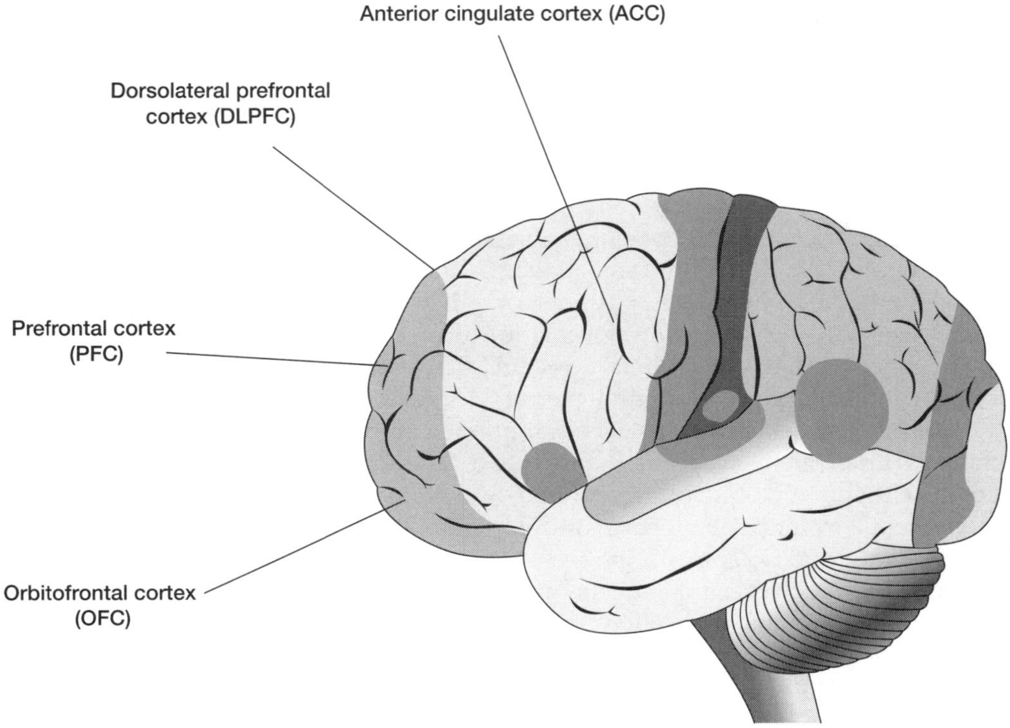

Figure 8.1 *Location of executive functioning in the brain.*

NEUROBIOLOGICAL AND GENETIC CONTRIBUTORS TO EXECUTIVE FUNCTIONING DIFFICULTIES AND DISORDERS

Neurobiological Factors

Some studies have used psychophysiological measures of the electrical activity of the nervous system, galvanic skin responses, and heart rate deceleration to identify neurobiological differences between children with ADHD and control children. When differences are found, they occur in the direction of diminished activity or arousability. The results of quantitative electroencephalographs and evoked-response potential measured during tests of attention have found increased slow wave or theta activity (particularly in the frontal lobe) and excess beta activity (Tannock, 1998). This is believed to be linked to the function of the PFC and is related to poorer performance on tests of attention and inhibition (Tannock, 1998). Children with ADHD have been found to have differences in brain structure, such as smaller right plana temporal regions of the temporal lobes, associated with auditory detection and analysis (Tannock, 1998). The posterior part or splenium region of the corpus callosum has also been found to be smaller in children with ADHD compared with control children (Semrud-Clikeman et al., 1994). In a study of the caudate nucleus, children with ADHD were found to have a smaller left caudate nucleus, and earlier studies found decreased blood flow in this region (Hynd et al., 1993). These studies had small sample sizes, however, and consequently low statistical power, and they have been hard to replicate in studies that also have small samples. In later studies with larger samples, other areas of the brain were found to be smaller in children with ADHD (Hynd et al., 1993). They included the caudate nucleus, but studies have varied as to whether the left or the right side tends to be smaller. Other studies have consistently found smaller right prefrontal cortical regions and smaller caudate volume (Hynd et al., 1993). Positron emission tomography (PET) analyses have found significant correlations between diminished metabolic activity in the left anterior frontal region and severity of ADHD symptoms in adolescents with ADHD (Zametkin et al., 1993). It is still difficult to determine the significance of these findings.

Tucker and Luu (2007) described the anterior cingulate cortex (ACC) as the crossroads of the dorsal and ventral networks for emotion regulation. Using electroencephalographic (EEG) event-related potential assessment of dorsal and ventral pathways in the ACC, Moadab, Gilbert, Dishion, and Tucker (2010) provided evidence for the theory that reduced dorsal control is related to undercontrolled symptoms (externalizing behaviors), whereas internalizing symptoms (overcontrol) are related to increased ventral control or overengagement of ventral limbic systems. This study was embedded in Eisenberg's notions of effortful control as a central part of the individual's capacity to regulate attention as well as emotion, extremes of which can presage internalizing or externalizing psychopathology (Eisenberg et al., 2001). Rothbart and Bates (2006) argued that individual differences in self-regulation (attention, emotion, and motor) result from interactions between temperamental factors and effortful control.

Dopamine and norepinephrine seem to be depleted in individuals with ADHD and other difficulties with executive functioning. Improvements in many children with ADHD who are given stimulant medications that enhance the production of these neurotransmitters support the theory of such neurotransmitter deficits in ADHD. Further direct evidence of decreased dopamine and norepinephrine function comes from studies of cerebral spinal fluid and blood and urinary metabolites (Zametkin & Rapoport, 1986).

Genetic Factors

Since the 1990s, significant progress has been made in genetic research on ADHD, but a specific gene or set of genes has not yet been identified. Because of the difficulties with relying on the categorical approach of *DSM-IV*, twin studies have relied on individual symptom domains of executive functioning. This approach estimates the genetic and environmental contributions to various symptoms of inattention, hyperactivity, and impulsivity by comparing twins who are genetically identical (monozygotic) and twins who share about 50% of genes (dizygotic). From a review of 20 of these studies, the heritability of ADHD was estimated to be as high as 76% (Faraone, 2004; Faraone et al., 2005). In another study, using teacher and parent ratings of monozygotic and dizygotic twins, further evidence was found for heritability of a common factor of 78% (Derks, Hudziak, Van Beijsterveldt, Dolan, & Boomsma, 2006). There is some suggestion from these twin studies that there might be some genetic differences among children with mild, moderate, and severe problems.

There have been fewer adoption studies than twin studies of ADHD, and in general the heritability coefficients found tend to be smaller. However, there is generally a higher incidence of ADHD in biological parents of children than in their adoptive parents, supporting the conclusion reached by twin studies that there is a strong genetic influence of the disorder (Sprich, Biederman, & Crawford, 2000). Family studies of children with ADHD have tended to consider children who also have a comorbid disorder. Family studies with large samples completed with children with ADHD, conduct disorder, and ODD have supported the position that an ADHD-aggressive (conduct) subtype might reflect a discrete phenotype and require further study (Jensen et al., 1997). Jensen (2001) also suggested that ADHD and overanxious disorder need to be considered as separate phenotypes for further study and noted that there is a higher risk of anxiety disorders in relatives with ADHD than those without ADHD. Also anticipated is a genetic relationship between ADHD and learning disabilities, with some studies suggesting a link between reading disorder, especially with inattentive symptoms (Willcutt, Pennington, & DeFries, 2000). On the other hand, studies of children with ADHD and depression suggest co-occurrence and no genetic connection.

Most of the molecular genetic studies of ADHD have concentrated on genes of the dopamine receptor system and those involved in dopamine transmission. The Multi-Center ADHD Gene Project analyzed 51 genes associated with the combined type of ADHD and found an association with ADHD and DRD5, one of a family of protein selectors involved in postsynaptic dopamine transmission (Lichter et al., 1993), and the monoamine oxidase A gene (Jiang et al., 2000). Studies are now looking beyond the dopaminergic system to consider the role of norepinephrine and the possible effects of three noradrenergic genes on ADHD (Comings et al., 1991).

Biological Contributions

Temperament

Effortful control allows a child to focus attention and inhibit an immediate or prepotent response such as delaying opening an attractive gift (Derryberry & Rothbart, 1997; Eisenberg, Hofer, & Vaughn, 2007; Rothbart, Ahadi, & Evans, 2000; Rothbart, Ellis, Rueda, & Posner, 2003). Effortful control includes automatic or nonconscious aspects of the control or containment of emotions. It is part of the temperament that the child is born with and similar to behavioral inhibition and the other traits of temperament described by Thomas, Chess, and Birch (1968). Research on effortful control was first introduced by Rothbart and colleagues, who described it as the child's capacity to "inhibit a dominant response and initiate a subdominant response" (Rothbart & Bates, 1998, p. 137). It is also related to the ability to focus or inhibit or activate a behavior in a way appropriate to the situation without actually desiring to do so (Dixon, Salley, & Clements, 2006). It emerges in the latter half of the first year, and some of the areas that relate to it include motivation, pleasure from low-intensity stimulation, and perceptual sensitivity (Murray & Kochanska, 2002; Olson, Sameroff, Kerr, Lopez, & Wellman, 2005). It is also believed to contribute to self-regulation by enabling the child to shift attention from threatening stimuli to soothing stimuli (Nigg, Goldsmith, & Sachek, 2004; Wolf & Bell, 2004). Good effortful control allows the individual to approach situations that she fears and inhibit actions that she desires. It can support the internalization of competence-related goals (e.g., school achievement and being kind to others) and the inhibition of immediate approach, with the goal of a larger reward later. Children who develop it often have better self-control and ability to deal with stress, concentration, and planning. It plays an important role in the development of moral thought and behavior, and children who are high on this temperament trait show empathy, guilt, and shame and are low on aggression. Effortful control has been found to have longitudinal stability and relate to a broad range of adaptive outcomes, such as agreeableness, social competence, ability to regulate emotions, and internalization of conscience (Chang & Burns, 2005; Eisenberg, Liew, & Pidada, 2004; Nigg et al., 2004; Wolfe & Bell, 2004). Poor effortful control has been related to impulsivity and externalizing behavior (Murray & Kochanska, 2002; Olson et al., 2005).

Traumatic Brain Injury

It is estimated that traumatic brain injury in children represents a significant public health problem in the United States and that 29,000 children annually experience disability as a result (Sesma, Slomine, Ding, McCarthy, & Children's Health after Trauma Study Group,

2008). Studies have found that children with traumatic brain injuries show impaired executive functioning not evident before the injuries (Sesma et al., 2008). The severity of impairment depends on the severity of the injury, functioning in various areas before the injury, age of the child when the injury occurred, and family functioning (Taylor, 2004; Schachar, Levin, Max, & Purvis, 2004). Some studies have found improvement over time (Anderson & Catroppa, 2005; Slomine et al., 2002). However, some of these improvements might relate to the practice effect of repeated administration of tests and the structured and distraction-free environment in which the tests are administered (Sesma et al., 2008; Silver, 2000). In a study conducted by Sesma et al. (2008), 18% to 38% of children from 5 to 15 years of age who sustained traumatic brain injury, compared with a group who had orthopedic fractures, were significantly more likely to have executive functioning problems, and these differences were evident 1 year after injury. Although traumatic brain injury is clearly related to executive functioning difficulties and ADHD generally, signs of brain damage are not detected in these children. However, a number of other risk factors are often identified.

Pregnancy and Birth Complications

Studies of children with ADHD have been mixed regarding the incidence of pregnancy and birth complications (Barkley, 1998; Valera & Seidman, 2006). Some studies have not found a history of more prenatal or birth complications in children with ADHD compared with normal controls. However, perinatal complications, such as toxemia or eclampsia, poor maternal health, or minor physical injuries to the developing fetus, might be associated with ADHD (Milberger, Biederman, Faraone, Guite, & Tsuang, 1997). Other studies have found a slightly higher incidence of difficult labor with fetal distress and low forceps delivery (Hartsough & Lambert, 1985). Yet large-scale epidemiological studies that have controlled for factors such as socioeconomic disadvantage and maternal smoking and substance use have not found a strong correlation between pregnancy and birth complications and ADHD (Goodman & Stevenson, 1989).

Prematurity and Low Birth Weight

Increased risk of ADHD has been found in children born preterm (Bhutta, Cleves, Casey, Cradock, & Anand, 2002; Foulder-Hughes & Cooke, 2003; Valera & Seidman, 2006). In a meta-analysis, Bhutta et al. (2002) found that children born preterm had a 2.64-fold higher risk of developing ADHD and having attention problems than control children not born preterm. Another study found that children aged 7 to 8 years who had been born preterm were more likely to have symptoms of inattention and impulsivity as well as a diagnosis of ADHD (Foulder-Hughes & Cooke, 2003). Working memory deficits were found in another study of premature children (Luciana, Lindeke, Georgieff, Mills, & Nelson, 1999).

Numerous studies have documented an association between low birth weight and ADHD and executive functioning difficulties (Mick, Biederman, Prince, Fischer, & Faraone, 2002). Low birth weight includes three groups of children: those with a birth weight of less than 2,500 grams (low birth weight) (Breslau et al., 1996), those with a birth weight of less than 1,500 grams (very low birth weight) (Botting, Powls, Cooke, & Marlow, 1998), and those with a birth weight of less than 1,000 g (extremely low birth weight) (Aarnoudse-Moens, Smidts, Oosterlaan, Duivenvoorden, & Weisglas-Kuperus, 2009; Esbjorn, Hansen, Greisen, & Mortensen, 2006; Taylor, Klein, Drotar, Schluchter, & Hack, 2006). Aarnoudse et al. (2009) suggested that impairment in executive functioning can contribute to challenges that children with extremely low birth weight experience throughout childhood. In a study that examined the impacts of low birth weight on ADHD while controlling for other factors, such as exposure to alcohol or cigarettes, parental ADHD, and social class, children with

ADHD were three times more likely to have been born with low birth weights (Mick et al., 2002). Extremely low birth weight places a child at greater risk, and it is likely that hypoxic or anoxic events during delivery, central nervous system damage, chronic lung disease, jaundice, and intraventricular hemorrhage contribute to these results (Taylor et al., 2006).

Smoking, Alcohol, and Substance Use During Pregnancy

Several retrospective studies have investigated whether maternal smoking is related to inattention and hyperactivity in children and found significant effects (Biederman, Faraone, Sayer, & Kleinman, 2002; Fried, 1995; Mick et al., 2002; Rodriguez & Bohlin, 2005). However, other studies have not found these effects (Wakschlag, Lahey, Loeber, Green, & Leventhal, 1997; Weitzman, Gortmaker, & Sobol, 1992). It is believed that methodological difficulties in many of the studies account for the discrepancies (Rodriguez & Bohlin, 2005). Studies with animals have found that prenatal nicotine exposure led to structural changes in the brain and caused dysfunction of the dopaminergic system, also found in children with ADHD (Ernst et al., 1999). In a prospective study, not confounded by sociodemographic factors, of 290 children from birth to age 7, smoking during pregnancy, particularly in early pregnancy, was associated with later symptoms of ADHD (Rodriguez & Bohlin, 2005).

The diagnosis of children prenatally exposed to alcohol is based on growth retardation, central nervous system impairment, and characteristic facial dysmorphology (Chasnoff, Wells, Telford, Schmidt, & Messer, 2010). More severe facial dysmorphology is correlated with more impaired levels of cognitive and neurodevelopmental deficits as well as increased brain dysfunction measured by MRI (Astley et al., 2009; Astley, Olson, Kerns, et al., 2009). Children with alcohol-related neurodevelopmental disorder (ARND) can have more pronounced executive functioning deficits than those with fetal alcohol syndrome (FAS; Connor, Sampson, Bookstein, Barr, & Streissguth, 2000; Kodituwakku, May, Clericuzio, & Weers, 2001). In fact, executive functioning difficulties are among the most common problems in children across the fetal alcohol spectrum, likely because they require the activation of interconnective neural circuits, some of which can become disrupted by alcohol use at any stage during fetal development (Bjorkquist, Fryer, Reiss, Mattson, & Riley, 2010; Chasnoff et al., 2010; Matson, Riley, Gramling, Delis, & Jones, 1998).

The effects of other drugs on the fetus have been difficult to determine because there is considerable variation in how different drugs affect development (Boris, 2009). Cocaine exposure can cause injury to fetal organs and the placenta and lead to preterm delivery, low birth weight, and neurobehavioral problems (Ren, Malanga, Tabit, & Kosofsky, 2004; Shankaran et al., 2007). It is also consistently associated with attentional, internalizing and externalizing, and total behavioral problems over time (Bada et al., 2007; Frank, Augustine, Knight, Pell, & Zuckerman, 2001).

Contributions of Parenting

Although parenting does not cause difficulties with executive functioning and ADHD, the interaction of genetics and parenting might contribute to about 10% of the variance. Even the most well-meaning parents can become locked in negative interactions with children with ADHD, which can set the stage for an escalation of negative behavior in the child. Intrusive, hostile, harsh, and coercive parenting, or withdrawn, unresponsive patterns of interaction, can exaggerate the child's symptoms and cause further difficulties. Parents who alternate among these types of parenting can further escalate the child's symptoms. Because children with ADHD find it difficult to organize and remain focused, a chaotic and unpredictable environment, as found in homes with parental depression, substance abuse, and family violence, can exaggerate symptoms of the child with executive functioning difficulties. Such children need structure, a predictable environment, and scaffolding to learn to regulate themselves. This can occur in containing and supportive interactions with parents. Parents with personality disorders and other mental health disorders often struggle to maintain positive interactions with their children and provide stable environments for them. Fathers can provide stability or, conversely, increase the risk of psychopathology in their children.

Children with executive functioning difficulties need two major types of support: emotional and instructional. Lack of support in these areas can exaggerate their difficulties. For example, a mother's responsiveness and warmth are believed to support the development of effortful control and various aspects of cognitive processing (Spinrad, Stifter, Donelan, McCall, & Turner, 2004). Warm maternal interactions were linked at 3.5 years to children's ability to shift attention (Gilliom, Shaw, Beck, Schoenberg, & Lukon, 2002). Spinrad et al. (2007) studied the longitudinal effects of supportive maternal interactions from 17 months to 30 months and found a positive link to effortful control over time. The researchers pointed out that supportive interactions can be particularly important for children with limited self-regulatory capacities. In research on 3-year-old twins focusing on parent–child interactions, maternal warmth and enjoyment were significantly linked to later attention regulation, task engagement, and general cognitive ability. Furthermore, in a sample of children born at medical risk, problem-solving ability at 5 years of age was associated with lower prenatal risk and responsive interactions with mothers (McGrath, Sullivan, & Seifer, 1998). Examining preschoolers' capacity to respond to parental requests and inhibit responses, researchers related these abilities to parents' co-regulation of behavior by engaging the child in conversation (Putnam, Spritz, and Stifter, 2002). These kinds of interaction have been associated with secure attachment, which has been linked, in turn, to later problem solving, competence, and resilience (Moss, Gosselin, Parent, Rousseau, & Dumont, 1997).

A number of strategies that provide instructional support have also been important (Hamre & Pianta, 2005). They include approaches such as scaffolding, directing the child's attention to relevant parts of the environment, providing guidance in breaking a task down, and encouraging private speech. They can be particularly important for children with difficulties with effortful control and executive functioning (Bjorklund & Pelligrini, 2002; Connor & Gross, 2003; Williams & Sternberg, 2002).

If a parent has ADHD, her own difficulties can make parenting more difficult, including problems reacting to tantrums, maintaining routines, and meeting other organizational needs. It can also make it more difficult for her to follow through with necessary treatment for her child, including getting him to multiple appointments (Weiss, Hechtman, & Weiss, 2000).

Case Study: Peter

Peter was described by his single mother as being in trouble in every area of his life. In school, he failed to concentrate on his work and had been aggressive to children on the playground. He also had problems completing homework and was failing his grade. He could not settle himself down at night without his mother lying with him until he fell asleep. Peter was diagnosed with ADHD, predominantly hyperactive impulsive type, and ODD and prescribed medication that was very successful in reducing his impulsivity and aggression and helping him to concentrate.

Executive functions affected included the following:

- Peter had problems with concentrating in the classroom and completing his schoolwork, seemingly due to his ADHD symptoms, particularly his hyperactivity and distractibility, but also his oppositionality toward those in authority.

- He found it very difficult to contain his emotions, particularly anger. His acting-out behavior frequently put himself and others at risk.
- Peter seemed to have little planning ability and acted impulsively without thinking about consequences. This resulted in his sister being hurt with scissors, windows being broken, and Peter putting himself and his family at risk when he grabbed the steering wheel of the car, nearly causing an accident.
- When he wanted something, he would nag his mother, who sometimes gave in, worn out by his nagging. It often focused on the same thing, such as a particular game on the computer. This perseveration on one idea could occur daily.
- When asked to do something in school, he often failed to follow through, seemingly unable to maintain instructions in WM.
- Peter failed most tasks requiring a sense of time.

Contributors to Peter's presentation included the following:

- Peter's mother admitted to drinking heavily and taking drugs during the first trimester of her pregnancy. She was also extremely anxious about her situation.
- No other complications with the pregnancy or delivery were noted, though his mother did admit to some postnatal depression and frequently ignoring Peter's crying during his early months.
- There was a strong genetic component to Peter's presentation as his father had been diagnosed with ADHD and was on medication for it. His mother probably also had some symptoms of ADHD, predominantly inattentive type. She found it difficult to provide an organized household despite efforts to do so.
- The marriage had been full of conflict before his parents broke up. Peter was often caught in the middle and blamed for the difficulties. After his father left, despite promises to pick Peter up, he failed to come on a number of occasions. When Peter visited him, he was left unattended on at least two occasions, and his mother had to rescue him.
- When he was asked to do a task or homework, no scaffolding was provided. He was expected to begin, focus on, and complete an activity with little support, an impossible task for him.
- Peter responded well and improved significantly after taking stimulant medication, suggesting a neurobiological cause of his difficulties.

It is assumed that ADHD contributed to most of Peter's difficulties, though some of his oppositional behavior seemed to be based on comorbidity with ODD, which led to many of his aggressive outbursts.

ASSESSING EXECUTIVE FUNCTIONING AND DISORDERS

Assessments of various executive functions have been available for decades. Previously, they were used primarily in neuropsychology assessments with adult clients who might have suffered brain damage. Now a number of standardized assessment tools have been developed for use with children. Because there are so many different executive functions, it is not possible to use a single measure. Consequently, assessment is used to identify problems and strengths. This then becomes the executive functioning profile of the child.

Informal Assessment

Observations

Observations of the child are best made across multiple situations, including in the school (classroom, playground, and special sessions) and in the home, assessing how competently the child can use various executive functions in these settings. It might be difficult, however, to determine *why* a child performs as he does because his performance can be affected by both parent and teacher behaviors. However, observations of his ability to inhibit a negative response can yield important information, and how well he can focus and hold instructions in mind can be inferred from classroom and home observations. If he is observed in more unstructured times during the school day, such as recess and lunchtime, on the playground, and in gym class, it is possible to determine how less structured time contributes to his presentation. Executive functions typically observed include task initiation, sustained attention and focus, response inhibition, flexibility and shifting, holding information in mind (WM), organization, and sense of time. Functional behaviors observed include time needed to begin a task, time spent on a task, and off-task behavior (Dawson & Guere, 2010). It is useful to collect both objective data, such as how long he stays focused, as well as a running record of his behavior during observation. McCloskey et al. (2009) provide the reproducible *Executive Function Student Observation (EFSO)* and *Executive Function Classroom Observation (EFCO)* forms on a CD that accompanies their book. They are very useful, particularly if the observer is not clear about which behaviors to observe in the classroom setting that relate to executive functioning. They also provide guidance on identifying issues with physical space and how the teacher supports or impedes the child's ability to manage school routines. The teacher can also provide a perspective on how representative the results of his behavior analysis are, particularly if the child made an unusual effort to behave.

Observations can also provide insights on how he obtains answers, the questions on timed tests that result in frustration or giving up, and his capacity to self-monitor performance, concentrate, and ignore distractions. His enjoyment, compliance, or anxiety can also be witnessed.

Case History and Interviews

Interviewing people who know the child best—parents, teachers, sometimes grandparents, other caregivers who spend considerable time with her—can provide important information as well. In addition to information gathering, interviewing parents can establish initial rapport with them and acknowledge their expertise regarding their child's history and current functioning. This includes how the child sees and thinks about the world and how she acts in her daily routines. His developmental history, including the pregnancy and birth; medical history; previous assessments and treatments; family history (including any trauma and current stress); and genetic history on both sides of the family, can yield important information. His school records can provide information on past and present functioning.

For eliciting information on specific executive functions, Dawson and Guere (2010) and McCloskey et al. (2009) provide interview forms that can be reproduced and used for conducting these interviews. The questions are organized around problem areas commonly found in children with executive functioning problems. For example, can the child plan tasks on her own and work independently? How are morning, schoolwork, and bedtime routines managed? How organized is the child, and how much supervision or support is needed for her to complete a task? How well can he control his behavior with peers and siblings, particularly when frustrated and stressed? How well can he look after his possessions? Older children and insightful younger ones can also be interviewed about similar behaviors. It can be interesting to see how well their answers agree with those given by parents, other caregivers, and teachers.

Behavioral Checklists or Rating Scales

Broad-Based Instruments

Checklists and rating scales comprise a critical component of a more formal assessment approach. Some instruments can be used to identify a number of social and emotional problems, including difficulties with attention and hyperactivity, anxiety, depression, aggression, and disruptive behavior. Given the incidence of comorbidity of children with executive dysfunction and ADHD, these instruments can provide valuable information on aspects of functioning and feelings that might be influencing the child's overall adjustment. They include the *Child Behavior Checklist* (*CBCL*; Achenbach, 2000) and the *Behavior Assessment System for Children*, 2nd ed. (*BASC-2*; Reynolds & Kamphaus, 2005).

Scales for Executive Functioning and Attention and Concentration

These measures include the *Behavior Rating Inventory of Executive Function* (*BRIEF*; Gioia, Isquith, Guy, & Kenworthy, 2000) and *Conners*, 3rd ed. (*Conners-3*; Conners, 2008).

Another screen is the *Brown Attention-Deficit Disorder Scales for Children and Adolescents* (Brown, 2001). There are parent and teacher scales available for children aged 3 to 7 and 8 to 2, and self-report versions are available for children aged 8 to 12 and 12 to 18. Those for younger children provide cluster scores for activation, attention, effort, affect, memory, and self-regulating action. The adolescent version does not include self-regulating action.

The *Executive Skills Questionnaire* (*ESQ*; Dawson & Guere, 2009) is included in their book. It is not recommended for use instead of the other measures as it is not norm referenced. It can be used to assess a number of executive functions and both strengths and weaknesses in order to design interventions with increased accuracy. There are teacher and parent versions for school-aged children and a student version to use with middle and high school children.

Academic tests and work samples from the classroom can also be used if the child is reported as having learning problems in school. It is helpful to use tests that are acceptable and used in the school district that the child attends.

Formal Assessment

Assessment of the Child

Assessments of various executive functions have been available for decades but for many years were used primarily in assessments of adults with brain damage. There are 25 different measures of attention, 15 of memory, and 20 of executive functioning, with most of the tests being multidimensional. Unlike tests specifically developed to assess intellectual capacity, language, and memory of children, many tests of executive functions were not developed for children and consequently are often not appealing to them. Also, many of them do not have sufficient normative data on children (Anderson, 1998).

Various executive functions are typically assessed using subtests designed to assess one particular function. But using subtests from various measures has limitations; because of the one to one situation, the examiner can cue the child when to begin and when to finish a task, so the subtest does not replicate the complexity or demands of the classroom and other activities that the child engages in daily. Nevertheless, it is important that part of the assessment is carried out directly with the child. McCloskey et al. (2009, p. 116) suggest the use of cascading production analysis, which "refers to a stepwise change in the effectiveness of task performance that occurs as the result of alterations in task demands."

If demands are increased, and the child's performance decreases, they call this cascading production decrement; if demands are decreased and the child's performance increases, they call this cascading production increment. The NEPSY Auditory Assessment Subtest increases executive functioning demand and often results in a significantly lower score for the second part of the test compared with the initial task. The WISC-IV Cancellation Structured and Cancellation Random test of visual processing also shows this type of demand increase.

Subtests That Measure Executive Functioning

Although somewhat controversial, formal neuropsychological test batteries such as the Halstead–Reitan (H-R) and Luria-Nebraska Neuropsychological Battery (LNNB) tend not to be used to assess executive dysfunctioning or ADHD. However, there are three tests that include a number of subtests of executive functioning that have been developed for children and can be used in addition to tests developed to assess specific executive functions. For each test, the complete battery can be administered, or subtests can be chosen on the basis of the executive functions believed to be compromised for a particular child.

A Developmental Neuropsychological Assessment, 2nd ed. (*NEPSY-II*; Korkman, Kirk, & Kemp, 2007) assesses the child across six domains from 3 to 16 years and 11 months of age. The domains assessed are executive functioning/attention, language, memory and learning, visuospatial processing, and social perception. A full assessment takes about 90 minutes for preschoolers and 2 to 3 hours for school-aged children. There are 32 subtests, with many suitable for the assessment of executive functioning. They can assess executive skills such as planning, cognitive flexibility, impulsivity, vigilance, auditory selective attention, monitoring, self-regulation, and problem solving.

The *Behavioral Assessment of the Dysexecutive Syndrome in Children* (*BADS-C*; Emslie, Wilson, Burden, Nimmo-Smith, & Wilson, 2003) was developed to provide an assessment of children's executive functioning from 7 to 16 years of age and takes about 40 minutes to complete. It has a number of subtests that are brief, varied, and fun for children, and they assess a number of executive functions and examine them for deficits.

The *Delis–Kaplan Executive Function System* (*D-KEFS*; Delis, Kaplan, & Kramer, 2001) assesses executive functions such as flexibility of thinking, inhibition, problem solving, planning, impulse control, concept formation, abstract thinking, and creativity in both verbal and spatial modalities. The age range for the test is 8 to 89. The game like format is engaging for the examinees and encourages optimal performance without providing feedback on whether the response was right or wrong. There is flexibility allowed in test selection, and if all nine subtests are used it takes about 90 minutes. The nine subtests stand alone, and there is no aggregate score. It has been used with children with a number of disorders, including ADHD.

Tests That Measure a Particular Executive Function

A wide range of executive functioning measures is available for use with children whose impairments interfere with normal maturation, cognition, and academic and social experiences.

Measures of Flexible Thinking

The *Wisconsin Card Sorting Test* (*WCST*; Heaton, 1981) measures flexibility of thinking or cognitive set shifting. There is a shortened 64-card version, the *Wisconsin Card Sorting Test 64* (*WCST-64*; Kongs, Thompson, Iverson, & Heaton, 2000), that can be used from 6.5 to 85 years of age. It consists of a set of cards with a small number of colored shapes such as two red squares or four blue circles. In the standard administration, the child has to match each consecutive response card to the examiner's stimulus cards according to the principle devised. The child is told that he is right or wrong without being told the active principle. He does not know that the sorting principle has been changed and must adapt the sorting according to the new rule. Perseveration errors suggest difficulty with inhibiting the previous response and shifting to a new response. Repetition errors are also seen as difficulty with self-monitoring.

The *Contingency Naming Task* (CNT; Anderson, Anderson, Northam, & Taylor, 2000) was modeled on the Stroop Color–Word Test (SCWT) and measures the ability to inhibit and switch a mental set. It uses color and shape stimuli with inner and outer shapes for each picture. The child is first asked to name a series of colored shapes by color and then to name the inner or outer shape on the drawing. The rules are given, and a learning period follows.

Measures of Working Memory

The Tower of Hanoi (TOH) (Simon, 1975) is primarily a test of WM but also assesses planning and behavioral inhibition. The child is required to place five disks of different sizes on three posts, with the largest on the bottom and the disks decreasing in size until the smallest is on the top. Only one disk can be moved at a time. There are computerized and noncomputerized versions, with research suggesting that the apparatus version is easier for children (Bishop, Asmodt-Leeper, Cresswell, McGurk, & Skuse, 2001). It has been used with children from 3 to 12 years of age. Because of concerns that the level of intellectual functioning was affecting the results on the *Tower of Hanoi,* the *Tower of London* (TOL) was developed and adapted for children. It uses colored balls and posts of different lengths, and children are to arrange the balls to match the picture (Shallice, 1982). Normative data on the test are available for children from age 7 to age 13 years, 11 months. In both tests, the child must retain a series of moves in mind. A number of other tests are available, including the *Tower* test on the *Delis–Kaplan Executive Function System* and the *Tower of London—Drexel University* (Culbertson & Zillmer, 2000), available commercially.

Span tests require the person to hold a certain amount of information in WM (Baddeley, 1996). The tests measure how much information can be remembered after a single presentation in correct order. The stimulus can be numbers, words, or letters. The digit span task on the *WISC-IV* is one of the most well known, with repeating the digits forward more related to auditory memory and the digits backward to WM. A difference of three or more digits between forward and backward spans is considered significant. Other *span Tests* include immediate repetition of visuospatial stimuli. They include tapping a sequence of blocks in a specific order, with successive trials of increasing length. The *NEPSY-II* includes a test of repeating a word list a number of times to see if the child can remember more words with repetition of them.

The Working Memory Test Battery for Children (*WMTB-C;* Pickering & Gathercole, 2001) is a standardized test for children from 4 to 15 years of age. The test battery includes eight subtests that assess various components of verbal and nonverbal WM. It is useful to identify children at risk of failing academically and assesses a child's capacity to learn. *The Automated Working Memory Assessment* (*AWMA;* Alloway, 2007) is a computer-based assessment of verbal and nonverbal WM skills. It can be used from 4 to 22 years of age. The scale is fully automated, so minimal training is required. It gives an interpretation of how the child will be affected in school. *The Working Memory Rating Scale* (*WMRS;* Alloway, Gathercole, & Kirkwood, 2008) can be used with children from 5 to 11 years of age. It is a behavioral rating scale for teachers. It has been conormed with the *AWMA* and can facilitate easy identification of children with WM deficits.

Measures of Attention

The *Test of Everyday Attention for Children* (*TEA-Ch*; Manly, Robertson, Anderson, & Nimmo-Smith, 1999) has nine subtests appealing to children, and administration takes about an hour. It is possible to use a four-subtest screener that takes about 20 minutes. It can be used with children from 6 to 16 years of age. The subtests measure visual, auditory, and sustained, attentional, and switching behavior.

The *Trail Making Test* (*TMT*; Reitan, 1986) began as a test for adults but was later adapted for children. It is one of the most used tests because it is sensitive to the shift, sustain, and inhibitory control aspects of attention. One version can be used with children from 9 to 14 years of age. It is a timed paper-and-pencil test with two parts. Part A requires the child to draw a line between numbered circles, and Part B is more complex and requires the child to draw a line alternating between numbers and letters in sequence. The time taken and number of errors are used to score the test. The *Delis–Kaplan Executive Function System* has a *Trail Making Test* that requires completion of five parts: visual scanning, number sequencing, letter sequencing, number–letter switching, and motor speed. This test allows the examiner to distinguish between ability with visual and/or motor components or in language sequences. The *Color Trails Tests* (*CTT*) was designed to be culture free and uses colored circles instead of letters, and the child alternates between colors and 25 numbers. Instructions can be presented non-verbally through gestures and sign language.

Visual search and cancellation tests are paper-and-pencil tests that require the child to search a random or organized array of stimuli and mark a target stimulus. Some of the stimuli searched for include letters, shapes, symbols, and words. These tests are used to see how well the child can focus on a particular visual stimulus without being distracted by other visual stimuli placed around it.

Continuous performance tests (CPT) are popular and widely studied forms of testing for executive functioning and ADHD (Barkley, 1998). They have been used with a number of variations, such as visual, auditory, numbers, and letters. The most common version is to have the child observe the computer screen while individual letters or numbers are flashed on it, and the child is asked to press a button when a certain number or letter or pair of stimuli in sequence appears. It assesses inattention and impulsivity without being impacted by other cognitive factors. Some commercially available *continuous performance tests* include *Conners's Continuous Performance Test* (Conners, 1995), *Gordon Diagnostic System* (*GDS*; Gordon, 1983), and *Test of Variables of Attention* (*TOVA*; Greenberg & Kindschi, 1996). The tests vary considerably in terms of the time that it takes, the type of stimulus used, and whether it is presented visually or auditorily.

Measures of Planning Ability

Tests such as the *Tower of Hanoi* (TOH; Simon, 1975) require planning of the moves that need to be made to successfully complete the task. Because only one disk can be moved at a time, and the child has only a certain number of moves to complete the task, some level of planning is required. The *Tower of London* (TOL), which requires children to arrange the balls to match a picture, also requires that the child plan the move ahead of time. A number of other tests are available, including the *Tower* test on the *Delis–Kaplan Executive Function System, Tower of London—Drexel University* (Culbertson & Zillmer, 2000), and the tower subtest from the first edition of the *NEPSY*, dropped in *NEPSY-II*.

The *Porteus Maze Test* (*PMT*; Porteus, 1965) measures planning and has been used in studies of ADHD because it is believed to measure something other than intelligence. The child draws a line from a starting point through increasingly difficult mazes. It has been used with children from 6 to 13 years of age. The total time needed to complete each maze is recorded.

The *Rey–Osterrieth Complex Figure Test* (ROCFT) (Corwin & Bylsma, 1992) measures planning ability and organizational skill and is a drawing test done with colored pens.

It can be used for children from 5 to 14 years of age. The child is asked to copy the Rey–Osterrieth figures either while observing the figure or after having copied it and then after 3 minutes or longer in a delayed recall trial. Each figure is scored for the 18 configuration elements of the drawing.

Measures of Selective or Focused Attention

The SCWT tests selective and focused attention (Lowe & Mitterer, 1982), the ability to shift from one set to another, and the ability to inhibit response and resist distraction (Lezak, 1995). The test requires the child to read words written in different colors and then switch to naming the colors instead of reading the words. This requires that the child inhibit the dominant response to read the words. It can be used with children from 6 years of age who can read. There are a number of versions, including the *Day–Night Stroop Test*, which includes two pairs of opposites (day/night and boy/girl) and requires the child to say the opposite as quickly as possible when a picture is presented on the computer screen. This assesses her ability to respond to one cue and ignore another and respond flexibly as directed.

Measures of Inhibiting

The *Matching Familiar Figures Test* (Kagan, 1966) measures impulsivity or the ability to inhibit a response. The examiner presents a picture of an object to a child, who has to match it to the identical object from various similar pictures. There are six items to choose from for 6- to 12-year-olds. There are 12 trials, and scores are obtained from initial response times and errors. It is useful to identify children who use a fast but inaccurate response strategy, as often found in children with ADHD.

Go–no go tasks measure the ability to inhibit and can reflect attention and concentration factors. There are various such tasks, a common one requiring the child to tap twice when the examiner taps once and to tap once if the examiner taps twice. In the next part of the test, the child is instructed to tap twice if the examiner taps once and to do nothing if the examiner taps twice. The number of times that these tasks are done can vary. In a similar test, the child is required to press a computer keyboard space bar when white crosses appear on the screen but not to respond to other shapes and then to switch to white squares and then to crosses again (Archibald & Kerns, 1999). This test measures the capacity for WM and inhibiting a dominant response.

Measures of Fluency

Tests of verbal fluency can test the ability to generate words in response to a letter cue, such as words beginning with "b," and the ability to produce words in response to a category cue, such as names of animals. They can require a verbal or written response. They require the ability to self-monitor, initiate, and shift and include a WM component. Many children produce a greater number of responses at the beginning than at the end. It can be particularly useful when children have a verbal learning disability and possible dyslexia to show the overlap between the two disorders.

TREATMENT OF DIFFICULTIES AND DISORDERS OF EXECUTIVE FUNCTIONING

Goal of Treatment

The goal of treating children with various kinds of executive functioning difficulties is to enable them, as far as possible, to cope at home, in school, and at community activities, supporting the use of strategies to function independently.

Principles of Treatment

- Treatment approaches need to be matched to the unique clinical needs of each child and family.
- Assessment findings and the child's "executive profile" should be matched to treatment strategies as far as possible.
- There is empirical evidence to support the use of certain interventions in some areas of executive functioning difficulties and with some comorbidities. However, in many situations, the evidence base to direct clinical intervention is thin, and clinicians need to use their experience with similar children instead.
- Stimulant medication has been shown to be the most effective single treatment approach for ADHD (Abikoff, 2001; Abikoff & Hechtman, 1996), likely because improvements in the child's behavior due to medication can improve parenting interactions and enhance teachers' strategies with the child in the classroom. However, some children with ADHD and certain comorbidities do not respond well to medication, or parents can be strongly opposed to its use. Also, in most cases, children do best with a combination of treatments.
- The education of parents on the diagnosis of executive functioning difficulties and the rationale for various treatment approaches are critical to increase parents' understanding of their child's difficulties and secure their cooperation with recommended treatments.
- Some children do best with a combination of treatments, including parent training, provision of strategies in the classroom, and training of various executive functions.
- With very young children, medication is often not used; instead, behavioral approaches are used, at least initially.
- Different combinations of ADHD and various comorbidities might need different approaches to treatment. For example, children with anxiety and ADHD might need different treatment approaches than children with ODD and ADHD.
- Many children, especially those in middle and high school, as cognitive and academic expectations increase, benefit from training in specific executive functions, such as organization, time management, and planning skills, to help them with the increasing complexity of their schoolwork.
- Training executive functioning skills directly is a relatively new but promising approach, and it is consistent with the belief that such focused interventions can make changes in brain functioning. If multimodal treatments are to be provided, then their order needs to be tailored to the severity and type of symptoms as well as parents' willingness to be involved.
- Capitalizing on the strengths of children, such as skills in sport, art, or music, can help to maintain their self-esteem as many become discouraged with managing their schoolwork.
- Improving executive functioning skills requires more than just imparting information because the ability needs scaffolding and practice.
- It is important to be realistic about expectations for the success of interventions for children with significant executive dysfunctions, for treatment is not easy. However, it is also critical to maintain and model hope, perseverance, and patience with the treatment plan.

Areas of Treatment and Specific Strategies

Medication

Major studies have proven the efficacy of stimulant medication for ADHD, reducing behavioral symptoms and improving academic and social functioning in about 50% to 90% of children (Barkley, 1998; Jensen, Abikoff, & Brown, 2009). Success often depends on whether other psychiatric and/or developmental disorders are present. In spite of the success in reducing inattention, impulsivity, and restless behavior, such medication usually needs to be combined with other treatments to maintain improvements long term.

Some difficulties with using medication include the following:

- Medication can adversely affect a comorbid disorder, or that disorder can reduce the effects of the medication on ADHD symptoms.
- Many parents are opposed to the use of medication, particularly for younger children.
- In a few cases, the positive effects of medication wear off over time, or the child finds that the effects are unpleasant.
- Side effects can include growth retardation related to appetite loss, sleep-onset problems and nightmares, dizziness or irritability, and, as the medication wears off, rebound symptoms. Occasionally, more serious side effects occur, including suicidal ideation, psychosis, and aggression.
- Interactions among medications can occur and reduce the effects of a prescribed medication.

The American Academy of Child and Adolescent Psychiatry has produced guidelines for the preferred order for a trial of medication in the treatment of ADHD. They include beginning with a stimulant, titrating upward to appetite suppression or intolerance, and monitoring for reduction of symptoms and side effects using standard questionnaires. If the first stimulant is ineffective or not tolerated, another stimulant is recommended. If it does not work, switching to an antidepressant such as atomoxetine, bupropion, or a selective serotonergic reuptake inhibitor (SSRI) or alpha adrenergic agonist (clonidine or guanfacine) is suggested.

Stimulants

Stimulants are believed to work by increasing the concentration of dopamine at the synapses (Wilens & Spencer, 1998, 2000). They primarily bind to the dopamine transporter protein and block its reuptake. The most common stimulants used for treating ADHD are methyphenidate (Ritalin, Methylin, and Metadate); dexmethylphenidate (Focalin); and amphetamines (dextroamphetamines, mixed amphetamine salts). With methylphenidate, the effects on behavior usually peak 1 to 2 hours after administration and wear off within 3 to 5 hours. It is more rapidly absorbed than Ritalin, and the effects are noticed sooner. There are a number of new stimulants that do not wear off as quickly. For children who cannot swallow tablets, there is now a system that delivers the dosage through patches on the skin that provide up to 12 hours of treatment. Concerta is a very popular medication, with effects peaking about 8 hours following administration. A single dose of this slow-release medication in the morning can last until the evening, and it has been shown to remain effective after 2 years of use. Concerta requires that the child swallow a large capsule, whereas some of the other formulations contain coated granules absorbed by the gut at different times. These capsules can be broken and mixed with juice or peanut butter, an easier approach for children who cannot swallow large capsules. Amphetamines also enhance dopaminergic transmissions and are available in a variety of formulations.

Atomoxetine

Atomoxetine, related to the antidepressants that block norepinephrine reuptake and increase availability of intrasynaptic norepinephrine, is considered a second-line treatment for ADHD. It is typically used when stimulants do not work or are not tolerated.

Some clinicians use it when there is comorbid anxiety because it does have some anxiolytic effect. It is not as effective as stimulants in reducing the primary symptoms of ADHD. Atomoxetine requires a gradual upward titration to the effective dose, taking several weeks to see its potential effect. It is sometimes used in addition to stimulants.

Other Medications

After unsuccessful trials of stimulants, bupropion and other antidepressants are occasionally recommended. Bupropion hydrochloride, used for the treatment of depression, is sometimes helpful but can exacerbate tics and cause irritability. Tricyclic antidepressants have also been used but have had less consistent success than stimulants and have adverse side effects such as dry mouth, hypotension, and possible cardiac effects. Other SSRIs are used less consistently. Clonidine has adrenergic agonist properties and does reduce the symptoms of ADHD but is less effective than stimulants. It has been effective when the child has conduct or oppositional defiant disorder and can reduce anxiety and hypervigilance in traumatized children. Because it tends to produce sedation, it is often prescribed at night, but if used in the day monitoring is needed to ensure that it does not induce drowsiness. For an extensive discussion of the use of medications with children with various comorbidities, see Prince and Wilens (2009).

There are three main approaches other than medication for treatment of children with executive functioning problems at home and school: short-term strategies to adapt the environment to support the child's executive functioning; approaches to support and teach the child various executive functions; and intense, focused coaching of executive functions that can enhance neurological functioning.

SHORT-TERM APPROACHES

Support for Various Executive Functions

For the child with executive functioning problems, the routine of the school day can be extremely challenging because it includes getting up on time and completing tasks such as getting dressed, eating breakfast, and packing the school bag with things needed for the day. Once at school, the child has to pay attention to the teacher, remember instructions and follow through with them, work quickly on timed tasks, complete assignments, and move from subject to subject. These are all difficult tasks for the child with executive functioning issues. Consequently, children with such difficulties need their environments and tasks to be adapted to their needs or what Barkley (2005) called a "prosthetic environment." This can be done by modifying the task that the child has to do and providing support to supplement her executive functioning. Helping her to have some success on a daily basis reduces the risk of her developing low self-esteem and a sense of being a failure. The level of support needed can be determined from an adequate assessment, and it should avoid buffering the child too much but needs to help her with skills that she cannot manage independently. The ultimate aim is for the child to understand the supports that she needs or provide them for herself. Parents can gradually scale back some of the supports, but they might be needed well into adolescence and even early adulthood. The aim is to help her repeat the behaviors enough so that they become automatic. It is important to experiment with her until she finds strategies that really work for her.

It is important to determine where the child is falling down with schoolwork and activities or tasks at home. For example, does he forget to write the assignment down and when it has to be handed in? Does he forget to bring the right books home? Does he not have enough time to complete the assignment or forget to hand it in? If there is an obvious pattern to his problems, then strategies can be put in place to overcome them. Using specific terms and making sure that he follows through with them are crucial. Where possible, using his ideas is important as doing so increases the likelihood that he will come up with ideas to help himself later in life. In rewarding behaviors, it is important to focus on desired outcomes and only reward them or progress toward them, for example, getting organized in the morning or completing schoolwork.

Providing Support for Each Executive Function

Initiating a Task

Typically, young children have difficulties with getting started on a number of tasks and need assistance from parents, whereas older children are gradually capable of taking on tasks independently. However, older children with executive functioning difficulties can continue to need strategies to help them get started on a task.

- Set up a schedule and make it clear to the child; refer to it frequently so that it becomes automatic for him. This can be an agenda, a visual or online calendar, or a chart on the fridge. Make it something realistic to a particular child. Put in specific times for tasks to be completed whenever possible. This will include routines, homework, and chores.
- Provide verbal reminders while referring to the written schedule.
- Make sure that the child understands the value of what is being done (e.g., completing homework so that she can eventually graduate from high school).
- Have something that the child likes to do as a reward. Give him a reward if he initiates something that has to be done without being reminded. If rewards are insufficient, occasionally taking away privileges can encourage greater effort to complete tasks.
- Use timers, alarms, and other technologies to cue the time to start.
- Ensure that the child spends enough time and does not rush through a routine or task to get it done but leaves it partially completed.
- It might be necessary to sit down with the child to make sure that she begins the task. Some children are very good at talking about what needs to be done and how important it is but never get around to doing it. Help her choose a topic and break it down into subtasks that can be scheduled over the time period allowed to complete the assignment.
- Sometimes having a tutor or an ADHD coach for the child can be helpful.

Planning and Organization

Some children struggle with planning and organizing tasks unless they have a structure and routine, which can involve organizing things in their heads, organizing their possessions, or planning to complete a longterm project. They might fail to hand in homework and underestimate the time needed on a project.

- Try to identify the reason for the project not being handed in on time and work on overcoming the problem.
- Find a strategy applicable to the child's problem. For some, getting started is difficult. Breaking the work down into manageable chunks can be helpful.
- Help the child to write reminders in his agenda.
- Go through the items/steps that need to be done to get the task completed. This process can be applied to routines such as cleaning the child's room and getting ready for bed. For younger children, providing pictures of the steps might enhance their attention.

Time Management

Time management allows the child to work out the time needed to complete a task and monitor her progress in order to finish it on time. It includes starting the task on time and not procrastinating.

- Give the child a schedule to follow and prompt him along the way.
- Set up a time limit for each step and remind him of the time still left.
- Use some of the cueing devices listed above, such as timers, bells, and alarms.

Working Memory

Some children have difficulty holding information in mind to perform the steps of a task. Verbal information can easily be lost, and they do better with concrete reminders.

- Give the child one instruction at a time and have him repeat it to make sure that he has remembered it. Repeat them by just saying the most relevant word, which might be easier to remember.
- Provide visual cues and schedules to support his memory.
- For younger children, use multisensory prompts such as singing or tapping out a rhythm as the words are said.
- If the instructions have to be given all at once, provide bulleted or numbered points and indicate that there are, for example, three things to do and name them by number.
- Chunk information so that the child can get one part of the work done without being overloaded by the whole assignment.
- Simplify instructions whenever possible, reducing unnecessary verbiage. Make the material as meaningful and familiar as possible and try to simplify the requirements. Encourage the child to request information if needed.
- Have cards showing the steps of a task, for example, in doing multiplication or planning an essay. Provide printed notes or a voice recorder that can store information that needs to be remembered.
- Teach the child to make and use lists and have him write down things as he thinks of them.

Focus/Effort

This refers to the ability to sustain attention and effort on a task until it is completed. This can be difficult if the child gets distracted or becomes tired or bored with what he is doing.

- Use incentives or rewards for task completion, especially for tasks that the child dislikes or when there is no intrinsic reward.
- The child will need one-to-one supervision and attention, feedback, and reinforcement.
- Break the task into shorter subtasks, rewarding each one, to prevent his giving up prematurely.

Flexibility and Shifting

Many children with executive functioning difficulties perseverate on one aspect of a task or get stuck on an idea and cannot get beyond it. They can also expect complete adherence to rules and routines and find any changes difficult. In other words, they lack flexibility and have problems with adapting to new situations or environments. If the first attempt to do something fails, they often have difficulty changing gears and trying something else.

- If change is anticipated, run through the new schedule beforehand, explaining to the child what to expect.
- Use social stories to go through situations and what will be expected of the child.
- Give her strategies for self-talk to reassure herself about the new situation (e.g., "I can manage this, I've managed things before").
- Recount situations that you have faced, going through the steps by which you overcame the difficulty.
- Teach the child ways to calm herself down if she finds herself becoming anxious or angry about a new situation.
- Brainstorm with her the things that she can do to feel less anxious about what is coming up.

Emotion Control

Some children with executive functioning difficulties have problems inhibiting emotional arousal and outbursts in order to complete a task and achieve goals.

- Teach coping strategies to help the child calm down, such as taking deep breaths before a test, using positive self-talk to reduce fear or frustration, or rehearsing scripts before an event.
- Use emotion coaching when he is becoming upset. Spend time acknowledging his feelings, stopping acting out, and problem solving with him.
- Reinforce efforts that he makes to control impulsive acting out or overcome fear about a certain situation, such as sleeping alone.
- See the section on behavior management, which gives ideas for disciplining the child who becomes angry and aggressive.

Inhibition

This is the capacity to think before acting and avoid acting impulsively, including saying things that the child should not and disobeying rules.

- With a younger child, an adult's supervision is often required to reduce impulsive and sometimes dangerous behavior.
- Repeat the rules and emphasize what the child did that was unacceptable.
- Restrict her from potentially dangerous situations and accompany her when needed.
- Teach rules about not interrupting conversations and encourage her to listen for a time when it is appropriate for her to talk.
- Cue the child with private signs, such as holding up your hand, to indicate when she needs to stop an action or not begin it.
- Ask her to repeat the agreed-upon rule for entering a group appropriately or keeping quiet.

Self-Monitoring

This refers to the ability to observe one's behavior and estimate whether it meets expected standards. Problems with self-monitoring include not checking work and behaving in ways that irritate classmates, such as not noticing how others might view the behavior.

- Provide external monitoring by reminding the child about the goals or consequences of his behavior.
- With an academic task, remind him about the purpose of a paper, rereading the instructions, writing an outline, and checking back on these components.

BEHAVIOR MANAGEMENT AND PARENT TRAINING

Behavior management systems are built on the principle that any behavior followed by a positive event is more likely to be repeated and any behavior followed by a negative event is less likely to occur. However, this must be consistent; if the negative behavior is not followed by the expected consequence even once, it is more likely to occur again. Any management plan is primarily about teaching and not about punishment. The goal is that the child will incorporate the desired behavior reliably, though routines need to be maintained. For children with executive functioning difficulties, having a behavior or discipline plan in place is important, though it is only one aspect of the support needed. Such a plan provides the child with the structure and support needed to see that her efforts and good behavior are noticed and rewarded. Collaboration between parents and teachers is important to ensure consistency and communication across settings. Consistent responses among the main caregivers are critical because disagreements and arguments in front of children can sabotage the whole system. If this occurs, couple therapy might be necessary before the plan can be put in place. Parents need to understand how the child feels and that lectures, threats, and yelling do not work. The plan can be done individually with one family or a group of parents, and parents will be expected to do homework between weekly sessions.

The first step in setting up a behavior plan is for the child's caregivers, typically the mother and father, to choose the rules and routines that they view as important for their child. These can include rules for *keeping the child safe,* such as crossing the road, not speaking to strangers, not playing with matches; *morals,* such as not hurting anyone physically, verbally, or emotionally; and *routines,* such as bedtime, mealtimes, homework, chores, and other aspects of family life seen to be important. The fewer the rules the better, because once in place, follow through needs to occur for the child to learn. Enforcement is easier the fewer the rules there are. Consequences for rule breaking need to be consistent and written out so that the child can see them. For children who find it difficult to regulate their behavior without step-by-step guidance, a comprehensive plan for expectations for the whole day might be needed. Sometimes it might be necessary to let the child experience the natural consequences of his behavior, such as having to sit out physical education that he likes because he forgot to bring clothing or equipment.

It is also critical to provide rewards for children when they make extra efforts with their homework, reduce negative behaviors, help someone in the family, try extra hard to organize their possessions, or bring home the right books for homework. Rewards can be more productive than consequences for children with self-esteem issues who can feel that they are continually being punished. Reward systems often work best if older children are involved in choosing the rewards or privileges that they will lose if they do not follow the rules or meet the standards. Reward systems often include what can be earned in a single day and how points can be saved over a longer time to secure a more salient reward. They can give children who have often felt like failures a sense of competence and filling an important place in the family.

Defiant Children (Barkley, 2005, 2006), Parent–Child Interaction (PCIT; Rayfield, Monaco, & Eyberg, 1999), Helping the Noncompliant Child (Forehand & McMahon, 1981), Incredible Years Program (Webster-Stratton et al., 2001), and Dina Dinosaur Program (Webster-Stratton & Reid, 2003) have shown efficacy in many randomized controlled trials and use the behavioral principles described above. These programs are most frequently used with groups of parents and follow a set program or structure from week to week for managing children in public places, using time-out and other disciplinary approaches, and designing a home-oriented token system. Yet many children do not respond to them and in addition require a treatment plan for children with executive functioning problems.

LONGER-TERM APPROACHES

Although children need scaffolding and constant supervision to strengthen their executive functioning and build a repertoire of self-management skills, once a child has learned strategies to enhance a particular executive function, the parent's or teacher's role changes. It should then focus on helping the child to become more independent and use these strategies on her own. Developing these skills requires constant repetition, to the point where they no longer require conscious effort. The supports can be gradually faded out. It is important to keep reviewing the strategies and do random checks to see that they are being maintained. Some long-term approaches are described below:

- The child should develop note taking when information is being given and use mnemonics or memory aids such as lists of useful spelling words, counters, memory cards, and audio recordings. These strategies can be used on an ongoing basis. Also use rhymes and pictures to enhance memory and ways to carry out tasks.
- Teach the child how to come up with solutions to problems. Determine whether she is trying to do so and if not ask questions to help her come up with solutions. If she cannot think of solutions, give suggestions and make sure that they are followed.
- Self-talk or private speech is used by preschool-aged children during problem solving to guide their activities. It also serves as a self-regulating function and can be helpful to encourage a child to keep trying. The development of private speech is positively related to scaffolding provided to the child during problem solving, particularly what is said to her to help her stay involved. Children internalize the speech of their caregivers and transform it into private speech. For that reason, talking about consequences, explaining tasks, and discussing events are crucial. Private speech can be used when a child is in a situation that produces fear or anger. Words and phrases that are encouraging can be containing and motivating for the child when a problem or challenge presents itself: "You can do it," "Good try," "You can manage it, I know you can," or "You have what it takes to do it" (Landy, 2009).
- Children who can complete tasks on time, follow rules, and make their own decisions usually feel in control and good about themselves. In part, this is because their behavior generally brings positive reactions from parents, teachers, and peers, making them feel competent and accepted, and reinforces their positive behaviors. Children with difficulties concentrating and problem solving often feel confused and rejected, which can significantly affect their self-esteem and cause them to exhibit more behavioral problems. Finding activities in the community that the child enjoys, such as Girl Guides, can give her recognition for development of skills. Some children might enjoy a sport, such as karate, especially if there is an emphasis on developing self-control.
- Children can be taught problem-solving strategies when they face a real-life situation, need to complete homework, or are becoming very upset. These are as follows:

    1. Ask questions that can help children to consider alternatives, remember things that worked yesterday, and notice the differences among things. Some researchers have noted that questions can help children to distance themselves in time and space from what they are doing to imagine things differently or consider possible solutions.
    2. Provide hints on how to do things and stay involved so that the child does not become discouraged. Make suggestions about how things might work better. Responses are left openended and are not intrusive but allow the child to remain focused.
    3. Model parts of how to do the task so that the child can do it herself and sometimes join in the task.

- Give instructions with words, pictures, or actions when the child is doing something wrong or really becomes stuck. Help him to focus on aspects of a task by labeling things and cueing him if attention lags.
- Teach the child to use a watch, schedules, and calendars to become organized. Some children might need a tutor or coach who can teach them about becoming organized for their assignments and other activities.
- Help the child with planning by verbalizing ahead what needs to be done first. Make sure that the necessary materials and tools are available to complete the task. Break it down into small component parts and make sure that they are ordered so that she can be successful.
- For children who consistently have difficulty with homework or other tasks, give them some steps to follow:

1. Decide what needs to be done.
2. Examine how the task can be done.
3. Focus on it. Spend time thinking about it and then begin.
4. Keep trying, and do not give up.
5. Find an answer or a strategy.
6. Determine whether the answer or strategy is correct.

The first few times that these strategies are used, parents can scaffold them by being available, asking questions, and supporting the child. As he becomes more confident, he can take over the steps himself. Sometimes writing the steps on a piece of cardboard that he keeps available can be helpful.

- If a child constantly fails to turn in homework and assignments, find out where things are breaking down. The child can be helped to build a strategy to overcome the problems. Perhaps she is not writing the assignment down, forgetting to bring home the required text, not turning in completed work, or starting too late and not anticipating the time needed to complete the task.
- For children who easily become overwhelmed, teach them techniques such as deep breathing to calm down or taking a time-out in a calming place or with an activity that helps her to calm down. Some children like to listen to music or sit in a bean bag chair. The child can also be helped to go to a favorite place in his head. The calming strategy will vary from child to child, and some children might need to have an activity such as jumping on a trampoline to help them deal with feeling anxious or being overwhelmed by noise or the presence of others.

Computer Training Programs

Computer-assisted cognitive training is a promising approach for helping students with ADHD gain self-control and improve attention, problem solving, and social skills. Although the studies generally show promising results, the number of children treated is small, and there have been serious methodological issues with some of the studies (Xu, Reid, & Steckelberg, 2002). Some of these studies are summarized below.

In one study Shalev et al. (2007) tested the effects of using the Computerized Progressive Attentional Training (CPAT) program with 20 6- to 13-year-old children with ADHD. The program targets different types of attentional problems and the children received the program twice a week over an 8-week period. The children showed a significant improvement in reading comprehension, passage copying, and in parents' reports of inattentiveness compared to a control group who did not receive the program. One study was conducted with adult subjects without any physical or mental health disorder who were given WM training and its effects evaluated by functional magnetic resonance imaging (fMRI). Training improved WM performance and resulted in increased brain activity in the dorsolateral prefrontal and parietal association cortices, indicating plasticity of the neural networks used in WM tasks even in older subjects (Klingberg et al., 2005). With children similar training of WM also found improvements using fMRI. Although the number of children treated was small the improvements were promising (Olesen, Westerberg, & Klingberg, 2004). In another study of 50 children between the ages of 7 and 12 who met criteria for ADHD, either combined type or predominantly inattentive type, the children performed 90 WM trials on each day of training over about 40 minutes. The level of difficulty was adapted to match the WM span of the child. The children in the treatment group improved significantly more than those in the comparison group, and at follow-up the treatment effect was still significant. Parent ratings demonstrated significant reduction of inattention and hyperactivity/impulsivity (Klingberg et al., 2005). In a more recent study with preschoolers using computerized training to improve WM and inhibition, the children improved in WM but not inhibition (Thorell, Lindqvist, Bergman, Bohlin, & Klingberg, 2008). The Fast ForWord computer program is primarily designed to develop "phonological awareness" but has also been found to be helpful in enhancing auditory processing and WM (Borman & Benson, 2006; Stevens, Fanning, Coch, Sanders, & Neville, 2008).

Another approach has been to use biofeedback training with children with ADHD (Baron-Faust, 2000; Condor, 2000). Using electromyography (EMG) feedback has been shown to reduce muscle tension levels. In addition, using EEG feedback, operant conditioning of brain wave activity can occur. Using EMG feedback, children were taught to calm down by observing how they can move a peak-to-peak microvolt meter pointer. This approach has been useful in the treatment of hyperactivity (Xu et al., 2002). In the other approach, EEG information is displayed using lights or sounds that show the children how much of each they are producing. Children are given feedback and trained to increase beta production and reduce slow wave theta activity. A number of case study reports indicate that children have improved academic performance and that hyperactivity and distractibility have been reduced. However, in some cases, children have received other treatments at the same time, making it impossible to determine the effectiveness of biofeedback training (Tansey & Bruner, 1983). Another concern with the studies is whether improvements are generalized to the classroom and other situations. Some studies have suggested generalization but have lacked adequate controls (Alhambra, Fowler, & Alhambra, 1995; Washwani, Radvanski, & Carmody, 1998). Several group studies have also reported improvements on measures of intelligence and achievement for children with ADHD using biofeedback. However, significant issues with the studies have made it difficult to determine whether biofeedback training actually contributed to the changes. At this time, there is cautious optimism that biofeedback training is a promising approach, possibly as an ancillary treatment to other approaches (Arnold, 1999). It is clear that these approaches are showing promise and that they will be used increasingly in the future.

Case Study: Treatment of Peter

Conduct problems, including ODD and aggression, account for a great deal of the comorbidity in children with ADHD. In fact, ODD and/or conduct disorder are found in 40% to 60% of children with ADHD (Newcorn, Halperin, & Miller, 2009). This comorbidity increases the risk of poor outcomes for children. As well, aggressive and impulsive behavior makes the children harder to manage. However, recognizing executive functioning difficulties does expand the treatments available for these children. Work with Peter and his mother largely took place in the home. This enabled the home visitor to work with his mother to set up strategies and routines required in the home environment. Ways to help Peter to use a number of strategies outlined previously were explained to Peter's mother and she used a lot of them on a nightly basis. A lot of work was also carried out in the classroom. Some of the early approaches to treatment are presented in Table 8.3.

Table 8.3 *Main Focus of Peter's Treatment*

Type of Treatment	Focus of Treatment
Providing education and information on the difficulties	It was important to provide Peter's mother with information about ADHD and discuss with her his difficulties, which included impulsivity that often put himself, his sister, and his mother at risk.
Behavior management and parent training	When ADHD was explained, Peter's mother immediately noted her own symptoms and revealed that she had been given that diagnosis as well. So it was very difficult for her to set up a consistent routine, structure, or behavior management plan. However, the importance of doing so was explained to her, and she was assisted in preparing a visual outline of the rules, consequences for not following them, and reward system when Peter did follow the rules and routines put in place. It was also suggested that his mother attend a parenting group, in which she learned a great deal about how to manage Peter without becoming too punitive.
Medication	Peter's mother agreed to the use of stimulants, and immediately Peter's aggressive behavior diminished and allowed his mother to put her behavior management plan in place without difficulty.
Lack of focus and motivation	One issue that Peter's mother found difficult was that Peter would not begin his homework without becoming aggressive and instead insisted on being on the computer for hours. With the medication, the behavior management plan, and a reward system in place at home, it was possible to include 15–20 minutes of homework in his evening routine. This improved his school performance significantly. Support in the classroom also helped to reduce his acting-out behaviors.
Initiating, planning, and organizing	It was important to set up a schedule with verbal and visual reminders of what was expected of Peter at school and home. It was important that he be reminded at school and home to complete his assignments and begin to experience some success.
Inhibiting	Peter's mother and his aide in the classroom were instructed that their physical presence was critical to monitor and interrupt his impulsiveness and aggression. It was also important to give Peter signs to use when he was becoming upset that allowed his mother and teacher to help him use strategies to calm down.

CONCLUSION

Working with children with executive functioning difficulties can be a delicate balance between providing support and building skills to give them independence. If no effort is made to help them or provide accommodation in the home and classroom, they will not succeed and remain at risk of becoming overwhelmed and demoralized. On the other hand, if there is no effort to encourage autonomy, they can become dependent and helpless. Parents particularly might have to experiment with the level of support that children need, letting them try to manage on their own but being ready to provide support and help if they become overwhelmed. It is also important to involve children in problem solving and finding solutions to their difficulties. In fact, one of the most important messages given to children is that they can create a sense of hope and, as Brooks (2006) has described it, find their "islands of competence."

Some websites that offer related programs and information are listed in Table 8.4.

Table 8.4 *Websites*

Website	Information on Website
www.developingchild.harvard.edu	A number of articles that "translate science into policy." Provides an excellent article that talks about the parts of the brain that are affected in ADHD.
www.aboutkidshealth.ca	Hospital for Sick Kids Toronto website that provides a multipart series on executive functioning and information on adapting the classroom for students with ADHD. Includes series by Dr. Philip David Zelazo on executive functioning, *Trusted Answers From the Hospital for Sick Children.*
www.chadd.org	Sponsored by Children and Adults with Attention Deficit/ Hyperactivity Disorder (CHADD). Provides bimonthly and annual conference.
www.add.org	This is the official website of the Attention Deficit Disorder Association.
www.DrThomasEBrown.com	Provides information on Dr. Brown's publications and websites and access to articles and a newsletter published four times a year.
www.promisingpractices.net/ programs.asp	Website of the Promising Practices Network on Children, Families, and Communities funded by the RAND Corporation. Provides information on proven and promising programs to improve outcomes for children.
www.help4adhd.org	Presents evidence-based information on ADD in children, adolescents, and adults.
www.ldonline.org	Website provides information and resources for the assessment and treatment of learning disabilities and ADHD.
http://guide.helpingamericasyouth .gov/programtool.ap.cfm	This is the website of Helping America's Youth, with an overview of 180 intervention programs.
www.parentsmedguide.org	Website developed by the American Psychiatric Association and American Academy of Child and Adolescent Psychiatry to provide information on medications for depression and ADHD.
http://research.aboutkidshealth .ca/teachadhd	Website of Teach ADHD that has a number of resources and fact sheets that provide a number of strategies that can be used for children with ADHD in classroom practice.

9

Difficulties and Disorders of Attachment and Social Development

Humans are social beings, and two important characteristics that we look for in children are their capacities to form relationships and have empathy for others. Without these essential aspects of development, children can grow up lonely and create anguish in their relationships. The most extreme social difficulties include psychopathy with antisocial behavior, lack of empathy for others, and withdrawal from social contact with others (Cillessen & Bellmore, 2004). There are many different pathways to the development of social difficulties, including some that are more obviously biological and genetic, such as with children on the autism spectrum disorder (ASD) or with fetal alcohol syndrome; others result from interpersonal trauma or failure to develop attachments with others.

Case Study: Ethan

Eleven-year-old Ethan was referred for treatment of his extreme behavioral difficulties. He had been diagnosed with oppositional defiant disorder. At referral, he had extreme acting-out and aggressive behaviors at home and school. He also engaged in impulsive and dangerous behaviors, such as trying to jump off the roof and interest in extreme sports. He also had problems with developing social competence. As described by his middle-class parents, the most alarming aspect of his behavior was that Michael appeared to have no empathy for others or remorse if he hurt someone. He was cruel toward his younger brother and unable to sustain friendships at school. Although he would initially make a friend, his friendships did not last because he would find ways to upset the other child, often in underhanded ways, sometimes embarrassing him in front of other children. This behavior resulted in Michael being isolated from peers, and he expressed a deep sense of loneliness. He was often suspended from school. Although at times he could be grandiose about his abilities, he was also depressed and described himself as "bad and worthless."

DEFINITIONS OF SOCIAL COMPETENCE

Social competence involves the skills that allow children to succeed in managing social situations and forming various relationships. The goals of social competence include being liked and accepted, having friends, and engaging in rewarding and reciprocal interactions with others. Social development begins with attachment relationships with parents and other caregivers. The desire and capacity to have friendships with peers begin to develop in the preschool years and become increasingly important in elementary school and when the child reaches adolescence. To have effective interactions and satisfying relationships, children need to be sensitive to social communications from others (Howes & James, 2004).

Empathy is also important and involves an affective response to another person's emotional state (Decety, 2007). Empathy can also be accompanied by personal distress and a self-focused reaction with an identical or a similar emotion to the one that the other person is experiencing, such as anxiety. Sympathy can also result that is other oriented and involves feeling concern or sadness for the other person and a desire to improve his or her emotional condition. Prosocial behavior includes caring behaviors such as sharing, helping, or comforting another person, and feeling concern over the distress of someone else. It also involves cooperating with others. Altruism refers to prosocial behavior that does not involve any personal gain but the desire to help others. Some individuals may feel guilty or unworthy if they do not carry out altruistic acts and feel pride if they do. Altruistic people may join movements such as helping the poor or working for human rights in countries throughout the world.

Another important social capacity is perspective taking or listening to and understanding others' points of view. This includes having a theory of mind (TOM) or understanding that others have thoughts and feelings different from one's own. As a result, social understanding and interaction improve (Hay & Cook, 2007). There are two main types of maladaptive social development: externalizing behaviors such as aggression and bullying, and internalizing behaviors such as avoidance, withdrawal, and passivity, which do not achieve the child's social goals (Rigby, 2004; Rubin, Burgess, & Coplan, 2004).

UNDERSTANDING SOCIAL DEVELOPMENT

Research on social development began in the late 1800s and early 1900s. At that time, social development was not identified as a distinct area of research, though there was interest in how it unfolds, and some researchers described observations in "baby diaries" (Shinn, 1990). After this initial period of study, collecting objective and verifiable data on the development of social competence became an emphasis. Toward the end of this early period, more studies on interactions with parents and collaborations with peers began to appear (e.g., Buhler, 1931; Gessell, 1928). However, through the influence of behaviorism and psychodynamic views, social learning theories emerged and meant a shift away from a maturationist perspective to an interest in the effect of the environment and particularly the influence of parents on social development (Bandura, 1977; Miller & Dollard, 1941).

The modern era has seen a significant shift toward recognition of the child as an active agent in social interactions, including increased interest in the influence of temperament on social development and bidirectionality of the parent–child dyad (Bell, 1968). Other new areas of research have included the effects of group care on children's development, including their social development. In addition, the influence of peers, particularly after 10 years of age, has become increasingly recognized. Other topics have included the effects of culture and mass media on social development. As well, use of neuroimaging to study the social brain has provided crucial information on neural mechanisms involved in processing social information. Interest has also expanded in identifying and evaluating treatments for children whose social development has not followed a typical trajectory.

An important area of research began in the 1930s on the effects of early experiences of deprivation on development, including social development. Much of this early research demonstrated how children who were extremely neglected did not obtain normal developmental abilities and in the most extreme cases died (Dennis, 1960; Hunt, 1961). Some early studies of children in institutions showed that few of them seemed to form attachments with caregivers in the institutions. This was due in part to the caregiver-to-child ratio and the policies of many institutions that caregivers were not allowed to develop close relationships with particular children. Although some of the children seemed clingy, many appeared to be emotionally detached (Tizard & Hodges, 1978; Tizard & Rees, 1975). Early studies of the development of children after placement in adoptive homes or foster homes demonstrated mixed findings, whereas more recent research has generally shown that outcomes vary for early-placed and later-placed adoptees. The intelligence of children adopted before 6 months of age showed no statistically significant difference from that of noninstitutionalized children. However, children adopted after 6 months of age showed lower intelligence compared with noninstitutionalized children. Also, in some studies, children adopted after 12 months of age were found to have difficulty with attachments and social relationships. Although many did become attached, the process was often slower than typical, and a larger percentage than in the general population had disorganized attachments. Also, differences in neurodevlopment have been found (Pollack, Nelson, Sclaak, Roeber, Wewerka, et al., 2010). These studies have demonstrated clearly the importance of early relational experience on development, attachment, and social capacity.

As well, with increasing awareness of the level of violence in society, interest in how to combat these trends by promoting social competence and empathy in children has grown. Equally important, new methodologies for researching social development have emerged. Also, a number of longitudinal studies in the United States and Europe have provided vital information on the duration and effects of early social experiences, different trajectories of social development, and importance of the timing of certain events.

ATTACHMENT THEORY AND RESEARCH

Attachment theory has been the "most visible and empirically grounded conceptual framework" for understanding social development (Cassidy & Shaver, 2008, p. xi). Although perhaps its primary focus has been on discussing the effects of early parent–child relationships on later development, there is a growing clinical literature on the effects of troubled or disrupted early relationships on later development, particularly social development.

Attachment theory originated in the 1950s when John Bowlby, a psychiatrist and psychoanalyst, proposed that an infant's attachment or tie to his mother (or substitute caregiver) is crucial. He saw attachment quality as formed from a number of behavioral systems that develop during the first year of life and ensure survival by attracting the attention of caregivers. By the time the child is 6 to 7 months old these behaviors become focused on caregivers or attachment figures who are involved in the care of the child. Bowlby formulated ideas on internal working models (IWMs) of attachment of the self and others. He believed that these models influence how the child sees himself and the world and that these first relationships became models for his subsequent relationships (Karen, 1994). Bowlby also proposed that disruption of the mother–child bond by physical separation or loss, or emotional unavailability of the caregiver, could lead to various disorders.

Mary Ainsworth, after conducting a series of research studies in the 1970s, made a significant contribution to attachment theory. Basing her work on Bowlby's theory, she conducted extensive home observations of mothers' interactions with their infants. She developed a system to classify the quality of the relationship between children and their caregivers using the terms "secure," "insecure–avoidant," and "insecure–ambivalent/resistant." She developed the *Strange Situation* as a way to measure attachment (Ainsworth, Blehar, Waters, & Wall, 1978). From her extensive home observations in Baltimore in the

United States and in Africa, Ainsworth determined that the quality of a child's attachment to her caregiver was related to how the caregiver responded to her signals in the first year of life (Ainsworth & Wittig, 1969). The parenting characteristics that she identified as being linked to the child's secure attachment were sensitivity to the child's cues, acceptance of the child, accessibility to the child, and cooperation in interactions. The *Strange Situation* measure that she developed of mothers' interactions with their infants is still used in current research to assess the child's quality of attachment.

Children from different attachment classifications behave differently when they are away from their parents in daycare or school. *Securely attached* children usually manage well away from their parents and are generally good problem solvers but seek the help of teachers in situations that they cannot manage alone. Their social skills and ability to manage conflict are more advanced and positive than those of insecurely attached children. Popular with peers, securely attached children develop more friendships. They also tend to be resilient under stress and have good self-control. *Insecure–avoidant* children also manage well away from parents but are more isolated from other children and place less value on having friends or seeking interactions with others. They can be angry and hostile and tend not to be liked by other children or adults. They do not do well with understanding or responding to other people's feelings and tend not to show their own. Some insecure–avoidant children are competent and can be in control in nonsocial situations. Others tend to be more noncompliant and disobey rules. If they have a problem, or are in pain or upset, they do not show it or ask for help and withdraw instead. *Insecure–ambivalent/resistant* children have more difficulty being away from parents and find it very hard to settle down. They can seem helpless, fearful, and tense as a result. In daycare and school, they often present as unhappy and whiney and show a high degree of neediness. When situations are frustrating or difficult they have problems coping and with coming up with a solution. They are intense and conflictual and switch between being angry one minute and helpless and seductive the next, often in quick succession. They have poor social skills and are often not well liked by other children, and teachers often become frustrated with them. Although insecure attachment is a risk factor for children's development, particularly social and emotional development, disorganized/disoriented attachment, described next, is more predictive of psychopathology.

Disorganized/disoriented children have very poor social skills and are often both bullies and victims. They might miss their parents and appear frightened when with them as well as away from them. They may show unusual, hard-to-understand behavior at times. Sometimes they may seem to dissociate, or freeze and present as frightened, and may show ambivalent behavior such as hitting after seeking to be close. They have low tolerance for frustration and poor self-control and are very disorganized and disoriented in their approaches to problems. They usually have behavioral difficulties and can be impulsive or show anxiety and depression.

Although there was already a vast literature on attachment in infancy and early childhood and significant research on attachment in adolescence and adulthood, the study of attachment from 7 to 12 years of age was neglected until the 2000s (Kerns, 2008). This was largely because there were few measures of attachment quality for this age group. The *Strange Situation* was designed for children from 12 to 24 months of age; measures were developed by the MacArthur preschool group for the preschool years; and the *Adult Attachment Interview* (AAI) was used for later adolescence and adulthood. It is now widely recognized that there are significant developmental shifts in the social worlds of children in middle childhood, with parental supervision shifting from parent directed to more parent–child coregulation. This in turn leads to changes in attachment behavior (Mayseless, 2005). In middle childhood, influences extend beyond the parent–child relationship as formal schooling begins and the social world expands. Peers take on greater importance in their lives, and children begin to have clear preferences for peers as playmates (Kerns, Tomich, & Kim, 2006). There are gains in perspective taking, understanding of self in relation to others, cognitive flexibility, and capacity for empathy and helping (Raikes & Thompson, 2005). Changes also take place in the attachment system in middle childhood from being less about "proximity" of the attachment figure to being more about "availability" (Ammaniti, van IJzendoorn, Speranza, & Fedele, 2005). It is still important for the child to get in contact or the parent to be available if the child is ill or hurt (Bowlby, 1969/1982). This shift parallels the child's increase in self-reliance and autonomy, being away from parents for increasing periods of time in school and at various community activities. Waters, Kondo-Ikemura, Posada, and Richters (1991) suggested that this represents a change to "mutual coregulation" in which the child takes more responsibility for communicating with the attachment figure about where she is going to be and any changes of plans.

One mechanism by which attachment quality shows continuity is the IWMs (Bretherton & Munholland, 2007). Recently, longitudinal studies followed children from infancy to adolescence and early adulthood and have provided information on how stable attachment is over time (Ammaniti, van IJzendoorn, Speranza, & Tambelli, 2000; Grossman, Grossman, & Waters, 2005; Sroufe, Egeland, Carlson, & Collins, 2005; Weinfeld, Whaley, & Egeland, 2004). With a large number of studies with unique findings, it has been challenging to come up with overall conclusions (Thompson, 2008), but a few are listed below:

- Children are less likely to develop secure attachments if a number of stresses accumulate in the first few years.
- Attachment can change from secure to insecure and vice versa but in relatively stable situations up to 80% of children's attachment quality will not change over time (Belsky & Fearon, 2002).
- Both early mother–child and father–child relationships are important for the child's development. Both influence the child's capacity to manage emotional conflict. The mother–child and father–child relationship both predict security in romantic relationships later. However, the father–child relationship has been shown to be the most important for developing children's peer relationships in middle childhood and social competence in middle childhood.

Generally, studies have found securely attached children in middle childhood or adolescence to be more socially competent and to get on well with other children. They are also more likely to show concern for other children (Denham, 1994; Kestenbaum, Farber, & Sroufe, 1989). Individual differences in emotion regulation have also been linked to differences in attachment (Laible & Thompson, 1998; Steele & Steele, 2005b). This probably occurs from parents' containment of the infant when he is upset and discussion of emotions with children in early and middle years (Laible & Thompson, 1998; Steele & Steele, 2005b; Steele, Steele, Croft, & Fonagy, 1999).

Little attention was paid in attachment research in the 1970s and 1980s to examining earlier relationships and psychopathology (DeKlyen & Greenberg, 2008). More recent, studies have considered various populations to examine possible links between attachment insecurity and disorganized attachment and later psychopathology. A number of low-risk, mainly middle-class samples have been examined for associations between insecure attachment and disruptive behavior and found no significant main effects between the two. DeKlyen and Greenberg (2009, p. 645), after reviewing this research, concluded that "main effect models will be of little interest in low-risk samples and are likely to provide little of value in understanding potential linkages between attachment and externalizing pathology."

On the other hand, studies of high-risk samples that have assessed early-attachment security and followed children for various time periods have shown that children in high-risk environments with early-insecure attachment are significantly more likely to have poor peer relationships, more symptoms of aggression, depression, and overall poorer adjustment than children with early security. These effects were stronger for boys than girls. The only study that has followed a sample from infancy to early adulthood was the Minnesota Parent–Child Project (Sroufe et al., 2005; Wienfeld, Sroufe, Egeland, & Carlson, 2008). The study has produced a number of follow-up reports that have tried to find links to certain disorders and to link different types of insecurity to different types of psychopathology.

In a longitudinal study with a high-risk sample beginning in early infancy, links between insecure and disorganized attachment and later behavioral patterns were found (Lyons-Ruth, Easterbrooks, Davidson, Cibella, & Bronfman, 1997). The researchers found that preschoolers rated as hostile with peers and adults by teachers were more likely to have been classified as insecure (and especially disorganized) as infants. In fact, 71% of hostile preschoolers had disorganized attachments at 18 months, whereas only 12% of hostile preschoolers had secure attachments. The researchers also found that a combination of low infant intelligence and insecure attachment was highly predictive of externalizing problems at age 7. However, neither factor alone was predictive of these outcomes. Internalizing problems were predicted only by avoidant attachment, and the symptoms met clinical levels only when the mother was depressed.

Shaw and Vondra (1995) studied a low-income sample and found that infant attachment insecurity predicted behavioral problems at age 3. When children were 5 years of age, insecure attachment at 12 months was associated with parent-rated problems. Disorganization was predictive of internalizing problems (Shaw, Keenan, Vondra, Delliquadri, & Giovannelli, 1997). Disorganized children were most likely to have elevated aggression (60%), whereas 31% of avoidant, 28% of ambivalent/resistant, and only 17% of secure infants did. When combined with parent ratings of difficult temperament at age 2, children with ratings of both disorganized attachment and difficult temperament scored at the 99th percentile for aggression.

In a study of children with cystic fibrosis or congenital heart defects not at social risk, infants in both medically diagnosed groups had lower rates of secure attachment at 12 to 18 months of age (Goldberg, Gotowiec, & Simmons, 1995). They were most likely to have disorganized attachment. Only children who had been avoidantly attached had higher internalizing and externalizing problems at age 4, whereas neither ambivalent nor disorganized children had higher rates of problems than secure infants.

Attachment and Clinical Groups

Other studies have considered the attachment classification of children in various clinical groups. Conduct problems in early childhood have been the most studied, and results indicate that children with avoidant and disorganized or controlling or coercive attachment patterns, according to Crittenden's (1992) system, are most likely to develop these problems. In a study of preschool children with oppositional defiant disorder, 80% were insecurely attached to their mothers, compared with 30% of the nonclinical sample. It was most associated with the avoidant and controlling classification. Similar attachment classifications were found with each parent (DeKlyen, Speltz, & Greenberg, 1998). Conclusions from these studies indicate that 20% of these clinic-referred children had secure attachments, so no one factor (including attachment) could fully explain the clinical problems.

Some studies have also found concurrent associations between insecure attachment and anxiety disorders, but the associations tend to be weak (Bosquet & Egeland, 2006; Warren, Huston, Egeland, & Sroufe, 1997). Disorganized and both avoidant and ambivalent–resistant classifications were related to anxiety disorders in some studies

(Manassis & Bradley, 1994). Children diagnosed with reactive attachment disorder (RAD) have also been diagnosed with depression. High concurrent rates of depression have been found in their parents as well (Abela et al., 2005).

There is insufficient longitudinal data to establish pathways between early-attachment types and psychopathology. Insecure attachment is not a form of psychopathology, but along with other risk factors in the child or family context it can lead to increased risk of either externalizing or internalizing psychopathology (Rutter, 1985). There is a tendency for children with an avoidant attachment classification to develop externalizing disorders and for children with an ambivalent–resistant classification to be associated with internalizing disorders, though data do not consistently support these pathways. Overall, avoidant children tend to have the greatest rate of psychopathology.

DISORDERS OF SOCIAL DEVELOPMENT AND THEIR PREVALENCE

In the *Diagnostic and Statistical Manual of Mental Disorders*, 5th edition (*DSM-5;* American Psychiatric Association [APA], 2013), there are a number of disorders in which children have problems with attachment and social difficulties as major symptoms.

Reactive attachment disorder (RAD) was first described in studies of young children raised in institutions, situations of extreme abuse and neglect, or who have experienced multiple changes of caregivers. As outlined previously, children at age 4 who had been raised in residential nurseries since birth were described as either withdrawn and unresponsive or indiscriminately friendly, attention seeking, and socially superficial. RAD was first described as a disorder in the third edition of the *DSM-III* (3rd ed.; APA, 1980). The disorder was revised in *DSM-IV* (4th ed.; APA, 1994); *The ICD-10 Classification of Mental and Behavioural Disorders* (World Health Organization, 1992); and unofficial nosologies such as *DC: 0-3R* (Zero to Three, 2005). In *DSM-5,* Reactive Attachment Disorder is limited to children who have experienced a pattern of "extremes of insufficient care" and who show minimal responsiveness to others and episodes of sadness, irritability or fearfulness that are not related to events in the environment. Another disorder, Disinhibited Social Engagement Disorder, has been added that describes a pattern of behavior in which the child approaches unfamiliar adults without appropriate caution or reticence. These behaviors are not limited to the impulsivity often associated with attention deficit/hyperactivity disorder (ADHD) but also include socially inhibited behavior.

RAD and Disinhibited Social Engagement Disorder are rare in community samples but more common in children in foster care, perhaps as high as 35% (Boris et al., 2004). It is readily identified in children raised in institutions (Smyke, Dumitrescu, & Zeanah, 2002). Because of the confusion among different diagnostic classification systems, some researchers and clinicians recommend using a continuum from secure, insecure, disorganized, RAD, to nonattached (Smyke et al., 2002).

Other *DSM-5* disorders characterized by impairment in social interactions include Autism Spectrum Disorder (ASDs), and various anxiety disorders including Separation Anxiety Disorder, Selective Mutism, Specific Phobia, Social Anxiety Disorder, and Generalized Anxiety Disorder, and Disruptive, Impulse-Control, and Conduct Disorders including Oppositional Defiant Disorder, Intermittent Explosive Disorder, and Conduct Disorder (oppositional defiant disorder and conduct disorder).

THE SOCIAL BRAIN

During the past decade, the field of social neuroscience has emerged. It uses a variety of approaches to increase understanding of the neural mechanisms used to process social information (Adolphs, 2003; Cozolino, 2006; Goleman, 2006; Insel & Fernald, 2004; Johnson et al., 2005; Siegel, 1999, 2007). There is no single site identified for the social brain, and the complex circuitry for it is coordinated throughout the brain (see Figure 9.1). The neural networks involved in particular social activities vary; those used for a conversation with a friend are different from those used for a mother's face-to-face interaction with her baby (Adolphs, 2003; Cozolino, 2002; Johnson et al., 2005). These complex networks gradually evolve during development and are strongly influenced by the child's interactions and experiences with parents and other caregivers (Cozolino, 2006; Porges, 2007). The brain is not a fixed structure and undergoes constant change and reconstruction across the lifespan, with neuroplasticity possible in some situations.

Our understanding of brain function in this area comes from research with animals, postmortem examinations of people with social problems, and functional neuroimaging techniques, which include functional magnetic resonance imaging (fMRI), positron emission tomography (PET), event-related potentials (ERP), electroencephalography (EEG), magnetoencephalography (MEG), and infrared spectroscopy (INRS) (Cameron, 2004; Gunnar & De Haan, 2009). See Figure 9.1 for an approximate schematic guide to the location of the brain structures involved in social functioning.

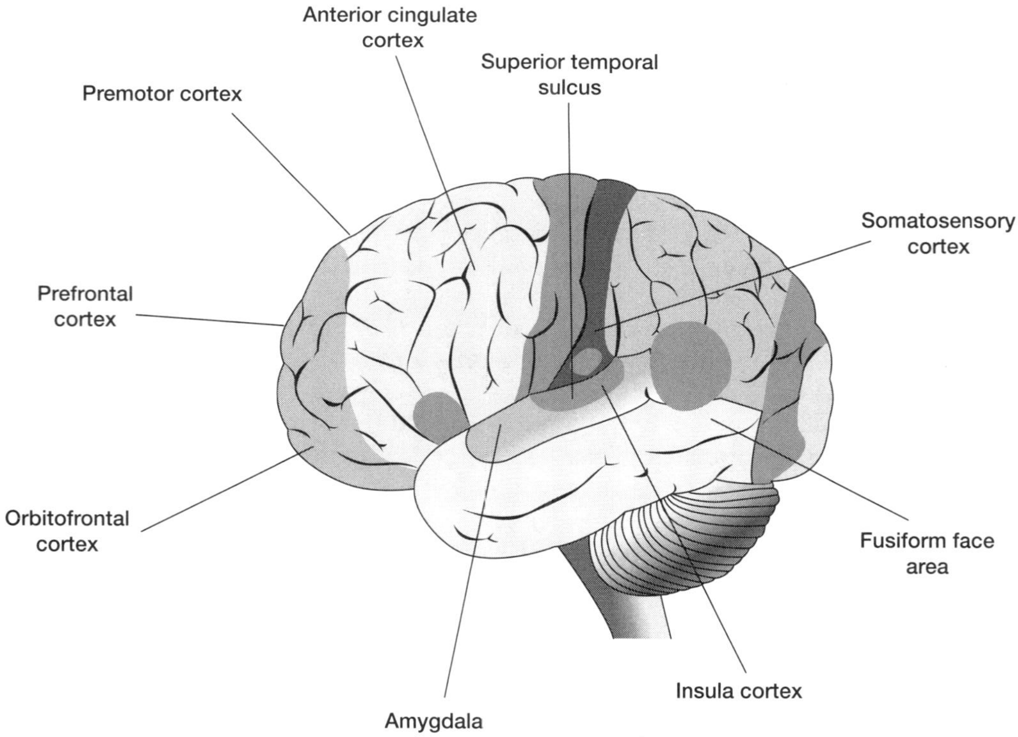

Figure 9.1 *Critical areas of the social brain.*

Although there is no one site in the brain where social functioning occurs, some key structures have been identified and described as interconnected and influencing one another. One of the most important is the *orbital medial prefrontal cortex*, located on the ventromedial surface of the frontal lobe. The area has connections with multiple brain regions and receives information on all aspects of internal and external environments. This information is used in the regulation of emotions and the development of goal-directed behavior (Barbas, 2007; Price, 2007). In monkeys, development of the orbital frontal cortex has been found to coincide with their ability to integrate information from current social interactions with memories of similar interactions and use this information to determine how to react (Machado & Bachevalier, 2003; Payne & Bachevalier, 2009).

One aspect of the brain explored recently in terms of social development and the effects of therapy has been *mirror neurons*. They were first discovered in monkeys in 1992. These neurons were activated when the monkey executed hand movements such as grasping an object but also when other individuals (monkeys or humans) carried out similar movements (Gallese, Fadiga, Fogassi, & Rizzolatti, 1996; Rizzolatti, Fadiga, Gallese, & Fogassi, 1996). They were discovered in the monkey's ventral premotor cortex and posterior parietal cortex. The mirror neurons did not respond to a tool, only to a person or monkey performing the same task, and were linked to initiating the movement and achieving a similar goal. Also, they did not respond to a hand doing an action without a goal or target. Researchers have since found evidence that a large proportion of the human motor system can be activated by observing an action performed by another person (Rizzolatti, Fadiga, Matelli, Bettinardi, Perani, & Fazio, 1996). The mirror system might also be important for a number of higher-level social processes. Because the actions of another person can influence one's own actions, they might also explain synchronized group behaviors such as dancing, emotional attunement, resonance, empathy, and mutual understanding. Consequently, they might also bridge the gap between the sender and the receiver (Jeannerod, 2001).

Certain neurochemicals are thought to regulate various social behaviors, such as attachment, pair bonding, empathy, and prosocial behavior. These neurochemicals relate to reward, decrease of pain, and feelings of well-being, and they are released by the social motivational system of the amygdala, anterior cingulate, and orbitofrontal cortex (OFC). Among the neuropeptide hormones implicated in social behavior are oxytocin, vasopressin, and corticotropin-releasing factor. The release of these neurochemicals stimulates activity, and the release of dopamine and endogenous opioids is believed to be associated with parent–infant attachment, formation of social bonds, and pleasure and physiological soothing (Bales & Carter, 2009; Cozolino, 2006; Kramer, Cushing, & Carter, 2003). Dopamine is also particularly important to the attachment system and goal-directed behavior and has been associated with reinforcement and pleasure.

CONTRIBUTORS TO DIFFICULTIES WITH SOCIAL FUNCTIONING

Neurological Contributors

Most of the research on the neurobiology of social development has been conducted on animals and focused on the neural underpinnings of social behavior and attachment (Coan, 2008). In more recent research, measures of autonomic nervous system (ANS) physiology, EEGs, glucocorticoid levels, and fMRIs have been used to study emotional and social behavior (Coan, 2008). Gunnar and de Haan (2009) review some of these new and more traditional methods of studying the developmental and neural underpinnings of social functioning.

Research on differences in neural circuits associated with secure, insecure, and disorganized attachment, and attachment disorders is rare. Most research has focused on the regulatory function of attachment relationships, especially when the person is under stress (Gunnar, 2005; Hofer, 1995). Infants with secure attachments to their mothers following the *Strange Situation*, which includes stressful separation from the parent, had lower cortisol levels than insecurely attached or disorganized infants (Hertsgaard, Gunnar, Erickson, & Nachmias, 1995; Thompson & Trevarthan, 2008). Also, studies with animals and infants have shown that nurturing behaviors can lower stress reactions in the ANS and hypothalamic–pituitary–adrenal (HPA) axis (e.g., Boccia, Reite, & Laudenslager, 1989). Similarly, for adults, physical contact with an attachment figure during a threat-based experiment reduced threat-responsive neural activity in affect-related action and arousal circuits (Coan, Shaefer, &

Davidson, 2008). In another study, women with autonomous and insecure or anxious attachments were asked to think about negative and positive relationship scenarios. Anxious attachment was associated with activity in the dorsal anterior cingulate cortex and the temporal pole but not the OFC. The research suggested that individuals with anxious attachment do not activate neural systems to help regulate their emotional responses.

As might be expected given the number of developmental areas impacted by autism, many areas of the social brain, as well as the neural networks connecting the cortex, limbic systems, and cerebellum, have been found to be abnormal (Baron-Cohen et al., 2000). Some areas of the brain most implicated in autism include the brainstem and cerebellum, which relate to the ability to shift attention, orient to a particular object, and hold joint attention (Courchesne, 1997; Harris, Courchesne, Townsend, Carper, & Lord, 1999). There is also evidence of decreased gray matter in the part of the cerebral cortex identified as containing the mirror neuron system (Oberman et al., 2005; Williams, Whiten, Suddendorf, & Perrott, 2001). The corpus callosum connecting the two cerebral hemispheres has also been found to be reduced (Vidal et al., 2006). Several areas of the brain, including the left frontal lobe, have been linked to difficulties with imitation found in autistic children. In these children, the right rather than left frontal lobe is activated when they are asked to imitate someone (Dawson, Warrenburg, & Fuller, 1985). Another area of impairment in autism is the deficit in social motivation that results in reduced attention to faces, voices, and hand gestures and contributes to a failure to develop the ability to process such stimuli (Dawson et al., 2002). Some of the brain areas implicated are the medial temporal lobe and orbitofrontal circuit. The fusiform face area in the occipital lobe, involved in the identification of faces, has also been proposed as being influential in this difficulty (Dalton et al., 2005; Kanwisher, McDermott, & Chun, 1997). The levels and processes of serotonin, opioid peptides (vasopressin and oxytocin), gamma-aminobutyric acid (GABA), and dopamine, which affect approach behavior, social attachment, social mastery, stereotypical behavior, learning, and memory, can be reduced in children with autism (Chugani, 2002; Insel, O'Brien, & Leckman, 1999). The neurochemical brain-derived neurotrophic factor has also been suggested as having relevance for brain development and function in autism (Bauman & Kemper, 2005).

Although social anxiety is one of the most prevalent anxiety disorders, little is known about its etiology (Beidel & Turner, 2005). Although somewhat speculative, neuroimaging studies of animals and humans have led to the identification of a tentative model of the neurocircuitry of anxiety disorders. It includes the notion that individuals with anxiety disorders have an exaggerated amygdala responsivity and/or a deficient top-down modulation of the amygdala response due to deficiencies in function within the ventromedial prefrontal cortex and/or the hippocampus (Rauch & Drevets, 2009; Shekhar, Sajyk, Gehlert, & Rainnie, 2003). Differences in the brains of subjects with social anxiety have been hard to identify, though one researcher found reduced striatal dopamine reuptake binding-site density in a social anxiety group. Lower dopamine levels might reduce the desire to approach others and the sense of well-being. Perhaps the hyperreactive amygdala leads to sustained interpersonal vigilance and an overestimation of danger (Baird et al., 1999; Schwartz, Jones, Shin, Kagan, & Rauch, 2003). Another brain structure beginning to attract attention in understanding social anxiety is the bed nucleus of the stria terminals that is close to but separate from the amygdala and unlike the amygdala does not activate a fight/flight response to the stimuli but results in a lower level of arousal experienced as anxiety (Davis, Taylor, Crawley, Wood, & Mikulis, 1997). It might be the structure that accounts for long-term anxiety and a sense of foreboding.

In children with conduct disorders, amygdala dysfunction and poor executive control are seen as core features of the difficulties (Blair, 2001, 2006; Frick & Marsee, 2006). Some researchers have considered that atypical activity in the OFC can contribute to difficulties with executive and behavioral control (Blair, 2001; Kiehl, 2006). This has not yet been identified at an anatomical level (Frick & Marsee, 2006; Lykken, 1995). However, some studies of emotional memory (Kiehl et al., 2001) have found reduced amygdala, anterior cingulate cortex, and medial OFC activity (Birbaumer et al., 2005; Kiehl et al., 2001). Other neural systems of the social brain have also been implicated, such as the insula, anterior and posterior cingulate cortex, parahippocampal gyrus, and superior temporal gyrus (Kiehl, 2006). However, research has shown that some cognitive functions that rely on these structures are intact in individuals with psychopathy. Another line of research has found lower autonomic reactions to punishment and negative stimulus cues in psychopathic individuals (Raine, 1996, 2013). They include autonomic arousal, electrodermal responses to distress cues (Hare, 1972), lower heart rate following punishment, and fewer skin conductance responses following punishment (Arnett, Howland, Smith, & Newman, 1993). In addition, low levels of serotonin are found in violent criminals and lower glucose metabolism in both lateral and medial portions of the frontal lobes (Raine et al., 1994).

Genetic Contributors

An important new area of study concerns possible genetic influences on disorganized attachment behaviors. Various approaches have been used, including behavioral genetics, molecular genetics, and gene–environment models, to examine a possible link (Lyons-Ruth & Jacobvitz, 2008). Some studies have found that nonshared factors, such as trauma and different parenting styles, are likely important in the etiology of disorganized attachment (Bokhorst et al., 2003). Some research using behavioral genetic methods to study high-risk alleles in twin pairs at 1 year of age has found that, when they are present, the incidence of disorganized attachment is higher. However, some studies have failed to replicate these findings (Bakermans-Kranenburg & van IJzendoorn, 2004; Spangler & Zimmerman, 2007). It has been concluded that genetic differences might play an indirect role in processes leading to the co-construction of attachment relationships.

There is strong evidence for genetic risk factors in autism. In twin studies, concordance rates for autism for monozygotic twins have ranged from 69% to 95%, whereas for dizygotic twins concordance rates were from 0% to 24% (Bailey et al., 1995; Ritvo, Freeman, Mason-Brothers, Mo, & Ritvo, 1985). Overall, evidence indicates that the interaction of multiple genes influences gene expression or changes in proteins that are part of a complex regulatory network. This increases susceptibility to autism. Various interactional factors affect the expression of these genes, suggesting that early intervention can alter gene expression (Dawson & Zanolli, 2003).

There is some suggestion that social anxiety disorder is familial, with an odds ratio of 4:7 between parental and child social phobia (Lieb et al., 2000). Behavioral genetic studies suggest that genetic factors influence susceptibility to social phobias (Hettema, Prescott, Myers, Necile, & Kendler, 2006). Behavioral inhibition (BI) is thought to predispose people to the disorder, and this trait might be linked to genes that encode for the corticotropin-releasing factor (Smoller, Rosenbaum, Biederman, 2003; Smoller et al., 2005).

It is clear at this time that no single gene can account for aggression and antisocial behavior. In the future, it might be possible to define more clearly the gene–environment interactions that contribute to aggressive disorders.

Biological Contributors

Vaughn, Bost, and van IJzendoorn (2008, p. 199), reviewing several decades of attachment research, concluded that the "fundamental individual differences distinction in attachment theory (i.e., security vs insecurity) could not be explained by major temperament approaches." They also concluded, however, that attachment or parent–child relationship constructs could not explain temperament characteristics or individual differences found by major theories. This conclusion also held for disorganized attachment and indiscriminate attachment behaviors as found in children in foster care or adopted from orphanages (van IJzendoorn, Schuengel, & Bakermans-Kranenburg, 1999; Lyons-Ruth & Jacobvitz, 1999, 2008). It was therefore concluded that attachment disorganization is not an inborn characteristic of the infant. There has been a suggestion that temperament might bias a child toward using avoidance or resistance to maintain proximity to the mother. However, this has not been fully explored (Hare & Fox, 2003).

One possible "trait" of autistic children is an impairment in social motivation or interest in socially relevant stimuli. For example, young children with autism are less likely to look at their mothers during social interaction (Dawson, Hill, Galpert, Spencer, & Watson, 1990) or show positive emotion during joint-attention episodes (Kasari, Sigman, Mundy, & Yirmiya, 1990). They are also not interested in social–linguistic stimuli (Klin, 1991; Kuhl, Coffey-Corina, Padden, & Dawson, 2004). This deficit might be due to dysfunction of the dopamine reward system, especially in social contexts (Dawson et al., 2009). Abnormalities in oxytocin and vasopressin activity have also been suggested as contributors to these difficulties. Other lines of research have considered mother's stress, viral infections, and immune system abnormalities during pregnancy as possible contributors (Ashwood & van de Water, 2004; Boucher, 2009).

In children with anxiety disorder, temperament studies have identified individual differences in reactivity, inhibition to the unfamiliar, and withdrawal (Kagan & Snidman, 2004). Research has found that these differences were present from early infancy and related to a lower threshold for arousal in forebrain areas, particularly the amygdala. Davidson and Fox found differences in frontal cortical activation (Davidson, 1993, 2000; Fox, 1991, 1994). Greater activity in the right rather than left prefrontal cortex predicted early inhibition and shyness and later social anxiety (Davidson, Marshall, Tomarken, & Henriques, 2000). Although this does not support a genetic link, it does show that tendencies toward social anxiety are present early and can show continuity, sometimes intensifying.

Two main types of temperament have been implicated in social anxiety: BI (Kagan, 2003; Pfeifer, Goldsmith, Davidson, & Rickman, 2002) and negative affectivity and emotional lability. BI describes the child's initial behavioral response to novelty or "behavioral inhibition to the unfamiliar" (Kagan, 1997, 2003; Kagan & Snidman, 2004). Children with BI typically withdraw from unfamiliar people, objects, and situations and can show signs of anxiety and distress. Inhibition is evident in toddlers and moderately consistent across early childhood (Asendorpf, 1994; Pfeifer et al., 2002). It is related to shyness, low sociability, timidity, and introversion, and it is usually consistent across different situations, such as the home and child care, and ages (Asendorpf, 1994; Daniels & Plomin, 1985). The most extremely inhibited children usually have low levels of social competence and high levels of social anxiety. Some (usually about 10%–15%) continue in the predicted pattern of inhibition beyond early childhood (Aksan & Kochanska, 2004; Calkins, Fox, & Marshall, 1996; Fordham & Stevenson-Hinde, 1999). Fox, Henderson, Rubin, Calkins, & Schmidt, 2001; Kagan, 2003; Kagan & Snidman, 2004; Theall-Honey & Schmidt, 2006). Children originally classified as inhibited were more likely to become uninhibited over time if they were in the middle of the sample distribution. If the BI is more extreme, it is predictive of anxiety disorders, but parenting and other factors, especially subsequent life events, can change the trajectory (Craske, Poulton, Tsao, et al., 2001; Kagan, 2003; Kagan & Snidman, 2004: Pfeifer et al., 2002; Theall-Honey & Schmidt, 2006). However, if anxiety is present in elementary school, 42% will be anxious in high school.

Aksan and Kochanska (2004) also found links between early inhibition to novelty and later effortful control, another characteristic of temperament, suggesting that nonimpulsive reactions to stimulation can become characteristic responses of the child. Shy children have been described by teachers as less prosocial and more withdrawn, and with behavioral observation they display more reticent behavior and parallel (rather than interactive) play (Coplan, Prakash, O'Neil, & Amur, 2004). So early shyness can lead to long-term social consequences, though most children outgrow it. Longitudinal studies suggest that persistently shy children are more likely to have anxiety disorders in adolescence (Prior, Smart, Sanson, & Oberklaid, 2000). The second temperament trait that might be linked to anxiety, negative affectivity and emotional lability, is less well researched but believed to be a predisposing factor for social anxiety disorders and depressed mood (Roberts & Kendler, 1999). Children who are also high in reactivity and negative affect can show heightened levels of attentional vigilance and orientation in novel situations. Due to their negative emotional biases, they find it hard to disengage from the threatening part of a situation and shift their attention to other things.

Inhibited children have greater activation in the right hemisphere associated with withdrawal emotions such as anxiety and depression (Davidson et al., 2000; Martin & Fox, 2006; Tillfors, Furmark, Marteinsdottir, & Fredrikson, 2002). Other researchers have explored individual differences in the thresholds of the limbic system substructures. Inhibited children have elevated levels of muscle tension, startle response, and pupil dilation when presented with novel stimuli. As well, they have higher and more stable heart rates and lower heart period variability as assessed by respiratory sinus arrhythmia (RSA) an index of the parasympathetic nervous system (Burgess, Marshall, Rubin, & Fox, 2003). Higher morning cortisol readings have also been found (Martin & Fox, 2006). A number of physiological responses to other people lead to an experience of the social world as dangerous. As discussed above, children with social anxiety have right-hemisphere activation shown to result in decreased metabolism in the Broca's area responsible for speech. This suggests that, the more anxious someone becomes, the more likely she is to have difficulty speaking (Bruder, Schneider, Stewart, McGrath, & Quitkin, 2004; Rauch, Shin, & Wright, 2003). This theory is highly speculative but might explain the link to selective mutism sometimes found in children with social anxiety. Dysfunction in the dopamine and serotonin systems has been found in adults with social phobias (Nutt, Bell, & Malizia, 1998; Potts, Book, & Davidson, 1996).

Some research has looked at the behavioral activation system as opposed to the BI system and suggests that exuberant children who develop behavioral problems might do so due to a lack of inhibition. Behavioral difficulties might also result from strong approach dispositions. Deficits in the vigilance system that involves norepinephrine input to the right lateral frontal lobe in the locus coeruleus might be implicated (Posner & Rothbart, 1991; Rothbart, Posner, & Boylan, 1990). Deficits in this system are also thought to underlie ADHD in children. It is believed that a combination of high surgency and low effortful control predicts elevated cortisol responses. This combination in one study predicted aggression and peer rejection (Gunnar, Sebanc, Tout, Donzella, & van Dulman, 2003).

Parenting Contributors

Reactive attachment disorder is rare even in disadvantaged populations of children (Boris et al., 2004; Egger, Kondo, & Angold, 2006). However, it is found in larger numbers in children coming into foster care (35%) and children living in institutions (75%) (Smyke et al., 2002; Zeanah, Smyke, Koga, Carlson, & BEIP Core Group, 2005). The caregiving or parenting associated with RAD includes severe social deprivation and neglect.

A child can have an extremely disturbed relationship with a caregiver and show vigilance/hypercompliance, role reversal, and risk taking, with self-endangerment, during interactions (Zeanah & Boris, 2000). In addition, children with disorganized/disoriented attachment are more likely to have concurrent and later psychopathology (Green & Goldwyn, 2002). The disorganized child generally experiences unpredictable caregiving. At times, the caregiver seems helpless, fearful, and unable to manage the situation; at other times, the caregiver seems angry, hostile, and self-referential/intrusive. These frightened/frightening (FR) behaviors, as they have been referred to, place the child in an unresolvable conflict. Lyons-Ruth and colleagues also described the mothers as showing "impaired ability to engage in well-attuned affective communication with their young children" or disrupted affective communication (Lyons-Ruth & Jacobvitz, 1999, p. 53). Such caregivers can be depressed, alcoholic, drug dependent, abusive, or traumatized, with a significant level of psychopathology, including character disorder, anxiety disorder, severe depression, sociopathic tendencies, and even psychosis. The parents of infants with disorganized attachment as well as various disorders have been found on the AAI to have unresolved loss or trauma (Lyons-Ruth, Bronfman, & Atwood, 1999; Moran, Forbes, Evans, Tarabulsy, & Madigan, 2008; Thalhuber, Jacobvitz, & Hazen, 1998). The incidence of disorganized attachment ranges from 13% to 85% in populations with serious parental psychopathology (Lyons-Ruth, Connell, Grunebaum, & Botein, 1990; Lyons-Ruth & Spielman, 2004; Solomon & George, 1999).

Little literature exists on parenting and disorganized attachment in middle childhood. One longitudinal study that examined subtypes of disorganized attachment at school age found that 68% of children had controlling attachments with their mothers. This pattern was either controlling–punitive or controlling–caregiving. For the former group, the child's interactions with the caregiver were hostile and aggressive and seemed to be intent on humiliating the parent. The controlling–caregiving child seemed motivated to orient or protect the parent by being extremely cheerful, polite, or helpful. Of the sample, 32% showed confusion or apprehension (Moss, St.-Laurent, Dubois-Comtois, & Cyr, 2005). Many disorganized children also experience the death of a parent or parental separation and divorce.

Several studies have found that children with autism and other forms of pervasive developmental disorders (PDDs) form secure attachments with their caregivers (Rogers, Ozonoff, & Maslin-Cole, 1993), though insecure and particularly disorganized attachments occur more frequently than with nonclinical children. Unusual behaviors typical of autism were disregarded during coding. A meta-analysis concluded that attachment security is compatible with autism at the rate found with typically developing children (53%) (Rutgers, Bakermans-Kranenburg, van IJzendoorn, & Beckelaer-Onnes, 2004). In a study of toddlers diagnosed with autism, severity of their symptoms was predictive of insecure attachment, and mental retardation comorbid with autism was predictive of disorganized attachment (Naber et al., 2007).

Early behaviors of the child with autism include the following:

- impairment in social initiations with others;
- less interest in faces, voices, and hand gestures;
- failure to establish joint attention;
- lack of interest in human speech and intentional communication;
- impairment in imitation; and
- restricted range of activities and repetitive behaviors.

Although lack of exposure to social information is not responsible for the abnormal brain development of the autistic child, early intervention that targets these domains of social functioning through enriched caregiver–child interactions can change the developmental trajectories of many of these children toward a more normal course (Faja & Dawson, 2006). This suggests that the parent–child interactions that often result from these early child behaviors might contribute to ongoing deterioration in children with autism.

Social learning in the family might be a factor in the development of social anxiety in children. One parent or both parents might have an anxiety disorder and attribute it to the parenting that they received. These adults have described family communication patterns, emphasizing shame, social isolation, and concern about the opinions of others (Bruch & Heimberg, 1994; Bruch, Heimberg, Berger, & Collins, 1989). In research with children and adolescents, two main parenting characteristics have been associated with social phobia. There seems to be a positive relationship between high levels of social anxiety and parents restricting their children's social interactions, being less socially active themselves, and being overprotective of their children (Bogels, van Oosten, Muris, & Smulders, 2001; Caster, Inderbitzen, & Hope, 1999). The other parenting characteristic associated with social anxiety in children is rejection, though it might be associated with other disorders in children. Hummel and Gross (2001) observed a sample of anxious children with a mean age of 11 years, 8 months with their parents completing a jigsaw puzzle with their parents. Overall, the parents used fewer verbal exchanges with their children and gave them less positive feedback. The children in turn showed more negative feedback and commands, suggesting negative reciprocal interactions.

There has been some disagreement over the effects of parenting on children with oppositional disorders because of contradictory views on the development of these disorders. However, all positions agree that, although certain brain dysfunctions contribute to the disorders, failure to respond to and learn from discipline is a factor. For many children with conduct disorders, discipline that relies on behavioral approaches does not arouse enough anxiety or discomfort to motivate improvements in their behavior.

Case Study: Ethan

Ethan's parents were caring, high-functioning people deeply concerned about their son and struggled to find suitable treatments for him. His presentation seemed to be a combination of an uninhibited temperament from early on, difficult early experiences with both parents, and anxiety and depression over his current situation. These factors are summarized below:

- Ethan had a difficult, "temperamentally exuberant" personality with low fear of new situations and impulsive approach behavior.
- Maternal depression and consequent trauma might have resulted in greater right-brain activation and hemispheric asymmetry. This could also have contributed to the storing of implicit trauma memories that could be triggered and result in aggressive outbursts at certain times.
- Ethan had insecure/disorganized attachment with both parents from early on. His attachment could best be described as disorganized, with a tendency to initially "approach" and then "move away" and become angry and frustrated with both parents.
- He had a negative sense of self and others that might have developed because of the punitive discipline that he had received from his father and the early trauma.
- Ethan probably had problems with development of the social brain, including the amygdala and parts of the prefrontal cortex (e.g., orbital medial prefrontal cortex and anterior cingulate cortex).
- He had lower autonomic reactions to rewards and punishments, making discipline less effective.
- There was inconsistent parenting by both parents, and Ethan needed more attachment-based discipline from early on. This had worsened before the referral.
- There was a possible genetic risk, with both his mother and maternal grandmother having had chronic anxiety and depression. Also, Ethan's paternal grandfather might have had ADHD; Phillip often talked about how his father was an alcoholic and cruel and at times violent toward his mother.

TYPICAL DEVELOPMENT OF SOCIAL COMPETENCE

Understanding social competence from a developmental perspective allows us to appreciate the early foundations or capacities that need to be in place for more sophisticated social behaviors to evolve. If one area is compromised, it can have significant influences on others. For example, the child who learns to talk early often has fewer temper tantrums, and the child who gains efficient control of his emotions is more likely to play with others. Knowing the level of development at which a child is functioning can determine the strategies to help develop social capacity. Social competence includes a number of capacities including attachment to caregiving figures, perspective taking, empathy, sharing, having friendships, negotiation, and conflict resolution. A child who is having difficulty with social skills or social competence can have difficulty in any or all of these capacities. When and how these capacities unfold is outlined in Table 9.1.

Assessing Social Competence and Disorders

The assessment of attachment beyond infancy has presented challenges for attachment researchers. Gradually, validated measures have become available for later ages. One problem with many of the measures is that they require extensive training to administer and score.

Attachment of Children From 12 Months to 2 Years

Attachment in infancy (from 12 to 20 months) has traditionally been assessed using the *Strange Situation*, an observational measure developed in the late 1970s (Ainsworth et al., 1978). The laboratory situation consists of eight 3-minute episodes with the child: (a) either alone, (b) with a parent, or (c) with a stranger (someone whom the child has never seen before). The episodes present the child with increasingly stressful situations so that the child's attachment-related behaviors can be observed (e.g., crying and seeking proximity). The child is classified in terms of attachment as secure, insecure–avoidant, insecure–ambivalent/resistant, or disorganized/disoriented, largely on the basis of behaviors shown on reunion (Ainsworth et al., 1978; Main & Solomon, 1990). Some of the behaviors used to determine the child's attachment classification include attention to the mother, exploring the room and toys, seeking proximity to the mother after separation, and how and when the child is calmed at reunion. The *Strange Situation* procedure has demonstrated adequate reliability with high intercoder agreement for trained coders within a laboratory (Ainsworth et al., 1978). Validity has been harder to establish, with assessments repeated too soon finding low stability and assessments completed more than 20 months apart showing less stability of classification (Cassidy, Berlin, & Belsky, 1990). The psychometric properties with fathers and other caregivers and in other cultures have been questioned.

Attachment of 3- to 4-Year-Old Children

The *Cassidy–Marvin Assessment of Attachment in Preschoolers* uses the *Strange Situation* procedure with slightly longer separations and different instructions for the caregiver (Cassidy & Marvin, 1992). It was developed by the MacArthur Working Group on Attachment. It is the preferred measure for assessment of attachment in 3- to 4-year-old children (Solomon & George, 2008). Classification is mainly based on the child's behavior toward the mother at reunion. The quality of the interaction, including talking and negotiating engaged in by parent and child around the separations, is also scored. The child is assigned to one of five groups: secure, avoidant, ambivalent, controlling/disorganized, and insecure/other.

Table 9.1 *Highlights of Typical Social Development and Parenting*

Age Range	Development	Parenting
Birth to 12 months	■ In the first year the child's social partners are primarily caregivers and parents ■ Interactions are close and intense and infants love the reciprocity and attunement they experience during engagements with others ■ Even in the first few months babies love to have "conversations" with and to connect with parents ■ Attachment is established by 7–8 months and becomes a prototype for later social relationships ■ Infants show interest in other babies and may show concern or empathy if another baby is upset and offer him toys ■ May show contagion from the emotion of another child or adults	■ Parent provides dyadic synchrony, and nonverbal behavior supports the development of a secure attachment and later social competence ■ Uses exaggerated "parentese" speech and positive emotionality to get the more withdrawn baby involved in interactions ■ Shows availability if the infant is seeking out interaction and makes sure she does not find it too intrusive or feel overwhelmed by it ■ Tries to present the child with a positive facial expression in interactions ■ Parent resonates and attunes to the infant's emotional state as much as possible ■ If child is upset parent uses various ways to calm her down using touch, rocking, voice, etc. ■ Indicates interest in what the child seems to be trying to communicate
12 to 24 months	■ Toddlers love to be around other children and like to play close to them and may engage in parallel play ■ Solitary play is still common as are struggles over toys and other possessions ■ Cooperation is only possible for brief periods of time ■ By 18 months children play for longer together and the play is a little more coordinated ■ There is an increase in sharing behavior and responding if another child is upset ■ Use social referencing and respond to emotion of another person ■ Begin to share with others gradually	■ Parent models ways to deal with intense emotions and helps child to use similar strategies ■ Makes sure the child has the opportunity to be around peers ■ Encourages the child to engage in pretend play as a way to interact with peers and to enjoy the play of others ■ Encourages sharing behavior during snack time and play time ■ Arranges to be around when other children are present and scaffolds some cooperative play if it is possible
2 to 4 years	■ Much more social and cooperative play with peers ■ Usually alternate between solitary, parallel, and social play ■ Early social games include chasing games and imitation of others ■ Can get in disagreements as sharing declines and "it's mine" increases for a while ■ Begin to have friendships and learn to enter a group and to stay involved with the play for a long period of time ■ Begin to be able to resolve conflicts and work together to reach a goal and solve a problem	■ Arranges play dates and time around other children outside the home and coaches the child to enter a group and interact with others ■ Encourages perspective taking if the child becomes angry and too intrusive with another child ■ Keeps social engagements relatively short and encourages structure sharing and cooperative interactions ■ Encourages sharing ■ Helps children solve conflicts that they are unable to solve themselves

(continued)

Table 9.1 *Highlights of Typical Social Development and Parenting (continued)*

Age Range	Development	Parenting
4 to 6 years	▪ Learn how to play cooperatively with others most of the time and to establish friendships ▪ Peer relationships and the ability to get along with others expands considerably ▪ Identify with peers and understand their perspective ▪ Learn conflict-resolution skills and interactive dialogue but disagreements are still common ▪ Begin to internalize representations of important friendships ▪ With support can show empathy for the less fortunate such as those living in poverty or with illnesses	▪ Supports child to play cooperatively with others and intervenes during conflict and teaches conflict-resolution skills ▪ If child is having difficulty playing with others parent will coach her to enter groups and to stay involved in the game ▪ Reads stories about friendships that children have and develop social stories about the child's own situation ▪ Encourages the child to have friends and make sure he is not feeling rejected or isolated
7 to 10 years	▪ Increasing desire to be recognized and accepted by the peer group ▪ Strength and depth of friendships increase and involve common values, commitment, and mutual support ▪ Show empathy and concern for other people, especially their special friends	▪ Makes sure the child has some positive and reciprocal friendships ▪ Tries to connect to parents of the child's friends so that similar rules can be put in place in the homes ▪ Makes sure child is not being a bully or a victim ▪ Shows model caring and altruistic behavior and tries to get child involved in this ▪ Connects with the child's sense of being a friend and talks about what this means to both the children
11 to 13 years	▪ Popularity and status in the peer group become very important to the child ▪ Peer pressure becomes a strong force in the child's life ▪ Growing interest in the opposite sex ▪ Child is still very self-focused although has capacity to see the views of others ▪ Tends to ignore the family in favor of time with peers for much of the time	▪ Offers help if the child seems to be rejected or is having difficulty making friends ▪ Monitors friendships, interactions with the opposite sex, and social gatherings attended by the child ▪ Checks that the child is not depressed or becoming more impulsive and engaging in excessive risk-taking behavior

Intercoder agreement has been between about 12% and 85%, with most reporting reliabilities of 85% or higher. Results have been compared with those on the *Attachment Q-Sort* (AQS) *Test,* based on attachment behaviors in the home (Posada, 2006; van IJzendoorn, Vereijken, Bakermans-Kranenburg, & Riksen-Walraven, 2004). Correspondence is high for children classified as secure and ambivalent or disorganized but not for children assessed as being avoidant and controlling. Continuity or stability of classifications over time has been somewhat low, especially for the avoidant group.

Attachment of 5- to 7-Year-Old Children

The *Main–Cassidy Attachment Classification for Kindergarten-Age Children* has found predictable differences between secure and insecure groups and ABCD groups. It is based on a 3- to 4-minute reunion after an hour of separation (Main & Cassidy, 1988). Intercoder reliability has ranged from 70% to 88%. Test–retest reliability has been 62% (Main & Cassidy, 1988). Links between classification at age 6 and social competence and peer acceptance at school have been found, with the secure group showing greater competence.

Attachment Measures Based on Symbolic Representations

The *Separation Anxiety Test* (SAT) was originally developed for adolescents and later modified for children from 4 to 7 years of age by Klagsbrun and Bowlby (1976). It consists of six photographs of attachment-related scenes, and the child is asked to describe how she feels about the situations and what she would do. Kaplan (1987) developed a classification system for the responses. Children are classified as being "resourceful" (B), "inactive" (A), "ambivalent" (C), or "fearful" (D). Correspondence with attachment classifications was 68% for the four groups. Slough and Greenberg (1990) used the SAT pictures and developed four scales from the Kaplan early system to rate attachment security.

Doll Play

The *Attachment Story Completion Task* (CASCT; Bretherton, Ridgway, & Cassidy, 1990) has the child enact stories using small human figures (mothers and children) and other props, and certain situations and issues are played out, such as spilling juice and departure. It was originally used with 4-year-olds. A classification system is used to identify the four main attachment groups. Secure children show coping behavior, avoidant children do not respond, ambivalent children show inconsistent patterns, and disorganized children show odd or disorganized responses.

Two other systems have been developed: *Incomplete Stories with Doll Family* and *Attachment Doll Play Assessment* (ADPA; George & Solomon, 2000). Validation of the measures is incomplete, but they are believed to have great potential. Currently, they are a rich source of children's thoughts and states of mind regarding attachment. Although the systems can identify the likely behavior of the secure infant and young child, it has been much more difficult to distinguish between the insecure group representations.

The *Attachment Q-Sort* (AQS) does not require extensive training to obtain reliability and reflects the child's behavior in the home. The Q-set consists of 90 items on cards designed to describe various attachment behaviors. The cards are sorted into nine piles from "least characteristic" to "most characteristic" of the child. The sorts are done by a parent or observer after 2 to 6 hours of observation in the home. It can be used for children from 12 to 60 months of age. Results are based on comparison with a criterion sort. The child's security score is the correlation coefficient between the observer's sort and the criterion sort. It has moderate associations with results on the *Strange Situation*. It has adequate validity across the United States and other cultural groups (Posada, 2006; van IJzendoorn et al., 2004).

Attachment of 8- to 12-Year-Old Children

Although there is an ample literature showing the critical importance of attachment figures in middle childhood, there is a lack of reliable and valid measures of attachment in this age group. Approaches have included questionnaires completed by the child, narrative discourse measures, analysis of family drawings, and observations of secure base behavior in a separation–reunion paradigm (Kerns, 2008; Kerns, Schlegelmilch, Morgan, & Abraham, 2005). For some methods, such as questionnaires and interviews, multiple measures are available. Some researchers have adapted measures first developed for early childhood, whereas others have tried to adapt measures used in adolescence. Unfortunately, there is limited valid data for most of the measures available (Kerns et al., 2005).

Child Questionnaires

In this approach, children complete a questionnaire about whom they see as their attachment figures and how they perceive the quality of their attachments. Kerns et al. (2005) suggested that, to establish their validity, results should be compared with information obtained from other individuals, such as teachers and trained observers.

The *Security Scale* is a 15-item questionnaire that measures the child's perception of his relationship with a parent (Kerns, Aspelmeier, Gentzler, & Grabill, 2001). It taps the degree to which the child sees his attachment figure as responsive and available, someone whom he would rely on when stressed, and someone with whom he has interest in communicating. The items are presented in a format developed by Harter (1985) for assessing self-esteem. The scale has adequate internal consistency, particularly for 10- to 12-year-olds. Two-week test–retest reliability was found to be adequate ($r = 0.75$) in a sample of children in Grades 4 and 5 (Kerns, Klepac, & Cole, 1996). It also has associations with other measures of attachment (Kerns et al., 2005).

Avoidant and Preoccupied Coping Strategies Questionnaires (Yunger, Corby, & Perry, 2005), of which a shorter version is available (Finnegan, Hodges, & Perry, 1996), measure preoccupied and avoidant attachment styles. High internal consistency and test–retest reliability have been found. The two scales have been evaluated on children from 8 to 13 years of age (Kerns et al., 2005; Yunger et al., 2005). The avoidant scale was negatively correlated with indicators of security and responsiveness, but the preoccupied scale did not correlate consistently with other attachment measures.

Narrative Methods

An interview format obtains more detailed information than can be obtained using questionnaires. The interviewer can begin a story that the child finishes verbally or by using dolls and other props, or for older children the AAI can be used.

The *Doll Story Completion Task* (Granot & Mayseless, 2001) is an upward extension of the Bretherton et al. (1990) story stem approach described previously. The five stories developed for younger children have been adapted for children from 9 to 12 years of age. The themes are the same, and coders rate them as secure or insecure using four criteria: open expression of emotions, nature of the parent–child relationship, positive resolution of events, and coherence of the narrative. Children are also rated as insecure, avoidant, ambivalent, or disorganized. Granot and Mayseless (2001) examined mother–child attachment with Israeli 9- to 11-year-olds and reported good observer agreement (0.78 to 0.85) and high test–retest reliability of 94% over 3 months. Results were related to results on the security scale and teacher ratings on the scale.

The *Separation Anxiety Test* (SAT; Klagsbrun & Bowlby, 1976) is a set of six pictures that require children to talk about the feelings and actions of the children in the pictures. Coders rate responses on 9-point scales (e.g., emotional openness, devaluing of attachment, and coherence). The child is assigned a classification of secure/valuing of attachment, dismissing/avoidance, or enmeshed/preoccupied/ambivalent. Adequate observer agreement has been found (Kerns et al., 2005). However, scores on this test at 11 years of age have not shown association with mother–infant attachment at 1 year using the *Strange Situation*. This test has the weakest evidence of validity of the tests for older children.

The *Child Attachment Interview* (CAI; Shmueli-Goetz, Target, Fonagy, & Datta, 2008) is a semi-structured interview in which children describe their relationships with primary caregivers. For school-aged children, the emphasis is on children's perceptions of attachment figures and relies on verbal and nonverbal communication. It is scored for the mother and father on nine scales (e.g., involving anger, idealization, dismissal, and overall state of mind) coded from 1 to 9. Children are identified as secure, dismissing, preoccupied, or disorganized. Reasonable stability was found over 3 months and 1 year. It also had sound discriminant validity supported by the predominance of insecure attachment in the clinical sample to which it was applied.

The *Attachment Interview for Childhood and Adolescence* (AICA; Ammaniti, van IJzendoorn, & Fedele, 2006) assesses children and adolescents from 10 to 14 years of age, and questions on the AAI were modified for children of these ages. Coding is similar to that of the AAI, and participants are assigned to secure (valuing of attachment), dismissing or preoccupied, and unresolved with respect to past trauma. Two longitudinal studies have been conducted on Italian children. Observer agreement (82%) on classifications was adequate. One study of children from 10 to 14 years of age found stability of 71%, the highest for secure and avoidant participants (Ammaniti et al., 2006).

The *Friends and Family Interview* (FFI; Steele & Steele, 2005b) is an open-ended interview designed to assess children's feelings about self, parents, siblings, and friends. Children are asked what they like least and most about themselves, and specific probes are used to access more information. Longitudinal studies have shown evidence of discriminate validity (Steele & Steele, 2005b).

Drawing Methods

Only one study using a family drawing technique for this age group has been found: *Family Drawing Techniques* (Fury, Carlson, & Sroufe, 1997). The children were 8- and 9-year-olds. Their drawings were evaluated for attachment classification (secure, avoidant, and resistant), signs of security, and quality (e.g., emotional distancing). In a longitudinal study of children seen in the *Strange Situation* at 12 and 18 months, results were compared with results from the *Family Drawing Techniques* at 8 to 9 years of age. There was evidence of discriminant validity, with results from the *Strange Situation* related to those from the *Family Drawing Techniques*. Coder agreement was also adequate.

Assessment of Appearance and Reality and Theory of Mind

Prior to developing a TOM, usually achieved by about 4 years of age, the child gradually acquires the ability to understand the physical and factual world and distinguish between appearance (i.e., the way things are perceived to be) and reality (i.e., the way things actually are). The child becomes aware of other people's thoughts, beliefs, and desires. This capacity allows him to understand that a person's mental world can be different from his own and the world of real situations and occurrences. Once this is acquired, the child can make a judgment from another person's perspective (Astington & Olson, 1995; Hala, Hug, & Henderson, 2003; Mitchell, 1997; Wellman, Cross, & Watson, 2001). As a consequence, he now has the capacity for perspective taking, empathy, and prosocial behavior.

Assessment of these capacities includes appearance and reality tasks and TOM or false-belief tasks. The former usually asks children to look at objects and name them. For example, the child is shown a rock that looks like a sponge, feels and explores it, and names it again. Children unable to pass the test continue to call the object a sponge. Another version is the Smarties or Band-Aid box that contains crayons instead of Smarties (small round candies) or Band-Aids. After inspection, some children still say that the box contains Smarties instead of crayons. Children are asked what their mothers would think is in the box if they came into the room.

In the Sally–Anne experiment (Wimmer & Perner, 1983), a child is shown a cartoon of Sally putting a marble into her basket and then another girl, Anne, coming along and moving the marble into her box while Sally is out for a walk. The child being assessed knows where the marble is, but Sally, when she comes back, expects to find the marble in her basket. The child is asked where Sally should look for her marble. The child with a TOM knows that Sally should look in the basket, whereas the child who has not developed that capacity says that she should look in the box. Enacting the Sally–Anne experiment with two dolls yields the same results, with 80% of autistic children failing the experiment. Firth (1989) also described an experiment in which one of the experimenters was given a coin and asked to hide it in one of three places and the child was asked to remember where the coin was put. While the experimenter was out of the room, another experimenter hid the coin in another place. He asked the child where the person outside the room would think the coin was and where he would look for it when he came back into the room. The same percentage of autistic children failed this test. Interestingly, children with autism can pass tests based on cartoon strips depicting a mechanical or behavioral entry story and only fail stories about other people's thoughts.

The Social Perception Domain on the *NEPSY*, second edition (*NEPSY-II*; Korkman, Kirk, & Kemp, 2007) has subtests of affect recognition and TOM that are useful.

Assessment of Perspective Taking

Perspective taking is the important ability "to perceive the intentions, actions, and dispositions of others" (Perlman, Vander Wyk, & Pelphrey, 2010). It allows the child to make accurate judgments about how to act in various social situations. It takes several years to develop as young children have difficulty seeing a situation from a point of view other than their own. This capacity can be further complicated if intense emotions are involved. Lack of perspective taking is referred to as egocentrism and characteristic of young children's thinking. Perspective taking is not fully achieved until about 11 to 12 years of age. Because many of the issues with perspective taking occur in social situations, tests of interpersonal problem solving can determine how children understand social conflicts, their perspectives on what is occurring, and other people's points of view.

Attributional Biases and Response Styles (Dodge & Frame, 1982) can be used from 3 years of age on. This test employs 10 picture stories that examine children's biases in interpreting peers' perspectives and intentions. The stories depict children in ambiguous situations, such as entering a group, being bumped into, or being hit by a ball. The stories can be scored for ability to see the other person's intent and for hostile or more positive evaluations of that intent.

The *What Happens Next Game* (*WHNG*; Shure, 1990) can be used with preschoolers and early-elementary-school children and measures the child's ability to consider different consequences for two interpersonal acts: grabbing a toy from a peer and taking something from an adult without asking. The procedure uses pictures and stick figures and can include questions about how the other person thinks and feels about what happened.

The assessment is scored for the total number of different relevant consequences for both interpersonal situations.

Assessment can also include observations of the child at home and school. Interviews with parents and children about the child's capacity to see the other person's perspective in various situations can also be revealing. Clearly, this is a capacity that can be absent or very distorted in all the disorders discussed in this chapter.

Assessment of Empathy and Prosocial Behavior

The first signs of the ability to show empathy and respond with the same emotion as the other person appear early in life. However, it is not until 5 or 6 years of age that the child's response is more other oriented and involves concern or sadness for the situation or emotional state of the other person and a desire to improve that person's condition (Hoffman, 2000). Empathy is likely to be linked to prosocial behavior, which includes cooperation and caring behaviors such as sharing, helping, and comforting.

The *Borke Test of Interpersonal Awareness* (Borke, 1971) can be used from 3 years and above. Part 1 uses stories depicting general situations that can make a child feel happy, sad, afraid, or mad. The child is asked to complete the picture by choosing pictures of happy, sad, afraid, or mad faces, the face that best shows how the child feels. Part 2 asks children to describe the subject as behaving in ways that might make the other child feel happy, afraid, sad, or mad. Children receive one point for each emotion that they identify correctly. The number obtained can be compared with norms in the child's age group. There are 21 items that take 10 minutes to complete.

The *Bryant Index of Empathy* (Bryant, 1982) can be used with children from 5 years and above. It asks children to answer yes or no to statements (e.g., "Sometimes I cry when I watch television"). In this way, the test emphasizes shared feelings. There are 22 items, which take 10 minutes to complete.

Assessment of Social Competence and Friendships

Social competence in children is reflected in their successful social functioning with peers and adults. It involves social skills that allow children to achieve goals such as being liked and accepted, having friends, and engaging in rewarding and reciprocal interactions with others.

The *California Preschool Social Competence Scale* (CPSCS; Levine, Elzey, & Lewis, 1969) is used with 3- to 6-year-olds and has teacher and parent rating scales. The items contain four descriptions of children that detail varying degrees of competence relative to the behaviors being measured.

The *Kohn Social Competence Scale* (Kohn, 1977) assesses the child's social competence in a childcare, preschool, or Kindergarten environment. The scale measures two opposing dimensions of social functioning: interest–participation versus apathy–withdrawal and cooperation–compliance versus anger–defiance. A scoring key takes about 3 minutes to complete.

A Measure of Peer Sociometric Ratings is used for preschool children in daycare or Kindergarten. Children are individually shown pictures of the other children in the class and asked to place the pictures on a happy, neutral, or sad face to indicate whether they like, neither like nor dislike, or dislike a classmate. Scores are then summarized across the responses to give a score for each child. The scores can be used to identify popular, rejected, or neglected (neither liked nor disliked) children.

The *Social Competence and Behavior Evaluation* (SCBE; LaFreniere & Dumas, 1995) can be used for preschool and elementary school children. These teacher rating scales measure social competence, emotional expression, and general adaptation of children. The obtained scores can be used to design classroom interventions to focus on the child's strengths and weaknesses.

The *Social Responsiveness Scale* (SRS; Constantino, 2002) assesses social awareness, social information processing, capacity for reciprocal social communication, and social anxiety/avoidance, and it can be used to identify autistic social impairment. It is used with children from 4 to 18 years of age.

The *Social Skills Rating System (Parent and Teacher Forms)* (SSRS-P, T; Gresham & Elliott, 1990) evaluates social skills and problem behaviors of school-aged children. Each behavior is rated in terms of frequency and perceived importance. The system measures cooperation, assertion, responsibility, empathy, and self-control. There are parent and teacher versions. It can be used to design interventions.

Assessment of Children With Disorders of Socialization

For children with RAD who are affected by trauma, social anxiety disorder, and conduct disorders, these abilities are highly compromised. For children with autism, a large percentage will fail basic TOM tests, whereas children with the other disorders might pass these tests but have difficulty in situations in which they are triggered or emotions are particularly high. Children with social anxiety or conduct disorders are likely to have very distorted views of what is going on in certain situations, with children with social anxiety believing that they are being criticized or seen as inadequate and children with antisocial tendencies seeing hostile intent. Children with RAD or the effects of trauma can often be triggered in social situations, see rejection, and act out without conscious control.

Assessment of Children Suspected of Having Reactive Attachment Disorder

There is currently no universally recognized measure or protocol available for diagnosing and assessing children suspected of having RAD. However, some promising approaches are using structured observations and interviews (Boris et al., 2004). Yet there are no procedures that can definitely diagnose or classify either the withdrawn/inhibited or the social/disinhibited pattern. Most researchers and clinicians agree that the following procedures should be used as part of assessment:

- observations of any difference in the child's responses toward caregivers and strangers;
- structured episodes that activate the wariness system, such as the *Strange Situation*, or procedures for older children that allow the clinician to observe behavior at reunion toward the caregiver, parent, and stranger;
- observation of free play with caregivers; and
- semi-structured interviews with caregivers that focus on difficulties such as indiscriminate friendliness and withdrawal and inhibition.

Other approaches have been developed, including one that uses a battery of tests that include child and parent clinical interviews and several global rating scales of attachment and behavior and two reactive attachment questionnaires (Sheperis et al., 2003). Boris et al. (2004) also developed a protocol using behavioral observation and a structured interview. They also used clinical observation of the child with a series of episodes giving them the opportunity to observe the child with an attachment figure and a stranger. The American Academy of Child and Adolescent Psychiatry (2005) Practice Parameters for diagnosing RAD recommend several observations of the child with caregivers and an unfamiliar adult as well as a thorough assessment of her early caregiving environment from other sources.

TREATMENT OF DIFFICULTIES AND DISORDERS OF ATTACHMENT AND SOCIAL DEVELOPMENT

Goal of Treatment

The goal of treating children with various kinds of social difficulties is to enable them, as far as possible, to manage in group settings, form friendships and relationships, and function in the community.

Principles of Treatment

- A thorough multidisciplinary assessment of children with significant social difficulties needs to be completed.
- Although it is important to use evidence-based approaches to treat social problems, typically parents and teachers are most interested in simple but effective strategies that can be used at home and school to prevent a negative behavior from occurring or, when it does, ways to react to eventually eliminate the behavior. Strategies to encourage adequate social abilities are also welcomed.
- Approaches originally developed for children with one disorder of socialization can often be used for children who have social difficulties but do not fully meet criteria for the disorder.
- In many instances, a developmental approach is important because children might be functioning in certain areas of social development at a much lower level than standard for their chronological age. Developing certain social abilities might be necessary before teaching various social skills.
- Behavioral strategies need to be attachment and relationship based and focused on enhancing the understanding of mental states and self-reflectivity of both the child and the parent for the child to make the necessary developmental gains.
- When children are referred for treatment because of attachment disorders, the effects of trauma, and developmental disorders such as autism, it might not be possible to eliminate their delays or symptoms. However, their social functioning can be significantly enhanced and in turn improve their ability to manage in school, sustain relationships, and secure employment later.
- For children with social difficulties, it is important to adapt the home or school environment so that the child can gradually adapt to being with other children and adults and interact socially. This will often include assessment of sensory processing by an occupational therapist.
- Although social skills can be taught, it is important to increase the social understanding that underlies the skill. This can support the transfer of skills from one situation to another, which is often a challenging task for children with autism and social anxiety.

Treating Children With Attachment Difficulties or Disorders

Treating Reactive Attachment Disorders and Disinhibited Social Engagement Disorder

Currently, there are no evidence-based treatments for children diagnosed with RAD (American Academy of Child and Adolescent Psychiatry, 2005; Rutter, 2008). A number of therapies for this population have been tried, including inducing anger and then using physical restraint to calm the child down (O'Connor & Zeanah, 2003). However, as pointed out by Rutter (2008), these approaches do not use attachment principles and are highly intrusive, even causing death in a few cases. Consequently, they have no evidence of effectiveness, are dangerous, and should never be used. Strategies suggested for children with disorganized attachment and outlined in Chapter 5 for children who have been traumatized can be useful.

Treating Disorganized/Disordered Attachment

Dyadic Approaches

A number of approaches have been used with children with disorganized/disordered attachment and their primary caregivers (typically their mothers) to develop secure attachments. The programs promote sensitive responsiveness of the caregiver and attempt to reduce disruptive behavior and improve communication in interactions. Helping the caregiver to understand the inner world of the child, and particularly her own past experiences and feelings and their effect on her caretaking, is important. This understanding can change the caregiver's attributions of her child so that their interactions are more positive. Appropriate interactions are modeled by the therapist and efforts made to increase the parent's self-reflectivity or understanding of her own thoughts and feelings. These approaches are *Child–Parent Psychotherapy* (CPP; Lieberman & Van Horn, 2008); *Circle of Security* (Powell, Cooper, Hoffman, & Marvin, 2009); *Modified Interactional Guidance* (Benoit, Madigan, Lecce, Shea, & Goldberg, 2001); and *Watch, Wait, and Wonder* (Cohen et al., 1999). Each has been successful in increasing the sensitivity of the mother's interactions with her child and consequently in reducing the incidence of disorganized/disoriented attachment. Another approach that has been used primarily to enhance the relationship of adopted or foster children with their carers is *Dyadic Developmental Psychotherapy* (DDP; Hughes, 2006). In this approach, the therapist works with the child, demonstrating the use of Playfulness, Acceptance, Curiosity, and Empathy (PACE) as well as attunement and responsiveness to the child and how it can contribute to a reduction in negative behaviors and an increase in attachment to the parent. This approach also emphasizes the reintegration of unconscious memories of trauma into explicit memories to reduce the child's triggered aggression, anxious reaction, and overall emotion dysregulation.

Large-scale community approaches successful with infants and young children to enhance attachment and prevent social and emotional problems later include the *Attachment and Biobehavioral Catch-Up Intervention* (Dozier, Lindhiem, & Ackerman, 2005), *New Orleans Interventions for Children in Foster Care* (Zeanah et al., 2005), *UCLA Family Development Project* (Heinicke et al., 2006), and *Minding the Baby* (MTB; Slade, 2002; Slade et al., 2007).

Individual Approaches

Brisch (2012) describes the integration of attachment principles into child therapy. He emphasizes the need for child therapists to provide nurturing, caring interactions to facilitate the child's secure attachment with caregivers, expression of emotional concerns, and development of positive IWMs of self and others. He suggests that "the patients' self and other representations mature within the therapeutic relationship as a result of changes in affect, cognition, and behavior" (p. 75). He describes the therapist as providing a secure base for the child and how different strategies might be needed with the child with avoidant, ambivalent/resistant, or disorganized attachment patterns to help her change her sense of self and others.

Goodyear-Brown (2010) explains that a significant role of the play therapist is to provide the child with an experience in the playroom as a safe place and the therapist as a safe person. This can be done by attunement processes and by what happens in the therapeutic space. The ways of providing a secure base for the child will vary with different children, and she describes her approach as "follow[ing] the child's *need* in doing this" rather than the child's *lead*, so this process can be very different for different children and even for the same child over time (p. 51). This might imply that the therapist needs to participate in the play of one child and provide joint attention and delight in what is happening, whereas another child, to feel less vulnerable and anxious, might need additional structure for the play. The play therapist can offer special activities or encourage certain types of play using toys in the playroom. Sometimes safety can be created by moving around the room with the child while she makes "it safe" or providing sensory materials such as Play-Doh that can be calming and reduce any anxiety that she is feeling.

Encouraging a Positive View of Self and Others

Children with disorganized/disoriented attachment or RAD, particularly if they have experienced loss or abuse, have very negative views of self and lack trust in others. Rebuilding these views into more positive ones can take years for some children, whereas others seem to be more open to changing working models of attachment and can do so earlier. Helpful strategies include the following:

- Provide a home and school in which there is some permanency and consistency in terms of routines and structures to give the child a sense of security and understanding of what to expect day to day.
- Establish clear rules and limits through visual cues and other reminders about acceptable behavior. Make it explicit that hurting anyone in the family or classroom, physically or emotionally, is not allowed because everyone must feel safe and protected.
- Make discipline attachment based so that, after the child is disciplined, the relationship is repaired by letting him know that you understand how hard it is for him but that the rules are there to keep everyone safe. It is important not to nag him, and ensure that consequences are not too harsh, and never threaten to send him away. The child should never be shamed or criticized but should be given ways to do better next time.
- Notice good behavior and empathic or prosocial responses; they need to be acknowledged as much as academic success.
- Find for each child approaches that can help her to feel relaxed and close to the caregiver. For some children, it might be deep touch or pressure; for another, it might be jumping on a trampoline. Sometimes the bedtime routine of reading a story and discussing anything upsetting for the child during the day can be helpful.
- Comfort the child when he is hurt, ill, upset, frightened, or lonely. Children with negative views of self and others might not expect this to happen and might not realize that they are feeling an emotion, especially if it is not significant at first. Try to catch the child before he gets very upset and let him know that you see he is sad, afraid, or frustrated, show empathy, and then suggest something helpful. The child will gradually realize that he and his thoughts and feelings are important to someone else, and this realization can help him to change his view of himself and others.

- Caregivers need to be aware of their own unresolved loss and trauma and how this can impact their interactions with their children and others. They need to be supported to seek counseling if they are repeating cycles of rejection or severe punishment or going too far in the opposite direction (e.g., not disciplining or setting limits because their parents were too strict and punitive).
- Talk about people in the child's immediate world who are doing things to help others, such as a teacher, minister, neighbor, or youth worker, so that he begins to realize that there are people who are helpful to others, especially the less fortunate. Also talk about and read books to him about important people in the world who are helping others.
- For children who have been abused and neglected, treatment might be necessary either with the caregiver or individually.

Encouraging Theory of Mind, Perspective Taking, and Understanding of Mental States

Social understanding and competence require that children be aware of the mental states of others or develop a TOM. Although difficulties with TOM and perspective taking are most noticeable in children on the autism spectrum, those with other difficulties, such as oppositional behaviors, attachment disorders, and social anxiety, can also have difficulties in these areas. As well, children who have not had synchronized interactions with caregivers and discussions on what is going on in their minds and those of their parents, can be compromised in the development of these capacities.

Encouraging the Development of a Theory of Mind

In children with autism, areas of the brain usually used for TOM tasks do not function normally (i.e., amygdala, insula, and anterior cingulate); however, when these tasks are taught to children with autism, they can learn them, and they are processed in the right side of the brain in an adjacent area instead (temporal lobe) (Happe et al., 1996). Programs have been developed in which children with autism have been taught the underlying social cognitive principles necessary to understand the mental states of others. Children improve on the tasks but do not always transfer the skills to other settings, so they might have to be taught again. A practical guide is available to teach children with autism these abilities, which can help them to have a TOM, and can be used with children with other social difficulties. The program was developed by Howlin, Baron-Cohen, and Hadwin (1999) and emphasizes teaching social understanding or learning to comprehend what another person is thinking and feeling

Encouraging Perspective Taking

Children can learn perspective taking when caregivers talk to them about the thoughts and feelings of others with whom they interact. Mental-state language refers to mind-related comments as opposed to those about behavioral or physical characteristics of people. Such comments can be about thoughts, desires, and feelings in the caregiver's mind, the child's mind, or another person's mind. Mental-state talk can take place during play, discipline, television watching, and reading. In mental-state discourse, the child is asked about how he is feeling and what he is thinking about so that his perspective as well as the other person's can be understood. When children hear this kind of discourse, reasoning about mental states is encouraged and internalized and can be used in their interactions.

Taking every opportunity to get the child to understand the perspectives of other people is important. For example, if she has a friend over to play and becomes bored and starts to do her own thing, after the visit, draw attention to how the other child likely felt.

Ask her how she feels when a child at school is mean to her or ignores her. When disciplining the child, repairing the relationship afterward and talking about how her behavior affected her friend emotionally is important. Avoiding doing this in a punitive way, and encouraging her input on what she thinks her friend thought and felt is useful.

To encourage perspective taking, a number of programs have been developed for play interactions between parent and child and to enhance play in young autistic children (Bornstein, Haynes, O'Reilly, & Painter, 1996). *Greenspan Floor Time Model* encourages parents to provide sensitive and responsive interactions with their infants, toddlers, and preschoolers. This approach has been used successfully with children with challenges with perspective taking to extend their play, encourage two-way interactions, and prompt them to socialize more (Greenspan & Wieder, 1998, 2007). It encourages children to communicate and take more initiative. In addition, the program helps parents who have difficult toddlers to interact more sensitively with them (DeGangi & Greenspan, 1997).

Encouraging Empathy and Prosocial Behavior

It is difficult to teach a child to show empathy and prosocial behavior, and the best way is to teach the social understanding basic to these behaviors, such as perspective taking and TOM. Modeling caring behavior when the child is upset and toward people outside the home or in the classroom is really helpful. The way that the caregiver responds to the child, in fact, might be the most crucial learning for her. Children learn not by being told to be caring but by how their caregivers respond to them. In other words, caring must be woven into the fabric of the home or classroom. The child who feels loved will have the energy and security to respond lovingly to others. Modeling prosocial and altruistic attitudes, such as not putting other people down and respecting others' points of view, can be very influential for children. Showing responsibility to the family, at the workplace, and in the community can also be excellent models.

Clearly, children need to be protected from a full understanding of the problems that other people face in the world. However, it is important to demonstrate concrete altruistic behavior toward families in the community who may be facing a tragedy or poverty, for example. It is helpful for children to see that the family has a commitment to some people in society beyond themselves. Children can be involved in caring activities, such as participating in a fund-raising campaign by selling things for a particular cause. Noticing a child's spontaneous helping behavior and acknowledging it can help improve it. Children often show caring behavior every day—protecting another child at school, comforting a friend, or sharing a treat with another person—and this behavior needs to be acknowledged as much as success in sport or in schoolwork. Playing cooperative games with children can also be helpful in encouraging cooperation rather than competition.

With more socially inhibited and shy children, it might be necessary to be more direct in getting them to show prosocial behavior, for their natural tendency is to be more passive and hang back. However, providing physical presence and support, clear directives, and praise for their efforts can increase children's capacity for showing caring and prosocial behaviors.

Case Study: Ethan

When Ethan was referred for treatment, his most concerning characteristics for his parents were what they saw as his lack of empathy and remorse when he hurt his brother or another child or engaged in behavior that was thoughtless of other people in the family or at school. They asked for suggestions to help him with these characteristics and for ideas to help him learn perspective taking. As often happens with children with a more disinhibited and impulsive temperament, Ethan's father, in an effort to gain more control over his behavior, became more punitive, and his mother became more helpless and frightened as she felt more out of control with him. Unfortunately, the frightening and frightened behaviors that they engaged in led to a disorganized attachment in Ethan, and his behavior escalated as he had no sense of a safe, secure relationship with either parent. This increased his need to feel in control of them and situations. His parents also asked for the best way to discipline him and noted that consequences did not seem to work for Ethan as they did for his brother. It was then thought that a number of strategies were necessary to reduce his aggressive behaviors and get his parents to believe that they could have a relationship with him. The following approaches allowed his parents to feel more in control of his behavior and increased Ethan's capacity for empathy, prosocial behavior, and remorse.

- It was important to report to the parents the significant findings from the multidisciplinary assessments. Although Ethan was of average intelligence overall, he had a number of developmental challenges. For example, his receptive and narrative language was 2 to 3 years behind his chronological age. In addition, he received very low scores on tests of working memory and other executive functions, and these deficits were significantly impacting his academic functioning and made it difficult for him to manage academic subjects and follow through with instructions.
- Ethan, unlike his brother, had a temperament at the extreme end of disinhibition and impulsiveness, and children of this temperament type do not respond to consequences as other children do. Therefore, the two most important parenting strategies that were used to help Ethan develop secure attachments and warm relationships with his parents were to be as warm and responsive to him as possible. This helped him to begin to want to please his parents and be more open to following rules and routines and to understanding the thoughts and feelings of others. Developing perspective taking and empathy made him less likely to hurt other people and begin to feel remorse.
- It was also important for Ethan's parents to believe that they could gain some control over his behavior by coming up with solutions and sticking to them. This was part of having them realize that Ethan could learn to respond differently and that it was hard for him to think that he could not be controlled.
- In some ways, he had been made to feel that he was "the center of the universe" in the family as the handsome and talented athlete. Strategies were needed to help him overcome this grandiosity and egocentricity by improving his perspective taking.
- His parents needed to decide on a few rules that they could enforce consistently and identify other, less important behaviors that they could ignore. They were supported to use a list of the rules with visual prompts where necessary. It was stressed that the new rules were for everyone, including his father. The consequences for not following them were also made clear.
- Then his parents were asked to come up with ideas on how they could develop a better relationship with Ethan, and it was emphasized that his father needed to stop being punitive and threatening and that his mother needed to remain firm and not be intimidated by his behavior.
- Efforts needed to be made to use mental-state talk with Ethan. When he hurt someone, his parents needed to discipline him using induction. In this approach, the child is constantly reminded of how his behavior made the other person feel and that it was like how he would feel in a similar situation. His parents were also encouraged to notice any empathic behavior and praise Ethan for it as well as his academic and sporting achievements.
- It was also suggested that his parents use emotion coaching or trying to catch him when he was starting to feel sad, angry, or frustrated and let him know that they noticed how hard it seemed for him and that they were available to help him in any way that they could.

These strategies and directions were very helpful for Ethan and his family, and gradually changes began to occur, though it was important to continue to model the strategies and provide ongoing support for the family for a number of months. For children with Ethan's temperament and parents with their backgrounds, it is crucial to work long enough to see significant changes and prevent reversion to previous patterns of interaction.

Teaching Social Skills and the Ability to Have Friendships

Effective approaches to enhancing social competence have been identified by comparing socially skilled and unskilled children and determining how the skilled children react in interactions with their peers (Borja-Alvarez, Zarbatany, & Pepper, 1991; Putallaz & Wasserman, 1990). Areas of focus have included competent play with peers, group entry, staying involved with friends, and conflict resolution (Cillessen & Bellmore, 2004). As well, more personal attributes of children have been studied, suggesting that, when they have more positive expectations about a social situation, they are more likely to be successful (Rabiner & Coie, 1989). Of course, with socially anxious children, and those with high-functioning autism, anxiety about social situations frequently impacts their ability to enter social situations and behave appropriately. Other research has found a concurrent relationship between emotion regulation and peer group acceptance. Findings show that expression of positive feelings is related to being liked by peers, whereas expression of anger is related to being disliked by peers (Denham, Bassett, & Wyatt, 2007; Walter & LaFreniere, 2000). As well, personal characteristics of children's social contextual variables at home and school have significant effects on children's social success (Putallaz & Wasserman, 1989). Some programs that can help with some of these issues are described next.

Giggle Time (Sonders, 2003) is a program primarily designed to develop the communication skills of children with ASD. However, it can be used for other children with social difficulties. The reciprocal, playful interactions outlined can encourage social turn taking, joint attention, and mutually satisfying social play. These are all parts of the basic foundation of perspective taking and understanding the other person. Also, because the games are repetitive and fun, they are likely to be rewarding and provide motivation to be engaged with others. The manual provides specific instructions on how to structure each play activity. The activities use rhyme and action to help get the child involved. In other words, rather than using toys and equipment, the approach uses people to engage children in shared affect and social connections. As such, it can engage children who have lacked early attachments or face-to-face interactions and children who find it difficult to trust others or are anxious in the company of others. Although these exercises are for young children, sometimes it is necessary to go back to early types of interaction to enhance the development of older children who have experienced trauma or are too anxious to reach out to others by themselves.

Social Decision-Making Strategies or Social Autopsies

After a child has had a problem or a meltdown in a social situation, helping him to identify the problem or mistake and to come up with alternative ideas for how he might have behaved can be critical.

1. After the event, help the child to identify who was involved and how it happened.
2. Brainstorm with him about other options that he could have used. This gets him involved in thinking about what happened and deciding on ways to act differently.
3. Consequences for each option generated can be discussed.
4. Options are prioritized according to whether he is comfortable with them and whether they can lead to something that he wants to happen.
5. Strategies chosen are written down, and a plan is developed.
6. The strategies are practiced by using imagery or acting them out.

Reciprocal Communication or Engagement

A child might tend not to discuss other children's topics and engage in a monologue about her own interests instead. This kind of behavior is common with children with Asperger's syndrome but can occur in younger children and those without perspective taking. The goal is to reduce her amount of speaking to allow an exchange to take place. A self-management package can be developed in which she is to ask a question of her partner and listen to and show interest in what he has to say. She can reflect on or acknowledge what the other person said. Teach her to request information and thank someone who has been helpful. Also encourage her to show sympathy by making comments about things that might be difficult for the other child. Encourage her to use simple manners, such as saying thank you, please, and excuse me, if she interrupts someone's conversation or has to leave the interaction. These simple strategies can make an important difference and leave a much better impression of the child.

Social Skills

Supporting Children at Group Entry

Group entry can be difficult for all children but particularly for children with attachment and other social difficulties. Typically, more than half of all entry attempts are rejected by other children. In trying to enter a group and initiate contact, children with mental health issues may use a number of strategies, which can include hanging back for more anxious children, to being aggressive, and pushing in for more aggressive children. Success in entry attempts appears to be related to three main elements.

1. *Observation*: Children need to be able to observe what is happening in the group play.
2. *Bid for entry*: The anxious child needs to learn how to reach out and ask to enter the group, and the aggressive child also needs to learn to ask if he can enter the group instead of pushing in or becoming aggressive.
3. *Manner of approach*: Children need to be helped to enter the group in a positive way as far as possible, avoiding being seen as shy and hanging back or being aggressive.

If a child has difficulty entering groups, coaching the child and encouraging other children to allow his group entry may be crucial. For younger children, activities can be set up that encourage interactive play. This may be necessary at home and at school in order for the child to experience some sense of success. Success can help children feel more confident and build self-esteem. For older children, giving the whole class similar instructions about acceptance of others and monitoring the behavior on the playground are important. Below are some strategies for helping children with group entry that can be used by teachers and parents.

- Have activities that encourage collaboration.
- Make sure toys and games are available that can encourage cooperation and interactive play (e.g., interactive board games).
- As far as possible, just having one other child for the child to play with at first can be helpful and then gradually introducing a third child.
- Although it is not helpful to hover over children all the time, it may be necessary at first to avoid a child getting overwhelmed and reacting negatively. It can also enable the child to experience some success and to increase self-esteem.

- In the child care or school where there are large groups of children, it is important to be available to comfort a child who becomes upset by being rejected. It is also important to offer suggestions to children who are having difficulties playing together, and praise children who are cooperating well.
- In some schools, a buddy system is in place in which a socially competent child supports another child on the playground who has more difficulty with social interactions.
- Pointing out any efforts children may be making to interact with a child and correcting any misconceptions about it can help the child who has social problems to gradually find new ways to process information about other children's behavior.
- Read children's stories in which a child is rejected or a child helped so that children can learn ways to work out things in a relationship.

Keeping Social Interactions Going

Some children want complete control over what is going on once they enter a group. In other words, they do not know how to interact *with* other children. Other children might not want to participate because they like being alone or become overwhelmed being around other children. Some strategies that can help include the following:

- Encourage communication skills, and model and practice them, so that the child can have a conversation. Discussion of everyone's social experiences around the dinner table can be helpful. Make sure that emotions are included in the conversation.
- Use coaching to improve social and friendship skills. Choose one skill to work on at a time until the child consistently experiences success with it. It is important to determine where the child is developmentally and start at that level and gradually teach the skills expected at the next age level.
- Show how agreeing with the other child at times can help to keep the interaction going.
- Use strategies from a social skills curriculum (e.g., Begun, 1995, 1996; Khalsa, 1996). These programs provide handouts as well as clear instructions on how to conduct the suggested activities. Coach children who talk too much or fail to communicate at all to listen to what other children are saying.

Using Approaches Throughout the Day

Power cards look like business cards and can be carried in the child's pocket or a knapsack. On them is a three-to-five-step strategy for solving a particular problem or scenario. Relevant pictures, photographs, and so on can be used, and the child refers to the card prior to an event that he might find problematic and is anxious about. Alternatively, the instructions can be put on his desk and referred to. More ideas of this kind can be found at www.lindamoodbell.com

Cartooning can be really useful if a child likes to draw. She can create a comic strip with characters showing their conversations during social events. She can depict situations about which she is anxious. Suggest to her what she can say and what effect it might have on the other child.

Visual cues and schedules on the desk or in a backpack can let the child know what is coming next. Provide a few pictures and sequential instructions on how things will happen in the morning before going to school and throughout the school day.

Encouraging Friendships

As with the skills for entering a play group, children might need to be coached to gain skills to make and keep friends. These skills include perspective taking, showing empathy, and helping others. Some ways to improve these skills follow.

- Help children to understand which behaviors affect their ability to make friends and keep them. Some children might not realize the effects of pushing another child or not listening when someone else is talking. Sometimes this information has to be repeated several times before the child can follow the suggestions. Balance this by commenting on any positive behaviors of the child.
- Notice if a child is upset because another child has rejected him; show empathy for how sad he might be feeling. However, also help him to understand what happened and problem solve how to prevent it from happening again and what he can do if it does.
- Some children do not understand what having a friend means and what both children need to do to keep the friendship going. Emphasize that having a friend means listening to her; a friend is someone to spend time with, share ideas with, show concern for, and help.

Teaching Conflict Resolution

Conflicts occur all the time when children, including siblings, are together. Conflicts at home and school are frustrating, of course, but they can play an important role in children's social development by forcing children to learn about other people's perspectives. Children must learn neither to act aggressively nor to use physical force but instead to use more indirect methods, such as discussion, to resolve conflicts.

Some children can settle conflicts themselves, whereas some children need help to learn effective conflict-resolution skills. Children frequently provide caregivers with excellent opportunities for teaching conflict resolution when there are fights or arguments occurring. The skills are best taught when or before a conflict occurs. Learning to resolve conflicts can involve two major strategies: helping the child to process and interpret the social cues or reactions of the other child better and correcting any misconceptions and learning actual conflict resolution skills.

Also teaching steps repeatedly that children need to go through to resolve conflicts can help children to gradually do them by themselves. Calming the upset child first before going through the steps is crucial whether he is sad or angry. Sometimes by doing this, a conflict can be avoided but if not the following steps should be gone through.

1. Ask each child to explain what they think is going on and why they are upset. Insist that the children try to use appropriate words and a pleasant tone of voice if possible.
2. Ask questions to clarify the issues further. Help each of the children to come up with a solution keeping the questions going until something useful is suggested. Try to get the children to agree on a solution by asking the children what caused the conflict and difficulty.
3. Select a solution that satisfies both sides.
4. Put the solution or plan in writing and with pictures. Adjust anything that is not working.

Using Social or Therapeutic Stories

Social stories can promote social interactions with peers. They are developed together with the child (Gray, 2000, 2002; Smith, 2002). They were originally developed for children with autism and are individualized for a particular child using her name, photographs of the child, and they describe the relevant components of social situations in which she has difficulties. The children are then taught appropriate responses to other children. They can be taught using repetitions of the stories and looking at the illustrations and photos of themselves incorporated into the stories. The stories are read daily to the child and can be referred back to if she has difficulty in a social situation. These social stories are sometimes used with videotaped examples of her interactions. Skills taught include entering a group, getting other children's attention, initiating comments and requests, and making contingent responses. Studies have shown that, when social stories are used, children have increased rates of social free play, social behavior, contingent responding, and social engagement. Some generalization of the skills across other contexts has been found as well (Barry & Burlew, 2004; Delano & Snell, 2006).

Therapeutic stories can also be developed, particularly for children who are very anxious and tend to withdraw from groups or those who are more aggressive and impulsive. Therapeutic stories are about emotional difficulties that get in the way of the child's overall functioning, whereas social stories are about dealing with difficult situations. Therapeutic stories are typically made into a book, and the child reads them daily to help integrate the ideas into his sense of self and others and to calm down. They begin by having the child identify things that make him become aggressive or lead him to feel anxious, and they introduce positive aspects of his capacities and suggest new ways in which he can cope. Sometimes they are used to externalize a child's outbursts, referred to as the "temper monster," which is described as coming up with thoughts to upset the child and ideas that can get him into trouble. He is then given ways to overpower the temper monster. Better answers are also given for his negative beliefs about himself. Other stories can be written about worries and how adults can look after the worries so that the child can stop worrying and trying to solve all the problems. These stories can be excellent therapeutic tools to help children reduce emotion dysregulation.

Cognitive Interventions and Treatments

It is important to get children with social cognition difficulties and separation and social anxiety to monitor their behavior and performance. This approach can be used with children with the capacity for self-understanding who are motivated to fit in with other children.

Child-focused cognitive-behavioral therapy (CBT) can be used with children with a wide range of mental health problems, including attachment difficulties and social anxiety. Although CBT with children has not been compared with other approaches and proven to be more successful than them, it is considered to be evidence based as a number of randomized controlled studies have shown its effectiveness. A number of manuals have been developed: *Coping Cat* for children with anxiety (Kendall, Stark, & Adam, 1990); *Stop and Think* for impulsive children (Kendall, 1992); *Keeping Your Cool: The Anger Management Work Book* for children with aggression (Nelson & Finch, 1996); *Think Good–Feel Good* for children who are anxious (Stallard, 2005). CBT can be focused on key cognitions assumed to underlie the child's problems. A significant part of CBT is related to the improvement of dysfunctional cognitions, which occur particularly in children with anxiety disorders, trauma disorders, and aggression and oppositional problems (Beidel & Turner, 2005).

Some children seem to live in a state of constant arousal and vigilance that contributes to their difficulties with social interactions. In fact, many children with social issues have high states of arousal and can benefit from learning strategies for "soothing the physiology" before other treatment approaches such as CBT are used (Goodyear-Brown, 2010). These calming strategies need to be adapted to the developmental age of the child using metaphors of animals or children pretending to do certain tasks. Other approaches include strategies in which tension and relaxation of muscles are demonstrated and practiced. Deep breathing as a way to calm down can also be used with young children if they are motivated to use the skill. Soothing guided imagery can also be used with children who can relax enough to use the strategy. Encouraging caregivers to use calming strategies with their children is crucial, and they can become part of bedtime routines.

Systematic desensitization or exposure has been used successfully, primarily with children with social anxiety. The hierarchy of exposure takes the child through looking at pictures of the fearful stimulus, watching it on television, and being close to it in reality.

Social skills groups can give a child strategies to use in socializing with others. The groups consist of structured-learning lessons and social activities. Children learn skills necessary for effective social functioning and then practice them in natural social situations. Difficult social events are discussed and alternative behaviors to use in them brainstormed. Role playing, modeling, and other techniques are used. Children with ASDs often benefit best from such social skills groups. Groups are considered very helpful by parents, teachers, and participants, and they often report improvements in social skills and self-confidence. The groups also provide opportunities for children with social difficulties to make social contacts and learn social activities (Howlin & Yate, 1999).

Use of Medication

Although medication is seldom the first-line approach for children with social skills difficulties, it can sometimes be useful to reduce the impulsivity or arousal that might be contributing to aggressive responses. Stimulant medication is an effective form of treatment to reduce impulsive responses. Although it is most commonly used for treatment of ADHD, such traits are not uncommon in children with ASD and disorganized attachments and trauma disorders. Such use is considered off label but is commonly used and has reasonable success. Caveats, such as clarifying family history of sudden cardiac death or arrhythmia or the side effect of appetite suppression, are important when using medication in this fashion.

Atypical or second-generation antipsychotics such as risperidone are also used for treatment of aggression, especially when psychosocial approaches have been unsuccessful or there is concern about placement breakdown. Because of the incidence of weight gain and the possibility of metabolic syndrome (which can predispose one to diabetes because of insulin resistance and elevation of blood cholesterol and lipids), these medications should ideally be used short term, primarily to allow the psychosocial approaches to be more effective.

Occasionally, antidepressants, such as the selective serotonin reuptake inhibitors, can be helpful in the treatment of very inhibited and anxious children as part of the psychosocial treatment. Long-term use of these medications requires monitoring to ensure continued effectiveness and absence of deleterious side effects, as with both stimulants and antipsychotics. For information on medication use in ASD, see Volker and Lopata (2008).

A new treatment of social skills difficulties and with empathic responding in children with ASD involves the use of oxytocin, sometimes called the "bonding hormone." It is still being researched but does show promise (Guastella et al., 2010).

CONCLUSION

Difficulties with socialization can have tremendous effects on children's ability to function in multiple settings, including home, school, and community. Most children referred for treatment have significant difficulties with socializing with peers, and these impairments can impact their later ability to have long-term relationships and be employable. However, a number of strategies can improve social outcomes for children and enhance their well-being and sense of acceptance by others. A diagnostic and categorical approach can be enriched when a functional developmental and dimensional approach is used as well.

Refer to Table 9.2 for more information about related programs and online sources.

Table 9.2 *Websites*

Website	Information on Website
www.rdiconnect.com	Website of Relationship Development Intervention Program for Autism Spectrum Disorders. Also used when the early relationship between parents and children has broken down for some reason.
www.jkp.com	Website of Jessica Kingsley Publishers who distribute a number of very useful publications on work with children with autism spectrum disorders and their social difficulties.
www.wiley.com/go/clinicIansguide	All worksheets and psychoeducational materials for Think Good–Feel Good Program of cognitive behavioral therapy for children are available here.
www.promisingpractices.net/programs.asp	Website of the Promising Practices Network on Children, Families, and Communities funded by the RAND Corporation. Offers information on proven and promising programs to improve outcomes for children.
www.pathstraining.com/index.html	Website for the Promoting Alternative THinking (PATH) program that teaches children ways to self-regulate their emotions and effective problem-solving strategies.
www.olweus.org/public/bullying_ prevention_program.page	Website for Olweus Bullying Prevention Program designed to prevent bullying and to reduce existing bullying problems and promote better peer relationships in the school.
www.findyouthinfo.gov/	Website of Helping America's Youth, with an overview of 180 intervention programs.
www.thereachinstitute.org	The Resource for Advancing Children's Mental Health (REACH) Institute helps parents, educators, and health professionals identify and treat children with emotional and behavioral challenges with effective therapies.
http://esrnational.org/professional-services/early-childhood-elementary-and-after-school-services/resolving-conflict-creatively-program	The Educators for Social Responsibility (ESR) website provides assistance with the Resolve Conflict Creatively Program (RCCP) and provides training and implementation. ESR is a comprehensive, school-based program for children from Kindergarten to Grade 8. The program teaches how to resolve conflicts in the classroom. Outcomes are positive.
www.projectachieve.info	"Stop and Think" social skills program that teaches children to stop and think of solutions before they act out and get out of control or withdraw.
www.wingsforkids.org	The "WINGS helping kids soar" program has a life-skills curriculum of 30 learning objectives and fun learning, social, and emotional skills. It also has an after-school group program for children to teach them skills that can be used throughout their daily lives.
www.parentingscience.com/preschool-social-skills.htm	A website primarily for parents with excellent summaries with useful strategies to help teach social skills to preschoolers.

10

The Integrated Approach to Intervention for Children With Multiple Mental Health Challenges

The model described in this book is explored further in this chapter through three case examples of children with complex challenges in multiple areas of functioning and in the environments around them. A dimensional, developmental, and functional understanding has been integrated with a categorical diagnostic approach to both understand and treat the children (Cicchetti & Toth, 2009; Helzer, Wittchen, Krueger, & Kraemer, 2008; Kraemer, 2008). The assessment and treatment of the children and how they were put back on positive trajectories are described. The interventions gave these children the possibility of completing their education and obtaining employment; maintaining satisfactory relationships; and, perhaps most important, developing positive views of their capabilities and hopes for the future. These were all considered impossible by their parents at the time of referral.

The children had a number of genetic, biological, trauma-related, attachment, and psychosocial issues that contributed to their presentations. It was not possible or helpful to tease apart which issue was contributing to which symptom. It was critical, however, to carry out an in-depth assessment of all the areas of development affected, integrate the findings, and make recommendations useful for parents, teachers, and other caregivers. The recommendations needed to be understandable, practical, and implementable at home and school. Although each child and his or her situation were unique, they shared the fact that their parents had been seeking support and help for years without success. During this time, the children had fallen further and further behind in school, and their symptoms had worsened. One problem was that, although a number of assessments had been conducted by various disciplines, they had often been done at different times, sometimes years apart, and the findings had not been integrated in a way that could be helpful in really understanding the child. In other words, they could not provide a coherent picture of what was happening for the child at the time of referral. A number of diagnoses had been suggested, though service providers had often disagreed about which ones were accurate. The parents felt burnt out, hopeless, and blamed by service providers who had implied that the child's difficulties were due to attachment problems or discipline issues.

Other writers have developed different models for treating multichallenged children, including Greene and Ablon (2006), Hughes (2006), Stein and Chowdbury (2006), and Ziegler (2005). These authors use different approaches but have all gone beyond traditional treatments, such as parent-management training, and have developed ways to work with children with complex issues to improve their development.

As outlined below, the strategies designed for the children discussed here focused on their delayed functioning in various dimensions of development. The strategies were intense, consistent, and repetitive in order to improve the child's capacities in the identified areas of difficulty. Also, as far as possible, the strategies were used at home and school.

Case Study 1: Jonathan

Reasons for Referral and Developmental and Family History

Ten-year-old Jonathan was referred by an agency in the community for assessment and treatment because current and past approaches did not seem to be helpful and were rejected by his parents. His difficulties were extreme dysregulation of emotions and behavior, resulting in a variety of symptoms at home and school. They included outbursts that involved hitting, kicking, and spitting at other students in school. At times, Jonathan had been suspended, creating a dilemma for his parents. Both were employed in high-level professional jobs and had no family members close by who could look after him. These outbursts also occurred in the home, mainly toward his mother. His younger brother, Mark, cried when he talked about being hit and hurt by his older brother and described how the attacks were unprovoked.

Jonathan's parents, Mario and Christina, had sought help for their son since he was 3 years of age, when they first became aware that his difficult behaviors were not going away and that his aggressive and acting-out behaviors, instead of lessening as would be expected at that age, were getting worse. Both parents at the time of referral were feeling out of control, with Mario often exploding and Christina ending up screaming at Jonathan in desperation. Since the first referral to an agency for children with multiple challenges, Jonathan and his parents had been seen multiple times for assessment and treatment. The assessments included evaluations by several pediatricians, several speech and language assessments and treatment for stuttering, and assessment for autism spectrum disorder. Blood and chromosomal tests were negative. An ophthalmologist had diagnosed Jonathan with right convergent strabismus and refractory error requiring glasses, which he wore consistently. There were no particular traumas identified. Jonathan had been diagnosed as having symptoms of autism spectrum disorder and oppositional defiant disorder (ODD), but the real nature of his difficulties remained a mystery. After these assessments, his parents hoped for an explanation or diagnosis and treatments that could reduce his symptoms and eliminate his extreme behaviors.

Jonathan was a planned and very much wanted baby. There were no problems identified during the pregnancy, birth, or early months following birth. At birth, his Apgars were 9 and 10. His mother described feeling very attached to him right away. They went home from the hospital at the normal time. Jonathan was breast-fed for 6 months, sucked well, and seemed to be a content baby. Christina said that she had felt more relaxed with Jonathan than with his younger brother, Mark, who had cried incessantly after going home from the hospital. However, as Jonathan entered toddlerhood, delays in acquiring language were noted, and an escalation of temper tantrums and aggressive outbursts had occurred.

Referral and Early Strategies

As part of his assessment and treatment, Jonathan was referred to a treatment center and classroom that specialized in developing strategies to treat children with mental health problems and complex presentations. A multidisciplinary team was available to assess him, including a psychiatrist, speech and language pathologist, occupational therapist, clinical psychologists, and specialist teachers. A case coordinator, assigned to the family, who was a social worker, integrated the various services provided, made home visits, and carried out treatment with the parents. The case coordinator, other specialists, and teachers also liaised with Jonathan's home school to introduce successful strategies to support Jonathan in the classroom and on the playground. His parents were not optimistic about the outcome of the referral, and as they talked it became clear that they were still searching for an explanation of and cure for his problems. It appeared that they had done little to use suggestions from the recent neuropsychological assessment report and other assessments done before the referral. Also, they made it clear that the strategies suggested in the parenting sessions that they had attended had not worked. They believed that his home school had done nothing to help Jonathan and were very critical of school staff.

Establishing the Goals and Process of Treatment

By the time of referral, Jonathan's parents and his home school placement were at a breaking point. His parents had begun to blame each other for his difficulties. A characteristic splitting between Jonathan and Mark was found, with Mark being seen as the good child and aligning himself with his parents against Jonathan. Jonathan was doing well on a soccer team, though occasionally he got into fights with the other children, but his coach was good at dealing with this and giving him appropriate consequences. It was necessary at the beginning of treatment to make two things clear to his parents: it was unlikely that one cause or treatment would be identified, and both parents would need to attend all treatment sessions to get the same message and support each other in implementing recommendations. The treatment occurred over 9 months and included the following elements:

- Assessment of Jonathan in all major areas of functioning was conducted by a multidisciplinary team. Integrating any past relevant and current findings and providing suggestions for treatment were crucial parts of the approach. A neuropsychological assessment had been completed just before referral, and Jonathan was under the care of a pediatrician whom he had seen regularly since infancy.
- Jonathan was placed in a specialized classroom that permitted identification of the triggers for his outbursts and what else was contributing to his unusual symptoms. It allowed the development of strategies to prevent the outbursts when possible and to quickly calm him down when they did occur as well as strategies to improve his learning and academic abilities.
- Home visits, with sessions around parenting and discipline, were provided. They included dealing with systemic issues in the family both between the parents and between the siblings.
- During the treatment, Jonathan continued to attend his home school for 1 half day a week that was gradually increased and the staff at his home school were given feedback about his assessment and strategies to defuse his aggressive responses and quickly bring Jonathan back to a baseline. Also, suggestions on how to support his learning were provided.
- Agencies in the community were located that could support Jonathan and continue to advise the family when the intensive intervention was completed.
- Training for teachers in Jonathan's home school was provided before he returned there full time.

Assessment of Jonathan

Assessment included direct testing of Jonathan by various disciplines, and multiple observations of him in the classroom, at different times of the day and when he had become aggressive or hyperaroused, and in the home. Various questionnaires were completed by his parents and teachers to screen for problems with executive functioning and other areas of difficulty and to collect data on areas in which difficulties were identified. These screening questionnaires included the *Child Behavior Checklist* (*CBCL*; Achenbach, 2000), *Conners-3* (Conners, 2008), *Behavior Rating Inventory Executive Function* (*BRIEF*; Gioia, Isquith, Guy, & Kenworthy, 2000), *Brown Attention-Deficit Disorder Scales for Children and Adolescents* (Brown, 2001), *Proactive and Reactive Aggression Parent and Teacher Rating Scales* (Brown, Atkins, Osborne, & Milnamow, 1996), *Occupational Therapy Screening Measure* (Sim, 2013), and *Children's Communication Checklist* (2nd ed.) (*CCC-2*; Bishop, 2003). A number of other assessment tools were used by the specialists who evaluated him.

Results From the Assessment of Jonathan

Conclusions from the various assessments were that Jonathan had several problems in a number of areas of functioning. In other words, as expected, his complex presentation could not be explained by one disorder, and he presented with subthreshold symptoms of many. It seemed likely that underlying his main difficulty of emotion and behavior dysregulation he had extreme physiological reactivity. A diagnosis of attention deficit/hyperactivity disorder (ADHD: combined type) was made by the neuropsychologist because in testing there was clear evidence of executive functioning problems and difficulties with frontal lobe functioning. No other diagnoses were made, though Jonathan had some symptoms of autism spectrum disorder, posttraumatic stress disorder (PTSD) (though no clear trauma was identified), and oppositional defiant disorder (ODD), as had been previously suggested. Areas of challenge included the following:

- In the *speech and language assessment*, a scattered profile of language development was identified, with difficulties with speech sounds, grammar, and sentence structure. Stuttering was also a problem at times. Jonathan also had auditory processing difficulties, making it hard for him to understand instructions and questions and retain and recall them when needed. He was found to have significant deficits with pragmatic language and social communication. All of these difficulties were extreme and affected his ability to gather, integrate, and apply verbal knowledge to solve problems and interpret situations. They also impacted his capacity for self-talk or inner speech. These issues also impacted negatively on his academic performance and social abilities.
- In the *cognitive assessment* using the *Wechsler Intelligence Scale for Children* (*4th ed.; WISC-IV*; Wechsler, 2004) Jonathan's full-scale IQ was in the borderline range, with verbal comprehension and processing speed his lowest scores. His perceptual reasoning or nonverbal reasoning was in the average range and of relative strength, and Jonathan was able to perform much better on tasks that required him to solve visual problems. He struggled with tasks that required him to solve problems verbally and process verbal information accurately and quickly. This is a common pattern for children with his profile of symptoms.
- An *academic assessment* found that Jonathan's reading age was 7 years, 8 months, well below his chronological age of 10 years, and his comprehension was even lower, at 7 years, 3 months. On a math test, Jonathan scored at 7 years of age. His spelling and reading speed were both in the normal range. These results suggested that some of his other difficulties were affecting his academic levels.
- Jonathan had difficulties performing a number of *executive functions,* including focusing and concentrating; being able to shift flexibly between tasks or concepts; generating new ideas or strategies; stopping himself from responding in an inappropriate way; integrating multiple streams of information; initiating a task without being prompted to do so; and planning and decision making. On the *NEPSY-II*, he was also found to have significant problems with the Attention and Executive Functioning domain particularly when he had to retain and manipulate verbal information.
- Jonathan had *problems with memory,* particularly verbal memory and working memory, when he had to hold facts in mind. He had particular difficulty as instructions became more complex. With nonverbal material such as pictures, his memory capacity was in the average range. On the *NEPSY-II* he had significant problems in the Memory and Learning domain.
- Jonathan had *difficulties in social situations,* particularly with peers. He could not monitor social situations, read nonverbal cues of others, and often thought that someone was responding negatively to him when in fact the person was not. He did not pass tests for having a theory of mind, but when tested with the *Autism Diagnostic Observation* System (ADOS) he did not fully meet criteria for a diagnosis of autism spectrum disorder, though he had several symptoms of high-functioning autism or Asperger's syndrome.
- An *occupational therapy* assessment found that Jonathan had problems with certain visual motor skills that impacted his ability to track objects fluently, especially across the midline. Difficulties were noted in proprioception, manual dexterity, upper limb coordination, and novel gross and fine motor tasks, thought to be the result of his poor motor planning, body awareness, and joint laxity. He also had poor postural tone, and his movements were uncoordinated. Jonathan had

significant sensitivities to visual, auditory, vestibular, and touch stimuli, which resulted in aggressive and avoidant behaviors. As a consequence, multisensory environments were overwhelming for him, for he was unable to filter out unwanted stimuli. It was thought that he engaged in sensory-seeking behaviors in an effort to self-soothe and "drown out" unwanted stimuli.

Results From the Questionnaires

The results on the *BRIEF* scales confirmed that Jonathan had problems with executive functioning or for inhibiting a response, flexibly shifting attention from one thing to another, working memory, planning and organizing, and monitoring his work and other tasks. On the Brown ADD scales, he had scores in the markedly atypical range on six of the clusters assessed. They were for effort (sustaining effort and processing speed), emotion (managing frustration and modulating emotion), memory (using working memory and recalling information), action (difficulty regulating behaviors and actions); focus (focusing, sustaining, and shifting attention to tasks), and activation (ability to organize and prioritize action on work and other tasks). This resulted in the ADD inattention total score and ADD combined total score being in the markedly atypical range as well. These results were consistent across home and school settings. Jonathan was found to have more reactive than proactive or planned aggression, consistent with his tendency to act out when he became hyperaroused.

Observations of Jonathan at School and Home

Observations of Jonathan in the classroom and on the playground showed that, though his behavior was extremely variable from day to day, there was consistently a pattern of dysregulation. Each day he engaged in behaviors that occurred with little thought. In the classroom, they included singing out loudly, swearing, and making remarks unrelated to what was going on. He also spoke in different voices and acted in silly ways, seemingly oblivious of what was going on around him. Jonathan also moved constantly, tapping his foot, moving around, clicking his fingers, and wriggling in his chair. On the playground, he was observed to run around making shooting actions in the air, laughing at nothing, and pretending to be hurt when no one was near him. These behaviors were annoying to the other children, who tended to move away from him, isolating him from healthy interactions. It was clear from these observations that Jonathan had little capacity to inhibit a response, had poor regulation of his emotions and behaviors, and was unable to monitor his behavior. During testing, he became disorganized and sometimes aggressive when faced with challenging tasks. Observations at home showed a boy who was isolated from other family members and tended to play repetitive games on the computer. At times, he would lose control, and some of his outbursts toward his mother and brother seemed to gain attention that was lacking. See Table 10.1 for a summary of these results.

Treatment

Working With the Family

One of the most critical aspects of Jonathan's treatment was to have his parents begin to understand his behavior in a different way and give up their search for *the* reason for his problems and with it their expectation of a miracle cure. This meant changing their attributions of their son, understanding that he was very compromised, and realizing that his issues were chronic and that he would need support for a long time. The first stage was for them to grieve the loss of their wished-for child. This was particularly difficult, for in the first 6 months of his life there had been no suggestion that he would have problems, and they had held on to this belief for a long time.

Another major focus was to work with the family system and the parents' relationship, which was at a breaking point. Each parent blamed the other for interacting with Jonathan in the wrong way or not doing enough to help him. Having both parents present during all sessions eventually

Table 10.1 *Summary of Jonathan's Assessment Results*

Genetic/Biological/Neurological Intrinsic Disorders →	Clusters of Symptoms ↔	Other Contributing Factors
Executive dysfunction/ADHD ▪ Difficulty with inhibiting an inappropriate response ▪ Difficulty with working memory or holding events in mind and working on them ▪ Problems with internalizing speech for problem solving and encouraging himself to keep trying ▪ Difficulty with self-regulation of affect and behavior ▪ Difficulty with analyzing behavior and creating new flexible responses ▪ Problems with shifting from one task or perspective to another ▪ Problems with initiating a task or getting going ▪ Difficulty with planning and problem solving ***Language disorders*** ▪ Difficulties with speech sounds ▪ Problems with grammar and sentence structure ▪ Receptive language problems, making it hard to understand instructions and questions and retain them ▪ Stuttered at times ▪ Use of inner speech compromised ▪ Limited comprehension of complex patterns of speech ▪ Reading comprehension below chronological age ***Auditory processing and memory problems*** ▪ Limited comprehension of speech ▪ Great deal of difficulty remembering complex instructions or ideas ▪ Problems with working memory and manipulating information ▪ Memory better for nonverbal material than verbal material	***Social and peer-relationship difficulties*** ▪ Missed facial expressions and other nonverbal cues of others ▪ Did not understand the perspectives of others and had difficulty with turn taking in conversation ▪ Failed theory-of-mind tasks ▪ Did not know how to enter a group and stay involved with the children ▪ Sensory sensitive, so became overwhelmed if there was too much noise or activity or too many sights ***Academic problems*** ▪ Below chronological age for reading and math ▪ Difficulty with concentrating ▪ Problems with following instructions and beginning tasks ▪ Difficulty with tracking words on the page ▪ Difficulty if asked to remember something and write a paragraph about it ▪ Difficulty with manual dexterity, so struggled with writing ***Sensory processing problems*** ▪ Problems with visual–motor integration ▪ Difficulty with tracking visual stimuli across the midline ▪ Difficulty with separating head and eye movements ▪ Low threshold for visual, auditory, vestibular, and touch and problems with multisensory processing ▪ Difficulty with dividing his attention between more than one task	***Other challenges*** ▪ Speech difficulties that began in early childhood ▪ Parents' initial lack of understanding and accepting his difficulties and challenges ▪ School very negative about Jonathan and his parents ▪ Below average intellectual capacity and learning problems in reasoning with words ▪ Insecure attachment resulting from his parents not knowing how to deal with him and consequently not being consistent with him ▪ High anxiety and poor self-esteem, might be at risk of depression because of isolation from peers ***Positives/strengths*** ▪ Did well with soccer and really liked to connect with other children ▪ Some areas of strength in learning (e.g., rote memory, spelling, reading speed) ▪ Could acquire new skills if they were taught and well practiced ▪ Parents' ultimate acceptance of his difficulties and desire to help him ▪ School personnel willing to put strategies in place once they realized how much Jonathan struggled ▪ Became able to ask for help when getting upset and use strategies to calm down

ensured agreement between them on how to deal with a particular issue and work together for improvement. Issues identified from testing were described and the rationale for interventions explained. Through discussion, the parents were eventually able to accept that, though the strategies were not a cure, with their help Jonathan could begin to use them, and they could make a significant difference to his long-term prognosis. During these discussions, a number of previous misconceptions were corrected.

- That Jonathan had borderline cognitive ability in many areas of functioning. It was explained that he had below average or borderline cognitive functioning in areas such as reasoning with words, processing instructions, and working memory. Other compromised areas included speech and language, reading, mathematics, perspective taking, and theory of mind. The significance of these difficulties was explained to the parents.
- Because Jonathan had average intelligence in perceptual or nonverbal intelligence it was assumed that he was naughty when he refused to do his homework or became dysregulated and acted out. It was explained that executive functions, such as planning, problem solving, and organizing, are just as important as cognitive ability and that problems with them impeded his learning. Also that he struggled with verbal comprehension was explained.
- That Jonathan was being disobedient when he failed to follow instructions. His parents believed that he understood everything that was said to him and were surprised to learn that often he could only remember the first or last instruction and could not hold all of the instructions in his head and carry them out. It was explained that this was due to auditory processing and working memory difficulties.
- That Jonathan was only angry and frustrated and that this was the reason for his aggression and noncompliance. It was explained to his parents that underneath this behavior he often felt anxious and sad and overwhelmed by what was going on around him because he had difficulty with understanding or interpreting what was happening and what was expected of him. He sometimes avoided the situation and switched off. At other times, he seemed to be hyperattentive and responded with outbursts or other inappropriate behaviors. Again it was emphasized that this behavior was physiological and reactive and not intentionally planned ahead to hurt others.
- That if Jonathan had average intelligence in one area he was just not trying. It was explained to his parents that in terms of speech and language and social and emotional development he was acting as a much younger child. These areas included the capacity for perspective taking and showing empathy. He also had difficulty in social situations with picking up nonverbal cues of others and needed instruction on how to observe and engage with other children to learn from them.
- That Jonathan was intentionally cruel to others. It was made clear that he did not have a theory of mind or understand the perspectives of others, and this impacted his interactions with his brother, his social abilities, and his capacities to form friendships.

Gradually, Mario and Christina realized that they needed to work with Jonathan and react to him in different ways so that he could learn to manage his environment at home and school.

Working With Jonathan

The specific strategies to help Jonathan cope at home and school are listed in Table 10.2.

Termination of Treatment

After more than 9 months of treatment, there were significant changes in how both Jonathan's parents and his home school understood Jonathan and worked with him. Integration of many of the recommendations for working with him at home and school began to result in significant changes

Table 10.2 *Behavioral, Emotional, and Social Issues: Suggested Strategies for Jonathan*

Issue	Reasons for Difficulty	Strengths	Strategies
Impulsive behavior, reacts to what is going on around him	▪ Does not think through the possible results of his impulsive behavior (e.g., blurting out, hitting other children) ▪ Can become triggered in a situation that is overwhelming in terms of noise, activity, or complexity ▪ Can respond negatively to lack of structure and supervision ▪ Difficult situations can lead him to act out ▪ Situation not calm enough for him to concentrate	▪ Can be taught how to behave in certain situations and follow through (e.g., remembering his "manners") ▪ Will cooperate in situations in which he is interested (e.g., playing soccer, rote learning) ▪ Responds to structures and limits	▪ Teach Jonathan how to behave in certain situations (e.g., going to the pool). ▪ Teach him self-talk or inner dialogue to think things through before he acts. ▪ Have him tell you why he acted as he did and what he can do to stop acting in that way. ▪ Review an incident in which Jonathan was aggressive to someone and let him know how dangerous it can be. Have him repeat it and draw a picture or find pictures about it. Talk about how it can feel to other people. ▪ Have him discuss his personality (e.g., brave and fearless, concerned and anxious when he feels rejected). Talk about how these aspects can work together for him. ▪ Have Jonathan use self-talk to calm down his physiological reaction: for example, "I can handle this, I can control my feelings, I've done it before and can do it again." ▪ After an impulsive episode, teach him four steps to problem-solve so that he can avoid acting impulsively the next time. These steps were: *1.* Slowing down: Talk about a situation in which Jonathan acted impulsively and ask him to stop and think about what happened. *2.* Perspective taking: Ask him how anyone involved in the situation must have felt and thought. *3.* Goal setting: Have him think about what he wants to do next time he is becoming upset. *4.* Choosing a solution: Have Jonathan think about what he can do differently next time.

Attention and concentration difficulties	■ ADHD, which involves impairments in certain parts of the brain and contributes to the difficulty ■ Becomes resistant and might act out when required to do something that he does not like doing or is not interested in ■ Easily distracted by stimuli around him (e.g., a child singing, things on his desk) ■ Can concentrate for only 10 minutes at a time for some tasks ■ Has difficulty with getting started on a task without any support or scaffolding	■ Can concentrate for some time on subjects in which he is interested ■ Responds to bursts of work with having frequent breaks ■ Can focus for some time when it is something that he likes doing	■ Make sure Jonathan is listening when giving instructions and makes eye contact; touch his arm to make sure he is listening. ■ Give instructions individually, check that he understands, and make sure that he follows through with what he has been asked to do. ■ Use novelty to get his attention, such as putting something in a box and getting him to guess what it is. ■ Present material in auditory, visual, and kinesthetic channels since auditory processing of instructions is difficult for Jonathan. ■ Provide cues for structure (e.g., visual guides for steps of a task). ■ Teach math concepts using things that Jonathan is interested in. ■ Gradually increase the time that he can sustain concentration and graph his progress. ■ Keep in mind that he can remember only the first two instructions without repetition. ■ Teach Jonathan to deep breathe and remind himself to focus so that he can be in a calm state for learning. ■ If he is not paying attention, ask him what is happening for him and support him to keep trying. ■ Use a timer that counts down and rings when an activity should be completed. This depersonalizes setting limits for a particular task. ■ Teach him self-talk or private speech by talking him through tasks so that he learns to do it by himself. Use encouraging statements such as "You can do it." This approach can also enhance his sense of competence. ■ Jonathan does best with hands-on activities and visual cues since he cannot hold information in his mind to work on. ■ Give him a lead into a difficult activity of something that he likes to do (e.g., completing a maze). ■ Provide short, achievable activities that can be done in 15 minutes. ■ Give small amounts of work with brief breaks. ■ Use reminder cards for work and upcoming routines or if Jonathan is becoming upset. ■ Use private signaling for Jonathan to attend (e.g., a tap on the shoulder). ■ Signal him when something important is coming up. ■ Show empathy and let him know that you understand it is hard for him and that you appreciate it when he does his best.

(continued)

Table 10.2 *Behavioral, Emotional, and Social Issues: Suggested Strategies for Jonathan (continued)*

Issue	Reasons for Difficulty	Strengths	Strategies
Aggression (physical and verbal)	▪ Lacks the capacity to control or contain his emotional reactions primarily due to his severe ADHD and an overreactive nervous system ▪ Can be triggered by a sense of rejection ▪ Can regress to a primitive, disinhibited, or disintegrated response because he reacts from the emotional center of his brain rather than the rational cognitive part ▪ Might want to act as if he is all powerful and in control to get what he wants	▪ At times can avoid getting caught up in the conflicts of other children ▪ Has internalized some idea that hurting others is not right	▪ Because not hurting others is one of the “absolute rules” at home and school, have consequences that have been agreed to if Jonathan is aggressive. ▪ Let him know that you will stop him to keep him and other people safe. ▪ If you can anticipate that he will become aggressive, try attuning to him and letting him know that you understand he is getting upset, asking him to tell you what is upsetting him, and problem solving how to avoid getting out of control. ▪ Praise him every time he manages not to become aggressive after being upset. ▪ Have Jonathan name the physical feeling that he has and link it to the emotion of anger. ▪ Make an anger thermometer and have him tell you where he is at on it. ▪ Teach Jonathan to become aware of his actions (e.g., ask him what led to the incident, how he felt, what he could have done differently). ▪ Try not to react in a fearful way and let him know that he will be restrained if necessary. ▪ If Jonathan is verbally aggressive, let him know that it is unacceptable and follow through with a consequence. ▪ Give him a signal that he can use to indicate that he is becoming upset; also look for subtle signs and change the situation if possible. ▪ Let him know how aggression makes other people feel and relate it to how he feels. ▪ Try to identify situations in which Jonathan is likely to become aggressive or have a meltdown and move back from an adversarial role and link with him before it happens. ▪ Try not to insist that he do things that are difficult for him and remember that he is still very needy of understanding and support. ▪ If he is becoming upset, use distraction and redirection (e.g., humor that is not a put down and that he can understand and enjoy). ▪ Teach Jonathan to down shift or calm down before he gets out of control. ▪ Remember that repetition is essential for him to use the strategies that he is taught and that there will be regressions at times.

Emotion regulation difficulties	■ Difficulty with using small emotions to know that he is becoming emotionally overwhelmed ■ Nervous system is hyperaroused frequently and he is hypervigilant, both of which can contribute to his anxiety and anger ■ Has sensory processing difficulties and is hypersensitive to some stimulation ■ Functions at a very young age emotionally and socially	■ Talks at times about being worried, providing an opportunity to support him to manage his emotions ■ Wants to have friends	■ Try to get Jonathan to discuss his emotional reactions; if he has difficulty, talk about what you think is going on (e.g., he must be feeling left out and sad). ■ Give all the children in the classroom a chance to earn a "holiday pass" as a reward for working hard. It can give him an opportunity for a break if he is feeling stressed rather than isolating him, which can make him feel different and get him really upset. ■ If he gets into a conflict with another child, have both children talk about what happened and how they feel and problem solve ways to deal with it without becoming aggressive. ■ Remember that Jonathan is functioning at a younger age in his emotional development and try to be understanding if he is upset and anxious. ■ Teach him to deep breathe when he is becoming upset. ■ Help him to think of something pleasant or calming when he is upset or have some fun with him. ■ Give him something that is calming for him that he can hold on to if he is getting upset. ■ Give him a gentle pat on the back or touch on the arm to calm him down before he loses control. ■ Use relaxation techniques, such as calming music, that work for Jonathan. ■ Practice labeling the emotions of people in pictures and photographs. ■ Play emotion charades in which he gets a card with the name of an emotion on it and has to act it out or guess the emotion when other people act it out. ■ If schoolwork is hard for him, let him know that you understand and will support him to complete it. ■ Use attachment-based interactions in which he learns that caregivers like him and notice his positive qualities.

(*continued*)

Table 10.2 *Behavioral, Emotional, and Social Issues: Suggested Strategies for Jonathan (continued)*

Issue	Reasons for Difficulty	Strengths	Strategies
Sensorimotor and sensory integration issues	▪ Has a number of sensory issues that contribute to his difficulties at school, including problems with eye tracking, fine motor control, and auditory processing ▪ Has a number of learning problems, so easy for him to get discouraged and give up ▪ Hypersensitive to noise in the classroom and other settings, such as the swimming pool ▪ Hypersensitive nervous system might contribute to his difficulties ▪ Seeks sensory input and might fidget or try to increase some sensations ▪ Difficulties with transitions, particularly if they have to be changed	▪ Can use visual cues to support his learning in other sensory areas	▪ Implement a sensory diet to help Jonathan regulate by increasing his tolerance to stimuli and provide ways to meet his sensory needs. ▪ Provide a quiet place in the classroom where he and other children can go when they are feeling overwhelmed. ▪ Educate his parents and teachers regarding “at risk” situations that can be triggering for Jonathan due to his sensory needs. Provide sensory activities prior to and during these times to help him cope and/or avoid such times if possible. ▪ Encourage Jonathan to engage in activities with strong proprioceptive feedback, such as climbing or swinging, that improve his overall strength and endurance. ▪ Worksheets might be accepted better by Jonathan if they do not contain too much work on each. ▪ Use clear physical and visual prompts and alert him to the connections among certain pieces of information. ▪ Try to use subject matter that interests him and can keep him trying hard. ▪ Use scanning and visual tracking activities such as the *Where's Wally* books (Handford, 1987), which Jonathan found calming. ▪ Try to adapt his desk and things that he uses for schoolwork to make it easier for him to manage (e.g., prescription of a specialized finger splint and pencil grip to improve handwriting, making sure that he uses his glasses for reading activities). ▪ Have Jonathan use a computer when writing is needed and for other activities as it can give him immediate rewards for success.
Hyperactivity	▪ ADHD compels him to move, fidget with his hands or feet, and/or talk incessantly ▪ Seeks sensation at times, which can lead to some of his movements ▪ Might become triggered and start to move to calm himself down	▪ Can stay still longer when it is something he is interested in	▪ Between short bursts of work, allow Jonathan to stand and walk around. ▪ Provide lessons that emphasize manual or physical expression to diffuse energy in a positive way. ▪ Give Jonathan frequent breaks and let him try something different and more active. ▪ Try giving him something that he can fiddle with that will not disturb others. ▪ Keep his hands busy (e.g., doodling). ▪ Try to determine which movement activities calm him rather than make him hyperaroused and use them often (e.g., swinging on a swing, jumping on a trampoline, swimming, drumming). ▪ Have him sit in a containing seat such as a bean bag chair while watching television; it can help to calm him down and keep him focused since it gives him firm touch.

Occasional premeditated acting out to get something	▪ Has learned that certain behaviors will get him sent home from school ▪ Apparent premeditated action might have been set off because something was so exciting that Jonathan found it difficult to stop	▪ When told firmly that his behavior is not going to work, calms down and stops it	▪ Jonathan must know that he will not be sent home for his extreme behavior. ▪ He must have immediate consequences that can deter him from dangerous behaviors that he finds exciting. ▪ When he starts with very negative behavior, make every effort to calm him down, distract him, or change the activity (e.g., use a joke). ▪ Try not to talk at him but ask him to tell you what is going on, listen to him, and try to calm him down. ▪ If Jonathan cannot be diverted from these behaviors, after he has calmed down, repair the relationship.
Low self-esteem and poor sense of self	▪ Because of several factors, has a sense that he cannot do a number of things ▪ Beneath the bravado and reckless behavior might be a feeling that he is bad and worthless ▪ People's responses to him can trigger memories of angry responses from his parents	▪ Does respond well when his achievements are noticed ▪ As suggested by his anxiety, has concerns about himself and others	▪ Give Jonathan a special job in the classroom doing something at which he can excel. ▪ Use positive labels such as "eagle eyes" when he finds something that no one else can see. ▪ Acknowledge that he has a difficulty and then praise him for his efforts to overcome it by doing something well. ▪ Give Jonathan a sense of belonging in the classroom by supporting him to participate in activities as much as possible. ▪ Use his strengths so that he has experiences of success, which will help to build his sense of competence. ▪ Have a "brag book" for Jonathan in which his achievements are written down and read to him. ▪ When he is feeling discouraged and says that he cannot do anything, remind him of things that he has done really well recently. ▪ Give him rewards and acknowledgments for small successes (e.g., only blurting out twice before recess). ▪ Remember that he can see rejection in certain body movements, tone of voice, facial expressions, or just being touched by accident in a line, so it is important to let him know what really occurred. ▪ It will be hard for Jonathan to develop a new view of himself, so it is critical to notice any small gains. ▪ Try to pair him with a positive child for activities as he is more likely to experience success and be supported to be cooperative. ▪ Realize that it can take several months for Jonathan to develop a more positive view of himself. ▪ Interactions are attachment based and involve positive involvement whenever possible.

(continued)

Table 10.2 *Behavioral, Emotional, and Social Issues: Suggested Strategies for Jonathan (continued)*

Issue	Reasons for Difficulty	Strengths	Strategies
Socialization difficulties	■ Finds it hard to see other people's perspectives ■ Can become verbally or physically aggressive if triggered ■ Finds it hard to play with another child for any period of time and sustain a friendship because of ADHD	■ Wants to play with other children and seeks them out ■ Does know how to behave in some situations, uses his "manners," and can be polite	■ Try role playing certain characters with Jonathan and then reverse the roles. ■ Have him cooperate with other students on an activity and scaffold it. ■ Teach social skills such as making eye contact, realizing nonverbal cues, understanding personal space, opening a conversation, and displaying manners. ■ Decide on one or two behaviors that Jonathan will work on during a week. Have him list them on a card and review them at the end of the week. ■ Videotape Jonathan playing with other children and play it back to him, noticing the interactions that worked well. ■ Teach him how to behave in various social situations and talk him through them, such as entering a group of children or going to visit family friends. ■ Make up a social story for him about what works for him socially. ■ Encourage perspective taking by reviewing social interactions with Jonathan and ask him what he thought about them and how he thought the other people experienced them. ■ If he does not have any ideas about what happened, prompt him until he does come up with some ideas about the results. ■ Talk to Jonathan about a social problem and give him a model of what he can do the next time. ■ Teach him to follow social cues by increasing his awareness of how others react to him and how he has to adjust his behavior accordingly. ■ Teach him the steps of conflict resolution when conflicts occur. ■ Coach him in how to join a group of children and how to stay involved in a positive way.

Dealing with perseveration around certain activities and constant questioning	▪ Occurs partly because of Jonathan's ADHD and need for constant talking ▪ Might also be anxious and want reassurance and "contact" with someone ▪ Likely that his narrow range of interests is familiar to him, gives him a sense of control, and can be calming	▪ Favorite subjects can be used to help him learn a number of school subjects ▪ Has a lot of knowledge in his areas of interest	▪ Provide structured routines at home and school to help Jonathan be aware of transitions. Visual organizers can be especially helpful. ▪ Sometimes a short time-out, not done as a punishment, can help him to shift gears and change the topic or activity. ▪ At times, if Jonathan is perseverating on asking a particular question, respond to any emotion such as fear or frustration and help him think about things to overcome it. ▪ Try to enlarge his areas of interest by using various strategies and supporting him in finding out about them. ▪ When he asks a question, answer it quickly and then immediately ask him a question that takes it in a somewhat different direction. ▪ Jonathan found it easier to focus on one task at a time, so limit his choices to one or two. ▪ He benefited from practice in shifting attention. Working on two or three familiar tasks and rotating them at regular intervals can help him to develop more flexibility and become more accustomed to shifting. ▪ Get Jonathan to learn by doing; this will assist him in not getting stuck on an idea so easily. For example, if he is to learn about trees, take him on a bike ride to learn about them.
Difficulty with social communication and pragmatic language	▪ Difficult for him to have a reciprocal conversation because he lacks pragmatic language ▪ Has difficulty with seeing and being interested in the perspectives of others	▪ Vocabulary can enable him to engage in reciprocal conversations ▪ Wants to relate to other children	▪ Teach Jonathan to notice what is going on with other people and particularly their nonverbal cues. This can be done by examining the facial expressions of others in group situations, using photos of other people, and examining his own facial expressions in the mirror. ▪ Help him to take turns in conversations and remain with the conversation of the other person. ▪ Coach him to talk with his brother and assist him by keeping the conversation going. ▪ Have conversations at the dinner table, giving everyone a chance to talk and then listen, and respond to the other people in the family. ▪ Encourage Jonathan to speak clearly and choose topics suitable for the setting and ages of the children with whom he is playing.

in his behavior and academic functioning. Although Jonathan still presented as an unusual child, he was able to contain his aggressive outbursts, complete his homework with scaffolding from his parents, and won the award for the most improved player on his soccer team. His parents were able to have a "friend" over to play with him, and Jonathan began to show an interest in "helping" small children in his extended family. They believed that they were now able to manage him on their own and became involved with some groups for Jonathan in the community. Post-tests showed significant improvement on the *Child Behavior Checklist* completed by both his parents and the school, reduction in aggression on the *Reactive and Proactive Aggression Scale*, reduction in parenting stress, improvement in the parent–child relationship, and reduction in symptoms on the *Conners-3.* As Mario and Christina put it on a *Consumer Satisfaction Questionnaire*, "We now understand Jonathan's problems better and how to help him and can see hope for a good future for him."

Case Study 2: Millie

Reasons for Referral and Developmental and Family History

Twelve-year-old Millie was referred by a clinical psychologist at a children's mental health center for assessment of and treatment for long-standing problems with disorganized behavior and difficulty with forming friendships. She was also noted to have poor social boundaries and impulsivity, and worries were raised about her safety as she matured into adolescence.

Millie lived with her single mother, Marjorie, in housing that was modest but adequate for their needs. Marjorie worked part time as a bookkeeper but devoted most of her time to her daughter. Her concerns were that Millie might not be employable because she was failing at school and that it was not safe for Millie to go out alone because she lacked common sense. She reported that Millie could not go to the shops alone just a block away and had been seen by a neighbor to cross the street without checking both directions and had nearly been run over.

Marjorie had been worried about Millie from early in the pregnancy when an ultrasound detected problems with her kidneys. The pregnancy, instead of being a joyous time, was worrying for Marjorie and her husband, Ron. Millie was born full term by emergency caesarean section due to fetal distress. She was quite sick at birth, had trouble breathing, and was placed in the intensive care nursery for a month as doctors monitored her lungs, kidneys, and possible spina bifida. Millie required surgery at 4 and 21 months to fix problems with her bladder and kidneys. These operations caused significant anxiety for Marjorie, who became depressed and required medication to lift her spirits. Millie could not be breast-fed since she refused breast milk, preferring to be bottle-fed. This was a disappointment for her mother. Ron was very supportive of Marjorie during this time and excited to have a child. However, he travelled a lot with his job, having to leave Marjorie alone for a great deal of the time to look after Millie.

Marjorie described Millie in the first few months as not wanting to be held and pushing her away. This seemed to be because she was in pain. She slept well at night but did not nap during the day, leaving Marjorie exhausted. In the first 12 months, Millie was boisterous and active, always moving and exploring. She used to bang her head on the cupboards, which worried her parents, and they tried to stop her, but she would become quite angry when they held her to stop her. Milestones were reached at normal times, and Millie walked at 12 months and started to say words in her second year. Marjorie described Millie at this time as more focused on toys than people. She required more surgery at 6 years of age for her eye. When she was 8 years of age, Millie developed a virus and was diagnosed with insulin-dependent diabetes, which often became unstable and needed to be monitored frequently. However, she was able to report that she was feeling strange when her blood sugar was low.

Since starting school at 4 years of age, Millie had problems with her behavior and socially with peers. She had also been bullied by older children, resulting in several moves of schools in an attempt to find a suitable one for her. Also her parents had frequent disagreements as to how to help Millie, which could become quite heated.

When Millie was 9 years of age, her father died suddenly from a heart attack that Millie witnessed. Since that time, Marjorie had suffered from significant anxiety and depression and found it hard to get out of bed in the mornings. Family history was positive for depression on the maternal side and possibly Asperger's syndrome.

Referral and Early Strategies

Millie was referred to a specialized classroom for a 4-week assessment and recommendations for strategies for her mother and her home school to use with her. She was assessed by a multidisciplinary team since she had not had any recent assessments, though her diabetes was being monitored on a regular basis by a specialist at the local hospital. There was also a support team for children with diabetes and their families to answer questions, and Marjorie was encouraged to phone the help line if she was worried. She used this resource frequently, finding it a wonderful support, and she was happy that it would continue during Millie's adolescence. Marjorie was overwhelmed by the thought of more assessments and having to transport her daughter to the school, some distance from her home. To relieve her stress, it was arranged that hospital transportation would pick up Millie for school and take her home at the end of the day. Marjorie could thus have a month when she did not have to wait anxiously by the phone for a call from the school to pick up Millie; the school assured her that it had nurses to deal with her diabetes and other staff trained to deal with difficult behaviors. Marjorie had not been referred to any parenting programs and thought that she had received little support in parenting her daughter. She was happy to know that during the day she would have a break from Millie, but it was unclear whether she would use any of the suggestions from the assessment in her home.

A case coordinator, a psychiatric nurse, was assigned to support Marjorie in putting in place suggestions from the assessments and work with teachers from Millie's home school, where there seemed to be significant issues with Millie in the classroom.

Establishing the Goals and Process of Treatment

Millie and her mother were understandably very close, and Marjorie was terrified of losing her daughter, especially because she had been so sick in the past. Millie had a similar worry about losing her mother and often had nightmares of her mother dying suddenly. Consequently, the atmosphere in the home was joyless. It seemed that neither mother nor daughter could tolerate the thought of Millie moving toward independence during adolescence. Treatment included the following elements:

- Millie was placed briefly in a specialized classroom mainly for assessment but also to test medication and other strategies to help overcome her most concerning symptoms and find ways to help her with her learning difficulties. Efforts to teach Millie about less academic subjects such as gardening and cooking were also provided in the school.
- The case coordinator conducted home visits to suggest strategies for Marjorie to use with Millie. Initial intervention focused on helping Marjorie with her grieving so that she could help Millie to gradually become more independent.
- The home school was given feedback on the assessments and support to improve Millie's learning, social ability, and adaptive behavior.
- The occupational therapist intervened in Millie's gross and fine motor difficulties, and an additional program helped Millie to learn life skills such as using public transportation, crossing roads, using money, shopping, and cooking.
- The case coordinator located additional services for Millie and Marjorie in the local community from which they were isolated, having moved several times in the previous years to find an appropriate school for Millie. An agency was also located that would help to support the family after the case was closed.

Assessment of Millie

Various questionnaires were completed by Marjorie and Millie's teachers to screen for Asperger's syndrome and identify the need for further assessment of speech and language and areas covered by occupational therapy such as gross and fine motor development and sensory processing. Millie was also screened for executive functioning, particularly impulsivity. The questionnaires used included the *Asperger Syndrome Diagnostic Scale* (*ASDS;* Myles, Jones-Block, & Simpson, 2001), *Child Behavior Checklist* (*CBCL*; Achenbach, 2001), *Behavior Rating Inventory Executive Function* (*BRIEF;* Gioia, Isquith, Guy, & Kenworthy, 2000), and *Brown Attention Deficit Disorder Scales for Children and Adolescents* (Brown, 2001). A number of other tests were used to directly assess Millie. She was screened for speech and language and occupational therapy (OT) difficulties and referred for a more intensive assessment.

Results From the Assessment of Millie

The overall conclusion from the various assessments was that Millie had a nonverbal learning disability, difficulties with a number of executive functions, and a pragmatic language disorder. She also had difficulties in a number of areas, including peer relationships, impulsivity and lack of planning and problem solving, some perseveration on certain subjects that worried her or calmed her, and academic achievement. Results of the assessments included the following.

- The *speech pathology assessment* found that Millie had strong language skills and average expressive and receptive vocabulary. However, she had severe pragmatic language or social communication problems and difficulties with higher-level language, such as problem solving and narrative.
- On the *cognitive assessment* using the *WISC-IV,* Millie's full-scale IQ was in the borderline range, and there were significant differences between her various index scores, which ranged from extremely low at the 1st percentile for perceptual reasoning to average at the 34th percentile for working memory. There was a difference of 20 points between her verbal comprehension and perceptual reasoning, with the lower score on perceptual reasoning indicating that Millie had a nonverbal learning disability. She struggled most with subtests that required spatial awareness and reasoning and visual coordination, eye–hand coordination, and short-term visual memory. This meant that her full-scale IQ did not represent her overall functioning well as there were significant differences among the indexes.
- An *academic assessment* found that Millie had a spelling age of 13 years, similar to her chronological age. On the other hand, her writing test showed that her ideas were not well developed or sequenced and that she needed support to produce her best efforts. Millie was found to be a capable reader, with a reading age of approximately 12 years. On a math test, she was at a Grade 6 level or 2 years behind her chronological age. She did better on tasks that were more concrete and had difficulty comprehending more complex instructions and questions. There were weaknesses in a number of areas assessed, which were likely to be related to her nonverbal learning disability.
- The *occupational therapy* assessment found that Millie had grasped many foundational skills, such as balance, postural control, handwriting skills, and reading skills, but she performed them at a slower pace than her peers. She had difficulty with motor planning and organizing herself in a logical and sequential manner. Assessment of activities of daily living indicated that her poor organizational skills impacted her ability to function at an appropriate level.

Results From Questionnaires and Direct Testing of Millie

From the questionnaires completed by her mother and teachers, Millie had a number of problems with various executive functions. However, direct testing and observation indicated a mixed picture.

She had difficulty with getting herself organized and starting her work and needed scaffolding to do so. She also had problems with self-monitoring of her work and behavior. Although on the questionnaires Millie seemed to have difficulty with working memory, on the Working Memory Index on the *WISC-IV* she obtained her best scores. She seemed to enjoy these tasks, and her rote memory was very good, allowing her to excel in repeating numbers on the digit span test. However, she had more trouble with repeating them in reverse. It was noticed during testing sessions that Millie had significant problems being consistent with her responses, and it often took some effort to bring her attention back to the task.

- In addition to the findings noted above, the occupational therapy assessment found that Millie had difficulties with oculomotor control, visual perception, spatial relation, and visual motor tests and was only at an 8-year-old level on these tasks. She also had difficulty with coordination, proprioception, kinesthetic tasks, and crossing the midline.
- On the *Autism Diagnostic Observation System* (*ADOS;* Lord, Rutter, DiLavore, & Risi, 1999) used to assess Millie for autism spectrum disorder, she presented with some symptoms of Asperger's syndrome but did not meet full criteria for it. Some of the behaviors indicating that Millie did not meet criteria for an autism diagnosis were consistent eye contact with the examiner and joint attention on several occasions with the examiner and her mother. Millie responded immediately when her name was called and smiled frequently at the examiner. She engaged in elaborate make-believe play themes both alone and with the examiner. In describing pictures and a story in a picture book, Millie was able to sum up what was happening and often used gestures to illustrate it. She occasionally asked questions about what was going on. She could answer questions in an appropriate way. She talked about being lonely and sad at times because she was teased and wished that she had a brother or sister or friend. She hoped to have a sleepover with one of the girls in the classroom. She also created a very imaginative story with small objects used in the test. There was no unusual intonation, her speech was not slow, jerky, or irregular, and it was very intelligible.
- Speech therapy assessment found that Millie had a pragmatic language disorder, tended to interpret language literally, and missed facial expressions as clues to how to continue with a conversation. She also did not understand sarcasm, humor, or threats. She sometimes kept talking about the same topic. However, she did well on the verbal scales on the *WISC-IV* and read well, with good comprehension.

Observations of Millie at School and Home

From observations of Millie in the classroom and on the playground, it was found that she was keen to make friends and always made every effort to play with her peers at recess and lunch. No aggressive outbursts were observed. However, she was very impulsive and tended to flit from one subject to another when having a conversation. Her topics of conversation tended to be repetitive and immature and not appealing to other children her age. She was found to do some things without thinking or regard for safety. For example, she would sometimes push one of the swings really high without realizing that it would come close to another child. At other times, she would go running down the hallway and bang into someone. The same kind of behavior was noticed at home, and she could not be trusted to cook since she would impulsively turn on the stove or almost get her finger caught in the mixer blades. Academically, the same kind of tendency was found when Millie was intent on completing a piece of work or some craft or art activity, she started instantly with no planning, and as a result things seldom worked out for her. Difficulties with understanding complexity also added to her impulsivity, for she would often hear only one of several instructions.

Millie's moods could shift rapidly from being very high and excited to being quite anxious and tense. This variance was due at times to her diabetes and at other times to perceived rejection or schoolwork that she found difficult. Sometimes she would become upset because a teacher helping her with her work moved away to assist another child, and she seemed to perceive this as rejection. She sometimes put her head on her desk, obviously sad and distressed. It was also noticed, however, that Millie could overcome these feelings and reengage when a child or teacher talked to her and showed interest in how she was feeling or what she was doing. Although aggressive behavior was not observed in the specialized setting, Millie would become angry or frustrated at times, especially if she thought that something was not fair or that she had not been treated in the way expected. At these times, it was somewhat more difficult to calm her down, and it was necessary to help her problem solve for this to happen.

On the other hand, Millie presented as likable and attractive, chatty, and interested in what was going on in other people's lives. She could be a little intrusive sometimes, but at other times her behavior was appropriate, and she showed sincere interest in others and concern and empathy for them. For example, a pet of one of the teachers was ill at one point, and Millie enquired about the pet's condition each morning and showed empathy for the pet and its owner. On a few occasions when she hurt someone's feelings or knew that one of the children was having a hard time, she would make something for them or create a card to cheer them up. This was done without any prompting by Marjorie, though she was supportive of Millie's efforts. See Table 10.3 for a summary of results.

Treatment

Working With the Family

One of the most important goals of Millie's treatment was to help her mother with her sadness and despair and the challenges of dealing with an often ill child with difficult behavior. Having a month when Marjorie knew that she would not be called to pick up Millie from school and did not have to get her at the end of the day gave Marjorie much-needed rest and time to meet with friends whom she had not seen for a long time.

During this time, assessments were completed and the findings interpreted to Marjorie, with suggestions on how to help Millie. Having concrete things to do that made sense to Marjorie gave her a feeling of having control over how Millie behaved. Marjorie was also informed that a diagnosis of nonverbal learning disability fit best with Millie's symptoms and that Millie did not have autism spectrum disorder. The implications were described in detail. For example, Marjorie was informed that Millie's problems in fine and gross motor functioning and reading nonverbal cues explained many of her difficulties socializing with peers. It was also explained that problems with pragmatic language and social communication were impacting her capacity to have friends.

The other important aspect of treatment was to involve Marjorie in some of the interventions, particularly the occupational therapy work on enhancing Millie's life skills and the speech and language intervention. This enabled Marjorie to better understand the supports and strategies that Millie needed and allowed her to have hope for her daughter as she saw some changes happening. The strategies to overcome impulsivity and help Millie problem solve were also described to Marjorie. The home school was also given the strategies (outlined in Table 10.4) to use.

Working With Millie

Specific strategies given to Marjorie and the school to help Millie are described in Table 10.4.

Termination of Treatment

At the end of treatment, there were a number of improvements for both Millie and her mother. However, it was clear that Millie would need ongoing support if she was to maintain a job and become independent enough to live on her own. Marjorie was very motivated for that to happen as she began to rebuild her life by expanding work hours and sometimes going out with friends. The strategies developed for Millie by her home school were very helpful. Teachers in the specialized

Table 10.3 *Summary Findings of Millie's Assessment Results*

Genetic/Biological/Neurological Intrinsic Disorders →	Clusters of Symptoms ↔	Other Contributing Factors
Nonverbal llearning disability ■ Difficulty with psychomotor coordination ■ Problems with nonverbal problem solving ■ Difficulties with understanding the incongruities and humor of others ■ Difficulty using visual information to know where things are in the environment ■ Impairment in social interactions ■ Poor coordination and visual perception	**Social and peer relationship difficulties** ■ Social awkwardness in language and in adapting to novel social situations ■ Rejection and teasing by peers ■ Immature and behavior may be impulsive ■ Talked incessantly about topics that are unsophisticated compared to interests of peers ■ Could not sustain friendships with peers and could go rapidly from being best friend to worst enemy	**Other challenges** ■ Medical problems that began in infancy and have persisted. ■ Lack of social support for family. ■ Maternal anxiety and depression. ■ Frequent changes of schools. ■ Borderline intellectual capacity and learning problems. ■ Trauma from frequent disagreement between her parents and observing her father's heart attack. ■ Eating problems from infancy. ■ Insecure attachment resulting from the many issues outlined above. ■ Poor self-esteem and may be at risk for depression about isolation from peers.
Executive dysfunction disorder/ADHD ■ Difficulty with inhibiting a response and shifting perspective ■ Difficulty with working memory or holding events in mind and working on them ■ Problems with internalizing speech for problem solving, etc. ■ Difficulty with self-regulation of affect and behavior ■ Difficulty with analyzing behavior and creating new flexible responses	**Impulsivity/lack of planning and problem solving** ■ Flitted from one subject to another in talking and in learning ■ Lacked cause-and-effect thinking and understanding ■ Extremely distractible and could go off on tangents ■ Placed herself at risk by her behavior in the neighborhood ■ Had unrealistic goals for what she wanted to have and to do	**Positives/strengths** ■ Friendly, tried hard to connect with people and wants to be accepted. ■ Used language to communicate with others. ■ Attractive child who could relate well if supported to do so. ■ Some areas of strength in learning (e.g., rote memory, vocabulary, reading, handwriting). ■ Could acquire new skills if they were taught and well practiced. ■ Mother's empathy and efforts to understand and support Millie.
Pragmatic language disorder ■ Did not understand sarcasm, humor, and even threats ■ Interpreted language literally ■ Missed facial expressions of others as clues to whether to continue the conversation ■ Did not understand the perspective of others and has difficulty with turn taking in conversation ■ Sometimes kept talking about the same topic	**Perseveration and fixation on certain subjects** ■ Became fixated on certain topics that she talked and thought about incessantly ■ Topics often included things in the family that she was anxious about (e.g., finances, school she will attend) ■ Struggled with trying to understand why peers did not like her despite being given information ■ Did not see the perspective of others or integrate it into her understanding of situations	
Diabetes mellitus ■ Transient episodes of deficiencies or excess blood sugar could affect Millie's behavior and academic functioning ■ Could cause anxiety and tension for Millie and her mother around managing her diet, testing of blood sugar, and stabilizing her blood sugar levels ■ Other emotional issues that are common in children with diabetes mellitus	**Academic problems** ■ Difficulties with mathematics ■ Significant difficulties with copying material from the board ■ Problems with time management ■ Difficulties with abstract reasoning making it hard for her to understand complex material ■ Significant difficulties with focusing and following through with her schoolwork	

Table 10.4 *Behavioral, Emotional, and Social Issues: Suggested Strategies for Millie*

Issue	Reasons for Difficulty	Strengths	Strategies
Difficulties with socialization	■ Difficulty with reading the nonverbal cues of others ■ Problems with pragmatic language and social communication ■ Behavior can be impulsive, might act out without thinking ■ Can misinterpret the intentions and behaviors of others as rejection ■ Can talk about a favorite subject without being aware that it is not of interest to another person ■ Might just be curious and run after something she sees	■ Can be taught how to behave in certain situations and follow through (e.g., ask people questions about themselves) ■ Is a very endearing child who can show interest in and empathy for another person ■ Wants to have friends ■ Is friendly to peers and adults and interested in what is going on with them	■ Due to nonverbal learning disability, need to teach Millie how to engage with other children. ■ This means making out a script for Millie with words to use, how to use gestures with the words, and how close to be to other children. ■ Teach Millie self-talk to think through the steps before she tries to enter a group. ■ Explain the behavior using a combination of pictures, videotaping the interaction and playing it back, and role playing. ■ Have Millie try a behavior and then discuss how the interaction went for her. ■ Practice with Millie what might happen next in an interaction to lessen the novelty of social situations. ■ Praise her when she shows attention to others, compliment them, and shows empathy, as she does at times, and encourage her to keep doing this. ■ Encourage her to think before she acts and be aware of safety issues. ■ Millie was told to inform her mother and the teacher about any bullying so that steps could be taken by the school to prevent it from happening again. ■ After an impulsive episode, teach Millie to problemsolve so that she can avoid acting impulsively next time. 1. Slowing down: Talk about a situation in which she acted impulsively and ask her to stop and think about what happened. 2. Perspective Taking: Ask her how anyone involved in the situation must have felt and thought. 3. Goal setting: Have her think about what she wants to do the next time she is becoming upset. 4. Choosing a solution: Have Millie think about what she will do differently the next time.

Fine and gross motor difficulties	■ Difficulty with gross motor abilities, including difficulty with coordination, spatial relations, and proprioceptive processing ■ Difficulties with oculomotor control, visual perception, visual motor tasks, and crossing the midline ■ Nonverbal reasoning extremely low and showed up in the areas outlined above	■ Keen to join in any gross motor activities such as jumping on the trampoline ■ Enjoys art and craft activities	■ Have a visual timetable on her desk to help Millie focus and deal with transitions. It can use words and pictures. ■ Use the trampoline and drumming activities, which Millie enjoys and which help to calm her down. ■ Support her handwriting with the right kind of pencil grip and have small bursts of activity so that she does not become overloaded. ■ Support her fine motor control through arts and crafts, which Millie enjoys a great deal.
Academic problems	■ Ideas in written essays not well developed or sequenced ■ Math concepts 2 years behind her chronological age ■ Difficulty with more complex instructions and questions ■ Struggles with abstract reasoning and more complex ideas ■ Can be impacted by problems with impulsivity and issues with working memory	■ Has excellent rote learning, reading, spelling, and vocabulary ■ Can acquire new skills when taught and rehearsed enough	■ Weaker subject areas must be supported and coached and independent work monitored. ■ Incentives and rewards for trying hard are important motivators. ■ Add to her word banks of sight words for topics in which she is interested. ■ Teach math concepts using things that Millie is interested in, such as animals and nature. ■ Millie can only remember the first two instructions without repetition, so use questioning to make sure that she has understood the instructions. ■ Use a timer that counts down and rings when an activity should be completed. This depersonalizes the setting of limits, putting it outside the person working with her on a particular task. ■ Teach Millie self-talk by talking her through tasks so that she learns to do them by herself. Use encouraging statements such as "You can do it." This can also enhance her sense of competence.

(continued)

Table 10.4 *Behavioral, Emotional, and Social Issues: Suggested Strategies for Millie (continued)*

Issue	Reasons for Difficulty	Strengths	Strategies
			■ Millie can be helped by using hands-on activities and having visual cues for some activities because she cannot hold information in her mind for long. ■ Give a lead into a difficult activity of something that she likes to do (e.g., finding animals in a book). ■ Provide short, achievable activities that can be done in 15 minutes. ■ Give her small amounts of work with brief breaks. ■ Show empathy and let Millie know that you understand it is hard for her and appreciate it when she does her best. ■ Use private signaling for her to attend (e.g., a tap on the shoulder). ■ Have Millie use the computer, which can give her immediate feedback and be a powerful reward and incentive for her to try hard on a task. ■ Support her with her math skills using visual props and a calculator. ■ Present only one concept at a time and provide frequent repetitions.
Difficulties with pragmatic language and social communication	■ Contributed to by nonverbal learning disability and impulsivity ■ Difficulties with understanding and using more complex language and ideas ■ Problems with auditory processing and working memory, making it difficult to understand the other person ■ Narrative tends to be disorganized and non-sequential ■ Has difficulty with understanding concepts without pictures and other objects to help clarify them ■ Sometimes cannot read the emotional expressions of another person	■ Is very interested in having conversations with others and does not get discouraged because it is difficult for her ■ Can engage in interactive conversations at times	■ Help Millie to come up with ideas for topics of conversation more suitable for her age group. ■ Use word-finding games on a certain topic. ■ Use barrier games to enhance auditory processing in which Millie has to put a counter on a certain person or object in a picture as described by the speech therapist. ■ Extend the topic of a conversation that Millie brings up to add richness beyond "who," "what," and "where" so that what is said flows better. ■ Use role playing expressing a certain emotion and trying to match the other person's emotion. Use a mirror for Millie to see her own facial expression and match it to that of the other person. ■ Act out the interactions using puppets or a miniature doll family or a variety of animals or children. Demonstrate the space to be left and what to say. ■ Use groups of children to do this.

Problems with impulsivity	▪ Difficulty with using small emotions to know that she is becoming emotionally overwhelmed ▪ Nervous system hyperaroused frequently, hypervigilant, both of which can contribute to anxiety and anger ▪ Has sensory integration difficulties and is hypersensitive to some stimulations ▪ Functioning at a very young age emotionally and socially	▪ Has some strengths that can be used to encourage planning and problem solving ▪ Can acquire new skills if taught and rehearsed enough ▪ At times will talk about being worried, giving an opportunity to support her ▪ Would like to be more independent	▪ After an impulsive episode, teach Millie to problem solve to avoid acting impulsively the next time. 1. Slowing down: Talk about a situation in which she acted impulsively and ask her to think about what happened. 2. Perspective taking: Ask her how anyone involved in the situation must have felt and thought. 3. Goal setting: Have her think about what she wants to do the next time she is becoming upset. 4. Choosing a solution: Have Millie think about what she will do differently the next time. ▪ Suggest other topics that she can think about if her thinking becomes rigid or her behavior repetitious. ▪ Remind Millie of any rule that she is disregarding when she behaves impulsively and explain how other children might view her behavior. ▪ Improve planning and organizing for Millie, having her break a task into small chunks, and reward her as she completes a section by the deadline. Prompt her to go on to the next one. ▪ Make a work plan and help Millie to follow it by providing cues to stay on task and check how she is doing. Fade out the support as she becomes more able to do it. ▪ If schoolwork is hard for her, let her know that you understand and will support her to complete it. ▪ Decide on a disinhibited behavior that needs to be eliminated or replaced, such as talking out in class or crossing the road without looking. ▪ Talk about the behavior that needs to be changed and why it seems to be happening, involving Millie in the discussion. Make it clear why the behavior has to be changed. ▪ Select a replacement skill to meet the same needs for her. ▪ Walk through the new skill and have Millie practice it enough so that she can be successful with it. ▪ Reward her for ignoring the disinhibited response and using a new one. ▪ Consider the use of medication and treatment for symptoms of past trauma.

(continued)

Table 10.4 *Behavioral, Emotional, and Social Issues: Suggested Strategies for Millie (continued)*

Issue	Reasons for Difficulty	Strengths	Strategies
Difficulties with life skills and protective behaviors	▪ Impulsive and naive behavior, placing her at risk as she enters adolescence ▪ Cannot judge if a situation is dangerous ▪ Needs supervision all the time, unaware at times of what is going on around her	▪ Very cooperative with any treatment offered and often asks for information about the world	▪ Give Millie information on planning with money and going to the bank to open a bank account. ▪ Teach her about going on public transportation, following a route on a map, buying a ticket, and figuring out where to get off and what to do if she misses the stop. ▪ Have her practice shopping, enquiring about a product, and paying for an item. ▪ Have her practice asking for directions and reading a map and signs ▪ Safety proof Millie and warn her about not speaking to strangers and whom she can approach for help. ▪ Teach her about areas where she can go and those to avoid and how to phone 911 or contact the police if she is in trouble. ▪ Go to the cinema with her and discuss the movies she should and should not see.
Enhancing self-esteem and sense of self	▪ Because of several factors, has a sense that she cannot do a number of things ▪ Often feels anxious and sad and that nobody likes her ▪ At times, people's responses to her trigger feelings and memories of loss and other negative experiences	▪ Responds well when her achievements are noticed ▪ Anxiety suggests that she has concerns about herself and others	▪ Give Millie a special job in the classroom doing something at which she can excel. ▪ Use positive labels such as "helpful" and "busy." ▪ Acknowledge that she has a difficulty and then praise her for doing something well. ▪ Give Millie a sense of belonging in the classroom by supporting her to participate in activities as much as possible. ▪ Use her strengths so that she has experiences of success that will help to build her sense of competence. ▪ When Millie is feeling discouraged and says that she cannot do anything, remind her of things that she has done really well recently. ▪ Give her rewards and acknowledgements for small successes (e.g., only blurting out twice before recess). ▪ Millie can see rejection in body movements, tones of voice, or facial expressions, so it is important to review what happened and let her know what really occurred.

			■ It will be very hard for her to develop a new view of herself, so it is critical to notice small gains. ■ Try to have Millie paired with a very positive child for some activities as she will be more likely to experience success and be supported to be cooperative. ■ Realize that it might take several months for Millie to develop a more positive view of herself
Supporting Millie with her diabetes	■ Can affect her moods ■ Makes Millie and her mother very anxious if sugar levels are low ■ Marjorie anxious about how to handle the disorder in the future	■ Excellent support system available for Marjorie and will continue to be available for Millie through adolescence ■ Several services available through the hospital for Millie and her mother	■ Regular monitoring of blood sugar levels was established. ■ Millie was trained to handle as much of her care as possible. ■ She attended groups and a camp for children with diabetes. ■ The school nurse met with Millie regularly to help her with her anxiety and blood sugar levels.
Dealing with perseveration around certain activities and constant questioning	■ Might be anxious and want reassurance and "contact" with someone ■ Narrow range of interests familiar to her, gives her a sense of control, can be calming	■ Favorite subjects can be used to help her learn a number of school subjects ■ Can sometimes use questions to make contact with other people	■ Sometimes a short time-out, not done as a punishment, can help Millie to shift gears and change the topic or activity. ■ At times, if she is perseverating on asking a particular question, respond to the emotion (e.g., when she keeps asking about airplanes, suggest that she worries about them crashing). Reassure her that the planes will be all right. ■ Play out some of the things that she talks about and give the play scene a good outcome. ■ Try to enlarge her areas of interest by using a variety of strategies and supporting her in finding out about them. ■ When Millie asks a question, answer it quickly and then immediately ask her something that takes it in a somewhat different direction. ■ See suggestions for closing the circle of communication in the main report.

school explained the strategies to the teacher in the home school. Also, her aide came into the specialized classroom to learn the strategies. Millie's academic performance and interactions with peers significantly improved as a result. One big challenge was that it was difficult for Millie to generalize what she learned in one setting to another, so the strategies had to be retaught in different settings. However, she continued to be a delightful child, gained in maturity, and was well liked by teachers and people in the community. There were no more aggressive outbursts, though Millie could still become dysregulated at times. Follow-up was carried out by a psychiatrist in the community who saw Millie alone to monitor her medication and tendency to become depressed. She also saw Marjorie occasionally and was available to see Millie more frequently if she did become depressed. However, with the new strategies, Millie was feeling more confident and less out of control, and her anxiety and sadness seemed to have decreased. She was also attending a social skills group in which many of the skills that she needed were taught, and she had joined the Girl Guides, in which she had earned a badge for cooking and art and had made a friend.

Case Study 3: Michael

Reasons for Referral and Developmental and Family History

Seven-year-old Michael was referred for assessment and treatment by a psychiatrist who was seeing him in private practice but thought that he needed to be managed by an agency that could provide more in-depth assessment and treatment. At the time of referral, Michael was described as having chronic disturbances of emotion and behavior. They included selective mutism, particularly in school; school refusal (with Michael having been at home for 2 months at the time of referral); difficult behavior at home and school that could include aggression; and most significant, severe anxiety. Michael was easily overwhelmed outside the home and avoided social interactions with peers. He found it very difficult to establish relationships with adults and children and to trust others. He also worried about losing his mother. His anxiety included separation anxiety, beginning at a young age, and social anxiety. At times, when he found schoolwork difficult, he would withdraw, become almost catatonic, and pretend to fall asleep, as if to avoid further contact.

Joanna's pregnancy with Michael was stressful because it was unplanned, and her partner was angry because he wanted only one child. There were issues in the ultrasound early in the pregnancy, but no abnormalities were found in the amniocentesis. Other incidents during the pregnancy included a fall (with no apparent injury) and at 7 months surgery for appendicitis with a postoperative wound infection. Michael was born at 40 weeks following a short labor with no complications. Joanna suffered from severe postnatal depression. Michael was a difficult baby, far different from his older brother, Sam, whom she described as an "easy" baby. Michael would often take 2 hours to fall asleep, and Joanna thought that she was unable to soothe him. She saw him as very difficult from an early age and wanting things done a certain way that she often had difficulty understanding. When he was 4 months old, Joanna had surgery because of tearing during delivery. She found it difficult to form an attachment or bond with him. When Michael was 2 years old, Joanna's partner left saying that he did not want and resented Michael. This left her devastated and made it even more difficult for her to interact with and attach to Michael.

Michael became anxious and increasingly difficult, and Joanna described everything as being a battle. He refused to get out of the car and walk to shops. He would flop on the floor and refuse to move, embarrassing Joanna, who sensed that everyone was looking at her and thinking what a terrible mother she was. Sometimes, in desperation, she would get into the car, start the engine, and threaten to leave him there. Because she could not drive away, Michael would win the battle and increase her frustration with and anger toward him. At this time, Joanna withdrew even more from Michael and spent more time with Sam, his older brother. Michael's behavioral problems and oppositionality increased, and Joanna became more depressed, wishing at times that she could "walk out and leave him."

Developmental history was relatively unremarkable. Michael walked a little late, at 15 months, with no speech or language issues identified. However, at 2 years of age, he began to refuse to talk outside the home. At about this time, Joanna, with Michael in the car, was first on the scene of a horrendous accident, but she did not believe that Michael saw much and did not seem upset by it. It was very upsetting for her.

From 1 to 4 years of age, Michael attended a child care center twice a week, while Joanna returned to work as a legal secretary. He cried at first when she left him but soon settled. He participated well in the routines and activities, and no aggressive behavior was identified. He did not want to interact with the other children, however, and he could be strong willed and hard to direct at times. Michael was also avoidant of staff and preferred to manage himself if he was upset and would not accept comforting by a staff member. At times, he showed selective mutism or refused to talk to anyone, and this was handled by the child care staff ignoring him.

In Kindergarten and Pre-Primary, this behavior increased, and a number of behavioral strategies (e.g., a behavior chart, 1, 2, 3, Magic, and time-out chair) and an educational assistant for 2 days a week were introduced. Michael continued to want to play alone. He responded well to his teacher, a male, the next year and developed a trusting relationship with him and still talks about him. However, the teacher left in the middle of the year due to illness, and Michael was devastated. He began to misbehave with relief teachers, and his behavior became more controlling and erratic. He was physically and verbally aggressive with staff and other children. This behavior continued in Year 1, and his new teacher adopted an authoritarian approach to discipline that did not work. Joanna was called every second day to pick him up, and in February an expulsion letter was sent home. After Michael returned to school, his anxiety, withdrawal, and stubbornness escalated, and an aggressive outburst in which he hurt another child resulted in a suspension until his management could be reviewed. When his favorite male teacher left on long service leave, Michael was very upset, and an escalation in his negative behavior occurred.

Medically, Michael was healthy. However, his gross motor skills were very delayed, he was clumsy, and had poor muscle tone, balance, and strength and endurance. Various medications, including Tegretol, Tofranil, fluoxetine, and clonidine (125 mg), were tried. The clonidine helped Michael to be less reactive and more able to self-regulate. The only identified disorders in the extended family were Joanna's depression and anxiety, and the biological father's brother (Michael's uncle) had severe Asperger's syndrome.

As was evident at referral, there had been ongoing concerns about Michael since he was 2 years of age. However, since that time, assessment and treatment had been sporadic, sometimes because Joanna had not followed through with treatment. There seemed to have been an emphasis on trying to find out which disorder Michael had without providing treatment that was convenient and acceptable to Joanna. Past assessments had ruled out autism spectrum disorder, and an electroencephalogram (EEG) had been normal. Joanna had attended a parenting group and had participated in 16 weeks of in-home mother–child play sessions. She also attended a parenting group on childhood anxiety.

Referral and Early Strategies

It was agreed that teachers at the specialized school would be available to help with information from the assessments and developing strategies to support Michael. Joanna was keen to learn the best ways to interact with him and was fully supportive of a full assessment. She also requested any ideas that she and the school could use to overcome his issues, particularly noncompliance and poor peer relationships. A multidisciplinary team—clinical psychologist, speech and language pathologist, and occupational therapist—began an assessment that was difficult to complete because Michael could be very challenging. The assessment was integrated with treatment provided by the occupational therapist and speech and language pathologist. Joanna felt discouraged because she had attended a number of parenting sessions but did not think that many gains had been made either in her relationship with Michael or in his behavior or emotional state. However, she was very supportive of what the school was doing and available as much as possible to attend appointments. She did not expect a cure but believed that, if she could learn to adjust her parenting to help Michael manage better, the family could move ahead.

Establishing the Goals and Process of Treatment

There was some splitting between Joanna and her two boys, with a tendency for her to feel much less connected to Michael and consequently far less confident disciplining him. With Sam, she felt confident setting limits and following through with them in a way that she could not do with Michael. She believed that this was because of his more difficult and stubborn temperament. She also admitted that she often threatened consequences for his behavior but in almost all cases gave up and did not follow through.

A case coordinator who was a very experienced psychologist was assigned to the family to work with Joanna to be more firm and consistent with discipline and more available emotionally to Michael. This had been difficult due to the circumstances of the conception, pregnancy, and early infancy. Joanna was dismissive of Michael, struggled to deal with his needs, and at times rejected him.

Treatment occurred over a year and included the following:

- The home school was supported as required to gradually reintegrate Michael. This included strategies for the educational assistant and teacher to use. They were based on assessment results, including observations of what eventually worked for him.
- Assessment of and treatment for speech and language difficulties, motor development, sensory processing, cognition, social ability, perspective taking, and academic level were provided. Consultation also took place with Michael's pediatrician and psychiatrist.
- Home visits included both family system work and support for Joanna's parenting.
- Joanna was supported to find resources in her local community as she was very social and had lost contacts and friends since her partner left and the problems with Michael began to escalate and affect her life significantly.

Assessment of Michael

Assessment included direct testing of Michael by various disciplines and multiple observations of him at school on different days and at home with his mother and brother. Various questionnaires were completed by his mother and teacher to screen for issues with executive functioning, anxiety and depression, externalizing behaviors such as noncompliance and conduct problems, and capacity for perspective taking and empathy. These questionnaires included the following: *Child Behavior Checklist* (*Parent and Teacher*) (*CBCL;* Achenbach, 2000, *Child Depression Inventory* (*CDI;* Kovacs & MHS Staff, 2003), *Revised Children's Manifest Anxiety Scale* (*RCMAS;* Reynolds & Richmond, 2003), *Trauma Symptom Checklist for Young Children* (*TSCYC;* Briere & PAR Staff, 1996), and *Conners-3* (Conners, 2008).

Results From the Questionnaires

Michael had high scores on the internalizing scales on the *CBCL* and for depression on the *CDI* and for anxiety on the *RCMAS*. He also had high scores for aggression on the *CBCL* completed by the school. He did not show high scores, however, on the *TSCYC*, probably because the trauma that he had experienced due to his mother's depression did not show up in symptoms identified as PTSD.

Results From the Assessment of Michael

Overall conclusions were that Michael was highly anxious and experienced extreme physiological arousal when he felt threatened by a task that he found difficult or did not want to do. He would become physically sick if pushed beyond a certain threshold and withdraw and shut down. He sometimes turned white and shook, and his eyes would widen as if in a fear reaction. This was not dissociative but appeared to be trauma related. Michael was aware of what was being said during that time and occasionally interjected with relevant comments. It was believed that his symptoms were caused by his anxiety about abandonment, leading to a need to be in control of the interaction.

It was noticed that Joanna, in her interactions with him, was very preoccupied with him but equally anxious, finding it difficult to take control of the situation. Diagnoses were made of generalized anxiety disorder and motor skills disorder, with learning problems, including a moderate language disorder. In the various assessments, it took considerable time to develop rapport and for Michael to concentrate and continue trying until he completed the tests. Results are listed below.

- On the *Wechsler Intelligence Scale for Children,* 4th edition (*WISC-IV*) or test of *cognitive ability,* Michael obtained a full-scale IQ in the average range at the 58th percentile. He did slightly better on perceptual reasoning than verbal comprehension, and his lowest scores were for working memory, but all were in the average to above average range of functioning. These results were surprising given his difficulties with a number of academic areas and suggested that his behavioral and emotional problems might have contributed to his results on the academic tests.
- On *academic testing,* Michael was 2 years behind his chronological age for reading (preliteracy level), spelling, writing, and math. These results were probably affected by frequent school absences, anxiety, and refusal to try activities. Handwriting was hard work for Michael and very tiring, but he had legible writing and correct spacing of words but difficulty with letter size and line spacing.
- The *speech assessment* found that Michael's expressive language scores were all below average. This assessment included vocabulary, formulating sentences, and word structure. Michael also had difficulty with receptive vocabulary, in the low-average range. He had severe problems with narrative skills and needed a significant level of scaffolding to engage in spontaneous conversation. He was assessed as having a moderate language disorder, and it was predicted that, because there would be more linguistic demand and complexity in the curriculum, it would be difficult for him. It was also believed that these difficulties contributed to his selective mutism.
- It was not possible to complete *projective tests* with Michael because he did not want to describe pictures or draw them himself. However, he did enjoy playing interactive games and could gradually take the part of a puppet called Scaredy Cat who eventually became bold and was able to "control the universe."
- Michael *lacked a theory of mind* and failed testing of it, including for the Sally–Anne experiment and the theory of mind subtest on the *NEPSY-II*.
- The *occupational therapy assessment* found that Michael had significant difficulties with visual tracking. He could converge his eyes but struggled with diverging them, so he had difficulty with visual accommodation, particularly at a distance. He also had difficulties isolating his head movements from his eyes. These problems might have contributed to Michael becoming tired and avoidant after visually intensive activities. He also had difficulty with proprioception or knowing the position of his body in space, which meant that he could be clumsy at times and had problems using his body to interact efficiently with his environment. He also had difficulty with motor planning, bilateral integration, and postural tone. Having low postural tone meant that he was floppy at times, and tasks such as handwriting could be difficult, leaving him fatigued at the end of the day. Michael did much better with fine motor tasks than gross motor tasks, such as running speed and agility and upper limb strength and coordination, which were below average. He also had problems crossing the midline, which resulted in greater effort and slower pace. Overall, on visual perceptual and visual motor integration skills, Michael performed well, and they were a relative strength for him. He had significant problems with and sensitivities to auditory, visual, vestibular, and touch sensations. He did not like messy activities and hated trips to the hairdresser and dentist.

Observations of Michael at School and Home

Michael was observed in his home school before he was expelled for an aggressive outburst. He obviously had great difficulty with schoolwork, refusing to do worksheets and anything requiring writing. When things became too difficult, he sat on the floor under his desk and refused to come out until the teacher stopped asking him to do the work. At one point, he was immobile under the desk and seemed to have fallen asleep. He also refused to talk to children and teachers or had symptoms of selective mutism. When it was time to go outside, he lined up with the other children but refused to engage them with eye contact or conversation. He did not become aggressive but presented as more withdrawn and anxious.

Initially, Michael presented in assessment sessions with the speech and language pathologist and occupational therapist as having problems separating from his mother. He was shy, would not talk, and was withdrawn, with minimal eye contact. He was also observed to avoid work that he perceived as challenging by hiding his eyes and pretending to fall asleep. He needed a lot of prompting and did not respond to rewards such as sweets or prizes but did love playing games with adults, especially when he brought a familiar game with him that he could play better than the examiners. He also wanted to control the assessment sessions and the teachers in the classroom. However, as testing and intervention proceeded, making spontaneous eye contact, being willing to attempt tests, problem solving, and relinquishing control all improved. See Table 10.5 for a summary of results.

Treatment

Working With the Family

It was difficult to work with Joanna to find appropriate strategies to support Michael, not because she was not open to trying suggestions, but because it took many sessions to identify successful ways to work with him, and the approaches that were successful changed significantly over time as he began to improve. It was important to explain to Joanna that, though Michael had average overall cognitive ability, he was very compromised by his level of anxiety, speech and language problems, and significant problems with fine and gross motor development. This explanation helped her to understand why he acted the way he did. It was important to support Joanna to choose rules that she could enforce consistently, such as not hurting others. However, she needed to avoid threatening a consequence that she could not follow through with or try to enforce rules that were not important and which led to Michael becoming oppositional and/or withdrawn.

The steps of the intervention are described next:

- At first, Joanna was helped to problem solve which limits were essential and which were not important and could be ignored if Michael was having a difficult day. Specifically, some rules were necessary to keep Michael safe, such as not being out alone at night. Others were about moral issues important to Joanna, such as nobody in the family being hurt emotionally or physically and not lying. Routines were also important for Michael to feel safe and secure. Helping Joanna to distinguish between when to enforce a behavior and when to let it go was helpful for her. She was encouraged to use the same rules and consequences for Sam. Sessions were also provided to support a new relationship between the boys and between Joanna and them.
- Joanna was helped to provide Michael with strategies to calm himself down when he was becoming anxious, such as deep breathing, thought stopping, and thinking positive thoughts. She herself found these approaches useful.
- Joanna wanted to have a better relationship with Michael as there were periods when she became very frustrated and angry with him or gave up when he withdrew from her. By helping her to be more firm, to have a consistent routine, and always to follow up with consequences, her anxiety, and in turn Michael's, were reduced.
- Joanna was helped to attune more to Michael rather than give up and become anxious herself. This was done through role playing and interactional guidance using videotape viewing.
- She also watched the sessions provided by the speech and language pathologist and occupational therapist and learned strategies to use with Michael.

Working With Michael

The specific strategies used for Michael are outlined in Table 10.6.

Table 10.5 *Findings of Michael's Assessment*

Genetic/Biological/Neurological Intrinsic Disorders →	Clusters of Symptoms ↔	Other Contributing Factors
Generalized anxiety disorder ▪ Some separation anxiety as a preschooler ▪ Became highly anxious when could not do something or was overwhelmed with sensory input ▪ School refusal and selective mutism ▪ Withdrew and became frozen and unable to function ▪ Became controlling in order to overcome anxiety **Motor skills disorder/sensory processing problems** ▪ Difficulty with motor planning and proprioceptive processing ▪ Difficulty with balance and postural control ▪ Problems with gross motor functioning ▪ Lack of strength in upper limbs ▪ Sensory sensitivities with touch, smell, and sound ▪ Issues with sensory processing and integration **Moderate language disorder** ▪ Expressive language well below average ▪ Problems with vocabulary, formulating sentences, and word structure ▪ Receptive vocabulary in the below-average range ▪ Problems with narrative skills or with telling a story ▪ Needed scaffolding to engage in a conversation ▪ As there was more linguistic demand and need for complexity with school curriculum, Michael increasingly struggled	**Social and peer relationship difficulties** ▪ Not interested in interacting with peers ▪ Ignored other children and was isolated from them ▪ Did not understand the perspective of others and had difficulty with turn taking in conversation ▪ Did not respond to cues from communication partner ▪ Pushed any children away who wanted to interact with him **Impulsivity and aggression** ▪ Could be physically aggressive at times toward otherchildren or adults if became overwhelmed ▪ Showed difficulty with controlling emotions, including anxiety and frustration ▪ Very controlling and used it to avoid doing things and to reduce anxiety **Low self-esteem and poor sense of self** ▪ Struggled with feelings of rejection ▪ Believed he could not do things and became overwhelmed and gave up trying ▪ Avoided trying, so did not experience success making things happen or completing things he set out to do ▪ Unfavorable comparison with his brother who was described as having an "easy" personality **Learning and academic problems** ▪ Significant difficulties with writing and with the content of his written work ▪ Problems with punctuation and running his ideas into each other ▪ Work not well organized or sequenced ▪ Needed ongoing teacher modeling, prompting, and visual aids to be able to complete his work ▪ Some delays in math and reluctant to complete problems and seemed overwhelmed by them	**Other challenges** ▪ Maternal depression and mental health issues earlier in Michael's life. ▪ Insecure attachment resulting from Michael's early difficult behavior and his challenging temperament. ▪ Mother was anxious and believed she could not control Michael. ▪ Helplessness and frightened behavior of mother exaggerated Michael's anxiety, control, and low self-esteem. ▪ Possibly experienced some small "t" trauma because of the situation when he was born and his mother's difficulty in responding to him. **Positives/strengths** ▪ Average intelligence and above average intelligence in one area. ▪ Responded to reinforcement at times. ▪ Had some areas of vulnerability that could be used to increase his capacity for empathy. ▪ Average to above average speech and language development. ▪ Some capacity for reciprocal social communication when not overwhelmed. ▪ Mother's capacity to understand Michael and to follow through with suggestions of ways to work with him. ▪ Mother provided a stable home and took time off to be able to attend all appointments.

Table 10.6 *Behavioral, Emotional, and Social Issues: Suggested Strategies for Michael*

Issue	Reasons for Difficulty	Strengths	Strategies
Generalized anxiety/selective mutism/school refusal	▪ Behavioral inhibition to novelty, leading to withdrawal from unfamiliar people and situations ▪ Possible genetic vulnerability to becoming anxious and distressed in stressful situations ▪ Difficulties with early mother–infant interactions in terms of being a difficult baby to soothe and mother having postnatal depression ▪ Became overwhelmed because there were so many tasks with which he struggled	▪ Eventually possible to calm down his anxiety and have him enjoy some fun time with the therapist ▪ Did see transfer from therapy sessions to the classroom	▪ Provide opportunities in a number of areas of development where Michael can experience success. ▪ Use activities that Michael enjoys, and encourage him to try them for a few minutes. ▪ Give him opportunities for gradual reintroduction into school ▪ Discuss transitions and changes to schedules ahead of time so that Michael is prepared for them. ▪ Design a visual timetable of upcoming activities for therapy sessions so that he knows what to expect and to work through what needs to be done. ▪ Use a melodic, soothing tone while giving him instructions ▪ Write a therapeutic story with Michael about what makes him anxious and how he can overcome it. ▪ Teach him to use self-talk to get through a difficult situation. ▪ Also teach him deep breathing to calm himself down when he feels himself becoming anxious and upset. ▪ Use child-focused cognitive behavioral therapy such as the Coping Cat program for children with anxiety. ▪ Teach him to calm himself down using metaphors of animals and relaxation of muscles. ▪ Use soothing, guided imagery for Michael to listen to before falling asleep.

Motor skills and sensory processing	▪ Difficulty with visual tracking ▪ Low postural tone, making handwriting difficult ▪ Running speed and agility, upper limb strength, and coordination below average ▪ Many sensory sensitivities	▪ Fine motor, visual perception, and visual integration skills strong	▪ Give Michael visual cues to help him manage his environment. ▪ Help him to develop basic skills, such as building strength by running even a short distance. ▪ Have him engage in regular exercises, such as climbing, swinging, and riding a bike, to encourage core muscle strength and improve postural muscle tone. ▪ Use graded tasks, such as starting with a larger ball and then moving to smaller balls for catching and starting with targets that are close and gradually moving them further away. ▪ Support practice with handwriting by providing the right kind of pencil grip and having small bursts of activity so that Michael does not become overloaded. ▪ Provide a sensory diet in the school so that he can tolerate it better, including a fiddle box and the Alert program.
Language disorder	▪ Expressive language well below average ▪ Problems with vocabulary, formulating sentences, and word structure ▪ Receptive language below average ▪ Problems with narrative skills ▪ Selective mutism, so not able to practice any language skills that he has	▪ Receptive language is stronger than expressive language and in the average range ▪ Mother committed to following through with suggestions to support his language development	▪ Work with Michael in a group of three students with language impairments. One child is very social and able to get Michael interacting and using language. ▪ Use puppets, for Michael seems to find it easier to use words through a puppet and especially likes being a shy puppet. ▪ Encourage language in a small social skills group that Michael attends at the school. ▪ Build up a word bank of animals that Michael saw at the farm school and of wild animals not at the farm. Also discuss words associated with the animals, what they like to do, and whether the animal is tame or wild. ▪ Encourage Michael to tell a story or create a narrative with drawings about an animal that he likes. ▪ Build up vocabulary around a story about a cat that is scared all the time but becomes brave one day when it helps children to escape from a fire during the night. ▪ As his reading improves, he is able to read a story aloud in the classroom; although very difficult for him at first, he is proud to get through it.

(*continued*)

Table 10.6 *Behavioral, Emotional, and Social Issues: Suggested Strategies for Michael (continued)*

Issue	Reasons for Difficulty	Strengths	Strategies
Difficulties with socialization and peer relationships	▪ Does not show interest in interacting with adults or children ▪ Very shy and inhibited about new situations and people ▪ Language and motor issues make it challenging for Michael to interact with other children ▪ Lacks a theory of mind and does not think past his own view of the world	▪ Can be taught how to behave in certain situations and follow through (e.g., ask people questions about themselves) ▪ Enjoys playing games with adults when they are things that he likes to do	▪ Michael enjoys games with the therapist once he becomes familiar with them. Adults need to be enthusiastic and encourage him to respond in a similar way. ▪ Work with him in a group of three children to teach social skills; each child receives positive feedback from the other children. ▪ Teach him self-talk to calm himself down before he speaks or plays with another child. ▪ Explain the behavior using pictures, videotaping the interaction and playing it back, and role playing. ▪ Return to basic levels of turn taking with Michael. ▪ Play games that are repetitive and fun, such as those in Theraplay. ▪ Practice with Michael what might happen next in an interaction to lessen the novelty of social situations. ▪ Teach him perspective taking and understanding other people with a great deal of scaffolding. ▪ Practice joint attention and social turn taking with him. ▪ Use "social autopsies" after Michael has a meltdown, becomes anxious and withdrawn, or acts aggressively; help him to review the situation and come up with alternative ways to behave. ▪ Help him to respond to children who might be encouraging him to join a group. ▪ Because Michael does not want to participate with peers, enlist an older child in the school to support him and involve him in games and how to enter a group.

Problems with impulsivity and aggression	■ Difficulty with using small emotions to know that he is becoming emotionally overwhelmed ■ Nervous system is frequently hyperaroused, which contributes to his anxiety and aggression at times ■ Sensory-integration difficulties, hypersensitive to some stimulation ■ Functioning at a very young age emotionally and socially ■ Very controlling and avoids doing things and following rules and routines	■ Some areas of academic strength that can be used to encourage planning and problem solving ■ Can acquire new skills if taught and rehearsed enough ■ Can engage in topics that interest him	■ After an impulsive episode, problem-solve to help Michael avoid acting impulsively the next time. ■ Discuss a situation in which he acted impulsively and ask him to stop and think about what happened. ■ Ask him how anyone else involved in the situation must have felt and thought (i.e., perspective taking). ■ Have him think about what he wants to do the next time he is becoming upset. ■ Remind Michael of any rule that he is disregarding when he behaves impulsively and explain how other children might view his behavior. ■ Improve planning and organizing by having him break a task into small chunks and reward him as he completes a section by the deadline. Prompt him to go on to the next section. ■ If schoolwork is hard for him, let him know that you understand and will support him to complete it. ■ Talk about the behavior that needs to be changed; involve Michael in the discussion if possible. Make it clear to him why the behavior has to be changed. ■ Reward him when he ignores the disinhibited response and uses a new one. ■ Consider using medication. ■ If Michael is becoming upset, encourage him to sit on a bean bag chair in the classroom. ■ Give him a card to keep in his pocket that has visual cues (words and pictures) that he can use to calm himself down or go through the steps of problem solving.

(*continued*)

Table 10.6 *Behavioral, Emotional, and Social Issues: Suggested Strategies for Michael (continued)*

Issue	Reasons for Difficulty	Strengths	Strategies
Enhancing self-esteem and sense of self	▪ Struggles with feelings of rejection ▪ Because of several difficulties, has a sense that he cannot do anything and refuses to try ▪ Avoids trying things, so ends up not having experiences of success or competence ▪ Unfavorable comparison with his brother, who is talked about as being a cooperative child	▪ Responds well when achievements are noticed ▪ Enjoys the attention of and activities engaged in with therapists	▪ Acknowledge that Michael has a difficulty and then praise him for doing something that he does well. ▪ As he is reintegrated into his home school, give him a sense of belonging in the classroom by supporting him to participate in activities as much as possible. ▪ Challenge him just enough so that he can experience some success with gross motor activities and narrative skills. ▪ When Michael is feeling very discouraged and says that he cannot do anything, remind him of things that he has done really well recently. ▪ He does not respond well to receiving rewards and praise but does to getting special time with therapists. ▪ Remember that Michael can be triggered easily by his sensory sensitivities. ▪ He can perceive rejection in body movements, tones of voice, or facial expressions, so review what happened and let him know what really occurred. ▪ It will be hard for Michael to develop a new positive view of himself and might take him several months, so make note of very small gains. ▪ He makes most gains and learns best when engaged in play; use humor and adult attention to help him persevere with tasks.

Academic problems	■ Significant difficulties with writing and the content of written work ■ Problems with punctuation and running ideas into each other ■ Work not well organized or sequenced ■ Difficulty with more complex instructions and questions ■ Struggles with abstract reasoning and complex ideas ■ Some delays in math, reluctant to complete problems, seems overwhelmed by them	■ Has average overall intelligence and some capacity for abstract reasoning, though it is just below average ■ Can acquire new skills when taught and rehearsed enough	■ Weaker subject areas must be supported and independent work monitored. ■ Fun time with adults is an important motivator for Michael. ■ He finds a word bank helpful when learning spelling and for reading and writing activities. ■ Teach math concepts using things that Michael is interested in, such as animals and nature. ■ Needs ongoing teacher modeling, prompting, and visual aids to complete work. ■ Provide as many visual cues as possible and allow extra time to introduce new tasks. A visual schedule on the desk can be helpful for Michael. ■ Use story boards and videos and photographs demonstrating the activity. ■ Teach Michael self-talk by talking him through tasks so that he learns to do it by himself. Use encouraging statements such as "You can do it." This can also enhance his sense of competence. ■ He can be helped by using hands-on activities and having visual cues for some activities as he cannot hold information in his mind for long. ■ Give a lead into a difficult activity of something that he likes to do (e.g., finding animals in a book). ■ Provide short, achievable activities that can be done in 15 minutes and let Michael have time with an adult to talk about the task. ■ Give him small amounts of work with brief breaks. ■ Prompt him to make sure that he listens to all instructions given in the classroom. ■ Provide scaffolding to help Michael retell a narrative.

(*continued*)

Table 10.6 *Behavioral, Emotional, and Social Issues: Suggested Strategies for Michael (continued)*

Issue	Reasons for Difficulty	Strengths	Strategies
Sensory integration and hypersensitivity issues	▪ Has a number of sensory sensitivities and anxiety, which contribute to his difficulties in school ▪ Seems to have a hypersensitive nervous system that might contribute to his difficulties ▪ Difficulties with transitions and changes in schedule ▪ Problems with integrating information from various types of stimulation	▪ Fine motor skills strong ▪ Can cope with noise or touch if he initiates it and has some control over it	▪ Have a visual timetable on his desk incorporating small pictures that can be referred to frequently so that he is aware of his schedule; it will help to contain his difficulties with transition. ▪ Provide individual support for handwriting and continue with occupational therapy sessions around this area of difficulty. ▪ Provide a place in the classroom for Michael to retreat to if he finds himself becoming overwhelmed. A bean bag chair can be used by any of the children in the classroom. ▪ Jumping on a trampoline or drumming can calm Michael down at different times of the day. ▪ Consider having Michael use a computer when writing is required and for other activities as doing so can give him immediate rewards. ▪ Provide him with a fiddle box or a doodling pad to keep his hands busy.

Termination of Treatment

Michael and his family were involved in treatment for about 9 months, during which time he was reintegrated successfully into his home school and attended for some months without incident. However, he had not made a friend up to that time but could participate with other children in group activities; that had not been possible before. He was also interacting more with other children in the extended family. His schoolwork improved dramatically, and he began to catch up with his grade level in some subjects. Also, with medication, Michael was less anxious and less resistant to attending school. He also spoke to others, albeit infrequently. It was suggested that as he got older he would benefit from more cognitive-behavioral therapy (CBT) to learn more strategies to overcome his anxiety and prevent him from becoming depressed. Michael also continued seeing a psychiatrist in the community whom he liked seeing and who provided some continuity over time for the family.

CONCLUSION

Treatment of multichallenged children needs to be intensive and adapted to their needs in various functional areas. It also needs to involve the environment around the child, particularly family and school contexts. Even with these kinds of treatment approaches, children often continue to have challenges in managing their emotions and behaviors. However, with enough focused and intense strategies, particularly when children become more able to manage them on their own, they can become independent and have fulfilling lives. Jonathan was able to maintain his improvements and continued to do much better at home and in school. His parents were happy with the changes and the improvements in their relationship and the family. Millie, to her delight, had a friend whom Marjorie really liked, and she was able to engage in some activities outside the home with her friend. With her strength in verbal areas, Millie was starting to consider employment options and helping out at the local news agency, where she was well liked and reliable. Marjorie was feeling much better, had returned to work, and was seeing friends more often. Michael continued to struggle with anxiety at times but was able to manage school and did not have any more aggressive outbursts. Joanna reported that at times she forgot how difficult things had been, and she was more relaxed and believed that, with the boys getting on much better together, they were now more of a family and could enjoy activities together.

In addition to this anecdotal evidence, in a recent evaluation of a program using this kind of model, not only was consumer satisfaction extremely high, but also pre- and post-test results showed statistically significant improvements on all the variables on the *CBCL*, with the variables no longer being clinically significant (Landy, 2012). There was also a trend toward improvements in parent self-esteem, parenting stress (difficult child), and parent–child interactions. Further evaluation with follow-up and a comparison group is planned.

For more details about various websites and programs that deal with child disorders, see Table 10.7.

Table 10.7 *Websites**

Website	Information on Website
www.developingchild.harvard.edu	Provides a number of articles that "translate science into policy." Also has a number of articles on issues that may contribute to the development of psychopathology in children such as maternal depression, toxic substances in utero, and other early experiences.
www.who.int/mental_health/en/	Website provides information on the incidence of mental and behavioral disorders throughout the world. A number of publications on the prevention of mental health disorders, promoting mental health, and emerging evidence on best practice are also available.
www.nimh.nih.gov/statistics/index.shtml	Website of the National Institute of Mental Health. Information on statistics and research on mental health are provided as well as a number of useful reports.
www.nami.org	This is the website of the National Alliance on Mental Illness, the largest grassroots mental health organization dedicated to supporting Americans affected by mental illness. It has a Child and Adolescent Action Center.
www.health.nih.gov	Website of the U.S. Department of Health and Human Services website provides public access to a number of articles and reports on mental and physical health.
www.aboutourkids.org	Website of the New York University Child Study Center that includes information on disorders and treatments, seeking professional help and participating in research.
www.ncbi.nlm.nih.gov/pubmed	PubMed website has more than 21 million citations for biomedical literature from MEDLINE, life science journals, and online books, some of which discuss contributors to mental disorders. Citations may include links to full-text content of the citations.
www.mentalhealthamerica.net	Website of Mental Health America. Provides information on a number of children's mental health resources.
www.aacap.org	Website of the American Academy of Child and Adolescent Psychiatry (AACAP), which addresses concerns about health care and socioeconomic issues affecting children. Has a number of articles on mental health topics by recognized professionals in the field. Also provides practice parameters for children of all ages.
www.nccp.org	Website for the National Center for Children in Poverty (NCCP). It emphasizes preventing or alleviating poverty as well as documenting its effects on development. A number of papers are available on these topics.
www.nicic.gov	Discusses the number of mentally ill persons in the correction system. Also the need for screening and services for youth aged 10 to 18 in the juvenile justice system.

*Other websites are listed in tables in Chapters 3, 4, 5, 6, 7, 8, and 9.

11

Working With Parents

In this chapter, we provide a theoretical framework for working with parents and a perspective of assisting parents with their children who have various behavioral, emotional, and social problems. The modern world has seen a significant rise in single-parent households, divorced and blended families, and unmarried teen parents. Biological, adoptive, and foster parents; siblings; grandparents; and institutional caregivers take care of children, and these interactions have significant influences on children's development.

Evidence shows that early experiences with caregivers, particularly relational experiences, have significant effects on the developing brain (Nelson & Bloom, 1997; Swain, Lorberbaum, Kose, & Strathearn, 2007). These effects in turn have been associated with the quality of children's attachment to their parents and various cognitive, emotional, and social capacities as well as specific disorders (Collins, Maccoby, Steinberg, Hetherington, & Bornstein, 2000).

Sensitive and responsive parenting provides appropriate levels of stimulation and involves synchrony in the interactions between parent and child. It has been associated with secure attachment, an important foundation for children's later development, and with domains such as self-esteem, positive peer interactions, and emotional and literacy development (Jones, Forehand, Brody, & Armistead, 2002; Zhou et al., 2002).

Caregiving that is intrusive, excessively stimulating, controlling, or unresponsive has been associated with insecure or disorganized attachment and more negative child development, including poor emotion regulation, socialization difficulties, behavioral problems, and difficulties in school (Belsky, 1999; Berlin & Cassidy, 1999; De Wolff & van IJzendoorn, 1997; Foreman & Davies, 2003; Ge, Brody, Conger, Simons, & Murray, 2002; Gibson-Davis & Gassman-Pines, 2010; Petit, Laird, Dodge, Bates, & Criss, 2001). For children with special challenges, specific strategies are needed to assist both parents and teachers in their interactions with these children.

Although nurturing is critical, parents also have other roles, including limit setter, teacher, and playmate. Parents vary in their level of comfort with these roles, and partners can emphasize different balances among them (Landy, 2009).

Parents have an enormous influence on their children, but children also affect their parents. When children develop mental health problems, they can have significant influences on parents' sense of competence, attributions of their children, and interactions and relationships with their children. Clearly, when children with multiple challenges are referred for treatment, parents often feel blamed and ineffective in their parenting. They have frequently sought suitable treatment services and felt that professionals have not understood them or their child.

THEORIES OF PARENTING

Many theories contribute to an understanding of parenting and working with parents, and the most widely used are described next.

Trauma theory has become one of the most important theories informing the treatment of children and their parents. The devastating effects of trauma on biochemical, neurological, and psychological functioning have become increasingly understood since the 1990s, with new findings regularly published. If trauma is unresolved and untreated, it can affect emotion regulation, memory, perception, and behavior and, when the effects are extreme, result in various symptoms and disorders that are difficult to treat. These include posttraumatic stress disorder (PTSD), depression, and borderline personality disorder. Trauma can include natural and human-caused disasters, medical procedures, and abuse and neglect. It can include parental non-responsiveness and lack of nurturance, called small "t" traumas, that can be difficult to identify but just as damaging if they happened in early childhood when the brain was being formed. Parents' unresolved trauma history can result in negative interactions and insecure relationships and attachments with their children. This history might not be remembered or even denied, particularly at the beginning of treatment. Therapists working with traumatized parents who are experiencing frequent emotion dysregulation or dissociation from the triggering of trauma memories often use Mindfulness-Based Stress Reduction (MBSR) or mindfulness practices such as meditation, breathing, and increasing mindfulness of the breath and body to provide the person with useful strategies to increase their sense of well-being and to reduce distressing symptoms (Corcoran, Farb, Anderson, & Segal, 2010). These "tools" are often taught to individuals who are receiving treatment for complex trauma and are included in Phase 1 of such treatment so that when trauma memories are accessed the person will have strategies to use to cope with their effects on their well-being and functioning.

Attachment theory is also relatively recent and has informed both the assessment and the treatment of interactional and relational difficulties between parent and child. The quality of attachment that the infant develops with her primary caregiver (most often her mother) influences her development, behavior, sense of self, and beliefs about others (Cassidy & Shaver, 2008). A number of parent–child interactional characteristics, originally identified by Ainsworth, that need to be considered in any assessment include parental sensitivity, acceptance of the child, responsiveness to her cues, cooperation with her needs, empathy with and understanding of her thoughts and feelings, and level of positive emotionality with her. A parent's capacity to reflect on her own and her child's inner experiences or for mentalizing has also been found to have an important influence on the child's quality of attachment and is considered during assessment (Fonagy & Target, 2005; Grienenberger, Kelley, & Slade, 2005; Oppenheim & Koren-Karie, 2002; Slade, 2005; Slade, Grienenberger, Bernbach, Levy, & Locker, 2005). Therapists working from this perspective use mentalisation-based therapies (MBT) particularly with parents with personality disorders such as borderline personality disorder. In about 80% of cases, the child's attachment classification will match that of the mother. Because parent–child interactions and the resulting attachment quality are so important for the child's development, when children have insecure or disorganized attachments interventions often focus on enhancing the mentalizing abilities of parents and increasing the synchrony of their responses to their child during parent–child interactions (Benoit & Parker, 1994; Fonagy, Steele, & Steele, 1991).

Psychoanalytic and psychodynamic theories emphasize the importance of unconscious memories on how parents interact with their children. Having a baby can be a powerful trigger that brings these memories to the surface and into consciousness. These resurfaced memories can dramatically influence how a parent interacts with a child from infancy into later childhood (Belsky, Conger, & Capaldi, 2009; Cohler & Paul, 2002). They can also result in the parent being depressed or frustrated in the parenting role and dramatically influence her interactions with her child. So it is important to assess the experiences of parents as they were growing up and their understanding of those experiences. It is also helpful to identify any negative patterns that might need to become a focus of intervention. In addition, defensive functioning, current adaptive behaviors and relationships, and any negative or positive interactions need to be considered. Intervention should help to integrate and make sense of any resurfaced memories so that the parent can begin to understand how they might be affecting her patterns of behavior in the present, particularly those affecting her child. Therapists working from this perspective also emphasize an emotional and not just a behavioral or concrete functional perspective. What happens in the intervention relationship or transference might also be considered to understand how a parent relates to others and the therapist.

Social learning theory also focuses on parent–child interactions as important contributors to child outcomes. Unlike attachment theorists, researchers from this perspective measure the behavioral components of parent–child interactions and how they can reinforce one another as well as how the parent's behavior becomes a model for the child's behavior. For example, when parents' interactions with their child are punitive, negative, and intensely emotional, the child is likely to respond negatively, which can increase his parents' negativity and in turn his risk of ongoing problems. It is believed that cycles of negativity increase through this process of mutual reinforcement. The child becomes increasingly reactive and acts out, while the parents' reactions become increasingly harsh and punitive (Patterson & Fisher, 2002; Scaramella & Leve, 2004). These coercive cycles of parent–child interaction affect the child's development of emotion regulation and social competence. Internalization of rules and compliance to parents' requests can also be affected. As well, punitive and harsh parental interactions have been linked to many of the difficulties discussed in this book (Rothbaum & Weisz, 1994). Social learning theorists describe how, from these repeated negative exchanges with parents, children develop attributional biases that influence how they view and remember events along with the world and their place in it (Dodge, 1993).

Social support theory considers the social context in which parents and children live that affects how they interact. This context includes the level and type of support in the immediate and extended family, the community in which they live, and any agencies and programs available to the family. Social support theory also emphasizes the need to empower parents by being involved in designing interventions that can enhance their children's development (Dunst, Trivette, & Thompson, 1991; Weissbourd, 1993). Assessment considers the level and type of services available to the family. Any cultural practices that might be influencing parenting practices are also considered. Intervention includes providing instrumental support as well as crisis intervention. The service provider is seen as part of the support system. Parents might be referred to appropriate agencies, programs, or courses to build competence.

Cognitive behavioral theory focuses on how people think and how changing cognitions can help parents with children with multiple challenges. The theory considers how parents' negative cognitions of their child or their perceptions, expectations, and interpretations of their child influence how they parent. Therapies based on this theory help to change parents' negative cognitions and attributions of their children and their situations. Cognitive behavioral therapy (CBT) is a psychotherapeutic approach that helps parents to challenge their patterns and beliefs and replace them with more adaptive ones. Emotional experiences are not ignored, but efforts to influence them take place through cognitive modification. Various skills can be taught, such as motivational self-talk, relaxation, desensitization, modeling, and minimizing negative or self-defeating thoughts. Beliefs about and attributions of a child are cognitions that influence parenting and can become the focus of interventions with parents when they are negative. These strategies can also be used with adults and children as young as 4 years of age (Hayes, Follette, & Follette, 1995).

Attribution theory is a social learning and cognitive theory that, as discussed above, emphasizes the importance of parents' attributions and expectations of their children and their effects on parenting and their children's development. Research has focused on parents identified as depressed and abusive. Depressed parents have often been found to have negative perceptions of their children. Research has also examined the attributions of abusive parents, and Bugental and colleagues found that abusive parents have "threat-oriented schemas" and attribute high control to their children and low control to themselves. She also suggested that they attribute hostile intent to their children. These schemas are believed to begin to operate automatically, especially in stressful situations and during difficult interactions with their children (Bugental, 1992). To cope with these interactions, the child might withdraw or become more difficult to control and increase the risk of abuse. Bugental and colleagues (Bugental, Ellerson, Lin, Rainey, Kokotovic, et al., 2002) have developed an intervention that works with parents to redefine their attributions to be less threat based and blaming and helps them to problem-solve in order to find ways to discipline their children and interact with them in more positive ways.

Behaviorism sees human beings as shaped by what goes on in the environment, particularly what happens in response to their behavior. Behavior modification approaches to discipline are used in parenting programs and schools to discourage and eliminate negative behaviors and reinforce and encourage positive behaviors. Parents and teachers use a set of rules and consequences for children who do not follow them. Noticing, acknowledging, and rewarding positive behavior lets the child know that efforts to behave are appreciated. This can bolster self-esteem and increase positive behavior.

Integrative theoretical approaches to assessment and treatment are recommended in this book. In assessing and treating children with complex mental health challenges, a number of professionals from a variety of disciplines with multiple theoretical perspectives are likely to be involved. Consequently, it is necessary to integrate these perspectives and strategies into one treatment plan. Some integrative theories can guide this process, including the transactional model, which considers the multiple contributors to the child's presentation and the dynamic interplay among them. The more risk factors there are, the greater the likelihood that negative transactional processes will be established and the child's development affected. In this book, we draw on the theory of *developmental psychopathology* and how difficulties and disorders can develop from different developmental trajectories across the life span (Cicchetti & Rogosch, 2002; Cicchetti & Sroufe, 2000; Rutter & Sroufe, 2000). This approach also addresses how competence and positive adaptation can occur despite exposure to multiple risk factors and adversity (Luthar & Cicchetti, 2000; Masten & Curtis, 2000; Sameroff, 2001).

Other integrative approaches examine the developmental *mechanisms* or processes that link parenting to various child outcomes. These approaches examine how psychopathology develops across time using various statistical approaches such as sequential regression analysis and nested path analysis, and they can inform ways to place development on a more appropriate path. Research has considered the development of violent behavior in adolescence and of conscience in young children (Dodge, Greenberg, Malone, & Conduct Problems Prevention Research Group, 2008; Kochanska, Barry, Askan, & Boldt, 2008; Yates, Obradovic, & Egeland, 2010).

CONTRIBUTORS TO PARENTING

The determinants of parenting are complex, but certain factors are particularly important. They include the social context in which children are raised, such as family income and neighborhood (Brady et al., 2003). The family system, if warm and supportive, can be a protective factor, but interparental conflict and particularly spousal abuse or domestic violence are likely to place children at risk of developing both internalizing and externalizing behavioral problems, social difficulties, and self-esteem problems (Kitzmann, Gaylord, Holt, & Kenny, 2003; Rhodes, 2008).

Parenting Knowledge, Beliefs, Attitudes, and Attributions of Children

Different levels of knowledge about and experience of child development and child rearing affect parenting. Parents' cognitions come from various sources, such as how parents themselves were parented, cultural values, level of education and socioeconomic status, religious beliefs, and influence of other family members. Of course, having children can change one's cognitions about child rearing and be affected by characteristics such as special needs or chronic illnesses (Landy & Menna, 2006).

Parenting knowledge is associated with parents' sense of competence and satisfaction with the parenting role (Bornstein et al., 2003). When parents have more knowledge, they are more likely to make more accurate attributions or interpretations of their children's behaviors (Bugental & Happaney, 2002). Accurate parenting knowledge has also been linked to children's better developmental outcomes and health and fewer behavioral problems. Mothers who know more about child development report more positive descriptions of their children, score higher in parenting skills, and behave in developmentally appropriate ways with them, even controlling for income and education (Grusec & Goodnow, 1994; Putnam, Sanson, & Rothbart, 2002). Research has shown that parenting knowledge that fits with ideas already held about parenting and with cultural or religious beliefs is more likely to be seen as useful and therefore used. Perhaps the parents' relationship with the intervenor or service provider is the most important factor (Landy & Menna, 2006). Parents' beliefs affect child outcomes by influencing parents' behavior with their children. Parents' attributions, which usually center on the reasons that their child develops and behaves in a certain way (e.g., is disobedient or anxious and shy), are believed to develop from parents' own experiences and observing other parents and children.

Intergenerational Transmission of Parenting

An interesting finding has been that, when the attachment classification of the mother is assessed during pregnancy using the *Adult Attachment Interview* (AAI), the attachment classification of the child at 12 months is the same in 75% to 80% of cases. Similar concordance has been found when the two measures are collected concurrently (Ainsworth & Eichberg, 1991; van IJzendoorn, Kranenburg, Zwart-Woudstra, Van Busschbach, & Lamberman, 1991; Zeanah et al., 1993) or when the infancy data are collected years earlier than the AAI (Grossman, Fremmer-Bombik, Rudolph, & Grossman, 1988; Main, Kaplan, & Cassidy, 1985).

A significant literature on the transmission of parenting across generations has considered how abusive and/or hostile, harsh parenting is transmitted. A smaller literature has examined the continuity of warm and supportive parenting. In general, though some continuity of parenting has been found, parenting experiences are not inevitably repeated. Kaufman and Zigler (1987) estimated the rate to be about 30%. Other researchers have found that parenting experienced growing up accounted for only about 14% to 16% of the variance (Belsky, Jaffee, Sligo, Woodward, & Silva, 2005; Capaldi, Pears, Patterson, & Owens, 2003; Conger, Neppl, Kim, & Scaramella, 2003). Recent research has explored the developmental outcomes that occur as a result of certain parenting. For example, Chen and

Kaplan (2001) found that positive, supportive, or constructive parenting resulted in the development of a competent child with success in interpersonal relationships and educational attainments. On the other hand, hostile parenting can predict aggressive behavior in childhood (Caspi & Elder, 1988; Neppl, Conger, Scaramella, & Optai, 2009). These child outcomes are also related to parenting behavior when the child becomes a parent and shows further transmission of parenting across another generation.

Parent Characteristics

Attachment theorists see the capacity for mentalization as the most important parenting characteristic that leads to the intergenerational concordance of the attachment classification. Parents with capacity for mentalization can "keep the baby in mind" (Slade, 2002, p. 10). They also treat the child as a person with a mind and feelings and respond to her behavior with feeling and mind-related comments (e.g., "Looks like you're feeling bored and lonely and would like to be held").

Mothers With Mental Illness

There is a significant literature showing the adverse effects of parental depression on child outcomes. Recent studies have found greater deficits in interactions of women with schizophrenia with their children compared with women with other disorders (Zahn-Waxler, Duggal, & Gruber, 2002). Parents with borderline personality disorder (BPD) are characterized by patterns of instability in interpersonal relationships, self-image, and emotions. Parenthood is a very difficult role for an individual with BPD. She might tend to experience child independence as rejection and struggle against child individuation. Her inconsistency, unpredictability, and uncontained rage result in the child feeling responsible for whether he will experience an affectionate response or a verbal or physical slap. Consequently, love and hate are frequently mixed and cause the child intense confusion. Female substance abusers who become pregnant have various risk factors (Lester, Boukydis, & Twomey, 2000). Many women who use drugs during pregnancy and after their infants are born suffer from depression, anxiety, and personality disorders that produce complex problems that need to be addressed in intervention. Parents addicted to drugs might use a variety of drugs and/or alcohol or combinations of them and become obsessed with the need to get money to buy them, and often they live in environments characterized by chaos, violence, and poverty. Substance abuse by pregnant women can affect the developing fetus and cause ongoing problems postpartum. Perhaps the best known and most understood effects of substance use during pregnancy are those of alcohol use (Stratton, Howe, & Battaglia, 1996). Parenting deficits as a result of substance abuse pose significant risks for children's development, particularly for poor impulse control, conduct problems, and poorer overall adjustment (Bornstein, Mayes, & Park, 1998). Teenage mothers generally have less optimal interactions and child-rearing patterns with their infants and young children. They tend to be less sensitive, responsive, and emotionally positive with them (Lester, 1992). In general, children of adolescent mothers have poorer outcomes than children of older mothers. These differences, which include cognitive functioning and psychosocial problems, first occur in the preschool years and continue into the elementary school years. By adolescence, school achievement is lower, and misbehavior and other school problems are markedly higher (Moore, Morrison, & Green, 1997). Parents with unresolved loss and trauma have representations of their children that are incoherent and distorted and are more likely to have children with disorganized attachment (Schechter et al., 2005). Unresolved loss or trauma can result in frightening and frightened behaviors of parents with their infants (Jacobvitz, Hazen, & Riggs, 1997; Thalhuber, Jacobvitz, & Hazen, 1998). More subtle maternal behaviors have also been identified as related to disorganized attachment. They include expressing extreme misattunement to infants' cues and communications and using competing caregiving strategies such as encouraging and then rejecting attachment-seeking behaviors. Some parents tend to shift between the two patterns, sometimes in the same interaction. Children with insecure attachment are less at risk of developing psychopathology but can have more dysfunctional patterns of relating, making it more difficult for them to develop secure and satisfying relationships with peers.

CONTRIBUTIONS OF THE CHILD

Developmental delays include those resulting from extreme prematurity or very low birth weight, especially if an infant has other medical complications (Rose, Feldman, Jankowski, & Van Rossen, 2005). Other biological and/or genetic conditions and chronic medical conditions and repeated illnesses are also related to later psychosocial difficulties (Stuber & Shemash, 2006). They can affect the parent–child interaction, making parenting more challenging. Difficult temperaments can also challenge parents' caregiving and result in punitive and harsh parenting within coercive cycles of parent–child interactions (Deater-Deckard & Petrill, 2004; Patterson & Fisher, 2002; Scaramella & Leve, 2004). An important new area of research examining genetic vulnerability has found that hereditary gene structure significantly affects the outcomes for children who experience adverse situations in early life (Bradley, 2005).

Interactions with peers become increasingly important in elementary school and beyond. Overassociation with deviant peers, partly due to lack of parental monitoring, has been found to predict adolescent deviant behavior (Dodge et al., 2008; Patterson, Reid, & Dishion, 1992; Simons, Wu, Conger, & Lorenz, 1994). Once part of a deviant peer group, a child is more likely to engage in antisocial behavior and become increasingly unacceptable to a peer group interested in academic, social, and age-appropriate activities. This is particularly true if the child struggles with school and has no positive mentors or identification figures in the family or neighborhood. Obviously, aggression, conduct problems, and oppositional defiant reactions can further isolate him.

TYPES OF PARENTING

There is growing consensus that, though genes provide the initial blueprint for the architecture of the brain, parenting, particularly in the early years, affects how neural circuitry actually develops. The physiological systems that influence a variety of biological functions are affected by early interactions. Abuse, neglect, and chaotic situations leave the child with little support to handle stress. Even harsh discipline or failure to notice or respond to her can lead to a stress system that is chronically aroused and responds to increasingly lower levels of stimulation. This can contribute to the development of stress-related diseases and psychopathology.

Harsh, Punitive, and Physical Discipline

Serious forms of physical abuse are associated with negative outcomes, but there is less consensus on the effects of spanking and slapping. According to a number of parent polls, corporal punishment is used with more than 90% of children in the United States. Some children are hit on a daily basis, and many parents believe that spanking a child is the only way to stop negative behavior and make him more obedient (Giles-Sims, Straus, & Sugarman, 1995). However, the research is clear that physical punishment negatively affects child development in a number of areas (Gershoff, 2002). It also negatively affects the parent–child relationship and can result in fear, anxiety, insecurity, and anger in younger children and depression, unhappiness, and hopelessness in older children and youth. Children are also less likely to develop a conscience and internalize moral values (Bender et al., 2007; Lopez, Bonenberger, & Schneider, 2001; Stormshak, Bierman, McMahon, & Lengua, 2000; Ulman & Straus, 2003).

Coercion

Poor parenting practices such as lack of monitoring, criticism and harshness, and inconsistent discipline lead to demanding and coercive behavior in the child. The parent might then give in, allowing her to "win." The child, as a consequence, continues to engage in these behaviors, and the parent continues with ineffective discipline, often escalating with angry and hostile responses. In this way, the child never learns skills to improve her behavioral responses and feels increasingly rejected and unsupported (Dishion, French, & Patterson, 1995; Patterson, 1982).

Mutual Responsiveness

Several researchers have discussed the importance of mutual responsiveness between parent and child. Kochanska and colleagues identified the "mutually responsive orientation" that is "positive, mutually binding and cooperative," as crucial for socialization, and predictive of internalized conscience and guilt later (Aksan, Kochanska, & Ortmann, 2006, p. 834). Behaviorally uninhibited and fearless children who do not respond to normal consequences respond best to this type of relationship (Kochanska, Aksan, & Koenig, 1995). Studies have also shown that parents' efforts to be more responsive and grant more autonomy lead to greater child compliance (Wahler & Bellamy, 1997).

Overprotection

Although much of the literature on parenting has been about children with externalizing behaviors and difficulties, much less has been written about children who are behaviorally inhibited and socially withdrawn, anxious, or depressed. One observation is that some parents themselves are anxious and overprotective with their children, sometimes giving them the message that the outside world is not safe and discouraging their independence (Williams, Degnan, Perez-Edgar, Henderson, Rubin, et al., 2009). Because of the bidirectional effects of parent behavior and child temperament with children high in behavioral inhibition, permissiveness and oversolicitous parenting can exaggerate the child's anxiety, whereas a style of parenting that supports more opportunities for socialization and independence might be critical.

Authoritarian, Authoritative, and Permissive

Diana Baumrind and associates followed preschoolers into middle childhood and adolescence and linked family interactions and discipline styles to a number of developmental outcomes (Baumrind, 1971, 1973; Baumrind & Black, 1967). They identified three primary styles of parenting: authoritarian, authoritative, and permissive. The authoritarian pattern is high in enforcing rules and low in responding to the child. This type of parent also restricts the child's sense of independence. Authoritative parenting includes the enforcement of rules and standards but allows for discussion with children and encourages their input into certain decisions. Permissive parents have few expectations or rules for the child, accept his negative behavior, and encourage age-inappropriate independence (Baumrind, 1971, 1973, 1989). In her original study, Baumrind (1971, 1973) found that by 8 or 9 years of age children who had received each kind of discipline had very different outcomes. Children in authoritative families were the most competent, more achievement oriented and independent, and more cooperative and friendly than those in the other two types, who had lower social and cognitive competence (Baumrind, 1973, 1989, 1991). Later research found similar results.

Parent Monitoring

The importance of parent monitoring was first acknowledged in the literature on predictors of delinquency (Forgatch, 1991; Loeber, Stouthamer-Loeber, Van Kamman, & Farrington, 1991; Patterson, 1982; Patterson et al., 1992). The influence of monitoring increases at about 10 years of age as children engage in more peer-related activities in preadolescence and adolescence (Loeber et al., 1991). In one study, improvements in monitoring were more predictive of children's outcomes than improvements in discipline. Cavell (2000) described it as multidimensional, including the following:

- limiting the degree to which children are involved with deviant peers and antisocial activities;
- increasing the extent to which children let their parents know where they are and the activities that they are involved in;
- imposing curfews, rules, and routines; and
- supervising activities across multiple settings (at school, after school, and with peers).

Warmth or Positive Emotionality

Positive emotionality has been widely recognized as an important influence on moral development. Warmth gives children a sense of being loved and respected, which encourages a tendency to comply with requests and identify with parents and other caregivers (Dix, 1991, 1992; Grusec, Goodnow, & Kuczynski, 2000; Kochanska 1995; Maccoby, 1983). Exposure to high amounts of positive emotion is believed to enhance mood induction, with children who experience this positivity from parents more likely to be attentive and to comply with parental requests (Dix 1991; Hoffman, 1983, 1988; Kochanska, 1997; Maccoby & Martin, 1983). This positive emotional climate in a home has also been called "flexibility within clear boundaries." A healthy emotional climate is one in which parents are caring and warm and love children unconditionally but also set clear boundaries letting children know what is acceptable and what is not. At the same time, children are encouraged to be independent and have a say in what goes on in the family. This is similar to the authoritative style of parenting described by Baumrind (1971, 1973, 1989).

TREATMENT OF FAMILIES WITH MULTI-CHALLENGED CHILDREN

Only a small percentage of families with children with behavioral and emotional problems actually attend mental health or early-intervention programs (Meltzer, Gatward,

Corbin, Goodman & Ford, 2003; Offord, Boyle, Racine, Fleming, Cadman, et al., 1992; U.S. Department of Health and Human Services, 1999). In addition, at least half of families who initially attend treatment drop out prematurely (Wierzbicki & Pekarik, 1993). The reasons for this lack of psychological readiness or resistance to being involved with services vary from family to family and can present significant challenges to treatment professionals. More retention of families in treatment needs to be a major emphasis of providing services to high-risk families with multi-challenged children.

Level of Motivation

Many families can be described as "hard to reach." In general, families approach participating in treatment programs with varying degrees of motivation. This can range from those who were mandated by child protection agencies to those who sought help because of concerns about their child's behavior and development or their parenting of or relationship with their child. As Prochaska (1999) pointed out, people go through a number of stages during the process of change. He therefore suggested that any service offered needs to be adapted to the parents' stage of readiness for change. Prochaska, DiClemente, and Norcross (1992) similarly pointed out that intervention has to be matched to parents' or other caregivers' stage of readiness. For example, for parents who have no intention to participate in interventions immediately, giving them information about their children's needs can encourage them to get involved in more in-depth interventions at a later time. Few families are believed to reach termination of treatment, in which they feel confident enough to stop intervention completely. Most families remain in a stage of maintenance for several years or return for support when difficult events arise in their lives or when a child reaches a challenging stage of development. Unfortunately, programs are seldom set up to accommodate these differences or the need for long-term support.

Reasons for Families Not Attending Services

Some of the reasons that families do not attend services can include the following issues. *Practical issues* that can prevent families from attending treatment include not having transportation to attend appointments. Or it might not be safe for the service provider to visit the home because of the possibility of being responded to violently or the visit negatively affecting safety for the parent in the home. Sometimes it is not possible to schedule visits at suitable times because of a parent's work schedule. Chaotic functioning of parents can also prevent their engagement in consistent and predictable ways.

Attitudinal issues are related to a belief of the parents that the service provider will interfere or not understand their child or the needs of the family. This belief can result from earlier experiences with service providers by whom they felt judged or who lacked empathy or were too intrusive. Many parents feel blamed for their child's problems and feel that it is seen as a result of their parenting. They also feel that no effort has been made to understand their child. Although some parents see it as "normal" to seek help from professionals for physical health issues, acknowledging that their child has a mental health issue can threaten their image of who they are and lead to profound feelings of shame and humiliation. Some can also think that child protection services will become involved if they disclose problems. They might fear that they will be told to parent in a certain way. This can be more upsetting if they have bad experiences with child protection services during childhood or in the more recent past. Some parents fear disclosing violent, illegal, or other negative activity within the family that can jeopardize their access to social assistance or housing. If illegal immigrants are discovered and reported, they can be deported. Some parents might be reluctant to become involved with services because they fear disclosure of private information regarding their health status, such as having HIV or schizophrenia. Parents can have concerns about possible stigmatization if such information becomes known in the immediate community. For some parents, it is uncomfortable or even intimidating to attend an office or center for services. Yet other parents can see a home visit as intrusive and fear losing control. They might also feel uncomfortable about the state of their home and that it will cause criticism.

Cultural issues can get in the way of the intervention when parents and interventionists speak different languages, for example. The use of interpreters can be difficult, and nuances of meaning can be lost. These issues can constrain the working alliance that the interventionist and parents are able to develop (Barrera & Corso, 2003). In a therapeutic context in which the focus is on the parents' attributions and beliefs about their child, themselves, and their relationship, this issue is particularly important. Cultural belief systems of parents affect how they attend to their children's behavior, how they interpret it, the goals that they hold for their children, and how they behave in relation to their children (Harkness & Super, 1996; Harwood, Miller, & Irizarry, 1995). Families also have cultural or religious beliefs about styles of dress, forms of greeting, body language, topics of discussion, and behavior in interaction. Without some awareness of these issues, an interventionist might offend a family or family member without even knowing it.

Building a Trusting Relationship With Parents

Building trust is the central task in developing a positive working relationship with parents and preventing them from prematurely dropping out of treatment (Prinz & Miller, 1994). Obstacles and disruptions in the development of trust likely reflect patterns developed in the past, and change might be possible only when a worker can contribute to creating a new relationship. Research with parents of aggressive children has shown that, when parents feel accepted, supported, and not blamed by professionals, they are more likely to reflect on their parenting styles (Levac, McCay, Merka, & Reddon-D'Arcy, 2008). Some of these characteristics of intervention are listed below:

- Respecting that the parents are doing the best that they can at the time.
- Responding reliably to the parents' communications.
- Helping to secure housing, food, resources, daycare, and school services, particularly in times of crisis.
- Empowering parents to be agents of change in their families.
- Working with parents as partners and respecting their wishes and needs.
- Acknowledging and empathizing with parents' positive and negative experiences.

TREATMENT OF PARENTS

Much of the parenting literature focuses on behavior management or discipline and on teaching parents how to impose consequences when children misbehave. In a search of the popular literature on parenting, Gottman, Katz, and Hooven (1997) found 1,412 references to "parents and discipline" and 69 references to "parents and emotion." Although compliance is important for most families, research on child development and studies on the treatment of multi-challenged children suggest that a broader set of parenting behaviors needs to be encouraged in therapeutic interventions if negative cycles of parent–child interactions are to be reduced or eliminated and children's positive development encouraged.

Treating Parents of Children With Externalizing Disorders

Most parenting programs to treat children with externalizing difficulties and disorders such as aggression, oppositional defiant disorder, and conduct disorder are provided in group settings. They are typically based on a behavioral and social-learning model of parent training, with a review of parent-training research finding that 89% of studies emphasized a behavioral approach (Rogers Wiese, 1992). One of the biggest influences has been coercion theory, which has focused on the patterns of parental discipline that contribute to "coercive parent–child exchanges." Although there are other coercion theories, that of Gerald Patterson and his colleagues at the Oregon Social Learning Center has been the most influential, partly because of the impressive research conducted on both the assessment of "coercive" parent–child interactions and the effectiveness of behavior management parent training. Chamberlain and Patterson (1995) researched coercive parent–child interactions and found four subtypes: inconsistent discipline; irritable, explosive, harsh, punitive discipline; low monitoring of and involvement with the child; and inflexible discipline, with parents relying on a limited number of strategies. These patterns of discipline are believed to result in the child learning to use arguing and tantrums to get what he wants from his parents.

To manage discipline, parents can develop a list of behaviors that they want to reduce in their child; choose rewards and punishments as incentives and disincentives to behave; and devise a system of charts with stars, stickers, tokens, or levels of success. A number of programs teach these skills in Phase 2; Phase 1 teaches parents to attend to their children in positive ways using play sessions in which they follow the child's lead and provide a running commentary on it. They are also taught to use praise and rewards such as hugs and kisses to increase specific behaviors and ignore other behaviors to decrease problems (Forehand & McMahon, 1981; McMahon & Forehand, 1984; Webster-Stratton & Hierbert, 1994). The program used by Patterson and colleagues (Horne & Patterson, 1980) does not emphasize play and attending to the positive behaviors of the child. These parent-training programs can be delivered using group didactic instructions or intense individual training methods.

To substitute for costly and time-consuming individualized training approaches, Webster-Stratton (1987) developed a videotape series of 250 vignettes that can be used in training groups or self-administered by parents in the home.

The results of parent training with children with behavioral problems are positive, with targeted behaviors being reduced, such as aggression, temper tantrums, and noncompliance (Hughes & Cavell, 1994; Serketich & Dumas, 1996). However, as noted by Patterson (1985, p. 1347), "a number of studies have failed to provide support for the efficacy of parent training for some families of oppositional children." One reason suggested for these difficulties is that instructors are not sufficiently trained, but this has been disproved in other studies (Webster-Stratton, 1990; Webster-Stratton, Kolpacoff, & Hollinsworth, 1988). Significant numbers of parents fail to attend parent management training, and 25% to 33% drop out after one or two sessions (Kazdin, Mazurick, & Bass, 1993; Scott & Dadds, 2009). Follow-up studies have also found that 30% to 50% of treated families fail to maintain the improvements over time (Webster-Stratton, 1990). Webster-Stratton (1990) has described the parents of nonresponsive children as more likely to be depressed, having antisocial traits and unresolved loss and trauma. Stressful family circumstances, such as marital discord, poverty, single-parent status, and social isolation, are also believed to contribute to these findings.

Although the bidirectional nature of parent–child interactions is generally accepted, many treatment programs ignore how certain characteristics of children can affect parents and their interactions with their children. Characteristics such as negative emotionality or irritability can lead to parent–child conflict (Sanson, Hemphill, & Smart, 2004). In a series of important studies, Kochanska (1995, 1997b) showed that fearless children do not respond well to a more gentle form of control or discipline but respond best to positive, mutually reciprocal, warm interactions with parents and to having secure attachment relationships.

TREATING CHILDREN WITH INTERNALIZING DISORDERS

Information on working with parents with children with internalizing disorders is limited, even though anxiety and depression, for example, are common childhood disorders and without treatment are likely to persist into adolescence and adulthood.

Children With Anxiety

Children who develop anxiety disorders typically have a temperament style described as behaviorally inhibited (Kagan, 2003). "Inhibited" describes their initial response to novelty, but they are typically shy, timid, and low on sociability at home and daycare. Vervoort et al. (2010) also found that anxious children are more likely to have automatic or unconscious threat-based reactions or interpretations of both negative and ambiguous stimuli than nonanxious children. Chorpita (2001) described the reason as a more easily triggered brain system or behavioral inhibition system. This neurological reaction leads to a narrowing of attention and increased central nervous system arousal. Children at the extreme end of the inhibited temperament, approximately 10% to 15%, show continuity of symptoms. Certain characteristics of parents of anxious or depressed children are more likely to contribute to continuity. They are more likely to be anxious or depressed themselves and show high control or overprotection, rejection, low warmth, negative communication, and anxious behavior (Ginsburg, Siqueland, Masia-Warner, & Hedtke, 2004; Moore, Whaley, & Sigman, 2004). These characteristics have been found in fathers as well as mothers of anxious children (Liber et al., 2008). These disorders are likely to persist if they are not treated and predispose children to anxiety disorders in adolescence and adulthood (Cresswell, Willetts, Murray, Singhal, & Cooper, 2008; Estelle, Mustillo, Erkanli, Keeler, & Angold, 2003; Gar & Hudson, 2009; Hirshfeld, Micco, Simoes, & Henin, 2008).

Cognitive-behavioral therapy has been efficacious for these disorders. However, given the contributions of parents to their child's presentation, many programs use family-based approaches with parents and children or parents alone. One representative program was used with 4- to 7-year-old children with anxiety disorders and their parents. It was evaluated using a randomized controlled trial (Hirshfeld-Becker et al., 2010). A manualized program based on the Coping Cat program was also used (Kendall, Kane, Howard, & Siqueland, 1992). Most of the children in the sample had anxiety disorders more common in young children, such as separation anxiety, social phobia, and specific phobia. Some had generalized anxiety disorder or agoraphobia. The program consisted of 17 sessions following a certain schedule. Parents were encouraged to allow the child space and protect her from danger. They were also encouraged to model coping and praise her for adaptive coping and not criticize or reinforce anxious behavior. Results showed that 59% of CBT children compared with 18% of controls were free of anxiety disorders at the end of the group. The children also showed an increase in coping capacity.

A program for children with anxiety that also incorporated parents into the treatment was developed by Barrett, Dadds, and Rapee (1996). It showed very positive results, particularly for children between 7 and 10 years of age.

Khanna and Kendall (2009) examined the efficacy of various parent-training techniques for child outcomes included in a family CBT program. They found that parent anxiety management and transfer of control to the child significantly contributed to improvements in her global functioning. However, improvements in her anxiety levels were not found from child report measures.

In another approach, Thienemann, Moore, and Tompkins (2006) worked with parents alone over 12 weeks using a manual-based therapy protocol that taught them to be lay therapists for their children. The program *Helping Your Anxious Child: A Step-by-Step Guide for Parents* (Rapee, Spence, Cobham, & Wignall, 2000) was very successful in reducing anxiety and impairment in children. It was most successful with separation anxiety and specific phobias. Parents reported that the strategies had been helpful in managing their own anxiety. It was a pilot study and did not use a randomized, controlled design.

Two studies examined how parent training was able to reduce child anxiety and in some cases improve child competence. One used quantitative data (Eisen, Raleigh, & Neuhoff, 2008), and the other qualitative data (Ben-Amitay, Rosental, & Toren, 2010). In the first study, only parents of children with separation anxiety received 10 individualized weekly sessions, which included education on how to teach their children self-control and other CBT skills. The children improved following the group and at 6-month follow-up, but only when the parents reported enhanced efficacy or satisfaction and reduced stress did the children achieve scores at the higher end of typical outcomes. A qualitative study examined the group process of 24 children from 6 to 13 years old and their 40 parents as it related to separation–individuation. Therapists used a cognitive-behavioral approach over 10 weeks with six child–parent dyads at a time. Group members engaged in a process believed to be therapeutic as the children shared anxieties with each other and parents recalled anxieties or events that were traumatic at the time. Children were able to "separate" from parents as they connected and began to identify with peers. The parent subgroup also confronted their anxieties and limitations.

Children With Depression

The treatment of children with depression has received even less attention than the treatment of children with anxiety. Treatments have also tended to be influenced primarily by cognitive and behavioral models similar to treatments for anxiety. They have focused on changing schemas or perceptions of self from being negative and hopeless to being more positive (Gladstone & Kaslow, 1995). Behavioral models have focused more on deficits in coping skills, particularly social problem solving. The approach that has the most empirical support is coping skill training (CST), especially for adolescents (Kazdin & Weisz, 1998). However, adding a parent-training component has not enhanced outcomes.

Kovacs et al. (2006) have developed a program, Contextual Emotion-Regulation Therapy (CERT), based on the development of improved emotion regulation. Although the program is targeted at improving children's cognitive and interpersonal capacities, parents are involved in it. Children and parents watch films of children coping or becoming overwhelmed with sadness and distress and discuss what helps them. Discussion also takes place on preventing bad feelings from getting out of hand and increasing children's resilience.

Fristad and colleagues developed and evaluated a "multifamily psychoeducational psychotherapy" (MF-PEP) of eight 90-minute sessions (Cummings & Fristad, 2007; Fristad, Goldberg-Arnold, & Gavazzi, 2003; Mendenhall & Fristad, 2009). The program combines psychoeducation, family systems, and cognitive-behavioral psychotherapy techniques (e.g., problem-solving skills and pleasant life-event scheduling) and has been used with children with depression and bipolar disorder. It has been successful in increasing positive family interactions, efficacy in seeking treatment, improved coping skills, and improved attitudes toward the child. Compared with treatment as usual and being on the waiting list, children who received MF-PEP had lower scores on the Mood Severity Index or an index of their total severity of manic and depressive symptoms. This was maintained 6 months later. The waiting-list group, when they received MF-PEP, experienced similar results.

Children With Other Disorders

Obsessive–compulsive disorder (OCD) occurs in about 1 in 200 children and adolescents and can cause severe and chronic impairment in academic, social, and family functioning (Whitestead & Jacobsen, 2010). Exposure and response prevention (ERP) have been the most researched treatments for adults and children. Various ways to administer the treatment have been tried; some are weekly sessions, others more intensive, with children receiving week-long sessions. This has been done by collapsing the traditional 8-week treatment into 10 sessions over 5 days (Abramowitz, Foa, & Franklin, 2003). The inclusion of parents in intensive treatment is consistent with the success of family-based approaches to OCD in children (Barrett, Healy-Farrell, & March, 2004). The intense program has three goals: to educate parents and children/adolescents on cognitive-behavioral understanding of OCD and treatment with ERP, to provide children/adolescents with initial symptom reduction, and to build the confidence of both child and parent to continue ERP after treatment sessions. The symptoms of OCD are significantly reduced after this intensive program.

Maltreating Parents

Children exposed to maltreatment are at high risk of developing behavioral problems and cognitive difficulties in childhood and in adolescence are at risk of dropping out of school, delinquency, substance abuse, and serious relational difficulties (Lau & Weisz, 2003; Widom, 2000). Recently, behavioral interventions, CBT, and family support have been the most common treatments used by child welfare (NSCAW Research Group, 2005). Also used are parent-training programs that aim to change parenting practices and promote consistent and contingent use of reinforcement, voluntary ignoring, and adequate punishment to increase a parent's sensitivity to the child, appropriate monitoring, and problem-solving skills. These programs have shown a decrease in the number of children and families who participate in protection services (Corcoran, 2000; Lau & Weisz, 2003). In a study of participation in the Incredible Years Parenting Program, parents were found to use less harsh discipline, more appropriate discipline, and more positive verbal discipline (Letarte, Normandeau, & Allard, 2010).

However, other authors have suggested that maltreatment is a problem of the parent–child relationship and that interventions should target this relationship (Tarabidsky, Pascuzzo, Moss, St-Laurent, Bernier, et al., 2008). Much of this attachment-focused work has been carried out with infants, young children, and parents and has focused on increasing their understanding of the behaviors, emotions, and signals of the children and responding to them sensitively (Cicchetti, Rogosch, & Toth, 2006; Madigan, Moran, & Pederson, 2006). Some approaches have used videotaping of parent–child interactions to draw attention to certain parts of these interactions.

Another approach uses parent–child interaction therapy (PCIT) to reduce harsh, violent, or neglectful parenting and increase positive and responsive interactions. The PCIT program has been used successfully in other populations (Thomas & Zimmer-Gembeck,

2007). The program integrates elements of attachment theory, traditional child psychotherapy, and behavioral techniques. There are two phases: child-directed interaction (CDI) and parent-directed interaction (PDI). Both phases begin with a parental teaching session followed by weekly sessions conducted around a dyadic play session between parent and child with the therapist as coach. In Phase 1, the child leads the play while the parent describes, reflects, and praises appropriate child behaviors, ignores inappropriate behaviors, and does not criticize, ask questions, or interfere. Once an appropriate CDI skill level is reached, PDI based on social learning theory is commenced, with the parent continuing the same behaviors and giving clear, direct, and developmentally appropriate verbal commands to the child while consistently applying specific consequences for the child's compliance (e.g., labeled praise) and noncompliance (e.g., time-out) (Chaffin et al., 2011). The sessions are conducted with the parent and child in a play therapy room and the therapist in another room behind a one-way mirror. The therapist and parent communicate through a bug-in-the-ear device. It allows direct coaching of the parent's interaction.

With the addition of strategies to increase parents' self-motivation, the program can reduce child welfare recidivism over 3 years. The parents involved had chronic and severe child welfare histories of abuse and neglect. With younger children (2–3 years of age), preschooler–parent psychotherapy, in which parent and child engage in therapy together, was more successful in decreasing negative maternal representations of the child compared with a group that received psychoeducational home visits (Toth, Maughan, Manly, Spagnola, & Cicchetti, 2002). The preschoolers in the study had been maltreated. As a result of the intervention, mothers were helped to process painful and adverse early experiences and link them to their current interactions with their children. This resulted in an increase in maternal empathy for the children, an increase in dyadic problem solving, and a reduction in maltreatment.

So, although parent-training interventions continue to dominate the literature, a number of other approaches show excellent outcomes and might be more successful than cognitive-behavioral approaches in enhancing the parent–child relationship and attachment.

WHEN STANDARDIZED TREATMENTS DO NOT WORK

As pointed out earlier, standardized and manualized treatments, especially for children with externalizing behaviors, often do not work. When this happens, other approaches from other theories can be used.

Enhancing Attributions of the Child

By the time that children have been referred for treatment, parents have typically developed extremely negative attributions of them. These attributions are often reinforced by teachers and descriptions of the child as "naughty," "bad," "lazy, "oppositional," and "disobedient." Parents and teachers often see the child as being deliberately difficult and do not consider the effects of trauma or loss or challenges in various areas of functioning. The child likely has been given a number of diagnoses, and parents might have tried a number of treatments. The approach endorsed in this book is a multidisciplinary assessment of the child. It influences how the parent understands the child, shifting attributions from negative to positive and helping the parent to have more empathy for the child. For example, the child seen as disobedient might have auditory processing or working memory difficulties and finds it almost impossible to follow more than one instruction because she cannot "hold them in mind." When such information is provided along with helpful strategies for the parent and teacher to use, their view of the child and how they connect with her are likely to improve.

Other authors have discussed similar approaches (e.g., Greene and Ablon, 2006). Lieberman (1999, p. 739) pointed out that parental attributions can "help determine whether or how the infant's behaviors are responded to, misinterpreted, or ignored." When attributions are negative, interaction and discourse with the child can be damaging to his sense of self and his emotional and behavioral manifestations of it. Two interviews have been developed to measure these attributions (see Slade, Aber, Berger, Bresgi, & Kaplan, 2003; Zeanah, Benoit, & Barton, 1993). Some research has found relationships between the results of these interviews and parenting behaviors and interactions with children.

Attribution theory emphasizes the importance of parents' attributions and expectations of their child on parenting behavior and child development. Work has also been carried out on the role of threat-based attributions in child abuse (Bradley & DeV Peters, 1991; Crittenden, 1985). Bugental has worked with parents to redefine attributions of their children to be less threat based and blaming and find new ways to interact with and discipline their children (Bugental et al., 2000). When Bugental used a cognitive-appraisal approach in the Healthy Families home visiting program, it had a significant impact on reducing child abuse (control group 36%, home visiting program 20%, and home visiting and cognitive appraisal approach only 4%). It was believed that engaging in cognitive appraisal opened up the possibility of stopping negative attributions; instead, the parent could consider the child and the reasons for his behavior as well as solutions to the problems.

Encouraging Reflective Functioning and Mentalising Abilities

Reflective functioning was introduced by Fonagy and colleagues in the 1990s and has been developed further since then (e.g., Fonagy, Gergely, Jurist, & Target, 2002; Fonagy et al., 1995). It refers to an individual's capacity to envision mental states in the self or others. Mental state refers to all mental experience: thoughts, feelings, desires, beliefs, and intentions. These researchers believe that this knowledge is central to understanding and containing otherwise overwhelming emotions. The ability to mentalize emotions is important for managing and expressing them (Fonagy et al., 2002). High mentalising ability in parents has been related to secure attachments in children and other aspects of their development, particularly emotion regulation. A similar concept, psychological mindedness, can predict attending and staying in therapy (Piper, McCallum, & Hassan, 1992).

Parents who lack the capacity for self-reflectivity often feel inadequate, helpless, and out of control. In the early stages of treatment, competence-based and supportive approaches are the most useful for these parents to help establish a therapeutic alliance and diminish resistance to intervention. Developing parents' capacity to think about their child's internal experience rather than just her behavior has been addressed in a number of publications. Slade (2006) identified a number of ways in which parents' self-reflectivity and mentalizing of can be enhanced.

Problem Solving and Planning

Not a day passes when parents do not have to make decisions and solve problems to maintain adequate daily structure and carry out the tasks of parenting. Areas most influenced by problem solving include disciplining, monitoring, supervising, setting up routines, and keeping people safe. Providing a routine can be extremely demanding for some parents, particularly those used to a chaotic lifestyle.

One of the most important aspects of the program for treating explosive children developed by Greene and Ablon (2006) is collaborative problem solving (CPS). It is used to facilitate adult–child problem solving, enabling parent and child to develop skills to resolve disagreements collaboratively. If this can be learned, it can diffuse conflicts and avoid aggressive outbursts from the child. The approach also teaches the child cognitive skills that are likely to be lacking. Research on the effectiveness of CPS, compared with parent training with children with attention deficit/hyperactivity disorder (ADHD), showed that CPS was equally effective and in some instances more effective than parent training in improving the sense of parent competence and child adaptability, reinforcing parents' efforts to connect with their children, and improving distractibility–hyperactivity (Greene et al., 2004).

Problem-solving skills training (Chendall & Braswick, 1985) combines cognitive and behavioral techniques to teach problem-solving skills such as generating alternative solutions and engaging in means–end thinking to manage interpersonal situations. Children practice the skills using role-playing with feedback. Parents are actively involved and observe the sessions, assisted by the therapist, and the use of problem-solving steps is fostered in the home. There are also written guidelines on how to prompt and assist the child. Between-session calls are also provided. In a research study compared with parent management treatment, both programs improved child functioning by reducing antisocial and delinquent behavior and increasing prosocial competence. However, the two approaches combined led to the most changes in child and parent functioning (Kazdin, Siegel, & Bass, 1992).

Emotion Coaching

Emotion regulation is the process by which people control or regulate internal reactions as well as outward expressions (Landy, 2009). The capacity to regulate emotions in an adaptive way is crucial for a sense of emotional well-being and the development of coping and resilience. Such a capacity can significantly affect parenting. Parents who have more difficulty with parenting, particularly dealing with their children's emotions, likely have mental illness, unresolved loss and trauma, are teenage parents, and have children with particularly difficult temperaments.

Gottman (1997) developed a five-step "emotion coaching" process that parents can use with their children to help them understand, cope with, and regulate their emotional worlds. Children whose parents use the approach have better cognitive, emotional, and social outcomes in adolescence. The steps of emotional coaching include the following:

1. noticing children's emotions, even if they are subtle and recognizing that an emotion can be an opportunity for intimacy and teaching;
2. listening empathetically and letting the child know that his feelings are valid;
3. helping the child to label the emotions that she is feeling;
4. setting limits while helping the child problem solve;
5. helping the child to choose a solution and supporting her to use it to see if it is workable.

The process also encourages effortful control or focusing on a problem and building positive attributions of self and others.

Emotional Reminiscing

Parents have also been trained in emotional reminiscing as part of parent management training. The approach trains parents in discussing past events with their children using emotion labels and "wh" questions about "what" happened and "why" and how they felt about it. In a pilot study using the approach, Salmon, Dadds, Allen, and Hawes (2009) found that parents increased discourse about emotions and that their children's conversations showed more elaborations and emotional references. This kind of conversation can be encouraged when children come home from school or at the family dinner table, for example.

Enhancing Parenting Knowledge

Parents have various cognitions about child development and child rearing that can affect their parenting and every aspect of their children's developmental outcomes. These cognitions include parenting knowledge, beliefs, attitudes, and attributions of why children do things.

Clearly, then, parents want information about parenting their children, particularly if a child has significant mental health issues and challenging behaviors. This information can be delivered either in group form or in individual sessions. However, timing will affect how well it is received and how successful it will be in changing parents' behavior.

Speaking for the child during a teachable moment in a home visit or clinic session can be used when a parent ignores or misinterprets the action of a child. The intervenor does not judge the parents' attribution but points out another way of seeing what the child is thinking or feeling. Information on his diagnosis or difficulty and how it relates to his behavior can be particularly useful. For example, a child with executive functioning difficulty or ADHD might have neurological issues that make getting started and focusing on an activity difficult. Providing information on mood disorders and cognitive-behavioral techniques can reduce mood symptom severity in the child and increase utilization of services (Mendenhall, Fristad, & Early, 2009). The aim is to adjust parents' attitudes toward and beliefs about their child to be more realistic and provide them with strategies to foster a positive relationship with their child and enhance his development. Appropriate information on strategies of discipline can also be introduced during these discussions.

Encouraging Acceptance of Children

In his approach of dyadic developmental psychotherapy, Daniel Hughes (2009) describes an attitude of PACE (**P**layfulness, **A**cceptance, **C**uriosity, **E**mpathy) or an interpersonal stance that can be used between parent and child and in other relationships. Playfulness is described as creating a space to simply be together with no set agenda and experience joy and fun together. Hughes describes Acceptance as being "accepted completely for who he is" (p. 78). He also emphasizes that discipline works best when it does not threaten the parent–child relationship or the child's sense of self-worth. Curiosity involves the parent in really trying to understand the reasons for the child's behavior and what is going on in his mind. Empathy includes providing support for more difficult and negative feelings through nonverbal and verbal expressions of feelings.

Cowell (2000, p. 100) has also described "parents' acceptance of children" and defined it as "any behavior that fosters in children a sense of autonomy while not threatening their relationship security." Examples are child-directed play, reflective listening, physical affection, showing understanding, and approving of behavior. This sense of acceptance can result in a parent–child relationship described by Kochanska and colleagues as a "mutually responsive orientation" crucial for socialization and predictive of internalized conscience and guilt later (Aksan et al., 2006, p. 834). See Cowell (2006) for a description of various strategies or skills of acceptance.

Providing Structure, Routines, and Limits

Although enhancing the relationship between parent and child is critical, many parents who seek services for their children, particularly when they have externalizing problems, want information on how to set limits on their children's behavior. For children to be safe and feel safe, there need to be predictable and consistent routines, rules, and limits in place; children need to know that their parents are in control and willing and able to contain them. Three things are paramount.

1. Rules are kept to a minimum and must emphasize stopping any aggressive, destructive, and dangerous behavior to keep everyone in the family safe. The rules must be clearly articulated to the whole family.
2. Consequences must be used consistently and harsh, punitive discipline stopped.
3. As well as consequences for negative behavior, it is critical to have rewards for positive behavior that include noticing any effort to be cooperative, helpful, and to reduce negative behavior. Although concrete rewards can be useful, positive time with a parent or praise can also enhance the relationship.

The choice of consequence for negative behavior is a difficult one but generally includes time-out and restriction or withdrawal of privileges. Both are often hard to enforce, but it is critical to persist.

Repairing the Relationship and Establishing Prosocial Values

Discussion of repairing the relationship can be more generic and includes the importance of stopping ongoing arguments and criticism of the child. Efforts need to focus on helping parents listen to their child, find out what is of concern to her, and replace criticism with encouragement and praise (Nichols, 2004). This approach can include setting aside time to talk, perhaps before bedtime, or discussing events of the day at dinner time.

Another important way to repair the relationship occurs after a rupture, often resulting from the child having been disciplined. Two things are important.

1. Allowing the child to express his feelings about what happened, and listening for the emotions being expressed. Sometimes the parent might apologize for becoming angry and yelling. Showing empathy for the child's feeling of frustration or sadness is particularly important.
2. It is critical, however, to make it clear how the child's behavior affected other people. Reminding the child how she feels when someone bullies her or upsets her, and explaining that this is how her behavior upset other members of the family is critical. This induction is seen as a vital aspect of encouraging internalization of rules and development of conscience (Hoffman, 1988, 1991). It can result in an increase of responsibility and feelings of guilt if the child misbehaves. This is particularly important if children show proactive or planned aggression and no remorse after it. Hughes (2009) discusses the need for repair following conflict, separation, misunderstanding, as well as discipline.

THE APPROACH RECOMMENDED IN THIS BOOK

When working with multi-challenged children, there is flexibility in the type of approach used in choosing the first steps or in how it begins. This is based on the readiness of the parents, their preference for receiving information initially, and the areas of child difficulty where intervention is most needed. The usual steps and types of intervention are described next, though their order can vary, and not all are needed depending on the family situation.

- Parents are given an opportunity to describe their child and his difficulties. A developmental history is usually taken, and questionnaires are completed. Appointments are made for any assessments to be completed by the multidisciplinary team.
- Working with parents also begins with an emphasis on forming a therapeutic relationship by sharing empathy for their difficulties with their child and their struggles to find support and helpful ways to work with her. Respect is shown for their efforts, dedication to their child, and helpful attitudes.
- Whenever possible, if there are two parents, appointments are made that both can attend. This is to make sure that they support each other in any new direction to be adopted and work together as far as possible.
- Feedback is then given on the multidisciplinary assessment of the child. The findings are used to explain some of his behavior and academic, emotional, and social difficulties. Clear ways to intervene with him are explained as well as how they can be implemented at home and/or in school. Efforts are made to develop empathy for the child and understanding that he is struggling with various developmental delays or areas of challenge.
- Discussion also takes place with both parents on how they would describe themselves as parents (e.g., strict, anxious, worn out, angry, and easygoing) and how their descriptions relate to how they were parented. Explaining that sometimes we parent how we were parented or go to the opposite extreme to avoid repeating patterns of parenting that were difficult for us can be helpful. Also inviting the parents to describe their own parents and any difficult events that occur during their own childhood can be helpful although it is important not to push for painful memories.
- The intervenor discusses with the parents the characteristics they would like their child to have. They typically include doing well in school, being kind and caring, being moral and doing the "right" thing, being strong and standing up for what she believes in, and being independent and competent. Asking parents which kind of parenting will develop these capacities allows the intervenor to correct any misconceptions and provide information on what research suggests is the best way to develop the characteristics chosen. The temperaments of the child and parents can be discussed if there appears to be a mismatch, such as a parent who is very outgoing and active and a child who is more shy and academic. Encouraging a better "fit" between the two can be helpful for the parent–child relationship.
- Discussion then takes place on the parenting needed to develop these abilities in the child. Rules and routines are important, as is parents being in charge. They need to provide their child with a sense of safety and consistency about what to expect. It is important to have as few rules as possible to establish the emotional and physical safety of the family. However, as pointed out by Greene and Ablon (2008), some behaviors can be ignored, whereas others must be given consequences. Ways to enforce the rules and provide consequences are decided on. If the child is more anxious than acting out, it is important to encourage her to be more independent and involved in discussing rules and consequences.
- Particularly with parents who tend to be more dismissive, ways of showing acceptance of the child and creating emotional moments with the child are discussed. Positive times with the child are also encouraged. Parents are taught the steps of emotion coaching that they need to go through. It is explained that criticism must be reduced and positive words used to encourage the child to do well. Efforts are made to encourage rational and calming thoughts and positive self-talk in the child. Parents are asked to have some fun time with their child and avoid conflict whenever possible for the next week or until the next session. For the child who is more anxious, especially if the parents are overprotective and oversolicitous, it is important to emphasize encouragement for the child to problem solve.

- Parents are often eager to point out that their child acted out and that it was not possible to avoid triggering by showing empathy. This can be when he was particularly aggressive, destructive of property, or engaged in other behaviors for which the parents had consequences. Parents often want an approach with clear instructions on what to do. Steps can include (1) for approximately 20 seconds, parents show him with their facial expressions and words how serious they saw the behavior to be; (2) they make sure not to shame him but explain his responsibility not to hurt others; (3) they repair the relationship by using induction to make him understand the perspective of the other person; and (4) parents consider what was most upsetting for them and connect it back to their own upbringings if appropriate. These steps are interchangeable, of course, and can be adapted to the challenges and strengths of the child and parents.

In Figure 11.1, the components of working with parents of multi-challenged children are summarized. Although some order is implied, the steps are not numbered as the intervener should move flexibly between the different components adapting them to the child's and parent's individual needs and sometimes needing to go back and redo some of the components. For example, if parents are extremely dismissive of the child's emotions the suggestions about using emotion coaching may need to occur early. Similarly, if parents are particularly chaotic and no rules and routines are in place, establishing these may need to be prioritized. If parents are overprotective helping them to encourage their child's independence may need to be an emphasis. Some clinicians may also choose to work through some of the main difficulties the parents are experiencing with their child one by one allowing them to choose the areas in which the parents are most motivated to improve. Either way it is important to address all the issues identified in Figure 11.1 at an appropriate time during the intervention.

See Table 11.1 for details about related programs and online sources.

Description of child and problems with him/her experienced by parents. Developmental history taken and any intake questionnaires and procedures completed	*Discuss results of multidisciplinary assessment* as soon as they are available. Explain how they can affect the child's functioning. *Provide clear ways to intervene on the basis of these results.*	Discuss with parents *setting up rules, routines and rewards.* Provide clear ways to choose rules and go through process of choosing only absolutes or rules that must be enforced.
Building a therapeautic relationship with parents is key. Showing respect for their previous efforts to find help for their child, and what they have tried. Give a sense of hope.	*Discussion of how parents are parenting, and how they were parented.* Discuss intergenerational repetition of parenting and what they want to do the same, and what they want to do differently, than their parents.	Explain that it is also crucial to *develop a relationship with their child by sharing emotional moments.* Introduce use of emotion coaching, fun times together, and times to connect around emotion.
Establish that *sessions involving both parents will be needed whenever possible.* This will avoid confusion for the child. Other members of the family may also be included.	*Discuss characteristics they want their child to have, and how they think they can develop them in their child.* Differences in temperament between parent and child discussed.	*When child does act out aggressively, becomes noncompliant, or withdraws, make it clear they need to let the child know their behavior is unacceptable* but afterward *repair the relationship* and help child know how others feel about it, and help them find a more positive way to cope.

Figure 11.1 *Working with parents with multi-challenged children: a flexible and integrative approach.*

Table 11.1 *Websites*

Website	Information on Website
http://livesinthebalance.org	A nonprofit organization founded by Dr. Ross Greene, child psychologist, author of the *Explosive Child* and *Lost at School* and originator of the Collaborative Problem Solving (CPS) approach for working in the home and school with children with "explosive behavior." Website has information on how to implement the model and includes a videotape and articles.
www.promisingpractices.net/programs.asp	Website of the Promising Practices Network on Children, Families, and Communities funded by the RAND Corporation. Information on proven and promising programs to improve outcomes for children.
www.pacer.org	Website for the PACER Minnesota Parent Training and Information center that is funded by the U.S. Department of Education Office of Special Education Program. It provides programs and resources for children with emotional or behavioral disorders.
www.pathstraining.com	Website for the provider of training and technical assistance for the Promoting Alternative Thinking (PATH) program that teaches children ways to self-regulate their emotions as well as effective problem-solving strategies.
www.starrtraining.org/trauma-and-children	Website of the Trauma and Loss Center (TLC), which provides information and training on treating grief and trauma reactions in children.
www.findyouthinfo.gov	Website of Helping America's Youth, provides an overview of 180 intervention programs.
www.thereachinstitute.org	The Resource for Advancing Children's Mental Health (REACH) Institute helps parents, educators, and health professionals identify and treat children with emotional and behavioral challenges with effective therapies.
www.danielhughes.org	Website of Daniel Hughes that provides information on Dyadic Developmental Psychotherapy, including dates of training and information on consultation on working with parents and traumatized children.

(continued)

Table 11.1 *Websites (continued)*

Website	Information on Website
www.projectachieve.info	"Stop and Think" social skills program teaches children to stop and think of solutions before they act out and get out of control or withdraw.
www.pcit.phhp.ufl.edu	Website for the parent–child interaction therapy (PCIT), which describes the program and identifies training opportunities to learn how to implement the program.
www.parentingscience.com/preschool-social-skills.html	A website primarily for parents, containing excellent summaries and useful strategies to help teach social skills to preschoolers.
www.challengingbehavior.fmhi.usf.edu.topics.html	Website for the Technical Assistance Center on Social Emotional interventions that provides information on evidence-based practices for young children with challenging behavior.
www.foundationsforsuccess.org	This is the website for Foundations for Success.
www.med.umich.edu/libr/yourchild/topics.html	Website of the University of Michigan Health System that provides information on child development and behavior resources for parents.
www.pacer.org	Website for PACER center that provides information sheets for parents about children with disabilities on a number of topics.
www.parenting.org	Website for Boys' Town that provides parents with a newsletter and articles and parenting guides.
www.cdc.gov/parents	Website of the Centers for Disease Control and Prevention that has parenting videos and articles on a number of topics "to keep your child healthy and safe."
www.childdevelopmentinfo.com	Child Development Institute's *Parenting Today* has a panel of experts, including pediatricians and psychologists, and features articles on a number of child development topics. It has been recommended by the American Psychological Association and *Psychology Today*.

12

A Developmental, Dimensional, Functional Approach to School-Based Mental Health Services

CLAUDIA KOSHINSKY CLIPSHAM

In addition to providing students with an academic education, schools are increasingly being called on to provide mental health services (Christner, Mennuti, & Whitaker, 2009; Lean & Colucci, 2010). This extension of the role of schools has developed in response to growing recognition of the needs of the children they serve. Reviewing data from epidemiological studies in the United States, Canada, and the United Kingdom, Waddell and her colleagues (Waddell, Offord, Shepherd, Hua, & McEwan, 2002) reported estimated prevalence rates of mental health disorders in children from 10% to 20%. Yet only 16% to 27% of these children receive specialized mental health services. Estimates of the percentages of children who receive special education services for these problems were 24% in Ontario and 50% in the United Kingdom. According to one study in the United States (Burns et al., 1995), 70% to 80% of children with mental health problems who receive services get them in the education system, and for the majority of these, the education sector is their sole source of service.

Embedding mental health services in the school setting makes sense, because children spend a substantial part of their everyday lives in that environment. Furthermore, academic learning is functionally interrelated with other aspects of development. Without adequate support, the difficulties experienced by children with social, emotional, and behavioral problems compromise their opportunities to learn and succeed in school (Center for Mental Health in Schools at UCLA, 2006). In a series of federally funded studies in the United States, educational, behavioral, and social outcomes for students with emotional and behavioral difficulties were found to be lower than those for students with other types of disability (Bradley, Henderson, & Monfore, 2004) and were described by one team of authors as "dismal" (Bradley, Doolittle, & Bartolotta, 2008). These poorer outcomes may be related, at least in part, to difficulties in accessing services. Students with emotional disturbances are identified as having special needs later than students with other disabilities, and they change schools more often because of reassignment by their school districts; moreover, their parents report being less satisfied with the educational services received by their children and having to make a greater effort to secure those services than parents of children with other disabilities (Wagner, Kutash, Duchnowski, Epstein, & Sumi, 2005). When a child does not receive support to address social, emotional, and behavioral problems, these difficulties can interfere with her learning; furthermore, if the child's difficulties are expressed in behavior that interrupts educational activities in the school, learning for other children may also be placed at risk. Lean and Colucci (2010) called this the "multiple-ripple effect."

Other children may be subject to factors that place them at risk for poor outcomes, even though they may not qualify for specific diagnoses or formal special needs identification (Adelman & Taylor, 1998). Such risk factors include individual differences that require personalization of instruction. Equally important are systemic and contextual risk factors that create barriers for children in accessing and becoming effectively engaged in their educational settings. These factors include poverty, living in out-of-home settings, lack of connection to community resources, exposure to community violence, and lack of access to health care. They also include direct or vicarious experiences in their families and cultural groups of oppression and disparity in power that make them hesitant to open themselves to relationships with outsiders. Problems may arise for these children, not simply because of their individual characteristics, but also because of the mismatch or lack of congruence between their characteristics and the demands of the school environment in which they are expected to function (Deno, 1989, 2005). Rather than waiting until children experiencing such risk factors have problems that become expressed in social, behavioral, and learning problems, and then locating these problems as "disorders" residing within the individual child, the delivery of educational services needs to be adapted proactively to address the situational risk and protective factors that affect students.

Adelman and Taylor (2009) suggest that although school policy development is currently directed toward two components, improving instruction and school management, a third component is also needed. They call this the "enabling component," stating that "a comprehensive, multifaceted, integrated continuum of enabling activity is essential in addressing the needs of youngsters who encounter barriers that interfere with their benefiting satisfactorily from instruction" (p. 28). This component includes activities such as enhancing regular classroom instructional strategies, facilitating connections with home and community, and supporting children and families through transitions. It also includes promoting social and emotional learning and development in students (Zins, Bloodworth, Weissberg, & Walberg, 2004). Schools are thus being called on to reduce barriers to learning; build on the strengths of each student; and promote the social, emotional, behavioral, and academic competencies of all their students in a comprehensive and integrated manner (Adelman & Taylor, 1998, 2006; Greenberg et al., 2003; Lean & Colucci, 2010; Repie, 2005).

SCHOOL-RELATED MENTAL HEALTH SERVICES

In the provision of school-related mental health services, program design and delivery typically involve professionals whose training and experience are rooted in education and/or mental health. Each of these orientations is guided by theoretical influences and emphases that are often different but potentially overlapping (Kutash, Duchnowski, & Lynn, 2006). For instance, the education system has focused on improving academic outcomes for students, addressing psychosocial barriers as a means of ensuring student success. In the mental health system, emotional, relational, and behavioral problems have often been the main areas of focus, with educational functioning being addressed as one, but sometimes not the primary, area of adaptation to be enhanced. Collaboration between the two perspectives can be facilitated by identifying the larger goal they have in common: enhancing the child's adaptation in all settings (Kutash et al., 2006).

Another area of commonality between education and mental health approaches is a conceptualization, based on public health models, of services on a continuum from less intensive to more intensive. From the children's mental health perspective, services are conceptualized on a continuum from prevention to treatment (Christner et al., 2009). The integrative framework developed by Weisz and colleagues for children's mental health services in general (Weisz, Sandler, Durlak, & Anton, 2005) is applicable to the specific context of school-based services (Kutash et al., 2006). In this model, interventions are positioned along the continuum between prevention and treatment according to the level of risk factors that they address. Five levels were defined as follows:

1. Health promotion/positive development strategies are directed at the whole population, attempting to enhance strengths to reduce risk for later problems and increase potential for positive outcomes.
2. Universal prevention strategies address risk factors in entire populations of children without identifying which individuals are at elevated risk.
3. Selective prevention strategies target groups identified as sharing a particular risk factor, and interventions are designed to counteract that risk.
4. Indicated prevention strategies provide intervention for individuals who exhibit symptoms of a disorder but do not currently meet criteria for a diagnosis.
5. Treatment intervention strategies target individuals with high symptom levels and/or diagnosable conditions.

From the education perspective, a similar continuum is conceptualized in the Response to Intervention (RTI) model (Mellard, McKnight, & Jordan, 2010; National Center on Response to Intervention, 2010). Three levels of instruction are identified (see Figure 12.1) as follows:

1. Tier 1 or "universal" services provide primary prevention-level, classwide, high-quality, general instruction to 100% of the population of students. In most RTI models, Tier 1 interventions should be adequate to support educational progress for approximately 80% of students. The 20% of students for whom this level of instruction is not adequate to support gains in learning are considered to be "nonresponders" to Tier 1 instruction.
2. For these Tier 1 nonresponders, more intense and specialized secondary prevention-level instruction is provided. The increased level of intensity of these Tier 2 or "targeted" interventions should be sufficient to support educational progress for another 15% of students, still leaving approximately 5% of students who are nonresponders to Tier 2 interventions.
3. For the 5% of students for whom Tier 2 interventions are not adequate to support gains in learning, more intense, specialized, individualized instruction at a tertiary-prevention Tier 3 (or "indicated") level is provided.

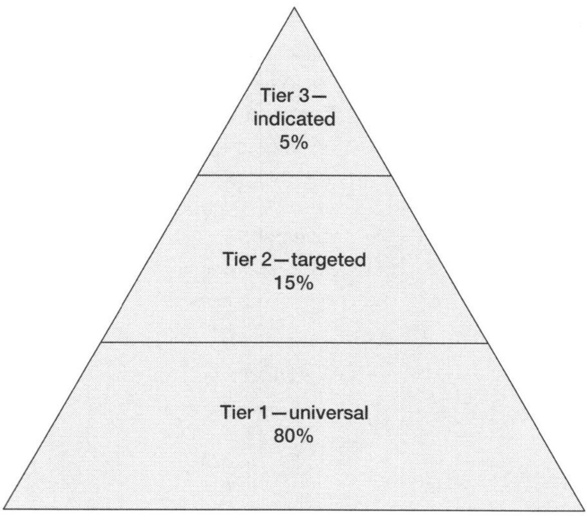

Figure 12.1 *RTI model.*
Adapted from Lean and Colucci (2010).

Thus, the guiding conceptualization for both educational and mental health perspectives is a continuum of services from less intense to more intense, based on a foundation of high-quality preventive interventions provided for all students. Inherent in this approach is a commitment to develop and use a range of practices and programs that are responsive to the needs of individual students and their families, that are effective in reaching across and breaking down barriers, and that promote the success of all students. Working from this vision, when an intervention or program is not used by specific children and families or by groups of children and families because they experience barriers to accessing it, they cannot be dismissed as being "not ready" to use services and allowed to "fall off the radar" of the education and mental health systems. Similarly, a standardized educational or mental health program provided to all students/clients may be adequate to allow a large proportion of them to make progress; however, children for whom it is not intense and individualized enough cannot be left to struggle and fail. Rather, a range of programs and services needs to be developed, with options that are flexible and responsive in order to adapt the services to the clients' needs rather than vice versa (Prince Inniss, Nesman, Mowery, Callejas, & Hernandez, 2009). This conceptualization applies at a macro-level in terms of service planning and program development for a community or school district; equally, it applies at the micro-level of the classroom or therapy room in interventions with small groups, individual families, and individual children.

Providing high-quality, population-wide, prevention programs is essential in the model, embraced by both educational and mental health orientations, which involves a continuum of services. Lean and Colucci (2010, p. 62) observed that when these preventive services are seriously attenuated or eliminated as a result of budget constraints, the difficulties experienced by children "become chronic and intractable." As a result, they estimated that 80% to 90% of the efforts of support service professionals in the school system are devoted to providing intensive Tier 3 interventions rather than prevention programs, in essence turning the conceptualization of tiered services upside down (see Figure 12.2).

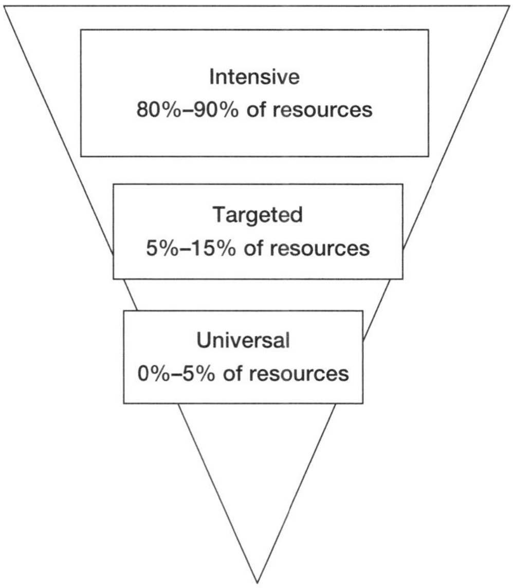

Figure 12.2 *Attenuated focus on prevention and the impact on service delivery.*
Adapted from Lean and Colucci (2010).

For both education and mental health approaches, less intensive prevention programs and more intensive treatment interventions often overlap and complement each other to serve a broad range of children and families. In both approaches, services can be situated in a range of contexts. Prevention and intervention can be located separately in distinct settings such as home, school, outpatient clinic, day-treatment program, or hospital; likewise, a range of services can be provided from the same base, such as a school setting. Even when services are all provided within the context of the school, the environments in which they are provided vary (Kutash et al., 2006). A school might be situated in a local neighborhood or in a specialized setting such as a hospital or juvenile justice facility. Some children might receive services in general education classrooms, whereas others might be placed in these classrooms with additional supports, either in class or in "pull-out" interventions for periods of the school day. Other children might receive services in more specialized, segregated classes. Regardless of location, services may be funded and administered by the educational system or the mental health system, and at times these may be partnered. For instance, a specialized classroom program might be offered jointly by educational and mental health services, working in collaboration with children and their families. A plan of treatment for a child/family might include both educational and mental health components, developed collaboratively by a "wrap-around" planning team.

Effective educational and mental health partnerships need to go beyond simply "co-locating" services in schools (Lean & Colucci, 2010). Programs and services are strengthened when educational and mental health perspectives are functionally integrated into a collaborative effort to enhance the adaptation of children in the many contexts in which they live—home, family, school, and community. Collaboration with the child welfare system is also essential for children who live in foster care placements (Weinberg, Zetlin, & Shea, 2009). In order for collaborative efforts to be effective when the systems attempting to work together are each so complex, their integrated functioning needs to be carefully planned and orchestrated; otherwise, well-intentioned efforts from the educational, mental health, and child welfare sectors can operate at cross-purposes at times. Programs and services are sometimes offered as disconnected packages, rather than in a well-considered, strategic, coherent manner. Organizational structures are required that bring operations together into coordinated, integrated, "interconnected systems" (Kutash et al., 2006). As Adelman and Taylor (2009, p. 39) put it, "structure follows function."

At the same time, the value of central organization needs to be balanced with adequate opportunity to adapt procedures and services to "local" conditions—in a family, neighborhood, school, cultural community, partnering service provider, or other source of influence that impacts service delivery and efficacy for a child. Furthermore, some diversity of philosophies and approaches to service needs to be supported, in order to offer clients choices rather than forcing them to "take or leave" the only intervention available. In fact, if central coordination of services leads to rigid standardization of service delivery, the flexibility needed to offer an effective "enabling" component can be jeopardized (Prince Inniss et al., 2009). For instance, a crucial consideration in engaging clients considered to be "hard to reach" is the opportunity to develop working alliances and relationships with them (Landy, Menna, & Clipsham, 2006); therefore, the systems within which educators and clinicians work must be designed to enhance opportunities for ongoing individualized connection and relational coherency rather than obscure working relationships in a maze of bureaucratic procedural priorities. Otherwise, when they are delivered without a relational context and on a scale that is too complex to be comprehended by the client, services become "hard to reach" for most people. (For further discussion of issues that make services and service systems "hard to reach," see Hughes, 2007. For a discussion of strategies to enhance the availability of culturally competent mental health services, see Prince Inniss et al., 2009.)

The challenges at the organizational level are substantial but not insurmountable, and considerable effort is being devoted to devising solutions. For instance, Adelman and Taylor (2009) and Lean and Colucci (2010) discuss the challenges involved in making the systemic changes needed, together with processes and models that could be used to guide these changes, in order to integrate mental health services more fully into educational systems. Van Acker and Mayer (2009, p. 101) call for a "significant paradigm shift" to redefine the roles of school and community agencies and allocate the financial and human resources necessary to effectively meet the academic, social, and emotional needs of children.

Whether they are working in a "new world" of better organized and integrated services, or doing their best to make existing systems function better, educators and mental health clinicians can work side by side to provide services to children and their families, in regular classes, special education classes, hybrid mental health treatment and education classes, and other specialized settings, such as hospitals, clinics, and treatment centers. In this chapter, the words *practitioner, educator, clinician, teacher, therapist, worker,* and *professional* are used interchangeably to recognize that interventions may be carried out by professionals from different disciplines, with affiliations in education or mental health or both. Furthermore, programs and practices are described as "mental health" and "education" interventions interchangeably, because the two are inextricably related.

A CHALLENGE FOR EDUCATORS AND CLINICIANS

Programs and practices implemented every day in regular classrooms can affect the development of students, for better or worse, depending on the extent to which they actually respond to each child's needs and strengths. In fact, professionals working in school-related education and/or mental health programs are routinely asked to provide services for children with a wide range of needs and strengths, many of whom have diagnosed or undiagnosed difficulties that affect their adaptation to school environments. Attempting to meet the diversity of strengths and needs presented by the children in a given school or classroom can be challenging. Educators and clinicians can feel "deskilled" when first asked to work with a child with a particular diagnosis with which they do not have extensive experience, asking themselves, "What do I know about meeting the needs of children with reactive attachment disorder or ADHD or autism?" Some children have been given multiple diagnostic labels, with multiple checklists of symptoms and accompanying recommendations, sometimes bringing a teacher or clinician to wonder, "What does all this mean for what I do, day by day, to meet the needs of this child?" Even when educators and clinicians do have previous experience in working with children with a given diagnostic label, they might still experience a sense of discrepancy in working with a new child, because children who have been given the same diagnostic label can differ from each other in important ways. Children with different diagnoses can also be similar in some ways, because diagnostic categories often overlap, involving difficulties in similar functional areas. Moreover, teachers and clinicians often sense that there are children in their classrooms and programs who might not have been given specific diagnoses, but who present with behaviors and difficulties that need to be addressed to enable them to be successful learners. Thus, educators and clinicians who are keenly aware of the diversity of needs, diagnosed and undiagnosed, of the children in their classrooms can at times feel that they are dealing with a confusing array of individuals who differ considerably from each other, each with a separate checklist of needs.

BENEFITS OF A DEVELOPMENTAL, DIMENSIONAL, FUNCTIONAL APPROACH

A developmental, dimensional, functional approach provides conceptual and practical support for school mental health practitioners in meeting the diverse needs of their students. The contributions made by this approach are evident at multiple levels, from planning practices and programs for specific students or classrooms to developing intervention programs for wider use. Some of these benefits are discussed below.

Individual differences can be conceptualized on a developmental continuum that informs practice, supporting a continuum of interventions within a classroom.

A major advantage of a functional dimensional developmental approach is that it provides a unifying framework within which individual differences among children in a classroom can be understood. If an educator/clinician is knowledgeable about the ways in which skills and abilities develop in each specific area, he can consider each child's present functioning and corresponding experiences and interactions that would likely support further progress. He can use this developmental perspective to understand how the child's functioning relates to the continuum of developmental progress in each area; furthermore, specific practices and interventions can also be seen on a developmental continuum, from those that promote early development in each area to those that support later development.

Often the principles that guide practices and teaching methods appropriate for children who have difficulties are the same ones that guide effective practice for most children; however, specific content and intensity are adjusted to match the child's developmental level. An educational practice that would be generally appropriate for children at a younger age can often be adapted to deal with an identified risk factor or difficulty for an older child. For instance, the same general principles recommended for teaching reading to typical learners are also valuable for children who are struggling: a child with severe difficulties in word decoding in Grade 3 may require intensive and explicit instruction and practice in the phonics skills and decoding strategies that some of his classmates mastered at an earlier age. The level of instruction that he would be given would thus be geared to his specific level of skill development. At the same time, both children with reading problems and their typically learning classmates benefit when higher-order skills such as comprehension of narratives are taught concurrently with explicit instruction in foundational skills. If the child with the reading problem has listening comprehension skills similar to those of others in his class, he might be able to participate along with his classmates in a lesson focused on enjoying and engaging with a story, provided that he has access to the text through an accommodation such as assistive technology or his teacher reading it aloud to the whole class (Expert Panel on Literacy and Numeracy Instruction for Students with Special Education Needs, Kindergarten to Grade 6, 2005).

An understanding of development in each area allows a teacher to develop a "class profile" of the range of functional levels of the students in each area (Expert Panel on Literacy and Numeracy Instruction for Students with Special Education Needs, Kindergarten to Grade 6, 2005). The design of the classroom environment and program can then be based on this profile, maximizing flexibility and inclusiveness to the extent possible. Within this context, specific adaptations of the overall practices in the class can be made to meet individual needs. The general question, "Which educational practices are effective in working with children with this diagnosis?" can be productively complemented by asking, "Given what is observed about this child's functional competencies and difficulties in each area, which experiences and inputs are needed to help her take the next steps in developing?" By reframing the planning process in developmental rather than strictly diagnostic terms, rather than trying to plan for a bewildering array of 20 or 25 conceptually separate individual learning plans in a class, a teacher can consider each student's needs and strengths in relation to a developmental continuum that provides an organizing, integrative frame of reference.

Case Study of Ms. Evans

For example, understanding the ways in which children develop skills in self-regulation and self-control helps Ms. Evans to design her classroom program to fit the overall needs of her Grade 2 students; furthermore, her awareness of the functional developmental levels of individual students with respect to self-regulation allows her to adapt what she does to meet individual needs within the larger group program.

In setting up her classroom, Ms. Evans is aware of the principles articulated by Shanker (2012, 2013) that self-regulation skills are essential for children to succeed in the school environment and that they develop these skills by being regulated by others. Thus, she designs her classroom environment and routines to promote regulation.

- Typical classrooms have instructional materials, schedules, and reminders covering the walls. Many adults have developed the skills to tune out the information that they do not need, and they can efficiently direct their attention to the specific picture or list or schedule needed at the moment; however, for many children who have not yet developed those skills, walls covered in stimuli can be very distracting and disorganizing. These children can have great difficulty picking out the information that they need when they need it. Similarly, although a room full of activity can be enlivening to an adult who has a mental framework for understanding it and the skill to focus on one activity without being drawn in by the sights, sounds, and actions of others, it may be almost impossible for some children to remain similarly focused and organized. Ms. Evans adjusts the amount of stimulation in the classroom environment to the level that the children can manage, to prevent their feeling more stressed and less safe.
- Based on her knowledge of the capacity for self-control that typical 7-year-olds exhibit, Ms. Evans provides a fair degree of external structure and predictability. For example, from the beginning, she clearly explains the day-to-day routines and schedules to all the students and posts them on the board. She provides frequent reminders to the students about them.
- Within the schedule, Ms. Evans includes times each day when children are allowed to make choices about what they will do. On the morning that we are observing, at free time she explains to the students that they can play a game of their choice from the shelf, work on a craft project, listen to a story on the computer, or play a science game. Some of them know what they want to do. Others have difficulties with choosing, and Ms. Evans invites and supports them to make decisions and get started on their activities. She moves around the classroom, quietly chatting with individual students, showing interest in what they are doing, and asking questions or making suggestions that allow them to expand on their chosen activities.

Ms. Evans includes structured group-learning activities in the schedule every day as well. While leading these activities, she continually monitors the students in the group.

- On the day that we are observing, she comments aloud on the positive listening skills that many students are exhibiting.
- At the same time, Ms. Evans provides support to four others whose attention is divided between arguing about who will be on whose team at recess and the group lesson, by asking questions that allow them to speak and stay engaged with the lesson and reminding them when needed about rules such as taking turns to speak.
- Over time, Ms. Evans has recognized that three children in the group have self-control skills more typical of somewhat younger children. She routinely provides additional supports for them by monitoring where they sit in the group so that distractions can be minimized and redirection offered to them without undue interruption to the group. She also plans group-learning activities that involve a high level of active participation to maintain their interest. Sometimes, if they are having difficulty staying focused through the whole lesson planned for the group, she breaks it up into several shorter segments, interspersed with other activities.
- Two students in the class have been identified as having significant difficulties with emotional regulation and self-control. A child-and-youth worker (CYW) who assists in the class for some

portions of the day stays close to them during group times, providing support for them to remain emotionally and behaviorally regulated and engaged in the group-learning activity. On the morning that we are observing, one child gets upset when another child calls him a name, and the CYW talks quietly with him in the corner to help him calm down and make a plan to deal with the situation. Together, they return to the group.

- One child in the classroom has severe and longstanding difficulties with following routines, sequencing her actions, inhibiting inappropriate actions, and shifting from one task to the next, and she has been assigned a one-to-one support worker to help her manage during the school day. Her understanding of the concepts and language used in the group lesson is commensurate with that of many other children in the class, and with support, prompting, and proactive intervention from her one-to-one worker, she can often participate productively in the group activity. However, at times when she becomes overwhelmed and agitated, her one-to-one worker might take her to another room where they can work together to help her calm down and reorient to the routine before returning to the group.

Thus, based on their knowledge of the development of self-control and self-regulation skills in children, together with an understanding of the children in their class, Ms. Evans and the classroom team offer a range of experiences that require more or less self-regulation, with fine-tuning to meet the needs of individual children. Of course, the extent to which they can meet this wide range of needs depends on the availability of resources, including the number of adults in the classroom.

A developmental understanding supports "thinking outside the box," to go beyond the immediate behavioral presentation of the child, to consider the ways in which less well-developed functional skills may be contributing to an observed problem in adapting to the classroom environment.

Ross Greene (2008) suggests that challenging behaviors are most likely to occur when the classroom environment places greater demands on the child's functional adaptation than her skills can support. An understanding of her developmental difficulties in the functional skill areas that underlie the behavioral problem allows the teacher or clinician to approach the child with more empathy. By helping her to learn and use the skills that she needs to function more adaptively, the barriers to her learning can be reduced, and she can participate more successfully in the educational program.

Case Study

For instance, Selena is a 9-year-old who has difficulties bringing to mind and organizing the separate pieces of information needed to mentally compose a response to a question. She often has difficulties with answering questions that her teacher asks in science class; she might hesitate and stumble over her words, provide an off-topic response, or even freeze, unable to respond. If her teacher, Mr. Khan, knows that Selena understands the basic individual concepts needed to answer the question, but does not fully appreciate the extent of her functional difficulty in retrieving and assembling the information quickly, he might assume that she is not trying or is oppositional. These attributions might lead him to increase demands on Selena in an attempt to teach her to try harder, which can increase her anxiety and further diminish her capacity to respond fluently to the question. Or he might quickly move on to ask another child in the class to provide the answer, leaving Selena to feel that once again, she has not been able to respond effectively in the classroom environment. But if Mr. Khan understands the developmental difficulty underlying her behavior, he can provide prompts and scaffolding to help her retrieve relevant concepts and organize her thoughts to compose a response. Selena's ongoing development of competency in self-expression would thus be enhanced rather than diminished, and her engagement in the science curriculum would be supported.

Going beyond surface behavioral presentation is especially important for children who have difficulties with attention and executive functioning. If teachers and parents are not aware of the difficulties that a child is experiencing, they might conclude that he is not motivated and not trying or applying himself to his studies. If the important adults in his life assume that he is choosing not to cooperate with requests and is being defiant, and respond in kind, a coercive pattern of interaction based on power and control rather than mutual cooperation might be established. The child is then placed at increased risk for academic underperformance or failure, with accompanying difficulties in emotional and behavioral regulation and a reluctance or even resistance to call on adults for help with his problems. Indeed, children who have been diagnosed with attention deficit/hyperactivity disorder (ADHD) are at higher risk for a number of other comorbid difficulties, including anxiety, depression, and other mood disorders, oppositional defiant and conduct disorders, and learning disabilities (Barkley, 2006). However, when the difficulties that a child exhibits with controlling, directing, planning, and organizing his attention and actions are recognized, and it is understood that he is not failing to follow through because he does not want to, but rather, because he does not have the self-regulatory skills to do so consistently, then appropriate supports can be put in place to mitigate some of the primary effects of his developmental difficulties with executive functioning; furthermore, some of the secondary negative effects on his learning and emotional development can be prevented or ameliorated (McCloskey, Perkins, & Van Divner, 2009).

A fine-grained understanding of the course of development in each area, the ways in which functioning is interrelated across areas, and the risk and protective factors that influence developmental pathways to particular outcomes can inform the design and development of programs and interventions.

A clear model of the factors that contribute to the development of behavioral problems makes it possible to specify targets and goals for interventions to prevent or treat them (Holmbeck, Greenley, & Franks, 2003; Lochman & Gresham, 2009). Although there may be a number of biologically based as well as broader contextual factors associated with a negative outcome that are relatively difficult to change, they may exert their influence through proximal mediating factors related to current functioning. These are identifiable, accessible, and more amenable to change, making them good targets to consider in designing interventions.

For instance, working from a contextual social–cognitive model of the development of aggressive behavior, Lochman and his colleagues (Lochman, Powell, Whidby, & Fitzgerald, 2006; Lochman & Wells, 2002; Lochman, Wells, & Lenhart, 2008) identified distortions in aggressive children's social–cognitive appraisals: in responding to a social interaction, aggressive children recall fewer social cues, selectively attend to hostile cues, and tend to focus on recent cues while forgetting those that occurred earlier in the sequence. They tend to attribute hostile attentions to others and underestimate their own aggressiveness while perceiving others as being more aggressive. On the other hand, empathy or recognition of the feelings of others is positively associated with prosocial behavior and negatively associated with antisocial behavior in school-aged children. Lochman and his associates also noted important deficiencies in the problem-solving processes of aggressive children: they tend to generate fewer verbal problem-solving strategies and more action-oriented strategies, and they evaluate aggressive strategies more positively. The child guidance practices used by parents are also considered in Lochman's model: harsh discipline, poor problem solving, vague directions, low monitoring of behavior, inconsistent parenting, and low parental involvement all contribute to the development of aggressive behavior in children. In turn, the aggressive and antisocial behavior of their children often contributes to parents' feelings of inefficacy and frustration, potentially decreasing the efficacy of parenting practices in the family.

Following from their understanding of these key factors in the development of aggression, Lochman and his colleagues developed the Coping Power program (Lochman et al., 2008; Wells, Lochman, & Lenhart, 2008) to address the social–cognitive processing and decision-making skills of aggressive children, together with the disciplinary practices used by their parents. The program was designed for use in Grades 3 to 7 as a preventive intervention for children who have high ratings by teachers and parents on aggressive behavior and as an intervention for children who meet criteria for diagnoses of oppositional defiant or conduct disorder. It has also been adapted for use as a treatment component within existing children's mental health programs (Elbe, Andrade, Schmidt, & Thomson, 2010). Groups are provided for children as well as their parents, with interrelated content (Lochman & Wells, 2004). The child groups deal with establishing group rules, identifying and practicing strategies to cope with angry feelings, training in social perspective taking and social problem solving, and practicing social skills such as negotiation and cooperation (Lochman et al., 2008). Although the children's groups typically occur before or after school or at lunch time, and thus are not part of the formal academic curriculum, the transfer of skills from group to classroom is promoted. The content of the parent groups includes identifying behavioral goals for children, rewarding positive child behavior, setting age-appropriate expectations, using appropriate consequences, developing family communication strategies, managing stress, and problem solving (Wells et al., 2008). When the Coping Power program was implemented with aggressive elementary school boys, during the year following the intervention, reductions were found in children's self-reported delinquent behavior and parent-reported alcohol and marijuana use by the child, together with improvements in teacher reports of the children's functioning in school (Lochman & Wells, 2002, 2004). Path analyses indicated that these effects were mediated by improvements in children's internal locus of control; parental consistency; and changes in children's attributions, person perceptions, and expectations regarding the outcomes of aggressive behaviors. For further discussion of the outcomes of the Coping Power program, see www.copingpower.com/ResultsBenefitsOutcomes.aspx.

A developmental perspective allows evidence-based practices and recommendations for working with children with specific diagnoses to be fine-tuned to meet the individual needs of each student.

At the level of program implementation, a model of the processes that typically lead to the development of a functional problem, and the risk and protective factors that mediate its effects on the child's functioning more generally, allow more structured, standardized intervention programs to be individualized to meet the specific needs of a child more effectively. For instance, Lochman and Gresham (2009) recommend a thorough assessment of children on entry in the Coping Power program to guide a comprehensive treatment plan. The specific factors considered in this assessment follow from the developmental model on which the program is based, such as the child's social information processing skills and attribution biases. From the understanding gained from this assessment, some aspects of the Coping Power program can be highlighted more than others to address specific strengths, deficits, and comorbid difficulties of individual children within the group.

Fine-tuning can also occur within the classroom. Educational practices generally found to be useful for students with specific diagnoses can be understood more fully by considering the functional developmental needs that they are designed to address, allowing them to be adapted to the individual child rather than being applied prescriptively. For example, visual supports such as picture schedules are often recommended for children diagnosed with autism spectrum disorders (Magyar, 2011). These tools highlight the stimuli relevant to the completion of a task; furthermore, they support the child in executing routines by providing prompts for each specific action to be completed, allowing him to sequence his behavior by matching his actions to each prompt, step by step. In this way, his behavioral organization is supported by reducing the demands on him to remember and mentally assemble information and use it to initiate actions on his own. However, some children who have been diagnosed with autism might have difficulties with interpreting relatively abstract pictorial symbols; for these children, more concrete objects might be needed as reminders. Other children might be stronger in reading than in interpreting pictures; for them, printed-word reminders might be more effective. In fact, regardless of the type of visual prompt used, children need adequate instruction and practice to allow them to reliably decode the meanings of the pictures or symbols and associate them with the actions to which they refer. Without such practice and repetition, the visual tool can add another layer of challenge to the task of completing the routine rather than making it easier. By understanding the developmental function of the tool, its use can be fine-tuned to the specific functional skills of the child. Also, its use can be extended to other children with similar functional difficulties. For example, a visual schedule might be useful for children who have working memory and organizational difficulties, even if they have not been diagnosed with autism.

A developmental perspective provides an informed place to start working when an evidence-based practice does not seem to be working for a specific child or when there are no evidence-based practices to guide intervention.

The importance of using evidence-based practices as opposed to those based on "instinct, hearsay, or teacher, parent, or Internet recommendation" (Lembke & Stormont, 2005) is widely embraced, with good reason. Educators and clinicians are accountable to the children and parents whom they serve as well as the funders who support their work to seek practices and programs that have been shown to be effective. However, as Fuchs and Deshler (2007, p. 132) remind us, no intervention is validated for all children at all times. When an intervention has been tested and found to be effective for most children, it can be considered a "good bet." However, even when an intervention results in an overall positive effect for a large group of children, some individuals within that group might possess single characteristics or clusters of characteristics that make the intervention less effective or even counterproductive for them. Although some of these characteristics may be identified and studied, others may not be explicitly recognized. They can increase the variability or "error variance" of the outcome data for the group to some extent, but often not enough to alter the overall main effect of the intervention demonstrated for the group as a whole (Cronbach, 1975). The negative effect of a particular constellation of individual characteristics on the outcome of an intervention that has generally been found to be a good bet can go undiscovered until the intervention is tried and found to be ineffective for an individual child. At these times, a clinician or educator may draw on an understanding of how the child's functional development in one area is impacted by risk and protective factors influencing functioning in other areas and develop hypotheses about why the intervention did not work. This understanding can then guide the treatment plan, either in selecting another intervention better suited to the child's particular constellation of needs and strengths, or in providing additional supports to mitigate the negative effects of the factors that are reducing the efficacy of the intervention for this specific child. Evidence-based interventions are optimized when they are applied thoughtfully, based on a consideration of the individual child's developmental context.

At times, practitioners are not able to use a well-researched intervention to meet the needs of a particular child, either because of lack of access to existing programs, or because specific interventions have not been developed and evaluated. For instance, few school-based intervention programs have been developed explicitly for children who have experienced problematic attachment relationships with their caregivers, nor are there many studies evaluating the efficacy of specific classroom practices for children with these difficulties. However, there is an extensive literature on the detrimental effects of attachment problems on developmental outcomes and on the factors that mediate these effects, including affect regulation skills, emotional communication skills, internal representations of relationships, coherence of narratives about relationship experiences, and behavior in the context of relationships. The developmental understanding afforded by this body of research highlights these mediating factors as potentially useful targets for intervention for children who have experienced difficult attachment histories. An educator/clinician who has an understanding of these developmental processes can make informed choices about practices that are likely to be helpful for specific children, based on a carefully developed formulation of the individual child's and family's characteristics. Careful, ongoing assessment of the individual's progress is needed to provide feedback on whether the practices and interventions chosen have been effective (Ollendick, King, & Chorpita, 2006).

Attachment theory provides a valuable lens in looking at the effects of teacher-student relationships on children's adaptation to school, with implications for day to day practice. Waters and Cummings (2000) posited that, as children develop increased capacities to represent relationships symbolically, they increase their abilities to make use of people outside their families, including friends and teachers, as "secure base figures of convenience." Although their parental attachment figures are not physically present at school, their teachers may be able to act as secure base figures (Cyr & van IJzendoorn, 2007; Kennedy & Kennedy, 2004, 2007; Pianta, 1999; Zionts, 2005). Pianta (1999) suggested that a teacher may act as a source of protection, help, and comfort, helping the child to meet challenges and use feedback constructively, and buffering the child when she experiences failure. The emotional support supplied to the child through a positive relationship with her teacher can allow her to cope with more challenging academic activities, enhancing her opportunities for learning. It can also support her social adaptation.

Pianta (1999) characterized teacher–student relationships in terms of their closeness (including warmth and open communication), conflict, and dependency (where the child exhibits a developmentally inappropriate negative reliance on the teacher). He and his colleagues have found relationships between these dimensions and outcomes for students.

- Children with close, warm relationships with their Kindergarten teachers were found to be better adjusted in Grade 2 than those with high-conflict, dependent relationships in Kindergarten (Pianta, Steinberg, & Rollins, 1995).
- These effects of the quality of teacher–child relationships on the child's school adaptation appear to persist over time. High levels of conflict and dependency with teachers in Kindergarten were related to children's behavioral and academic outcomes in Grade 8, especially for those with behavioral problems and for boys in general (Hamre & Pianta, 2001).
- When teachers interact in a warm and positive manner with students in their classes, when they are responsive to the needs of individual children, and when they provide clear feedback to children as part of high-quality instruction, children's academic and social competencies are enhanced (Curby, LoCasale-Crouch, et al., 2009; Pianta, Belsky, & Vandergrift, 2008; Stuhlman & Pianta, 2009; Wilson, Pianta, & Stuhlman, 2007).
- The influence of conflict was demonstrated by Crosnoe et al. (2010), who found that children who enter school with low, average, or high levels of math skills tend to maintain separate but parallel trajectories of achievement right up through Grade 5. However, low starters were able to narrow the gap between their trajectories and those of other students if they were given more challenging, inference-based instruction and if they did not have conflictual relationships with their teachers. This improved rate of progress was found neither in students who were provided a less challenging instructional program limited to basic skills nor in students with elevated levels of conflict with their teachers.

Interpreting these findings in attachment terms, when teachers have warm, positive, and close relationships with their students, they are able to provide emotional support to the children as needed, allowing them to feel secure enough and emotionally regulated enough to engage and adapt in the classroom environment, develop positive social relationships, and meet academic challenges. On the other hand, when teacher–child relation ships are characterized by high levels of conflict and negative dependency, children may be less able to effectively signal their needs and get the reassurance that they need to feel safe; rather, they are more likely to be caught up in relational struggles that leave them feeling vulnerable and less able to engage freely and confidently with learning and social environments.

For children who are subject to factors that place them at increased risk for school difficulties, their relationships with teachers can moderate the impacts of these risk factors and support developmental pathways to more positive outcomes (Kennedy & Kennedy, 2004; Myers & Pianta, 2008; Pianta, 1999; Zionts, 2005). Zionts (2005) highlighted the potential for positive teacher–child relationships to act as buffers, preventing and reducing negative outcomes for children at risk for aggression and externalizing behavior due to factors such as disorganized attachment relationships with their primary caregivers. Supporting evidence comes from several studies as listed below:

- Ladd and Burgess (2001) found that for children at risk for behavioral problems such as aggression, a high level of conflict with teachers is an added stressor leading to a range of negative outcomes, whereas a close relationship with teachers is protective.
- Hughes and Cavell (1999) reported that for children identified as aggressive in Grades 2 and 3, positive relationships with teachers were related to lower levels of aggression in the following year; furthermore, these teacher–student relationships were found to be most beneficial for children whose parents reported histories of rejection by their own parents.
- In a study exploring the extent to which teacher–child relationships can buffer the effects of insecure attachment to caregivers, Buyse, Verschueren, and Doumen (2011) found that less secure parent–child relationships in Kindergarten were associated with higher levels of aggression in Grade 1; however, children with less secure parental relationships who had close relationships with their Grade 1 teachers were no longer at risk for more aggressive behavior. Furthermore, although less securely attached children were more at risk for lower levels of closeness with their teachers when the teachers' behavior was rated as low in sensitivity, when the teachers' behaviors were high in sensitivity, the less securely attached children were no longer at risk for low closeness to their teachers.
- Essex, Armstrong, Burk, Goldsmith, and Boyce (2011) found a moderating effect of children's behavioral reactivity on the connection between teacher–child relationships in Grade 1 and children's mental health in Grade 7. In their study, behaviorally inhibited children exhibited the most severe mental health symptoms in Grade 7 when their relationships with their Grade 1 teachers were high in conflict and the least severe mental health symptoms when their earlier relationships were low in conflict. For these inhibited children, their level of closeness to their Grade 1 teachers was not related to their level of symptoms in Grade 7. In contrast, behaviorally disinhibited children developed more severe symptoms by Grade 7 when their relationships with their Grade 1 teachers were low in closeness and the lowest level of later symptoms when their earlier relationships were high in closeness, with no effect of conflict.

Characteristics of children and teachers have a transactional effect on their relationships. For instance, the relationship between teacher–child conflict and the child's aggressive behavior is bidirectional: early aggressive or antisocial behavior by the child leads to a higher level of conflict with his teacher, which in turn leads to an escalation of aggression or a reduction in prosocial behavior (Birch & Ladd, 1998; Doumen et al., 2008). In a study examining contributions to relational conflict from factors in the teacher, child, and context, Mantzicopoulos (2005) found that teacher–child conflict in Kindergarten was higher for students rated higher with respect to hyperactivity and lower for children whose levels of achievement were higher. The level of conflict reported by children was also related to the developmental appropriateness of the instructional approach taken by the teacher and to the teacher's involvement in the transition of the child to school. Teacher reports of the difficulty of their teaching assignments were also related to higher reports of relationship conflict.

Summarizing the findings on the potential impacts of teacher–student relationships, Myers and Pianta (2008) observed that close positive relationships between teachers and students promote positive outcomes, but when students have difficulty forming positive relationships, the risk of negative outcomes is increased. Furthermore, recent findings suggest that the level of closeness in the teacher–child relationship is especially influential on outcomes for behaviorally disinhibited children, whereas the level of conflict is a more potent influence for better or worse for inhibited children.

Because teacher–student relationships can provide a strategically useful target for intervention, it is worth considering some factors that can influence relationship quality (Kennedy & Kennedy, 2004; Myers & Pianta, 2008; Pianta, 2006; Zionts, 2005). Although some of these influences are related to characteristics within the individual child or teacher, they are likely to exert effects on both partners through their ongoing dyadic interactions. Other potential influences arise from the context, including ecological factors in the child's family and the school setting. Following are some factors that have been hypothesized to influence the quality of teacher–child relationships.

- Children may have predisposing characteristics that make them harder to soothe and more challenging to respond to in a manner that is effective for affect regulation. Children with high negative emotional reactivity, low self-regulation, and low adaptability are likely to exhibit more behavioral difficulties that require teacher intervention and guidance (Myers & Pianta, 2008).
- These characteristics are particularly challenging in a school setting, where difficulties in following instructions and dysregulated behavior are hard to tolerate. Beliefs and attributions of teachers can play a role in how they respond to children exhibiting these characteristics. To the extent that teachers see their main role as providing instruction to support academic and social skill development, they might be more likely to respond negatively to children who do not achieve as expected or who seem unmotivated, aggressive, and disruptive. Conversely, they might be more inclined to respond positively and have warmer, closer relationships with children with high positive emotional reactivity, self-regulation, and adaptability (Myers & Pianta, 2008).
- Children who have experienced attachment disruptions or maltreatment have been found to engage in higher levels of negative, dependent help seeking from teachers and disruptive behavior (Kobak, Little, Race, & Acosta, 2001). Teachers can perceive the behaviors as inappropriate and respond in ways that are less supportive if they do not understand the needs that the child is attempting to communicate through these behaviors.
- Highly entrenched internal working models make children less likely to respond quickly to efforts to support them. They might refuse support or give signals that they do not want closeness and help. They might act in a controlling and coercive manner, inviting the teacher to respond in kind and play out the role according to the child's predictions. When a teacher can respond in a way that does not confirm the child's expectations, by not withdrawing and getting caught up in the power struggles that the child expects but continuing to offer support, the potential for change is enhanced. The child has a new relationship experience. However, it might take many experiences of contradiction of the old patterns and repetition of the new patterns before the child begins to change the expectations that he automatically brings to a new interaction. It might take even more repetitions to change his patterns of emotional processing. For a teacher who is trying hard to help him make the change, it can feel discouraging and disheartening when change is so slow and after so many tries, the child still responds based on predictions and patterns built up over a lifetime.
- Teachers also bring their own relationship histories and internal working models of attachment relationships to their interactions with their students (Kennedy & Kennedy, 2004). They bring their own predispositions to interpret children's behavior and attribute intentions to children according to their own life experiences. Although there is little direct research on teachers' attachment-related internal working models to support this claim, a parallel literature exists in the work of Mary Dozier and her colleagues

with foster parents (Dozier et al., 2009; Dozier, Higley, Albus, & Nutter, 2002; Dozier & Sepulveda, 2004). When dealing with children who have severe difficulties with attachment relationships related to histories of maltreatment and relationship disruption, even foster parents who have secure states of mind with respect to attachment need support in interpreting the child's behavior and not responding in ways that confirm her worst expectations. When children act in negatively provocative or avoidant ways, it often takes a conscious effort not to respond in kind. For foster parents who have less secure mental representations, it is even harder to provide the nurturance that the child needs without getting caught up in the negative cycles that can easily follow from her avoidant or provocative behavior. Like those of foster parents, teachers' responses to students are likely influenced by their own attachment histories and representations of relationships. Their prior experiences as teachers also inform the representations of their relationships with children that guide their actions in the classroom (Pianta, 1999).
- The organization of school schedules, where children might interact with a number of teachers in a day, can make it more difficult for one teacher to develop a close relationship with a child that can help to anchor him and supply him with a secure base in his school day (Pianta, 1999).

To promote positive teacher–child relationships, some suggestions have been offered with respect to design of the school environment.

- Provide continuity of relationships by keeping groups of children together, keeping children in the same building for several years, and keeping children with the same teacher or teachers for several years (Bergin & Bergin, 2009; Pianta, 1999).
- Facilitate transitions to new schools or teachers by promoting visits and opportunities to see the new school, meet the teacher, and identify an activity that the child can look forward to participating in at the new school (Bergin & Bergin, 2009).
- Reduce the number of teachers and transitions that the child needs to make, day by day, in the classroom (Bergin & Bergin, 2009; Pianta, 1999). Having to move from place to place in the school, dealing with different teachers each time, can be very challenging for children who need predictability and consistency and have difficulties with adjusting to new people. Limiting these shifts where possible, by having specialists come into the classroom rather than pulling children out, can be one way to reduce these transitions.

Providing teachers with information and support for reflection to help them develop positive relationships with children has been suggested.

- Providing training and consultation in child development and attachment theory can help teachers to further develop skills in noticing, interpreting, and responding to children's cues (Bergin & Bergin, 2009; Cyr & van IJzendoorn, 2007; Kennedy & Kennedy, 2007; Kobak et al., 2001; Schwartz & Davis, 2006). Helping a teacher to recognize that a child's behavior might reflect her attachment history, and to realize that she might be using strategies learned from previous life experiences to communicate her needs, allows the teacher to step outside the child's expectations and provide a new experience of relationship. For instance, where appropriate, helping teachers to reframe disruptive behavior as an expression of the child's need for connection and relationship can support consideration of a wider range of possible responses.
- Dozier and her colleagues (Dozier et al., 2002, 2009; Dozier & Sepulveda, 2004) have shown that training, support, and reflection can help foster parents to respond according to children's needs rather than their negative expectations. Providing a similar opportunity for teachers to reflect on their own cognitive and affective representations (Cyr & van IJzendoorn, 2007; Kennedy & Kennedy, 2004; Pianta, 1999) might

help them to respond positively to students who behave in controlling, coercive, and negatively dependent ways, rather than get drawn into power struggles and high-conflict interactions. In this way, they are more likely to be able to avoid confirming the negative expectations of children who have had difficult attachment histories.

Following are some examples of interventions to support the development of positive teacher–student relationships. Most are adaptations of approaches that have been used successfully in supporting parent–child relationships.

- Banking Time (Driscoll & Pianta, 2010) is a dyadic intervention designed to promote supportive relationships between teachers and preschool children. The name is intended to convey the message that teacher–student relationships are resources for children, and teachers can invest in building them up in one-on-one sessions with children. These relational resources yield dividends when they can be used to support the child's adaptation and day-to-day problem solving in the classroom. The one-to-one meetings take place on a regular basis according to a plan agreed on in advance. During each meeting, the child chooses an activity and leads the session while the teacher observes and narrates the child's actions, labels his feelings, and conveys supportive messages to the child regarding relationship themes. The goal is to build stronger supportive relationships between teachers and children who might be experiencing difficulties in the school environment. In an exploratory study using this intervention (Driscoll & Pianta, 2010), teachers reported increased feelings of closeness with the children and improved classroom behavior.
- Teacher–Child Interaction Therapy (McIntosh, 2010; McIntosh, Rizza, & Bliss, 2000) is an adaptation of the Parent–Child Interaction Therapy program developed by Eyberg (1988). Teachers and preschool-aged children meet one on one for weekly coaching sessions as well as daily 5-minute Special Time periods. The program involves two phases. In the first, child-directed phase, the teacher receives training and coaching in letting the child lead the play. The teacher is taught to use DRIP skills: "describing the child's activities, reflecting what the child was saying, imitating the child's actions, and praising the child" (McIntosh, Rizza, & Bliss, 2000, p. 456). The teacher is also trained not to use questions or give commands and to ignore the child's inappropriate behaviors in this phase. The goal of this child-directed phase is to enhance the positive relationship between teacher and child. In the second, teacher-directed phase, the teacher is taught how to give commands, follow up when the child is noncompliant, and increase consistency in responding to her behaviors. The purpose of this phase is to decrease disruptive behavior and increase positive social interaction in the classroom. Interactive behaviors of teacher and child are observed and coded on an ongoing basis using a time-sampling procedure, and these observations are used to help the teacher develop a treatment plan with effective strategies to change behaviors. Gershenson, Lyon, and Budd (2010) adapted the intervention, calling it Teacher–Child Interaction Training, for use in the classroom with groups of children.
- Child–Teacher Relationship Training (Morrison & Helker, 2010) is a play-based intervention for teachers and preschoolers adapted from Landreth and Bratton's (2006) Child–Parent Relationship Therapy program. Teachers are trained in play therapy skills, including following the child's lead, listening reflectively, recognizing feelings, and facilitating creative play. Following training, they choose one child to work with in weekly play sessions that are videotaped. These videotapes are used for supervision. In the next phase, the teachers practice the relationship-building skills that they have learned with small groups of children in the classroom, again with supervision and skill building. A pilot study suggested that teachers of preschoolers could transfer the relationship-building skills that they learned to their work in the general classroom, and the externalizing behaviors of the children whom they taught were reduced.

- Pianta (1999) suggested that videotaping interactions between a teacher and student for the teacher to review later with a consultant can promote reflection. Providing the opportunity for the teacher to narrate the interaction allows her to observe and label patterns and trace connections among her own feelings, beliefs, attributions, assumptions, interpretations, and actions. The video provides feedback that can inform the reflective process.

A differentiated and integrated *understanding of the individual child's functioning across areas can inform strategic educational and treatment planning.*

Although relevant evidence-based interventions may be available to choose in working with a specific child or family, they are often directed at specific factors and outcomes. Recommendations and evidence regarding their use as components in more comprehensive treatment plans for children and families with multiple difficulties are scarce. Of course, there are exceptions. For instance, Multisystemic Therapy addresses multiple factors influencing a youth and his family, and careful planning occurs in order to provide multiple treatment components in an integrated and strategic manner (Schoenwald, Brown, & Henggeler, 2000). However, educators and clinicians who work with children and families with multiple problems are often left to devise a strategic treatment plan on their own, without a strong base of evidence or a set of specific recommendations regarding which interventions to use when.

A functional developmental model is helpful in dealing with this challenge. By considering the child's strengths and difficulties in different areas, and the interplay between them in her day-to-day functioning, a detailed and holistic understanding of the child can be developed. Functional influences on the child's development from risk and protective factors operating in the wider context—family, school, neighborhood, and cultural/social milieu—can be more fully appreciated. By considering details of her development in specific areas, and integrating them into a coherent understanding of her overall functioning and adaptation to her environment, more strategic choices can be made about interventions and their sequence.

Case Study: Gregory

Gregory is an 8-year-old new in the school this year. He talks nonstop and can be very engaging, but he has difficulty with reading. He can connect some sounds with letters and recognize some simple three-letter words, but sounding out words is a struggle for him. Gregory exhibits severe difficulties in his Grade 3 classroom with directing his attention, controlling his actions, and regulating his feelings. Instead, he engages in disruptive behavior during group activities, refuses to cooperate with instructions, resists attempts to get him to focus on his individual work, tears up his books when asked to read, and flies into a rage if told to stop playing with the toys that he brings from home. On the playground, he has tried to run away from school on a few occasions when he has been particularly angry. Some children are afraid of Gregory because of his angry outbursts when they do not do what he wants them to do. In fact, this morning he hit another child on the head with a hockey stick when the child called him a name.

The principal and social worker set up an appointment to talk with his parents about the severity of this behavior and his likely suspension from school as a result. In this meeting, they learn that these are Gregory's foster parents, that Gregory experienced severe neglect during his early childhood, and that he was placed in foster care at the age of 4. Several foster placements broke down because of his aggressive and destructive behavior and tantrums. Although his current foster parents have done their best to provide a safe and calm environment for him, he is disobedient, defiant, and argumentative with them. He often yells, "You aren't the boss of me!" He will not sleep at night, and if they do not monitor him, he wanders around the house at night, turning on the computer and taking food from the kitchen all over the house, making a mess. Although Gregory can be quite engaging at times, he often meets their attempts to give him affection and support with anger and resentment. They are starting to worry that they do not have what it takes to provide a good home for him, and even though they feel guilty, they also feel so worn out that they are considering asking for him to be moved to another home.

At their meeting, Gregory's teacher, principal, social worker, and foster parents talk openly with each other about their frustrations and worries. They each have some ideas about practices that might help:

- a meeting with Gregory, his teacher, and his parents to plan his re-entry to school after the suspension;
- a program in the classroom with a chart to track behaviors and an incentive system for positive behaviors;
- extra tutoring in reading;
- a psychiatric consultation to consider whether medication would help Gregory to focus and be less aggressive;
- a referral to a group provided at the school for children at risk for aggressive behavior;
- a referral for a psychological assessment;
- a referral to the special needs consultant at the school for suggestions to help Gregory be more successful in learning;
- his teacher spending 10 minutes a day with him playing a game that he likes, regardless of his behavior in the classroom that day;
- his foster parents looking for a therapist at the local children's mental health center to work with them with Gregory, to help them have more fun with him, express feelings more clearly, and increase communication and cooperation; and
- his foster parents seeking support from child welfare services to help them in caring for Gregory.

The school staff and foster parents think that the list includes many good ideas, some of which involve evidence-based interventions; however, they think that they lack a guiding plan. How can they decide where to start?

One guiding principle that might help them is to consider the interrelationships among developmental areas. They can draw on Perry's (2006, 2009) discussions of the sequential development of levels of regulation "from the bottom up" (2009, p. 242). Although the main goals at school might be for Gregory to develop stronger reading and academic skills, social skills, and behavioral self-control, these rely on a developmental foundation of sensorimotor and affective regulation. To the extent that Gregory has difficulties with regulating himself in these basic ways, he is dependent on the world around him to help him do so. This external regulation can be supplied to some extent by designing his environment to be calm, clear, and structured enough to support his functioning. In addition, Gregory and children like him need stable supportive attachment relationships with adults who mediate between them and their environments, supporting and soothing and protecting them from being overwhelmed, and helping them to direct and control their behavior. As Gregory receives this external support over time, he can begin to internalize it, building the foundation for the development of higher-level skills, including metacognitive strategies to organize his own goal-directed behaviors, social insights, and academic skills.

An appreciation of the central role of relationships with adults who can help Gregory to feel regulated at a sensory and affective level provides an overarching organizing principle for their treatment plan. Taking the steps necessary to enable his foster parents to continue to care for him is a high priority. This may include practical support, such as having some respite services to give them a break, as well as informational validation of their experiences, such as training in understanding the behaviors of children who have experienced neglect. Therapeutic support can also be helpful, including interactional work that involves sensory play and attunement, to help Gregory gradually become more receptive to the emotional communication and supportive direction that his foster parents provide. The therapist can also help his parents to devise strategies for dealing with his behavior at home to maintain a calmer atmosphere there and support his ongoing sense of safety and trust in their developing relationship. Consultations with a psychiatrist, psychologist, and occupational therapist can help them to develop a better understanding of his needs. The foster parents clearly need a great deal of support to keep in mind that many repetitions of positively regulating relational experiences will likely be needed before Gregory can reliably regulate his feelings or change his expectations of others.

Similarly, the overarching importance of providing Gregory with the external regulation and support that he needs in the classroom is clear. This can be done by designing a calm environment with enough structure and cues to support his functioning. A key component will be the provision of stable, supportive relationships with adults, such as his teacher or CYW, who can help to soothe and regulate him, provide direction and cuing, and facilitate his successful engagement within the complex environment of the classroom. Scheduling some positive relationship-building time with him during which they follow his lead can allow him to begin to shift his negative expectations of them. When Gregory has angry explosions when they attempt to connect with him, they will likely need support to remain calm and soothing rather than confirming his worst expectations. This support can take the form of empathy from co-workers, opportunities for breaks when needed, self-care to reduce stress and maintain good physical health, and a nonjudgmental peer or supervisor to listen when they wish to reflect on their experiences with Gregory.

Higher-level functional goals can and should still be addressed. For example, a small number of clearly stated behavioral expectations, with recognition when Gregory meets them, can help him to experience a greater sense of control over his own actions; however, without help in regulating his feelings at a more basic level, he will likely have difficulty with successfully meeting these behavioral goals. Also, given his severe difficulties with reading, there is no time to waste in providing high-quality, intensive instruction and support in reading and literacy skills. However, he can likely access this instruction only if it is embedded in an overall program that takes into account his severe difficulties with fundamental self-regulation. Similarly, supporting his development of more effective social problem-solving strategies is essential, but if his basic need for support in self-regulation is not considered, he will likely have difficulty in using these strategies.

The sense of safety that the foster parents and teachers try to convey in their separate environments will likely be enhanced if Gregory can see that they work together well and trust each other. A sense of continuity and containment that bridges home and school environments can allow him to gradually change his negative expectations that adults cannot be trusted to work together to anticipate and respond to his needs.

By taking into account this child's development in each functional area, and considering the ways in which progress in one area rests on functioning in interrelated areas, a strategic plan for intervention can be organized. That is, the foundational areas on which further development in other areas rests can be appropriately emphasized rather than marginalized. This point is especially important in school settings, where the primary goals typically involve higher-level skills (in the sense that Perry defined them) such as thinking and problem solving, using language, understanding social interactions, and developing metacognitive strategies for academic success. Children who have not developed sufficient foundational self-regulation skills to negotiate the classroom environment might not be able to take part in these higher-level learning activities, even if the content is appropriate to their academic skill levels, unless they have the external supports that they need to remain regulated. Often this means adapting the expectations for self-regulation placed on these children to a level commensurate with their current functioning, providing emotional and behavioral supports to allow the child to successfully engage in the academic curriculum, and promoting his internalization of those externally provided regulatory supports to better enable him to maintain equilibrium in the future.

Although most educators and clinicians would endorse the importance of adapting their expectations to the level of functioning of the child, some express a worry that it might not serve the child's long-term interests. For instance, when a child with longstanding and severe affect regulation problems similar to those of Gregory has an explosive and disruptive tantrum in response to a request, the clinician or teacher might be asked to consider soothing him first, as one might with a much younger child, rather than immediately trying to teach him by "consequencing" him for his behavior, working to "process" what happened to get him to "accept responsibility" for his actions, or leaving him alone until "he is ready" to do what has to be done. Some clinicians worry that, by giving him the attention he needs to soothe him, they will "reinforce" his negative behavior. Some worry that, by soothing first rather than quickly using this "teachable moment" to make him "accountable" for his actions, they will not give him a "realistic" picture of the demands that will be placed on him when he moves on to a higher grade or a less supportive classroom setting. A developmental approach speaks to these worries by specifying the ways in which a child's future adaptation depends on the foundational skills that are being developed in the present. By failing to provide the external support that the child needs in the present to recover from emotional upheavals, the likelihood that he will develop the internalized affect regulation skills needed to support self-control and insight into his own behavior in the future is reduced rather than enhanced, just as surely as the likelihood of success at reading in the future is diminished if a child is not given the support that she needs to develop basic skills in the present. The key is the continual match between the support provided and her level of functioning, staying within her "proximal zone of development" (Vygotsky, 1978) by providing just enough help to allow her to do today what she will be able to do on her own in the future. This depends on the educator and clinician being able to gauge the child's skills at any given moment and maintain an awareness of her progress, in order to ensure that the level of support they are providing is indeed promoting development and competency rather than stagnation or frustration. Accurate assessment and progress monitoring are necessary to support this awareness.

APPROACHES TO ASSESSMENT

If interventions and practices are to be carefully selected and adapted to meet the needs of individual students, based on an understanding of their developmental functioning in each area, then assessment is essential to inform that understanding. Furthermore, once an intervention or program is selected, whether it is evidence based or not, the child's progress needs to be carefully monitored and evaluated to provide feedback regarding the efficacy of the intervention for that child, and to support ongoing adjustment and adaptation of the intervention to maximize its utility to the child (Deno, 2005). This is true whether the intervention is an educational program or a clinical treatment. In fact, information gained from assessments may be needed to fulfill various functions in providing services for individual children, including the following:

1. to monitor a child's progress with respect to a particular intervention or program, in order to evaluate the efficacy for that child;
2. to provide ongoing feedback while an intervention is being provided, to suggest ways in which it can be adapted and individualized to be more effective for the child;
3. to support problem solving when difficulties arise;
4. to identify a child who needs more targeted and intensive services;
5. to identify a child's particular constellation of functional strengths and difficulties in each developmental area to inform treatment/educational planning; and
6. to identify proximal and distal treatment goals and select appropriate interventions and practices, implemented in a developmentally appropriate sequence, to reach those goals.

In the field of school psychology, a main function of assessment has often been the determination of eligibility for special education services (Deno, 2005). When teachers and parents observe that a child is having difficulties, she is referred for psychoeducational assessment. Often this process is lengthy, involving normative assessments of cognitive functioning and processing, academic achievement, and behavior. These "snapshots" of her functioning at the time of assessment are used to make diagnostic and educational decisions regarding placement and services to be provided.

In the field of children's mental health, a similar Refer–Assess–Treat model is common (Doll & Haack, 2005). A child who comes to the attention of adults because of difficulties is referred for an assessment. In most cases, though his history is considered, the assessment itself focuses on his current or recent presentation. The assessment might be (a) symptom focused, to ascertain whether he meets criteria for a specific diagnosis or diagnoses; (b) development focused, to assess his developmental functioning in a number of areas; or (c) both, because they are not mutually exclusive. Based on the resulting diagnosis and/or developmental formulation, recommendations regarding treatment are made. Further assessment in the future may be recommended, but follow-up treatment monitoring (if it exists) is often not systematically linked to the assessment process.

In both educational and mental health settings, then, the Refer–Assess–Treat model has guided assessments. Children are referred for assessments when they are having difficulties. The focus of those assessments is often to ascertain whether children meet criteria for specific interventions, including placement in special education settings or referral for specific therapeutic mental health programs. Recommendations regarding the overall content of those interventions may be made, and repeating the assessment in the future may be recommended; however, integration of findings from earlier to later assessments or treatment monitoring is typically not systematic (if done at all).

The Refer–Assess–Treat model has been criticized from several points of view. It has been called a "Wait to Fail" model because the child has to exhibit difficulties before investigation and subsequent adaptive alteration of the teaching program occur (Vaughn & Fuchs, 2003, p. 139). Because waiting lists for assessments can be lengthy, the child often may struggle for a considerable period of time before receiving the support that she needs. Children who are subject to environmental or situational factors that place their development "at risk" often do not receive specialized services until they develop behavioral problems, rather than receiving services proactively to prevent problems from developing (Doll & Haack, 2005). Also, some children who are having difficulties can be missed because they do not come to the attention of adults. For instance, with respect to social and emotional problems, internalizing problems are often missed because they are less noticeable than externalizing problems, especially in group situations.

The value of in-depth, one-time, "snapshot" assessment using normative measures has also been criticized on the grounds that it does not provide relevant information to guide intervention. For instance, Fuchs and Deshler (2007) caution that more research is needed to explore whether or how assessments of cognitive processing can increase the efficacy of educational instruction. Furthermore, a one-time assessment does not provide information about a child's response to an intervention because it does not show change—or lack of it—as a function of treatment received. Without this feedback, the intervention cannot be systematically adjusted and tailored to the needs of the individual child.

To address difficulties with assessments that are directed at identification and placement, Stanley Deno (1989, 2005) proposed an alternative "problem-solving" approach to inform planning and decision making during the intervention process. He defined problem solving as working to reduce the discrepancy between a student's current level of skill development and the level expected in the child's environment. Rather than locating problems within individuals, this definition positions them in situations, in the mismatch between individual characteristics and environmental demands. A proposed solution to a problem is a hypothesis, to be confirmed or disconfirmed and revised, based on feedback regarding whether the solution worked to effectively reduce the discrepancy between performance and expectation. In the model articulated by Deno, there are five stages, each of which involves assessment or the gathering and evaluation of information.

1. In the problem identification stage, the student's performance is observed and recorded to decide whether a problem exists.
2. In the problem definition stage, the discrepancy between the student's performance and the level of performance expected is quantified to evaluate the importance of the problem.
3. In the intervention designing and planning stage, possible alternative strategies or solutions to reduce the discrepancy between expectations and performance are considered. These "solution hypotheses" (Deno, 2005, p. 25) are evaluated in order to identify the solution that will be tried.
4. In the intervention implementation stage, the solution or intervention chosen is put into practice. The fidelity of implementation and response of the student are monitored, in order to evaluate the extent to which the solution is being implemented as planned.
5. In the problem solution stage, the discrepancy between student performance and expectation is re-quantified, in order to decide whether the problem is being successfully solved by implementing the chosen solution.

The process is iterative: that is, the cycle can be repeated until an effective intervention is found and the discrepancy is minimized. A variety of information-gathering and evaluation strategies or approaches to assessment can be used to support the problem-solving process (Brown-Chidsey, 2005). Two examples are functional behavioral assessment and curriculum-based measurement.

Functional behavioral assessment (Steege & Brown-Chidsey, 2005) attempts to identify the characteristics of an individual student and her school environment that lead to behavior that interferes with her success in the classroom. Data may be gathered indirectly, through the reports of teachers, parents, and the student herself, as well as directly through observation. These data are used to define the interfering behavior concretely, measure its magnitude, and identify its antecedents and consequences. From these observations, hypotheses are formulated regarding the functional relationships between contextual features and the behavior in question. These hypotheses are tested by systematically manipulating the environmental variables thought to be contributing to the behavior, and assessing the extent to which behavior changes as a result of this intervention. Based on the feedback, hypotheses and interventions can be refined, and further testing can occur.

Curriculum-based measurement (Deno, 1986, 1989, 2003, 2005; Shinn & Bamonto, 1989) attempts to evaluate a student's response to an instructional program or intervention as it is delivered. Standardized measures of basic skills in a curriculum area are administered repeatedly. These measures are often fluency based, short, and sensitive to change. If the student's fluency increases at a rate commensurate with the level of skill development identified as a goal for that student, then the level of instruction offered may be judged to be effective for her. However, if the rate of growth is lower than that expected, then the instruction might be modified. Most often, the intensity of instruction is increased. Progress continues to be monitored to evaluate the extent to which the change in instruction is effective. If the rate of progress is still not adequate to support the student in reaching her goal, then further alterations in instruction might be made, and her skill level will continue to be monitored.

Curriculum-based measurement is often used in conjunction with the RTI model described earlier. When a student receives a program of instruction found to be effective for the general population of students in a school or district (Tier 1), his progress is tracked using a curriculum-based measurement approach. If his skill development is not progressing at the rate needed to successfully reach his goal in a timely manner, then his instructional program is adjusted, and he may be provided with a more intensive (Tier 2) program. If his skill development is still not progressing at a rate commensurate with his goal, then further adjustments and intensification of his instructional program are implemented, and if needed, a yet more intensive, individualized (Tier 3) intervention will be provided.

Approaches such as curriculum-based measurement and functional behavioral analysis have a clear role to play in providing the information needed to support the implementation of educational and mental health interventions. In contrast to the "snapshot" of a moment in time in traditional assessments, they reflect change over time before, during, and after intervention. The dynamic view thus afforded by problem-solving approaches seems to be particularly suited to supporting the first four functions listed previously: (1) monitoring a child's progress with respect to a particular intervention, (2) suggesting ways in which a particular intervention can be individualized, (3) supporting problem solving, and (4) identifying the need for more intensive intervention in a specific functional area (Deno, 2005; Steege & Brown-Chidsey, 2005). They can also provide in-depth information relevant to the last two functions mentioned: (5) identifying a child's particular constellation of functional strengths and difficulties in each developmental area to inform treatment/educational planning and (6) identifying proximal and distal goals in the treatment of the child and selecting appropriate interventions and practices, implemented in a developmentally appropriate sequence, to reach the goals. However, for children with very complex developmental profiles, these last two functions can at times require more comprehensive assessment across a wider range of developmental areas to complement data gained from problem-solving approaches.

A DEVELOPMENTAL PERSPECTIVE ON LEARNING DISABILITIES

Current thinking in the area of learning disabilities illustrates the value of a functional developmental perspective in understanding, assessing, and providing intervention for children with difficulties. In their conceptualization of learning disabilities, Fletcher, Lyon, Fuchs, and Barnes (2007) placed the construct solidly within a developmental context, drawing heavily on the extensive literature on reading disabilities as well as the less extensive but growing bodies of research on writing and math disabilities. They emphasized that the same theories that describe the typical development of academic skills are also useful in understanding why some children have difficulties developing those skills; furthermore, learning difficulties occur along a dimension of severity that is continuous with typical skill development, rather than being qualitatively distinct. Fletcher and colleagues argued that the primary manifestations of learning disabilities are academic skill deficits that may be exhibited in different educational domains, such as reading, writing, and arithmetic. In their overarching model of factors that influence the development and variability of academic skills, they included the following:

- neurobiological factors, including genetic factors as well as brain structure and function;
- core cognitive processes, such as phonemic awareness;
- behavioral and psychosocial factors such as motivation, attention, or depression; and
- environmental factors, including quality of the school and interventions provided.

These factors exert effects directly on academic skill development as well as indirectly through their influences on each other.

Implications of a Developmental Perspective in Defining and Identifying Learning Disabilities

This developmental perspective carries implications for definitions and procedures for identifying learning disabilities (Fletcher et al., 2007).

- If the main manifestation of a learning disability is an academic skill deficit, and if academic skills are distributed on a continuous dimension, then the identification of a specific cut-off line demarcating the boundary between typical skill development and a learning disability is arbitrary. Moreover, any single score assessing skill development is subject to measurement error.
- In many commonly used definitions of learning disabilities, behavioral, psychosocial, and environmental factors are specified as exclusionary factors. However, given that they are acknowledged contributors to the development of academic deficits, specifying them as exclusionary precludes the identification of some children who are indeed struggling learners in need of academic interventions. Furthermore, the vectors of influence between learning and these other factors are often bidirectional, and children may well have comorbid learning, emotional, and behavioral problems, with circular effects among their difficulties in each domain. In fact, because of the complex transactions among all of the factors that potentially influence the development of academic skills over the course of a child's lifetime, it is virtually impossible to distinguish the effects of behavioral, psychosocial, and environmental "causes" of skill deficits from those due to other factors. Although these factors may make academic problems more severe, and are certainly important to address in treatment, Fletcher and colleagues argued that they do not qualitatively change the basic need for interventions directed at academic skill development, the response to such interventions, or the means by which those interventions work. Therefore, using them as exclusionary factors has little empirical or conceptual justification in a developmental model of learning disabilities. In contrast, Fletcher and colleagues note that differentiating learning disabilities from learning problems due to mental retardation, sensory disorders, or linguistic diversity is reasonable because individuals with these difficulties do require different interventions. (However, the learning needs and effective interventions for some students in these categories might overlap to some extent with those for students with learning disabilities. For example, see Caffrey & Fuchs, 2007, for a discussion of the differences between students with mild mental retardation and those with learning disabilities.) In essence, the value of any definition of the construct of learning disabilities is its power to support a differential classification of low achievers that is reliable and valid and that corresponds to their intervention needs.

The core feature that does define the construct of learning disabilities is unexpected underachievement. Although some models of identifying learning disabilities attempt to index "unexpectedness" based on a discrepancy between achievement and IQ or on intraindividual cognitive skill differences, Fletcher et al. (2007) provide compelling evidence that these approaches do not adequately differentiate learning disabilities from other types of low achievement, nor do they provide information that is useful in designing interventions. Instead, they propose an assessment and evaluation process that focuses on the direct functional assessment of academic skills. However, rather than assessing achievement at one point in time, they maintain that "No person can be defined as learning disabled in the absence of evidence of a lack of adequate response to instruction that is effective for most students" (p. 5). Therefore, academic skills are tracked across time, and unexpectedness is indexed by an inadequate response to an intervention that has been shown to be effective for most learners.

Another central feature of learning disabilities is their heterogeneity. Five subgroups supported in the research cited by Fletcher et al. (2007) are the following:

1. reading disability as exhibited in word recognition and spelling difficulties;
2. reading disability as exhibited in comprehension difficulties;
3. reading disability as exhibited in difficulties with fluency and automaticity;

4. mathematics disability as exhibited in difficulties with computation and problem-solving; and
5. written expression disability as exhibited in difficulties with handwriting, spelling, and/or composition.

These can be differentiated with respect to the skill domains that are affected as well as intervention needs presented; therefore, in the assessment of learning disabilities, the direct functional assessment of skills specific to each area is needed.

Response to Intervention and Curriculum-Based Measurement

Fletcher et al. (2007) discussed the value of curriculum-based measurement in an RTI model to identify students with learning disabilities. For students who do not show what is considered to be an adequate response to successively intense, high-quality interventions, further assessment is done to explore potential reasons for a lack of response, and identification of a learning disability can be considered. Just as academic skill scores fall on a continuum, so too does "responsiveness" to instruction. Therefore, defining a cutoff pointt below which the response is judged to be "inadequate" is, at some level, arbitrary. Furthermore, where different methods and criteria are used to determine inadequate response, different subsets of children may be identified (Fuchs, 2003; Fuchs & Deshler, 2007). If the final level of achievement at the end of the school year is used as the sole criterion, students who start at a low level and progress at a high rate, but do not reach benchmarks by that time, could be identified as non esponders, even though their rate of growth suggests that they might well continue to make progress if the intervention level is maintained during the following school year. On the other hand, if rate of growth is the sole criterion, then students who progress slowly might be identified even if they have managed to catch up to the skill level expected for their grade by the end of the year. Therefore, Fletcher and colleagues suggest the use of the dual discrepancy method proposed by Fuchs and Fuchs (1998), whereby both rate of progress and final skill status are used. The student's response to instruction is classified as "inadequate" only when both criteria are met. At the same time, Fletcher and colleagues and Fuchs and Deshler (2007) also point out that further research is needed to examine implications arising from using different methods to gauge responsiveness to instruction.

Fuchs and Deshler (2007) also raised the question of the types of assessment that lead to more effective teaching and learning. It is often argued that a formal, lengthy, multidisciplinary assessment is not necessary and that a multitiered response to instruction process can provide the information needed to understand the academic needs of an individual student. Fuchs and Deshler commented that this position fails to recognize that, for students who are chronically unresponsive to increasingly intense levels of instruction, this might not be true. Another widely held position is that formal testing of cognitive processes such as working memory and processing speed does not provide added value in designing instructional interventions for struggling learners, and therefore, such cognitive processes do not need to be assessed. Although Fuchs and Deshler noted that this argument "resonates," they concluded that further research is needed to explore whether and how such assessment can inform instruction.

The contention that assessing working memory skills is not necessary to inform instructional interventions for learning difficulties might indeed warrant further examination, especially in light of the emphasis on considering working memory limitations in the literature on teaching children with executive functioning and attention problems, many of whom have comorbid learning problems (Kaufman, 2010; Martinussen,

Tannock, McInnes, & Chaban, 2006). Several possible arguments might speak to these seemingly contradictory positions. One is that considerations involving working memory limitations might be more relevant to managing the classroom environment and routines within which instructional programs are embedded, as opposed to the academic instructional programs themselves. Another is that many of the recommended practices for high-quality instruction, both for typical learners and for children with learning problems, are already designed to be low in demands on working memory; that is, they are already designed to be explicit and direct, with high levels of practice and review as well as explicit training in transferring skills to new contexts. Additional information about an individual's working memory limitations might be redundant in some sense, because a reduction in demand on working memory is already built into the academic instructional practices that are recommended. On the other hand, an appreciation of a child's working memory limitations is sometimes helpful in shifting the qualities that adults attribute to the child, helping them to understand his difficulties rather than interpreting his actions as lazy or oppositional. These shifts can transform teacher–child and parent–child relationships, and with them, the child's engagement with learning and possibly his response to instruction.

The value of feedback on students' responses to instruction gained from curriculum-based measurement is underlined by the positive effects on academic skill performance when teachers use curriculum-based measurement to support decision making in their instructional planning (Fletcher et al., 2007). One way in which this can be done is to raise the goals for individual students when their actual rates of growth exceed the rate expected by the teacher. Conversely, when the actual growth rate for a student is lower than that expected by the teacher, the data support the decision to modify the student's program of instruction, most often increasing intensity to facilitate progress.

A Continuum of Interventions: Increasing Instructional Intensity

In most academic areas, the same principles that guide instruction are similar whether the child is a typical learner or a struggling learner. These principles are grounded in the evidence base describing how children develop skills in each area. What varies is the intensity of instruction provided. A primary value of a response-to-instruction approach, supported by data from a curriculum-based measurement approach to assessment, is that a continuum of instructional levels of intensity can be provided and their effects evaluated. Mellard et al. (2010) discussed the following key variables that can be modified to increase instructional intensity:

- increasing the dosage, including the minutes of instruction provided to each student, the frequency of instruction, and the duration of instruction;
- decreasing group size, ranging from whole class to small groups to one-to-one instruction;
- increasing the amount of immediate, positive, corrective feedback to students;
- adjusting the pace of instruction to the individual student's mastery level, allowing a slower pace for a student who needs it rather than moving on when most of the students in the class have mastered a specific lesson;
- increasing the frequency of response opportunities that allow the student to practice a skill and respond to feedback on his performance;
- reducing the number of transitions between content areas or classes, prolonging the focus on one skill;

- breaking down broad goals into more specific, focused elements; and
- using instructors with high levels of professional development, experience, and skill in handling instructional challenges.

Recommendations for Teaching Children With Learning Problems

From an extensive review of the literature, Fletcher et al. (2007) distilled the following essential recommendations for intervention with learning disabilities.

- A range of evidence-based strategies needs to be available, and supports for implementing them with fidelity are needed.
- Early intervention is recommended to prevent the development of some learning problems and reduce the severity of difficulties experienced by students with learning disabilities. For instance, Peer-Assisted Learning Strategies (PALS; Fuchs, Fuchs, Mathes, & Simmons, 1997) is a classroom-level peer-tutoring intervention that can be used to support Tier 1-level teaching programs in order to prevent the development of learning problems. Students are paired, typically matching a student with stronger skills with one who is less skilled. The partners work together on learning activities, and the student designated as the "coach" assists the "player" in learning a skill. This approach supports student engagement in practicing skills while receiving scaffolding and support.
- Interventions for students with learning problems should increase instruction time, by adding on to the instruction that is already being provided, rather than replacing it.
- Interventions that have been shown to be effective teach academic content in the specific domain being targeted. Interventions that target processing or aspects of brain function without teaching academic skills have not been shown to produce improved outcomes for students with learning problems. Furthermore, interventions targeting one academic domain do not lead to improvement in other domains if explicit instruction in the skills involved in those domains is not provided.
- Instructional programs need to be balanced and integrated to cover all of the competencies that are required to be proficient in a given academic area. Foundational skills are best taught in concert with higher-order skills. For example, in reading programs in which instruction in word recognition, fluency, and comprehension are integrated, as the child acquires word-recognition skills, higher-order comprehension skills and strategies can be taught. Similarly, instruction in math calculation needs to be integrated with explicit teaching of problem-solving skills. It is not necessary or helpful to wait until students have acquired foundational skills before higher-order skills are incorporated.
- Instructional approaches that are explicit (where the content is directly and clearly presented, rather than relying on the student's ability to infer it), well organized, and systematic are most helpful for students with learning disabilities. Effective instruction profits from inclusion of both skill and strategy instruction. Ample opportunities for review of what has already been learned, together with explicit instruction in transferring what was learned in one context to be applied in another, are needed. Instructional practices should include extensive opportunities for active engagement and responding by students, both to practice and to receive feedback on skills being learned.
- Self-regulation strategies in which students set goals for and monitor their own academic performance are effective in enhancing learning.
- Frequent monitoring of progress is essential at all levels to inform instruction and intervention. All assessments should be implemented to support intervention.
- Further research is needed to identify and evaluate practices that are appropriate for subgroups of students with learning disabilities, including those with skill deficits in specific areas and those who have co morbid difficulties such as ADHD.

Case Study: Gregory

In order to clarify the potential value of different approaches to assessment, consider again the example of Gregory, described previously. Curriculum-based measurement can provide clear feedback regarding Gregory's response to the reading instruction currently offered. An intensification of instruction is probable from such an assessment, and this recommendation would likely be available to guide instruction long before a traditional psychoeducational assessment to diagnose a learning disability could be completed (especially if the wait list for psychological assessments in his school district is lengthy). In addition, a functional behavioral analysis of his disruptive outbursts in class can yield effective strategies for his teachers to use to help him engage more successfully in day to day activities in the school setting. It might also provide clues regarding factors influencing his behavior that might not be obvious at first glance in the classroom. Although both approaches can make invaluable contributions to his current functioning in school, by themselves, they are not likely to provide a complete understanding of the multiple interacting factors preventing Gregory from functioning adaptively at home and school. A more comprehensive assessment of his development in each functional area, including sensorimotor development, emotional regulation, behavioral regulation, social/attachment/relational development, attentional regulation and executive functioning, and speech/language/cognitive functioning, while considering the impacts of his life experiences, including possible effects of trauma, disrupted relationships, and unpredictable caregiving, can provide an understanding of Gregory that is both broad and deep. Full consideration of the demands placed on him at home and school can afford the opportunity to identify areas of mismatch that make his adaptation less successful.

Through such in-depth assessment and formulation, the strategic planning necessary to meet Gregory's educational and mental health needs can be supported. It might be true, as Fuchs and Deshler (2007) warned, that assessing his working memory might not provide specific recommendations to guide the ways in which Gregory is taught to read. But understanding how emotional hyperarousal limits his attempts to hold in mind the steps involved in completing a routine and apply strategies and concepts that he has learned to new situations is informative when devising ways to manage the classroom to allow him to be successful. Appreciating the potential for sensory overload in areas in which he is particularly sensitive can be very helpful in supporting his regulation. Understanding the relational patterns that Gregory has learned from his life experiences so far allows a teacher or foster parent to avoid acting in ways that confirm his worst expectations. Appreciating the effort that it takes for Gregory to maintain emotional control when he feels threatened, and the sense of danger that he feels when asked to allow adults to direct him instead of seizing control of situations himself, makes it possible to plan strategies in the classroom and at home to provide the emotional support and sense of safety that he needs. Recognizing his strengths allows them to be capitalized on to support his development. For instance, once Gregory becomes somewhat more able to use the soothing and regulation provided by adults, his strengths in oral language suggest that he may make good use of instruction and practice in self-talk strategies to guide his own reactions and behaviors.

An understanding of the ways in which all of these factors influence Gregory day to day in the classroom can be gained from an assessment that includes a review of his history, psychometric testing in some specific functional areas, observations, behavioral ratings, and interviews with him, his parents, and his teacher. Such a comprehensive assessment can provide a context within which the results of a curriculum-based measurement approach to assessing his reading skills or a functional behavioral analysis approach to solving a particular behavioral problem can be used; indeed, the broader understanding can inform the implementation of these more specific assessment/intervention components of his treatment plan, increasing the likelihood of success. Recognizing the factors contributing to Gregory's behavior can allow his foster parents and teachers to respond to him with greater compassion and containment rather than reactivity. It may enable them to have some greater sense of compassion and understanding for themselves as well, because the demanding nature of the work they are doing with him, day by day, is validated.

In fact, the two models of assessment—comprehensive in-depth and problem solving—can be integrated to serve children with intensive needs. Rather than waiting for children to fail, progress monitoring and problem solving need to be activated early. No child should be left to struggle with learning problems while waiting for a comprehensive assessment to identify a learning disability; rather, every child's progress should be monitored and instructional programs should be provided that match the level needed by the child to develop academic skills. Similarly, rather than waiting for a comprehensive traditional assessment to provide suggestions regarding a child's difficulties with behavioral control in the classroom, the functional relationships among antecedents, characteristics of the child, and consequences of the behavior should be identified sooner rather than later, in order to generate possible interventions. For many children, assessments/interventions directed at solving problems in specific areas might be all that they need to move forward successfully. However, to inform strategic treatment planning for children with complex presentations and severe problems, influenced by multiple risk and protective factors, comprehensive developmental assessment and formulation are invaluable. As Gregory's case illustrates, a developmental formulation based on a careful and comprehensive assessment can suggest targets for intervention, identifying priorities at the outset. It can also highlight strengths that can be capitalized on to support progress. However, as Deno (2005) pointed out, formulations and recommendations are hypotheses that need to be tested. If assessment stops once recommendations for treatment are made, then the feedback needed to support ongoing treatment planning and intervention is missing. On the other hand, if the child's progress and response to the interventions provided are monitored, then opportunities to evaluate their efficacy and fine-tune their delivery according to the child's needs are supported.

CONCLUSION

I have sketched ways in which a developmental, dimensional, functional perspective defines a common goal toward which service providers in both educational and children's mental health systems can work collaboratively to enhance children's functional adaptation across contexts and domains. An understanding of development in each area, the ways in which functioning is interrelated across areas, and the risk and protective factors that influence developmental pathways to particular outcomes can inform the design and development of programs and interventions. At the individual level, a differentiated and integrated understanding of the child's functioning across areas can inform strategic educational and treatment planning. A continuum of services can be developed to respond to the continuum of individual developmental differences that clients and students bring to the school and clinic. High-quality support can be offered, and the effects of this support can be monitored on an ongoing basis. When the level of support offered is not adequate to allow the child to adapt successfully—academically, socially, emotionally, or behaviorally—programs and practices can be adapted to provide support better matched to her strengths and needs. Every time that we do so—by changing an intervention or increasing its intensity—we have an opportunity to contribute to the assessment process, by recording with fidelity what we did to intervene, and by monitoring the child's progress in response. This feedback on the child's response to the intervention provides an evidence base to support an evaluation of what is effective for her. Furthermore, if we aggregate these data across individuals, we can contribute to a greater understanding of what works for whom, child by child.

The reader may refer to Table 12.1 for details about related programs and websites.

Table 12.1 *Websites*

Website	Information on Website
http://rtckids.fmhi.usf.edu/sbmh/default.cfm	Provides information on school-based Mental Health Services, Research & Training Center for Children's Mental Health, University of South Florida.
www.smhp.psych.ucla.edu	The Center for Mental Health in Schools, University of California at Los Angeles (UCLA).
http://csmh.umaryland.edu	The Center for School Mental Health, University of Maryland, School of Medicine.
www.schoolmentalhealth.org	School Mental Health Connection.
www.casel.org	Collaborative for Academic, Social, and Emotional Learning (CASEL).
www.hfrp.org	Harvard Family Research Project: Harvard Graduate School of Education.
www.promisingpractices.net/default.asp	Promising Practices Network on Children, Families, and Communities funded by the RAND Corporation.
www.anxietybc.com/parent/index.php	Anxiety BC (British Columbia).
www.kc.vanderbilt.edu	Vanderbilt Kennedy Center.
www.pbis.org	Positive Behavioral Interventions and Supports Center.
www.livesinthebalance.org	Collaborative Problem Solving.
www.interventioncentral.org	Intervention Central.
http://research.aboutkidshealth.ca/teachadhd	Teach ADHD.
www.ccyp.vic.gov.au/childsafetycommissioner/downloads/calmer_classrooms.pdf	Calmer Classrooms: A Guide to Working with Traumatized Children.
www.schoolmentalhealth.org/Resources/FostCare/ResFost.html	Resources for Working With Youth in Foster Care, School Mental Health.org.
www.rti4success.org	National Center on Response to Intervention.
www.studentprogress.org	National Center for Student Progress Monitoring.

(continued)

Table 12.1 *Websites (continued)*

www.directbehaviorratings.com	Direct Behavior Ratings: Assessment, Communication, Intervention.
www.colorado.edu/cspv	Center for the Study and Prevention of Violence, Institute of Behavioral Science, University of Colorado at Boulder.
www.prevnet.ca	Promoting Relationships and Eliminating Violence.
www.prevention.psu.edu/projects	The Prevention Research Center for the Promotion of Human Development, Penn State University.
www.olweus.org/public/bullying_ prevention_program .page	Website for Olweus Bullying Prevention Program.
www.esrnational.org/es/rccp.htm	The Educators for Social Responsibility (ESR) website provides assistance with the Resolve Conflict Creatively Program (RCCP) and provides training and implementation. ESR is a comprehensive, school-based program for children from Kindergarten to Grade 8. The program teaches how to resolve conflicts in the classroom. Outcomes are positive.
www.projectachieve.info	"Stop and Think" social skills program that teaches children to stop and think of solutions before they act out and get out of control or withdraw.
www.wingsforkids.org/wings/why-it-matters/learning-social-and-emotional-skills-missing-piece-education	The "WINGS helping kids soar" program has a life skills curriculum of 30 learning objectives and fun learning, social, and emotional skills. It also has an after-school group program for children to teach them skills that can be used throughout their daily lives.
www.self-regulation.ca	Website of the Canadian Self-Regulation Initiative.

13

Effective Prevention and Early Intervention

This book discusses the assessment and treatment of children with a complex array of difficulties, often with parents and social situations that present multiple challenges. Not uncommonly at the time of referral, situations are at breaking points, with children being expelled from school and the parents' relationship in serious trouble. Many parents talk about their child having had problems from early infancy, such as extreme irritability and difficulties settling into routines of sleeping and eating. They describe toddlers who could not attend group care because they refused to separate or had extreme tantrums, could not play with peers, or follow daily routines. As the child became a preschooler, the behavior often worsened, and parents describe everything, including a trip to the shopping mall or visiting friends, as being a battle and feeling exhausted as a result.

Some parents sought professional support and treatment early, whereas others hoped that their child would improve as he got older. They were given advice by friends and family, who often suggested opposite approaches. Some went to parenting groups, but nothing seemed to work. If they sought other treatment, they often felt blamed by service providers, the perceived message being that their parenting or relationship with the child was causing the problems. Sometimes there were significant contributing factors, but the family lacked an adequate assessment of the main causes of the child's symptoms and suggestions to treat the complex array of causative mechanisms that could be identified. Too often a diagnosis of oppositional defiant disorder (ODD) or attention deficit/hyperactivity disorder (ADHD) was made, but there were few attempts to understand the uniqueness of the child. As a consequence, some of the evidence-based treatments for a particular diagnosis might not have met the needs of the child who had, for example, speech and language delays and sensorimotor difficulties.

As illustrated in the case examples in Chapter 10 and in the other chapters in Section 2, many of the children treated made significant gains, and their parents were then hopeful that their children would complete school, become employed, and have successful relationships. However, if parents and their children had received support and treatment during the early years, some of the children's difficulties could have been minimized and the development of negative and coercive parenting patterns prevented. Although some degree of neuroplasticity is possible at any age, the younger the child the greater the probability that changes can occur in neural pathways. This chapter reviews how functional difficulties can appear in infancy and preschool years and outlines some of the established treatments. It also describes some of the most effective approaches to prevention and early intervention for particular groups of parents. Current knowledge of neuroplasticity is also briefly described.

DISORDERS IN OLDER CHILDREN AND ADULTS

Studies have documented an increase in the prevalence of various mental health disorders in both children and adults in recent years. Longitudinal and epidemiological studies in a number of countries of the incidence of social, emotional, and behavioral disorders have found that approximately 20% of children and adolescents between the ages of 4 and 16 throughout the world have one or more mental health disorders (Brandenberg, Friedman, & Silver, 1990; Friedli, 2009; World Health Organization, 2001, 2002). Of these children a significant percentage face multiple challenges. There has also been a significant rise throughout the Western world since the 1950s in the prevalence of eating disorders, depression, substance abuse, crime, and conduct disorders (Campbell, 2002).

DISORDERS IN INFANCY AND EARLY CHILDHOOD

There has been a long debate about the appropriateness of using diagnostic approaches for infants and young children. *The Diagnostic and Statistical Manual of Mental Health Disorders,* 5th edition (DSM-5; American Psychiatric Association [APA], 2013) does not include a section on "Disorders Usually First Diagnosed in Infancy, Childhood and Adolescence." Some diagnoses are noted to apply to certain age groups.

Two approaches have been used to overcome this lack of adequate diagnostic criteria for infants and preschoolers. The first approach has been called a "top-down approach" and is that taken by the Task Force on Research Diagnostic Criteria Infancy and Preschool (RDC-PA) (2003). The task force, using parent interview data and factor analysis, found that symptoms reflecting disorders such as ADHD, ODD, depression, and anxiety had an overall community prevalence in preschoolers of 10% to 15%. They concluded that the common forms of child and adolescent psychopathology are already in place by 2 years of age. It was pointed out, however, that these criteria cannot be used for children under 2 years of age (Egger & Angold, 2006; RDC-PA, 2003; Sterba, Egger, & Angold, 2007, 2009.

The second approach, the *Diagnostic Classification of Mental Disorders of Infancy and Early Childhood: 0–3* (Rev. Ed.; *DC-03R*), aims to classify disorders in infants and toddlers that are not covered in *DSM-IV* (4th ed.; APA, 1994) (Emde, 2003; Zero to Three Press, 2005). It classifies mental health disorders to 3 years of age using a developmental and dimensional framework rather than a diagnostic approach and is often used for children from birth to 5 years of age. It includes different versions of the *DSM-IV* diagnoses and new diagnostic categories such as regulatory and parent–child relationship disorders. The criteria used lack validation, but the classification is widely used in service settings, indicating a need among clinicians for clearer classification of behavioral and emotional difficulties in young children.

Prevalence of Disorders in Infants and Preschoolers

As noted previously, there is an overall prevalence of psychopathology of 10% to 15% in preschool children (not including infants and toddlers under 2 years of age). In a study in Denmark that looked at younger children, 16% to 18% of children had mental health problems at 18 months of age. The most common disorders were difficulties with emotion and behavior regulation and eating, and left untreated there was a major risk of ongoing psychopathology (Skovgaard, Houmann, Christiansen, Landorph, Jorgensen, & CC 2000 Study Team, 2007). These findings suggest that this population deserves treatment in its own right (Warner & Pottick, 2006).

Some of the most common mental health problems identified in infancy and early childhood include failure to thrive, sleeping and eating problems, aggression, oppositional defiance and other disruptive behavior, posttraumatic stress disorder, and anxiety and depression. There has also been an increase in children diagnosed with an autism spectrum disorder and ADHD in the early years (Campbell, 1996, 2002; Luby, 2006). Some of these disorders can be extremely serious. For example, failure to thrive accounts for 6% to 30% of infants seen in ambulatory care and inner-city emergency rooms and 15% of infant hospitalizations. It can be associated with recurrent infections, multiple developmental delays, lower scores on IQ tests, and emotional and behavioral problems (Esparo, Canals, & Jane, 2004).

Chronicity of Early Difficulties

Ongoing difficulties are common, particularly if children do not receive treatment in the preschool years. Sleeping and eating problems are common in the first 3 years of life and can cause significant anxiety and frustration for parents (Benoit, 2009; Owens & Burnham, 2009). Twelve percent of parents report child sleep problems by 2 years of age, and they are associated with later psychopathology (Lam, Hiscock, & Wake, 2003; Ong, Wickramaratne, Tang, & Weissman, 2006; Wake, Morton-Allen, Poulakis, Hiscock, & Wake, 2003). The prevalence of feeding problems ranges from 25% to 35% in typically developing children, and those that are not resolved by 2 years of age can predispose children to eating disorders in adolescence and early adulthood (Chatoor & Khushlani, 2006). Rates of aggression and other externalizing disorders are high in preschoolers, and surveys suggest that they are as high as 4% to 12%, or equivalent to rates for older children. When severe behavioral problems emerge among children in the preschool period, without intervention, as many as 65% are likely to have ongoing difficulties (Campbell, 2002; Campbell, Shaw, & Gilliom, 2000; Pfeifer, Goldsmith, Davidson, & Rickman, 2002). Another group of children who have significant difficulties are inhibited, anxious preschoolers who have early separation anxiety and tend to withdraw from new people, objects, and situations. They are more likely to be anxious in follow-up studies (Luby & Belden, 2006). Anxious children tend to have greater physiological reactivity to stress, and this is an indicator of later pathology (DeGangi, 2000). Similarly, mood disorders such as depression have been validated in numerous case studies and data from samples of preschoolers (Luby, 2009a, b). Although longitudinal studies have not yet been conducted, early extreme sadness or anhedonia or inability to enjoy activities and play likely predicts mood disorders at later ages (Zeman, Shipman, & Suveg, 2002).

There is increasing awareness that a significant percentage of children with severe difficulties in the early years who do not receive treatment will continue to have difficulties in later years (Fonagy, Target, Cottrell, Phillips, & Kurtz, 2000; Meltzer, Gatward, Corbin, Goodman, & Ford, 2003). Most disorders diagnosed later in life had their origins in early childhood and are understood to arise from a complex interaction of biological or temperamental factors in the child and his early rearing environment, of which parents are the most essential components. Because many mental disorders become increasingly difficult to treat the longer they exist, and because of the heavy burden that they impose on the individual, family, and society, there is growing recognition that the solution lies in early identification and intervention. Treating disorders once they are well established is not only difficult and partially effective but also requires significant investments from the treating agencies and individuals and families who are afflicted.

INFANCY AND EARLY CHILDHOOD PROBLEMS

Throughout Section 2 of this book, difficulties and disorders in a number of functional areas as contributors to problems were described. The treatment of children with severe difficulties in each functional area was discussed. Treatment of many older children can be long and difficult and not always successful. Signs of problems often occur at an early age, and treatment in the preschool years is most likely to be successful.

Discussed in Chapter 3 were difficulties with fine and gross motor functioning, balance and proprioception, and sensory processing. These can be identified early and often contribute to difficulties with parent–child interactions and attachments and might lead to extreme emotional and behavioral reactions. Warning signs in the first 3 to 6 years indicate that the child is experiencing difficulties with fine or gross motor functioning or sensory processing. It is important to provide treatment as soon as delays are identified because the child learns about the environment using sensorimotor skills. If problems with sensory processing are extreme, they can contribute to problems with eating and sleeping and engaging in a number of adaptive behaviors; activities with other children; and outings to busy or noisy venues such as the shopping mall. Because many areas of the brain are responsible for motor activities and are developed early, intervention as soon as possible is important to promote healthy brain development. A number of approaches to early intervention were provided in the chapter. One occupational therapy intervention for extremely low birth weight babies between 6 and 12 months of age, for example, included enhancing motor control and coordination. Many of the strategies discussed in the chapter to overcome hyperarousal and hyperreactive behavior can be used with infants and preschoolers. They include Wilbarger's brushing protocol, estimating "engine speed," adapting the environment to support the easily aroused child, and designing a sensory diet for the child. Chronic hyperarousal of her central nervous system can be avoided, and, with support, she will gradually be able to manage a wider range of activities and attend school without constant triggering.

As described in Chapter 4, basic vocabulary, grammar, and phonology are usually mastered by 3 years of age. However, a number of disorders can affect the development of these abilities, resulting in communication and language impairments. Specific language impairment (SLI) or language difficulties can include expressive, receptive, and phonological disorders. Language impairment is linked to problems with behavior and emotion regulation and is a major symptom of autism spectrum disorders. Delays and other language difficulties are usually identified in toddler and preschool years when language is being acquired. However, difficulties with social communication, pragmatic language, and stuttering can become obvious later. Although the literature on the efficacy of intervention with young children with language disorders is sparse, there is evidence that improvements are clinically significant when intervention occurs in preschool years and is provided by clinicians and trained parents and teachers.

Chapter 5 examined the effects of trauma such as abuse and neglect and exposure to violence; when trauma is severe and chronic, it can cause pervasive difficulties across the lifespan. The predominant effect of trauma can best be described as a severe dysregulation of behavior and emotion (Ford, Albert, & Hawke, 2009). As a result, children severely affected by trauma display a number of symptoms and are often diagnosed with a variety of disorders or comorbidities, such as ODD, conduct disorder (CD), generalized anxiety disorder (GAD), depression, ADHD, adjustment disorders, separation anxiety, and phobic disorder (van der Kolk, 2005). Their symptoms are frequently misunderstood, and the child can be wrongly labeled, for example, as "naughty," "bad," "lazy," and "oppositional" without understanding the underlying biology of their behaviors. Trauma experienced in infancy and early childhood can be particularly devastating because it alters the structure, organization, and chemistry of the brain, causing the resulting symptoms and personality characteristics. Because brain development is sequential, early trauma has more effects than trauma experienced in later childhood, adolescence, or adulthood. Trauma that results in strong and prolonged activation of the hypothalmic–pituitary–adrenal (HPA) axis can cause persistent elevations of stress hormones and altered levels of other key brain chemicals, such as serotonin and epinephrine. Perry et al. (1995) suggested that repetitive triggering of the fear networks can retain maladaptive neural circuits instead of more adaptive ones. Continuous stimulation of the stress-response system can also affect the immune system and other metabolic regulatory mechanisms, leading to a lower threshold for their activation throughout life. Persistent activation of the stress system in early childhood can affect organization of the brain and lead to difficulties with learning, memory, and self-regulation. There is also evidence that maltreated children have smaller brain volumes, fluid-filled cavities in the brain, and smaller areas of connection between left and right sides of the brain (De Bellis, 2002; De Bellis et al., 2000). The stress-response system can become hypersensitive, resulting in acting-out symptoms, hypervigilance, or withdrawal and dissociation (Friedman & Schnurr, 1995). Genes can be turned on or off by early experiences. One of these genes is responsible for controlling the stress hormone cortisol, and it can be turned off by traumatic experiences, also contributing to the hypersensitivity and overreactive triggering described above (Meaney, 2010). On the other hand, some traumatized children become hyporesponsive (Repetti, Taylor, & Saxby, 2007).

Given the potential of trauma in the first 5 years of life to affect development and functioning across the lifespan, three major approaches have been developed to reduce its effects: (1) evidence-based prevention services for at-risk children and their families, including home visiting programs to improve parenting and reduce abuse; (2) working with parents whose infants or young children have experienced trauma to recognize events that trigger fear reactions in their children and to protect them from such events as much as possible; and (3) working directly with the child using play therapy or cognitive-behavioral therapy (CBT) for young children and, if parents are equally traumatized, approaches to enhance parent's attributions and interactions with their children.

Chapter 6 described various factors beginning in early infancy that contribute to difficulties with emotion regulation. These include factors within the child that influence his ability to maintain attention and state regulation, which then affects his capacity to engage in synchronous interactions with caregivers (Feldman, 2007b, 2009). Mental health difficulties in the parents, abuse, and stress also interfere with his capacity to be attuned and engage in the synchronous interactions that predict vagal control and later attention and emotion regulation. Because this area is relatively new, there is comparatively little research on interventions in infancy and early childhood. However, it is logical that support for parents with infants with state-regulation difficulties, as well as parents who have been abused or neglected or are depressed, should be a priority. Interactions that emphasize parents' understanding of their child's feelings should form a basis for such efforts. Some of the approaches discussed in Chapter 6 are designed for young children and their parents.

Chapter 7, on difficulties and disorders of behavior regulation, noted that problems such as aggression and oppositional behavior can begin in the preschool period for some children and remain over time and development. There has been a great deal of debate about identifying these behaviors early because they overlap with normative misbehaviors of early childhood (Wakschlag, Briggs-Gowan, Carter, Hill, Danis, et al., 2007). However, disruptive-behavior problems can be difficult to deal with and are the most common reason for referral of young children (Wakschlag & Danis, 2009). Also, in a number of cases, the child's early problems with behavior regulation and anger modulation significantly increased the risk of impairment later. In fact, about 50% of children with early disruptive-behavior problems continue to exhibit disruptive behavior (Campbell, 2002; Kim-Cohen et al., 2005). It is therefore important to identify these children early and provide support for their parents and teachers to prevent these long-term trajectories.

As with behavior-regulation problems in older children, treating children effectively in the preschool period can also be challenging. Obviously, some of the parent-training and child-focused programs recommended for older children are not suitable for the preschool period. The Incredible Years Group Parenting Program has demonstrated effectiveness in improving parents' use of successful behavior management and child behavior strategies (Webster-Stratton & Reid, 2003; Webster-Stratton & Taylor, 2001). Parent training is often provided for individual families, allowing a focus on their particular issues. Some of the approaches discussed in Chapter 7 can be used with younger children and include changing parents' negative attributions of their child and increasing responsiveness and sensitivity in their interactions with him.

Because these children are still developing in a number of functional areas that can bring their behavior under control, encouraging this development can be a major focus of intervention. For example, strategies to develop conscience and empathy, or improve emotion regulation and problem solving, can be important approaches. There is also an extensive literature on infant–parent and toddler–parent psychotherapies that can be applicable to preschoolers with behavioral problems. Most adopt a nondirective approach based on psychodynamic, object relations, and attachment theories (Lieberman, Van Horn, & Ghosh Ipsen, 2005).

There is a great deal of evidence of the success of center-based interventions, with and without home visiting, in preventing the development of antisocial behavior and disorders such as conduct disorder and improving a number of child outcomes. Other programs for older children with conduct problems include classroom-based interventions. However, there has been little research on daycare-based programs for preschoolers with mental health issues, which is unfortunate because they can be optimal places for interventions.

As described in Chapter 8, ADHD and other difficulties with executive functioning are typically viewed as disorders beginning in elementary school-aged children. As a consequence, there is little literature on preschool-aged children with these difficulties. It has therefore been hard to estimate the prevalence of ADHD in the preschool years (Steinhoff et al., 2006). Diagnostic criteria in *DSM-5* for ADHD do not specify a minimum age for the disorder so it could be diagnosed in children from 3 to 6 years of age who can show symptoms of the disorder, though in some instances it is difficult to distinguish the symptoms from typical behavior (APA, 2013). Also, other disorders that can present in preschool years can make it more difficult to diagnose symptoms of ADHD. They include speech and language disorders, auditory processing problems, pervasive developmental disorders, and aggression.

Evidence suggests that, when children meet criteria for ADHD at 3 years of age, it is predictive of ADHD at age 9 in 48% of cases (Campbell & Ewing, 1990; Lahey et al., 2004). In *DSM-IV* field trials of children diagnosed with ADHD before 6 years of age, these younger children were found more likely to be diagnosed as having the hyperactive–impulsive subtype. There is little evidence of successful treatment of ADHD in preschool years.

Parents can use a number of strategies to encourage their preschoolers to concentrate and reduce any hyperactivity and impulsiveness. These strategies include the following:

- scaffolding the child to begin and complete a task such as coloring a picture, painting, or learning some letters and numbers;
- teaching the child to use self-talk to support her performance on various tasks;
- giving the child a movement break before completing a task;
- giving children a clear schedule of their day and discussing any changes in advance, and also making rules and consequences clear to them;
- breaking tasks down into smaller parts if the child has difficulty with concentrating and rewarding parts of the task as they are completed;
- encouraging the child to practice moving slowly like a tortoise instead of fast like a deer;
- structuring activities so that the child can experience success and making sure that he has the satisfaction of completing it himself;
- helping the child with planning ahead for a certain task and problem solving along the way;
- helping the child to learn about the sequence of events by going over events that have happened or are planned; and
- noticing any efforts to concentrate on something that the child finds hard to do and giving positive feedback.

Chapter 9 discussed the development of social competence and identified a number of possible issues or disorders that contribute to children having challenges with socialization. These are anxiety disorders (particularly social anxiety), attachment disorders, conduct disorders, and autism spectrum disorders.

Attachment is developed in the child by the end of the first year and formed from the interactions between mother (and other primary caregivers) and child that occur during the early months. The child's attachment style or quality is determined by the degree of sensitivity and responsiveness shown by the caregiver, particularly when the infant is hurt, ill, upset, or emotionally aroused. From these early experiences, the child has expectations about how she and others interact, feel, and behave. These interactions are laid down as internal working models of attachment and can continue to influence the child into adulthood, particularly in social interactions with others. These early interactions and the resulting attachment can provide a child with a sense of being able to cope with stress and reduce the reactivity of the HPA axis and the production of cortisol and serotonin. If these sensitive, containing interactions are not provided and the child instead experiences rejection or abuse, the HPA axis can easily be triggered and become overreactive, contributing to various types of psychopathology (Gunnar, 2007).

If the child's quality of attachment is secure or insecure, it indicates that the child has developed an organized strategy to deal with unfamiliar and stressful or threatening situations, separations, and illnesses. The type of attachment that the child develops is associated with later social and emotional development. Research has shown that insecure and disorganized attachment is associated with later psychopathology. There is a slight trend for children with avoidant attachment classifications to develop externalizing disorders and ambivalent–resistant classifications to be associated with internalizing disorders, though these pathways are not always found (DeKlyen & Greenberg, 2008). Disorganized attachment relationships are characterized by the breakdown of an organized strategy in stressful situations (Lyons-Ruth & Jacobvitz, 2008). Infants with disorganized attachments act in unpredictable ways, and their behavior seems to lack a goal, intention, or explanation. They frequently display aggressive behavior toward parents and avoidant and atypical movements. These children are also more likely to develop later psychopathology.

In a meta-analysis of data from 80 studies, it was found that in low socioeconomic families 34% met criteria for a disorganized attachment relationship, 43% of children had substance-abusing mothers, and 77% of children had maltreating parents (van IJzendoorn, Schuengel, & Bakermans-Kranenburg, 1999). The percentage is highest when the child also has a difficult temperament (Lyons-Ruth & Jacobvitz, 2008). The most pathological classification is that of reactive attachment disorder (RAD), in which attachments have failed to develop because the child was raised in seriously disturbed and atypical caregiver environments. They include orphanages, frequent changes of caregivers (as can result from changes in foster care), and extreme neglect and/or abusive caregiving. Symptoms of RAD are of two types: indiscriminate/disinhibited and emotionally withdrawn/inhibited. Both types of attachment are linked to various types of psychopathology (Zeanah & Smyke, 2009).

Given the importance of the attachment relationship, many early-intervention programs focus on improving mother–child interactions to encourage development of a secure attachment and thus enhance child outcomes and reduce psychopathology in children, adolescents, and adults. Given that attachment is in place by the first year, the earlier that these approaches can be provided the better, particularly when atypical interactions are present. Some of these approaches focus on altering the interactional processes in the attachment dyad and consequently the attachment quality of the child. Autism spectrum disorders are also discussed in Chapter 9. Although research on the effectiveness of intervention for children with these disorders is somewhat sketchy, and some widely used approaches have not been adequately researched, a few conclusions can be made from the existing research. Behavioral approaches have been the best researched. Children with higher IQs and fewer symptoms of aggression and self-abuse, for example, are more likely to make changes with treatments (Boucher, 2009). There is also evidence that interventions provided early are more likely to have positive outcomes. For higher-functioning children, changes in social skills and language have been found as a result of focused intervention, and there is optimism that more targeted and sustained interventions can change outcomes for children (Carr & Lord, 2009; Lord et al., 2006). These positive results have been found particularly with children with pervasive developmental disorder—not otherwise specified (PDD—NOS; Turner & Stone, 2007). In toddlers and preschool children, the strongest predictors of positive outcomes are nonverbal cognitive skills, motor skills, and receptive language abilities (Butter, Wynn, & Mulick, 2003; Corsello, 2005; Dawson & Zanolli, 2003).

Children with separation and social anxiety typically have inhibited temperaments. They tend to withdraw from unfamiliar people, objects, and situations and can show signs of anxiety and distress. This type of temperament is related to low sociability, timidity, and introversion and has been found to be consistent across situations such as the home and daycare and across ages. In one study, it was found that, if inhibition is evident in toddlers as a reaction to novelty, impulsivity, and inhibitory control at 9, 14, 22, 33, and 45 months, then it is likely to continue at older ages. Children with the most extreme inhibition have low levels of social competence and high levels of social anxiety. They are also high in reactivity and attentional vigilance. Those with overcontrolling or oversolicitous parenting are more likely to continue their inhibited styles. These children can cause stress for their parents and elicit parental irritation or withdrawal of contact. Their anxiety can also foster withdrawal from peers. However, a number of parenting strategies used in the early years can support children to become less anxious and more social and independent.

For children who are more anxious and inhibited, it is important for the parent to insist on a time-limited trial of an activity if she believes that it fits with the child's interests or abilities. It might be important to stay around the first time until the child is comfortable but then to support her by praising her for her initiative in attending alone. With the child who is more self-absorbed and withdrawn, using enthusiasm and animated interactions can draw her out. Activities such as playing with a balloon or bubbles can be helpful. With the child who finds change difficult, it is important to warn her about the change, talk about upcoming events, and give her a chance to ask questions. Using visual cues and schedules, such as calendars, to prepare her for changes and new experiences is useful. Giving warnings about transitions can also be helpful (Landy & Menna, 2006, 2009).

Young children benefit from interactions with peers (Ladd & Pettit, 2002). For children who are anxious about socializing with other children, it is important for parents to provide them with opportunities to interact with other children outside the home. This can be through the parents' own social networks, going to the park, or in preschool. Ladd and Hart (1992) found that parents who were "high initiators" of peer contacts had children who had more playmates and more frequent play experiences. The children were also more able to initiate more of their own peer contacts.

It might also be necessary to support play between the child and peers if this is difficult for him to initiate himself. This can be done by engaging in peer play as a partner and by observing rather than being directly involved. In the first approach, parents are directly involved in the play and encourage turn taking, prompt appropriate peer behaviors, and deal with conflicts. Some studies have shown that children obtain higher levels of social competence when mothers are involved directly in the play of young children (Bhavnagri & Parker, 1991). In the second type of intervention, when the mother is an observer from outside the group, it facilitates cooperation and helps to maintain interaction.

Children who are more socially anxious need to be taught social skills such as entering a group and being able to remain involved and cooperate with the other children (Landy, 2009). Again it is often important to scaffold the play by providing toys that can be used cooperatively, giving the child words to use to request group entry, and correcting any misattributions that the child might have about the behavior of another child in the group. Sometimes a more socially competent or older child can be recruited as a buddy to help a child who is having difficulty entering a group. Using social stories written by a parent or professional and individualized to the child and that teach the relevant components of a social situation that the child is having difficulty with or can be confused about can be helpful. The stories emphasize cues that the child needs to look out for and appropriate responses to them. His input is integrated into the story by asking him to describe what he finds difficult about the situation and teaching him how to interact in a more positive way. The stories are read to the child at least once a day and can be gone over frequently if he continues to have difficulty with the situation. A number of studies have found that, when social stories are used, children have increased social free play, rates of social behavior, contingent responding, and social engagement. Some generalizations to other settings have also been found (Barry & Burlew, 2004; Delano & Snell, 2006; Thiemann & Goldstein, 2001).

RISK AND PROTECTIVE FACTORS

Risk factors place an individual at risk of later poor outcomes, including developmental delays and various mental and physical disorders. In Chapter 1 and the chapters describing various disorders and difficulties, various contributors were described. Protective factors have been described by some writers as the opposite of risk factors and are seen as falling into similar categories. Rutter (1987) also identified four protective mechanisms or processes that can be set in place and account for individual variations in outcome: reducing the impact of a difficult situation, promoting the child's self-esteem, providing support in the environment for the child, and providing support for a child facing a difficult situation. Also described in Chapter 1 were the effects of cumulative risks studied by Belsky and Isabella (1988). In general, studies have found that children exposed to four or more risk factors, especially if they are more significant ones, will likely have compromised development. There is thus evidence that children growing up in families with multiple risk factors are the most likely to develop problems. These are families, often with few protective factors, in which the interactions between parent and child are most compromised, intergenerational problems have become entrenched, and the child might be at risk of abuse. It has been suggested that these extremely high-risk families might constitute only about 8% to 10% of families but result in 70% of child difficulties and use a similar proportion of the costs for mental health, criminal justice, and welfare services (Greenspan, 1986; Scott, Knapp, Henderson, & Maughan, 2001).

EFFECTIVE PREVENTION AND EARLY INTERVENTION

Evaluation Research

The widely published success of certain early-intervention programs has contributed to belief in the importance of prevention and early intervention. These programs have been seen as a window of opportunity through which to enhance the development of all infants and young children. As a result, there has been a significant increase in funding for certain early-intervention initiatives in the United States, Canada, England, and many other developed countries. Efforts have been made to develop a system with different levels of intervention, including universal prevention strategies and more intense interventions for children and families at high risk and treatment for children and families with identified difficulties. See Figure 13.1 for a model of prevention and early-intervention services.

The term "prevention" refers to any program or approach used to prevent later difficulties and enhance the cognitive, behavioral, emotional, social, and physical development of children from pregnancy to 6 years of age. Prevention programs are often offered to whole communities, especially high-risk ones. Early intervention, on the other hand, refers to programs provided when a child or parents are already identified as significantly at risk or the child is showing some type of difficulty, placing his development at risk. There are four typical approaches to providing early intervention: child focused, parenting programs that intervene with the parent–child interaction or relationship, parent focused, and two-generation programs in which both children and parents are the focus (St. Pierre & Layzer, 1998). Some programs are provided in both home and center settings. To add to the complexity, though enhancement of child development is the primary goal of most programs, various other factors have been considered as research outcomes: improving the birth weights of infants, reducing child abuse, enhancing parenting interactions, encouraging secure attachments, and enhancing parents' sense of personal and parenting competence. In longitudinal studies, outcomes assessed in adolescents and adults included employment, fewer arrests, and positive relationships.

Universal prevention services offer the whole population information about parenting infants and young children, parenting groups to prevent stress and support parents as they deal with the challenges of bringing up children, and drop-in centers where they can meet other parents. As shown in Figure 13.1, as we go up the triangle to levels 3 and 4, fewer children and families are served, but the services provided need to be more specialized and intense. We need service providers from all disciplines bringing their specialized knowledge and expertise if we are to effect change. However, we must remember that the difficulties faced by many children are profound and have long-lasting impacts on development. Yet many children strive toward growth, and evidence shows that, with the right program, there can be positive outcomes for many of these children over time.

A number of well-researched programs have carried out extensive pre- and post-testing using a number of outcome measures and compared them with control groups that do not receive the service. These programs have demonstrated significant improvements for children and families in the program compared with those in a control group. Many of these evaluation studies have measured outcomes a number of times, beginning immediately

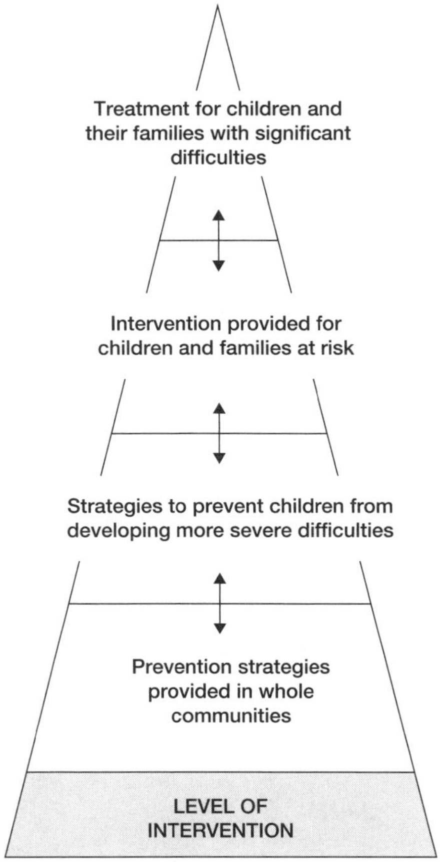

Figure 13.1 *Model of prevention and early-intervention services.*

after the program has ended and at later times, even into adulthood. An indication of the importance of these questions is the large number of reviews of early interventions carried out recently, primarily focusing on the state of knowledge concerning long-term effects on young children at high risk and their families (e.g., Landy & Menna, 2006a, 2006b; Mrazek & Brown, 2002; Webster-Stratton & Taylor, 2001; Westhues, Nelson, & MacLeod, 2003). Some of these programs and their outcomes are discussed below.

Home Visiting Programs

Gomby (2005) reviewed the evidence of the effectiveness of home visiting programs. Home visiting is a widely used approach to help families with young children in developed and developing countries. This is an important strategy because it can bring support to socially or geographically isolated families when it is difficult for the mother to leave the house, and the services can be tailored to meet the needs of individual families. It is also crucial to engage some of the most traumatized families who have a great deal of difficulty trusting service providers and typically feel more in control on their "home turf" and might be more likely to become involved in the service. These programs can be delivered to families with pregnant women, infants, toddlers, and young children under 5 years old. Home visiting can also be part of center-based programs. A number of these programs have demonstrated positive outcomes for families who were visited compared with those who did not receive the intervention (Sweet & Applebaum, 2004). Some successful programs are listed in the text that follows:

- **Elmira Prenatal and Early Infancy Program** (Olds, Hill, Robinson, Song, & Little, 2000). The home visits were provided by trained nurses, and families received an average of 30 home visits during pregnancy and until the child was 2 years of age. The population comprised young, single, first-time mothers from low socioeconomic groups. Families that received the intervention had lower rates of child abuse, and the children by 15 years of age had fewer arrests, less running away, and lower rates of smoking and drinking. Mothers had decreased welfare use and engaged in less criminal behavior.
- **Florida Parent Education Infant and Toddler Program** (Jester & Guinagh, 1983). Trained paraprofessionals provided weekly home visiting for children from 3 months to 3 years of age to low-income families, with several participants being teenage mothers. At age 15, the children had higher IQs and school achievement and lower school dropout rates than those not receiving the intervention.
- **Verbal Interaction Project** (Levenstein, O'Hara, & Levenstein, 1984). Home visits were provided by paraprofessionals who emphasized improvement of language. Families were primarily African American living in low-income housing with less than a year of education and semi-skilled jobs. The children received visits beginning when the child was 21 to 35 months for 3 years. The children were followed up in Grade 7 and had significantly higher IQ scores, had better grade retention, and required less special education than those who did not receive the intervention.
- **Infants at Social Risk Program** (Lyons-Ruth, Connell, Grunebaum, & Botein, 1990). Families were referred from social service agencies because of concerns about the child-rearing environment. Weekly home visits and group meetings were provided for 13 months. Home-visited infants had higher scores on the Bayley Mental Scale and increased rates of secure attachment, and fewer infants were in the disorganized attachment category than those in a comparison group.

Other programs were not successful. Researchers concluded that they had not been intensive enough due to lack of funding, had been provided by intervenors without suitable training and experience, and in some cases had not included a center-based initiative.

Center-Based Programs

A number of other programs have provided a center-based or nursery school intervention for the children with or without home visiting, and many have had significant effects on a number of child outcomes. Some of the best known and most successful programs are described below.

- **The Carolina Abecedarian Project** (Campbell & Ramey, 1994, 2002). Participants were African American families whose infants were at risk due to poverty. The children attended a full-day, year-round preschool program that began soon after birth and had a low student–teacher ratio. At follow-up when the children were 15, intervention-group children had much higher IQs and better scores on mathematics and reading. The mothers in the intervention group were less likely to be unemployed and were better educated.
- **Perry Preschool Program** (Schweinhart et al., 2005). The program was for children with IQ scores less than 85 who received a daily preschool program. By 40 years of age, the

participants were less likely to have been arrested and were earning more than those in the control group. They were more likely to have graduated from high school and to have required less special education.

- **Yale Child Welfare Research Project** (Seitz & Apfel, 1994). This was a daycare program provided for families with incomes below the poverty line from pregnancy to 30 months. Children by Grade 8 had better school attendance and less special education, and mothers had higher levels of education and were more likely to be self-supporting.
- **The Chicago Child–Parent Centers (CPC)** has served children in high-risk neighborhoods since 1967 (Reynolds, Temple, Robertson, & Mann, 2002). This preschool program ran for 8 hours a day, 5 days a week, and provided educational and family support services to children between 3 and 5 years of age. Outreach services were also provided. A longitudinal study of over 1,000 children who attended the program for 2 years from 3 to 5 years of age between 1983 and 1985 compared the results for these children with a comparison group that did not attend the program. Recently, long-term benefits were found for CPC children at 21 years of age (Reynolds et al., 2002). Adults in the intervention group were more likely to have completed school and less likely to need special education services. They were also less likely to have had juvenile arrests.
- **The Infant Health and Development Program (IHDP)** (Benasich & Black, 1994) was an intensive 3-year program for low-birth-weight infants. The children received high-quality, center-based care, and parent home visits by center-based staff were provided weekly for the first year and every other week for the second and third years. The program had beneficial effects for children's development, and mothers were more likely to have returned to work early and be employed (McCormick et al., 2006).
- **Early Head Start (EHS)** is a federally funded program in the United States that began in 1994 as a two-generation program to enhance children's health and development and strengthen family and community partnerships of low-income families with pregnant women, infants, and toddlers. EHS provides a combination of home visiting and center-based child care from the prenatal period to age 3. The most recent national evaluation of the short-term effects showed that EHS enhances child cognitive test scores and positive behaviors at ages 2 and 3 (Love et al. 2002).

In general, programs that provide center-based interventions for children have the best child outcomes, especially when infants and young children are already showing signs of developing significant delays or disorders, parents are at extremely high risk, and very negative parent–child interactions are present. The direct intervention that the child receives in a nursery or daycare setting might be a necessary component of the programs to improve child outcomes because the more intense, targeted strategies that the child receives are more likely to improve brain structure and organization and consequently development and functioning.

Targeted Short-Term Interventions

Some researchers have assessed the effects of specific interventions and compared them to other approaches to treatment. Studies have compared varied approaches such as psychodynamic, health promotion, and CBT. Strategies have focused on improving the interaction at a behavioral level (e.g., interactional coaching), enhancing parental mental representations or attributions (e.g., videotape viewing or interactional guidance), enhancing social support (e.g., referral to parent drop-in centers), and enhancing parental mental health and sense of self-efficacy (e.g., various types of counseling and parenting groups) (Landy & Menna, 2006b; McDonough, 2000). The findings from some of these evaluation studies are outlined next.

- **Coaching the Interaction** (van den Boom, 1994, 1995). One hundred mothers and infants were selected on the basis of infant irritability assessed at 15 days postpartum. The intervention focused on enhancing maternal sensitivity to infants' cues and encouraging mothers to imitate their infants and soothe them when they were upset. The sessions were provided between 6 and 9 months by a female psychologist. When the infants were 1 year of age, the following behaviors were more positive in the intervention group: maternal responsiveness and degree of stimulation, visual attentiveness to the infant, infant sociability, infants' ability to soothe themselves, and level of exploratory behavior. Infants were more likely to be securely attached. These outcomes were still evident when the children were 3 years of age.
- **Use of Soft Baby Carriers** (Anisfeld, Casper, Noyce, & Cunningham, 1990). Low-income, teenage mothers were given a soft baby carrier or a hard infant seat to use daily after going home from the hospital. At 13 months of age, infants of mothers who used the soft baby carriers rather than the hard infant seats were significantly more likely to be securely attached, and their mothers were more sensitive and contingently responsive to them.
- **Effectiveness of Infant Massage** (Field, 1998a, 1998b, 2000; Field, Hernandez-Reif, Diego, Feijo, Vera, & Gil, 2004). Infants of high-risk mothers and infants of mothers not at risk participated, and the infant was massaged using a firm touch. In some cases, the mother provided the massage following instruction from the massage therapist. Positive effects were found in a number of studies for infant state organization, weight gain, and developmental level. High-risk mothers who carried out the massage also benefited in terms of interactions with their infants and reduction in maternal depression. It is believed that massage enhances food absorption hormones, leading to stimulation of growth in the infant.
- **Interactional Guidance** (e.g., Robert-Tissot et al., 1996). Children under 30 months of age with sleeping, eating, behavior, and separation and attachment problems were assigned to interactional guidance or psychodynamic therapy. Interactional guidance consisted of up to 12 sessions, which included a 20-minute videotaped interaction played back and discussed with the mother to encourage her self-reflectivity and empathy for and understanding of her child. At follow-up 1 year later, both interventions were successful in treating child symptoms, and maternal sensitivity and self-esteem improved. Interactional guidance was more successful than the other intervention in increasing maternal sensitivity.
- **Watch, Wait, and Wonder (WWW)** (Cohen, Lojkasek, Muir, Muir, & Parker, 2002). Infants from 12 to 30 months old with feeding, sleeping, and behavior-regulation problems or difficulties with bonding participated. In a child-led play interaction, the parent was instructed to get down on the floor and play with her child and watch him, wait before responding, and wonder what was happening for him. This was followed by discussion between the parent and a therapist (psychologist or social worker) about the interaction and any issues that came up as a result of playing with her child. This intervention was compared with a more standard family intervention. Infants in the WWW intervention were more likely to be securely attached and less likely to have disorganized attachment. Symptoms were also more likely to be reduced, interactions were more attuned, and parent stress was more reduced.
- **The Incredible Years** (Webster-Stratton & Hammond, 1997). Parent and child groups are provided for young children with behavioral problems to enhance the interactions of parents with their children. Short- and longer-term improvements have been found.
- **Pathways to Competence for Young Children Parenting Program** (Landy, 2009; Landy & Menna, 2006a, 2006b; Landy & Thompson, 2006). The Pathways to Competence has been used with parents who have abused their children, mothers who have recently

left a violent situation, and parents of aggressive preschoolers. The program has shown positive outcomes, including increases in parents' sensitivity and responsiveness to their child, parenting knowledge, parenting self-esteem, and positive parent attributions and parent–child relationships, and reductions in child symptoms and parenting stress.

- **Infant–Parent Psychotherapy** (Lieberman & Van Horn, 2008). Parents of infants with insecure attachment at 12 months of age were provided with a nondirective, psychodynamic intervention with the mother and child present in which the interventionist responded to the emotional experiences of the mother. The intervention lasted for 12 months. At 2 years of age, the infants in the psychotherapy group were more likely to be securely attached, and the mothers were more sensitive and responsive to their infants than those of a control group who did not receive the intervention. The results on the outcome measures were similar to measures obtained from a sample of securely attached infants and their mothers.

Conclusions of Evaluation Research

From this research, it appears that many approaches to prevention and early intervention are successful in enhancing a number of child, parent, or interactional outcomes. Perhaps the most important findings, however, are that, when two or more approaches are compared, each approach is more successful in improving some outcomes than others and that some approaches work better with certain populations than others (Guralnick, 1997). Consequently, adequate assessment and formulation of cases are crucial so that the best interventions can be provided in each case. However, when programs are not intense or focused, positive outcomes might not occur. Because development is multidetermined and families at highest risk face multiple challenges, multisystemic and comprehensive approaches are the most effective for high-risk children and families (Conduct Problems Prevention Research Group, 1992; Greenspan, Weider, Nover, Lieberman, Lourie, & Robinson, 1987; Henggeler, Schoenwald, Rowland, & Cunningham, 2002; Kurtz, 2004; Wachs, 2000).

PRINCIPLES OF PREVENTION AND EARLY-INTERVENTION SERVICES

Overall Suggestions

- Outreach through home visiting is an essential component of programs for the most high-risk families to enable them to access programs. It can be critical for immigrant populations to have home visitors from the same cultural background who can speak the language used by the parents. For very disadvantaged families, providing incentives such as transportation to attend groups might be necessary.
- It is important to distinguish between services for high-risk and more low-risk families and to ensure success for both. Many programs have shown improvements in various factors for less at-risk families. When families are at high risk, the same strategies are usually not successful, and more focused and intensive services are required.
- As with older children, as research has shown that interventions focused on areas of difficulty are the most successful, the first stage of intervention should include an assessment to choose the most suitable interventions to enhance the child's development. Repeating the initial screening tool is also necessary to see whether adjustments in the intervention need to occur.
- Programs that begin earlier in a child's life, either during pregnancy or at birth, have been shown to be more successful than programs that begin after the child is 1 or 2 years

of age. Early plasticity of the brain allows opportunities to optimize brain structure and biochemistry. Also, intervening early avoids negative, especially coercive, parent–child interactions to be developed.

- When an outcome is targeted in a particular patient population, interventions shown to be effective with that population need to be used (e.g., group approaches for teenage mothers, attachment-based approaches for parents who find their relationships with their children difficult).
- Services are usually most effective with high-risk as opposed to low-risk or very high-risk families. Families that can help themselves usually show fewer benefits from prevention and home visiting programs. Families at high risk will suffer more without services and are more likely to show improvements compared with those that do not receive services. However, children in families at highest risk whose development is in jeopardy have the greatest need for services and are most likely to have negative outcomes without appropriate interventions.
- Children at highest risk need intensive, focused, and well-funded programs for interventions to be successful. Some of these interventions can be short term if provided by experienced intervenors. Although it might be hard to achieve significant long-term changes, children are more likely to have negative outcomes without the interventions.

Economic Benefits of Early-Intervention Programs

There is growing evidence that investment in prevention and early-intervention programs in the early years can save significant dollars later. These savings include the costs for welfare, incarceration, special education, substance-abuse treatment, and treatment of various disorders and developmental disabilities. The difference between these costs over a lifetime compared with the costs of early-intervention is enormous, and it is now well documented that early-intervention programs can have significant economic benefits for society. For example, James Heckman (2000, 2004), Nobel Prize-winning economist from the University of Chicago, among others, has demonstrated that investments in early-childhood programs have greater long-term economic benefits than program investments for older children, adolescents, and adults (see Figure 13.2).

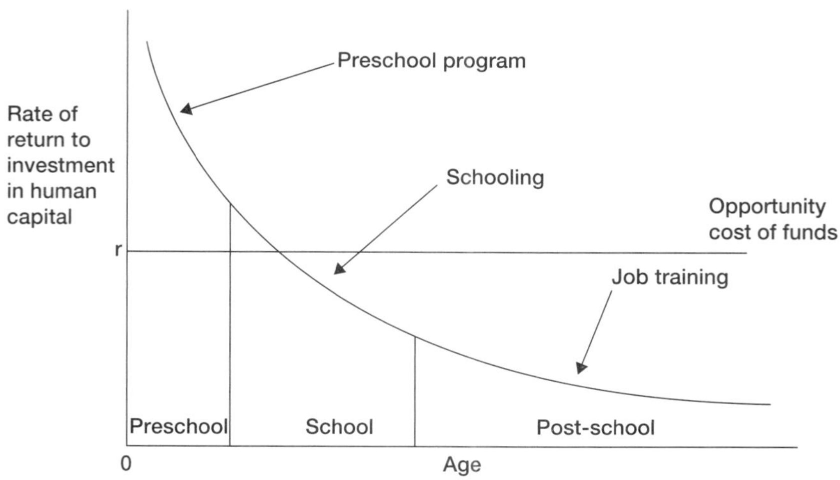

Figure 13.2 *Rates of return to human capital investment in disadvantaged children.*
Source: Heckman and Masterov (2007). Reprinted with permission.

Despite the ambitious goals of many prevention and early-intervention programs, the resources allocated to intervene with very high-risk families are usually woefully inadequate. Society provides primary and secondary education to children from 5 to 18 years of age at significant annual cost per child. It is important to provide at least comparable resources for high-quality early-childhood programs that have been shown to be more effective than money invested later in life.

However, to be successful, these programs must have the intensity or special focus of model programs with demonstrated positive long-term outcomes for children. For these positive outcomes to occur, programs serving at-risk children and those with identified problems and their families must be adequately funded to meet the extreme needs of this population. Table 13.1 provides examples of the funding levels of successful prevention and early-intervention programs.

Table 13.1 *Costs of Successful Programs for Children Aged 0 to 4 and Their Families*

Program Name	Average Cost per Child per Year ($)	Number of Years	Total Program Cost per Child ($)
Carolina Abecedarian*	20,000	5	100,000
IHDP*	23,582	3	70,747
CCDP*	10,800	5	54,000
Early Head Start*	10,100	3	30,300
Perry Preschool*	15,069	2	30,138
Chicago Child–Parent Centers*	7,617	2	15,234
Elmira Nurse Home Visitation*	5,250	2.5	13,125

*Indicates programs with at least one significant long-term positive effect.
CCDP: Comprehensive Child Development Program; IHDP: Infant Health and Development Program.

ISSUES TO BE ADDRESSED

Unfortunately, a number of children are raised in situations likely to impact negatively on their development. Many grow up in families without adequate support systems and in communities without family members, friends, or other networks where they can find information, advice, help, and emotional support. Despite society's relative affluence, many children grow up in poverty, and many more are exposed to traumatic events such as domestic and community violence, abuse, and neglect. At this time, despite a number of successful prevention and early-intervention initiatives available for infants and children at risk, in many communities there is no integrated system for referral and identification of those at risk and no intensive program to meet the mental health needs of high-risk families and their young children.

NEUROPLASTICITY: RESEARCH LINKING EXPERIENCES AND INTERVENTIONS TO CHANGES IN BRAIN FUNCTION

As discussed previously, it is important to identify children with developmental delays and early symptoms of disorders or difficulties in various functional areas as early as possible. Once problems have been identified, it is critical for the appropriate treatment to be as intense, focused, and repetitive as possible to effect changes. There is growing evidence that neuroplasticity is possible and that brain anatomy is not fixed and hard wired (Doidge, 2010). The evidence is primarily anecdotal or case based and in most areas lacks randomized, controlled trials. Yet some well-researched evidence is emerging in certain areas, such as the use of brain-based training programs. There is also a significant body of research using animals, particularly in studying neuroplasticity following brain damage. Also, some of the greatest skeptics in the scientific world who denied that neuroplasticity is possible for most of their careers have now acknowledged that they were wrong. For example, Torsten Wiesel, who won a Nobel Prize for establishing where visual processing occurs in the brain and who believed that once the connections are in place they cannot be changed, published an article in 1999 admitting that he was wrong and that adult neuroplasticity does occur.

Information on neuroplasticity tends to be organized in the following areas of study.

1. There is evidence that, when certain parts of the brain do not function due to disorder or damage, other parts can be retrained to take over the function. For example, autistic children who fail theory-of-mind tasks do not to show activity in the expected region of the brain, the dorsal lateral prefrontal cortex, as is seen in normal controls. However, after the autistic children were trained to complete the task, another part of the brain was activated (inferior temporal gyrus) and performed the same task for the child (Jolliffe & Baron-Cohen, 1999). In another line of research with individuals who have had strokes, a blood clot in a brain artery cuts off oxygen to the brain tissues, which then die. As a result, stroke victims can be left with a permanent disability. Before recent breakthroughs, it was believed that, unless a patient can gain back the use of his limbs within a short period of time, nothing can be done. However, following years of research with animals, Edward Taub developed constraint-induced (CI) movement therapy. It involves behavioral techniques that shape the damaged limbs through gradual and incremental approaches to relearn the tasks that they can no longer perform. During treatment, the functioning limbs are constrained through the use of slings. The patients are drilled in the incremental tasks for 6 hours a day for 10 to 15 days at a time. Studies have demonstrated that CI therapy can lead to extensive changes in brain structure that can occur long after the stroke in some patients (Kopp et al., 1999; Liepert et al., 1998).
2. In another group of studies, certain types of brain training have enabled people to start using parts of the brain normally used for an activity that did not function adequately previously. A number of controlled trials have been conducted using the Fast ForWord program, developed for language-impaired and dyslexic children. The program exercises brain function involved in language, and research has found that training in the program for 1 hour and 40 minutes a day compared with a similar computer game increased performance on speech, language, and auditory-processing tasks. Before the training, the children used different parts of their brains for reading than normal children. However, after using the Fast ForWord program, their brains began to normalize, and they developed increased activity in the left temporo-parietal cortex, and brain scans were similar to those of children who had no reading problems (Temple, et al., 2003). Another example of this kind of change is cochlear implants. The cochlear implant places a microphone inside the ear of an individual who is deaf because her cochlea is profoundly damaged and nonfunctional. The implant replaces the cochlea and provides the input needed to be able to encode speech. That this is possible proves that the auditory cortex of the brain is indeed plastic. Due to the increasing number of aging people, researchers have been developing programs to exercise five areas of the brain that are most likely to deteriorate in old age. Posit Science has developed memory

exercises and controlled studies to show functional improvements from the exercises. In one study, positron emission tomography (PET) scans of functioning before and after training showed metabolic changes in the right parietal lobes of the brains with computer-based cognitive training (Jagust et al., 2006; Mahncke et al., 2006).

3. Other evidence of brain plasticity comes from individuals who, through job demands, exercise their brains with skills shown to enlarge parts of the brain responsible for these skills. For example, London taxi drivers who received extensive practice in learning the locations of places in the city have been found to have larger volumes in the hippocampus, which stores spatial representations (Maguire et al., 2000). People who engage frequently in meditation, such as monks, have been found to have thicker insula or cortical thickening (Lazar et al., 2005). Also somewhat related are reports that the more musicians practice, the more changes that occur in the corresponding areas of the brain (Elbert, Pantev, Wienbruch, Rockstroh, & Taub, 1995).
4. Most important for this book are the impacts of various types of therapy on brain function that correlate with improvement in symptoms. Cognitive-behavioral therapy that corrects the extreme negative thinking of people with major depressive episodes has been shown to modulate cortical–limbic pathways and results in fewer relapses (Goldapple et al., 2004). Similarly, people with obsessive-compulsive disorder (OCD) who receive treatment that involves helping them to overcome what is described as "brain lock" have shown unlocking of the circuits thought to underlie the brain lock: that is, connections among the orbital frontal cortex, cingulate gyrus, and caudate nucleus. Brain scans after treatment showed that the three parts of the brain in OCD were now firing separately in a normal way (Schwartz & Begley, 2002: Schwartz, Stoessel, Baxter, Martin, & Phelps, 1996). Interpersonal therapy has also been linked with decreased metabolism in the frontal cortex believed to be linked to less rethinking and reappraisal or diminishing of rumination in depressed individuals (Brody et al., 2001).

In conclusion, though obviously it is important to identify problems as early as possible, in certain areas of functioning, probably far more than is known at this time, if children are adequately assessed and appropriate strategies provided, change can occur functionally and neurologically. Consequently, there is hope that, with the interventions outlined in this book, improvement is possible in children and, in many cases, parents.

See Table 13.2 for more information on related programs and online sources.

Table 13.2 *Websites*

Website	Information on Website
www.evidencebasedprograms.org	Website of the Coalition for Evidence-Based Policy that has information on evidence-based social programs including prevention and early-intervention programs.
www.nichcy.org	Website for the National Dissemination Center for Children with Disabilities (NICHCY) which has articles and a newsletter providing information on infants and children with disabilities and the Education Act (IDEA), the law authorizing early intervention and special education services.
www.promisingpractices.net/programs.asp	Website of the Promising Practices Network on Children, Families, and Communities funded by the RAND Corporation. Offers information on proven and promising programs to improve outcomes for children.
www.nectac.org	Website for National Early Childhood Technical Assistance Centre (NECTAR), U.S. Department of Education, which supports infant, toddler, and preschool programs for children with disabilities. It has resources on early childhood evidence-based practice.
www.jhsph.edu/research/centers-and-institutes	Website for Johns Hopkin's Bloomberg School of Pubic Health that disseminates research on prevention and treatment of mental disorders in children and adolescents.
www.ciu20.org/students-parents/docs/EI-Speech-and-language-Guide.pdf	Website of the Pennsylvania Office of Child Development and Early Learning. It has a report entitled, *Early Intervention for Infants, Toddlers, and Preschoolers and Their Families: Guidelines for Speech and Language Services.*
www.wsipp.wa.gov/	Website of the Washington State Institute for Public Policy, which has a number of reports on the benefits and costs of prevention and early intervention programs for youth. Describes a number of effective programs such as juvenile offenders programs and programs for preventing truancy and school dropout.

www.zerotothree.org	National nonprofit organization that informs, trains, and supports professionals, policymakers, and parents in their efforts to improve the lives of infants and toddlers. Their mission is "to promote the health and development of infants and toddlers.
www.pcit.phhp.ufl.edu	Website for the parent–child interaction therapy (PCIT) that describes the program and identifies training opportunities to learn the program. The program can be used with young children.
www.parentingscience.com/preschool-social-skills.html	A website primarily for parents with excellent summaries with useful strategies to help teach social skills to preschoolers.
www.challengingbehavior.fmhi.usf.edu	Website of the Technical Assistance Center on Social and Emotional Intervention for Young Children. Offers evidence-based teaching tools for young children with challenging behavior.
www.healthychildcare.org	Healthy Child Care America (HCCA) is supported by the American Academy of Pediatrics, with the Department of Health and Human Services, the Child Care Bureau, and the Maternal and Child Health Bureau. The Healthy Child Care America Campaign provides resources for parents and early-childhood educators.
www.excellence-earlychildhood.ca/home.asp	Website of the Centre of Excellence for Early Childhood Development. Access is given to the *Encyclopedia of Early Child Development,* which contains short articles that provide information on a number of topics related to child development written by experts in the field.

References

Aarnoudse-Moens, C. S., Smidts, D. P., Oosterlaan, J., Duivenvoorden, H. S., & Weisglas-Kuperus, W. (2009). Executive function in very preterm children in early school age. *Journal of Abnormal Child Psychology, 37,* 981–993.

Abela, J. R. Z., Hankin, B. L., Haigh, E. A. P., Adams, P., Vinokaroff, T. S., & Treyhorn, L. (2005). Interpersonal vulnerability to depression in high risk children: The role of insecure attachment and resonance seeking. *Journal of Clinical Child and Adolescent Psychology, 34,* 182–192.

Abikoff, H. (2001). Tailored psychosocial treatment for ADHD: The search of a good fit. *Journal of Clinical Child Psychology, 30,* 122–125.

Abikoff, H., & Hechtman, L. (1996). Multimodal therapy and stimulants in the treatment of children with ADHD. In P. Jensen & E. D. Hibbs (Eds.), *Psychosocial treatment for child and adolescent disorders: Empirically based approaches* (pp. 341–369). Washington, DC: American Psychological Association.

Abramowitz, J. S., Foa, E. B., & Franklin, M. E. (2003). Exposure and ritual prevention for obsessive-compulsive disorder: Effects of intensive versus twice-weekly sessions. *Journal of Consulting and Clinical Psychology, 71,* 394–398.

Achenbach, T. M. (2000). *Child Behavior Checklist (CBCL).* Burlington, VT: ASEBA, University of Vermont.

Achenbach, T. M. (2001). *The child behavior checklist manual and revised child behavior profiles.* Burlington, VT: Department of Psychiatry, University of Vermont.

Achenbach, T. M., Bernstein, A., & Dumenci, L. (2005). DSM-oriented scales and statistically based syndromes for ages 18 to 59: Linking taxonomic paradigms to facilitate multitaxonomic approaches. *Journal of Personality Assessment, 84,* 429–466.

Achenbach, T. M., & Rescorla, L. A. (2000). *Manual for the Child Behavior Checklist (1½–5 years), Achenbach System of Empirically Based Assessment (ASEBA).* Burlington, VA.

Ackerman, H., Vogel, M., Peterson, D., & Poremba. (1992). Speech deficits in ischaemic cerebellar lesions. *Journal of Neurology, 239,* 223–227.

Adams, C. (2004). Intervention for developmental pragmatic language impairments. *Aula Abierta, 82,* 79–96, eScholarID:1d1o142.

Adams, C. (2005). Social communication interventions for school-age children: Rational and description. *Seminars in Speech and Language, 26,* 181–188.

Adelman, H. S., & Taylor, L. (1998). Reframing mental health in schools and expanding school reform. *Educational Psychologist, 33,* 135–152.

Adelman, H. S., & Taylor, L. (2006). Mental health in schools and public health. *Public Health Reports, 121,* 294–298.

Adelman, H. S., & Taylor, L. (2009). Ending the marginalization of mental health in schools: A comprehensive approach. In R. W. Christner & R. B. Mennuti (Eds.), *School-based mental health: A practitioner's guide to comparative practices* (pp. 25–54). New York: Routledge, Taylor & Francis Group.

Adnams, C. M., Kodituwakku, P. A., Hay, A., Molteno, C. D., Viljoen, D., & May, P. A. (2001). Patterns of cognitive-motor development in children with fetal alcohol syndrome from a community in South Africa. *Alcoholism: Clinical and Experimental Research, 25,* 557–562.

Adolphs, R. (2003). Cognitive neuroscience of human social behavior. *Nature Reviews Neuroscience, 4*, 165–178.

Adrian, M., Zeman, J., Erdley, C., Lisa, L., Homan, K., & Sim, L. (2009). Social contextual links to emotion regulation in an adolescent inpatient population: Do gender and symptomatology matter? *Journal of Child Psychology and Psychiatry, 50*(11), 1428–1436.

Adrien, J. L., Lenoir, P., Martineau, J., Perrot, A., Hameury, L., Larmande, C., Sauvage, D. (1993). Blind ratings of early symptoms of autism based upon home movies. *Journal of the American Academy of Child and Adolescent Psychiatry, 32*, 617–626.

Agid, O., Shapira, I., Zislin, J., Ritsner, M., Hanin, B., & Murad, H., ... Lerer, B. (1999). Environment and vulnerability to major psychiatric illness: A case control study of early parental loss in major depression, bipolar illness and schizophrenia. *Molecular Psychiatry, 4*, 163–172.

Ainsworth, M. D. S., Blehar, M. C., Waters, E., & Wall, S. (1978). *Patterns of attachment: A psychological study of the Strange Situation*. Mahwah, NJ: Lawrence Erlbaum Associates.

Ainsworth, M. D. S., & Eichberg, C. (1991). Effects on infant-mother attachment of mother's unresolved loss of an attachment figure or other traumatic experience. In C. M. Parkes, J. Stevenson-Hinde, & P. Marris (Eds.), *Attachment across the life cycle* (pp. 160–183). London: Tavistock/Routledge.

Ainsworth, M. D. S., & Wittig, B. A. (1969). Attachment and exploratory behavior in one-year-olds in a strange situation. In B. M. Foss (Ed.), *Determinants of infant behavior* (Vol. 4, pp. 129–173). London: Methuen.

Aksan, N., & Kochanska, G. (2004). Links between systems of inhibition from infancy to preschool years. *Child Development, 75*, 1477–1490.

Aksan, N., Kochanska, G., & Ortmann, M. R. (2006). Mutually responsive orientation between parents and their children: Towards methodological advances in the science of relationships. *Developmental Psychology, 42*, 833–848.

Alhambra, M., Fowler, T., & Alhambra, A. (1995). EEG biofeedback: A new treatment option of ADD/ADHD. *Journal of Neurotherapy, 1*, 39–43.

Alink, L. R. A., Cicchetti, D., Kim, J., & Rogosch, F. A. (2009). Mediating and moderating processes in the relation between maltreatment and psychopathology: Mother-child relationship quality and emotion regulation. *Journal of Abnormal Child Psychology, 37*, 831–843.

Alloway, T. P. (2007). *The Automated Working Memory Assessment (AWMA)*. San Antonio, TX: Pearson.

Alloway, T. P., Gathercole, S. E., & Kirkwood, H. J. (2008). *The Working Memory Rating Scale (WMRS)*. San Antonio, TX: Pearson.

American Academy of Child and Adolescent Psychiatry. (2005). Practice Parameters for the assessment and treatment of children and adolescents with Reactive Attachment Disorder of infancy and early childhood. *Journal of the American Academy of Child and Adolescent Psychiatry, 44*, 1206–1219.

American Academy of Child and Adolescent Psychiatry. (2010). *ADHD—A guide for families*. Washington, DC: American Academy of Child and Adolescent Psychiatry.

American Academy of Pediatrics, Committee on Substance Abuse and Committee on Children with Disabilities. (2000). Fetal alcohol syndrome and alcohol-related neurodevelopmental disorders. *Pediatrics, 106*, 358–361.

American Psychiatric Association. (1968). *Diagnostic and statistical manual of mental disorders* (2nd ed.). Washington, DC: Author.

American Psychiatric Association. (1980). *Diagnostic and statistical manual of mental disorders* (3rd ed.). Washington, DC: Author.

American Psychiatric Association. (1987). *Diagnostic and statistical manual of mental disorders* (3rd ed., rev.). Washington, DC: Author.

American Psychiatric Association. (1994). *Diagnostic and statistical manual of mental disorders* (4th ed.). Washington, DC: Author.

American Psychiatric Association. (2000). *Diagnostic and statistical manual of mental disorders* (4th ed., text rev.). Washington, DC: Author.

American Psychiatric Association. (2013). *Diagnostic and statistical manual of mental disorders* (5th ed.). Washington, DC: Author.

American Speech-Language-Hearing Association (ASHA). (1993). *Definitions of Communication disorders and variations* [Relevant Paper]. Retrieved from www.asha.org/policy

American Speech-Language-Hearing Association (ASHA). (1996). *Central auditory processing disorder*. [Technical Report]. Retrieved from www.asha.org/policy

American Speech-Language-Hearing Association (ASHA). (2005). *Central auditory processing disorder*. [Technical Report]. Retrieved from www.asha.org/policy

American Speech-Language-Hearing Association (ASHA). (2007). *Motor speech disorders: Dysarthria*. Retrieved from http://www.asha.org/public/speech/disorders/dysarthria.htm

Ammaniti, M., Speranza, A. M, & Fedele, S. (2005). Attachment in infancy and in early and late childhood: A longitudinal study. In K. A. Kerns & R. A. Richardson (Eds.), *Attachment in middle childhood* (pp. 115–136). New York: Guilford Press.

Ammaniti, M., van IJzendoorn, M. H., Speranza, A. M, & Fedele, S. (2005). Attachment in infancy and in early and late childhood: A longitudinal study. In K. A. Kerns & R. A. Richardson (Eds.), *Attachment in middle childhood* (pp. 115–136). New York: Guilford Press.

Ammaniti, M., van IJzendoorn, M. H., Speranza, A. M. & Tambelli, R. (2000). Internal working models of attachment during late childhood and early adolescence: An exploration of stability and change. *Attachment and Human Development, 2*, 328–342.

Anderson, P., Anderson, V., Northam, E., & Taylor, H. G. (2000). Standardization of the Contingency Naming Test (CNT) for school-aged children: A measure of reactive flexibility. *Clinical Neuropsychological Assessment, 1*, 247–273.

Anderson, S. W., Bechara, A., Damasio, H., Tranel, D., & Damasio, A. R. (1999). Impairment of social and moral behavior related to early damage in human prefrontal cortex. *Nature and Neuroscience, 2*, 1032–1037.

Anderson, V. (1998). Assessing executive functions in children: Biological, psychological, and developmental considerations. *Neuropsychological Rehabilitation, 8*, 319–349.

Anderson, V., & Catroppa, C. (2005). Recovery of executive skills following pediatric traumatic brain injury (TBI): A 2 year follow-up. *Brain Injury, 16*, 759–772.

Anderson, V., Levin, H., & Jacobs, R. (2002). Executive functions following frontal lobe injury: A developmental perspective. In D. T. Stuss & R. T. Knight (Eds.), *Principals of frontal lobe function* (pp. 504–527). New York: Oxford University Press.

Andrews, G., Charney, D. S., Sirovatka, P. J., & Regier, D. A. (Eds.). (2009). *Stress-induced and fear circuitry disorders: Advancing the research agenda for DSM-V.* Arlington, VA: American Psychiatric Association.

Angold, A., & Costello, E. J. (2009). Nosology and measurement in child and adolescent psychiatry. *Journal of Child Psychology and Psychiatry, 50*, 9–15.

Angold, A., Costello, E. J., Farmer, E. M. Z., Burns, B. J. & Erkanli, A. (1996). Impaired but undiagnosed. *Journal of the American Academy of Child and Adolescent Psychiatry, 38*(2), 129–137.

Angrilli, A., Mauri, A., Palomba, D., Flor, H., Birbaumer, N., Sartori, G., … di Paola, F. (1996). Startle reflex and emotion modulation impairment after a right amygdala lesion. *Brain, 119*, 1991–2000.

Anisfeld, E., Casper, V., Nozyce, M., & Cunningham, N. (1990). Does infant carrying promote attachment? An experimental study of the effects of increased physical contact on the development of attachment. *Child Development, 61*, 1617–1627.

Appleyard, K., Yang, C., & Runyan, D. K. (2010). Delineating the maladaptive pathways of child maltreatment: A mediated moderation analysis of the rates of self-perception and social support. *Development and Psychopathology, 22*, 337–352.

Archer, J. (2004). Sex differences in aggression in real world settings: A meta-analytic review. *Review of General Psychology, 8*, 291–322.

Archibald, S., & Kerns, K. A. (1999). Identification and description of new tests of executive functioning in children. *Child Neuropsychology, 5*, 115–129.

Arnett, P. A., Howland, E. W., Smith, S. S., & Newman, J. P. (1993). Autonomic responsivity during passive avoidance in incarcerated psychopaths: Personality and individual differences. *Personality and Individual Differences, 14*, 173–184.

Arnold, L. E. (1999). Treatment alternatives for attention-deficit/hyperactivity disorder. *Journal of Attention Disorders, 3*, 30–48.

Arnold, L. E. (2001). Alternative treatments for adults with attention-deficit hyperactivity disorder (ADHD). *Adult Attention Deficit Disorder Annals of the New York Academy of Sciences, 931*, 310–341.

Arseneault, L., Tremblay, R. F., Boulerice, B., Seguin, R., & Saucier, J. F. (2000). Minor physical anomalies and family adversity as risk factors for violent delinquency in adolescence. *American Journal of Psychiatry, 157*, 917–923.

Arsenio, W. F., Adams, E., & Gold, J. (2009). Social information processing, moral reasoning, and emotion attributions: Relations with adolescents' reactive and proactive aggression. *Child Development, 80*, 1730–1755.

Asendorpf, J. B. (1994). The malleability of behavioral inhibition: A study of individual developmental functions. *Developmental Psychology, 30*, 912–919.

Ashwood, P., & van de Water, J. (2004). Is autism an autoimmune disease? *Autoimmunity Reviews, 3*, 557–562.

Astington, J. W., & Jenkins, J. M. (1999). A longitudinal study of the relation between language and theory of mind development. *Developmental Psychology, 35*, 1311–1320.

Astington, J. W., & Olson, D. R. (1995). The cognitive revolution in children's understanding of mind. *Human Development, 38*, 179–189.

Astley, S. J., Aylward, E. H., Olson, H. C., Kerns, K., Brooks, A., Coggins, T. E. ... Richards, T. (2009). Magnetic resonance imaging outcomes from a comprehensive magnetic resonance study of children with fetal alcohol spectrum disorders. *Alcoholism: Clinical Experimental Research, 33*, 1671–1689.

Astley, S. J., Olson, H. C., Kerns, K., Brooks, A., Aylward, E. H., Coggins, T. E., Richards, T. (2009). Neuropsychological and behavioral outcomes from a comprehensive magnetic resonance study of children with fetal alcohol spectrum disorders. *Canadian Journal of Clinical Pharmacology, 16*, 178–201.

Audet, L., & Ripich, D. (1994). Psychiatric disorders and discourse problems. In D. N. Ripich & N. A. Creaghead (Eds.), *School discourse problems* (pp. 191–227). San Diego, CA: Singilar Publishing.

Augimeri, L. K., Farrington, D. P., Koegel, C. J., & Day, D. M. (2007). The under 12 project: Effects of a community based program for children with conduct problems. *Journal of Child and Family Studies, 16*, 799–807.

Ayres, A. J. (1963). The ELEANOR Clark Slagle Lecture. The development of perceptual-motor abilities: A theoretical basis for treatment of dysfunction. *American Journal of Occupational Therapy, 27*, 221–225.

Ayres, A. J. (1972a). *Sensory integration and learning disorders*. Los Angeles, CA: Western Psychological Services.

Ayres, A. J. (1972b). Types of sensory integrative dysfunction among disabled learners. *The American Journal of Occupational Therapy, 26*(1) 13–18.

Ayres, A. J. (1977). Cluster analyses of measures of sensory integration. *The American Journal of Occupational Therapy, 31*(6), 362–366.

Ayres, A. J. (1989). *Sensory integration and praxis tests*. Los Angeles, CA: Western Psychological Services.

Ayres. J. (2005). *Sensory integration and the child: Understanding hidden sensory challenges*. Los Angeles, CA: Western Psychological Services.

Babinski, L. M., Hartsough, C. S., & Lambert, N. M. (1999). Childhood conduct problems, hyperactivity-impulsivity, and inattention as predictors of adult criminal activity. *Journal of Child Psychiatry and Psychiatry, 34*, 347–355.

Bach-y-Rita, P. (1981). Brain plasticity as a basis of the development of rehabilitation procedures for hemiplegia. *Scandinavian Journal of Rehabilitation Medicine, 16*, 73–83.

Bada, H. S., Das, A., Bauer, C. R., Shankaran, S., Lester, B., LaGasse, L., ... Higgins, R. (2007). Impact of prenatal cocaine exposure on child behavior problems through school age. *Pediatrics, 119*, 348–359.

Baddeley, A. D. (1996). The fractionation of working memory. *Proceedings of the National Academy of Science, USA, 93*, 968–1037.

Bailey, A., Le Couteur, A., Gottesmann, I., Bolton, P., Siminoff, E., Yuzda, E., & Rutter, M. (1995). Autism as a strongly genetic disorder: Evidence from a British Twin study. *Psychological Medicine, 25*, 63–77.

Baird, A. A., Gruber, S. A., Fein, D. A., Maas, L. C., Steingard, R. J., Renshaw, P. F., ... Yurgelun-Todd, D. A. (1999). Functional magnetic resonance imaging of facial affect recognition in children and adolescents. *Journal of the American Academy of Child and Adolescent Psychiatry, 38*, 195–199.

Baker, L., & Cantwell, D. P. (1987). A prospective psychiatric follow-up of children with speech/language disorders. *Journal of the American Academy of Child and Adolescent Psychiatry, 26*, 546–553.

Baker, L., & Cantwell, D. P. (1992). Attention deficit disorder with and without hyperactivity: A review and comparison of matched groups. *Journal of the American Academy of Child and Adolescent Psychiatry, 31*, 432–438.

Baker, S. D., Lang, R., & O'Reilly, M. (2009). Review of video modelling with students with emotional and behavioral disorders. *Education and Treatment of Children, 32*, 403–420.

Bakermans-Kranenburg, M. J., & van IJzendoorn, M. H. (2004). No association of dopamine D4 receptor (DR04) and 521 C/T promoter polymorphisms with infant attachment disorganization. *Attachment and Human Development, 6*, 211–218.

Bakermans-Kranenburg, M., J., & van IJzendoorn, M. H. (2011). Differential susceptibility to rearing environment depending on dopamine-related genes: New evidence and a meta-analysis. *Development and Psychopathology, 23*, 39–52.

Bakermans-Kranenburg, M. J., van IJzendoorn, M. H., Pijlman, F., Mesman, J., & Juffer, F. (2008). Experimental evidence for differential susceptibility: Dopamine D4 receptor polymorphism (DRD4 VNTR) moderates intervention effects of toddlers' externalizing behavior in a randomized control trial. *Developmental Psychology, 44*, 293–300.

Bales, K. L., & Carter, L. S. (2009). Neuroendocrine mechanisms of social bonds and child-parent attachment from the child's perspective. In M. de Haan & M. R. Gunnar (Eds.), *Handbook of developmental social neuroscience* (pp. 246–264). New York: Guilford Press.

Ball, J., & Khan, F. (2009). Communication and childhood complex trauma. Acquiring knowledge. *Speech, Language and Hearing, 3*, 144–148.

Baltaxe, C. (2001). Emotional, behavioral and other psychiatric disorders of childhood associated with communication disorders. In T. Layton, E. Crais, & L Watson (Eds.), *Handbook of early language impairment in children; Nature* (pp. 63–125). Albany, NY: Delmar Publishers.

Bandura, A. (1977). *Social learning theory*. Morristown, NJ: General Learning Press.

Baranek, G. T. (1998). Sensory processing in persons with autism and developmental disabilities: Considerations for research and clinical practice. *Sensory Integration Special Interest Section Newsletter, American Occupational Therapy Association, 21*(2), 1–4.

Baranek, G. T. (1999). Autism during infancy: A retrospective video analysis of sensory-motor and social behaviours at 9–12 months of age. *Journal of Autism and Developmental Disorders, 29*, 213–224.

Baranek, G. T. (2002). Efficacy of sensory and motor interventions in autism. *Journal of Autism and Developmental Disorders, 32*(5), 397–422.

Baranek, G. T., Foster, L. G., & Berkson, G. (1997). Tactile defensiveness and stereotyped behaviors. *American Journal of Occupational Therapy, 51*, 91–95.

Barbas, H. (2007). Specialized elements of orbitofrontal cortex in primates. *Annals of the New York Academy of Sciences, 1121*, 54–71.

Bardige, B., & Segal, M. (2004). Conversations in child care. *Zero to Three, 25*, 16–22.

Barfield, S., & Gaskill, R. (2005). *Positive impact of the neurosequential model of therapeutics in high risk children in a therapeutic pre-school setting*. Lawrence, KS: University Press of Kansas.

Barish, K. (2009). *Emotions in child psychotherapy*. Oxford: New York.

Barkley, R. A. (1990). The nature of ADHD. In R. A. Barkley (Ed.), *Attention deficit hyperactivity disorder. A handbook for diagnosis and treatment* (pp. 3–39). New York: Guilford Press.

Barkley, R. A. (1997). *Defiant children: A clinician's manual for assessment and parent training* (2nd ed.). New York: Guilford Press.

Barkley, R. A. (1998). *Attention-deficit hyperactivity disorder: A handbook for diagnosis and treatment* (2nd ed.). New York: Guilford Press.

Barkley, R. A. (2002). Major life activity and health outcomes associated with attention-deficit/hyperactivity disorder. *Journal of Clinical Psychiatry, 63*, 10–15.

Barkley, R. A. (2005). *ADHD and the nature of self-control*. New York: Guilford Press.

Barkley, R. A. (2006). *Attention-deficit hyperactivity disorder: A handbook for diagnosis and treatment* (3rd Ed.). New York: Guilford Press.

Barletta, J., & O'Mara, B. (2006). A review of the impact of marital conflict in child adjustment. *Australian Journal of Guidance and Counselling, 16*, 91–105.

Barnes, K., Vogel, K. A., Beck, A. I., Schoenfeld, H., & Owens, S. V. (2008). Self regulation strategies of children with emotional disturbance. *Physical & Occupational Therapy in Pediatrics, 28*, 369–387.

Barnett, A., Henderson, S. E., Scheib, B., & Schulz, J. (2007). *Detailed Assessment of Speed of Handwriting (DASH).* London, Pearson Education Inc.

Baron, I. S. (2004). *Neuropsychological evaluation of the child.* New York: Oxford University Press.

Baron-Cohen, S., Ring, H. A., Bullmore, E. T., Wheelright, S., Ashwin, C., & Williams, S. C. (2000). The amygdala theory of autism, *Neuroscience and Biobehavioral Reviews, 24,* 355–364.

Baron-Faust, R. (2000). Biofeedback widens its role in medicine. *CNN Community Health.*

Barrera, I., & Corso, R. M. (2003). *Skilled dialogue: Strategies for responding to cultural diversity in early childhood.* Baltimore, MD: Paul H. Brookes Publishing Co.

Barrett, P. M., Dadds, M. R., & Rapee, R. M. (1996). Family treatment of childhood anxiety: A controlled trial. *Journal of Consulting and Clinical Psychology, 64,* 333–342.

Barrett, P. M., Healy-Farrell, L., & March, J. S. (2004). Cognitive-behavioral family treatment of obsessive-compulsive disorder: A controlled trial. *Journal of the American Academy of Child and Adolescent Psychiatry, 43,* 46–62.

Barry, J. G., Yasmin, L., & Bishop, D. V. M. (2007). Heritable risk factors associated with language impairments. *Genes, Brain and Behavior, 6,* 66–76.

Barry, L. M., & Burlew, S. B. (2004). Using social stories to teach choice and play skills in children with autism. *Focus on Autism and Other Developmental Disabilities, 19,* 45–51.

Bates, J. E., & Petit, G. S. (2007). Temperament, parenting and socialization. In J. E. Grusec and P. D. Hastings (Eds.), *Handbook of socialization: Theory and research* (pp. 153–180). New York: Guilford Press.

Batshaw, M., Shapira, B., & Farber, L. (2007). Developmental delay and intellectual disability. In M. Batshaw, L. Pellegrino & N. Roizen (Eds.), *Children with disabilities* (6th ed., pp. 245–261). Baltimore, MD: Paul H. Brooks.

Baum, S. R., & Dwivedi, V. D. (2003). Sensitivity to prosodic structure in left- and right-hemisphere-damaged individuals. *Brain and Language, 87,* 278–289.

Bauman, M. I., & Kemper, T. L. (2005). *The neurobiology of autism.* Baltimore: Johns Hopkins University Press.

Baumeister, R. F., Smart, L., & Boden, J. M. (1996). Relation of threatened egotism to violence and aggression: The dark side of high self-esteem. *Psychological Review, 103,* 5–33.

Baumrind, D. (1971). Current patterns of parental authority. *Developmental Psychology, 4,* 1–103.

Baumrind, D. (1973). The development of instrumental competence through socialization. In A. D. Pick (Ed.), *Minnesota symposium on child psychology* (Vol. 7, pp. 3–46). Minneapolis: University of Minnesota Press.

Baumrind, D. (1989). Rearing competent children. In W. Damon (Ed.), *Child development today and tomorrow* (pp. 349–378). San Francisco: Jossey-Bass.

Baumrind, D. (1991). Rearing competent children. In W. Damon (Ed.), *Child development today and tomorrow* (pp. 349–378). San Francisco: Jossey-Bass.

Baumrind, D., & Black, A. E. (1967). Socialisation practices associated with dimensions of competence in preschool boys and girls. *Child Development, 38,* 291–327.

Baving, L., Laucht, M., & Schmidt, M. (2002). Frontal brain activation in anxious school children. *Journal of Child Psychology and Psychiatry, 43,* 265–274.

Baxendale, J., & Hasketh, A. (2003). A comparison of effectiveness of the Hanen Parent Programme and traditional clinic therapy. *International Journal of Language and Communication Disorders, 38,* 397–415.

Bayley, N. (2006). *Bayley scales of infant development* (3rd ed.) (Bayley III). San Antonio, TX: Pearson Assessment.

Beach, S. R. A., Brody, G. H., Gunter, T. D., Packer, H., Wernett, P., & Philibert, R. A. (2010). Child maltreatment moderates the association of MAOA with symptoms of depression and antisocial personality disorder. *Journal of Family Psychology, 24*(1), 12–20.

Beardslee, W. R., Versage, E. M., & Gladstone, T. R. G. (1998). Children of affectively ill parents: A review of the past 10 years. *Journal of the American Academy of Child and Adolescent Psychiatry, 37,* 1134–1141.

Beare, P., Togerson, C., & Creviston, C. (2008). Increasing verbal behavior of a student who is selectively mute. *Journal of Emotional and Behavioral Disorders, 16,* 248–255.

Bechara, A., Damasio, A. R., Damasio, H., & Anderson, S. W. (1994). Insensitivity to future consequences following damage to human prefrontal cortex. *Cognition, 50,* 7–15.

Beery, K. E., & Buktenica, N. A. (2010). *Developmental test of visual motor integration (rev. ed.)*. Chicago, IL: Follett Educational Corporation.

Begun, R. W. (Ed.). (1995). *Ready-to-use social skills lessons and activities for Grades PreK-K*. West Nyack, NY: The Center for Applied Research in Education.

Begun, R. W. (Ed.). (1996). *Ready-to-use social skills lessons and activities for Grades 4–6*. West Nyack, NY: Center for Applied Research in Education.

Beidel, D. C., & Turner, S. M. (2005). *Childhood anxiety disorders: A guide to research and treatment*. New York: Routledge.

Beitchman, J. H., Hood, J., Rochon, L., & Peterson, M. (1989). Empirical classification of speech/language impairment in children: Behavioral characteristics. *Journal of the American Academy of Child and Adolescent Psychiatry, 28*, 118–123.

Beitchman, J. H., Wilson, B., Johnson, C. J., Atkinson, L., Young, A., Adlaf, E., ... Douglas L. (2001). Fourteen year follow-up of speech/language impaired children and control children: Psychiatric outcome. *Journal of the American Academy of Child and Adolescent Psychiatry, 40*, 75–82.

Bell, C. C., & Jenkins, E. J. (1995). Community violence and children in the south side of Chicago. *Psychiatry, 56*, 46–54.

Bell, R. Q. (1968). A reinterpretation of the direction of effects in studies of socialization. *Psychological Review, 32*, 921–924.

Bellak, L., & Bellak, S. S. (1980). *Manual for the Children's Apperception Test (CAT)* (7th ed.). Larchmont, NY: CPS.

Bellini, S., Akullian, J., & Hopf, A. (2007). Increasing social engagement in young children with autism spectrum disorders using video self-modelling. *School Psychology Review, 36*, 80–90.

Belsky, J. (1999). Interactional and contextual determinants of attachment security. In J. Cassidy & P. Shaver (Eds.), *Handbook of attachment: Theory, research, and clinical applications* (pp. 249–264). New York: Guilford Press.

Belsky, J., Conger, R. D., & Capaldi, D. M. (2009). The intergenerational transmission of parenting: Introduction to the special section. *Developmental Psychology, 45*, 1201–1204

Belsky, J., & Fearon, R. M. (2002). Infant-mother attachment security, contextual risk, and early development: A moderational analysis. *Developmental Psychopathology, 14*, 293–310.

Belsky, J., & Isabella, R. (1988). Maternal, infant, and social-contextual determinants of attachment security. In J. Belsky & T. Nezworski (Eds.), *Clinical implications of attachment* (pp. 41–94). Mahwah, NJ: Lawrence Erlbaum Associates.

Belsky, J., Jaffee, S. R., Sligo, J., Woodward, L., & Silva, P. A. (2005). Intergenerational transmission of warm-sensitive-stimulating parenting: A prospective study of mothers and fathers of 3-year-olds. *Child Development, 76*, 384–396.

Belsky, J., Pasco-Fearon, R. M., & Bell, B. (2007). Parenting, attention and externalizing problems: Testing mediation longitudinally, repeatedly, and reciprocally. *Journal of Child Psychology and Psychiatry, 48*, 1233–1242.

Ben-Amitay, G., Rosental, B., & Toren, P. (2010). Brief parent-child group therapy for childhood anxiety disorders: A developmental perspective on cognitive behavioral group treatment. *International Journal of Group Psychotherapy, 60*, 389–406.

Benasich, A., & Black, G. W. (1994). The effects of early intervention on maternal employment, public assistance, and health insurance: The Infant Health and Development Program. *American Journal of Public Health, 84*, 924–931.

Bender, H. H., Allen, J. P., Boykin, K., McElhaney, K. B., Antonishak, J., Moore, C. M., ... Davis, S. M. (2007). Use of harsh physical discipline and developmental outcomes in adolescence. *Development and Psychopathology, 19*, 227–242.

Benner, G. J., Nelson, J. R., & Epstein, M. H. (2002). Language skills of children with EBD: A literature review. *Journal of Emotional and Behavioral Disorders, 10*, 43–59.

Bennett, D., Bendersky, M., & Lewis, M. (2002). Children's intellectual and emotional-behavioral adjustment at 4 years as a function of cocaine exposure, maternal characteristics, and environmental risks. *Developmental Psychology, 38*, 648–658.

Benoit, D. (2001). Modified interaction guidance. *IMPrint, 32*, 6–10.

Benoit, D. (2009). Feeding disorders, failure to thrive, and obesity. In C. H. Zeanah, Jr. (Ed.), *Handbook of infant mental health* (3rd ed., pp. 377–391). New York: Guilford Publishers.

Benoit, D., Madigan, S., Lecce, S., Shea, B., & Goldberg, S. (2001). Atypical maternal behavior toward feeding-disordered infants before and after intervention. *Infant Mental Health Journal, 22*, 611–626.
Benoit, D., & Parker, K. H. (1994). Stability and transmission of attachment across three generations. *Child Development, 65*, 1444–1456.
Benton, A. (1968). Differential behavioral effects in frontal lobe disease. *Neuropsychologia, 6*, 53–60.
Bergin, C., & Bergin, D. (2009). Attachment in the classroom. *Educational Psychology Review, 21*, 141–170.
Bergman, R. L., Piacentini, J., & McCracken, J. T. (2002). Prevalence and description of selective mutism in a school based sample. *Journal of the American Academy of Child and Adolescent Psychiatry, 41*, 938–946.
Berk, L. E., & Potts, M. K. (1991). Development and functional significance of private speech among attention deficit hyperactivity disordered and normal boys. *Journal of Abnormal Child Psychology, 19*, 357–377.
Berlin, L., & Cassidy, J. (1999). Relations among relationships: Contributions from attachment theory and research. In J. Cassidy & P. R. Shaver (Eds.), *Handbook of attachment: Theory, research, and clinical applications* (pp. 688–712). New York: Guilford Press.
Bernier, A., Carlson, S. M., & Whipple, N. (2010). From external regulation to self-regulation: Early parenting precursors of young children's executive functioning. *Child Development, 81*(1), 325–339.
Bernstein, J. H., & Waber, D. P. (2003). Pediatric neuropsychological assessment. In T. E. Feinberg & M. J. Farah (Eds.), *Behavioral neurology and neuropsychology* (2nd ed., pp. 773–781). New York: McGraw-Hill.
Bertand, J. (2009). Interventions for children with fetal alcohol spectrum disorders (FASDs): Overview of findings for five innovative research projects. *Research in Developmental Disabilities, 30*, 986–1006.
Bertrand, J., Floyd, R. L., & Weber, M. K. (2004). *Fetal alcohol syndrome guidelines for referral and diagnosis*. Atlanta: Centers for Disease Control and Prevention.
Betteheim, B. (1974). *A home for the heart*. New York: Alfred P. Knopf.
Beutler, L. E., & Malik, M. L. (2002). *Rethinking the DSM: A psychological perspective*. Washington, DC: American Psychological Association.
Bhavnagri, N., & Parker, R. D. (1991). Parents as direct facilitators of children's peer relationships: Effects of age of child and sex of parents. *Journal of Social and Personal Relationships, 8*, 423–440.
Bhutta, A. T., Cleves, M. A., Casey, P. H., Cradock, M. M., & Anand, K. J. (2002). Cognitive and behavioral outcomes of school-aged children who were born preterm: A meta-analysis. *Journal of the American Medical Association, 288*, 728–737.
Biederman, J., Faraone, S. V., Sayer, J., & Kleinman, S. (2002). Case-control study of attention-deficit hyperactivity disorder and maternal smoking, alcohol use, and drug use during pregnancy. *Journal of the American Academy of Child and Adolescent Psychiatry, 41*, 378–385.
Biederman, J., Mick, E., & Faraone, S. V. (2002). Influence of gender on attention deficit hyperactivity disorder in children referred to a psychiatric clinic. *American Journal of Psychiatry, 159*, 36–42.
Biederman, J., & Spencer, T. (1999). Attention-deficit/hyperactivity disorder (ADHD) as a noradrenergic disorder. *Biological Psychiatry, 46*, 1234–1242.
Bigelow, H. J. (1850). Dr. Harlow's case of recovery from the passage of an iron bar through the head. *American Journal of the Medical Sciences, 34*, 2–22.
Binder, J. R. (1997). Neuroanatomy of language processing studied with functional MRI. *Clinical Neuroscience, 4*, 87–94.
Birbaumer, N., Viet, R., Lotze, M., Erb, M., Hermann, C., Grodd, W., & Flor, H. (2005). Deficient fear conditioning in psychopathy: A functional magnetic resonance imaging study. *Archives of General Psychiatry, 62*, 799–805.
Birch, S. H., & Ladd, G. W. (1998). Children's interpersonal behaviors and the teacher-child relationship. *Developmental Psychology, 34*, 934–946.
Bishop, D. (2003). *Children's Communication Checklist—Revised* (CCC—2). Harcourt Assessment.
Bishop, D. (2003). *Test for the Reception of Grammar* (2nd ed.) (TROG-2). San Antonio, TX: The Psychological Corporation.
Bishop, D. (2004*). The Expressive, Receptive and Recall Narrative Instrument* (ERRNI). Pearson.
Bishop, D. V. M. (1992). The underlying nature of SLI. *Journal of Child Psychology and Psychiatry, 33*, 3–66.

Bishop, D. V. M. (2003). *Children's Communication Checklist (2nd ed.) (CCC-2) Manual.* Minneapolis, MN: Pearson Assessment.

Bishop, D. V. M., Adams, C. V., & Norbury, C. F. (2005). Distinct genetic influences on grammar and phonological short term memory: Evidence from 6 year old twins. *Genes, Brain and Behavior 5*(2), 158–169.

Bishop, D. V. M., Adams, C. V., & Rosen, S. (2006). Resistance of grammatical impairment to computerized training in children with specific and non-specific language impairments. *International Journal of Language and Communication Disorders, 41*, 19–40.

Bishop, D. V. M., Asmodt-Leeper, G., Creswell, C., McGurk, R., & Skuse, D. H. (2001). Individual differences in cognitive planning on the Tower of Hanoi task: Neuropsychological maturity or measurement error? *Journal of Child Psychology and Psychiatry, 42*, 551–556.

Bishop, D. V. M., & Baird, G. (2001). Parent and teacher report of pragmatic aspects of communication: Use of the Children's Communication Checklist in a clinical setting. *Developmental Medicine and Child Neurology, 43*, 809–818. doi:10.1017/S0012162201001475

Bishop, D. V. M., North, T., & Donlan, C. (1995). Genetic basis of specific language impairment: Evidence from a twin study. *Developmental Medical Child Neurology, 37*, 56.

Bissell, J., Fisher, J., Owens, C., & Polcyn, P. (1998). *Sensory motor handbook: A guide for implementing and modifying activities in the classroom.* California: Sensory Integration International.

Bjorklund, D. F., & Pelligrini, A. D. (2002). *The origins of human nature: Evolutionary developmental psychology.* Washington, DC: American Psychological Association.

Bjorkqvist, K., Osterman, K., & Kaukiainen, A. (1992). The development of direct and indirect aggressive strategies in males and females. In K. Bjorkqvist & P. Niemela (Eds.), *Of mice and women: Aspects of female aggression* (pp. 51–64). San Diego, CA: Academic Press.

Bjorkquist, O. A., Fryer, S. L., Reiss, A. L., Mattson, S. N., & Riley, E. P. (2010). Cingulate gyrus morphology in children and adolescents with fetal alcohol spectrum disorders. *Psychiatric Research, 181*, 101–107.

Black, B., & Uhde, T. W. (1995). Psychiatric characteristics of children with selective mutism: A pilot study. *Journal of the American Academy of Child and Adolescent Psychiatry, 34*, 847–856.

Blair, R. J. R. (1995). A cognitive developmental approach to morality: Investigating the psychopath. *Cognition, 57*, 1–29.

Blair, R. J. R. (1999). Responsiveness to distress cues in the child with psychopathic tendencies. *Personality and Individual Differences, 27*, 135–145.

Blair, R. J. R. (2001). Neuro-cognitive models of aggression, the antisocial personality disorders, and psychopathy. *Journal of Neurology, Neurosurgery, and Psychiatry, 71*, 727–731.

Blair, R. J. R. (2004). The roles of the orbital frontal cortex in the modulation of antisocial behavior. *Brain and Cognition, 55*, 198–208.

Blair, R. J. R. (2006). The emergent of psychopathy: Implications for the neuropsychological approach for developmental disorders. *Cognition, 101*, 414–442.

Blair, R. J. R., Budhani, S., Colledge, E., & Scott, S. K. (2005). Deafness to fear in boys with psychopathic traits. *Journal of Child Psychology and Psychiatry, 46*, 327–336.

Blair, R. J. R., Colledge, E., Murray, L., & Mitchell, D. G. (2001). A selective impairment in the processing of sad and fearful expressions with psychopathic tendencies. *Journal of Abnormal Child Psychology, 29*, 491–498.

Blanche, E., & Burke, J. P. (1991a). Combining neurodevelopmental and sensory integration approaches in the treatment of the neurologically impaired child. Part 1. *Sensory Integration Quarterly, 19*(1), 1–2.

Blanche, E., & Burke, J. P. (1991b). Combining neurodevelopmental and sensory integration approaches in the treatment of the neurologically impaired child. Part 2. *Sensory Integration Quarterly, 19*(1), 1–6.

Blank, M., Rose, S. A., & Berlin, L. J. (2003). *Preschool language assessment instrument* (2nd ed.) (PLAI-2). PRO-ED.

Bloom, L., & Lahey, M. (1978). *Language development and language disorders.* New York: John Wiley and Sons.

Bloomquist, M. L., & Schnell, S. V. (2002). *Helping children with aggression and conduct problems: Best practices for intervention.* New York: Guilford Press.

BMA Board of Science. (2006). *Child and adolescent mental health. A guide for health care professionals.* London: British Medical Association.

Boccia, M. T., Reite, M., & Laudenslager, M. (1989). On the physiology of grooming in a pigtail macaque. *Physiology and Behavior, 45*, 667–670.

Bogels, S. M., van Oosten, A., Muris, P., & Smulders, D. (2001). Familial correlates of social anxiety in children and adolescents. *Behavior Research and Therapy, 39*, 273–287.

Bokhorst, C. L., Bakermans-Kranenburg, M. J., Fearon, R. M. P., van IJzendoorn, M. H., Fonagy, P., & Schuengel, C. (2003). The importance of shared environment in mother-infant attachment security: A behavioral genetic study. *Child Development, 74*, 1769–1782.

Booth-LaForce, C., Rubin, K. H., Rose-Krasnor, L., & Burgess, K. B. (2005). Attachment and friendship predictors of psychosocial functioning in middle childhood and the mediating roles of social support and self-worth. In K. A. Kerns & R. A. Richardson (Eds.), *Attachment in middle childhood* (pp. 161–1880). New York: Guilford Press.

Boris, N. W. (2009). Parental substance abuse. In C. H. Zeanah, Jr. (Ed.), *Handbook of infant mental health* (3rd ed., pp. 171–179). New York: Guilford Press.

Boris, N. W., Hinshaw-Fuselier, S. S., Smyke, S. T., Scheering, M. S., Heller, S. S., & Zeanah, C, Jr. (2004). Comparing criteria for attachment disorders: Establishing reliability and validity in a high-risk sample. *Journal of the American Academy of Child and Adolescent, 43*, 568–577.

Borja-Alvarez, T., Zarbatany, L., & Peppers, S. (1991). Contributions of male and female guests and hosts to group entry. *Child Development, 62*, 1079–1090.

Borke, H. (1971). Borke test of interpersonal awareness: Interpersonal perception of young children. Egocentrism or empathy. *Developmental Psychology*, 203–269.

Borman, G. D., & Benson, J. (2006). *Can brain research and computers improve literacy? A randomized controlled trial of the Fast Forword Language computer-based training program*. University of Wisconsin School of Education.

Bornstein, M. H., Haynes, O. M., O'Reilly, A. W., & Painter, K. W. (1996). Solitary and collaborative pretence play in early childhood: Sources of individual variation in the development of representational competence. *Child Development, 70*, 2910–2929.

Bornstein, M. H., Hendricks, C., Hahn, C.-S., Haynes, O. M., Painter, K. M., & Tamis-LeMonda, C. S. (2003). Contributors to self-perceived competence, satisfaction, investment, and role balance in maternal parenting: A multivariate ecological analysis. *Parenting: Science and Practice, 3*, 285–326.

Bornstein, M. H., Mayes, L. C., & Park, J. (1998). Language, play, emotional availability, and acceptance in cocaine-exposed and non-cocaine exposed children and their mothers. *Parole, 1*, 7–8.

Bosquet, M., & Egeland, B. (2006). The development and maintenance of anxiety symptoms from infancy through adolescence in a longitudinal sample. *Development and Psychopathology, 18*, 517–550.

Botting, N., Powls, A., Cooke, R. W., & Marlow, N. (1998). Cognitive and educational outcome of very-low-birth-weight children in early adolescence. *Developmental Medical Child Neurology, 40*, 652–660.

Boucher, J. (2009). *The autistic spectrum: Characteristics, causes, and practical issues*. London, UK: Sage Publishers Ltd.

Bowers, L., Huisingh, R., Barrett, M., Orman, J., & LoGiudice, C. (1994). *Test of Problem Solving-Elementary-3* (TOPS-3 Elementary). PRO-IDEA.

Bowlby, J. (1969/1982). *Attachment and loss: Vol. 1: Attachment*. New York: Basic Books.

Boyce, W. (2006). Symphonic causation and the origins of childhood psychopathology. In D. Cicchetti, & D. Cohen (Eds.), *Developmental psychopathology: Vol. 2. Developmental neuroscience* (2nd ed., pp. 797–817). New York: Guildford Press.

Bradley, E. J., & DeV. Peters, R. (1991). Physically abusive and non-abusive mothers' perceptions of parenting and child behavior. *American Journal of Orthopsychiatry, 61*, 455–460.

Bradley, R., & Corwyn, R. (2002). Socioeconomic status and child development. *Annual Review of Psychology, 53*, 371–399.

Bradley, R., Henderson, K., & Monfore, D. A. (2004). A national perspective on children with emotional disorders. *Behavioral Disorders, 29*, 211–223. Bradley, R., Doolittle, J., & Bartolotta, R. (2008). Building on data and adding to the discussion: The experiences and outcomes of students with emotional disturbance. *Journal of Behavioral Education, 17*, 4–23.

Bradley, S. (2000). *Affect regulation and the development of psychopathology*. New York: Guilford Press.

Bradley, S. (2005). Can we prevent mental illness? An essay. *IMPrint, 44*, 6–8.

Brandenberg, H. A., Friedman, R. M., & Silver, S. E. (1990). The epidemiology of childhood psychiatric disorders: Prevalence findings from different studies. *Journal of the American Academy of Child and Adolescent Psychiatry, 29*, 76–83.

Bremner, J. D. (2001a). A biological model for delayed recall of childhood abuse. *Journal of Aggression, Maltreatment, and Trauma, 14,* 165–183.

Bremner, J. D. (2001b). Hypotheses and controversies related to the effects of stress on the hippocampus: An argument for stress-induced damage to the hippocampus in patients with posttraumatic disorder. *Hippocampus, 11,* 75–81.

Brendgen, M., Boiven, M., Vitaro, F., Girard, A. Dionne, G., & Perusse, D. (2008). Gene-environment interaction between peer victimization and child aggression. *Development and Psychopathology, 20,* 455–471.

Brennan, P. A., Grekin, E. R., & Mednick, S. A. (1999). Maternal smoking during pregnancy and adult male criminal outcomes. *Archives of General Psychiatry, 56,* 215–219.

Brennan, P. A., Grekin, E. R., Mortensen, E., & Mednick, S. (2002). Relationship of maternal smoking during pregnancy with criminal arrest and hospitalisation for substance abuse in male and female offspring. *American Journal of Psychiatry, 159,* 48–54

Breslau, N., Brown, G., Del Dotto, Kumar, S. Ezhuthachen, S., Andreski, P., & Hufnagle, K. G. (1996). Psychiatric sequelae of low birth weight at six years of age. *Journal of Abnormal Child Psychology, 24,* 385–400.

Breslau, N., Chilcoat, H. D., Johnson, E. O., Andreski, P., & Lucia, V. C. (2000). Neurologic soft signs and low birth weight: Their association and neuropsychiatric implications. *Biological Psychiatry, 47,* 71–79.

Bretherton, I., & Munholland, K. A. (2007). Internal working models of attachment relationships: Elaborating a central construction of attachment theory. In J. Cassidy & P. R. Shaver (Eds.), *Handbook of attachment research, theory, and clinical research* (2nd ed., pp. 102–130). New York: Guilford Press.

Bretherton, I., & Munholland, K. A. (2008). Internal working models of attachment relationships: Elaborating a central construction of attachment theory. In J. Cassidy & P. R. Shaver (Eds.), *Handbook of attachment research, theory, and clinical research* (2nd ed., pp. 102–130). New York: Guilford Press.

Bretherton, I., Ridgway, D., & Cassidy, J. (1990). Assessing internal working models of the attachment relationship: An attachment story completion task for 3-year-olds. In M. T. Greenberg, D. Cicchetti, & E. M. Cummings (Eds.), *Attachment in the preschool years* (pp. 273–308). Chicago, IL: University of Chicago Press.

Bricker, D., & Squires, J. (1999). *Ages and stages questionnaires (ASQ): A parent completed parent monitoring system* (3rd ed.). Baltimore, MD: Paul H. Brookes Publishing Co. Ltd.

Briere, J. (1996). *Trauma Symptom Checklist for Children (TSCC).* Lutz, FL: Psychological Assessment Resources (PAR).

Briere, J. (2007). *Trauma Symptom Checklist for Young Children (TSCYC),* PAR: Lutz, FL.

Briere, J., & Elliott, D. (2003). Prevalence and psychological sequelae of self-reported childhood physical and sexual abuse in a general population sample of men and women. *Child Abuse and Neglect, 27,* 1205–1222.

Briere, J., & Scott, C. (2006). *Principles of trauma therapy: A guide to symptoms, evaluation, and treatment.* Thousand Oaks, CA: Sage Publications.

Brinkmeyer, M., & Eyberg, S. M. (2003). Parent-child interaction therapy for oppositional children. In A. E. Kazdin & J. R. Weisz (Eds.), *Evidence-based psychotherapies for children and adolescents* (pp. 204–225). New York: Guilford Press.

Brinton, B., & Fujiki, M. (1993). Language, social skills, and socioemotional behavior. *Language, Speech, and Hearing Services in Schools, 24,* 194–198.

Brisch, K. H. (2012). *Treating attachment disorders: From theory to therapy* (2nd ed.). New York: Guilford Publishers.

Brody, A. L., Saxena, S., Stoessel, P., Gillies, L. A., Fairbanks, L. A., Alborzian, S., ... Baxter, L. R. Jr. (2001). Regional metabolic changes in patients with major depression treated with either paroxetine or interpersonal therapy: Preliminary findings. *Archives of General Psychiatry, 58,* 631–634.

Brody, G. H., Ge, X., Kim, S. Y., Murray, V. M., Simons, R. L., Gibbons, F. X., et al. (2003). Neighbourhood disadvantage moderates associations of parenting and older sibling problem attitudes and behavior with conduct disorders in African American children. *Journal of Consulting and Clinical Psychology, 71,* 211–222.

Broidy, M., Nagin, D. S., Tremblay, R. E., Brame, B., Dodge, K., Fergusson, D., ... Vitaro, F. (2003). Developmental trajectories of childhood disruptive behaviors and adolescent delinquency: A six site cross-national study. *Developmental Psychology, 39*, 222–245.

Bronfman, E. T., Parsons, E., & Lyons-Ruth, K. (2000). *Atypical Maternal Behavior Instrument for Assessment and Classification (AMBIANCE)—Manual for coding disrupted affective communication*. Unpublished manuscript, Harvard Medical School, Boston, MA.

Brooks, D. (2006). *Search for islands of competence: A metaphor of hope and strength*. Retrieved from www.drrobertbrooks.com

Brooks-Gunn, J., McCormick, M. E., Shapiro, S., Benasich, A. A., & Black, G. W. (1994). The effects of early education intervention on maternal employment, public assistance, and health insurance: The Infant Health and Development Program. *American Journal of Public Health, 84*, 924–931.

Brown, E. J., & Goodman, R. F. (2005). Childhood traumatic grief: An exploration of the construct in children bereaved on September 11. *Journal of Clinical Child & Adolescent Psychology, 34*, 248–259.

Brown, G. G., Kindermann, S. S., Siegle, G. J., Granholm, E., Wong, E. C., & Buxton, R. B. (1999). Brain activation and pupil response during covert performance of the Stroop Color Word Task. *Journal of the International Neuropsychological Society, 5*, 308–319.

Brown, G. T., Rodger, S., & Davis, A. (2003). Test of visual perceptual skills revised: An overview and critique. *Scandinavian Journal of Occupational Therapy, 10*, 3–15.

Brown, J., Cohen, P., Johnson, J., & Salzinger, D. C. (1998). Memory, trauma, treatment and the law: A longitudinal analysis of risk factors for child maltreatment: Findings of a 7 year prospective study of official records and self-reported child abuse and neglect. *Child Abuse and Neglect, 22*, 1065–1078.

Brown, K., Atkins, M. S., Osborne, M. L., & Milnamow, M. (1996). A revised teacher rating scale for reactive and proactive aggression. *Journal of Abnormal Child Psychology, 24*, 473–480.

Brown, L., & Unger, A. (1992). *Sentence Completion Series (SCS)*. Odessa, FL: Psychological Assessment Resources (PAR).

Brown, T. E. (2001). *Brown attention-deficit disorder scales for children*. Minneapolis, MN: Pearson.

Brown, T. E. (2005). *Attention deficit disorder: The unfocused mind in children and adults*. New Haven, CT: Yale University Press.

Brown, T. E. (Ed.). (2009). *ADHD comorbidities: Handbook for ADHD complications in children and adults*. Arlington: VA: American Psychiatric Association.

Brown, W. H., & Conroy, M. A. (2002). Promoting peer-related social communication competence in pre-school children. In H. Goldstein, L. Kaczmarek, and K. English (Eds.), *Promoting social communication: Children with developmental disabilities from birth to adolescence. Communication and intervention series* (Vol. 10, pp. 173–210). Baltimore, MD: Paul H Brooks Publishers.

Brown-Chidsey, R. (2005). *Assessment for intervention: A problem-solving approach*. New York: Guilford.

Bruch, M. A., & Heimberg, R. G. (1994). Differences in perceptions of parental and personal characteristics between generalized and non-generalized social phobics. *Journal of Anxiety Disorders, 8*, 155–168.

Bruch, M. A., Heimberg, R. G., Berger, P., & Collins, T. M. (1989). Social phobia and perceptions of early parental and personal characteristics. *Anxiety Research, 2*, 57–63.

Bruder, G. E., Schneider, F. R., Stewart, J. W., McGrath, P. J., & Quitkin, F. (2004). Left hemisphere dysfunction during verbal dichotic listening test in patients who have social phobia with and without comorbid depressive disorder. *American Journal of Psychiatry, 161*, 72–78.

Bugental, D. B. (1992). Affective and cognitive processes within threat-oriented family systems. In I. E. Sigel, A. V. McGillicuddy-Delisi, & J. J. Goodnow (Eds.), *Parental belief systems: The psychological consequences for children* (2nd ed., pp. 219–248). Mahwah, NJ: Lawrence Erlbaum Associates.

Bugental, D. B., Blue, J., & Cruzcosa, M. (1989). Perceived control over caregiving outcomes: Implications for child abuse. *Developmental Psychology, 25*, 532–539.

Bugental, D. B., Ellerson, P. C., Lin, E. K., Rainey, B., Kokotovic, A., & O'Hara, N. (2002). A cognitive approach to child abuse prevention. *Journal of Family Psychology, 16*, 243–258.

Bugental, D. B., & Happaney, K. (2002). Parenting attributions. In M. H. Bornstein (Ed.), *Handbook of parenting: Vol. 3. Status and social conditions of parenting* (2nd ed., pp. 509–535). Mahwah, NJ: Erlbaum.

Bugental, D. B., & Johnson, C. (2000). Parental and child cognition in the context of the family. *Annual Review of the Family, 61*, 315–344.

Bugental, D. B., Kokotovic, A., O'Hara, N., Holmes, D., Ellerson, P. C., Lin, et al. (2000). *A cognitive approach to child abuse prevention*. Unpublished manuscript. University of California, Santa Barbara.

Bugental, D. B., Lyon, J. E., Krantz, J., & Cortez, V. (1997). Who's the boss? Differential accessibility of dominance ideation in parent-child relationships. *Journal of Personality and Social Psychology, 72,* 1297–1369.

Buhler, C. (1931). The social behavior of the child. In C. Murchison (Ed.), *A handbook of child psychology* (pp. 374–416). Worcester, MA: Clark University Press.

Bundy, A. C., Lane, S. J., & Murray, E. A. (2002). *Sensory integration: Theory and practice* (2nd ed.). Philadelphia, PA: F. A. Davis Company.

Burgess, K. B., Marshall, P. J., Rubin, K. H., & Fox, N. A. (2003). Infant attachment and temperament as predictors of subsequent externalising problems and cardiac physiology. *Journal of Child Psychology and Psychiatry, 44,* 819–831.

Burns, B. J., Costello, E. J., Angold, A., Tweed, D., Stangl, D., Farmer, E. M., & Erkanli, A. (1995). Children's mental health service use across sectors. *Health Affairs, 14,* 147–159.

Burtner, P. A., Wilhite, C, Bordegaray, J., Moedl, D., Roe, R. J., & Savage, A. R. (1997). Critical review of visual perceptual tests frequently administered by pediatric therapists. *Physical and Occupational therapy in Pediatrics, 17,* 39–61.

Bushman, B. J., & Baumeister, J. F. (1998). Threatened egotism, narcissism, self-esteem, and direct and displaced aggression: Does self-love or self-hate lead to violence? *Journal of Personality and Social Psychology, 75, 219–229.*

Butter, E., Wynn, J., & Mulick, J. (2003). Early intervention critical to autism treatment. *Paediatric Annals, 32,* 677–684.

Buyse, E., Verschueren, K., & Doumen, S. (2011). Preschoolers' attachment to mother and risk for adjustment problems in kindergarten: Can teachers make a difference? *Social Development, 20,* 33–50.

Bzoch, K. R., League, R., & Brown, V. L. (1991*). Receptive-Expressive Emergent Language Test* (3rd ed.) (REEL-3). PRO-ED.

Cabrera, M. P., & Martinez, P. B. (2001). The effects of repetition, comprehension checks, and gestures, on primary school children in an EFL situation. *ELT Journal, 55,* 281–288.

Caffrey, E., & Fuchs, D. (2007). Differences in performance between students with learning disabilities and mild mental retardation: Implications for categorical instruction. *Learning Disabilities Research and Practice, 22,* 119–128.

Cahill, S. M. (2006). Classroom management for kids who won't sit still and other "bad apples". *Teaching Exceptional children Plus. 3 (1) Article 6.* Retrieved November 29, 2010, from http://escholarship.bc.edu/education/tecplus/vol3/iss1/art6/

Cairney, J., Hay, J. A., Faught, B. E., & Hawes, R. (2005). Developmental coordination disorder and overweight and obesity in children aged 9–14. *International Journal of Obesity, 29,* 369–372.

Calkins, S. (2002). Does aversive behaviour during toddlerhood matter: The effects of difficult temperament on maternal perceptions and behaviour. *Infant Mental Health Journal, 23,* 381–402.

Calkins, S., Fox, N., & Marshall, T. (1996). Behavioural and physiological antecedents of inhibition in infancy. *Child Development, 67,* 523–540.

Calkins, S. D., & Keane, S. P. (2009). Developmental origins of early antisocial behavior. *Development and Psychopathology, 21*(4), 1095–1110.

Camaioni, L., Aureli, T., Bellagamba, F., & Fogel, A. (2003). A longitudinal examination of the transition to symbolic communication in the second year of life. *Infant and Child Development, 12,* 1–26.

Cameron, J. L. (2004, June). *The use of animal models for mechanistic and developmental studies.* Paper presented at the NIMH workshop on the prevention of depression in children and adolescents. Rockville, MD.

Campbell, D. G., & Brewer, D. (1991). *Rhythms of learning: Creative tools for developing lifelong skills.* Tucson, AZ: Zephyr Press.

Campbell, F. A., & Ramey, C. T. (1994). Effects of early intervention on intellectual and academic achievement: A follow-up of children from low income families. *Child Development, 65,* 684–698.

Campbell, F. A., & Ramey, C. T. (2002). Early childhood education: Young adult outcomes from the Abecedarian Project. *Applied Developmental Science, 6,* 42–57.

Campbell, S. B. (1987). Parent-referred problem three-year-olds: Developmental changes in symptoms. *Journal of Child Psychology and Psychiatry, 28,* 835–846.

Campbell, S. B. (Ed.). (1996). Introduction to the special section young children at risk for psychopathology: Developmental and family perspectives. *Journal of Clinical Child Psychology, 25*(4), 372–375.

Campbell, S. B. (2002). *Behavior problems in preschool children: Clinical and developmental issues* (2nd ed.). New York: Guilford Press.

Campbell, S. B., & Ewing, L. J. (1990). Follow-up of hard-to-manage preschoolers: Adjustment at age 9 predictors of continuing symptoms. *Journal of Child Psychology and Psychiatry and Allied Disciplines, 31,* 871–889.

Campbell, S. B., Shaw, D. S., & Gilliom, M. (2000). Early externalizing behavior problems: Toddlers and preschoolers at risk for later maladjustment. *Development and Psychopathology, 12,* 467–488.

Cantwell, D. (1981). Foreword. In R. A. Barkley, *Hyperactive children: A handbook for diagnosis and treatment.* New York: Guilford Press.

Cantwell, D. P., & Baker, L. (1987). Clinical significance of childhood communication disorders: Perspectives from a longitudinal study. *Journal of Child Neurology, 2,* 257–264.

Capaldi, D., Pears, K., Patterson, G., & Owen, L. (2003). Continuity of parenting practices across generations in an at-risk sample: A prospective comparison and mediated associations. *Journal of Abnormal Child Psychology, 31,* 127–142.

Card, N. A., Stucky, D., Sawalani, G. M., & Little, T. D. (2008). Direct and indirect aggression during childhood and adolescence: A meta-analytic review of gender differences, intercorrelations, and relations to maladjustment. *Child Development, 79,* 1185–1229.

Carlson, S. M., Moses, L. J., & Breton, C. (2002). How specific is the relation between executive function and theory of mind: Contributions from inhibitory control and working memory. *Infant and Child Development, 11,* 73–92.

Carlson, S. M., & Wang, T. S. (2007). Inhibitory control and emotion regulation in preschool children. *Cognitive Development, 22,* 489–510.

Carr, J. L., Agnihotri, & Keightley, M. (2010). Sensory processing and adaptive behavior deficits of children across the fetal alcohol spectrum disorder continuum. *Alcohol Clinical Experience Research, 34(6),* 1022–1032.

Carr, T., & Lord, C. (2009). Autism spectrum disorder. In C. H. Zeanah, Jr. (Ed.), *Handbook of infant mental health* (3rd ed., pp. 301–317). New York: Guilford Press.

Carrow-Woolfolk, E. (1996). *Oral and Written Language Scales* (OWLS).

Carrow-Woolfolk, E. (1999a). *Test of Auditory Comprehension of Language* (3rd ed.) (TACL-3). PRO-ED.

Carrow-Woolfolk, E. (1999b). *Comprehensive Assessment of Spoken Language* (CASL). San Antonio, TX: Psychological Corporation.

Case, L., & Gang, B. (1999). *People with developmental disabilities as parents.* Toronto, Ontario: Front Porch Publications.

Case-Smith. J. (2001). Development of childhood occupations. In *Occupational therapy for children.* Mosby. St Louis: Missouri.

Casey, B. J., Giedd, J. N., & Thomas, K. N. (2000). Structural and functional brain development and its relation to cognitive development. *Biological Psychology, 54,* 241–257.

Caspi, A., & Elder, G. H. (1988). Emergent-family patterns: The intergenerational construction of problem behavior and relationships. In R. Hinde & J. Stevenson-Hinde (Eds.), *Relationships within families* (pp. 218–240). Oxford, England: Oxford University Press.

Caspi, A, McClay, J., Moffitt, T. E., Mill, J., Craig, I. W., Taylor, A., … Poulton, R. (2002). Role of genotype in the cycle of violence in maltreated children. *Science, 297,* 851–854.

Caspi, A., & Moffitt, T. E. (1995). The continuity of maladaptive behavior: From description to understanding in the study of antisocial behavior. In D. Cicchetti & D. J. Cohen (Eds.), *Developmental psychopathology. Volume 2. Risk, disorder, and adaptation* (pp. 472–511). New York: Wiley.

Caspi, A. Sugden, K., Moffitt, T. E., Taylor, A., Craig, I. W., Harrington, H., ... Poulton, R. (2003). Influence of life stress on depression: Moderation by a polymorphism in the 5-HTT gene. *Science, 301,* 386–389.

Cassidy, J., Berlin, L, & Belsky, J. (1990, April). *Attachment organization at 3 years: Antecedent and concurrent correlates.* Paper presented at the biennial meeting of the International Conference on Infant Studies, Montreal, Quebec, Canada.

Cassidy, J., & Marvin, R. S. with the MacArthur Attachment Working Group. (1992). *Attachment organization in preschool children: Coding guidelines* (4th ed.). Unpublished manuscript, University of Virginia.

Cassidy, J., & Shaver, P. R. (Eds.). (2008). *Handbook of attachment: Theory, research, and clinical applications* (2nd ed.). New York: Guilford Press.

Cassidy, J., Woodhouse, S. S., Sherman, L. J., Stupia, B., & Lejuez, C. W. (2011). Enhancing infant attachment security: An examination of treatment efficacy and differential susceptibility. *Development and Psychopathology, 23,* 131–148.

Caster, I., Inderbitzen, H., & Hope, D. (1999). Relationship between youth and parent perception of family environment and social anxiety. *Journal of Anxiety Disorders, 13,* 237–251.

Catts, H. W., Fey, M., Zhang, X., & Tomblin, J. B. (1999). Language basis of reading and reading disabilities: Evidence from a longitudinal study. *Studies in Reading, 3,* 331–361.

Catts, H. W., Hogan, T. P., & Adolf, S. M. (2005). Developmental changes in reading and reading disabilities. In H. W. Catts & A. G. Kamhi (Eds.), *The connections between language and reading disabilities* (pp. 25–40). Mahwah, NJ: Lawrence Erlbaum.

Cavell, T. A. (2000). *Working with parents of aggressive children.* Washington, DC: American Psychological Association.

Center for Mental Health in Schools at UCLA. (2006). The current status of mental health in schools: A policy and practice analysis. http://smhp.psych.ucla.edu/currentstatusmh/htm

Center on the Developing Child at Harvard University. (2007). *A science-based framework for early childhood policy: Using evidence to improve outcomes in learning, behavior, and health for vulnerable children.* http://www.developingchild.harvard.edu

Center on the Developing Child at Harvard University. (2009). *Maternal depression can undermine development of young children: Working Paper No. 8.* http://www.developingchild.harvard.edu

Centers for Disease Control and Prevention. (2007). Preventing alcohol use during pregnancy. www.cdc.gov/ncbddd/fasd/research_tracking.htm

Cermak, S. (1988a). The relationship between attention deficit disorder and sensory integration disorders. Part 1: Theory. *Sensory Integration Special Interest Section Newsletter, 11,* 1–4.

Cermak, S. (1988b). The relationship between attention deficit disorder and sensory integration disorders. Part 2: Treatment. *Sensory Integration Special Interest Section Newsletter, 11(3), 3–4.*

Cermak, S. (2009). Deprivation and sensory processing in institutionalized and postinstitutionalized children: Part 1. *Sensory Integration: Special Interest Section Quarterly, 32*(2), 1–4.

Cha, C. B., & Nock, M. K. (2009). Emotional intelligence is a protective factor against suicidality. *Journal of the American Academy of Child and Adolescent Psychiatry, 48,* 422–430.

Chabardes, S., Kahane, P., Minotti, L., Hoffman, D., & Benabid, A.-L. (2002). Anatomy of the temporal pole region. *Epileptic Disorders, 4*(Suppl.1), 9–16.

Chaffin, M., Funderburk, B., Bard, D., Valle, L.A., & Gurwitch, R. (2011). A combined motivation and parent-child interaction therapy package reduces child welfare recidivism in a randomized dismantling field trial. *Journal of Consulting and Clinical Psychology, 79,* 84–95.

Chaffin, M. S., Silovsky, J. F., Funderburk, B., Vallee, L. A., Brestan, E. V., Balschova, T., ... Bonner, B. L. (2004). Parent-child interaction therapy for physically abusive parents: Efficacy for reducing future abuse reports. *Journal of Consulting and Clinical Psychology, 72,* 500–510.

Chamberlain, P., & Patterson, G. R. (1995). Discipline and child compliance in parenting. In M. H. Bornstein (Ed.), *Handbook of parenting: Vol. 4, Applied and practical parenting* (pp. 205–225). Mahwah, NJ: Erlbaum.

Chang, F., & Burns, B. M. (2005). Attention in preschooler: Association with effortful control and motivation. *Child Development, 76,* 247–263.

Chaplin, T. M., & Cole, P. M. (2005). The role of emotion regulation in the development of psychopathology. In B. L. Hankin & J. R. Z. Abela (Eds.), *Development of psychopathology: A vulnerability-stress perspective* (pp. 49–74). Thousand Oaks, CA: Sage Publications.

Chapparo, C. (2009). *Understanding visual perceptual skills in children: Workshop manual.* Perth, Western Australia: Developmental Occupational Therapy Inc.

Chapparo, C., & Ranka, J. (2004). *The perceive, recall, perform and plan system of task analysis workshop.* Perth, Western Australia.

Chasnoff, I. R., Wells, A. M., Telford, E., Schmidt, C., & Messer, G. (2010). Neurodevelopmental functioning in children with FAS, PFAS, and ARND. *Journal of Developmental and Behavioral Pediatrics, 31,* 192–201.

Chatoor, I., & Khushlani, D. (2006). Eating disorders. In J. L. Luby (Ed.), *Handbook of preschool mental health: Development, disorders, and treatment* (pp. 115–136). New York: Guilford Press.

Chen, Z., & Kaplan, H. (2001). The intergenerational transmission of constructive parenting. *Journal of Abnormal Child Psychology, 31,* 127–142.

Chess, S. (1960). Diagnosis and treatment of the hyperactive child. *New York State Journal of Medicine, 60*, 2379–2385.

Children's Defense Fund. (2002). *The state of America's union: A 2002 action guide to leave no child behind.* Washington, D.C.: Author.

Chorpita, B. (2001). Control and the development of negative emotions. In M. W. Vasey & M. R. Dadds (Eds.), *The developmental psychopathology of anxiety* (pp. 112–142). New York: Oxford University Press.

Christner, R. W., Mennuti, R. B., & Whitaker, J. S. (2009). An overview of school-based mental health practice from system service to crisis intervention. In R. W. Christner & R. B. Mennuti (Eds.), *School-based mental health: A practitioner's guide to comparative practices* (pp. 3–22). New York: Routledge Taylor & Francis Group.

Chu, J. A. (1992). The therapeutic roller-coaster: Dilemmas in the treatment of childhood abuse survivors. *Journal of Psychotherapy: Practice and Research, 1*, 357–370.

Chu, J. A. (2012). *Rebuilding shattered lives: The responsible treatment of complex post-traumatic and dissociative disorders* (2nd ed.). New York: Wiley.

Chu, S. (1996). Evaluating the sensory integrative functions. *British Journal of Occupational Therapy, 59*(10), 465–474.

Chudley, A. E., Conry, J., Cook, J. L., Loock, C., Rosales, T., & LeBlanc, N. (2005). Fetal alcohol spectrum disorder: Canadian guidelines for diagnosis. Retrieved from http://www.cmay.cafegi/contentfull,17251/suppl

Chugani, D. C. (2002). Role of altered brain serotonin mechanisms in autism. *Molecular Psychiatry, 7*, 516–517.

Cicchetti, D. (1984). The emergence of psychopathology. *Child Development, 55*, 1–7.

Cicchetti, D. (2003a). Forward. In S. S. Luthar (Ed.), *Resilience and vulnerability: Adaptation in the context of childhood and adversities* (pp. xix–xxxi). New York: Cambridge University Press.

Cicchetti, D. (2003b). Neuroendocrine functioning in maltreated children. In D. Cicchetti & E. F. Walker (Eds.), *Neurodevelopmental mechanisms in psychopathology* (pp. 35–365). New York: Cambridge University Press.

Cicchetti, D., Ackerman, B. P., & Izard, C. E. (1995). Emotions and emotion regulation in developmental psychopathology. *Development and Psychopathology, 7*, 1–10.

Cicchetti, D., & Rogosch, F. A. (1996). Equifinality and multifinality in developmental psychopathology. *Development and Psychopathology, 8*, 597–600.

Cicchetti, D., & Rogosch, F. A. (2001). Diverse patterns of neuroendocrine activity in maltreated children. *Development and Psychopathology, 13*, 755–1048.

Cicchetti, D., & Rogosch, F. A. (2002). A developmental psychopathology perspective on adolescence. *Journal of Consulting and Clinical Psychology, 70*, 6–20.

Cicchetti, D., Rogosch, F. A., & Toth, S. L. (2006). Fostering attachment in infants in maltreating families through preventive interventions. *Development and Psychopathology, 4*, 489–493.

Cicchetti, D., & Sroufe, A. L. (2000). The past of prologue to the future: The times they've been a changin'. *Development and Psychopathology, 12*, 255–264.

Cicchetti, D., & Toth, S. L. (2009). The past achievements and future promises of developmental psychopathology: The coming of age of a discipline. *Journal of Child Psychology and Psychiatry, 50*, 16–25.

Cillessen, A. H. N., & Bellmore, A. D. (2004). Social skills and interpersonal perception in early and middle childhood. In P. K. Smith & C. M. Hart (Eds.), *Childhood social development* (pp. 355–374). Oxford, UK: Blackwell Publishing.

Clark, C. A. C., Woodward, L. J., Horwood, L. J., & Moor, S. (2008). Development of emotions and behavior in extremely preterm and very preterm infants: Biological and social influences. *Child Development, 79*, 1444–1462.

Clegg, J., Hollis, C., Mawhood, L., & Rutter, M. (2005). Developmental language disorders—A follow-up in later adult life. Cognitive, language, and psychosocial outcomes. *Journal of Child Psychology and Psychiatry, 46*, 128–149.

Clinton, G.T., & Jenkins-Monroe, V. (1994). Rorschach responses of sexually abused children: An exploratory study. *Journal of Child Sexual Abuse, 3*, 67–83.

Clipsham, C. K. (2006). Reaching and engaging hard-to-reach families. In S. Landy & R. Menna, *Early intervention with multi-risk families: An integrative approach* (pp. 179–197). Baltimore, MD: Paul H. Brookes.

Coan, J. A. (2008). Toward a neuroscience of attachment. In J. Cassidy & P. R. Shaver (Eds.), *Handbook of attachment research, theory, and clinical research* (2nd ed., pp. 241–265). New York: Guilford Press.

Coan, J. A., Shaefer, H. S., & Davidson, R. J. (2008). Lending a hand: Social regulation of the neural response to threat. *Psychological Science, 17*, 1032–1039.

Coccaro, E. F., Kavoussi, R. J., Sheline, Y. I., Berman, M. E., & Csernansky, J. G. (1997). Impulsive aggression in personality disorder correlates with platelet 5-HT2a receptor binding. *Neuropharmacology, 1*, 211–216.

Cocks, N., Barton, B., & Donelly, M. (2009). Self concept of boys with developmental coordination disorder. *Physical and Occupational Therapy in Pediatrics, 29*(1), 6–22.

Coggins, T. E., Timler, G. R., & Olswang, L. B. (2007). A state of double jeopardy: Impact of prenatal exposure and adverse environments on the social communicative abilities of school age children with fetal alcohol spectrum disorder. *Language, Speech and Hearing Services in Schools, 38*, 117–127.

Cohen, E. (2009). Parenting in the throes of traumatic events: Risks and protection. In D. Brom, R. Pat-Horenczyk, & J. D. Ford (Eds.), *Treating traumatized children: Risk, resilience, and recovery*, (pp. 72–84). New York: Routledge.

Cohen, J. A., Berliner, L., & Mannanno, A. F. (2000). Treating traumatized children: A research review and synthesis. *Trauma, Violence, and Abuse: A Review Journal, 1*, 29–46.

Cohen, N. J. (2001). *Language impairment and psychopathology in infants, children and adolescents*. California: Sage Publications.

Cohen, N. J., & Duvall, J. D. (1996). *The family attachment program: An innovative program for working with families adopting older children*. Toronto, ON: C. M. Hincks Institute.

Cohen, N. J., Davine, M., Horodezky, N., Lipsett, L. & Isaacson, L. (1993). Unsuspected language impairment in psychiatrically disturbed children: Prevalence and language and behavioral characteristics. *Journal of the American. Academy of. Child and Adolescent. Psychiatry, 32*, 595–603.

Cohen, N. J., Lojkasek, M., Muir, E., Muir, R., & Parker, C. J. (2002). Six month follow-up of two mother-infant therapies: Convergence of therapeutic outcomes. *Infant Mental Health Journal, 23*, 361–380.

Cohen, N. J., Menna, R., Vallance, D. D., Barwick, M. A., Im, N., & Horodezky, N. B. (1998). Language, social cognitive processing, and behavioral characteristics of psychiatrically disturbed children with previously identified and unsuspected language impairments. *Journal of Child Psychology and Psychiatry, 39*, 853–864.

Cohen, N. J., Muir, E., Lojkasek, M., Muir, R., Parker, C. J., Barwick, M. B., & Brown, M. (1999). Watch, Wait, and Wonder: Testing the effectiveness of a new approach to mother–infant psychotherapy. *Infant Mental Health Journal, 20*, 429–451.

Cohen, W., Hodson, A., O'Hare, A., Boyle., J., Durrani, T., McCartney, E., … Watson, J. (2005). Effects of computer based interventions using acoustically modified speech (Fast ForWord) in severe mixed receptive–expressive language impairment: Outcomes from a randomized controlled trial. *Journal of Speech, Language & Hearing Research, 48*, 715–729.

Cohen, W., Parmelee, A., Beckwith, L., & Sigman, M. (1992). Behavior problems and social competence during early adolescence in children born preterm. In S. Friedman & M. Sigman (Eds.), *The psychological development of low-birth weight children* (pp. 239–257). Norwood, NJ: Ablex Publishing Company.

Cohler, B. J., & Paul, S. (2002). Psychoanalysis and parenthood. In M. H. Bornstein (Ed.), *Handbook of parenting* (2nd ed.). *Vol. 3. Being and becoming a parent* (pp. 563–599). Mahwah, NJ: Lawrence Erlbaum Associates.

Cole, P. M., & Tan, P. Z. (2007). Emotion socialization from a cultural perspective: In J. E. Grusec & P. D. Hastings (Eds.), *Handbook of socialization: Theory and research* (pp. 516–542). New York: Guilford Press.

Collins, W. A., Maccoby, E. E., Steinberg, L., Hetherington, F. M., & Bornstein, M. H. (2000). Contemporary research on parenting: The case for nature and nurture. *American Psychologist, 55*, 218–232.

Colvin, C. R., Block, J., & Funder, D. C. (1995). Overly positive self-evaluations and personality: Negative implications for mental health. *Journal of Personality and Social Psychology, 68*, 1152–1162.

Comings, D. E., Comings, B. G., Muhleman, D., Dietz, G., Shahbarami, B., Tast, D., … Flanagan, S. D. (1991). The dopamine D2 receptor locus as a modifying gene in neuropsychiatric disorders. *The Journal of the American Medical Association, 266*, 1793–1800.

Condor, B. (2000). Getting feedback on attention deficit disorder. *Chicago Tribune Internet Edition*.

Conduct Problems Prevention Research Group. (1992). A developmental and clinical model for the prevention of conduct disorder: The FAST Track Program. *Development and Psychopathology, 4,* 509–527.

Conduct Problems Prevention Research Group. (1999a). Initial impact of the FAST Track prevention trial for conduct problems: 1. The high risk sample. *Journal of Consulting and Clinical Psychology, 67,* 631–647.

Conduct Problems Prevention Research Group. (1999b). Initial impact of the FAST Track prevention trial for conduct problems: II. Classroom effects. *Journal of Consulting and Clinical Psychology, 67,* 648–657.

Conger, R., McLoyd, V., Wallace, L., Sun, Y., Simons, R., & Brody, G. (2002). Economic pressure in African-American families: A replication and extension of the family stress model. *Developmental Psychology, 38,* 179–195.

Conger, R. D., Neppl, T., Kim, K. J., & Scaramella, L. (2003). Angry and aggressive behavior across three generations: A prospective longitudinal study of parents and children. *Journal of Abnormal and Child Psychology, 31,* 143–160.

Connell, A. M., & Goodman, S. H. (2002). The association between psychopathology in fathers versus mothers and children's internalizing and externalizing behavior problems: A meta-analysis. *Psychological Bulletin, 128,* 746–773.

Conners, C. K. (1995). *The conners continuous performance test.* North Tonawanda, NY: Multi-Health Systems.

Conners, C. K. (1997). *Conners' rating scales-revised technical manual.* North Tonawanda, NY: Multi-Health Systems (MHS) Inc.

Conners, C. K. (2008). *Conners* (3rd ed.) (Conners-3). North Tonawanda: NY: Multi-Health Systems.

Connor, D. B., & Gross, D. R. (2003). Longitudinal analysis of the presence, efficacy, and stability of maternal scaffolding during informal problem-solving interactions. *British Journal of Developmental Psychology, 21,* 315–334.

Connor, D. F. (2002). *Aggression and antisocial behavior in children and adolescents: Research and treatment.* New York: Guilford Press.

Connor, D. F., Melloni, R. J. Jr., & Harrison, R. J. (1998). Overt categorical aggression in referred children and adolescents. *Journal of the American Academy of Child and Adolescent Psychiatry, 37,* 66–73.

Connor, P. D., Sampson, P. D., Bookstein, F. L., Barr, H. M., & Streissguth, A. P. (2000). Direct and indirect effects of prenatal alcohol damage on executive function. *Developmental Neuropsychology, 18,* 331–354.

Constantino, J. N. (2002). *Social Responsiveness Scale (SRS) Manual.* Los Angeles, CA: Western Psychological Services.

Conti-Ramsden, G., & Botting, N. (2004). Social difficulties and victimization in children with SLI at 11 years of age. *Journal of Speech, Language, and Hearing Research, 47,* 145–161.

Cook, A., Spinazzola, J., Ford, J., & Lanktree, C., ... van der Kolk, B. (2005). Complex trauma in children and adolescents. *Psychiatric Annals, 35,* 390–399.

Cooper-Kahn, J., & Dietzel, L. (2008). *Late, lost, and unprepared: A parents' guide to helping children with executive functioning.* Bethesda, MD: Woodbine House.

Coplan, I. (1990). *Early Language Milestone Scale Complete (ELM Scale-2) Manual.* New York: Slosson Educational.

Coplan, J. (1993). *Early language milestone scale* (2nd ed.) *(ELM Scale-2).* Austin, TX: PRO-ED.

Coplan, R., Bowker, A., & Cooper, S. (2003). Parenting, daily hassles, child temperament and social adjustment in preschool. *Early Childhood Research Quarterly, 18,* 376–395.

Coplan, R. J., Prakash, K., O'Neil, R., & Armur, M. (2004). Do "you want" to play? Distinguishing between conflicted shyness and social disinterest in early childhood. *Developmental Psychology, 40,* 244–258.

Corcoran, J. (2000). Family interventions with child physical abuse and neglect: A critical review. *Children and Youth Services Review, 22,* 563–591.

Corcoran, K. M., Farb, N., Anderson, A., & Segal, Z. V. (2010). Mindfulness and emotion regulation: Outcomes and possible mediating mechanisms. In A. M. Kring & D. M. Sloan (Eds.), *Emotion regulation and psychopathology: A transdiagnostic approach to etiology and treatment* (pp. 339–353). New York: Guilford Press.

Corkum, P., Humphries, K., Mullane, J. C., & Theriault, F. (2008). Private speech in children with ADHD and their typically developing peers during problem-solving and inhibition tasks. *Contemporary Educational Psychology, 33*, 97–115.

Correll, C. U., & Carlson, H. E. (2006). Endocrine and metabolic adverse effects of psychotropic medications in children and adolescents. *Journal of the American Academy of Child and Adolescent Psychiatry*, 45(7), 771–791.

Corsello, C. (2005). Early intervention in autism. *Infants and young children, 18*, 74–85.

Corwin, J., & Bylsma, F. W. (1992). Translation of excerpts from Andre Rey's "Psychological Examination of Traumatic Encephalopathy" and F. A. Osterrieth's "The Complex Figure Copy Test." *Clinical Neuropsychology, 7*, 3–15.

Coull, J. T. (1998). Neural correlates of attention and arousal: Insights from electrophysiology, functional neuroimaging and psychopharmacology. *Progress in Neurobiology, 55*, 343–361.

Couperus, J. W., & Nelson, G. A. (2006). Early brain development and plasticity. In K. McCarney & D. Phillips (Eds.), *Blackwell handbook of early childhood development* (pp. 85–105). Malden, MA: Blackwell Publishing.

Courchesne, E. (1997). Brainstem, cerebellar, and limbic neuroanatomical abnormalities in autism. *Current Opinion in Neurobiology, 7*, 269–278.

Courtois, C. A. (2004). Complex trauma, complex reactions: Assessment and treatment. *Psychotherapy, Theory, Research, Practice, and Training, 41*, 412–425.

Cowell, T. A. (2000). *Working with parents of aggressive children: A practitioner's guide*. Washington, DC: American Psychological Association.

Cozolino, L. (2002). *The neuroscience of psychotherapy: Building and rebuilding the human brain.* New York: W. W. Norton & Co.

Cozolino, L. (2006*). The neuroscience of human relationships: Attachment and the developing social brain.* New York: W.W. Norton & Co. Inc.

Craig, A., & Tran, Y. (2006a). Epidemiology of stuttering in the community across the entire lifespan. *Journal of Speech, Language and Hearing Research, 45*, 1097–1105.

Craig, A., & Tran, Y. (2006b). Fear of speaking: Chronic anxiety and stammering. *Advances in Psychiatric Treatment, 12*, 63–68.

Craig, H. K., & Gallagher, T. M. (1984). Gaze and proximity as turn regulators within three-party and two-party child conversations. *Journal of Speech and Hearing Research, 25*, 65–75.

Crais, E., Douglas, D. D., & Campbell, C. C. (2004). The intersection of the development of gestures and intentionality. *Journal of Speech, Language and Hearing Research, 47*, 678–694.

Crais, E., & Lorch, N. (1994). Oral narratives of school aged children. *Topics in Language Disorders, 14*, 13–28.

Crais, E., Roy, V., & Free, K. (2006). Parents and professionals perceptions of the implementation of family centred practices in child and adolescent assessments. *American Journal of Speech–Language Pathology, 15*, 365–377.

Craske, M. G., Poulton, R., Tsao, J. C. I., & Plotkin, D. (2001). Paths to panic disorder/agoraphobia: an exploratory analysis from 3 to 21 in an unselected birth cohort. *Journal of the American Academy of Child and Adolescent Psychiatry, 40*, 556–563.

Cresswell, C., Willetts, L., Murray, L., Singhal, M., & Cooper, P. (2008). Treatment of child anxiety: An exploratory study of the role of maternal anxiety and behaviors in treatment outcome. *Clinical Psychology and Psychotherapy, 15*, 38–44.

Crick, N. R. (1995). Relational aggression: The role of intent attributions, feelings of distress, and provocation type. *Development and Psychopathology, 7*, 313–322.

Crick, N. R. (1997). Engagement in gender normative versus non-normative forms of aggression: Links to social–psychological adjustment. *Development and Psychopathology, 9*, 610–617.

Crick, N. R., & Dodge, K. A. (1994). A review and reformulation of social information-processing mechanisms in children's social adjustment. *Psychological Bulletin, 115*, 74–101.

Crick, N. R., & Dodge, K. A. (1996). Social information processes in reactive and proactive aggression. *Child Development, 67*, 993–1002.

Crick, N. R., & Grotpeter, J. K. (1995). Relational aggression, gender, and social psychological adjustment. *Child Development, 66*, 710–722.

Crittenden, P., Lang, C., Claussen, A., & Partridge, M. (2000). Relations among mothers' dispositional representations of parenting. In P. Crittenden & A. Claussen (Eds.), *The organization of attachment relationships: Maturation, culture and context* (pp. 214–233). Cambridge, UK: Cambridge University Press.

Crittenden, P. M. (1985). Maltreated infants: Vulnerability and resilience. *Journal of Child Psychology and Psychiatry, 26*, 85–96.

Crittenden, P. M. (1992). Quality of attachment in the preschool years. *Development and Psychopathology, 4*, 209–241.

Cronbach, L. J. (1975). Beyond two disciplines of scientific psychology. *American Psychologist, 30*, 116–127.

Crosbie, S., Teitzel, T., Ozanne, A., McIntosh, B., & Dodd, B. (2000). *Preschool and primary inventory of phonological awareness* (PIPA). Pearson.

Crosnoe, R., Morrison, F., Burchinal, M., Pianta, R., Keating, D. Friedman, S. L., ... The Eunice Kennedy Shriver National Institute of Child Health and Human Development Early Child Care Research Network. (2010). Instruction, teacher-student relations, and math achievement trajectories in elementary school. *Journal of Educational Psychology, 102*, 407–417.

Crosnoe, R., & Needham, B. (2004). Holism, contextual variability and the study of friendships in adolescent development. *Child Development, 75*, 264–279.

Crowe, S. L., & Blair, R. J. R. (2008). The development of antisocial behavior: What can we learn from functional neuroimaging studies? *Development and Psychopathology, 20*, 1145–1159.

Crystal, D. (2002). *The English language: A guided tour of the language* (2nd ed.). London: Penguin Books.

Culbertson, W. C., & Zillmer, E. A. (2000). *Tower of London—Drexel University*. Chicago, IL: Multisystem Health Systems.

Cullerton-Sen, C., Cassidy, A. R., Murray-Close, D., Cicchetti, D., Crick, N. R, & Rogosch, F. A. (2009). Childhood maltreatment and the development of relational and physical aggression: The importance of a gender-informed approach. *Child Development, 79*, 1736–1751.

Cummings, E., & Cummings, J. (2002). Parenting and attachment. In M. Bornstein (Ed.), *Handbook of parenting: Vol. 5. Practical issues in parenting* (2nd ed., pp. 35–58). Mahwah, NJ: Lawrence Erlbaum Associates.

Cummings, E. M., Schermerhorn, A. C., Davies, P. T., Goeke-Morey, M. C., & Cummings, J. S. (2006). Interparental discord and child adjustment: Prospective investigations of emotional security as an explanatory mechanism. *Child Development, 77*, 132–152.

Cummings, S., & Fristad, M. A. (2007). Medications prescribed for children with mood disorders: Effects of a family-based psycho-education program. *Experimental Clinical Psychopharmacology, 15*, 555–562.

Cummins, A., Piek, J. P., & Dyck, M. J. (2005). Motor coordination, empathy and social behaviour in school aged children. *Developmental Medicine and Child Neurology, 47(7)*, 437–442.

Curby, T. W., LoCasale-Crouch, J., Konold, T. R., Pianta, R. C., Howes, C. Burchinal, M., ... Barbarin, O. (2009). The relations of observed pre-k classroom quality profiles to children's achievement and social competence. *Early Education & Development, 20*, 346–372.

Cyr, C., & van IJzendoorn, M. H. (2007). Attachment in the schools: Toward attachment-based curricula. *Journal of Early Childhood and Infant Psychology, 3*, 95–117.

D'Andrea, W., Spinazzola, J., & van der Kolk, B. (2009). Phenomenology and nosology of symptoms following interpersonal trauma exposure in children: A review of literature on symptoms, biology, and treatment. Under review.

Daal, J. V., Verhoeven, L., & Balkom, H. (2007). Behavior problems in children with language impairment. *Journal of Child Psychology and Psychiatry, 48*, 1139–1147.

Dada, S., & Alant, E. (2009). The effect of aided language stimulation on vocabulary acquisition in children with little or no functional speech. *American Journal of Speech and Language Pathology, 18*, 50–64.

Dadds, M. R., Fraser, J., Frost, A., & Hawes, D. J. (2005). Disentangling the underlying dimensions of psychopathy and conduct problems in childhood. A community study. *Journal of Consulting and Clinical Psychology, 73*, 400–410.

Dadds, M. R., Hawes, D. J., Frost, A. D. J., Vassallo, S., Bunn, P., Hunter, K., & Merz, S. (2009). Learning to "talk the talk": The relationship of psychopathic traits to deficits in empathy across childhood. *The Journal of Child Psychology and Psychiatry, 50*(5), 599–606.

Dadds, M. R., Mullins, M. J., McAllister, R. A., & Atkinson, E. (2003). Attributions, affect, and behavior in abuse-risk mothers: A laboratory study. *Child Abuse and Neglect, 27*, 21–45.

Dadds, M. R., Perry, Y. Hawes, D. J., Merz, S., Riddell, A. C., Haines, D. J., ... Abeygunawardane, A. I. (2006). Look in the eyes: Fear recognition in child psychopathy. *British Journal of Psychiatry, 189*, 180–181.

Dahl, R. E. & Gunnar, M. R. (2009). Heightened stress responsiveness and emotional reactivity during pubertal maturation: Implications for psychopathology. *Development and Psychopathology 21*(1), 1–6.

Dale, P. S., Price, T. S., Bishop, D. V. M., & Plomin, R. (2003). Outcomes of early language delay: I. Predicting persistent and transient language difficulties at 3 and 4 years. *Journal of Speech, Language, and Hearing Research, 46*, 544–560.

Dalton, K. M., Nacewicz, B. M., Johnstone, T., Schaefer, H. S., Genbaucher, M. A., & Goldsmith, H. H. (2005). Gaze fixation and the neural circuitry of face processing in autism. *Nature Neuroscience, 8*, 519–526.

Daniels, D., & Plomin, R. (1985). Origins of individual differences in infant shyness. *Developmental Psychology, 21*, 118–121.

Davidson, R. J. (1993). The neuroscience of emotion and affective style. In M. Lewis & J. M. Haviland (Eds.), *Handbook of emotions* (pp. 143–154). New York: Guilford Press.

Davidson, R. J. (2000). Affective style, psychopathology, and resilience: Brain mechanisms and plasticity. *American Psychologist, 55*, 1196–1214.

Davidson, R. J. (2002). Anxiety and affective style: Role of the prefrontal cortex and amygdale. *Biological Psychiatry, 51*, 68–80.

Davidson, R. J., & Begley, S. (2012). *The emotional life of the brain*. New York, NY: Hudson Street Press.

Davidson, R. J., Marshall, J. R., Tomarken, A. J., & Henriques, J. B. (2000). While a phobic waits: Regional brain electrical and autonomic activity in social phobics in anticipation of public speaking. *Biological Psychiatry, 47*, 85–95.

Davies, D. (2004). *Child development* (2nd ed.). New York: Guilford Press.

Davies, P. L., & Gavin, W. J. (2007). Validating the diagnosis of sensory processing disorders using EEG technology. *American Journal of Occupational Therapy, 61*, 176–189.

Davies, P. T., Harold, G. T., Goeke-Morey, M. C., Cummings, E. M., Shelton, K., & Rasi, J. A. (2002). Child emotional security and inter-parental conflict. *Monographs of the Society for Research in Child Development, 67*(3, Serial No. 270), 41–62.

Davis, K. D., Taylor, S. J., Crawley, A. D., Wood, M. L., & Mikulis, D. L. (1997). Functional and attention-related activations in the human cingulate cortex. *Neurophysiology, 77*, 3370–3380.

Davis, M., & Whalen, P. J. (2001). The amygdala: Vigilance and emotion. *Molecular Psychiatry, 1*, 13–34.

Dawson, G., Carver, L., Meltzoff, A. N., Panagiotides, H., McPartland, J. & Webb, S. (2002). Neural correlates of face and object recognition in young children with autism spectrum disorders, developmental delays, and typical development. *Child Development, 73*, 700–717.

Dawson, G., Hill, D., Galpert, L., Spencer, A., & Watson, L. (1990). Affective exchanges between young autistic children and their mothers. *Journal of Abnormal Child Psychology, 18*, 335–345.

Dawson, G., Warrenburg, S., & Fuller, P. (1985). Left hemisphere specialization for facial and manual imitation in children and adults. *Psychophysiology, 22*, 237–243.

Dawson, G., Webb, S., & McPartland, J. (2005). Electrophysiological studies of face processing: Implications for understanding the nature of social impairments in autism. *Developmental Neuropsychology, 27*, 403–424.

Dawson, G., & Zanolli, K. (2003). Early intervention and brain plasticity in autism. In *Autism: Neural basis and treatment possibilities* (pp. 266–280). Chichester: Wiley and Sons for the Novartis Foundation.

Dawson, P., & Guare, R. (2010). *Executive skills in children and adolescents: A practical guide to assessment and intervention*. New York: Guilford Press.

De Angelis, T. (2007). A new diagnosis for childhood trauma? *Monitor on Psychology, 38*, 32–34.

De Bellis, M. D. (2001). Developmental truamatology: The psychobiological development of maltreated children and its implications for research, treatment, and policy. *Development and Psychopathology, 13*, 539–564.

De Bellis, M. D. (2002). Superior temporal gyrus volumes in maltreated children and adolescents with PTSD. *Biological Psychiatry, 51*, 544–552.

De Bellis, M. D., Keshaven, M. S., Clark, D. B., Casey, B. J., Giedd, J. N., Boring, A. M., ... Ryan, N. D. (1997). Developmental traumatology. Part 2: Brain development. *Biological Psychiatry, 45,* 1271–1284.

De Bellis, M. D., Keshaven, M. S., Shifflett, H., Ivengar, S., Beers, S. R., Hall, J., & Moritz, G. (2000). Brain structure in pediatric maltreatment related post-traumatic stress disorder: A sociodemographically matched study. *Biological Psychiatry, 52,* 1066–1078.

De Gangi, G. A. (2000). *Pediatric disorders of regulation in affect and behavior: A therapist's guide to assessment and treatment.* San Diego, CA: Academic Press.

De Gangi, G. A. & Greenspan, S. I. (1989). The assessment of sensory functioning in infants. *Physical Occupational Therapy in Pediatrics, 9,* 21–33.

De Gangi, G. A., & Greenspan, S. I. (1997). The effectiveness of short-term interventions in the treatment of inattention and irritability in toddlers. *Journal of Developmental and Learning Disorders, 1,* 277–298.

De Gangi, J. A., Breinbauer, C., Roosevelt, J. D., Porges, S., & Greenspan, S. (2000). Prediction of childhood problems at three years in children experiencing disorders of regulation during infancy. *Infant Mental Health Journal, 21*(3), 156–175.

De Lange, F. P., Haggart, P., & Toni, I. (2005). Neural topography and content of movement representations. *Journal of Cognitive Neuroscience, 17(1),* 97–112.

de Wied, M.,Goudena, P. P., & Malthys, W. (2005). Empathy in boys with disruptive behavior disorders. *Journal of Child Psychology and Psychiatry and Allied Disciplines, 46,* 867–880.

De Wolff, M. S., & van IJzendoorn, M. H. (1997). Sensitivity and attachment: A meta-analysis on parental antecedents of infant attachment. *Child Development, 68,* 571–591.

Deater-Deckard, K., & Petrill, S. A. (2004). Parent-child dyadic mutuality and child behavior problems: An investigation of gene-environment processes. *Journal of Child Psychology and Psychiatry, 45,* 1171–1179.

Decety, J. (2007). A social cognitive neuroscience model of human empathy. In E. Harmen-Jones, & F. Winkielman (Eds.), *Social neuroscience: Integrating biological and psychological explanations of social behavior* (pp. 237–260). Cambridge, UK: Cambridge University Press.

Degnan, K. A., Calkins, S. D., Keane, S. P., & Hill-Soderlund, A. L. (2008). Profiles of disruptive behavior across early childhood: Contributions of frustration reactivity, physiological regulation, and maternal behavior. *Child Development, 79,* 1357–1376.

DeKlyen, M., & Greenberg, M. T. (2008). Attachment and psychopathology in childhood. In J. Cassidy & P. R. Shaver (Eds.), *Handbook of attachment: Theory, research, and clinical applications* (2nd ed., pp. 637–665). New York: Guilford Publishers.

DeKlyen, M., Speltz, M., & Greenberg, M. T. (1998). Fathers and early starting conduct problems: Positive and negative parenting, father-son attachment, and the marital context. *Clinical Child and Family Psychology Review, 1,* 3–21.

Delano, M., & Snell, M. E. (2006). The effect of social stories on social engagement of children with autism. *Journal of Positive Interventions, 8,* 29–42.

Delis, D., Kaplan, E., & Kramer, J. H. (2001). *Delis-Kaplan executive function system.* San Antonio, Texas: Psychological Corporation.

DeLuca, C. R., Wood, S. J., Anderson, K., Buchanan, J. A., Proffitt, T. M., Mahony, K., & Pantelis, C. (2003). Normative data from the Cantab: 1. Development of executive function over the lifespan. *Journal of Clinical and Experimental Neuroscience, 25,* 242–254.

Démonet J. F., Thierry, G., & Cardebat, D. (2005). Renewal of the neurophysiology of language: Functional neuroimaging. *Physiology Review, 85,* 49–95.

Demyltenaere, K., Briffaerts, R., & Posada-Villa, J. (2004). Prevalence, severity, and unmet need for treatment of mental disorders in the World Health Organization World Mental Health Surveys. *The Journal of the American Medical Association, 291,* 2581–2590.

Denckla, M. B. (1991). Attention deficit hyperactivity disorder: Residual type. *Journal of Child Neurology, 6,* 44–50.

Denham, S. A. (1994). Mother-child emotional communication and preschoolers' security of attachment and dependency. *Journal of Genetic Psychology, 155,* 119–121.

Denham, S. A. (1998). *Emotional development in young children.* New York: Guilford.

Denham, S. A., Bassett, H., & Wyatt, T. (2007). The socialization of emotional competence. In J. E. Grusec & P. D. Hastings (Eds.), *Handbook of socialization: Theory and research* (pp. 614–636). New York: Guilford Press.

Dennis, T. A., & Hajcak, G. (2009). The late positive potential: A neurophysiological marker for emotion regulation in children. *Journal of Child Psychology and Psychiatry, 50*(11), 1373–1383.

Dennis, W. (1960). Causes of retardation among institutionalized children. *Journal of Genetic Psychology, 99*, 47–59.

Deno, S. L. (1986). Formative evaluation of individual student programs: A new role for school psychologists. *School Psychology Review, 15*, 358–374.

Deno, S. L. (1989). Curriculum-based measurement and special education services: A fundamental and direct relationship. In M. R. Shinn (Ed.), *Curriculum-based measurement: Assessing special children* (pp. 1–17). New York: Guilford.

Deno, S. L. (2003). Developments in curriculum-based measurement. *The Journal of Special Education, 37*, 184–192.

Deno, S. L. (2005). Problem-solving assessment. In R. Brown-Chidsey (Ed.), *Assessment for intervention: A problem-solving approach* (pp. 10–40). New York: Guilford.

Derks, E. M., Hudziak, H., van Beijsterveldt, C. E. M., Dolan, C. V., & Boomsma, D. I. (2006). Genetic analyses of maternal and teacher ratings on attention problems in 7-year-old Dutch twins. *Behavioral Genetics, 36*, 833–844.

Derryberry, D., & Rothbart, M. K. (1997). Reactive and effortful processes in the organization of temperament. *Development and Psychopathology, 9*, 633–652.

Dickman, Z. V., & Allen, J. J. (2000). Error monitoring during reward and avoidance learning in highand low-risk socialized individuals. *Psychophysiology*, 37, 43–54.

Dishion, T. J., French, D. C., & Patterson, G. R. (1995). The development and ecology of antisocial behavior. In D. Cicchetti & D. J. Cohen (Eds.), *Developmental psychopathology: Vol. 2, Risk, disorder, and adaptation* (pp. 421–471). New York: Wiley.

Dishion, T. J., Patterson, G. R., Stoolmuller, M., & Skinner, M. L. (1991). Family, school, and behavioral antecedents to early adolescent involvement with antisocial peers. *Developmental Psychology, 27*, 172–180.

Dix, D. (1992). Parenting on behalf of the child: Empathic goals in the regulation of responsive parenting. In E. Sigel, A. V. McGillicuddy-Delisi & J. J. Goodnow (Eds.), *Parental belief systems: The psychological consequences for children* (2nd ed., pp. 319–340). Mahwah, NJ: Lawrence Erlbaum Associates.

Dix, T. H. (1991). The affective organization of parenting: Adaptive and maladaptive processes. *Psychological Bulletin, 110*, 3–25.

Dixon, W., & Smith, P. (2003). Who's controlling whom? Infant contributions to maternal play behaviour. *Infant and Child Development, 12*, 177–195.

Dixon., W. F., Salley, B., & Clements, A. D. (2006). Temperament, distraction, and learning in toddlerhood. *Infant Behavior and Development, 29*, 342–357.

Dockrell, J. E. (2001). Assessing language skills in pre-school children. *Child Psychology and Psychiatry Review, 6*, 74–83.

Dodge, D. (2004). Human capital, early child development, and economic growth. In R. E. Tremblay, R. G. Barr, & R. DeV. Peters (Eds.), *Encyclopedia of early child development.* Montreal, Quebec: Centre for Excellence for Early Child Development.

Dodge, K. (1993). Social-cognitive mechanisms in the development of conduct disorder and depression. *Annual Review of Psychology, 44*, 559–584.

Dodge, K. A. (1991). The structure and function of reactive and proactive aggression. In D. J. Pepler & K. H. Rubin (Eds.), *The development and treatment of childhood aggression* (pp. 201–218). Hillsdale, NJ: Lawrence Erlbaum Associates.

Dodge, K. A. (1993). Social-cognitive mechanisms in the development of conduct disorder and depression. *Annual Review of Psychology, 44*, 559–584.

Dodge, K. A. & Frame, C. (1982). Social cognitive biases and deficits in aggressive boys. *Child Development, 53*, 620–635.

Dodge, K. A., Greenberg, M. T., Malone, P. J., & Conduct Problems Prevention Research Group (2008). Testing an idealised dynamic cascade model of the development of serious violence in adolescence. *Child Development, 79*, 1907–1927.

Dodge, K. A., & Rabiner, D. (2004). Returning to roots: On social information processing and moral development. *Child Development, 75*, 1003–1008.

Doherty, G. (2001). *Zero to Six: The basis for school readiness.* Hull, Quebec: Applied Research Branch, Human Resources Development Canada.

Doidge, N. (2010). *The brain that changes itself (rev. ed.).* Victoria, Australia: Scribe Publications Limited.

Dole, N., Savitz, D. A., Hertz-Picciotto, L., & Siega-Riz, A. M. (2003). Maternal stress and preterm birth. *American Journal of Epidemiology, 86*, 715–725.

Doll, B., & Haack, M. K. (2005). Population-based strategies for identifying school wide problems. In R. Brown-Chidsey (Ed.), *Assessment for intervention: A problem-solving approach* (pp. 82–102). New York: Guilford.

Domitrovich, C. E., Cortes, R., & Greenberg, M. T. (2007). Improving young children's social and emotional competence: A randomized trial of the Preschool "PATHS" curriculum. *The Journal of Primary Prevention, 28*, 67–91.

Donnellan, M. B., Trzesniewski, K. H., Robins, R. W., Moffitt, T. E., & Caspi, A. (2006). Low self-esteem is related to aggression, antisocial behavior, and delinquency. *Psychological science, 16*, 328–335.

Donzella, B., Gunnar, M. R., Krueger, W. K., & Alwin, J. (2000). Cortisol and vagal tone responses to competitive challenges in preschoolers: Associations with temperament. *Developmental Psychobiology, 37*, 209–220.

Douglas, V. I. (1972). Stop, look, and listen: The problem of sustained attention and impulse control in hyperactive and normal children. *Canadian Journal of Behavioural Science, 4*, 259–282.

Douglas, V. I. (1980). Higher mental processes in hyperactive children: Implications for training. In R. Knights & D. Bakker (Eds.), *Treatment of hyperactive and learning disordered children* (pp. 65–92). Baltimore: University Park Press.

Douglas, V. I., & Peters, K. G. (1979). Toward a clearer definition of the attentional deficit of hyperactive children. In G. A. Hale & M. Lewis (Eds.), *Attention and the development of cognitive skills* (pp. 173–248). New York: Plenum.

Doumen, S. Verchueren, K., Buyse, E., Germeijs, V., Luyckx, K., & Soenens, B. (2008). Reciprocal relations between teacher-child conflict and aggressive behavior in kindergarten: A three-wave longitudinal study. *Journal of Clinical Child and Adolescent Psychology, 37*, 588–599.

Downey. L. (2007). *Calmer classrooms: A guide to working with traumatized children*. Melbourne, Victoria, Australia: Child Safety Commissioner.

Dozier, M., Higley, E., Albus, K. E., & Nutter, A. (2002). Intervening with foster infants' caregivers: Targeting three critical needs. *Infant Mental Health Journal, 23*, 541–554.

Dozier, M., Lindhiem, O., & Ackerman, J. P. (2005). Attachment and biobehavioral catch-up. In L. J. Berlin, Y. Ziv, L. Amaya-Jackson, & T. Greenberg (Eds.), *Enhancing early attachments: Theory, research, and policy* (pp. 178–194). New York: Guilford Press.

Dozier, M., Lindhiem, O., Lewis, E., Bick, J., Bernard, K., & Pelosa, E. (2009). Effects of a foster parent training program on young children's attachment behaviors: Preliminary evidence from a randomized clinical trial. *Child and Adolescent Social Work Journal, 26*, 321–332.

Dozier, M., & Rutter, M. (2008). Challenges to the development of attachment relationships faced by young children in foster and adoptive care. In J. Cassidy & P. R. Shaver, *Handbook of attachment: Theory, research, and clinical applications* (pp. 698–717). New York: Guilford Press.

Dozier, M., & Sepulveda, S. (2004). Foster mother state of mind and treatment use: Different challenges for different people. *Infant Mental Health Journal, 25*, 368–378.

Drabick, D. A., Gadow, K. D., & Sprafkin, J. (2006). Co-occurrence of conduct disorder and depression in a clinic-based sample of boys with ADHD. *Journal of Child Psychology and Psychiatry, 47*, 766–774.

Driscoll, K. C., & Pianta, R. C. (2010). Banking time in Head Start: Early efficacy of an intervention designed to promote supportive teacher-child relationships. *Early Education and Development, 21*, 38–64.

Ducharme, J. M., Atkinson, L., & Poulton, L. (2000). Success-based noncoercive treatment of oppositional behavior in children from violent homes. *Journal of the American Academy of Child and Adolescent Psychiatry, 39*, 995–1004.

Ducharme, J. M., Folino, A., & Derosie, J. (2008). Errorless acquiescence training: A keystone approach to building social skills in children with anti-social behavior. *Behavior Modification, 2*, 39–60.

Dunford, C., Missiuna, C., Street, E., & Sibert, J. (2005) Children's perceptions of the impact of developmental coordination disorder on activities of living. *British Journal of Occupational Therapy, 68*(5), 207–214.

Dunn, B. (1993). Growing up with a schizophrenic mother: A retrospective study. *Journal of Orthopsychiatry, 63*, 177–189.

Dunn, J. (2007). Siblings and socialization. In J. E. Grusec & P. D. Hastings (Eds.), *Handbook of socialization: Theory and research* (pp. 309–327). New York: Guilford Press.

Dunn, J., Brown, J. R., & Beardsall, L. A. (1991). Family talk about emotions, and children's later understanding of others' emotions. *Developmental Psychology, 27*, 448–455.

Dunn, L. M., & Dunn, L. M. (2007). *Peabody Picture Vocabulary Test* (4th ed.) (PPVT-4). San Antonio, TX: Pearson.

Dunn, W. (1997). The Sensory Profile: A discriminating measure of sensory processing in daily life. *Sensory Integration Quarterly, 20*, 1–3.

Dunn, W. (1999) *Sensory profile: User's manual*. San Antonio, TX: Psychological Corporation.

Dunn, W. (2000). Habit: What's the brain got to do with it? *The Occupational Therapy Journal of Research, 20*, 6–20.

Dunn, W. (2001). The sensation of everyday life: Empirical, theoretical, and pragmatic considerations. *The American Journal of Occupational Therapy, 55*(6), 608–620.

Dunn, W. (2002). *Infant Toddler Sensory Profile Manual*. San Antonio, TX: Psychological Corporation.

Dunn, W. (2004). A sensory processing approach to supporting infant-caregiver relationships. In Sameroff, A. J., McDonough, S. L., & Rosenblur, K. L. (Eds.), *Treating parent-infant relationship problems: Strategies for intervention* (pp. 152–187). New York: Guilford Press.

Dunn, W. (2006). *Sensory profile-school companion manual*. San Antonio, TX: PsychCorp.

Dunn, W., & Bennett, D. (2002). Patterns of sensory processing in children with Attention Deficit Hyperactivity Disorder. *Occupational Participation and Health, 22*, 4–15.

Dunst, C., Trivette, C. M. & Thompson, R. B. (1991). Supporting and strengthening family functioning: Towards a congruence between principles and practice. *Prevention in Human Services, 9*, 19–43.

Earlscourt and Family Centre. (2001). *SNAP children's group manual*. Toronto, ON: Earlscourt Child and Family Centre.

Eckert, M. A, Leonard, C. M., Richards, T. L., Aylward, E. H., Thomson, J., & Berninger, V. W. (2003). Anatomical correlates of dyslexia: Frontal and cerebellar findings. *Brain, 126*, 482–494.

Edwards, S. L., Rapee, R. M., & Kennedy, S. (2010). Prediction of anxiety symptoms in preschool-aged children: Examination of maternal and paternal perspectives. *Journal of Child Psychology and Psychiatry and Allied Disciplines, 51*, 313–321.

Egger, H. L., & Angold, A. (2006). Common emotional and behavioural disorder in preschool children: Presentation, nosology, and epidemiology. *Journal of Child Psychology and Psychiatry and Allied Disciplines, 142*, 313–337.

Egger, H. L., & Angold, A. (2009). Classification of psychopathology in early childhood. In C. H. Zeanah, Jr. (Ed.), *Handbook of infant mental health* (3rd ed., pp. 285–300). New York: Guilford Publishers.

Egger, H. L., Erkanli, A., Keeler, G., Potts, E., Walter, B. K., & Angold, A. (2006). Test-retest reliability of the Preschool Age Psychiatric Assessment (PAPA). *Journal of the American Academy of Child and Adolescent Psychiatry, 45*, 538–549.

Egger, H. L., Kondo, D., & Angold, A. (2006). The epidemiology and diagnostic issues in preschool ADHD: A review. *Infants and Young Children, 19*, 106–122.

Eisen, P. R., Raleigh, H., & Neuhoff, C. C. (2008). The unique impact of parent training for separation anxiety disorder in children. *Behavior Therapy, 39*, 195–206.

Eisenberg, N., Cumberland, A., Spinrad, T. L., Fabes, R. A., Shepard, S. A., & Reiser, M. (2001). The relations of regulation and emotionality to children's externalizing and internalizing problem behavior. *Child Development, 72*, 1112–1134.

Eisenberg, N., Hofer, C., & Vaughan, J. (2007). Effortful control and its socioemotional consequences. In J. J. Gross (Ed.), *Handbook of emotion regulation* (pp. 287–306). New York: Guilford Press.

Eisenberg, N., Liew, J., & Pidada, S. U. (2004). The longitudinal relationship of regulation and emotionality to quality of children's socioemotional functioning. *Journal of Personality and Child Social Psychology, 78*, 136–157.

Eisenberg, N., Valiente, C., Spinrad, T. L., Cumberland, A., Liew, J., Reiser, M., … Cumberland, A. (2009). Longitudinal relations of children's effortful control, impulsivity, and negative emotionality to their externalizing, and co-occurring behavior problems. *Developmental Psychology, 45*, 988–1008.

Elbe, S., Andrade, B., Schmidt, N. L., & Thomson, D. (2010). *The evaluation of Coping Power within CONNECT: The effectiveness of an evidence-based treatment for aggressive behavior as implemented within an existing children's mental health program*. Report submitted to Provincial Centre for Excellence in Children's Mental Health, Ontario.

Elbert, T., Pantev, C., Wienbruch, C., Rockstroh, B., & Taub, E. (1995). Increased cortical representation of the fingers of the left hand of string players. *Science, 270*, 305–307.

Ellis, B. J., Boyce, W. T., Belsky, J., Bakermans-Kranenburg, M. J., & Van IJzendoorn, M. H. (2011). Differential susceptibility to the environment: An evolutionary-neurodevelopmental theory. In B. J. Ellis & W. T. Boyce (Eds.), *Special section: Differential susceptibility to the environment*. In D. Cicchetti (Ed.), *Development and Psychopathology, 23*(1), 7–28.

Ellis, W. E., & Zarbatany, L. (2007). Peer group status as a moderator of group influence on children's deviant aggressive and prosocial behavior. *Child Development, 78*, 1240–1254.

Emde, R. N. (2003). RDC—PA: A major step forward on some issues. *Journal of the American Academy of Child and Adolescent Psychiatry, 42*, 1513–1576.

Emslie, G. J., Portteus, A. M., Kumar, E. C., & Hume, J. H. (2004). Antidepressants: SSRIs and novel atypical antidepressants—An update on psychopharmacology. In H. Steiner (Ed.), *Handbook of mental health interventions in children and adolescents: An integrated developmental approach* (pp. 318–362). San Francisco, CA: Jossey-Bass.

Emslie, H., Wilson, F. C., Burden, V., Nimmo-Smith, I., & Wilson, B. A. (2003). *Behavioral Assessment of the Dysexecutive Syndrome in Children* (BADS-C). San Antonio, TX: Pearson.

Engel, S. (1995). *The stories children tell: Making sense of the narrative of children*. New York: W. H. Freeman and Co.

English, D. J., Upadhyaya, M. P., Litrownik, A. J., Marshall, J. M., Runyan, D. K., Graham, J. C., & Dubowitz, H. (2005). Maltreatment's wake: The relationship of maltreatment dimensions to child outcomes. *Child Abuse & Neglect Special Issue: Longitudinal studies of child abuse and neglect (LONGSCAN), 29*, 597–619.

Ernst, M., Zametkin, A. J., Matochik, J. A., Pascualvaca, D., Jones, P. H., & Cohen, R. M. (1999). High midbrain (18F) DOPA accumulation in children with attention deficit hyperactivity disorder. *American Journal of Psychiatry, 156*, 1209–1715.

Ernst, M., & Zametkin, J. (1995). The interface of genetics, neuroimaging, and neurochemistry in attention-deficit hyperactivity disorder. In F. Bloom & D. Kupfer (Eds.), *Psychopharmacology: The fourth generation of progress* (pp. 1643–1652). New York: Raven Press.

Esbjorn, B. H., Hansen, B. M., Greisen, G., & Mortensen, E. L. (2006). Intellectual development in a Danish cohort of prematurely born preschool children: Specific or general difficulties? *Developmental and Behavioral Pediatrics, 27*, 477–484.

Eslinger, P., Biddle, K., & Grattan, L. (1997). Cognitive and social development in children with prefrontal lesions. In N. Krasnegor, G. Lyon, & P. Goldman-Rakic (Eds.), *Development of the prefrontal cortex: Evolution, neurobiology, and behaviour* (pp. 295–336). Baltimore, MA: Paul H. Brookes Publishing.

Esparo, G., Canals, J., & Jane, C. (2004). Feeding problems in nursery school children: Prevalence and psychosocial factors. *Acta Paediatrica, 93*, 663–668.

Espelage, D. L., Holt, M. K., & Henkel. R. (2003). Examination of peer-group contextual effects on aggression during early adolescence. *Child Development, 74*, 205–220.

Essau, C. A., Sasagawa, S, & Frick, P. J. (2006). Callous-unemotional traits in a community sample of adolescents. *Assessment, 13*, 454–469.

Essex, M. J., Armstrong, J. M., Burk, L. R., Goldsmith, H. H., & Boyce, W. T. (2011). Biological sensitivity to context moderates the effects of the early teacher-child relationship on the development of mental health in adolescence. *Development and Psychopathology, 23*, 149–161.

Estes, E. L. (2010). Listening, language and learning skills of highly qualified listening and spoken language specialists in educational settings. *The Volta review, 110*, 169–178.

Etkin, A., & Wagner, T. D. (2007). Functional neuroimaging of anxiety: A meta-analysis of emotional processing in PTSD, social anxiety disorder, and specific phobia. *American Journal of Psychiatry, 164*, 1476–1488.

Eyberg, S. (1988). Parent-Child Interaction Therapy: Integration of traditional and behavioral concerns. *Child and Family Behavior Therapy, 10*, 33–46.

Fabes, R. A., Poulin, R. E., Eisenberg, N., & Madden-Derdich, D. A. (2002). The coping with children's negative emotions scale (CCNES): Psychometric properties and relations with children's emotional competence. *Marriage and Family Review, 34*(3/4), 285–311.

Faja, S., & Dawson, G. (2006). Early intervention for autism. In J. Luby (Ed.), *Handbook of preschool mental health: Developmental disorders and treatment* (pp. 388–416). New York: Guilford Press.

Faraone, S. V. (2004). Genetics of adult attention-deficit/hyperactivity disorder. *Psychiatric Clinics of North America, 27,* 303–321.

Faraone, S. V., Perlis, R. H., Doyle, A. E., Smoller, J. W., Goralnick, J., Holmgren, M. A., & Sklar, P. (2005). Molecular genetics of attention-deficit/hyperactivity disorder. *American Journal of Psychiatry, 158,* 1052–1057.

Faraone, S.V., Sergeant, J., Gillberg, C., & Biederman, J. (2003). The worldwide prevalence of ADHD; is it an American condition? *World Psychiatry, 2,* 104–113.

Farb, N. A., Anderson, A. K., Mayberg, H., Bean, J., McKeon, D., & Segal, Z. V. (2010). Minding one's emotions: Mindfulness training alters the neural expression of sadness. *Emotion, 10,* 25–33.

Farrant, B. M., Fletcher, J., & Maybery, T. (2006). Specific language impairment, theory of mind and visual perspective taking: Evidence for simulation theory and the developmental role of language. *Child Development, 77,* 1842–1853.

Farrar, M. J., & Maag, L. (2002). Early Language Development and the emergence of theory of mind. *First Language, 22,* 197–213.

Farrell, A., & Bruce, S. (1997). Impact of exposure to community violence on violent behavior and emotional distress among urban adolescents. *Journal of Clinical Child Psychology, 24,* 26–43.

Faught, B. E., Hay, J. A. Cairney, J., & Flouris, (2005). Increased risk for coronary vascular disease in children with developmental coordination disorder. *Journal of Adolescent Health,* 37, 376–380.

Fearon, R. P., Bakersmans-Kranenburg, M. J., van IJzendoorn, M. H., Lapsley, A-M., & Roisman, G. I. (2010). The significance of insecure attachment and disorganization in the development of children's externalizing behavior: A meta-analytic study. *Child Development, 81,* 435–456.

Feingold, B. (1975). *Why your child is hyperactive.* New York: Random House.

Feldman, H. M. (2005). Evaluation and management of language and speech disorders in preschool children. *Pediatrics in Review, 26,* 130–141.

Feldman, R. (2007a). Maternal versus child risk and the development of parent-child and family relationships in five high-risk populations. *Development and Psychopathology, 19*(2), 293–312.

Feldman, R. (2007b). Parent-infant synchrony and the construction of shared timing: Physiological precursors, developmental outcomes and risk conditions. *Journal of Child Psychology and Psychiatry, 48*(3/4), 329–354

Feldman, R. (2009). The development of regulatory functions from birth to 5 years: Insights from premature infants. *Child Development 80*(2), 544–561.

Felitti, V. J., Anda, R. F., Nordenberg, D., Williamson, D. F., Spitz, A. M., Edwards, V., … Marks, J. S. (1998). Relationship of childhood abuse and household dysfunction to many of the leading causes of death in adults: The Adverse Childhood Experiences (ACE) Study. *American Journal of Preventive Medicine, 14*(4), 245–258.

Fellitti, V. J., Anda, R. F., Nordenberg, D., Williamson, D. F., Spitz, A. M., Edwards, V., ... Marks, J. S. (1997). Relationship of childhood abuse and household dysfunction to many of the leading causes of death in adults: The Adverse Childhood Experiences (ACE) Study. *American Journal of Preventive Medicine, 14,* 245–258.

Fenson, L., Marchman, V. A., Thal, D., Dale, P. S., Resnick, I. S., & Bates, E. (2006). *MacArthur-Bates Communicative Development Inventories* (CDIs) (2nd ed.). Baltimore, MD: Paul H. Brookes Publishing.

Fergusson, D. M., & Lynskey, M. T. (1997). Early reading difficulties and later conduct problems. *Journal of Child Psychology and Psychiatry, 38,* 899–907.

Fertel-Daly, D., Bedell, G., & Hinojosa, J. (2001). Effects of a weighted vest on attention to task and self-stimulatory behaviors in preschoolers with pervasive developmental disorders. *American Journal of Occupational Therapy, 55,* 629–640.

Fey, M. E., Catts, H. W., Proctor-Williams, K., Tomblin, J. B., & Zhang, X. (2004). Oral and written story composition skills of children with language impairment. *Journal of Speech, Language and Hearing Research, 47,* 1301–1318.

Fey, M. E., Cleare, P., Long, S., & Hughes, D. (1993). Two approaches to the facilitation of grammar in children with language impairment: an experimental evaluation. *Journal of Speech and Hearing Research, 36,* 141–157.

Field, T., Hernandez-Reif, M., & Diego, M. (2006). Intrusive and withdrawn depressed mothers and their infants. *Developmental Review, 26,* 15–30.

Field, T., Hernandez-Reif, M., Diego, M., Feijo, L., Vera, Y., & Gil, K. (2004). Massage therapy by parents improves early growth and development. *Infant Behavior and Development, 27,* 435–442.

Field, T. M. (1998a). Maternal depression effects on infants and early interventions. *Preventive Medicine, 27*, 200–203.
Field, T. M. (1998b). Touch therapies. In R. R. Hoffman, M. F. Sherrick, & J. J. Warm (Eds.), *Viewing psychology as a whole: The integrative science of William N. Dember* (pp. 603–624). Washington, DC: American Psychological Association.
Field, T. M. (2000). Infant massage therapy. In C. H. Zeanah, Jr. (Ed.), *Handbook of infant mental health* (2nd ed., pp. 494–500). New York: Guilford Press.
Filipek, P. A., Semrud-Clikeman, M., Steingard, R. J., Renshaw, P. F., Kennedy, D. N., & Biederman, J. (1997). Volumetric MRI analysis comparing subjects having attention-deficit hyperactivity disorder with normal controls. *Neurology, 48*, 589–601.
Finnegan, R. A., Hodges, E. V. E., & Perry, D. G. (1996). Preoccupied and avoidant coping during middle childhood. *Child Development, 67*, 1318–1328.
Firth, U. (1989). *Autism: Explaining the enigma*. Oxford: Blackwell Publishing.
Fisher, A., Murray, E., & Bundy, A. (1991). *Sensory integration: Theory and practice*. Philadelphia: F. A. Davis.
Fisher, S. E., & DeFries, J. C. (2002). Developmental dyslexia: Genetic dissection of a complex cognitive trait. *Nature Review Neuroscience, 3*, 767–780.
Flanagan, D. P., & Ortiz, S. O. (2007). *Essentials of cross-battery assessment*. Hoboken, NJ: John Wiley & Sons, Inc.
Fletcher, J. M., Lyon, G. R., Fuchs, L. S., & Barnes, M. A. (2007). *Learning disabilities: From identification to intervention*. New York: Guilford.
Fletcher, K. E. (1992). *Dimensions of Traumatic Events (DOSE). Exposure questionnaire*. Available from Kenneth.Fletcher@umassmed.edu
Fletcher, K. E. (2003). Childhood posttraumatic stress disorder. In E. J. Mash & R. A. Barkley (Eds.), *Child psychopathology* (2nd ed., pp. 330–371). New York: Guilford Press.
Folio, M. R., & Fewell, R. R. (2000*). Peabody developmental motor scales (2nd edition) (PDMS-2)*. Western Psychological Services: Torance, CA.
Fonagy, P. (1999). *Transgenerational consistencies of attachment: A new theory*. Retrieved from www.dspp.com/papers/fonagy
Fonagy, P., Gergely, G., Jurist, E. L., & Target, M. (2002). *Affect regulation, mentalisation, and the development of the self*. New York: Other Press.
Fonagy, P., Steele, H., & Steele, M. (1991). Maternal representations of attachment during pregnancy predict the organisation of infant-mother attachment at one year of age. *Child Development, 62*, 891–905.
Fonagy, P., Steele, H., Steele, M., Leigh, T., Kennedy, R., Mattoon, G., & Target, M. (1995). Attachment, the reflective self, and borderline states: The predictive specificity of the Adult Attachment Interview and pathological emotional development. In S. Goldberg, R. Muir, & J. Kerr (Eds.), *Attachment theory: Social, developmental, and clinical perspectives* (pp. 233–278). New York: Analytic Press.
Fonagy, P., Steele, M., Steele, H., Moran, G. S., & Higgit, A. C. (1991). The capacity for understanding mental states: The refl ective self in parent and child and its signifi cance for security of attachment. *Infant Mental Health Journal*, 12, 201–218.
Fonagy, P., & Target, M. (2005). Bridging the transmission gap: An end to an important mystery of attachment research. *Attachment and Human Development, 7*, 333–343.
Fonagy, P., Target, M., Cottrell, D., Phillips, J., & Kurtz, Z. (2000). *A review of the outcomes of psychiatric disorder in childhood: MCH 17–33. Final report to the National Health Service Executive*.
Fontaine, N. M. G., Carbonneau, R., Vitaro, F., Barker, E. D., & Tremblay, R. E. (2009). Research review: A critical review of studies on the developmental trajectories of antisocial behavior in females. *The Journal of Child Psychology and Psychiatry, 50*, 363–385.
Fontaine, N. M. G., Rijsdijk, F. V., McCrary, E. J. P., & Viding, E. (2010). Etiology of different developmental trajectories of callous-unemotional traits. *Journal of the American Academy of Child & Adolescent Psychiatry, 49*, 656–664.
Ford, J. D. (2005). Treatment implications of attuned neurobiology, affect regulation, and information processing following child maltreatment. *Psychiatric Annals, 35*, 410–421.
Ford, J. D., Albert, D. B., & Hawke, J. (2009). Interventions for traumatized children: Restoring children's capacity for self-regulation. In D. Brom, R. Pat-Horenczyk, & J. D. Ford (Eds.), *Treating traumatized children: Risk, resilience, and recovery* (pp. 197–209). New York: Routledge.

Ford, J. D., Mahoney, K., Juste, M. C., & Hennessey, L. P. C. (2005). Target-A-Life Skills program. TARGET@Psychiatry.uchc.edu

Ford, J., & Milosky, L. (2008). Inference generation during discourse and its relation to social competence: An on-line investigation of abilities of children with and without language impairment. *Journal of Speech, Language, and Hearing Research, 51*, 367–380.

Fordham, K., & Stevenson-Hinde, I. (1999). Shyness, friendship quality, and adjustment during middle childhood. *Journal of Child Psychology and Psychiatry, 40*, 757–768.

Forehand, R. L., & McMahon, R. J. (1981). *Helping the non-compliant child: A clinician's guide to parent training*. New York, NY: Guilford Publishing.

Forgatch, M. S. (1991). The clinical science vortex: A developing theory of antisocial behavior. In D. Peplar & R. H. Rubin (Eds.), *The development and treatment of childhood aggression* (pp. 291–315). Hillsdale, NJ: Erlbaum.

Forgatch, M. S., & de Garmo, D. S. (1999). Parenting through change: An effective prevention program for single mothers. *Journal of Consulting and Clinical Psychology, 67*, 711–724.

Forman, E.M., & Davies, P.T. (2003). Family instability and young adolescent maladjustment: The mediating effects of parenting quality and adolescents appraisals of family security. *Journal of Clinical Child and Adolescent Psychology, 32*, 94–105.

Fosha, D. (2003). Dyadic regulation and experiential work with emotion and relatedness in trauma and disorganized attachment. In M. E. Solomon & D. J. Siegel (Eds.), *Healing trauma: Attachment, mind, body, and brain* (pp. 221–281). New York: W.W. Norton.

Foss, A., Swinth, Y., McGruder, J., & Tomlin, G. (2003). Sensory modulation dysfunction and the Wilbarger Protocol: An evidence review. *OT Practice, 8*(12), 1–8.

Foulder-Hughes, L. A., & Cooke, R. W. (2003). Motor, cognitive, and behavioral disorders in children born very preterm. *Developmental Medicine and Child Neurology, 5*, 97–103.

Fowles, D. C., & Kochanska, D. S. (2000). Temperament as a moderator of pathways to conscience in children: The contribution of electrodermal reactivity to emotional signals. *Psychophysiology, 37*, 788–795.

Fox, N. A. (1991). If it's not left, it's right: Electroencephalogram asymmetry and the development of emotion. *American Psychologist, 46*, 863–872.

Fox, N. A. (1994). Dynamic cerebral processes underlying emotion regulation. In N. A. Fox (Ed.), The development of emotion regulation: Biological and behavioral considerations. *Monographs of the Society for Research in Child Development, 59*(2–3, Serial No. 240), 152–166.

Fox, N. A., Henderson, H. A., Rubin, K. H., Calkins, S. D., & Schmidt, L. A. (2001). Continuity and discontinuity of behavioral inhibition and exuberance: Psycho-physiological and behavioral influences across the first 4 years of life. *Child Development, 72*, 1–12.

Fraiberg, S. (1980). *Clinical studies in infant mental health*. New York: Basic Books.

Francks, C., Fisher, S. E., Marlow, A. J., MacPhie, I. L., Taylor, K. E., Richardson, A. J., ... Monaco, A. P. (2003). Familial and genetic effects on motor coordination, laterality and reading-related cognition. *American Journal of Psychiatry, 160*, 1970–1977.

Frank, D. A., Augustine, M., Knight, W. G., Pell, T., & Zuckerman, P. (2001). Growth, development, and behaviour in early childhood following prenatal cocaine exposure: A systematic review. *The Journal of the American Medical Association, 285*, 1613–1625.

Franklin, L., Dietx, J., Jirikowic, T., & Astley, S. (2008). Children with fetal alcohol spectrum disorders: Problem behaviours and sensory processing. *The American Journal of Occupational Therapy, 62*, 265–273.

Fredrickson, B. L. (2001). The role of positive emotions in positive psychology: The Broaden-and-Build Theory of positive emotions. *American Psychologist, 56*(3) 218–226.

Freud, S. (1919/1954). *Introduction to psychoanalysis and the war neuroses*. Translated and edited by Strachey. London, UK: Hogarth Press.

Frick, P. J. (1998). *Conduct disorders and severe antisocial behavior*. New York: Plenum Press.

Frick, P. J. (2006). Developmental pathways to conduct disorder. *Child Psychiatric Clinics of North America, 15*, 311–332.

Frick, P. J., Bodin, S. D., &, Barry, C. (2000). Psychopathic traits and conduct problems in community and clinic-referred samples of children: Further development of the Psychopathy Screening Device. *Psychological Assessment, 12*, 382–393.

Frick, P. J., Cornell, A. H., Bodin, S. D., Dane, H. A., Barry, C., & Loney, B. R. (2003). Callous-unemotional traits developmental pathways to severe aggressive and antisocial behavior. *Developmental Psychology, 39*, 246–260.

Frick, P. J., & Hare, R. D. (2001). *Antisocial Process Screening Device (APSD): Technical Manual*. North Tonawanda, NY: Multi-Health Systems (MHS) Inc.

Frick, P. J., & Marsee, M. A. (2006). Psychopathy and developmental pathways to antisocial behavior in youth. In C. J. Patrick (Ed.), *Handbook of psychopathy* (pp. 355–374). New York: Guilford Press.

Frick, P. J., & Morris, A. S. (2004). Temperament and developmental pathways to conduct problems. *Journal of Clinical child and Adolescent Psychology, 33*, 54–68.

Frick, P. J., & Viding, E. (2009). Antisocial behavior from a developmental psychopathology perspective. *Development and Psychopathology 21*(4), 1111–1132.

Frick, P. J., & White, S. F. (2008). Research review: The importance of callous-unemotional traits for developmental models of aggressive and antisocial behavior. *Journal of Child Psychology and Psychiatry, 49*, 359–375.

Fried, P., & Watkinson, B. (2000). Visuo-perceptual functioning differs in 9- to 12-year olds prenatally exposed to cigarettes and marijuana. *Neurotoxicology and Teratology, 22*, 11–20.

Friederici, A. D. (2004). Event-related brain potential studies in language. *Current Neurological Neuroscience Reports, 4*, 466–470.

Friederici, A. D., Opitz, B., & von Cramon, D. Y. (2000). Segregating semantic and syntactic aspects of processing in the human brain: An fMRI investigation of different word types. *Cerebral Cortex, 10*, 698–705.

Friedli, L. (2009). *Mental health, resilience, and inequalities*. World Health Organization Europe. http://mentalhealth.org.uk/welcome

Friedman, M., & Schnurr, P. (1995). The relationship between trauma, post-traumatic stress disorder, and physical health. In Friedman, M., Charney, D., & Deutch, A. (Eds.), *Neurobiological and clinical consequences of stress: From normal adaptation to PTSD* (pp. 518–524). Philadelphia: Lippincott-Raven Publishers.

Friedman, M. J., & McEwen, B. S. (2004). PTSD, allostatic load, and mental illness. In P. P. Schnurr & B. I. Green (Eds.), *Trauma and health consequences of exposure to extreme stress* (pp. 157–188). Washington, DC: American Psychological Association.

Frijda, N. H. (1993). Moods, emotion episodes, and emotions. In M. Lewis and J. M. Haviland (Eds.), *Handbook of emotions* (pp. 381–403). New York: Guilford Press.

Fristad, M. A., Goldberg-Arnold, J. S., & Gavazzi, S. M. (2003). Multi-family psycho-education groups in the treatment of children with mood disorders. *Journal of Mental Family Therapy, 29*, 491–504.

Fuchs, D., & Deshler, D. D. (2007). What we need to know about responsiveness to intervention (and shouldn't be afraid to ask). *Learning Disabilities Research & Practice, 22*, 129–136.

Fuchs, D., Fuchs, L. S., Mathes, P., & Simmons, D. (1997). Peer-assisted learning strategies: Making classrooms more responsive to student diversity. *American Educational Research Journal, 34*, 174–206. Fuchs, LS., & Fuchs, D. (1998). Treatment validity: A simplifying concept for re-conceptualizing the identification of learning disabilities. *Learning Disabilities Research & Practice, 4*, 204–219.

Fuchs, L. S. (2003). Assessing intervention responsiveness: Conceptual and technical issues. *Learning Disabilities Research & Practice, 18*, 172–186.

Fujiki, M., Brinton, B., & Clarke, D. (2002). Emotion regulation in children with specific language impairment. *Language, Speech, and Hearing Services in Schools*, 33, 102–111.

Fujiki, M., Brinton, B., Morgan, M., & Hart, C. H. (1999). Withdrawn and sociable behavior of children with specific language impairment. *Language, Speech and Hearing Services in Schools, 30*, 183–195.

Fujiki, M., Brinton, B., & Todd, C. M. (1996). Social skills of children with specific language impairment. *Language, Speech, and Hearing Services in Schools, 27*, 195–202.

Fujiki, M., Spackman, M. P., Brinton, B., & Illig, T. (2008). Ability of children with language impairment to understand emotion conveyed by prosody in a narrative passage. *International Journal of Language and Communication Disorders, 43, 330–345.*

Fury, G., Carlson, E. A. & Sroufe, A. (1997). Children's representations of attachment relationships in family drawings. *Child Development, 68*, 1154–1164.

Gahagan, S. (2006). Failure to thrive: A consequence of undernutrition. *Pediatrics in Review, 27*. E1-e11. doi: 10.154z/pir.27-1-e1

Galantino, M., Galbavy, R., & Quinn, L. (2008). Therapeutic effects of yoga for children: A systematic review of the literature. *Pediatric Physical Therapy, 20*, 66–80.

Gallagher, T. M. (1996). Social-interactional approaches to child language intervention. In J. H. Bietchman, N. Cohen, M. M. Konstantareas, & R. Tannock (Eds.), *Language, learning and behavior disorders: Developmental, biological and clinical perspectives* (pp. 418–435). Cambridge, UK: Cambridge University Press.

Gallese, V., Fadiga, L., Fogassi, L., & Rizzolatti, G. (1996). Action recognition in the premotor cortex. *Brain, 119*, 593–609.

Gao, Y., Raine, A., Venables, P. H., Dawson, M. E., & Mednick, S. A. (2010). Reduced electrodermal fear conditioning from ages 3 to 8 years is associated with aggressive behavior at age 8 years. *The Journal of Child Psychology and Psychiatry, 51*, 550–558.

Gar, N. S., & Hudson, J. L. (2009). The association between maternal anxiety and treatment outcome for childhood anxiety disorders. *Behavior Change, 26*, 1–15.

Gartstein, M., & Fagot, B. (2003). Parental depression, parenting, family adjustment and child effortful control: Explaining externalising behaviours for preschool children. *Journal of Applied Developmental Psychology, 241*, 143–177.

Gascoigne, M. (2006). *Supporting children with speech, language and communication needs within integrated children's services*. [RCSLT Position Paper, RCSLT: London]. Retrieved from www.rcslt.org

Ge, X., Brody, G. H., Conger, R. D., Simons, R. L., & Murray, V. M. (2002). Contextual amplification of pubertal transition effects on deviant peer affiliation and externalising behavior among African American children. *Developmental Psychology, 38*, 42–54.

Geller, E., & Foley, G. M. (2009). Expanding the "Ports of Entry" for speech-language pathologists: A relational and reflective model for clinical practice. *American Journal of Speech-Language Pathology, 18*, 4–21.

George, C., Kaplan, N., & Main, M. (1996). *Adult attachment interview: Interview protocol* (3rd ed.). Unpublished manuscript, University of California at Berkeley.

George, C., & Solomon, J. (1990/2000). *Six year old attachment doll play classification system*. Unpublished manuscript, Mills College, Oakland, CA.

Gershenson, R. A., Lyon, A. R., Budd, K. S. (2010). Promoting positive interactions in the classroom: Adapting parent-child interaction therapy as a universal prevention program. *Education and Treatment of Children, 33*, 261–287.

Gershoff, E. T. (2002). Physical punishment by parents and associated child behaviors and experiences: A meta-analytic and theoretical review. *Psychological Bulletin, 128*, 539–579.

Gessell, A. (1928). *Infancy and human growth*. New York: Macmillan.

Ghaziuddin, M, Tsai, L., & Ghazuiddin, N. (1994). Clumsiness a marker for Asperger's Syndrome? *Journal of Intellectual Disability Research, 38*, 519–527.

Ghosh Ippen, C., Ford, J., Racusin, R., Acker, M., Bosquet, M., Rogers, K., ... Edwards, J. (2002). *Traumatic events screening inventory-parent report revised C*. Dartmouth, VT: National Center for PTSD Dartmouth Child Trauma Research Group.

Gibson-Davis, C. M., & Gassman-Pines, A. (2010). Early childhood family structure and mother-child interactions: Variation by race and ethnicity. *Developmental Psychology, 46*, 151–164.

Gidden, J. (1991). School children with emotional problems and communication deficits: Implications for speech language pathologists. *Language Speech and Hearing Services in Schools, 22*, 291–295.

Gifford-Smith, M. E., & Rabiner, D. L. (2004). Social information processing and children's social competence: A review of the literature. In K. A. Dodge, & J. Kupersmidt (Eds.), *Children's peer relations: From development to intervention to policy* (pp. 61–80). Washington, DC: APA.

Gil, E. (2006). *Helping abused and traumatized children: Integrating directive and non-directive approaches*. New York: Guilford Press.

Gilbertson, M. W., Shenton, M. E., & Ciszewski, A. (2002). Smaller hippocampal volume predicts pathologic vulnerability to psychological trauma. *Nature and Neuroscience, 5*, 1242–1247.

Giles-Sims, J., Straus, M. A., & Sugarman, D. B. (1995). Child, maternal and family characteristics associated with spanking. *Family Relations: Journal of Applied Family and Child Studies, 44*, 170–176.

Gill, C. B., Klecan-Aker, J., Roberts, T., & Fredenburg, K. A.,(2003). Following directions: Rehearsal and visualization strategies for children with specific language impairment. *Child Language Teaching and Therapy, 19*(1) 88–103.

Gilliom, M., Shaw, D. S., Beck, J. F., Schoenberg, M. A., & Lukon, J. L., (2002). Anger regulation in disadvantaged preschoolers: Strategies, antecedents, and the development of self-control. *Developmental Psychology, 38,* 222–235.

Gilmour, J., Hill, B., Place, M., & Skuse, D. H. (2004). Social communication deficits in conduct disorder: A clinical and community sample. *Journal of Child Psychology and Psychiatry, 45,* 967–978.

Ginsburg, G. S., Siueland, L., Masia-Warner, C., & Hedtke, K. A. (2004). Anxiety disorders in children: Family matters. *Cognitive and Behavioral Practice, 11,* 28–43.

Gioia, G. A., Isquith, P. K., Guy, S. C., & Kenworthy, L. (2000) *BRIEF: Behavior Rating Inventory of Executive Function: Professional manual.* Lutz, FL: Psychological Assessment Resources (PAR).

Gioia, G. A., Isquith, P. K., Kenworthy, L., & Barton, R. M. (2002). Profiles of everyday executive function in acquired and developmental disorders. *Child Neuropsychology, 8,* 121–137.

Girolametto, L., & Weitzman, E. (2007). Working with children with families with young children with communication and language impairment: Intervention promoting peer interaction skills. *Topics in Language Disorders, 27,* 93–120.

Gladstone, T. R., & Kaslow, N. J. (1995). Depression and attributions in children and adolescents: A meta-analytic review. *Journal of Abnormal Child Psychology, 23,* 597–606.

Gleason, M. M., Egger, H. L., Emslie, G. J., Greenhill, L. L., Kowatch, R. A., Lieberman, A. F., … Zeannah, C. H. (2007). Psychopharmacological treatment for very young children: Contexts and guidelines. *Journal of the American Academy of Child and Adolescent Psychiatry, 46*(12), 1532–1572.

Godwin-Emmons, P., and McKendry-Anderson, L. (2005). *Understanding sensory dysfunction: Learning, development and sensory dysfunction in autism spectrum disorders, ADHD, learning disabilities and bipolar disorders.* Philadelphia: Jessica Kingsley Publishers.

Goldapple, K., Segal, Z., Garson, C., Lau, M., Bieling, P., Kennedy, S., & Mayberg, H. (2004). Modulation of cortical-limbic pathways in major depression: treatment specific effects of cognitive behavior therapy. *Archives of General Psychiatry, 61,* 34–41.

Goldberg, E. (2001). *The executive brain: Frontal lobes and the civilized mind.* New York: Oxford University Press.

Goldberg, S., Gotowiec, A., & Simmons, R. J. (1995). Infant-mother attachment and behavior problems in healthy and chronically ill preschoolers. *Development and Psychopathology, 7,* 267–282.

Goldberg, S., MacKay-Soroka, J., & Rochester, J. (1994). Affect, attachment, and maternal responsiveness. *Infant Behavior and Development, 17,* 334–339.

Goldman, R., & Fristoe, M. (2000). *Goldman-Fristoe test of articulation* (2nd ed.) (G-F-TA-2). NCS-Pearson.

Goldstein, H., Kaczmarek, & English. (2002). *Promoting social communication: Children with developmental disabilities from birth to adolescence.* Baltimore, MD: Paul H. Brookes Publishers.

Goleman, D. (2006). *Social intelligence: The new science of social relationships.* London: Hutchinson.

Gomby, D. S. (2005). *Home visitation in 2005: Outcomes for children and parents.* Invest in Kids Working Paper No. 7, Toronto, ON.

Gondoli, D. M., & Braungart-Rieker, J. M. (1998). Constructs and processes in parental socialization of emotions. *Psychological Inquiry, 9,* 283–285.

Goodman, R., & Stevenson, J. (1989). A twin study of hyperactivity: The aetiological role of genes, family relationships and perinatal adversity. *Journal of Child Psychology and Psychiatry, 30,* 691–709.

Goodman, S. H., & Gotlieb, I. H. (2002). *Children of depressed parents: Mechanisms of risk and implications for treatment.* Washington, DC: American Psychological Association.

Goodyear-Brown, P. (2010). *Play therapy with traumatized children: A prescriptive approach.* Hoboken, NJ: John Wiley & Sons.

Gordon, M. (1983). *The Gordon diagnostic system.* DeWitt, NY: Gordon Systems.

Gorman-Smith, D., Henry, D. B., & Tolan, P. H. (2004). Exposure to community violence and violence perpetration: The protective effects of family functioning. *Journal of Clinical and Adolescent Psychology, 33,* 439–444.

Gottman, J. (1997). *Raising an emotionally intelligent child: The heart of parenting*. New York: Simon & Schuster.

Gottman, J. M., Katz, L. F., & Hooven, C. (1997). *Meta-emotion: How families communicate emotionally*. Mahwah, NJ: Lawrence Erlbaum Associates.

Gould, J. M., & Matz, P. S. (2010). Otitis Media. *Pediatrics in Review, 31*, 102–116.

Goyen, T-A., Lui, K., & Woods, R. (1998). Visual-motor, visual-perceptual, and fine motor outcomes in very-low-birthweight children at 5 years. *Developmental Medicine and Child Neurology, 40*, 76–81. [PubMed: 9489494]

Granot, D., & Mayseless, O. (2001). Attachment security and adjustment to school in middle childhood. *International Journal of Behavioral Development, 25*, 530–541.

Gravel, J. S., & Wallace, I. F. (1992).Effects of Otitis Media: Listening and language at 4 years of age. *Journal of Speech and Hearing Research, 35*, 588–595.

Gray, C. (2000). *The new social story book*. Future Horizons, Texas.

Gray, C. (2002). *My new social story book*. London, UK: Jessica Kingsley.

Gray, J. A. (1991). The neuropsychology of temperament. In J. Strelau & A. Angleitner (Eds.), *Explorations in temperament: International perspectives on theory and measurement* (pp. 105–128). New York: Wiley.

Gray, M., Prigerson, H., & Litz, B. T. (2004). Conceptual and definitional issues in traumatic grief. In B. Litz (Ed.), *Early intervention for trauma and loss in children and adults: Evidence-based directions* (pp. 65–84). New York: Guilford Press.

Green, B. L. (1993). Disasters and posttraumatic stress. In J. R. T. Davidson & E. B. Foa (Eds.), *Posttraumatic stress disorder: DSM-IV and beyond* (pp. 79–97). Washington, DC: American Psychiatric Association.

Green, D., Baird, G. & Sugden, D. (2006). A pilot study of psychopathology in developmental coordination disorder. *Child: Care Health and Development, 32*, 741–750.

Green, J., & Goldwyn, R. (2002). Annotation: Attachment disorganization and psychopathology: New findings in attachment research and their potential implications for developmental psychopathology in childhood. *Journal of Child Psychology and Psychiatry, 43*, 835–846.

Greenberg, L. M., & Kindschi, C. L. (1996). *Test of Variables of Attention (T.O.V.A.): Clinical guide*. St. Paul, MN: TOVA Research Foundation.

Greenberg, M. T., Kusche, C. A., Cook E. T., & Quamma, J. P. (1995). Promoting emotional competence in school-aged children: The effects of the PATHS Curriculum. *Development and Psychopathology, 7*, 117–136.

Greenberg, M. T., Weissberg, R. P., O'Brien, M. U., Zins, J. E., Fredericks, L, Resnik, H. & Elias, M. J. (2003). Enhancing school-based prevention and youth development through coordinated social, emotional, and academic learning. *American Psychologist, 58*, 466–474.

Greene, R. W. (2008). *Lost at school: Why our kids with behavioral challenges are falling through the cracks and how we can help them*. New York: Scribner.

Greene, R. W., & Ablon, J. S. (2006). *Treating explosive kids: The collaborative problem-solving approach*. New York: Guilford Press.

Greene, R. W., Ablon, J. S., Monuteaux, M. C., Goring, J. C., Henin, A., Raezer-Blakely, L., … Rabbitt, S. (2004). Effectiveness of collaborative problem-solving in affectively dysregulated children with oppositional-defiant disorder: Initial findings. *Journal of Consulting and Clinical Psychology, 72*, 1157–1164.

Greenough, W., & Black, J. (1992). Induction of brain structure by experience: Substrates for cognitive development. In M. Gunnar & C. Nelson (Eds.), *Developmental behavioural neuroscience: The Minnesota symposium on child psychology* (Vol. 24, pp. 155–200). Hillsdale, NJ: Lawrence Erlbaum Associates.

Greenspan, S. I. (1986). Developmental morbidity in infants in multirisk families: Clinical perspectives. *Public Health Reports, 97*, 18–23.

Greenspan, S. I., & Weider, S. (1993). Regulatory disorders. In C. H. Zeanah (Ed.), *Handbook of infant mental health* (pp. 280–290). New York: Guilford Press.

Greenspan, S. I., & Wieder, S. (1998). *The child with special needs: Encouraging intellectual and emotional growth*. Reading, MA: Addison-Wesley.

Greenspan, S. I., & Wieder, S. (2000). Principles of clinical practice for assessment and intervention. In *The Interdisciplinary Council of Developmental and Learning Disorders, Clinical practice guidelines: Redefining the standards of care for infants, children, and families with special needs* (pp. 55–84). Bethesda, MD: ICDL Press.

Greenspan, S. I., & Wieder, S. (2001). The developmental individual-difference, relationship-based (DIR/Floortime) model approach to autism spectrum disorders. In E. Hollander & E. Anagnostou (Eds.), *Clinical manual for the treatment of autism* (pp. 179–210). Washington, DC: American Paychiatric Publishing Inc.

Greenspan, S. I., & Weider, S. (2006). Infant and early childhood mental health: A comprehensive developmental approach to assessment and intervention. Arlington, VA: American Psychiatric Publishing Inc.

Greenspan, S. I., Wieder, S., Nover, R. A., Lieberman, A. F., Lourie, R. S., & Robinson, M. E. (1987). *Infants in multirisk families: Case studies in preventive intervention.* Madison, CT: International Universities Press.

Greenwald, R. (1997). *Child and Parent Reports of Post-traumatic Symptoms (CROPS & PROPS).* Copyrighted instruments.

Greenwald, R. (2006). Eye movement desensitization and reprocessing with traumatized youth. In N. B. Webb (Ed.), *Working with children and youth in child welfare* (pp. 246–266). New York: Guilford Press.

Gresham, F., Sugai, G., & Horner, R. (2001). Interpreting outcomes of social skills training for students with high-incidence disabilities. *Exceptional Children, 67*, 331–344.

Gresham, F. M., & Elliott, S. N. (1990). *Social skills rating system manual.* Circle Pines, MN: American Guidance Service.

Grienenberger, J., Kelley, K., & Slade, A. (2005). Maternal reflective functioning, mother-infant affective communication, and infant attachment: Exploring the link between mental states and observed care giving behavior in the intergenerational transmission of attachment. *Attachment and Human Development, 7*, 299–311.

Grinker, R. R., & Spiegel, J. J. (1945). *Men under stress.* New York: McGraw-Hill.

Groenewegen, H. J., & Uylings, H. B. (2000). The prefrontal cortex and the integration of sensory, limbic, and autonomic information. *Progress in Brain Research, 126*, 3–28.

Gross, H. E., Shaw, D. S., Burwell, R. A., & Nagin, D. S. (2009). Transactional processes in child disruptive behavior and maternal depression: A longitudinal study from early childhood to adolescence. *Development and Psychopathology, 21*, 139–156.

Grossman, K., Fremmer-Bombik, E., Rudolf, J., & Grossman, K. E. (1988). Maternal attachment representations as related to patterns of infant-mother attachment and maternal care during the first year. In R. A. Hinde, & J. Stevenson-Hinde (Eds.), *Relationships within families: Maternal influences* (pp. 241–260). Oxford: Clarendon Press.

Grossman, K. E., Grossman, K., & Waters, E. (Eds.). (2005). *Attachment from infancy to adulthood: The major longitudinal studies.* New York: Guilford Press.

Gruber, P., & Reynell, J. K. (1990). *Reynell developmental scales.* Los Angeles, CA: Western Psychological Services.

Grusec, J. E., & Goodnow, J. J. (1994). Impact of parental discipline methods on the child's internalization of values: A reconceptualization of current points of view. *Developmental Psychology, 30*, 4–19.

Grusec, J. E., Goodnow, J. J., & Kuczynski, L. (2000). New directions in analyses of parenting contributions to children's acquisition of values. *Child Development, 71*, 205–211.

Guastella, A. J., Einfeld, S. L., Gray, K. M., Rinehart, N. J., Tonge, B. J., Lambert, T. J., & Hickie, I. B. (2010). Intranasal oxytocin improves emotion recognition for youth with Autism Spectrum Disorders. *Biological Psychiatry, 67*, 692–694

Gump, B. B., Reihman, J., Stewart, P., Lonky, E., Durvill, T., Granger, D. S., & Matthews, K. A. (2009). Trajectories of maternal depressive symptoms over her child's life span: Relation to adrenocortical, cardiovascular, and emotional functioning in children. *Development & Psychopathology, 21*, 207–225.

Gunnar, M. (2007). Stress effects on the developing brain. In D. Romer & E. F. Walker (Eds.), *Adolescent psychopathology and the developing brain: Integrating brain and prevention science* (pp. 127–147). New York: Oxford University Press.

Gunnar, M., & Donzella, B. (2002). Social regulation of cortisol levels in early human development. *Psychoneuroendocrinology, 27*, 199–220.

Gunnar, M. R. (2005). Attachment and stress in early development: Does attachment add to the potency of social regulators of early stress? In C. S. Carter, L. Ahnert, K. E. Grossman, S. B. Hardy, M. E. Lamb, S. W. Porges, & N. Sachsher (Eds.), *Attachment and bonding: A new synthesis* (pp. 245–255). Cambridge, MA: MIT Press.

Gunnar, M. R. (2006). Social regulation of stress in early child development. In K. McCartney & D. Phillips (Eds.), *Early childhood development* (pp. 106–126). Malden, MASS: Blackwell Publishers.

Gunnar, M. R., & de Haan, M. (2009). Methods in social neuroscience: Issues in studying development. In M. de Haan & M. R. Gunnar (Eds.), *Handbook of developmental and neuroscience* (pp. 13–37). New York: Guilford Press.

Gunnar, M. R., Sebanc, A. M., Tout, K., Donzella, B., & van Dulman, M. M. H. (2003). Peer rejection, temperament and cortisol activity in preschoolers. *Developmental Psychology, 43*, 346–358.

Guralnick, M. J. (1997). Second-generation research in the field of early intervention. In M. J. Guralnick (Ed.), *The effectiveness of early intervention* (pp. 3–20). Baltimore: Paul H. Brookes Publishing Co.

Guthrie, R., & Bryant, R. (2005). Auditory startle response in firefighters before and after trauma exposure. *American Journal of Psychiatry, 162*, 283–290.

Hala, S., Hug, S., & Henderson, A. (2003). Executive function and false-belief understanding in preschool children: Two tasks are harder than one. *Journal of Cognition and Development, 4*, 275–298.

Halligan, S. L., Herbert, J., Goodyear, J., & Murray, L. (2007). Exposure to postnatal depression predicts elevated cortisol in relevant offspring. *Biological Psychiatry, 55*, 376–381.

Hammer, E. F. (1967). *Clinical applications of projective drawings*. Springfield, IL: Charles C. Thomas.

Hammill, D. D., & Newcomer, P. L. (2008). *Test of Language Development—Intermediate* (4th ed.) (TOLD-I-4). Austin, TX: Pro-Ed., Inc.

Hammill, D. D., & Newcomer, P. L. (2008). *Test of Language Development—Primary* (4th ed.) (TOLD-P-4). Austin, TX: Pro-Ed., Inc.

Hammill, D. D., Pearson, N. A., & Voress, J. K. (1993). *Developmental Test of Visual Perception* (2nd ed.) San Antonio, TX: PsychCorp.

Hamre, B. K., & Pianta, R. C. (2001). Early teacher-child relationships and the trajectory of children's school outcomes through eighth grade. *Child Development, 72*, 625–638.

Hamre, B. K., & Pianta, R. C. (2005). Can instructional support and emotional support in the first grade classroom make a difference for children at risk for school failure? *Child Development, 76*, 949–967.

Hancock, K., Craig, A., McCready, C., Costello, D., Campbell, K., & Gilmore, G. (1998). Two to six year controlled trial stuttering outcomes for children and adolescents. *Journal of Speech, Language and Hearing Research, 41*, 1242–1252.

Hancock, T., B., & Kaiser, A. P. (2006). Enhanced milieu teaching. In R. McCauley & M. Fey (Eds.), *Treatment of language disorders in children*. Baltimore, MD: Paul H. Brookes Publishers.

Handford, H. A., Mayes, S., Mattison, R., Humphrey, F., Bagnato, S., Bixler, E., … Kales, J. D. (1986). Child and parent reaction to the Three Mile Island nuclear accident. *Journal of the American Academy of Child and Adolescent Psychiatry, 25*, 346–356.

Handford, M. (1987). *Where's Wally*? London, UK: Walker Books.

Hanft, B. E., Miller, L. J., & Lane, S. J. (2000). Toward a consensus in terminology in sensory integration theory and practice: Part 3: Observable behaviors. *Sensory Integration Special Interests Section Quarterly, 23*, 1–4.

Happe, F., Ehlers, S., Fletcher, P., Frith, U., Johansson, M., Gillberg, C., … Frith, C. (1996). "Theory of mind" in the brain: Evidence from a PET scan study of Asperger Syndrome. *NeuroReport, 8*, 197–201.

Haradon, G., Bascom, B., Drogomir, C., & Scripcaru, V. (1994). Sensory functions of institutionalized Romanian infants: A pilot study. *Occupational Therapy International, 1*, 250–260.

Hardin, R. (2001). Conceptions and explanations of trust. In K. S. Cook (Ed.), *Trust in society* (pp. 3–39). New York: Russell Sage.

Hardon, A. Y., Minshew, N. J., Melham, N. M., Srihari, S., Jo, B., Bansal, R., … Stanley, J. A. (2008). An MRI and proton spectroscopy study of the thalamus in children with autism. *Psychiatry Research, 163*, 97–105.

Hare, R. D. (1972). Psychopathy and physiological responses to adrenaline. *Journal of Abnormal Psychology, 29*, 138–147.

Hare, R. D. (1996). Psychopathy a clinical construct whose time has come. *Criminal Justice and Behavior, 23*, 25–54.

Hare, R. D., & Fox. (2001). Psychopaths and their nature. In A. Raine & J. Sanmartin (Eds.), *Violence and psychopathy* (pp. 5–34). Berlin, Germany: Springer Publishers.

Haring, T. G., & Breen, C. G. (1992). A peer-mediated social network intervention to enhance the social integration of persons with moderate and severe disabilities. *Journal of Applied Behavior Analysis, 25*, 319–333.

Hariri, A. R., & Forbes, E. E. (2007). Genetics of emotion regulation. In J. J. Gross (Ed.), *Handbook of emotion regulation* (pp. 110–132). New York: Guilford Press.

Harkness, S., & Super, C. M. (Eds.). (1996). *Parents' cultural belief systems: Their origins, expressions, and consequences*. New York: Guilford Press.

Harlow, J. M. (1868). Recovery after severe injury to the head. *Publication of the Massachesetts Medical Society, 2*, 327–346.

Harris, D. B. (1963). *Children's drawings as measures of intellectual maturity*. New York: Harcourt, Brace, and World.

Harris, D. B. (1968). *Goodenough–Harris Drawing Test Manual*. New York: Harcourt, Brace, & World Inc.

Harris, N. S., Courchesne, E., Townsend, Carper, R., & Lord, C. (1999). Neuroanatomic contributions to slowed orienting of attention in children with autism. *Brain Research and Cognitive Brain Research, 8*, 61–71.

Harris, P. (1996). *Theories of theories of mind*. In P. Carruthers & P. K. Smith (Eds.). Cambridge: Cambridge University Press.

Harter, S. (1985). *Self Perception Profile for Children (SPPC)*. Denver, CO: University of Denver Press.

Hartley, C. A., & Phelps, E. A. (2010). Changing fear: The neurocircuitry of emotion regulation. *Neuropsychopharmacology Reviews, 35*, 136–146.

Hartsough, C. S., & Lambert, N. M. (1985). Medical factors in hyperactive and normal children: Prenatal, developmental, and health history findings. *American Journal of Orthopsychiatry, 55*, 190–210.

Harwood, R. L., Miller, J. G., & Irizarry, N. L. (1995). *Culture and attachment: Perceptions of the child in context*. New York: Guilford Press.

Hassen, N., & Botting, N. (2010). Dynamic assessment of children with language impairments: A pilot study. *Child Language Teaching and Therapy*, 6, 249–272.

Hassen, N., & Joffe, V. (2007). The case for dynamic assessment in speech and language therapy. *Child Language Teaching and Therapy, 23*, 19–25

Hassink, J. M., & Leonard, L. B. (2010). Within-treatment factors as predictors of outcomes following conversational recasting. *American Journal of Speech-Language Pathology*. doi:10.1044/1058-0360 (2010/09-0083)

Haugaard, J. (2004). Recognizing and treating uncommon behavioral and emotional disorders in children and adolescents who have been severely maltreated: Introduction. *Child Maltreatment, 9*, 123–130.

Havighurst, S. S., Harley, A. & Prior, M. (2004). Building preschool children's emotional competence: A parenting program. *Early Education & Development, 15*(4), 423–448.

Hay, D. F., & Cook, K. V. (2007). The transformation of prosocial behaviour from infancy to childhood. In C. A. Brownell & C. B. Kopp (Eds.), *Socioemotional development in the toddler years: Transitions and transformations* (pp. 100–131). New York: Guilford Press.

Heaton, R. K. (1981). *Wisconsin Card Sorting Test manual*. Odessa, FL: Psychological Assessment Resources.

Heberlein, A. S., & Adolphs, R. (2007). Neurobiology of emotion recognition. In E. Harmon-Jones & P. Winkielman (Eds.), *Social neuroscience: Integrating biological and psychological explanations of social behavior* (pp. 31–55). New York: Guilford.

Hechtman, L. (2009). ADHD in adults. In T. E. Brown (Ed.), *ADHD comorbidities: Handbook of ADHD complications in children and adults* (pp. 81–94). Washington, DC: American Psychiatric Publishing, Inc.

Heckman, J. J. (2000). Policies to foster human capital. *Research in Economics, 54*, 3–56.

Heckman, J. J. (2004). Investing in the very young. In R. E. Tremblay, R. G. Barr, & R. DeV. Peters (Eds.), *Encyclopedia of early child development*. Montreal, Quebec: Centre for Excellence for Early Child Development.

Heckman, J. J., & Masterov, D. V. (2007). Rates of return to human capital investment in disadvantaged children. *Review of Agricultural Economics, 29*(3), 446–493.

Heinicke, C. M., Goorsky, M., Levine, M., Ponce, V., Ruth, G., Silverman, M., et al. (2006). Pre- and postnatal antecedents of a home-visiting intervention and family developmental outcome. *Infant Mental Health Journal, 27,* 91–119.

Helzer, J. E., Kraemer, H. C., & Krueger, R. F. (2006). The feasibility and need for dimensional psychiatric diagnosis. *Psychological Medicine, 36,* 1671–1680.

Helzer, J. E., Wittchen, H-U, Krueger, R. F., & Kraemer, H. C. (2008), Dimensional options for DSM-V: The way forward. In J. E. Helzer, H. C. Kraemer, H-U. Wittchen, P. J. Sirovatka, et al. (Eds.), *Dimensional approaches in diagnostic classification: Refining the research agenda for DSM-V* (pp. 115–128). Arlington, VA: American Psychiatric Association.

Henderson, H. A., Marshall, P. J., Fox, N. A., & Rubin, K. H. (2004). Psychophysiological and behavioural evidence for varying forms and functions of non-social behaviour in preschoolers. *Child Development, 75,* 251–263.

Henderson, S. E., Sugden, D. A., & Barnett, A. L. (2009). *The movement assessment battery checklist* (2nd ed.) (MABC – 2). London, UK: Pearson.

Henggeler, S. W., Schoenwald, S. K., Borduin, C. M., Rowland, M. D., & Cunningham, P. B. (1998). *Multisystemic treatment of antisocial behavior in children and adolescents.* New York: Guilford Press.

Henggeler, S. W., Schoenwald, S. K., Rowland, M. D., & Cunningham, P. C. (2002). *Serious emotional disturbance in children and adolescents: Multisystemic therapy.* New York: Guilford Press.

Henry, J., Sloane, M., & Black-Pond, C. (2007). Neurobiology and neurodevelopmental impact of childhood traumatic stress and Prenatal Alcohol Exposure. *Language, Speech and Hearing Services in Schools, 38*(2), 99–107.

Herman, J. L. (1992). Complex PTSD: A syndrome in survivors of prolonged and repeated trauma. *Journal of Traumatic Stress, 5,* 377–391.

Herman, J. L. (1997). *Trauma and recovery: The aftermath of violence-from domestic abuse to political terror* (2nd ed.). New York: Basic Books.

Herpertz, S. C., Huebner, T., Marx, I., Vloet, T. D., Fink, G. R., Stoecker, T., … Herpertz-Dahlmann, B. (2008). Emotional processing in male adolescents with childhood-onset conduct disorder. *The Journal of Child Psychology and Psychiatry, 49,* 781–791.

Herron, N., van der Kolk, B. A., & Hostetler, A. (1994). The history of trauma in psychiatry. *Psychiatric Clinics of North America, 17,* 583–600.

Herstsgaard, L., Gunnar, M., Erickson, M. F., & Nachmias, M. (1995). Adrenocortical responses to the Strange Situation in infants with disorganized/disoriented attachment relationships. *Child Development, 66,* 1100–1106.

Hertzman, C., & Power, C. (2003). Health and human development: Understandings from life course research. *Developmental Neuropsychology, 3,* 719–744.

Hervey, A. S., Epstein, J., & Curry, J. F. (2004). The neuropsychology of adults with attention deficit hyperactivity disorder: A meta-analytic review. *Neuropsychology, 18,* 485–503.

Hettema, J. M., Neale, M. C., & Kendler, K. S. (2001). A review and meta-analysis of the genetic epidemiology of anxiety disorders. *American Journal of Psychiatry, 158,* 1568–1578.

Hettema, J. M., Prescott, C. A., Myers, J. M., Neale, M. C., & Kendler, K. S. (2005). The structure of genetic and environmental risk factors for anxiety disorders in men and women. *Archives of General Psychiatry, 62,* 182–189.

Hill, K. W., & Coufel, K. L. (2005). Emotional/behavioural disorders: A retrospective examination of social skills, linguistics, and student outcomes. *Communication Disorders Quarterly, 3.*

Hinduja, S., & Patchin, J. W. (2009). *Bullying beyond the schoolyard: Preventing and responding to cyberbullying.* Thousand Oaks, CA: Sage Publications.

Hinshaw, S. P. (2002). Process, mechanism, and explanation related to externalizing behavior problems. *Journal of Abnormal Child Psychology, 30,* 431–445.

Hirshfeld, D. R., Micco, J. A., Simoes, N. A., & Henin, A. (2008). High risk studies and developmental antecedents of anxiety disorders. *American Journal of Medical Ethics, Part C (Seminar in Medical Genetics), 148,* 99–117.

Hirshfeld-Becker, D. R., Biederman, J., Calltharp, S., Rosenbaum, E. D., Faraone, S. V., & Rosenbaum, J. F. (2003). Behavioral inhibition and disinhibition as hypothesized precursors to psychopathology: Implications for pediatric bipolar disorders. *Society of Biological Psychiatry, 53,* 985–999.

Hirshfeld-Becker, D. R., Masek, B., Henin, A., Blakely, L. R., Pollock-Wurman, R. A., McQuade, J., … Biederman, J. (2010). Cognitive behavioral therapy for 4- to 7-year-old children with anxiety disorders: A randomized clinical trial. *Journal of Consulting and Clinical Psychology, 78*, 498–510.

Hofer, M. A. (1995). Hidden regulation: Implications for a new understanding of attachment, separation, and loss. In S. Goldberg, R. Muir, & J. Kerr (Eds.), *Attachment theory: Social, developmental, and clinical perspectives* (pp. 203–232). Hillsdale, NJ: Analytic Press.

Hoffer, W. (2007). Development before birth. In M. Batshaw, L. Pellegrino, & N. Roizen (Eds.), *Children with disabilities* (6th ed., pp. 23–34). Baltimore, Maryland: Paul H. Brooks.

Hoffman, M. L. (1983). Affective and cognitive processes in moral internalisation. In E. T. Higgins, D. N. Ruble, & W. W. Hartup (Eds.), *Social cognition and social development: A socio-cultural perspective* (pp. 236–274). New York: Cambridge University Press.

Hoffman, M. L. (1988). Moral development. In M. Bornstein & M. Lamb (Eds.), *Developmental psychology: An advanced textbook* (pp. 497–548). Mahwah, NJ: Lawrence Erlbaum Associates.

Hoffman, M. L. (1991). Empathy, social cognition and moral action. In W. M. Kurtines & J. L. Gewirtz (Eds.), *Handbook of moral behavior and development: Vol. 1. Theory* (pp. 275–301). Mahwah, NJ: Lawrence Erlbaum Associates.

Hoffman, M. L. (2000). *Empathy and moral development: Implications for caring and justice.* New York: Cambridge University Press.

Hoffmann, S. G., & Bitran, S. (2007). Sensory Processing in social anxiety disorder: Relationship to harm avoidance and diagnostic subtypes. *Journal of Anxiety Disorders, 21*(7), 944–954.

Holmbeck, G. N., Greenley, R. N., & Franks, E. A. (2003). Developmental issues and considerations in research and practice. In A. E. Kazdin & J. R. Weisz (Eds.), *Evidence-based psychotherapies for children and adolescents* (pp. 21–41). New York: Guilford.

Homes (2002). In Farrant, B. M., Fletcher, J., & Maybery, T. (2006). Specific language impairment, theory of mind and visual perspective taking: Evidence for simulation theory and the developmental role of language. *Child Development, 77*(6), 1842–1853.

Horne, A. M., & Patterson, G. R. (1980). Working with parents of aggressive children. In R. R. Abidin (Ed.), *Parent education and intervention handbook* (pp. 159–184). Springfield, IL: Thomas.

Horowitz S. M. (1986). *Stress response syndromes* (2nd ed.). Northvale, NJ: Jason Aronson.

Horowitz S. M., Briggs-Gown, M. J., Storfer-Isser, A., & Carter, A. (2007). Prevalence and correlates and persistence of maternal depression. *Journal of Women's Health, 16*, 678–691.

Howard, L. (1997). Developmental coordination disorder: Can we measure our intervention? *British Journal of Occupational Therapy, 60*(5), 219–220.

Howe, M. L. (1997). Children's memory for traumatic experiences. *Learning and Individual Differences, 9*, 153–174.

Howes, C., & James, J. (2004). Children's social development within the socialization context of childcare and early childhood education. In P. K. Smith & C. H. Hart (Eds.), *Blackwell handbook of childhood development* (pp. 137–156). Malden, MA: Blackwell Publishing.

Howlin, F., Baron-Cohen, S., & Hadwin, J. (1999). *Teaching children with autism to mind-read: A practical guide for teachers and parents.* New York: John Wiley and Sons.

Howlin, F., & Yate, P. (1999). The potential effectiveness of social skills groups for adults with autism. *Autism, 3*, 299–307.

Huddy, C. L. J., Johnson A, & Hope P. L. (2001). Educational and behavioral problems in babies of 32–35 weeks gestation. *Archives of Disease in Childhood, 85*, 23–28. [PubMed: 11420317]

Hudley, C. A., Britsch, B., Wakefield, W. D., Smith, T., Demorat, M., & Cho, S. (1998). An attribution retraining progrsm to reduce aggression in elementary school children. *Journal of the American Academy of Child and Adolescent Psychiatry, 39*, 469–476.

Hudziak, J. J., Achenbach, T. M., Althoff, R. R., & Pine, D. S. (2008). A dimensional approach to developmental psychopathology. In J. E. Helzer, H. C. Kraemer, R. F. Krueger, H-U. Wittchen, P. J. Sirovatka, et al. (Eds.), *Dimensional approaches in diagnostic classification: Refining the research agenda for DSM-V* (pp. 101–114). Arlington, VA: American Psychiatric Association.

Hughes, D. A. (2006). *Building the bonds of attachment: Awakening love in deeply troubled children* (2nd ed.). Lanham, MD: Jason Aronson.

Hughes, D. A. (2009). *Attachment-focused parenting: Effective strategies to care for children.* New York: W. W. Norton & Co.

Hughes, J. N., & Cavell, T. A. (1994). Enhancing competence in aggressive children. In G. Cartledge & J. F. Milburn (Eds.), *Teaching social skills to children: Innovative approaches* (3rd ed., pp. 199–236). New York: Pergamon.

Hughes, J. N., & Cavell, T. A. (1999). Influence of the teacher-student relationship in childhood conduct problems: A prospective study. *Journal of Clinical Child and Adolescent Psychology, 28*, 173–174.

Hughes, J. N., Cavell, T. A., & Grossman, P. B. (1997). A positive view of self: Risk or protection for aggressive children? *Development and Psychopathology, 9*, 75–94.

Hughes, M. (2007). *Every child matters: Setting the context for the "hard to reach" children: Improving access, participation, and outcomes* (pp. 1–29). Chichester, West Sussex: John Wiley & Sons.

Huizink, A. J., Robles de Medina, P. G., Mulder, E. J. H., Visser, G. H. A., & Buitelaar, J. K. (2003). Stress during pregnancy is associated with developmental outcome in infancy. *Journal of Child Psychology and Psychiatry and Allied Disciplines, 44*, 810–818.

Hulme, C, Muter, C., & Snowling, M. (1997). *The Phonological Abilities Test (PAT)*. San Antonio. TX: PsychCorp.

Hummel, L. J., & Prizant, B. M. (1993). Language and social skills in the school-age population: A socioemotional perspective for understanding social difficulties of school-age children with language disorders. *Language, Speech, and Hearing Services in Schools, 24*, 216–224.

Hummel, R. M., & Gross, A. M. (2001). Socially anxious children: An observational study of parent-child interaction. *Child & Family Behavior Therapy, 31*, 548–555.

Hunt, I. M. (1961). *Intelligence and experience*. New York: Ronald Publishers.

Huppert, J. D., Foa, E. B., McNally, R. J., & Cahill, S. P. (2009). Role of cognition in stress-induced and fear circuitry disorders. In G. Andrews, D. S. Charney, P. J. Sirovatka, & D. A. Regier *(Eds.), Stress-induced fear circuitry disorders: Refining the research agenda for DSM-V* (pp. 175–193). Arlington, VA: American Psychiatric Association.

Hyman, S., & Towbin, K. (2007). Autism spectrum disorder. In M. Batshaw, L. Pellegrino, & N. Roizen (Eds.), *Children with disabilities* (6th ed., pp. 325–444). Baltimore, Maryland: Paul H. Brooks.

Hynd, G. W., Hern, K. L., Novey, E. S., Eliopulos, D., Marshall, R., Gonzalez, J. J., & Voeller, K. K. (1993). Attention deficit – hyperactivity disorder and asymmetry of the caudate nucleus. *Journal of Child Neurology, 8*, 339–347.

Ingram, R. E., & Price, J. M. (2001). The role of vulnerability in understanding psychopathology. In R. E. Ingram & J. M. Price (Eds.), *Vulnerability to psychopathology: Risk across the lifespan*. New York: Guilford Press.

Insel, T. R., & Fernald, R. D. (2004). How the brain processes social information: searching for the social brain. *Annual Review of Neuroscience, 27*, 697–722.

Insel, T. R., & O'Brien, D. J., & Leckman, J. F. (1999). Oxytocin, vasopressin, and autism: Is there a connection? *Biological Psychiatry, 45*, 145–157.

Isen, A. M. (2004). Some perspectives on positive feelings and emotions: Positive affect facilitates thinking and problem solving. In A. S. Manstead, N. Frijda, & A. Fischer (Eds.), *Feelings and emotions: The Amsterdam Symposium* (pp. 263–281). Cambridge: Cambridge University Press.

Izard, C. E., Trentacosta, C. J., King, K. A. & Mostow, A. J. (2004). An emotion-based prevention program for Head Start children. *Early Education and Development, 15*, 407–422.

Jacobvitz, D., Hazen, N., & Riggs, S. (1997, April). Disorganised mental processes in mothers' frightening/frightened care giving and disoriented/disorganised attachment in infancy. In D. Jacobvitz (Chair), *Caregiving correlates and longitudinal outcomes of disorganised attachment in infants*. Symposium conducted at the biennial meeting of the Society for Research in Child Development, Washington, DC.

Jagust, W., Mormino, B., DeCarli, C., Kramer, J., Barnes, D., & Reed, B. (2006). *Metabolic and cognitive changes with computer-based cognitive therapy for MCI*. Poster presentation at the Tenth International Conference on Alzheimer's and Related Disorders, Madrid, Spain, July 15–20.

James, B. (1994). *Handbook for treatment of attachment and trauma problems in children*. New York: Free Press.

Janet, P. (1889). *L'Automatisme psychologique*. Paris: Alcan.

Jeannerod, M. (2001). Neural stimulation of action: A unifying mechanism for motor cognition. *NeuroImage, 14*, 5103–5109.

Jemerin, J. M., & Boyce, W. T. (1990). Psychobiological differences in childhood stress response. II. Cardiovascular markers or vulnerability. *Journal of Developmental and Behavioral Pediatrics, 11,* 140–150.

Jensen, P. S. (2001). ADHD comorbidity and treatment outcomes in the MTA. *Journal of American Academy of Child and Adolescent Psychiatry, 40,* 1134–1136.

Jensen, P. S., Abikoff, H., & Brown, T. E. (2009). Tailoring treatment for individuals with ADHD and their families. In T. E. Brown (Ed.), *ADHD comorbidities: Handbook for ADHD complications in children and adolescents* (pp. 415–428). Washington, DC: American Psychiatric Publishing, Inc.

Jensen, P. S., Martin, D., & Cantwell, D. P. (1997). Comorbidity in ADHD: Implications for research, practice and DSM-V. *Journal of the American Academy of Child and Adolescent Psychiatry, 36,* 1065–1079.

Jernberg, A., & Booth, P. (1999). *Theraplay: Helping parents and children build better relationships through attachment-based play* (2nd ed.). San Francisco, CA: Jossey Bass.

Jerome, A. C., Fujiki, M., Brinton, B., & James, S. L. (2002). Self-esteem in children with specific language impairment. *Journal of Speech Language, and Hearing Research, 45,* 700–714.

Jester, R. E., & Guinagh, B. J. (1983). The Gordon Parent Education Infant and Toddler Program. In Consortium for Longitudinal Studies (Ed.), *As the twig is bent: Lasting effects of preschool programs* (pp. 103–132). Hillsdale, NJ: Lawrence Erlbaum Associates.

Jiang, S., Xin, R., Lin, S., Qian, Y., Tan, G., Wang, D., & Wu, X. (2000). Linkage studies between attention-deficit hyperactivity disorder and the monoamine oxidase genes. *American Journal of Medicine Genetics, 105,* 783–788.

Jirikowic, T., Carmichael. H, & Kartin, D. (2008). Sensory processing, school performance, and adaptive behaviour of young school-age children with fetal alcohol spectrum disorders. *Physical and Occupational Therapy in Pediatrics, 28*(2), 117–136.

Johnson, M. H., Griffin, R., Csibra, G., Halit, H., Farroni, T., de Haan, M., ... Richards, J. (2005). The emergence of the social brain network: Evidence from typical and atypical development: Integrating cognitive and affective neuroscience and developmental psychopathology (Special issue). *Development and Psychopathology, 17,* 609–615.

Jolliffe, & Baron-Cohen. (1999). A test of coherence theory: Linguistic processing in high functioning adults with autism or Asperger Syndrome: Is local coherence impaired? *Cognition, 71,* 149–185.

Jones, D. J., Forehand, R., Brody, G. H., & Armistead, L. (2002). Positive parenting and child psycho-social adjustment in inner-city single-parent African American families: The role of maternal optimism. *Behavior Modification, 26,* 464–481.

Jones, N., Field, T., & Davalos, M. (2000). Right frontal EEG asymmetry and lack of empathy in preschool children of depressed mothers. *Child Psychiatry and Human Development, 30,* 189–204.

Jongmans, N., Mecurin. E., De Vries., L., Dubowitz. L., & Henderson, S. (1997). Minor neurological signs and perceptual-motor difficulties in prematurely born children. *Archives Diseases in Childhood? 76,* 9–14.

Joseph, R. (2003). Emotional trauma and childhood amnesia. *Journal of Consciousness and Emotion, 4,* 151–178.

Joussetmet, M., Vitaro, F., Barker, E. D., Cote, S., Nagin, D. S., Zoccolillo, M., ... Tremblay, R. E. (2008). Controlling parenting and physical aggression during elementary school. *Child Development, 79,* 411–425.

Juffer, F., Bakermans-Kranenburg, M., & van IJzendoorn, M. H. (2005). Enhancing children's socioemotional development: A review of intervention studies. In D. M. Teti (Ed.), *Handbook of research methods in developmental psychology* (pp. 213–232). Oxford: Blackwell Publishing.

Juffer, F., Bakermans-Kranenburg, M. J., & van IJzendoorn, M. H. (2008). Earlier is better: A meta-analysis of 70 years of intervention improving cognitive development in institutionalized children. *Monographs for the Society for Research in Child Development, 73,* 279–293.

Juvonen, J., & Graham, S. (2001). *Peer harassment in school: The plight of the vulnerable and victimized.* New York: Guilford Press.

Kagan, J. (1966). Reflection-impulsivity: The generality and dynamics of conceptual tempo. *Journal of Abnormal Psychology, 71,* 17–24.

Kagan, J. (1997). Temperament and the reactions to unfamiliarity. *Child Development, 68,* 139–143.

Kagan, J. (2003). The limitations of concepts in developmental psychology. *Merrill-Palmer Quarterly, 50,* 291–298.

Kagan, J., & Snidman, N. (2004). *The long shadow of temperament*. Cambridge, MA: Harvard University Press.

Kagan, R. (2007). *Real life heroes: A life story book for children* (2nd ed.). New York: The Haworth Press.

Kalmanson, B., & Seligman, S. (2006). Process in an integrated model of infant mental health and early intervention practice. In G. M. Foley & J. D. Hochman (Eds.), *Mental health in early intervention: Achieving unity in principles and practice* (pp. 245–265). Baltimore, MD: Paul H. Brookes Publishing.

Kandel, E., & Mednick, S. (1991). Perinatal complications predict violent offending. *Criminology, 29*, 519–529.

Kanwisher, N., McDermott, J., & Chun, M. M. (1997). The fusiform face area: A module in human extrastriate cortex specialised for face perception. *Journal of Neuroscience, 17*, 4302–4311.

Kaplan, N. (1987). *Individual differences in six-year-olds' thoughts about separation: Predicted from attachment to mother at one year of age*. Unpublished doctorial dissertation. University of California at Berkeley.

Kardiner, A. (1941). *The traumatic neurosis of the war*. New York: Hoeber.

Karen, R. (1994). *Becoming attached: Unfolding the mystery of infant-mother bond and its impact on later life*. New York: Warner Books.

Kasari, C., Sigman, M., Mundy, P., & Yirmiya, N. (1990). Affective sharing in the context of joint attention interactions of normal. Autistic, and mentally retarded children. *Journal of Autism and Developmental Disorders, 20*, 87–100.

Kaufman, C. (2010). *Executive function in the classroom: Practical strategies for improving performance and enhancing skills for all students*. Baltimore, MD: Paul H. Brookes.

Kaufman, J., & Zigler, E. (1987). Do abused children become abusive parents? *American Journal of Orthopsychiatry, 57*, 186–192.

Kazdin, A. E. (2002). The state of child and adolescent psychotherapy research. *Child and Adolescent Mental Health, 7*, 53–59

Kazdin, A. E. (2005). *Parent management training: Treatment for opposition, aggressive, and antisocial behavior in children and adolescents*. New York: Oxford University Press.

Kazdin, A. E., Mazurick, J. L, & Bass, O. (1993). Risk for attrition in treatment of anti-social children and families. *Journal of Clinical Child Psychology, 22*, 2–16.

Kazdin, A. E., Siegel, T. C., & Bass, D. (1992). Cognitive problem-solving skills training and parent management training in the treatment of anti-social behavior in children. *Journal of Consulting and Clinical Psychology, 60*, 733–747.

Kazdin, A. E., & Weisz, J. R. (1998). Identifying and developing empirically supported child and adolescent treatments. *Journal of Consulting and Clinical Psychology, 66*, 18–35.

Kendall, P. C. (1992). *Stop and think workbook* (2nd ed.). Ardmore, PA: Workbook Publishing.

Kendall, P. C. (2006). Guiding theory for therapy for children and adolescents. In P. C. Kendall (Ed.), *Child and adolescent therapy* (3rd ed., pp. 243–294). New York: Guilford Press.

Kendall, P. C., Kane, M., Howard, B., Siqueland. (1992). *Cognitive-behavioral therapy for anxious children: Therapist manual*. Aardmore, PA: Workbook.

Kendall, P. C., Stark, K. D., & Adam, T. (1990). Cognitive deficits or cognitive distortion in childhood depression. *Journal of Abnormal Child Psychology, 18*, 155–270.

Kennedy, J. H., & Kennedy, C. E. (2004). Attachment theory: Implications for school psychology. *Psychology in Schools, 41*, 247–259.

Kennedy, J. H., & Kennedy, C. E. (2007). Applications of attachment theory in school psychology. *Journal of Early Childhood and Infant Psychology, 3*, 7–25.

Kennedy, S. H., Konarski, J. Z., Segal, Z. V., Lau, M. A., Bieling, P. J., McIntyre, R. S. & Mayberg H. S. (2007). Differences in brain glucose metabolism between responders to CBT and venlafaxine in a 16-week randomized controlled trial. *American Journal of Psychiatry, 164*, 778–788.

Keren, M., & Tyano, S. (2009). A developmental approach: Looking at the specificity of reactions to trauma in infants. In D. Brom, R. Pat-Horenczyk., & J. D. Ford (Eds.), *Treating traumatized children: Risk, resilience, and recovery* (pp. 85–101). New York: Routledge.

Kerns, K. A. (2008). Attachment in middle childhood. In J. Cassidy & P. R. Shaver (Eds.), *Handbook of attachment research, theory, and clinical research* (2nd ed., pp. 366–382). New York: Guilford Press.

Kerns, K. A., Aspelmeier, J. E., Gentzler, A. L., & Grabill, C. M. (2001). Parent-child attachment and monitoring in middle childhood. *Journal of Family Psychology, 15*, 69–81.

Kerns, K. A., Klepac, L., & Cole, A. K. (1996). Peer relationships and preadolescents' perceptions of security in the child-mother relationship. *Developmental Psychology, 32*, 457–466.

Kerns, K. A., Schlegelmilch, A., Morgan, T. A., & Abraham, M. M. (2005). Assessing attachment in middle childhood. In K. A. Kerns & R. A. Richardson (Eds.), *Attachment in middle childhood* (pp. 46–70). New York: Guilford Press.

Kerns, K. A., Tomich, P. L., & Kim, P. (2006). Normative trends in children's perceptions of availability and utilization of attachment figures in middle childhood. *Social Development, 15*, 1–22.

Kessler, J. W. (1980). A history of minimal brain dysfunction. In H. Rie & E. Rie (Eds.), *Handbook of minimal brain dysfunction: A critical view* (pp. 18–52). New York: Wiley.

Kessler, R. C. (2000). Posttraumatic stress disorder: The burden to the individual and to society. *Journal of Clinical Psychiatry, 61*, 4–14.

Kessler, R. C., Adler, L., Ames, M., Barkley, R. A., Birnbaum, H., Greenberg, P., ... Ustün, T. B. (2005). The prevalence and effects of adult attention deficit/hyperactivity disorder on work performance in a nationally representative sample of workers. *Journal of Occupational Environmental Medicine, 47*, 565–572.

Kessler, R. C., Berglund, P., Demler, O., Jin, R., Koretz, D., Merikangas, K. R., ... Wang, P. S. (2003). The epidemiology of major depressive disorder: Results of the National Comorbidity Survey Replication (NCS-R). *Journal of the American Medical Association, 289*, 3095–3105.

Kessler, R. C., Sonnega, A., Bromet, E., Hughes, M., & Nelson, C. B. (1995). Posttraumatic stress disorder in the national comorbidity survey. *Archives of General Psychiatry, 51*, 1048–1060.

Kessler, R. C., & Ustun, T. B. (2004). The World Health (WMH) Survey Initiative Version of the World Health Organization (WHO) Composite International Diagnostic Interview (CIDI). *International Journal of Methods in Psychiatric Research, 13*, 93–121.

Kestenbaum, R., Farber, E.A., & Sroufe, A. (1989). Individual differences in empathy among preschoolers: Relation to attachment history. *New Directions for Child Development, 44*, 51–64.

Khalsa, S. S. (1996). *Group exercises for enhancing social skills and self-esteem*. Sarasota, FL: Professional Resource Press.

Khanna, M. S., & Kendall, P. C. (2009). Exploring the role of parent training in the treatment of childhood anxiety. *Journal of Consulting and Clinical Psychology, 77*, 981–986.

Kiehl, K. A. (2006). A cognitive neuroscience perspective on psychopathy: Evidence for paralimbic system dysfunction. *Psychiatric Research, 142*, 107–128.

Kiehl, K. A., Smith, A. M., Hare, R. D., Mendrek, A., Forster, B. B., Brink, J.,_& Liddle, P. F. (2001). Limbic abnormalities in affective processing by criminal psychopaths as revealed in functional magnetic resonance imaging. *Biological Psychiatry, 50*, 677–684.

Kiesner, J., Cadinu, M., Poulin, F., & Bucci, M. (2002). Group identification in early adolescence: Its relation with peer adjustment and its moderator effects on peer influence. *Child Development, 73*, 196–208.

Kilbride, H. W., Thorstadt, K., & Daily, D. K. (2004). Preschool outcomes of less than 801 gram preterm infants compared with full term siblings. *Pediatrics, 113*, 742–747.

Kim-Cohen, J., Arseneault, L., Caspi, A., Tomas, M. P., Taylor, A., & Moffitt, T. E. (2005). Validity of DSM-IV conduct disorder in 4 ½-5-year-old children: A longitudinal epidemiological study. *American Journal of Psychiatry, 162*, 1108–1117.

Kimball, J. G., Lynch, K. M., Stewart, K. C., Williams, N. E., Thomas, M. A., & Atwood, K. D. (2007). Using salivary cortisol to measure the effects of a Wilbarger protocol- based procedure on sympathetic arousal: A pilot study. *American Journal of Occupational Therapy, 61*(4), 406–413.

Kimonis, E. R., Frick, P. J., Boris, N. W., Smyke, A. T., Cornell, A. H., Farrell, J. M., & Zeanah, C. H. (2006). Callous-unemotional features, behavioral inhibition, and parenting: Independent predictors of aggression in a high risk preschool sample. *Journal of Family Studies, 15*, 745–756.

Kinnealey, M., & Fuiek, M. (1999). The relationship between sensory defensiveness, anxiety, depression and perception of pain in adults. *Occupational Therapy International, 6*(3), 195–206.

Kinniburg, K. J., Blaustein, M., Spinazzola, J., & van der Kolk, B. A. (2005). Attachment, self-regulation and competency: A comprehensive intervention framework for children with complex trauma. *Psychiatric Annals, 35*, 5.

Kinsbourne, M., & Bemporad, B. (1984). Internalization of emotion: A model and the evidence. In N. A. Fox & R. J. Davidson (Eds.), *The psychology of affective development* (pp. 259–292). Hillsdale, NJ: Erlbaum.

Kirby, A., & Drew, S. (2003). *Guide to dyspraxia and developmental coordination disorder.* London, UK: Fulton Publishers.

Kitzmann, K. M., Gaylord, N. K., Holt, A. R., & Kenny, E. D. (2003). Child witnesses to domestic violence: A meta-analytic review. *Journal of Consulting and Clinical Psychology, 71*, 339–352.

Klagsbrun, M., & Bowlby, J. (1976). Responses to separations from parents: A clinical test. *Projective Psychology, 21*, 7–21.

Klin, A. (1991). Young autistic children's listening preferences in regard to speech: A possible characterization of the symptom of social withdrawal. *Journal of Autism and Developmental Disorder, 21*, 29–42.

Klingberg, T., Fernell, E., Olesen, P. J., Johnson, M., Gustafsson, P., Dahlstrom, K., ... Westerberg, H. (2005). Computerized training of working memory in children with ADHD–A randomized controlled trial. *Journal of the American Academy of Child and Adolescent Psychiatry, 44*, 177–186.

Kobak, R., Little, M., Race, E., & Acosta, M. C. (2001). Attachment disruptions in seriously disturbed children: Implications for treatment. *Attachment and Human Development, 3*, 243–258.

Kochanska, G. (1995). Children's temperament, mothers' discipline, and security of attachment: Multiple pathways to emerging internalization. *Child Development, 66*, 597–615.

Kochanska, G. (1997a). Multiple pathways to conscience for children with different temperament: From toddler to age five. *Developmental Psychology, 33*(2), 228–240.

Kochanska, G. (1997b). Mutually responsive orientation between mothers and their young children: Implications for early socialization. *Child Development, 68*, 94–112.

Kochanska, G. (1998). Mother-child relationship, child fearfulness, and emerging attachment: A short-term longitudinal study. *Developmental Psychology, 34*, 480–490.

Kochanska, G. (2002). Committed compliance, moral self, and internalization: A meditational model. *Developmental Psychology, 38*, 339–351.

Kochanska, G., & Aksan, N. (2006). Children's conscience and self-regulation. *Journal of Personality, 74*, 1587–1617.

Kochanska, G., Aksan, N., & Joy, M. C. (2007). Children's fearlessness as moderator of parenting in early socialization: Two longitudinal studies. *Developmental Psychology, 43*, 222–237.

Kochanska, G., Aksan, N., & Koenig, A. (1995). A longitudinal study of the roots of preschoolers' conscience: Committed compliance and emerging internalisation. *Child Development, 66*, 1752–1769.

Kochanska, G., Barry, R. A., Aksan, N., & Boldt, L. J. (2008). A developmental model of maternal and child contributions to disruptive conduct: The first six years. *The Journal of Child Psychology and Psychiatry, 49*, 1220–1227.

Kochanska, G., Forman, D. R., Aksan, N., & Dunbar, S. B. (2005). Pathways to conscience: Early mother-child mutually responsive orientation and children's moral emotion, conduct, and cognition. *Journal of Child Psychology and Psychiatry, 46*, 19–34.

Kochanska, G., Murray, K., & Coy, K. (1997). Inhibitory control as a contributor to conscience in childhood: From toddler to early school age. *Child Development, 68*, 263–277.

Kochanska, G., Philibert, R. A., & Barry, R. A. (2009). Interplay of genes and early mother-child relationships in the development of self-regulation from toddler to preschool age. *The Journal of Child Psychology and Psychiatry, 50*, 1331–1338.

Kochenderfer, B. J., & Ladd, G. W. (1996). Peer victimization: Manifestations and relationship to school adjustment in kindergarten. *Journal of School Psychology, 34*, 267–283.

Kodituwakku, P. (2007). Defining the behavioral phenotype in children with fetal alcohol spectrum disorders: A review. *Neuroscience and Behavioral Reviews, 31*, 192–201.

Kodituwakku, P. W., May, P. A., Clericuzio, C. L., & Weers, D. (2001). Emotion-related learning in individuals prenatally exposed to alcohol: An investigation of the relation between set shifting, extinction of responses, and behavior. *Neuropsychologia, 39*, 699–708.

Koenen, K. C., Harley, R. M., & Lyons, M. J. (2002). A twin registry study of familial and individual risk factors for trauma exposure and posttraumatic stress disorder. *Journal of Nervous and Mental Disorders, 190*, 209–218.

Koenen, K. C., Lyons, M. J., & Goldberg, J. (2003). A high risk study of combat-related PTSD comorbidity. *Twin Research, 218*, 218–226.

Kohn, M. (1977). The Kohn Social Competence Scale and Symptom Checklist for the Preschool Child: A follow-up report. *Journal of Abnormal Child Psychology, 5*, 249–263.

Kolassa, I-T., Kolassa, S., Ertl, V., Papassotiropoulos, A., & De Quervain, D. J-F. (2010). The risk of Posttraumatic Stress Disorder after trauma depends on traumatic load and the Catechol-O-Methyltransferase Val158Met polymorphism. *Biological Psychiatry, 67*, 304–308.

Kongs, S. K., Thompson, L. L., Iverson, G. L., & Heaton, R. K. (2000). *Wisconsin Card Sorting Test-64 Card Version (WCST-64)*. Odessa, FL: Psychological Assessment Resources.

Koomar, J. A. (2009). Trauma and attachment-informed SI assessment and intervention. *Special Interest Section Quarterly: American Occupational Therapy Association, 32*(4), 1–4.

Kopp, B., Kunkel, A., Muhlnickel, W., Villringer, K., Taub, E., & Flor, H. (1999). Plasticity in the motor system related to therapy-induced improvement of movement after stroke. *NeuroReport, 10*, 807–810.

Kopp, C. B. (1989). Regulation of distress and negative emotions: A developmental view. *Developmental Psychology* 25, 343–354.

Kopp, S., & Gillberg, C. (1997). Selective mutism: A population based study: a research note. *Journal of Child Psychology and Psychiatry, 38*, 257–262.

Koppitz, E. M. (1970). Brain damage, reading ability in Bender Gestalt Test. *Journal of Learning Disabilities, 2, 429–433.*

Korkman, M., Kirk, U., & Kemp, S. (2007). *NEPSY-II*. San Antonio, TX: Psychological Corporation.

Koshinsky Clipsham, C. K. (2006). Reaching and engaging hard-to-reach families. In S. Landy & R. Menna (Eds.), *Early intervention with multi-risk families: An integrative approach* (pp. 179–198). Baltimore, MD: Paul H. Brookes Publishing Co.

Kovacs, M., & MHS staff. (2003). *Child Depression Inventory* (CDI). Multi Health Systems.

Kovacs, M., Sherrill, J., George, C. J., Pollock, M., Tumuluru, R. V., & Ho, V. (2006). Contextual Emotional Regulation Therapy for childhood depression: Description and pilot testing of a new intervention. *Journal of the American Academy of Child and Adolescent Psychiatry, 45*, 892–903.

Kraemer, H. C. (2008). DSM categories and dimensions in clinical and research contexts. In J. E. Helzer, H. C. Kraemer, R. F. Krueger, H-U. Wittchen, P. J. Sirovatka, et al. (Eds.), *Dimensional approaches in diagnostic classification: Refining the research agenda for DSM-V* (pp. 5–18). Arlington, VA: American Psychiatric Association.

Kramer, K. M., Cushing, B. S., & Carter, C. S. (2003). Developmental effects of oxytocin on stress response: Single versus repeated exposure. *Physiology and Behavior, 79*, 775–782.

Krantz, P. J., & McClannahan, L. E. (2005). *Teaching conversation to children with autism: Scripts and script fading*. Bethesda, MD: Woodbine House.

Krishnakumar, A., Buehler, C., & Barber, B. K. (2003). Interparental conflict, ineffective parenting, and youth problems in European American and African American families. *Journal of Personal and Social Relationships, 20*, 239–260.

Kristtensen, H. (2000). Selective mutism and comorbidity with developmental disorder/delay, anxiety disorder, and elimination disorder. *Journal of the American Academy of Child and Adolescent Psychiatry, 39*, 249–256.

Krol, N., Morton, J., & De Bruyn, E. (2004). Theories of conduct disorder: A causal modeling analysis. *Journal of Child Psychology and Psychiatry, 45*, 727–742.

Krueger, R. F. (2002). Psychometric perspectives on co-morbidity. In J. E. Helzer & J. J. Hudziak (Eds.), *Defining psychopathology in the 21st century: DSM-V and beyond* (pp. 41–54). Arlington, VA: American Psychiatric Publishing.

Kruger, F., Moll, R., Zahn, A., Heinecke, A., & Grafman, J. (2007). Event frequency modulates the processing of human medial prefrontal cortex. *Cerebral Cortex, 17*, 2346–2353.

Kuhl, P., Coffey-Corina, S., Padden, D., & Dawson, G. (2004). Links between social and linguistic processing of speech in preschool children with autism: Behavioral and electrophysiological measures. *Developmental Science, 7*, 19–30.

Kuhlman, A., Little, D., & Sekuler, R. (2006). An interactive test of serial behavior: Age and practice alter executive function. *Journal of Clinical Experimental Neuropsychology, 28*, 126–144.

Kujala, T., Karma, K., Ceponiene, R., Belitz, S., Turkkila, P., Tervaniemi, M., & Näätänen, R. (2001). Plastic neural changes and reading improvement caused by audiovisual training in reading-impaired children. *Proceedings of the National Academy of Science, 98*, 10509–10514.

Kumpulainen, K., Rasanen, E., Henttonen, L., Almquist, F., Kresanor, K., Linna, S.-L., & Tamminen, T. (1998). Bullying and psychiatric symptoms among elementary school-age children. *Child Abuse and Neglect, 22,* 705–717.

Kumpulainen, K., Rasanen, E., Raaska, H., & Somppi, V. (1998). Selective mutism among second graders in elementary school. *European Journal of Child Adolescent Psychiatry, 7,* 24–29.

Kurtz, Z. (2004). *What works in promoting children's mental health.* Nottingham: Sure Start.

Kutash, K., Duchnowski, A. J., & Lynn, N. (2006). *School-based mental health: An empirical guide for decision-makers.* Tampa, FL: University of South Florida, The Louis de la Parte Florida Mental Health Institute, Department of Child and Family Studies, Research and Training Centre for Children's Mental Health.

Lachar, D., & Gruber, C. P. (1991). *Manual for the Personality Inventory for Children-Revised* (PIC-R). Los Angeles, CA: Western Psychological Services.

Ladd, G. W., & Burgess, K. B. (2001). Do relational risks and protective factors moderate the linkages between childhood aggression and early psychological and school adjustment? *Child Development, 72,* 1579–1601.

Ladd, G. W., & Hart, C. H. (1992). Creating informal play opportunities: Are parents' and preschoolers' initiations related to children's competence with peers? *Developmental Psychology, 28, 1179–1187.*

Ladd, G. W., & Pettit, G. S. (2002). Parenting and the development of children's peer relationships. In M. H. Bornstein (Ed.), *Handbook of parenting: Vol. 5, Practical issues in parenting* (pp. 269–309). Mahwah, NJ: Lawrence Erlbaum Associates.

LaFreniere, P. J., & Dumas, J. E. (1995). *Social competence and Behavior Evaluation* (CSBE). Los Angeles, CA: Western Psychological Services.

Lahey, B. B., Applegate, B., McBurnett, K., Brederman, J., Greenhill, L., Hynd, G. W., … Baumann, B. (2004). DSM-IV trials for Attention Deficit Hyperactivity Disorder for younger children. *Journal of the American Academy of Child and Adolescent Psychiatry, 37,* 695–702.

Lahey, B. B., Hart, E. L., Pliszka, A., Applegate, B., & McBurnett, K. (1993). Neurophysiological correlates of conduct disorder: A rationale and a review of research. *Journal of Clinical Child Psychology, 22,* 141–153.

Lahey, B. B. & Waldman, I. D. (2003). A developmental propensity model of the origins of conduct problems during childhood and adolescence. In B. B. Lahey, T. E. Moffitt, & A. Caspi (Eds.), *Causes of conduct disorder and juvenile delinquency* (pp. 76–117). New York: Guilford Press.

Laible, S. J., & Thompson, R. A. (1998). Attachment and emotional understanding in preschool children: A short term longitudinal study. *Developmental Psychology, 34,* 1038–1045.

Lam, P., Hiscock, H., & Wake, M. (2003). Outcomes of infant sleep problems: Behavior and maternal well-being. *Pediatrics, 111,* e203-e207.

Landreth, G. L., & Bratton, S. C. (2006*). Child-Parent Relationship Therapy (CPRT): A 10-session filial therapy model.* New York: Routledge,

Landry, S. H., Smith, K. E., Swank, P. R., & Guttentag, C. (2008). A responsive parenting intervention: The optimal timing across early childhood for impacting maternal behaviors and child outcomes. *Developmental Psychology, 44,* 1335–1353.

Landy, S. (2009). *Pathways to competence: Encouraging healthy social and emotional development in young children* (2nd ed.). Baltimore, MD: Paul H. Brookes Publishing Company.

Landy, S. (2012). *Family pathways: Characteristics of the program, the families, and preliminary outcome data.* Princess Margaret Hospital for Children, Perth, WA: The Government of Western Australia.

Landy, S., & Menna, R. (2006a). An evaluation of a group intervention for parents with aggressive young children: Improvements in child functioning, maternal confidence, knowledge and attitudes toward parenting. *Early Child Development and Care, 16,* 203–211.

Landy, S., & Menna, R. (2006b). *Early intervention with multi-risk families: An integrative approach.* Baltimore: Paul H. Brookes Publishing Co.

Landy, S., Menna, R., & Clipsham, C. K. (2006). Reaching and engaging hard-to-reach families. In S. Landy & R. Menna (Eds.), *Early intervention with multi-risk families: An integrative approach* (pp. 179–197). Baltimore, MD: Paul H. Brookes.

Landy, S., & Thompson, E. (2006). *Pathways to competence: A parenting program*. Baltimore, MD: Paul H. Brookes Publishing Co.

Lane, S. J., Miller, L.J, & Hanft, B. E. (2000). Toward a consensus in terminology in sensory integration theory and practice: Part 2: Sensory Integration Patterns of function and dysfunction. *Sensory Integration Special Interests Section Quarterly, 23*, 1–3.

Lane, S. J., & Schaaf, R. C. (2010). Examining the neuroscience evidence for sensory driven neuroplasticity: Implication for sensory based occupational therapy for children and adolescents. *The American Journal of Occupational Therapy, 64*, 375–390.

Lanza, S. T., Rhoades, B. L., Nix, R. L., Greenberg, M. T., & The Conduct Problems Prevention Research Group (2010). Modeling the interplay of multilevel risk factors for the future academic and behavior problems: A person-centered approach. *Development and Psychopathology, 22*, 313–335.

Lau, A. S., & Weisz, J. R. (2003). Reported maltreatment among clinic-referred children: Implications for presenting problems, treatment attrition, and long term outcomes. *Journal of the American Academy of Child and Adolescent Psychiatry, 42*, 1327–1334.

Laufer, M., & Denhoff, E. (1957). Hyperkinetic behavior syndrome in children. *Journal of Pediatrics, 50*, 463–474.

Law, Campbell, Roulstone, Adams, C., & Boyle, J. (2008). Mapping practice onto therapy: The speech and language practitioners construction of receptive language impairment. *International Journal of Communication Disorders, 43*, 245–263.

Law, J., Garrett, Z., & Nye, C. (2004). The efficacy of treatment for children with developmental speech and language delay/disorder: A meta-analysis. *Journal of Speech, Language and Hearing Research, 48*, 1114–1117.

Law, J., & Roy. (2008). Parental report of infant language skills: A review of the development and application of the Communicative Development Inventories. *Child and Adolescent Mental Health, 13*, 198–206.

Law, J., Rush, R., Schoon, I., & Parson, S. (2009). Modeling developmental language difficulties from school entry into adulthood: Literacy, mental health, and employment outcomes. *Journal of Speech, Language, and Hearing Research, 52*, 1401–1416.

Law, K., Stroud, L., LeGasse, L., Niaura, R., Jing, L., & Lester, B. (2003). Smoking during pregnancy and newborn neurobehavior. *Pediatrics, 111*, 1318–1323.

Lazar, S. W., Kerr, C. E., Wasserman, R. H., Gray, J. R., Greve, D. N., Treadway, M. T., … Fischl, B. (2005). Meditation experience is associated with increased cortical thickness. *NeuroReport, 16*, 1893–1897.

Lazarus, R. S., & Folkman, S. (1984). *Stress, appraisal and coping*. New York: Springer.

Le Grand, R., Mondloch, C. K., Mauer, D., & Brent, H. P. (2003). Expert face processing requires visual input to the right hemisphere during infancy. *Nature Neuroscience, 6*, 1108–1112.

Le Normand, M. T., & Cohen, H. (1999). The delayed emergence of lexical morphology in preterm children: The case of verbs. *Journal of Neurolinguistics, 2*, 235–246.

Lean, D. S., & Colucci, V. A. (2010). *Barriers to learning: The case for integrated mental health services in the schools*. Toronto: Rowman & Littlefield.

LeDoux, J. (2002). *Synaptic self: How we are who we are*. New York: Penguin Books.

Leerkes, E. M., Blankson, A. N. & O'Brien, M. (2009). Differential effects of maternal sensitivity to infant distress and nondistress on socio-emotional functioning. *Child Development, 80*(3), 762–775.

Leitao, C., Allan, L., & Phillips, M. (2004), *Peter and the cat* (2nd ed.). Black Sheep Press.

Lembke, E. S., & Stormont, M. (2005). Using research-based practices to support students with diverse needs in general education. *Psychology in the Schools, 42*, 761–763.

Lemirise, E., & Arsenio, W. (2000). An integrated model of emotion process and cognition in social information processing. *Child Development, 71*, 107–118.

Leonard, C., Eckert, M., Given, B., Virginia, B., & Eden, G. (2006). Individual differences in anatomy in predicting reading and oral language impairments in children. *Brain, 129*, 3329–3342.

Leonard, L. B. (1991). Specific language impairment as a clinical category. *Language, Speech, and Hearing Services in Schools, 22*, 66–68.

Leonard, L. B. (1998). *Children with specific language impairment*. Cambridge, MA: Bradford.

Leonard, L. B. (2009). Is expressive language disorder an accurate diagnostic category? *American Journal of Speech Language Pathology, 18*, 115–123.

Lester, B. M., Bagner, D. M., Liu, J., LaGasse, L. L. Seifer, R., Bauer C. R., … Das, A. (2009). Infant neurobehavioural dysregulation: Behaviour problems in children with prenatal substance exposure. *Pediatrics, 124*, 1355–1361.

Lester, B. M., Boukydis, C. F. Z., & Twomey, J. E. (2000). Maternal substance abuse and child outcome. In C. H. Zeanah, Jr. (Ed.), *Handbook of infant mental health* (2nd ed., pp. 161–175). New York: Guilford Press.

Letarte, M-J., Normandeau, S., & Allard, J. (2010). Effectiveness of a parent training program "Incredible Years" in a child protection service. *Child Abuse and Neglect, 34*, 253–261.

Levenstein, O'Hara, & Levenstein. (1984). Home again. *Child Development, 55*, 636–647.

Levine, K. J. (1994). *Fine motor dysfunction: Therapeutic strategies in the classroom.* Tucson, AZ: Therapy Skill Builders.

Levine, S., & Alpert, M. (1959). Differential maturation of the central nervous system as a function of early experience. *A.M.A. Archives of General Psychiatry, 19591*, 403–405.

Levine, S., Elzey, F., & Lewis, M. (1969). *California preschool social competency scale.* Palo Alto, CA: Consulting Psychologists Press.

Levy, F., Hay, D. A., Bennett, K. S., & McStephen, M. (2005). Gender differences in ADHD subtype morbidity. *Journal of the American Academy of Child and Adolescent Psychiatry, 44*, 368–376.

Lewis, B. A., Freebairn, L. A., & Taylor, H. G. (2003). Academic outcomes in children with histories of speech sound disorders. *Journal of Communication Disorders, 33*, 11–30.

Lewis, B. A., Shriberg, L. D., Freebaim, L. A., & Hansen, A. J. (2006). The genetic basis of speech sound disorders: Evidence from spoken and written language. *Journal of Speech, Language, and Hearing Research, 49*, 1294–1312.

Lewis, L. L., & Maurer, D. (2009). Effects of early deprivation on visual development. *Optometry and Vision Science, 86*, 640–646.

Lezak, M. (1995). *Neuropsychological assessment* (3rd ed.). New York: Oxford University Press.

Liber, J. M., Van Widenfelt, B. M., Goedhart, A. W., Utens, E. M., van der Leeden, A. J., Markus, M. T., & Treffers, P. D. (2008). Parenting and parental anxiety and depression as predictors of treatment outcome for childhood anxiety disorders: The role of father has been underestimated? *Journal of Clinical Child & Adolescent Psychology, 34*, 747–758.

Lichter, D. G., & Cummings, J. L. (Eds.). (2001). *Frontal-subcortical circuits in psychiatric and neurological disorders.* New York: Guilford Press.

Lichter, J. B. (1993). Comparative genomic hybridization: Uses and limitations. *Seminars in Hematology, 37*, 346–347.

Lichter, J. B., Barr, C. L., Kennedy, J. L., Van Tol, H., Kidd, K. K., & Levak, K. J. (1993). A hypervariable segment in the human dopamine receptor P4 (DRD4) gene. *Human Molecular Gene, 2*, 767–773.

Lidz, C. S. (2003). *Early childhood assessment.* Hoboken, NJ: John Wiley & Sons, Inc.

Lieb, R., Wittchen, H. U., Hofler, M., Fuetsch, M., Stein, M. B., & Merikangs, K. R. (2000). Parental psychopathology, parenting styles, and the risk of social phobia in offspring. *Archives of General Psychiatry, 57*, 859–865.

Lieberman, A. F. (1991). Attachment theory and infant-parent psychotherapy: Some conceptual, clinical and research considerations. In D. Cicchetti, & S. L. Toth (Eds.), *Rochester symposium on developmental psychopathology: Vol. 3. Models and integrations* (pp. 261–287). Rochester, NY: University of Rochester Press.

Lieberman, A. F. (1999). Negative maternal attributions: Effects on toddlers' sense of self. *Psychoanalytic Inquiry, 19*, 737–750.

Lieberman, A. F., Ghosh Ippen, C., & Van Horn, P. (2006). Child-parent psychotherapy: A six month follow-up of a randomized controlled trail. *Journal of the American Academy of Child and Adolescent Psychiatry, 45*, 913–918.

Lieberman, A. F., Silverman, R., & Pawl, J. H. (2000). Infant-parent psychotherapy: Core concepts and current approaches. In C. H. Zeanah, Jr. (Ed.), *Handbook of infant mental health* (2nd ed., pp. 472–484). New York: Guilford Press.

Lieberman, A. F., & Van Horn, P. (2005). *"Don't hit my mommy!" A manual for child-parent psychotherapy with young witnesses of family violence.* Washington, DC: ZERO TO THREE Press.

Lieberman, A. F., & Van Horn, P. (2008). *Psychotherapy with infants and young children: Repairing the effects of stress and trauma in early attachment.* New York: Guilford Press.

Lieberman, A. F., Van Horn, P., & Ghosh Ipsen, C. (2005). Towards evidence-based treatment: Child-parent psychotherapy with preschoolers exposed to marital violence. *Journal of the American Academy of Child and Adolescent Psychiatry, 44,* 1241–1248.

Liepert, J., Miltner, W. H. R., Bauder, H., Sommer, M., Dettmers, C., Taub, E., ... Weiller, C. (1998). Motor cortex plasticity during constraint-induced movement therapy in stroke patients. *Neuroscience Letters, 250,* 5–8.

Lindsay, G., & Dockerell, J. (2002). Meeting the needs of children with speech, language and communiation needs: A critical perspective on inclusion and collaboration. *Child Language and Teaching Therapy, 18,* 91–101.

Linver, M., Brooks-Gunn, J., & Kohen, D. (2002). Family process as pathways from income to young children's development. *Developmental Psychology, 38,* 719–734.

Liotti, G. (1997). Disorganized/disoriented attachment in the psychotherapy of dissociative disorders. In S. Goldberg, R. Muir & J. Kerr (Eds.), *Attachment theory: Social, developmental and clinical perspectives* (pp. 343–363). Hillsdale, NJ: The Analytic Press.

Lochman, J. E. (1992). Cognitive-behavioral interventions with aggressive boys: Three year follow-up and prevention effects. *Journal of Consulting and Clinical Psychology, 60,* 426–432.

Lochman, J. E., & Gresham, F. M. (2009). Intervention, development, assessment, planning, and adaptation: The importance of developmental models. In M. M. Mayer, R. Van Acker, J. E. Lochman, & F. M. Gresham (Eds.), *Cognitive-behavioral interventions for emotional and behavioral disorders: School-based practice* (pp. 29–57). New York: Guilford.

Lochman, J. E., Powell, N. R., Whidby, J. M., & Fitzgerald, D. P. (2006). Aggressive children: Cognitive-behavioral assessment and treatment. In P. C. Kendall (Ed.), *Child and adolescent therapy: Cognitive-behavioral procedures* (3rd ed., pp. 33–81). New York: Guilford.

Lochman, J. E., & Wells, K. C. (2002). Contextual social-cognitive mediators and child outcome: A test of the theoretical model of the Coping Power program. *Development and Psychopathology, 14,* 971–993.

Lochman, J. E., & Wells, K. C. (2004). The Coping Power program for preadolescent aggressive boys and their parents: Outcome effects at the one-year follow-up. *Journal of Consulting and Clinical Psychology, 72,* 571–578.

Lochmann, J. E., Wells, K. C., & Lenhart, L. A. (2008). *Coping power child group program: Facilitator guide.* Oxford, UK: Oxford University Press.

Loeber, R., Green, S. M., Lahey, B. B., & Stouthamer-Loeber, M. (1991). Differences and similarities between children, mothers, and teachers as informants on disruptive child behavior. *Journal of Abnormal Child Psychology, 19,* 75–95.

Loeber, R., Stouthamer-Loeber, M., Van Kammen, W. B., & Farrington, D. P. (1991). Initiation, escalation, and desistance in juvenile offending and their correlates. *Journal of Criminal Law and Criminology, 82,* 36–82.

Lohmann, H., & Tomasello, M. (2003). The role of language in the development of false belief understanding: A training study. *Child Development, 74,* 1130–1144.

Lombardino, L. J., Lieberman, R. J., & Brown, J. C. (2005*). Assessment of Literacy and Language (ALL): Examiner's Manual*. Pearson.

Lonigan, C. J., Elbert, J. C., & Johnson, S. B. (1998). Empirically supported psychosocial interventions for children: An overview. *Journal of Clinical Child Psychology, 27,* 138–145.

Lonigan, C. J., Vasey, M. W., Phillips, B. M., & Hazen, R. A. (2004). Temperament, anxiety, and the processing of threat-relevant stimuli. *Journal of Child and Adolescent Psychology, 33,* 8–20.

Lopez, N. L., Bonenberger, J. I., & Schneider, H. G. (2001). Parental disciplinary history, current levels of empathy and moral reasoning in young adults. *North American Journal of Psychology, 3,* 193–204.

Lord, C., & Paul, R. (1997). Language and communication in autism. In D. J. Cohen & F. R. Volkmar (Eds.), *Handbook of autism and pervasive developmental disorders* (pp. 195–225). New York, NY: John Wiley & Sons, Inc.

Lord, C. Risi, S., DiLavore, P., Shulman, C., Thurm, A., & Pickles, A. (2006). Autism from 2 to 9 years of age. *Archives of General Psychiatry, 63,* 694–701.

Lord, C., Rutter, M., Dilavore, P., & Risi, S. (1999). *Autism Diagnostic Observation Schedule (ADOS).* Western Psychological Services, Torrance, CA.

Lord, C., Rutter, M., DiLavore, P. C., & Risi, S. (2000). *Autism Diagnostic Observation Schedule (ADOS)*. Los Angeles, CA: Western Psychological Services.

Lord, C., Rutter, M., & LeCouteur, A. (1994). Autism diagnostic interview—Revised: A revised version of the diagnostic Interview for caregivers of individuals with possible pervasive developmental disorder. *Journal of Autism and Developmental Disorders, 24*, 659–685.

Lounds, J., Borkowski, J., Whitman, T., Maxell, S., & Weed, K. (2005). Adolescent parenting and attachment during infancy and early childhood. *Parenting, Science and Practice, 5*, 91–137.

Love, J. M., Kisker, E. E., Ross, C. M., Schochet, P. Z., Brooks-Gunn, J., Paulsell, D., ... Brady-Smith, C. (2002). *Making a difference in the lives of infants and toddlers and their families: The impacts of Early Headstart, Vol. 1: Final Technical Report.* Washington, DC: U.S. Department of Health and Human Services, Administration for Children and Families, Head Start Bureau. Prepared by Mathematica Policy Research under Contract DHHS-105-95-1936.

Lovejoy, M. C., Graczyk, P. A., O'Hare, E., & Neuman, G. (2000). Maternal behavior and parenting behavior: A meta-analytic review. *Clinical Psychology Review, 20*, 561–592.

Lowe, D. G., & Mitterer, J. O. (1982). Selective and divided attention in a Stroop task. *Canadian Journal of Psychology, 36*, 684–700.

Lowe, M., & Costello, A. J. (1998). *Symbolic play test* (2nd ed.). London, UK: GL Assessment.

Luby, J. L. (2009a). Depression. In C. H. Zeanah, Jr. (Ed.), *Handbook of infant mental health* (3rd ed., pp. 409–420). New York: Guilford Publishers.

Luby, J. L. (2009b). Early childhood depression. *American Journal of Psychiatry, 166*, 975–979.

Luby, J. L., & Belden, A. C. (2006). Mood disorders: Phenomenology and a developmental emotion reactivity model. In J. L. Luby (Ed.), *Handbook of preschool mental health: Development, disorders, and treatment* (pp. 209–230). New York: Guilford Press.

Luciana, M., Lindeke, L., Georgieff, M., Mills, M., & Nelson, C. A. (1999). Neurobehavioral evidence of working memory deficits in school-aged children with histories of prematurity. *Developmental Medicine and Child Neurology, 41*(8), 521–533.

Lundberg, O. (1993). The impact of childhood living conditions on illness and mortality in adulthood. *Social Science and Medicine, 36*, 1047–1052.

Lurito, J. T., & Dzemidzic, M. (2001). Determination of cerebral hemisphere language dominance with functional magnetic resonance imaging. *Neuroimaging Clinics of North America, 11*, 355–363.

Lutcke, H., & Frahm, J. (2008). Lateralized anterior cingulated function during error processing and conflict monitoring as revealed by high-resolution fMRI. *Cerebral Cortex, 18*, 508–510.

Luthar, S. S., & Cicchetti, D. (2000). The construct of resilience: Implications for intervention and social policy. *Developmental and Psychopathology, 12*, 857–885.

Luxemberg, T., Spinazzola, J., Hidalgo, J., Hunt, C., & van der Kolk, B. A. (2001). Complex trauma and disorders of extreme stress (DESNOS) Part 2: Treatment. *Directions in Psychiatry, 21*, 395–415.

Lykken, D. T. (1995). *The antisocial personalities*. Hillsdale, NJ: Erlbaum.

Lyons-Ruth, K., Bronfman, E., & Atwood, G. (1999). A relational diathesis model of hostile-helpless states of mind: Expressions in mother-infant interaction. In J. Solomon & C. George (Eds.), *Attachment disorganization* (pp. 33–70). N.Y.: Guilford Press.

Lyons-Ruth, K., Connell, D. B., Grunebaum, H. U., & Botein, S. (1990). Infants at social risk: Maternal depression and family support services as mediators of infant development and security of attachment. *Child Development, 61*, 85–98.

Lyons-Ruth, K., Easterbrooks, M. A., & Cibelli, C. F. (1997). Infant attachment security and maternal predictors of early behavior problems: A longitudinal study of low-income families. *Journal of Abnormal Child Psychology, 23*, 335–357.

Lyons-Ruth, K., Easterbrooks, M. A., Davidson, Cibelli, C. F., & Bronfman, F. C. (1995, April). *Predicting school-age externalizing symptoms from infancy: Contributions of disorganized attachment strategies and mild mental lag*. Paper presented at the biennial meeting of the Society for Research in Child Development. Indianapolis, IN.

Lyons-Ruth, K., & Jacobvitz, D. (1999). Attachment disorganization: Unresolved loss, relationship violence, and lapses in behavioral and attenional strategies. In J. Cassidy & P. R. Shaver (Eds.), *Handbook of attachment research, theory, and clinical research* (pp. 520–554). New York: Guilford Press.

Lyons-Ruth, K., & Jacobvitz, D. (2008). Attachment disorganization: Genetic factors, parenting contexts, and developmental transformation from infancy to adulthood. In J. Cassidy & P. R. Shaver (Eds.), *Handbook of attachment research, theory, and clinical research* (2nd ed., pp. 666–677). New York: Guilford Press.

Lyons-Ruth, K., Melnick, S., Bronfman, E., Sherry, S., & Llanas, L. (2004). Hostile-helpless relational models and disorganised attachment patterns between parents and their young children: Review of research and implications for clinical work. In L. Atkinson & S. Goldberg (Eds.), *Attachment issues in psychopathology and intervention* (pp. 65–94). Mahwah, NJ: Lawrence Erlbaum Associates.

Lyons-Ruth, K., & Spielman, E. (2004). Disorganized infant attachment strategies and helpless-fearful profiles of parenting: Integrating attachment research with clinical intervention. *Infant Mental Health Journal, 25*, 318–335.

Lyons-Ruth, K., Yellin, C., Melnick, S., & Atwood, G. (2005). Expanding the concept of unresolved mental states: Hostile/Helpless states of mind on Adult Attachment Interviews are associated with disruptive mother-infant communication and infant disorganization. *Development and Psychopathology, 17*, 271–301.

Lyons-Ruth, K., Zoll, D., Connell, D., & Grunebaum, H. U. (1989). Family defiance and family disruption in childhood: Associations with maternal behavior and infant maltreatment during the first years of life. *Development & Psychopathology, 1*, 219–236.

Maccoby, E.E. (1983). Let's not over attribute the attribution process: Comments on social cognition and behavior. In E.T. Higgins, D.N. Ruble & W.W. Hartup (Eds.), *Social cognition and social development* (pp. 356–370). New York: Cambridge Press.

Maccoby, E. E., & Martin, J. (1983). Socialisation in the context of the family: Parent-child interaction. In P. H. Mussen (Series Ed.) & E. M. Hetherington (Vol. Ed.), *Handbook of child psychology: Vol. 4. Socialisation, personality, and social development* (pp. 1–101). New York: Wiley.

Machado, C. J., & Bachevalier, J. (2003). Non-human primate models of childhood psychopathology: The promise and the limitations. *Journal of Child Psychology and Psychiatry, 44*, 64–87.

Machover, K. (1952). *Personality projection in the drawing of the human figure*. Springfield, IL: Charles C. Thomas.

Mackie, J., Cicchetti, D., & Toth, S. L. (2001). Dissociation in maltreated versus nonmaltreated preschool-aged children. *Child Abuse and Neglect, 25*, 1253–1267.

Madden, J., O'Hara, J., & Levenstein, S. (1984). Home again: Effects of the Mother-Child Home Program on mother and child. *Child Development, 55*, 636–647.

Madigan, S., Hawkins, E., & Goldberg, S., & Benoit, D. (2006). Reduction of disrupted caregiver behavior using modified interaction guidance. *Infant Mental Health Journal, 27*, 509–527.

Madigan, S., Moran, G., & Pederson, D. R. (2006). Unresolved states of mind, disorganized attachment relationships, and disrupted interactions of adolescent mothers and their infants. *Developmental Psychology, 42*, 293–304.

Madigan, S., Moran, G., Scheungel, C., Pederson, D., & Otten, R. (2007). Unresolved maternal attachment representations, disrupted maternal behavior and disorganized attachment in infancy: Links to toddler behavior problems. *Journal of Child Psychology and Psychiatry, 48*, 1042–1050.

Magalhaes, L. C., Missiuna, C., & Wong, S. (2006). Terminology used in research reports of developmental coordination disorder. *Developmental Medicine and Child Neurology, 48*(11), 937–941.

Maguire, E. A., Gadian, D. G., Johnsrude, I. S., Good, J. D., Ashburner, J., Frackowiak, R. S. J., & Frith, C. D. (2000). Navigation-related structural change in the hippocampi of taxi drivers. *Proceedings of the National Academy of Sciences, USA, 97*, 4398–4403.

Magyar, C. I. (2011). *Developing and evaluating educational programs for children with autism*. New York: Springer.

Mahncke, H. W., Connor, B. B., Appelman, J., Ahsanuddin, J. L., Hardy, J. L., Wood, R. A., ... Merzenich, M. M. (2006). Memory enhancement in healthy older adults using a brain plasticity-based training program: A randomized controlled study. *Proceedings of the National Academy of Sciences, USA, 103*, 12523–12528.

Main, M. (1995). Recent studies in attachment: Overview, with selected implications for clinical work. In S. Goldberg, R. Muir, & J. Kerr (Eds.), *Attachment theory: Social, developmental and clinical perspectives* (pp. 407–474). Hillsdale, NJ: Analytic Press.

Main, M., & Cassidy, J. (1988). Categories of response to reunion with the parent at age 6: Predictable from infant attachment classifications and stable over a one month period. *Developmental Psychology, 24,* 415–426.

Main, M., Hesse, E., & Kaplan, N. (2005). Predictability of attachment behavior and representational processes at 1, 6, and 19 years of age: The Berkeley longitudinal study. In K. E. Grossman, K. Grossman, & E. Waters (Eds.), *Attachment from infancy to adulthood: The major longitudinal studies* (pp. 245–304). New York: Guilford Press.

Main, M., Kaplan, N., & Cassidy, J. (1985). Security in infancy, childhood, and adulthood: A move to the level of representation. In I. Bretherton & E. Waters (Eds.), Growing points of attachment theory and research. *Monographs of the Society for Research in Child Development*, 50 (1–2, serial No. 209), 66–104.

Main, M., & Solomon, J. (1990). Procedures for identifying infants as disorganized/disoriented during the Ainsworth Strange Situation. In M. T. Greenberg, D. Cicchetti, & E. M. Cummings (Eds.), *Attachment in the preschool years: Theory, research, and intervention* (pp. 121–160). IL: University of Chicago.

Malbin, D. (2002). *Fetal alcohol spectrum disorders: Trying differently rather than harder* (2nd ed.). Oregon; FASCETS, Inc.

Malchiodi, C. A. (2008). *Creative interventions with traumatized children*. New York: Guilford Press.

Manassis, K. (2008). *Keys to parenting your anxious child* (2nd ed.). Hauppauge, NY: Baron's Educational Series, Inc.

Manassis, K. (2009). *Cognitive behavioral therapy with children: A guide for the community practitioner*. New York: Routledge.

Manassis, K., & Bradley, S. (1994). The development of childhood anxiety disorders: Toward an integrated model. *Journal of Applied Developmental Psychology, 15,* 345–366.

Mandich, A. D., Polatajko, H.J, Macnab, J. J., & Miller, L. T. (2001). Treatment of children with developmental coordination disorder: What is the evidence? *Physical Occupational Therapy in Paediatrics, 20, 51–68.*

Mangeot, S. D., Miller, L. J., McIntosh, D. N., McGrath-Clarke, J., Simon, J., Hagerman, R. J. (2001) Sensory modulation dysfunction in children with ADHD. *Developmental Medicine and Child Neurology, 43,* 399–406.

Manian, N., & Borenstein, M. H. (2009). Dynamics of emotion regulation in infants of clinically depressed and non-depressed mothers. *Journal of Child Psychology and Psychiatry, 50*(11), 1410–1418.

Manly, T., Robertson, I. H., Anderson, V., & Nimmo-Smith, I. (1999). *The test of everyday attention for children: Manual.* Bury St. Edmunds, UK: Thames Valley Test Company.

Mantzicopoulos, P. (2005). Conflictual relationships between kindergarten children and their teachers: Associations with child and classroom context variables. *Journal of Child Psychology, 43,* 425–442.

March, J. S. (2009). The future of psychotherapy for mentally ill children and adults. *Journal of Child Psychology and Psychiatry, 50,* 170–179.

Margolin, G., & Gordis, E. B. (2000). The effects of family and community violence on children. *Annual Review of Psychology, 51,* 445–479.

Marko, J., & Merchbach, H. (2004). Traumatic stress, brain changes, and memory deficits: A critical note. *The Journal of Nervous and Mental Disease, 192,* 548–553.

Martens, W. H. J. (2005). Shame and narcissism: Therapeutic relevance of conflicting dimensions of excessive self-esteem, pride, and pathological vulnerable self. *Annals of the American Psychotherapy Association, 8,* 10–27.

Martin, N. (2006). *Test of visual perceptual skills* (3rd ed.). Novato, CA: Academic Therapy Publications.

Martin, N. A., & Brownell, R. (2000). *Expressive One-Word Picture Vocabulary Test—4th ed.* (EOWPVT-4). Torrance, CA: Western Psychological Services.

Martin, T., & Fox, N. A. (2006). Temperament: In K. McCartney & D. Phillips (Eds.), *Blackwell handbook of early childhood development* (pp. 127–146). Malden, MA: Blackwell Publishing.

Martinez, C. R., & Forgatch, M. S. (2001). Preventing problems with boy's noncompliance: Effects of a parent training intervention for divorcing mothers. *Journal of Consulting and Clinical Psychology, 69,* 416–428.

Martinussen, R., Tannock, R., McInnes, A., & Chaban, P. (2006). *Teach for success: Teach ADHD: Teacher's resource manual.* Toronto, ON: TV Ontario.

Marwitt, S. J., & Stenner, A. J. (1972). Hyperkinesis: Delineation of two patterns. *Exceptional Children, 38*, 401–406.
Mason, A. & Frick, P. J. (1994). The heritability of antisocial behavior: A meta-analysis of twin and adoption studies. *Journal of Psychopathology and Behavioral Assessment, 16*, 301–323.
Masten, A. S., & Powell, J. L. (2005). A resilience framework for research, policy, and practice. In S. S. Luthar (Ed.), *Resilience and vulnerability: Adaptation in the context of adversities* (pp. 1–25). New York: Cambridge University Press.
Masten, C. L., Eisenberger, N. I., Borofsky, L. A., McNealy, K., Pfeifer, J. H., & Dapretto, M. (2011). Subgenual anterior cingulate responses to peer rejection: A marker of adolescents' risk for depression. *Development and Psychopathology, 23*, 283–292.
Masten, P. S., & Curtis, W. J. (2000). Integrating competence and psychopathology: Pathways towards a comprehensive science of adaptation in development. *Development and Psychopathology, 12*, 529–550.
Matson, S. N., Riley, E. P., Gramling, L. J., Delis, D. C., & Jones, K. L. (1998) Neurological comparison of alcohol-exposed children with and without physical features of fetal alcohol syndrome. *Neuropsychology, 12*, 146–153.
Maughan, B., & Cicchetti, D. (2002). The impact of child maltreatment and inter-adult violence on children's emotion regulation abilities. *Child Development, 73*, 1525–1542.
May-Benson, T. A., & Koomar, J. A. (2010). Systematic review of research evidence examining the effectiveness of interventions using sensory integrative approach for children. *The American Journal of Occupational Therapy, 64*, 403–414.
Mayseless, O. (2005). Ontogeny of attachment in middle childhood: Conceptualization of normative changes. In K. A. Kerns & R. A. Richardson (Eds.), *Attachment in middle childhood* (pp. 1–23). New York: Guilford Press.
McBurnett, K., Lahey, B. B., Rathouz, P. J., & Loeber, R. (2000). Low salivary cortisol and persistent aggression in boys referred for disruptive behavior. *Archives of General Psychiatry, 57*, 38–43.
McCallie, M., Blum, C., & Hood, C. (2006). Progressive muscle relaxation. *Journal of Human behaviour in the Social Environment, 13*, 51–66.
McCartney, K., Owen, M. T., Booth, C. L., Clarke-Stewart, A., & Vandell, D. L. (2004). Testing a maternal attachment model of behavior problems in early childhood. *Journal of Child Psychology and Psychiatry, 45*, 756–778.
McClosky, G., Perkins, L. A., & Van Divner, B. (2009). *Assessment and intervention for executive function difficulties*. New York: Routledge.
McCormick, M. C., Brooks-Gunn, J., Buka, S. L., Goldman, J., Yu, J., Salganik, M., ... Casey, P. H. (2006). Early intervention with low birth weight premature infants: Results at 18 years of age for the Infant Health and Development Program. *Pediatrics, 117*, 771–780.
McDonough, S. C. (2000). Interaction guidance: An approach for difficult to engage families. In C. H. Zeanah, Jr. (Ed.), *Handbook of infant mental health* (2nd ed. pp. 485–493). New York: Guilford Press.
McEwen, B. (2000a). Allostasis and allostatic load: Implications for neuropsychopharmacology. *Neuropsychopharmacology, 22*, 108–124.
McEwen, B. (2000b). Allostasis, allostatic load and the aging nervous system: Role of excitatory amino acids and excitotoxicity. *Neurochemical Research, 25*, 1219–1231.
McEwen, B. (2002). Protective and damaging effects of stress mediators: The good and bad sides of the responses to stress. *Metabolism, 51*, 2–4.
McEwen, B., & Schmeck, H. (1994). *The hostage brain*. New York: Rockefeller University Press.
McGaha, C. (2002). Development of parenting skills in individuals with an intellectual impairment: An epigenetic explanation. *Disability and Society, 17*, 81–91.
McGhee, R. L., Ehrier, D. J., & DiSimi, F. (1978). *Token test for children*, 2nd ed. (TTFC-2).
McGrath, M. M., Sullivan, M. C., & Seifer, R. (1998). Maternal interaction patterns and preschool competence in high risk children. *Journal of Nursing Research, 47*, 309–317.
McInnes, A., Fung, D., Manassis, K., Fiksenbaum, L., & Tannock, R. (2004). Narrative skills in children with selective mutism: An exploratory study. *American Journal of Speech Language Pathology, 13*, 304–315.
McIntosh, D. (2010). Treating disruptive classroom behaviors of preschoolers through teacher-child interaction therapy. In A. A. Drewes & C. E. Schaefer (Eds.), *School-based play therapy* (2nd ed., pp. 197–218). Hoboken, NJ: Wiley.

McIntosh, D. E., Rizza, M. G., & Bliss, L. (2000). Implementing empirically supported interventions: Teacher-child interaction therapy. *Psychology in the Schools, 37*, 453–462.

McIntosh, D. N., Miller, L. J., Shyu, V., & Hagerman, R. J. (1999). Sensory modulation disruption, electrodermal responses and functional behaviours. *Developmental Medicine and Child Neurology, 41*, 608–615.

McKown, C., Gumbiner, L. M., Russo, N. M., & Lipton, M. (2009). Socio-emotional learning skill, self-regulation and social competence in typically developing and clinically referred children. *Journal of Clinical Child & Adolescent Psychology, 38*(6), 858–871.

McLeer, V., Callaghan, M., Henry, D., & Wallen, J. (1994). Psychiatric disorders in sexually abused children. *Journal of the American Academy of Child and Adolescent Psychiatry, 33*, 313–319.

McLoyd, V. (1998). Socioeconomic disadvantage and child development. *American Psychologist, 53*, 185–204.

McLoyd, V., & Wilson, L. (1991). The strain of living poor: Parenting, social support and child mental health. In A. Huston (Ed.), *Children in poverty* (pp. 105–135). New York: Cambridge University Press.

McMahon, R. J., & Forehand, R. (1984). Parent training for the noncompliant child: Treatment outcome, generalization, and adjunctive therapy procedures. In R. F. Dangel & A. Polster (Eds), *Parent training: Foundations of research and practice* (pp. 298–328). New York: Guilford Press.

McMahon, R. J., & Forehand, R. (2003). *Helping the noncompliant child: Family-based treatment for oppositional behavior* (2nd ed.). New York: Guilford Press.

McNab, F., Varrone, A., Farde, L., Jucaite, A., Bystritsky, P., Forrsberg, H., & Klingberg, T. (2009). Changes in cortical dopamine D1 receptor binding associated with cognitive training. *Science, 323*, 800–802.

Mead, H. K., Beauchaine, T. P., & Shannon, K. E. (2010). Neurobiological adaptations to violence across development. *Development and Psychopathology, 22*(1), 1–22.

Meaney, M. (2010). Epigenetics and biological definition of gene x environment interactions. *Child Development, 81*, 41–79.

Meaney, M. J., & Szyf, M. (2005). Maternal care as a model for experience-dependent chromatin plasticity? *Trends in Neurosciences, 28*, 456–453.

Mednick, S. A., Volavka, J., Gabrielli, W. F., & Intil, T. (1998). EEG as a predictor of antisocial behavior. *Criminology, 19*, 219–231.

Mellard, D., McKnight, M., & Jordan, J. (2010). RTI tier structures and instructional intensity. *Learning Disabilities Research & Practice, 25*, 217–225.

Meltzer, H., Gatward, R., Corbin, T., Goodman, R., & Ford, T. (2003*). Persistence, onset, risk factors, and outcome of childhood mental health disorders.* London: TSO.

Mendenhall, A. N., Fristad, M. A., & Early, T. J. (2009). Factors influencing service utilization and mood symptom severity in children with mood disorders: Effects of multi-family psycho-education groups (MFPGs). *Journal of Consulting and Clinical Psychology, 77*, 463–473.

Menkes, J. H., Sarnat, H. B., & Maria, B. L. (2006). *Child neurology* (7th ed.). Lippincott, Williams & Wilkins.

Merzenich, M. M., Jenkins, W. M., Johnston, P., Schreiner, C., Miller, S. L., & Tallal, P. (1996). Temporal processing deficits of language-learning impaired children ameliorated by training. *Science, 271*, 77–81.

Mesulam, M.-M. (2000). Brain, mind, and the evolution of connectivity. *Brain and Cognition, 42*, 4–6.

Mesulam, M.-M. (2002). The human frontal lobes: transcending the default mode through contingent encoding. In T. Stuss & R. T. Knight (Eds.), *Principals of frontal lobe function* (pp. 8–30). New York: Oxford University Press.

Meyer, M., Alter, K., Friederici, A. D., Lohmann, G., & von Cramon, D. Y. (2002). fMRI reveals brain regions mediating slow prosodic modulations in spoken sentences. *Human Brain Mapping, 17*, 73–88.

Mezulis, A., Hyde, J., & Clark, R. (2004). Father involvement moderates the effect of maternal depression during a child's infancy on child behaviour problems in kindergarten. *Journal of Family Psychology, 18*, 575–588.

Mezzacappa, F. E., Kindlon, D., Saul, J. P., Arseneault, L., Pihl, R. O., & Earls, F. (1996). Relationship of aggression and anxiety to autonomic regulation of heart rate variability in adolescent males. *Annals of the New York Academy of Science, 794*, 376–379.

Mezzacappa, F.E., Kindlon, D., Saul, J.P., & Earls, F. (1998). Executive and motivational control of performance task behavior and autonomic heart rate regulation in children: Physiologic validation of two-factor solution inhibitory control. *Journal of Child Psychology and Psychiatry, 39*, 525–533.

Michelson, L., Sugai, D., Wood, R., & Kazdin, A. (1983). *Social skills assessment and training with children: An Empirically Based Approach*. New York, NY: Plenum Press.

Mick, E., Biederman, J., Prince, J., Fischer, M. J., & Faraone, S. V. (2002). Impact of low birth weight on attention deficit/hyperactivity disorder. *Journal of Developmental and Behavioral Pediatrics, 23*, 16–22.

Milberger, S., Biederman, J., Faraone, S., Guite, J., & Tsuang, M. (1997). Pregnancy, delivery, and infancy complications and ADHD: Issues of environmental interactions. *Biological Psychiatry, 41*, 65–75.

Miller, B. L., & Cummings, J. L. (Eds.). (2006). *The human frontal lobes: Functions and disorders* (2nd ed.). New York: Guilford Press.

Miller, C. (2006). Developmental relationships between language and theories of mind. *American Journal of Speech-Language Pathology, 15*,142–154.

Miller, D. C. (2007). *Essentials of school neuropsychological assessment*. Hoboken, NJ: John Wiley & Sons, Inc.

Miller, L. J. (2006). *Miller function and participation scales* (M-FUN-PS). San Antonio, TX: The Psych. Corp.

Miller L. J., Anzalone, M. E., Lane, S. J., Cermak, S. A., Osten, E. T. (2007). Concept evolution in sensory integration: A proposed nosology for diagnosis. *The American Journal of Occupational Therapy, 61*(2), 135–140.

Miller, L. J., & Lane, S. J. (2000, March). Toward a consensus in terminology in sensory integration theory and practice: Part 1: Taxonomy of neurophysiological processes. *Sensory Integration Special Interests Section Quarterly, 23*, 1–4.

Miller, L. J., McIntosh, D. N., McGrath, J., Shyu, V., Lampe, M., Taylor, A. K., ... Hagerman, R. J. (1999). Electrodermal response to sensory stimuli in individuals with fragile x syndrome: A preliminary report. *American Journal of Medicinal Genetics, 83, 268–279.*

Miller, N. E., & Dollard, J. (1941). *Social learning and imitation*. New York: McGraw-Hill.

Miller-Kuhaneck, H., Henry, D. A., Glennor, T. J., & Mu, K. (2007). Development of the Sensory Processing Measure–School: Initial studies of reliability and validity. *American Journal of Occupational Therapy, 61*, 170–175.

Milner, B. (1963). Some effects of different brain lesions on card sorting. *Archives of Neurology, 9*, 90–100.

Milner, B. (1982). Some cognitive effects of frontal lobe lesions in man. *Philosophical Transactions of the Royal Society of London B: Biological Sciences, 298*, 211–226.

Mirsky, A. F., & Duncan, C. C. (2001). A nosology of disorders of attention. In J. Wasserstein, L. Wolff, & F. F. LeFever (Eds.), *Adult attention disorder: Brain mechanisms and life outcomes*. New York: Annals of New York Academy of Sciences.

Miskovic, V., Schmidt, L. A., Georgiades, K., Boyle, M., & MacMillan, H. L. (2010). Adolescent females exposed to child maltreatment exhibit atypical EEG coherence and psychiatric impairment: Linking early adversity, the brain and psychopathology. *Development and Psychopathology, 22*(2), 419–432.

Missiuna, C. (2001). Strategies for success: working with children with developmental coordination disorder. *Physical Occupational Therapy in Pediatrics, 20*, 1–4.

Missiuna, C. (2003). *Children with developmental coordination disorder: At home and in the classroom. Canadian Child Centre for Childhood Disability Research*. Mc Master University.

Mitchell, D., & Blair, R. J. R. (2000). State of the art: Psychopathy. *Psychologist, 13*, 356–360.

Mitchell, P. (1997). *Introduction to theory of mind: Children, autism, and apes*. New York: St. Martin's Press.

Miyahara, A., Tsuji, M., Hori, M., Nakanishi, K., Kageyama, H., & Sugiyama, T. (1997). Brief report: Motor in coordination in children with Asperger syndrome and learning disabilities. *Journal of Autism and Developmental Disorders, 27, 597–603.*

Moadab, I., Gilbert, T., Dishion, T.J., & Tucker, D.M. (2010). Frontalolimbic activity in a frustrating task: Covariation between patterns of coping and individual differences in externalizing and internalizing behavior. *Development and Psychopathology, 22*, 391–404.

Moffitt, T. E. (1990). Juvenile delinquency and attention deficit disorder: Boys' developmental trajectories from age 3 to age 15. *Child Development, 61,* 893–910.

Moffitt, T. E., Caspi, A., Harrington, H., & Milne, B. (2002). Males on the life-course persistent and adolescent-limited antisocial pathways: Follow-up at age 26. *Development and Psychopathology, 14,* 179–207.

Moffitt, T. E., Caspi, A., Rutter, M., & Silva, P. A. (2001). *Sex differences in antisocial behavior* (pp. 237–239). Cambridge, U.K. Cambridge University Press.

Moffitt, T. E., & Henry, B. (1991). Neuropsychological studies of juvenile delinquency and violence: A review. In J. Milner (Ed.), *The neuropsychology of aggression* (pp. 67–91). Norwell, MA: Kluwer Academic Publishers.

Monahan, K. C., Steinberg, L., & Cauffman, E. (2009). Affiliation with antisocial peers, susceptibility to peer influence, and antisocial behavior during the transition to adulthood. *Developmental Psychology, 45,* 1520–1530.

Monk, C. S. (2008). The development of emotion-related neural circuitry in health and psychopathology. *Development and Psychopathology, 20*(1), 1231–1250.

Moore, G. A. (2009). Infants' and mothers' vagal reactivity in response to anger. *Journal of Child Psychology and Psychiatry, 50*(11), 1392–1400.

Moore, K. A., Morrison, D. R., & Greene, A. D. (1997). Effects on the children born to adolescent mothers. In R. A. Maynard (Ed.), *Kids having kids: Economic costs and social consequences of teen pregnancy.* Washington, DC: Urban Institute.

Moore, P. S., Whaley, S. E., & Sigman, M. (2004). Interactions between mother and children: Impacts of maternal and child anxiety. *Journal of Abnormal Child Psychology, 113,* 471–476.

Moran, G., Forbes, L., Evans, E., Tarabulsy, G., & Madigan, S. (2008). Both maternal sensitivity and atypical maternal behavior independently predict attachment security and disorganisation in adolescent mother-infant relationships. *Infant Behavior and Development, 31,* 316–320.

Morgan, C. A., Wang, S., & Southwick, S. M. (2000). Plasma neuropeptide-Y concentrations in humans exposed to military survival training. *Biological Psychiatry, 47,* 902–909.

Moroney, R. M. (1992). Social support systems: Families and social policies. In S. L. Kagan, B. Weissbord, & E. Zigler (Eds.), *America's family support programs: Perspective and prospectives* (pp. 31–37). London: Yale University Press.

Morrison, M. O., & Helker, W. P. (2010). Child-teacher relationship training: Using the power of the child-teacher relationship as a school-based mental health intervention. In A. A. Drewes & C. E. Schaefer (Eds.), *School-based play therapy* (2nd ed., pp. 181–195). Hoboken, NJ: Wiley.

Morse, B. A., Miller, P. T., & Cermak. S. A. (1995). Sensory processing in children with FAS. *Alcoholism: Clinical and Experimental Research, 19,* 588.

Moss, E., Gosselin, C., Parent, S., Rousseau, D., & Dumont, M. (1997). Attachment and joint problem-solving experiences in the preschool period. *Social Development, 6,* 1–17.

Moss, E., Smolta, N., Cyr, C., Dubois-Comtois, K., Mazzarello, T., & Berthiaume, C. (2006). Attachment and behavior problems in middle childhood as reported by adult and child informants. *Development and Psychopathology, 18,* 425–444.

Moss, E., St.-Laurent, D., Dubois-Comtois, K. & Cyr, C. (2005). Quality of attachment at school-age: Relations between child attachment behaviors, psychosocial functioning, and school performance. In K. A. Kerns & R. A. Richardson (Eds.), *Attachment in middle childhood* (pp. 189–211). New York: Guilford Press.

Mpofu, E., & Conyers, L. M. (2003). Neurochemistry in the co-morbidity of conduct disorders of childhood and adolescence: Implications for counseling. *Counseling Psychology Review, 16,* 37–41.

Mrazek, P. J., & Brown, C. H. (2002). *An evidence-based literature review regarding outcomes in psychosocial prevention and early intervention in young children.* Technical Report. Toronto, ON: Invest in Kids Foundation.

MTA Cooperative Group. (1999a). A 14-month randomized clinical trial of treatment strategies for attention-deficit/hyperactivity disorder: Multimodal Treatment Study of Children with ADHD. *Archives of General Psychiatry, 56,* 1073–1086.

MTA Cooperative Group. (1999b). Effects of comorbid anxiety, poverty, session attendance, and community medication in treatment outcome in children with attention deficit/hyperactivity disorder. *Archives of General Psychiatry, 56,* 1088–1096.

Mueller, L. J., Sommer, M., Wagner, V., Lange, K., Taschler, H., Roder, C. H., ... Hajak, G. (2003). Abnormalities in emotion processing within cortical and subcortical regions in criminal psychopaths: Evidence from a functional magnetic resonance imaging study using pictures with emotional content. *Biological Psychiatry, 54*, 152–162.

Muir, E., Lojkasek, M., & Cohen, N. J. (1999). *Watch, Wait, and Wonder: A manual describing a dyadic infant-led approach to problems in infancy and early childhood.* Toronto: Hincks-Dellcrest Institute.

Munns, E. (2000). *Theraplay: Innovations in attachment-enhancing play therapy.* Northvale, NJ: Jason Aronson Inc.

Munoz, L. C., Frick, P. J., Kimonis, E. R., & Aucoin, K. J. (2008). Verbal ability and delinquency: Testing the moderating role of psychopathic traits. *The Journal of Child Psychology and Psychiatry, 49*, 414–421.

Murray, K. T., & Kochanska, G. (2002). Effortful control: Factor structure and relation to externalizing and internalizing behaviors. *Journal of Abnormal Child Psychology, 30*, 503–514.

Murray-Close, D., Ostrov, J. M., & Crick, N. R. (2007). A short-term longitudinal study of growth of relational aggression during middle childhood: Associations with gender, friendship intimacy, and internalizing problems. *Development and Psychopathology, 19*, 187–203.

Myers, S. S., & Pianta, R. C. (2008). Developmental commentary: Individual and contextual influences on student-teacher relationships and children's early problem behaviors. *Journal of Clinical Child and Adolescent Psychology, 37*, 600–608.

Myles, B., Jones-Block, S., & Simpson, R. (2001). *Asperger Syndrome Diagnostic Scale (ASDS).* North Tonawanda, NY: Multi-Health Systems, Inc.

Naber, E., Swinkels, S., Buitelaar, J., Dietz, C., Bakermans-Kranenburg, M., van IJzendoorn, M., ... Van Engeland, H. (2007). Attachment in toddlers with autism and other developmental disorders. *Journal of Autism and Developmental Disorders, 202*, 37, 1123–1138.

Nader, K. (1997). Childhood traumatic loss: The interaction of trauma and grief. In C. R. Figley, B. E. Bride, & N. Mazza (Eds.), *Death and trauma: The traumatology of grieving* (pp. 17–41). London: Taylor & Francis.

Nader, K. (2008). Risk and resilience factors: Trauma's mediator, moderator, or outcome variables. In K. Nader (Ed.), *Understanding and assessing trauma in children and adolescents: Measures, methods, and youth in context* (pp. 107–135). New York: Routledge.

National Center on Response to Intervention. (2010). *Essential components of RTI: A closer look at response to intervention.* Washington, DC: US Department of Education, Office of Special Education Programs, National Center on Response to Intervention.

National Institute for Clinical Excellence (ICE). (2005). *Post-traumatic stress disorder: The management of PTSD in adults and children in primary and secondary care.* (No. Clinical Guidelines 26). London: Author.

National Institute of Deafness and Other Communication Disorders (NIDCD). (2010). *Auditory processing disorders in children.* http://www.nidcd.nih.gov/health/voice/auditory.html

National Organization on Fetal Alcohol Syndrome. (2004). Fetal alcohol syndrome: Guidelines for referral and diagnosis.

National Scientific Council on the Developing Child. (2007). *The science of early childhood development: Closing the gap between what we know and what we do.* Cambridge, Massachusetts: National Scientific Council on the Developing Child.

National Scientific Council on the Developing Child. (2008). *Mental health problems in early childhood can impair learning and behavior for life: Working paper No. 6.* National Scientific Council on the Developing Child: Harvard University.

Natsuaki, M. N., Ge, X., Reiss, D., & Neiderhiser, J. M. (2009). Aggressive behavior between siblings and the development of externalizing problems: Evidence from a genetically sensitive study. *Developmental Psychology, 45*, 1009–1018.

Neale, M. D. (1999). *Neale analysis of reading ability: Manual (3rd ed.).* Melbourne, VICT, Australia: ACER Press.

Neilson, R. (2003a). *The Sutherland Phonological Awareness Test—Revised* (SPAT-R). Melbourne, VICT, Australia: ACER Press.

Neilson, R. (2003b). *Astronaut Invented Spelling Tests* (AIST). Jamberoo, NSW, Australia: Language, Speech, and Literacy Services.

Nelson, C. (2000). The neurological bases of early intervention. In J. Shonkoff & S. Meisels (Eds.), *Handbook of early childhood intervention* (pp. 204–229). New York: Cambridge University Press.

Nelson, C. A., & Bloom, F. E. (1997). Child development and neuroscience. *Child Development, 68,* 970–987.

Nelson, J. R., Benner, G. J., & Rogers-Adkinson, D., L. (2003). An investigation of the characteristics of K-12 Students with co-morbid emotional disturbance and significant language deficits in public school settings. *Behavioral Disorders, 29,* 25–33.

Nelson, N. (2011). The relevance of rhetoric. In D. Lapp & D. Fisher (Eds.), *Handbook of research on teaching the English/language arts* (pp. 290–297). New York: Routledge.

Nelson, W. M., & Finch, A. J. (1996). *"Keeping your cool": The anger management work book.* Ardmore, PA: Workbook Publishing.

Neppl, T. K., Conger, R. D., Scaramella, L. U., & Optai, L. L. (2009). Intergenerational continuity in parenting behavior: Mediating pathways and child effects. *Developmental Psychology, 45,* 1241–1256.

Newbury, D. F., Fisher, S. E., & Monaco, A. P. (2010). Recent advances in the genetics of language impairment. *Genome Medicine, 2,* 6. doi: 10.1186/gm127

Newcorn, J. H., Halperin, J. M., & Miller, C. J. (2009). ADHD with oppositionality and aggression. In T. E. Brown (Ed.), *ADHD comorbidities: Handbook for ADHD complications in children and adolescents* (pp. 157–187). Washington, DC: American Psychiatric Publishing Co.

Nguyen, D., Smith, L. M., LaGasse, L. L., Derauf, C., Grant, P., Shah, R., ... Lester, B. M. (2010). Intrauterine growth of infants exposed to prenatal methamphetamine: results from infant development, environment and lifestyle study. *The Journal of Pediatrics, 157,* 337–339.

NICHD Early Child Care Research Network. (2005). *Child care and child development: Results from the NICHD study of early child care and youth development.* New York: Guilford Press.

Nichols, M. P. (2004). *Stop arguing with your kids.* New York: Guilford Press.

Nigg, J. T. (2006). Temperament and developmental psychopathology. *Journal of Child Psychology and Psychiatry, 47*(3/4), 395–422.

Nigg, J. T., Goldsmith, H. H., & Sachek, J. (2004). Temperament and attention deficit hyperactivity disorder: The development of a multiple pathway model. *Journal of Clinical Child and Adolescent Psychology, 33,* 42–53.

Nijenhuis, E., van der Hart, O., & Steele, K. (2002). The emerging psychobiology of trauma-related dissociation and dissociative disorders. In H. D'Haenen, J. den Boer, & P. Willner (Eds.), *Biological psychiatry* (pp. 1079–1098). New York: John Wiley & Sons.

Nikopoulis, C. K., & Keenan, M. (2003). Promoting social initiation in children with autism using video modeling. *Behavioral Interventions, 18,* 87–108.

Nippold, M. A., Hesketh, L. J., Duthie, J. K., & Mansfield, T. C. (2005). Conversational versus expository discourse: A study of syntactic development in children, adolescents, and adults. *Journal of Speech, Language, and Hearing Research, 48,* 1048–1064

Nippold, M. A., & Schwartz, I. E. (2002). Do children recover from specific language impairment? *Advances in Speech Language Pathology, 4,* 41–49.

Noble, K., Tottenham, N., & Casey, B. (2005). Neuroscience perspectives on disparities in school readiness and cognitive achievement. *The Future of the Children, 15,* 71–89.

Nol, J. G., Shenk, C. E., Yeh, M. T., Ji, J., Putnam, F. W., & Trickett, P. K. (2010). Receptive language and educational attainment for sexually abused females. *Pediatrics, 126,* 3.

Nomura, Y., Rajendran, K., Brooks-Gunn, J., & Newcorn, J. H. (2008). Roles of perinatal problems on adolescent antisocial behaviors among children born after 33 completed weeks: A prospective investigation. *The Journal of Child Psychology and Psychiatry, 49,* 1108–1117.

Norris, C. J., & Cacioppo, J. T. (2007). I Know How You Feel: Social and emotional information processing in the brain. In E. Harmon-Jones & P. Winkielman (Eds.), *Social neuroscience: Integrating biological and psychological explanations of social behavior* (pp. 84–105). New York: Guilford.

NSCAW Research Group. (2005). *National survey of child and adolescent well-being (NSCAW) CPS sample component wave 1 data analysis report, April 2005.* Washington, DC: Department of Health and Human Services, Administration for Children, Youth and Families.

Nutt, D. J., Bell, C. J., & Malizia, A. L. (1998). Brain mechanisms of social anxiety disorder. *Journal of Clinical Psychiatry, 59,* 4–11.

O'Connor, T., Heron, J., Golding, J., Glover, V., & AL SPAC Study Team. (2003). Maternal antenatal anxiety and behavioural/emotional problems in children: A test of a programming hypothesis. *Journal of Child Psychology and Psychiatry, 44,* 1024–1036.

O'Connor, T. G., & Zeanah, C. H. Jr. (2003). Attachment disorders: Assessment strategies and treatment approaches. *Attachment and Human Development, 5,* 321–326.

O'Hare, A. (2009). Autism spectrum disorder: Diagnosis and management. *Archives of Disease in Childhood Education and Practice, 94,* 161–168.

O'Leary, C., Zubrick, S. R., Taylor, C. L., Dixon, G., & Bower, C. (2009). Prenatal exposure and language delays in 2-year-old children: The importance of dose and timing on risk. *Pediatrics, 123,* 547–554.

Oberman, L. M., Hubbard, E., McCleery, J. P., Altschuler, E., Ramachandran, V. S., & Pinada, J. A. (2005). EEG evidence for mirror neuron dysfunction in autism spectrum disorders. *Cognitive Brain Research, 24,* 190–198.

Ochsner, K. N., & Gross, J. J. (2007). The neural architecture of emotion regulation. In J. J. Gross & R. Buck (Eds.), *The handbook of emotion regulation* (pp. 87–109). New York: Guilford Press.

Offord, D. R., Boyle, M. H., Racine, Y. A., Fleming, J. E., Cadman, D. T., Blum, H. M., ... MacMillan, H. L. (1992). Outcome prognosis and risk in a longitudinal follow-up study. *Journal of the American Academy of child and Adolescent Psychiatry, 31,* 916–923.

Olds, D. L., Hill, P., Robinson, J., Song, N., & Little, C. (2000). Update on home visiting for pregnant women and parents of young children. *Current Problems in Pediatrics, 30,* 107–144.

Olds, D. L., Robinson, J., Song, N., Little, C., & Hill, P. (1999). *Replacing risks for mental disorders during the first five years of life: A review of preventive interventions.* Report submitted to the Center for Mental Health Services, University of Colorado, Health Sciences Center.

Olds, D. L., Sadler, L., & Kitzman, H. (2007). Home visiting: Recent program evaluations: Analysis and recommendations. *The Future of Children, 9,* 4–26.

Olesen, P., Westerberg, H., & Klingberg, T. (2004). Increased prefrontal and parietal brain activity after training of working memory. *Nature Neuroscience, 7,* 75–79.

Ollendick, T. H., King, N. J., & Chorpita, B. F. (2006). Empirically supported treatments for children and adolescents. In P. C. Kendall (Ed.), *Child and adolescent therapy: Cognitive-behavioral procedures* (3rd ed., pp. 492–520). New York: Guilford.

Olson, H. C., Streissguth, A. P., Sampson, P. D., Barr, H. M. Bookstein, F. L., & Thiede, K. (1997). Association of prenatal exposure with behavioral and learning problems in early adolescence. *Journal of the American Academy of Child and Adolescent Psychiatry, 36,* 1187–1194.

Olson, S. L., & Sameroff, A. J. (2009). *Regulatory processes in the development of childhood behavioral problems* (2nd ed.). Cambridge, UK: Cambridge University Press.

Olson, S. L., Sameroff, A. J., Kerr, D. R., Lopez, W. L., & Wellman, H. M. (2005). Developmental foundations of externalizing problems in young children: The role of effortful control. *Development and Psychopathology, 17,* 25–45.

Olweus, D. (1994). Bullying at school: Long term outcomes for the victims and an effective school-based program. In L. R. Huesmannn (Ed.), *Aggressive behavior: Current perspectives* (pp. 97–130). New York: Plenum Press.

Ong, S. H., Wickramaratne, P., Tang, M., & Weissman, M. M. (2006). Early childhood sleep and eating problems as predictors of adolescent and adult mood and anxiety disorders. *Journal of Affective Disorders, 96,* 1–8.

Oon, P. P. (2010). Playing with Gladys: A case study integrating drama therapy with behavioral interventions for the treatment of selective mutism. *Clinical Child Psychology and Psychiatry, 16,* 215–230.

Oppenheim, D. (2006). Child, parent, and parent-child emotional narratives: Implications for developmental psychopathology. *Development and Psychopathology, 18*(3), 771–790.

Oppenheim, D., & Korie-Karie, N. (2002). Mothers' insightfulness regarding their children's internal worlds: The capacity underlying secure mother-child relationships. *Infant Mental Health Journal, 23,* 593–605.

Orr, S. P., Metzger, L. J., & Muller, M. W. (2004). Psychophysiological assessment of PTSD. In J. P. Wilson & T. M. Keene (Eds.), *Assessing psychological trauma and PTSD* (2nd ed., pp. 289–343). New York: Guilford Press.

Osofsky, J. (Ed.). (1998). *Children in a violent society.* New York: Guilford Press.

Osterling, J., & Dawson, G. (1994). Early recognition of children with autism: A study of first birthday home videotapes. *Journal of Autism and Developmental Disorders, 24,* 247–257.

Ostrov, J. M., & Godleski, S. A. (2007). Relational aggression, victimization, and language development: Implications for practice. *Topics in Language Disorders, 27*, 146–166.

Owens, J., & Burnham, M. M. (2009). Sleep disorders. In C. H. Zeanah, Jr. (Ed.), *Handbook of infant mental health* (3rd ed., pp. 362–376). New York: Guilford Publishers.

Ozen, S., Ece, A., Oto, R., Tirasci, Y., & Goren, S. (2005). Juvenile delinquency in a developing country: An example in Turkey. *International Journal of Law and Psychiatry, 28*, 430–441.

Ozonoff, S., Heung, K., Byrd, R., Hansen, R., & Hertz-Picciotto, I. (2008). The onset of autism: Patterns of symptom emergence in the first years of life. *Autism Research, 1*, 320–328.

Pabhakaran, V., Narayanan, K., Zhao, Z., & Gabrieli, J. D. E. (2000). Integration of diverse information in working memory within the frontal lobe. *Nature Neuroscience, 3*, 85–90.

Pajer, K. A., Gardner, W., Rubin, R. T., Perel, J., & Neal, S. (2001). Decreased cortisol levels in adolescent girls with conduct disorder. *Archives of General Psychiatry, 58*, 297–302.

Pardini, D., & Loeber, R. (2008). Interpersonal callousness trajectories across adolescence: early social influence and adult outcomes. *Criminal Justice Behavior, 35*, 244–262.

Pardini, D., Obradovic, J., & Loeber, R. (2006). Interpersonal callousness, hyperactivity/impulsivity, inattention, and conduct problems as precursors to delinquency persistence in boys: A comparison of three grade-based cohorts. *Journal of Clinical Child and Adolescent Psychology, 35*, 46–59.

Parham L. D., Cohn E. S., Spitzer S., Koomar J. A., Miller L. J., Burke J. P., et al. Fidelity in sensory integration intervention research. *The American Journal of Occupational Therapy*, 61, 216–227.

Parham, L. D., Ecker, C., Miller-Ruhaneck, A., Henry, D. A., & Glennon, T. J. (2007). *Sensory processing measure*. Los Angeles, CA: Western Psychological Services.

Parham, L. D., & Mailloux, Z. (2005). Sensory Integration. In J. Case-Smith (Ed.), *Occupational therapy for children* (5th ed., pp. 356–409). St Louis, Missouri: Mosby Inc.

Patrick, M. R., Snyder, J., Schrepferman, L. M., & Snyder, J. (2005). The joint contribution of early parental warmth, communication and tracking, and early child conduct problems on monitoring in late childhood. *Child Development, 76*, 999–1014.

Patterson, G. R. (1982). *Coercive family process*. Eugene, OR: Castalia.

Patterson, G. R. (1985). Beyond technology: The next stage in developing an empirical base for parent training. In L. L'Abate (Ed.), *Handbook of family psychology: Vol. 2* (pp. 1344–1379). Homewood, IL: Dorsey.

Patterson, G. R., & Fisher, P. A. (2002). Recent developments in our understanding of parenting: Bidirectional effects, causal models, and the search for parsimony. In M. H. Bornstein (Ed.), *Handbook of Parenting: Vol. 5. Practical issues in parenting* (2nd ed., pp. 59–88). Mahwah, NJ: Lawrence Erlbaum Associates.

Patterson, G. R., Forgatch, M. S., Yoerger, K. L., & Stoolmiller, M. (1998). Variables that initiate and maintain early-onset trajectories of juvenile offending. *Development and Psychopathology, 10*, 531–547.

Patterson, G. R., Reid, J. B., & Dishion, T. (1992). *Antisocial boys*, Vol. 4, Eugene, OR: Castalia.

Paul, R. (1995). *Language disorders from infancy through adolescence: Assessment and intervention*. Mosby: Elsevier Health Science.

Paul, R. (2006). *Language disorders from infancy through adolescence: Assessment and intervention* (3rd ed.). Mosby: Elsevier Health Sciences.

Pavlov, I. P. (1926). *Conditioned reflexes: An investigation of the physiological activity of the cerebral cortex*. New York: Dover Publications.

Pawl, J., & Milburne, L. A. (2006). Family and relationship-centered principles and practices. In G. M. Foley & J. D. Hochman (Eds.), *Mental health in early intervention: Achieving unity in principles and practice*. Baltimore, MD: Paul H. Brookes Publishing.

Payne, C., & Bachevalier, J. (2009). Neuroanatomy of the developing social brain. In M. De Haan & M. R. Gunnar (Eds.), *Handbook of developmental social neuroscience* (pp. 38–59). New York: Guilford Press.

PDM Task Force. (2006). *Psychodynamic diagnostic manual*. Silver Spring, MD: Alliance of Psychoanalytic Organizations.

Peden, M., Oyegbite, K., Ozanne-Smith J., Hyder, A. A., Branche, C., Rahman, AKM F., … Bartolomeos, K. (2008). *World report on child injury prevention*. Geneva, Switzerland: World Health Organization.

Peers, P. V., Ludwig, C. J. H., Rorden, C., Cusack, R., Bonfigiglioli, C., Bundersen, C., … Duncan, J. (2005). Attentional functions and parietal and frontal cortex. *Cerebral Cortex, 15*, 1469–1484.

Pelcovitz, D., van der Kolk, B. A., Roth, S., Mandel, F., Kaplan, S., & Resnick, P. (1997). Development of a criteria set and a structured interview for disorders of extreme stress (SIDES). *Journal of Traumatic Stress, 10*, 3–16.

Pelphrey, K. A., & Carter, E. J. (2008). Charting the typical and atypical development of the social brain. *Development and Psychopathology, 20*(4), 1081–1102.

Pennington, B. F. (2002). *The development of psychopathology: Nature and nurture*. New York: Guilford Press.

Pennington, B. F. (2009). How neuropsychology informs our understanding of developmental disorders. *Journal of Child Psychology and Psychiatry, 50*, 72–78.

Pepler, D., Jiang, D., Craig, W., & Connolly, J. (2008). Developmental trajectories of bullying and associated factors. *Child Development, 79*, 325–338.

Perlman, S. B., Vander Wyk, B. C., & Pelphrey, K. A. (2010). Brain mechanisms in the typical and atypical development of social cognition. In P. D. Zelazo, M. Chandler, & E. Crone (Eds.), *Developmental social cognitive neuroscience* (pp. 99–124). New York: Psychological Press.

Perry, B. (2000). Traumatised children: How childhood trauma influences brain development. *The Journal of the California Alliance for the Mentally Ill, 11*, 2–10.

Perry, B. (2005), Applying principles of neurodevelopment to clinical work with traumatized children: The neurosequential model of therapeutics. In N. B. Webb, *Working with traumatized youth in child welfare* (p. 44). New York: Guilford Publishing.

Perry, B., Pollard, R., Blakley, T., Baker, W., & Vigilanti, D. (1995). Childhood trauma, the neurobiology of adaptation and "use-dependent" development of the brain: How "states" become "traits". *Infant Mental Health Journal, 10*, 271–291.

Perry, B. D. (1997). Incubated in terror: Neurodevelopmental factors in the "cycle of violence." In J. Osofsky (Ed.), *Children in a violent society* (pp. 124–148). New York: Guilford Press.

Perry, B. D. (2002). Childhood experience and the expression of genetic potential: What childhood neglect tells us about nature and nurture. *Brain and Mind, 3*, 79–100.

Perry, B. D. (2006). Applying principles of neurodevelopment to clinical work with maltreated and traumatized children: The neurosequential model of therapeutics. In N. B. Webb (Ed.), *Working with traumatized youth in child welfare* (pp. 27–52). New York: Guilford Press.

Perry, B. D. (2008). Child maltreatment: The role of abuse and neglect in developmental psychopathology. In T. Beauchaine & S. Henshaw (Eds.), *Child and adolescent psychopathology* (pp. 93–128). New York: Wiley.

Perry, B. D. (2009). Examining child maltreatment through a neurodevelopmentally informed approach to clinical work with maltreated children. *Reclaiming Children and Youth: The Journal of Strength-Based Interventions.*

Perry, B. D., & Hambrick, E. (2008). Introduction to the neurosequential model of therapeutics: A neurodevelopmentally informed approach to clinical work with maltreated children. *Reclaiming Children and Youth: The Journal of Strength-Based Interventions.*

Peterson, L. W., & Hardin, M. (1997). *Children in distress: A guide for screening children's art*. New York: W. W. Norton.

Peterson, R. L., Pennington, B. F., Shriberg, L. D., & Boada, R. (2009). What influences literacy in children with speech sound disorder? *Journal of Speech, Language, and Hearing Research, 52*, 1175–1185.

Petit, G. S., Laird, R. D., Dodge, K. A., Bates, J. E., & Criss, M. M. (2001). Antecedents and behavior problem outcomes of parental monitoring and psychological control in early adolescence, *Child Development, 72*, 583–598.

Pfefferbaum, B., Nixon, S. J., Tucker, P. M., Tivis, R. D., Moore, V. L., Gurwitch, R. H., … Geis, H. K. (1999). Posttraumatic stress responses in bereaved children after the Oklahoma City bombing. *Journal of the American Academy of Child and Adolescent Psychiatry, 38*, 1372–1379.

Pfeifer, M., Goldsmith, H. H., Davidson, R. J., & Rickman, M. (2002). Continuity and change in inhibited and uninhibited children. *Child Development, 73*, 1474–1485.

Pfeiffer, B., & Kinnealey, M. (2003). Treatment of sensory defensiveness in adults. *Occupational Therapy International, 10*, 175–184.

Pfeiffer, B., Koenig, K., Kinnealey, M., Sheppare, M., & Henderson, L. (2011). Effectiveness of sensory integration interventions in children with autism spectrum disorders: A pilot study. *The American Journal of Occupational Therapy, 65*, 76–85.

Phelps, E. A., & LeDoux, J. E. (2005). Contributions of the amygdala to emotion processing: From animal models to human behavior. *Neuron, 48*, 175–187.

Pianta, R. C. (1999). *Enhancing relationships between children and teachers.* Washington, DC: American Psychological Association.

Pianta, R. C. (2006). Classroom management and relationships between children and teachers: Implications for research and practice. In C. M. Evertson & C. S. Weinstein (Eds.), *Handbook of classroom management: Research, practice, and contemporary issues* (pp. 685–709). Mahwah, NJ: Lawrence Erlbaum.

Pianta, R. C., & Belsky, J., & Vandergrift, N. (2008). Classroom effects on children's achievement trajectories in elementary school. *American Educational Research Journal, 45*, 365–397.

Pianta, R. C., Steinberg, M. S., & Rollins, K. B. (1995). The first two years of school: Teacher-child relationships and deflections in children's classroom adjustment. *Development and Psychopathology, 7*, 295–312.

Pickering, S. J., & Gathercole, S. E. (2001). *The Working Memory Test Battery for Children* (WMTB-C). London: Harcourt.

Picton, T. W., Alain, C., & Knight, A. R. (2002). The theatre of the mind: Physiological studies of the human frontal lobes. In T. Stuss & R. T. Knight (Eds.), *Principals of frontal lobe function* (pp. 109–126). New York: Oxford University Press.

Piek, J. P., Pitcher, T. M., & Hay, D. A. (1999). Motor coordination and kinaesthesis in boys with attention deficit-hyperactivity disorder. *Developmental Medicine and Child Neurology, 41*, 159–165.

Pietrini, P., Guazzelli, M., Basso, G., Jaffe, K., & Grafman, J. (2000). Neuronal correlates of imaginal aggressive behavior assessed by positron emission tomography in healthy subjects. *American Journal of Psychiatry, 157*, 1772–1781.

Pine, D. S., Bruder, G. E., Wasserman, G. A., Miller, L. S., Musabegovic, A., & Watson, J. B. (1997). Verbal dichotic listening in boys at risk for behavior disorders. *Journal of the American Academy of Child and Adolescent Psychiatry, 36*, 1465–1473.

Pine, D. S., Shaffer, D., Schonfeld, I. S., & Davies, M. (1997). Minor physical anomalies: Modifiers of environmental risks for psychiatric impairment? *Journal of the American Academy of Child and Adolescent Psychiatry, 36*, 395–403.

Piper, W. E., McCallum, M., & Hassan, F. A. A. (1992). Psychological mindedness and psychodynamic work. In W. E. Piper, M. McCallum, & F. A. A. Hassan (Eds.), *Adaptation to loss through short-term group psychotherapy* (pp. 169–190). New York: Guilford Press.

Piven, J., Palmer, P., Jacobi, D., Childress, D., & Arndt, S. (1997). Broader Autism phenotype: Evidence from a family history study of multiple Autism incidence in families. *American Journal of Psychiatry, 154*, 185–190.

Plenk, A. M., Hinchey, F. S., & Davies, M. U. (1985). *Plenk Storytelling Test.* Salt Lake City, UT: The Children's Center.

Plessinger, M. A., & Woods, J. R. Jr. (1993). Maternal placental, and fetal pathophysiology of cocaine exposure during pregnancy. *Clinical Obstetrics and Gynecology, 36*, 267–278.

Pliszka, S. R., Sherman, J. O., Barrow, M. V., & Irick, S. (2000). Affective disorder in juvenile offenders: A preliminary study. *American Journal of Psychiatry, 157*, 130–132.

Plomin, R., & Crabbe, J. (2000). DNA. *Psychological Bulletin, 126*, 806–828.

Pluess, M., & Belsky, J. (2009). Differential susceptibility to rearing experience: The case of childcare. *Journal of Child Psychology and Psychiatry and Allied Disciplines, 50*, 396–404.

Polanczyk, G. V., de Lima, M. S., Horta, B. L., Biederman, J., & Rohde, L. A. (2007). *The worldwide prevalence of ADHD: A systemic review and metaregression analysis. American Journal of Psychiatry, 164*, 942–948.

Polatajko. H. J., & Cantin, N. (2010). Exploring the effectiveness of occupational therapy interventions, other than the sensory integration approach, with children and adolescents experiencing difficulty processing and integrating sensory information. *The American Journal of Occupational Therapy, 64*, 415–429.

Polatajko, J. J., & Mandich, A. (2004). *Enabling Occupation in Children: The Cognitive Orientation to daily Occupational Performance (COOP) approach.* Ontario, Canada: CAOT Publications ACE.

Pollack, N., Lockhart, J., Blowes, B., Semple, K., Webster, M., et al. (2009). *Handwriting assessment protocol* (2nd Ed). Retrieved from http://www.canchild.ca/en/measures/handwritingassessment.asp

Pollock, S. D., Nelson, C. A., Schlaak, M. F., Roeber, B. J., Wewerka, S. S., Wiil, K. L., ... Gunnar., M. R. (2010). Neurodevelopmental effects of early deprivation in postinstitutionalized children. *Child Development, 81*(1) 224–236.

Popescu, M., Fey, M. E., Lewine, J. D., Finestack, L. H., & Popescu, E. (2009). N400 responses of children with primary language disorder: Intervention effects. *Cognitive Neuroscience and Neuropsychology, 20*, 1104–1108.

Porges, S. W. (1988). Neonatal vagal tone: Diagnostic and prognostic implications. In P. N. Vietze & H. G. Vaughn, H. G. (Eds.), *Early identification of Infants with developmental disabilities* (pp. 147–159). Philadelphia, PA: Gruen Stratton.

Porges, S. W. (1995). Orienting in a defensive world: Mammalian modifications of our evolutionary heritage. A polyvagal theory. *Psychophysiology, 35*, 301–318.

Porges, S. W. (2007). The polyvagal perspective. *Biological Psychology, 74*, 116–143.

Porteus, S. D. (1965). *The porteus maze test: Fifty years application*. New York: The Psychological Corporation.

Posada, G. (2006). Assessing attachment security at age three: Q-sort home observations and the MacArthur Strange Situation adaptation. *Social Development, 15*, 644–658.

Posner, M. I., & Rothbart, M. K. (1991). Attentional mechanisms and conscious experiences. In M. Rugg & A. D. Miner (Eds.), *The neuropsychology of consciousness* (pp. 91–112). London: Academic Press.

Posner, M. I., & Rothbart, M. K. (2000). Developing mechanisms of self-regulation. *Development and Psychopathology, 12*, 427–441.

Post, R., Weiss, S., & Smith, M. (1995). Sensitisation and kindling: Implications for the evolving neural substrates of posttraumatic stress disorder. In M. Friedman, D. Charney, & A. Deutch (Eds.), *Neurological and clinical consequences of stress: From normal adaptation to PTSD* (pp. 203–224). Philadelphia: Lippincott-Raven.

Post, R. M., Weiss, B., Smith, M., He, Li, & McCann, L. (1997). Kindling versus quenching: Implications for the evolution and treatment of posttraumatic stress disorder. In R. Yehuda & A. McFarlane (Eds.), *Psychobiology of posttraumatic stress disorder* (pp. 285–296). New York: New York Academy of Sciences.

Potts, N. L. S., Book, S., & Davidson, J. R. T. (1996). The neurobiology of social phobia. *International Clinical Psychopharmacology, 11*, 43–48.

Powell, B., Cooper, G., Hoffman, K., & Marvin, R. S. (2009). The circle of security. In C. H. Zeanah, Jr. (Ed.), *Handbook of infant mental health* (3rd ed., pp. 450–467). New York: Guilford Press.

Preston, J. L., Frost, S. J., Mencl, W. E., Fullbright, R. K., & Landi, N. (2010). Early and late talkers: School age language, literacy and neurolinguistic differences. *Brain, 133*, 2185–2195.

Price, J. I. (2007). Definition of the orbital cortex in relation to specific connections with limbic and visceral structures and other cortical regions. *Annals of the New York Academy of Sciences, 1121*, 54–71.

Price, J. M., & Lento, J. (2001). The nature of child and adolescent vulnerability. In R. E. Ingram & J. M. Price (Eds.), *Vulnerability to psychopathology: Risk across the lifespan* (pp. 20–38). New York: Guilford Press.

Prince Inniss, J., Nesman, T., Mowery, D., Callejas, L. M., & Hernandez, M. (2009). Serving everyone at the table: Strategies for enhancing the availability of culturally competent mental health services. Tampa: University of South Florida, College of Behavioral and Community Sciences, Louis de la Parte Florida Mental Health Institute, Department of Child and Family Studies, Research and Training Center of Children's Mental Health. http://rtckids.fmhi.usf,edu

Prince, J. B. (2008). Catcholamine dysfunction in attention-deficit/hyperactivity disorder: An update. *Journal of Clinical Psychopharmacology, 28*, 39–45

Prince, J. B., and Wilens, T. E. (2009). Pharmacotherapy with ADHD and comorbidities. In T. E. Brown (Ed.), *ADHD comorbidities: Handbook for ADHD complications in children and adolescents.* (pp. 339–384). Washington, DC: American Psychiatric Publishing, Inc.

Prinz, R. J., & Miller, G. E. (1994). Family-based treatment for childhood antisocial behavior: Experimental influences on dropout and engagement. *Journal of Consulting and Clinical Psychology, 62*, 645–650.

Prior, M. R., Smart, D., Sanson, A. V., Oberklaid, F. (2000). Longitudinal predictors of behavioral adjustment in pre-adolescent children. *The Australian and New Zealand Journal of Psychiatry, 35*, 297–307.

Prochanska, J. O., & DiClemente, C. C., & Norcross, J. C. (1992). In search of how people change: Application to addictive behaviors. *American Psychologist, 47*, 1102–1114.

Prochaska, J. O. (1999). How do people change, and how can we change to help many more people? In M. A. Hubble, B. L. Duncan, & S. D. Miller (Eds.), *The heart and soul of change: What works in therapy?* (pp. 227–255). Washington, DC: American Psychological Association.

Propper, C., Moore, G. A., Mills-Koonce, W. R., Halpern, C. T., Hill-Soderlund, A. L., Calkins, S. D., ... Cox, M. (2008). Gene-environment contributions to the development of infant vagal reactivity: The interaction of dopamine and maternal sensitivity. *Child Development, 79*(5), 1377–1394.

Prutting & Kirchner. (1987). A clinical appraisal of the pragmatic aspects of language. *Journal of Speech and Hearing Disorders, 52*, 105–119.

Pulkkinen, L. (1996). Proactive and reactive aggression in early adolescence as precursors to anti-and prosocial behaviors in young adults. *Aggressive Behavior, 22*, 241–257.

Putallaz, M, & Wasserman, A. (1989). Children's naturalistic entry behavior and sociometric status: A developmental perspective. *Developmental Psychology, 25*, 297–305.

Putnam, S. P., Sanson, A. V., & Rothbart, M. K. (2002). Child temperament and parenting. In M. H. Bornstein (Ed.), *Handbook of parenting: Vol. 1. Children and parenting* (2nd ed., pp. 255–277). Mahwah, NJ: Erlbaum.

Putnam, S. P., Spritz, B. L., & Stifter, C. A. (2002). Mother–child co-regulation during delay of gratification at 30 months. *Infancy, 3*, 209–225.

Puttallaz, M., & Wasserman, A. (1990). Children's entry behavior: A developmental perspective. In S. R. Asher & J. D. Coie (Eds.), *Peer rejection in childhood* (pp. 60–89). New York: Cambridge University Press.

Quay, H. C. (1993). The psychobiology of undersocialized aggressive conduct disorder: A theoretical perspective. *Development and Psychopathology, 5*, 165–180.

Rabiner, D., & Coie, J. D. (1989). Effect of expectancy inductions on rejected children's acceptance by unfamiliar peers. *Developmental Psychology, 23*, 450–461.

Radke-Yarrow, M., & Klimes-Dougan, M. (2002). Parental depression and offspring disorders: A developmental perspective. In S. Goodman & I. Gotlib (Eds.), *Children of depressed parents: Mechanisms of risk and implications for treatment* (pp. 155–173). Washington, DC: American Psychological Association.

Raikes, H. A., & Thompson, R. A. (2005). Relationships past, present, and future: Reflections on attachment in middle childhood. In K. A. Kerns & R. A. Richardson (Eds.), *Attachment in middle childhood* (pp. 255–282). New York: Guilford Press.

Raine, A. (1989). Evoked potentials and psychopathy. *International Journal of Psychophysiology, 8*, 1–16.

Raine, A. (1993). *The psychopathology of crime*. San Diego, CA: Academic Press.

Raine, A. (1996). Autonomic nervous system factors underlying disinhibited, antisocial, and violent behaviour: Biosocial perspectives and treatment implications. *Annals of the New York Academy of Sciences, 794*, 46–59.

Raine, A. (2002). Annotation: The role of prefrontal deficit, low autonomic arousal, and early health factors in the development of antisocial and aggressive behavior in children. *Journal of Child Psychology and Psychiatry, 43*, 417–434.

Raine, A., Buchsbaum, M. S., Stanley, J., Lottenberg, S., Abel, L., & Stoddard, J. (1994). Selective reductions in prefrontal glucose metabolism in murderers. *Biological Psychiatry, 36*, 365–373.

Raine, A., Venables, P. H., & Mednick, S. A. (1997). Low resting heart rate at age 3 years predisposes to aggression at age 11 years: Evidence from the Mauritius Child Health Project. *Journal of the American Academy of Child and Adolescent Psychiatry, 36*, 11457–1464.

Raine, A., Venables, P. H., & Williams, M. (1990). Relationship between central and autonomic measures of arousal at age 15 years and criminality at age 24 years. *Archives of General Psychiatry, 47*, 1003–1007.

Raine, S. (2013). *The anatomy of violence: The biological roots of crime*. NY: Pantheon Books.

Rais-Bahrain, M. L. K., & Short, B. L. (2006). Premature and small-for-date infants. In M. L. Batshaw, L. Pellegrino, & N. J. Raizen (Eds.), *Children with disabilities* (6th ed., pp. 107–124). Baltimore, MD: Paul H. Brooks Publishing Co.

Ramos, M., Guerin, D., Gottfried, A., Bathurst, K., & Oliver, P. (2005). Family conflict and children's behaviour problems: The moderating role of child temperament. *Structural Equation Modeling: A Multidisciplinary Journal, 12*, 278–298.

Rapee, R. M., Spence, S., Cobham, C., & Wignall, A. (2000). *Helping your anxious child: A step-by-step guide for parents*. Oakland, CA: New Harbinger.

Rapin, I., & Dunn, M. (2003). Update on the language disorders of individuals on the autistic spectrum. *Brain and Development, 25*, 166–172.

Rauch, S. L., & Drevets, W. C. (2009). Neuroimaging and neuroanatomy of stress-induced and fear circuitry disorders. In G. Andrews, D. S. Charney, P. S. Sirovatka, & D. A. Regier (Eds.), *Stress-induced and fear circuitry disorders: Refining the research agenda for DSM-V* (pp. 215–254). Arlington, VA: American Psychiatric Association.

Rauch, S. L., Shin, A. M., & Wright, C. I. (2003). Neuroimaging studies of amygdala function in anxiety disorders. *Annals of the New York Academy of Sciences, 985*, 389–410.

Rauch, S. L., van der Kolk, B. A., Fisler, R. E., Alpert, N. M., Orr, S. P., Savage, C. R., ... Pitman, R. K. (1996). A symptom provocation study of post-traumatic stress disorder using positron emission tomography and script-driven imagery. *Archives of General Psychiatry, 33*, 380–387.

Rayfield, A., Monaco, L., & Eyberg, S. M. (1999). Parent-child interaction therapy with oppositional children: Review and clinical findings. In S. W. Ollendick & T. H. Ollendick (Eds.), *Handbook of psychotherapies with children and families* (pp. 327–344). New York, NY: Kluwer Academic/Plenum Publishers.

Reich, W. (2000). Diagnostic Interview for Children and Adolescents (DICA*). Journal of the American Academy of Child and Adolescent Psychiatry, 39*, 59–66.

Reid, J. B., Eddy, J. M., Fetrow, R. A., & Stoolmiller, M. (1999). Description and immediate impact of a prevention intervention for conduct problems. *American Journal of Community Psychology, 27*, 483–517.

Reitan, R. M. (1986). *Trail-making test: Manual of administration and scoring*. Tucson, AZ: Neuropsychology Press.

Remschmidt, H., Poller, M., Herpertz-Dahlman, B., Hennighausen, K., & Gutenbruner, C. (2001). A follow-up study of 45 patients with elective mutism. *European Archives of Psychiatry and Clinical Neuroscience, 251*, 284–296.

Ren, J. Q., Malanga, C. S., Tabit, E., & Kosofsky, B. E. (2004). Neuropathological consequences of prenatal cocaine exposure in the mouse. *International Journal of Developmental Neuroscience, 22*, 309–320.

Renfrew, C. E. (1998). *Renfrew Language Scales-Action Picture Test-bus Story Test-Word Finding Vocabulary Test*. Winslow Publisher.

Repetti, R., Taylor, S. E. & Saxe, D. (2007). The influence of early socialization experiences on the development of biological systems. In J. Grusec & P. D. Hastings (Eds.), *Handbook of socialization: Theory and research* (pp. 124–152). New York: Guilford Press.

Repie, M. S. (2005). A school mental health issues survey from the perspective of regular and special education teachers, school counselors, and school psychologists. *Education and Treatment of Children, 28*, 279–298.

Rescorla, L. (2005). Age 13 language and reading outcomes in late-talking toddlers. *Journal of Speech, Language, and Hearing Research, 48*, 459–472.

Reynell, J., & Huntley, L. (1985). *Reynell language scale—2nd ed. NFER Nelson.*

Reynolds, A. J., & Richmond, B. O. (2003). *Revised Children's Manifest Anxiety Scale* (RCMAS) (2nd ed.*)*. Los Angeles: CA: Western Psychological Services.

Reynolds, A. J., Temple, J. A., Robertson, D. L., & Mann, E. A. (2002). Age 21 cost-benefit analysis of the Title 1 Chicago Child-Parent Centers. *Educational Evaluation and Policy Analysis, 24*, 267–303.

Reynolds, C. R., & Kamphaus, R. (2004). *Behavioral assessment for children manual*. Circle Pines, MN: American Guidance Service.

Reynolds, C. R., & Kamphaus, R. W. (2005*). Behavior assessment system for children manual*, 2nd ed. (BASC-2) Minneapolis, MN: Pearson.

Rhee, S. H., & Waldman, L. D. (2002). Influences on antisocial behavior: A metaanalysis of twin and adoption studies. *Psychological Bulletin, 128*, 490.

Rhodes, K. A. (2008). Children's responses to interparental conflict: A meta-analysis of their associations with child adjustment. *Child Development, 79*, 1942–1956.

Rice, M. L., Taylor, C. L., & Zubrick, S. R. (2008). Language outcomes of 7-year-old children with or without a history of late language emergence at 24 months. *Journal of Speech, Language, and Hearing Research, 51, 394–407.*

Rice, M. L., & Warren, S. F. (Eds.). (2004). *Developmental language disorders: From phenotypes to etiologies.* Mahwah, NJ: Erlbaum.

Richard, G., & Fahy, J. (2005). *The source for development of executive functions.* East Moline, IL: LinguiSystems, Inc.

Rieffe, C., Oosterveld, P., Miers, A. C., Terwogt, M. M., & Ly, V. (2008). Emotion awareness and internalizing symptoms in children and adolescents: The Emotion Awareness Questionnaire revised. *Personality and Individual Differences, 45,* 756–761.

Riek, E. F., & Anderson, D. (2009). Adolescent/adult sensory profile and obsessive compulsive disorder. *The American Journal of Occupational Therapy, 63,* 138–145.

Rigby, K. (2004). Bullying in childhood. In P. K. Smith & C. H. Hart (Eds.), *Handbook of childhood social development* (pp. 549–568). Malden, MA: Blackwell Publishers.

Riggs, P. D., Baker, S., Mikulich, S. K., Young, S. E., & Crowley, T. J. (1995). Depression in substance-dependent delinquents. *Journal of the American Academy of Child and Adolescent Psychiatry, 34,* 764–771.

Riley, E. P., & Mc Gee, C. L. (2005). Fetal alcohol spectrum disorders: An overview with emphasis on changes in brain and behaviour. *Exp Bio Med,* 230, 35–365.

Rinaldi. (2001). Long term outcomes of parent training and predictors of adolescent adjustment. *Dissertation Abstract International, 62*(05), 2498 (UMI No. 3014016).

Ringwalt, S. (2008). *Developmental screening and assessment instruments.* Chapel Hill, NC: National Early Childhood Technical Assistance Center.

Riorden, D., Appleby, L., & Faragher, B. (1999). Mother-infant interaction in post-partum women with schizophrenia and affective disorders. *Psychological Medicine, 29,* 991–995.

Ritvo, E. R., Freeman, B. J., Mason-Brothers, A., Mo, A., & Ritvo, A. M. (1985). Concordance for the syndrome of autism in 40 pairs of afflicted twins. *American Journal of Psychiatry, 142,* 74–77.

Riva, D., & Giorgi, C. (2000). The cerebellum contributes to higher functions during development: Evidence from a series of children surgically treated for posterior fossa tumours. *Brain, 123,* 1051–1061

Rizzolatti, G., Fadiga, L., Gallese, V., & Fogassi, I. (1996). Premotor cortex and the recognition of motor actions. *Cognitive Brain Research, 3,* 131–141.

Rizzolatti, G., Fadiga, L., Matelli, M., Bettinardi, V., Perani, D., & Fazio, F. (1996). Localization of grasp representations in humans by PET, 1. Observation versus execution. *Experimental Brain Research, 111,* 246–252.

Robert-Tissot, C., Cramer, B., Stern, D. N., Serpa, S. R., Bachmann, J. P., Palacio-Espasa, F., … Mendiguren, G. (1996). Outcome evaluation in brief mother-infant psychotherapies: Report on 75 cases. *Infant Mental Health Journal, 17,* 97–114.

Roberts, G. E., & Gruber, C. (2005). *Roberts-2 manual.* Los Angeles, CA: Western Psychological Services.

Roberts, S. B., & Kendler, K. S. (1999). Neuroticism and self-esteem as indices of the vulnerability to major depression in women. *Psychological Medicine, 29,* 1101–1109.

Robichon, F., Bouchard, P., Demonet. J., & Habib, M. (2000). Developmental dyslexia: Re-evaluation of the corpus callosum in male adults. *European Journal of Neurology, 43,* 233–237.

Robins, L., Marcus, L., Reich, W., Cunningham, R., & Gallagher, T. (1996). *The diagnostic interview schedule IV.* St. Louis: Washington University.

Robins, R. W., Tracy, J. L., & Shaver, P. R. (2001). Shamed into self-love: Dynamics, roots, and functions of narcissism. *Psychological Inquiry, 13,* 230–236.

Robinson, E. A., & Eyberg, S. M. (1981). The dyadic parent-child interaction coding system: Standardization and validation. *Journal of Consulting and Clinical Psychology, 49,* 245–250.

Rodger, S. & Brandenburg, J. (2009). Cognitive Orientation to (daily) Occupational Performance (CO-OP) with children with Asperger's syndrome who have motor-based occupational performance goals. *Australian Journal of Occupational Therapy, 56*(1), 41–50.

Rodriguez, A., & Bohlin, G. (2005). Are maternal smoking and stress during pregnancy related to ADHD symptoms in children? *Journal of Child and Adolescent Psychology and Psychiatry, 46,* 246–254.

Rogers, S. L., Gordon, C. Y., Schanzenbacher, K. E., & Case Smith M. J. (2001). Common diagnosis in pediatric occupational therapy practice. In J. Case-Smith (Ed.), *Occupational therapy for children.* Mosby Inc. St Louis, Missouri.

Rogers, S., Ozonoff, S., & Maslin-Cole, C. (1993). Developmental aspects of attachment behavior in young children with pervasive developmental disorders. *Journal of American Academy of Child and Adolescent Psychiatry, 32,* 1274–1282.

Rogers Weise, M. R. (1992). A critical review of parent training research. *Psychology in the Schools, 29,* 229–236.
Roisman, G., & Fraley, R. (2006). The limits of genetic influence: A behavioural-genetic analysis of infant-caregiver relationship quality and temperament. *Child Development, 77,* 1656–1667.
Rose, R., & Philpot, T. (2005). *The child's own story: Life story work with traumatized children.* London, UK: Jessica Kingsley Publishers.
Rose, S. A., Feldman, J. F., Jankowski, J. T., & Van Rossen, R. (2005). Pathways from prematurity and infant abilities to later cognition. *Child Development, 76,* 1172–1184.
Rose, S. L., Rose, S. A., & Feldman, J. F. (1989). Stability of behavior problems in young children. Development and Psychopathology, 1, 5–19.
Rosenkoetter, S. E., & Walness, S. B. (2006). Relationships at the heart of early language and literacy. In J. Knapp-Philo & S. E. Rosenkoetter (Eds.), *Learning to read the world: Language and literacy in the first three years* (pp. 81–100). Washington DC: ZERO TO THREE PRESS.
Rosenzweig, M. R. (1966). Environmental complexity, cerebral change, and behaviour. *American Psychologist, 21, 321–332.*
Rosenzweig, M. R., Krech, D., Bennett, E. L & Diamond, M. C. (1962). Effects of environmental complexity and training on brain chemistry and anatomy: A replication and extension. *Journal of Comparative and Physiological Psychology, 55,* 429–437.
Rossetti, L. (1990). *Rossetti infant-toddler language scale.* East Moline, IL: LinguiSystems.
Rothbart, M. K., Ahadi, S. A., & Evans, D. E. (2000). Temperament and personality: Origins and outcomes. *Journal of Personality and Social Psychology, 78,* 122–135.
Rothbart, M. K., & Bates, J. E. (1998). Temperament. In W. Damon & N. Eisenberg (Eds.), *Handbook of child psychology: Vol. 3, Social and emotional and personality development* (5th ed., pp. 105–176). New York: Guilford Press.
Rothbart, M. K., & Bates, J. E. (2006). Temperament. In W. Damon (Series Ed.) & N. Eisenberg (Vol. Ed.), *Handbook of social psychology: Vol. 3, Social, emotional, and personality development* (6th ed., pp. 99–166). New York: Wiley.
Rothbart, M. K., Ellis, L. K., Rueda, M. R., & Posner, M. I. (2003). Developing mechanisms of temperamental effortful control. *Journal of Personality, 71,* 1113–1143.
Rothbart, M. K., Posner, M., & Boylan, A. (1990). Regulatory mechanisms in infant development. In J. T. Enns (Ed.), *The development of attention: Research and theory* (pp. 3–79). Oxford, UK: North Holland.
Rothbaum, F., & Weisz, J. R. (1994). Parental caregiving and child externalizing behavior in non-clinical samples: A meta-analysis. *Psychological Bulletin, 116,* 55–74.
Rotter, J., & Rafferty, J. (1950). *The manual for the Rotter Incomplete Sentences Blank.* New York: Western Psychological Corporation.
Rottnek, F., Searight, H. R., & Abby, S. L. (2001). Conduct disorder: Diagnosis and treatment in primary care. *American Academy of Family Physicians.* Retrieved from www.aafp.org/afp/20010415//1579.pdf
Rowe, R., Maughan, B., Moran, P., Ford, T., Briskman, J., & Goodman, R. (2010). The role of callous-unemotional traits in the diagnosis of conduct disorder. *The Journal of Child Psychology and Psychiatry, 51,* 688–695.
Rowe, R., Rijsdijk, F. V., Maughan, B., Hosang, G. M., & Eley, T. C. (2008). Heterogeneity in antisocial behaviours and comorbidity with depressed mood: A behavioural genetic approach. *The Journal of Child Psychology and Psychiatry, 49,* 526–534.
Royeen, C. B. (1989). Commentary on "Tactile functions in learning-disabled and normal children: Reliability and validity considerations." *Occupational Therapy Journal of Research, 9,* 16–23.
Rubin, K., Burgess, K., Dwyer, & Hastings, P. (2003). Predicting preschoolers' externalising behaviours from toddler temperament, conflict and maternal negativity. *Developmental Psychology, 39,* 164–176.
Rubin, K. H., Burgess, K. B., & Coplan, R. J. (2004). Social withdrawal and shyness. In P. K. Smith & C. H. Hart (Eds.), *Blackwell handbook of childhood development* (pp. 329–352). Malden, MA: Blackwell Publishing.
Ruchkins, V. V., Schwab-Stone, M., Koposov, R., Vermeiren, K., & Steiner, H. (2002). Violence exposure, posttraumatic stress, and personality in juvenile delinquents. *Journal of the American Academy of Child and Adolescent Psychiatry, 4,* 322–329.
Ruffman, T., Slade, L., & Crowe, E. (2002). The relation between children's and mother's mental state language and theory-of-mind understanding. *Child Development, 73,* 734–751.

Ruiz, R., & Avant, K. (2005). Effect of prenatal stress: A synthesis of literature. *Advances in Nursing Science, 28*, 345–355.

Russo, N., Foxe, J. J., Brandwein, A. B., Altschuler, T., Gomes, H., & Molholm, S. (2010). Multisensory processing in children with autism: High-density electrical mapping of auditory-somatosensory integration. *Autism Research, 3*(5), 253–257. doi: 10.1002/aur.152

Rutgers, A., Bakermans-Kranenburg, M., van IJzendoorn, M., & Beckelaer-Onnes, I. (2004). Autism and attachment: A meta-analytic review. *Journal of Child Psychology and Psychiatry, 45*, 1123–1134.

Rutter, M. (1985). Resilience in the face of adversity: Protective factors and resistance to psychiatric disorder. *British Journal of Psychiatry, 147*, 598–611.

Rutter, M. (1987). Psychosocial resilience and protective mechanisms. *American Journal of Orthopsychiatry, 57*, 316–331.

Rutter, M. (2000). Psychosocial influences: Critiques, findings and research needs. *Developmental Psychopathology, 12*, 375–405.

Rutter, M. (2002). Commentary: Nature and nurture interplay in emotional disorders. *Journal of Child Psychology and Psychiatry, 44*, 934–944.

Rutter, M. (2008). Implications of attachment theory on research for childcare policies. In J. Cassidy & P. R. Shaver (Eds.), *Handbook of attachment: Theory, research, and clinical implications* (2nd ed., pp. 958–974). New York: Guilford Press.

Rutter, M. (2009). Understanding and testing risk mechanisms for mental disorders. *Journal of Child Psychology and Psychiatry, 50*, 72–78.

Rutter, M., Giller, H., & Hagell, A. (1998). *Antisocial behavior by young people*. Cambridge, England: Cambridge University Press.

Rutter, M., Kim-Cohen, J., & Maughan, B. (2006). Continuities and discontinuities in psychopathology between childhood and adult life. *Journal of Child Psychology and Psychiatry, 47*, 276–295.

Rutter, M., MacDonald, H., Le Couteur, A., Harrington, R., Bolton, P., & Bailey, A. (1990). Genetic factors in child psychiatric disorders: II. Empirical findings. *Journal of Child Psychology and Psychiatry, 31*, 39–83.

Rutter, M., & Rutter, M. (1993). *Developing minds: Challenge and continuity across the life span*. New York: Basic Books.

Rutter, M., Sillberg, J., O'Connor, T., & Simonoff, E. (1999). Genetics and child psychiatry: II Empirical research findings. *Journal of Child Psychology and Psychiatry, 40*, 19–55.

Rutter, M., & Sroufe, A. L. (2000). Developmental psychopathology: Concepts and challenges. *Development and Psychopathology, 12*, 265–296.

Saarni, C. (2000). The social context of emotional development. In M. Lewis and J. M. Haviland-Jones (Eds.), *Handbook of emotions* (2nd ed., pp. 306–322). New York: Guilford Press.

Saigh, P. A., Mrouch, M., & Bremner, J. D. (1997). Scholastic impairments among traumatized adolescents. *Behavior Research and Therapy, 35*, 429–436.

Salmivalli, C., & Isaacs, J. (2005). Prospective relations among victimization, rejection, and friendliness, and children's self and peer perspectives. *Child Development, 76*, 1161–1171.

Salmon, K., Dadds, M. R., Allen, J., & Hawes, D. J. (2009). Can emotional language skills be taught during parent training for conduct problem children? *Child Psychiatry and Human Development, 40*, 485–498.

Salmon, P., & Calderbank, S. (1996). The relationship of childhood physical and sexual abuse to adult illness behaviour. *Psychosomatic Research, 40*, 329–336.

Salt, A., & Redshaw, M. (2005). Neurodevelopmental follow-up after preterm birth: Follow up after two years. *Early Human Development, 82*, 185–197.

Sameroff, A. J. (1983). Developmental systems: Contexts and evolution. In W. Kessen (Ed.), *Handbook of child psychology: Vol. 1. History, theories and methods* (pp. 238–294). New York: Wiley.

Sameroff, A. J. (2001). Developmental systems and psychopathology. *Development and Psychopathology, 12*, 297–312.

Sameroff, A., & Fiese, B. (1990). Transactional regulation and early intervention. In S. Meisels & J. Shonkoff (Eds.), *Handbook of early childhood intervention* (pp. 119–149). New York: Cambridge University Press.

Sameroff, A. J., & Fiese, B. S. (2000). Transactional regulation: The developmental ecology of early intervention. In J. D. Shonkoff & S. J. Meisels (Eds.), *Handbook of early childhood intervention* (pp. 135–159). Cambridge, UK: Cambridge University Press.

Sameroff, A. J., & Mackenzie, J. (2003). Research strategies for capturing transactional models of development: The limits of the possible. *Development and Psychopathology, 15,* 613–640.

Sameroff, A. J., McDonough, S., & Rosenbaum, K. (Eds.). (2004). *Treating parent-infant relationship problems: Strategies for intervention.* New York: Guilford Press.

Sanders, M. R. (2008). Triple P-Positive parenting program as a public health approach to strengthening parenting. *Journal of Family Psychology, 22,* 506–517.

Sanson, A., Hemphill, S. A., & Smart, D. (2004). Connection between temperament and social development: A review. *Social Development, 13,* 142–170.

Sapolsky, R.M. (1994). Why zebras don't get ulcers: *A guide to stress-related disorders and coping.* New York: Freeman.

Saylor, C. F., & Swenson, C. C. (1999). The Pediatric Emotional Distress Scale: A brief screening measure for young children exposed to traumatic events. *Journal of Clinical Child Psychology, 28,* 70–81.

Scaramella, L. V., & Leve, L. D. (2004). Clarifying parent-child reciprocities during early childhood: The early childhood coercion model. *Clinical Child and Family Psychology Review, 7,* 89–107.

Schaaf, R. C., & Davies, P. L. (2010). Evolution of the sensory integration frame of reference. *The American Journal of Occupational Therapy, 64,* 363–367.

Schachar, R., Levin, H. S., Max, J. E., & Purvis, K. (2004). Attention deficit hyperactivity disorder symptoms and response inhibition after closed head injury in children: Do preinjury behaviour and injury severity predict outcome? *Developmental Neuropsychology, 25,* 79–188.

Schechter, D. (2004). How posttraumatic stress affects mothers' perceptions of their babies: A brief video feedback intervention makes a difference. *Zero to Three, 24,* 43–49.

Schechter, D. S., Coots, T., Zeanah, C. H., Davies, M., Coates, S. W., Kimberley, A. T. ... Myers, M. M. (2005). Maternal mental representations of the child in an inner-city clinical sample: Violence related post traumatic stress and reflective functioning. *Attachment and Human Development, 7,* 313–331.

Schechter, D. S., Myers, M. M., Brunelli, S. A., Coates, S. W., Zeanah, C. H., Davies, M., ... Liebowitz, M. R. (2006). Traumatized mothers can change their minds about their toddlers: Understanding how a novel use of videofeedback supports positive change of maternal attributions. *Infant Mental Health Journal, 27,* 429–447.

Scheeringa, M. (2009). Posttraumatic stress disorder. In C. H. Zeanah, Jr. (Ed.), *Handbook of infant mental health* (3rd ed., pp. 345–361). New York: Guilford Publishers.

Scheeringa, M., Salloum, A., Arnberger, R., Weems, C., Amaya-Jackson, L., & Cohen, J. A. (2007). Feasibility and effectiveness of cognitive-behavioral therapy for post-traumatic stress disorder in preschool children: Two case studies. *Journal of Traumatic Stress, 20,* 631–636.

Scheeringa, M. S., Peebles, C. D., Cook, C. A., & Zeanah, C. H. (2001). Towards establishing procedural criterion, and discriminant validity for PTSD in early childhood. *Journal of the American Academy of Child and Adolescent Psychiatry, 40,* 52–60.

Scheeringa, M. S., & Zeanah, C. H. (2001). A relational perspective on PTSD in early childhood. *Journal of the American Academy of Child and Adolescent Psychiatry, 55,* 685–691.

Scheeringa, M. S., Zeanah, C. H., Myers, L., & Putnam, F. (2003). New findings on alternative criteria for PTSD in preschool children. *Journal of the American Academy of Child & Adolescent Psychiatry, 42,* 561–570.

Scheeringa, M. S., Zeanah, C. H., Myers, L., & Putnam, F. (2004). Heart period and variability findings in preschool children with posttraumatic stress symptoms. Journal of the American Academy of Child & Adolescent Psychiatry, 44, 899–906.

Scheeringa, M. S., Zeanah, C. H., Myers, L., & Putnam, F. (2005). Predictive validity in a prospective follow-up of PTSD in preschool children. *Journal of the American Academy of Child & Adolescent Psychiatry, 55,* 685–691.

Schiffer, F. (2000). Can different cerebral hemispheres have distinct personalities? Evidence and its implications for theory and treatment of PTSD and other disorders. *Journal of Trauma and Dissociation, 1,* 83–84.

Schiffer, F., Teicher, M., & Papanicolau, A. (1995). Evoked potential evidence for right brain activity during the recall of traumatic memories. *Journal of Neuropsychiatry and Clinical Neurosciences, 71,* 169–175.

Schmidt, L. A. & Fox, N. A. (1998). Electrophysiological studies: I Quantitative electroencephalography. In C. E. Coffey & R. A. Brumback (Eds.), *Textbook of pediatric neuropsychiatry* (pp. 315–329). Washington, DC: American Psychiatric Press.

Schmidt, L. A., Fox, N. A., & Schulkin, J. (1999). Behavioral and psychophysiological correlates of self-representatives in temperamentally shy children. *Developmental Psychobiology, 35*, 119–135.

Shmueli-Goetz, Y., Target, M., Fonagy, P., & Datta, A. (2008). The Child Attachment Interview: A psychometric study of reliability and validity. *Developmental Psychology, 44*, 939–956.

Schneider, B. H. (1992). Didactic methods for enhancing children's peer relations: A quantitative review. *Clinical Psychology Review, 12*, 363–382.

Schneider, M. L., Moore, C. F., Barnhart, T. E., Larson, J. A., DeJesus, O. T., Mukherjee, J., ... Kraemer, G. W. (2005). Moderate level prenatal alcohol exposure alter striatal dopamine system function in rhesus monkeys. *Alcohol Clinical Research, 29*, 1685–1697.

Schneider, M. L., Moore, C. F., Larson, J. A., Barr, C. S., DeJesus O. T., & Roberts, A. D. (2009). Timing of moderate level prenatal alcohol exposure influences gene expression of sensory processing behaviour in rhesus monkeys. *Frontiers in Integrative Neuroscience, 3*, 1–9. Retrieved from www.frontiersin.org

Schoenwald, S. K., Brown, T. L., & Henggeler, S. W. (2000). Inside multisystemic therapy: Therapist, supervisory, and program practices. *Journal of Emotional and Behavioral Disorders, 8*, 113–127.

Schonfeld, A., Mattson, S., Lang, A., Delis, D. & Riley, E. (2001). Verbal and non-verbal fluency in children with heavy prenatal alcohol exposure. *Journal of Studies on Alcohol, 62*(2), 239–246.

Schonfeld, A. M., Pasley, B., Frankel, F., & O'Connor, M. S. (2006). Executive functioning predicts social skills following prenatal alcohol exposure. *Child Neuropsychology, 12*, 439–452.

Schore, N. A. (1994). *Affect regulation and the origin of the self: The neurobiology of emotional development.* Mahwah, NJ: Erlbaum.

Schore, N. A. (1997). Early organization of the nonlinear right brain and development of a predisposition to psychiatric disorders. *Development and Psychopathology, 9*, 595–631.

Schore, N. A. (1998). The experience-dependent maturation of an evaluative system in the cortex. In K. Pribram (Ed.), *Brain and values: Is a biological science of values possible* (pp. 337–358). Mahwah, NJ: Erlbaum.

Schore, N. A. (2001). The effects of a secure attachment relationship on right brain development, affect regulation, & infant mental health. *Infant Mental Health Journal, 22*, 7–66.

Schore, N. A. (2001). The effects of early relational trauma on right brain development, affect regulation, and infant mental health. *Infant Mental Health Journal, 22*(1–2), 201–269.

Schore, N. A. (2003). *Affect dysregulation and disorders of the self.* New York: Norton.

Schteingart, J., Molnar, J., Klein, T., Lowe, C., & Hartmann, A. (1995). Homelessness and child functioning in the context of risk and protective factors monitoring child outcomes. *Journal of Clinical Child and Adolescent Psychology, 24*, 320–331.

Schubiner, H., Scott, R., & Tzelepis, A. (1993). Exposure to violence among inner-city youth. *Journal of Adolescent Health, 14*, 214–219.

Schuder, M. R., & Lyons-Ruth, K. (2004). "Hidden trauma" in infancy: Attachment, fearful arousal, and early dysfunction of the stress response system. In J. D. Osofsky (Ed.), *Young children and trauma: Intervention and treatment* (pp. 69–106). New York: Guilford Press.

Schuetze, P., Lawton, D., & Eiden, R. D. (2006), Prenatal cocaine exposure and infant sleep at 7 months of age: The influence of the caregiving environment. *Infant Mental Health Journal, 27*, 383–404.

Schwab-Stone, M. J., Jones, S. M., Henrich, C. C., Lechman, P., & Ruchkin, V. (2003). No safe haven III: Disentangling the impact of involvement in violence from violent exposure. *Journal of the American Academy of Child and Adolescent Psychiatry, 38*, 359–367.

Schwartz, D., & Proctor, L. J. (2000). Community violence exposure and children's social adjustment in the school peer group: The mediating roles of emotion regulation and social cognition. *Journal of Consulting and Clinical Psychology, 68*, 670–683.

Schwartz, E., & Davis, A. S. (2006). Reactive attachment disorder: Implications for school readiness and school functioning. *Psychology in Schools, 43*, 471–479.

Schwartz, E., Wrignt, C., Shin, L. M., Kagan, J., & Rauch, S. L. (2003). Inhibited and uninhibited infants grown-up: Adult amygdala response to novelty. *Science, 300*, 1952–1953.

Schwartz, J. M., & Begley, S. (2002). *The mind and the brain: Neuroplasticity and the power of mental force.* New York: HarperCollins Publisher.
Schwartz, J. M., Stoessel, P. W., Baxter, L. R., Martin, K. M., & Phelps, M. E. (1996). Systematic changes in cerebral glucose metabolic rate after successful behavior modification treatment of obsessive-compulsive disorder. *Archives of General Psychiatry, 53,* 109–113.
Schweinhart, L. J., Montie, J., Xiang, Z., Barnett, W. S., Belfield, C. R., & Nores, M. (2005). *Lifetime effects: The High/Scope Perry Preschool study through age 40* (Monographs of the High/Scope Educational Research Foundation, 14). Ypsilanti, MI: High/Scope Press.
Scott, S. & Dadds, M. R. (2009). Practitioner review: When parent training doesn't work: theory-driven clinical strategies. *Journal of Child Psychology and Psychiatry, 50,* 1441–1450.
Scott, S., Knapp, M., Henderson, J., & Maughan, B. (2001). Financial costs of social exclusion: Follow-up study of antisocial children into adulthood. *British Medical Journal, 323,* 1–5.
Seifer, R., & Dickstein, S. (2000). Parental mental illness and infant development. In C. H. Zeanah, Jr. (Ed.), *Handbook of infant mental health* (2nd ed., pp. 145–160). New York: Guilford Press.
Seitz, V., & Apfel, N. H. (1994). Parent-focused interventions: Diffusion effects on siblings. *Child Development, 65,* 677–683.
Self-Brown, S., LeBlanc, M., & Kelley, M. L. (2004). Effects of violence exposure and daily stressors on psychological outcomes in urban adolescents. *Journal of Traumatic Stress, 1,* 519–527.
Semel, E., Wigg, E. H., & Secord, W. (2004). Clinical Evaluation of Language Fundamentals, 4th ed. (CELF-4). San Antonio, TX: The Psychological Corporation.
Semel, E., Wiig, E. H., & Secord, W. (2006). *Clinical Evaluation of Language Fundamentals—Preschool,* 2nd ed. (CELF-P-2). Pearson.
Semel, E., Wiig, E. H., & Secord, W. (2006). *Clinical evaluation of Language Fundamentals,* 4th ed. (CELF-4). Pearson.
Serketich,W. J., & Dumas, J. E. (1996). The effectiveness of behavioral parent training to modify antisocial behavior in children: A meta-analysis. *Behavior Therapy, 27,* 171–186.
Sesma, H. W., Slomine, B. S., Ding, R., McCarthy, M. L., & Children's Health after Trauma Study Group (CHAT). (2008). Executive functioning in the first year after pediatric brain injury. *Pediatrics, 121,* 1686–1695.
Shalev, L., Tsal, Y., & Mevorach, C. (2007). Computerized progressive attentional training (CPAT) program: Effective direct intervention for children with ADHD. *Child Neuropsychology, 13,* 382–388
Shallice, T. (1982). Specific impairments of planning. *Philosophical Transactions of the Royal Society of London, 298,* 199–209.
Shankaran, S., Lester, B. M., Abhik, D., Bauer, C. R., Bada, H. S., & Lagasse, L. (2007). The impact of maternal substance use during pregnancy on childhood outcome. *Seminars in Fetal and Neonatal Medicine, 12,* 143–150.
Shanker, S. (2012). Building healthy minds: It takes a village. In S. Olfman & B. D. Robbins (Eds.), *Drugging our children: How profiteers are pushing antipsychotics on our youngest, and what we can do to stop it.* Santa Barbara, CA: Praeger.
Shanker, S. (2013). *Calm, alert and learning: Classroom strategies for self-regulation.* Pearson, Canada: Don Mills, ON.
Shapiro, F. (2001). *Eye movement desensitization and reprocessing: Basic principles, protocols, and procedures* (2nd ed.). New York: Guilford Press.
Shapiro, F. (2002). EMDR twelve years after its introduction: Past and present research. *Journal of Clinical Psychology, 58,* 1–22.
Sharma, M. Purdy, S. C. & Kelly, A. S. (2009). Comorbidity of auditory processing, language and reading disorders. *Journal of Speech, Language and Hearing Research, 52,* 706–727.
Shaw, D. S., Keenan, K., Vondra, J. I., Delliquadri, E., & Giovannelli, J. (1997). Antecedents of preschool children's internalizing problems: A longitudinal study of low-income families. *Journal of the American Academy of Child and Adolescent Psychiatry, 36,* 1760–1767.
Shaw, D. S., & Vondra, J. I. (1995). Infant attachment security and maternal predictors of early behavior problems: A longitudinal study of early behavior problems families. *Journal of Abnormal Child Psychology, 23,* 335–357.
Shear, K., Belnap, B. H., Mazumdar, S., Houck, P., & Rollman, B. L. (2006). Generalized Anxiety Disorder Severity Scale (GADSS): A preliminary validation study. *Depression and Anxiety, 23,* 77–82.

Shekhar, A., Sajdyk, T. J., Gehlert, D. R., & Rainnie, D. G. (2003). The amygdala, panic disorder, and cardiovascular responses. *Annals of the New York Academy of Sciences, 985*, 308–325.

Shelby, J. S., & Felix, E. D. (2005). Posttraumatic play therapy: The need for an integrated model of directive and nondirective approaches. In L. Reddy, T. M. Files-Hall, & C. E. (Eds.), *Empirically based play interventions for children* (pp. 79–103). Washington, DC: American Psychological Association.

Sheperis, C. J., Doggett, R. A., Hoda, N. E., Blanchard, T., Renfero-Michel, E. L., Holdiness, S. H., & Schlagheck, R. (2003). The development of an assessment protocol for reactive attachment disorder.*Journal of Mental Health Counselling, 25*, 291–310.

Shields, A. & Cicchetti, D. (1998). Reactive aggression among maltreated children: The contributions of attention and emotion dysregulation. *Journal of Clinical Child Psychology 27*(4), 381–395.

Shields, A., & Cicchetti, D. (2001). Parental maltreatment and emotion dysregulation as risk factors for bullying and victimization in middle childhood. *Journal of Clinical Child Psychology, 30*, 349–363.

Shinn, M. (1990). *Biography of a baby*. Boston: Houghton Mifflin.

Shipman, K. L. & Zeman, J. (2001). Socialization of children's emotion regulation in mother-child dyads: A developmental psychopathology perspective. *Development and Psychopathology 13*, 317–336.

Shoal, G. D., Giancola, P. R., & Kirillova, G. P. (2003). Salivary cortisol, personality, and aggressive behavior in adolescent boys: A 5 year longitudinal study. *Journal of the American Academy of Child and Adolescent Psychiatry, 42*, 1101–1107.

Shonkoff, J. P., Boyce, W. T., & McEwen, B. S. (2009). Neuroscience, molecular biology, and the childhood roots of health disparities: Building a framework for health promotion and disease prevention. *The Journal of the American Medical Association, 301*, 2252–2259.

Shortt, J. W., Stoolmiller, M., Smith-Shine, J. N., Eddy, J. M., & Sheeber, L. (2010). Maternal emotion coaching, adolescent anger regulation, and siblings' externalizing symptoms. *Journal of Child Psychology and Psychiatry and Allied Disciplines, 51*, 799–808.

Shriberg, L. O., Tomblin, B. J., & McSweeny, J. L. (1999). Prevalence of speech delay in 6-year-old children and comorbidity with language impairment. *Journal of Speech, Language, and Hearing Research, 42*, 1461–1481.

Shure, M. D. (1990). *The What Happens Next Game (WHNG) Manual*. Philadelphia, PA: Department of Mental Health Sciences, Hahnemann University.

Siegel, D. J. (2003). An interpersonal neurobiology of psychotherapy: The developing mind and the resolution of trauma. In M. E. Solomon & D. J. Siegel (Eds.), *Healing trauma: Attachment, mind, body, and brain* (pp. 1–56). New York: W.W. Norton.

Siegel, D. J. (2007). *The mindful brain: Reflection and attunement in the cultivation of well-being*. New York: W.W. Norton & Co.

Siegel, L. S. (1982). Reproductive perinatal and environmental factors as predictors of the cognitive and language development of preterm and full-term infants. *Child Development, 53*, 963–973.

Sigmundson, H. (2003). Perceptual deficits in clumsy children: Inter and intra-modal matching approach—A window into clumsy behavior. *Neural Plasticity, 10*, 27–38.

Silk, J. S., Ziegler, M. S., Whalen, D. J., Dahl, R. J., Ryan, N. D., Dietz, L. J., … Williamson, D. E. (2009). Expressed emotion in mothers of currently depressed, remitted, high-risk, and low-risk youth: Links to child depression status and longitudinal course. *Journal of Clinical Child and Adolescent Psychology, 38*(1), 36–47.

Silman, A. J., Haskard, D., & Day, S. (1986). Distribution of joint mobility in normal populations results of the use of fixed torque measuring devices. *Annual of the Rheumatic Diseases, 45*(1), 27–30.

Silva, R. C. (2004). *Posttraumatic stress disorders in children and adolescents*. New York: W.W. Norton.

Silver, C. H. (2000). Ecological validity of neuropsychological assessment in childhood traumatic brain injury: Developmental neuropsychology. *Journal of Head Trauma Rehabilitation, 15*, 973–988.

Sim, E. (2013). *Occupational therapy screening questionnaire*. In S. Landy & S. Bradley (Eds.), *Children with multiple mental health challenges: An integrated approach to intervention* (pp. 91–93). New York: Springer Publishers.

Simon, C. S. (1986). *Evaluating communicative competence: A functional pragmatic procedure*. Tucson, TX: Communication Skill Builders.

Simon, H. A. (1975). The functional equivalence of problem solving skills. *Cognitive Psychology, 7,* 268–288.

Simons, R. L., Wu, C., Conger, R. D., & Lorenz, F. O. (1994). Two routes to delinquency: Differences between early and late starters on the impact of parenting and deviant peers. *Criminology, 33,* 141–172.

Simos, P. G., Fletcher, J. M., Bergman, E., Breier, J. I., Foorman, B. R., Castillo, E. M., ... Papanicolaou, A. C. (2002). Dyslexia-specific brain activation profile becomes normal following successful remedial training. *Neurology, 58,* 120–1213.

Simpson, G. A., Colpe, L., & Greenspan, S. (2003). Measuring functional developmental delays in infants and young children: Prevalence rates from the NHIS-D. *Pediatrics & Perinatal Epidemiology, 17,* 68–80.

Singer, J. L., Singer, D. G., & Schweder, A. E. (2004). Enhancing preschooler's language and school readiness through imaginative play with parents and teachers. In R. Clements & L. Florentino (Eds.), *The child's right to play: A global approach* (pp. 35–47). Westport, CT: Greenwood Publishers.

Skarakis-Doyle, E., & Dempsey, L. (2008). The detection and monitoring of comprehension errors by preschool children with and without language impairment. *Journal of Speech, Language, and Hearing Research, 51,* 1227–1243.

Skovgaard, A. M., Houmann, T., Christiansen, E., Landorph, S., Jorgensen, T., and the CC 2000 Study Team (2007). The prevalence of mental health problems in children 1 ½ years of age—The Copenhagen Child Cohort 2000. *Journal of Child Psychology and Psychiatry and Allied Disciplines, 48,* 113–149.

Slade, A. (2002). Keeping the baby in mind: A critical factor in perinatal mental health. *Zero to Three, 22,* 11–16.

Slade, A. (2005). Parental reflective functioning: An introduction. *Attachment and Human Development, 7,* 269–281.

Slade, A., Aber, J. L., Berger, B., Bresgi, I., & Kaplan, M. (2003). *Parent Development Interview Revised* (PDI-R2-S). City College of New York, NY.

Slade, A., Grienenberger, J., Bernbach, E., Levy, D., & Locker, A. (2005). Maternal reflective functioning, attachment, and the transmission gap: A preliminary study. *Attachment and Human Development, 7,* 283–298.

Slade, A., Sadler, L. S., DeDios-Kenn, C., Webb, D., Currier-Ezepchick, J., & Mayes, L. (2005). Minding the Baby: A reflective parenting program. *Psychoanalytic Study of the Child, 60,* 74–100.

Slomine, B. S., Gerring, J., Grados, M. A., Vasa, K. D., Brady, K. D., Christensen, J. R. & Denckla, M. B. (2002). Performance on measures of "executive function" following pediatric traumatic brain injury. *Brain Injury, 16,* 759–772.

Slough, V. M., & Greenberg, M. T. (1990). Five-year-olds' representations of separation from parents: Responses from the perspective of self and other. *New Directions for Child Development, 48,* 67–84.

Slutske, W. S., Heath, A. C., Dinwiddie, S. H., Madden, P. A., Bucholz, K. K., Dunne, M. P., ... Martin, N. G. (1998). Common genetic risk factors for conduct disorder and alcohol dependence. *Journal of Abnormal Psychology, 107,* 363–374.

Smart, D., Sanson, A., & Prior, M. (1996). Connections between reading disability and behavior problems: Testing causal and temporal hypotheses. *Journal of Abnormal Child Psychology, 24,* 363–383.

Smith, C. (2002). *Writing and developing social stories: Practical interventions in autism.* Milton Keynes, UK: Speechmark Publishing Ltd.

Smits, M., Visch-Brimk, E., Schraa-Tam, C. K., Eng, M., Koudstaal, P. J., & van der Lugt, A. (2006). Functional MR imaging of language processing: An overview of easy-to-implement paradigms for patient care clinical research. *Radiographics, 26,* 145–158.

Smoller, J. W., Rosenbaum, J. F., & Biederman, J. (2003). Association of a genetic marker at the corticotropin-releasing hormone locus with behavioral inhibition. *Biological Psychiatry, 54,* 1376–1381.

Smoller, J. W., Yamaki, L. H., Fagerness, J. A., Biederman, J., Racette, S., Laird, N. M., ... Sklar, P. B. (2005). The corticotropin releasing hormone gene and behavioral inhibition in children at risk for panic disorder. *Biological Psychology, 57,* 1485–1492.

Smyke, A. T., Dumitrescu, A. S., & Zeanah, C. M. (2002). Attachment disturbances in young children. 1: The continuum of caretaking casualty. *Journal of the American Academy of Child and Adolescent Psychiatry, 41,* 972–982.

Snyder, J., Cramer, A., Afrank, J., & Patterson, G. R. (2005). The contributions of ineffective discipline and parental hostile attributions of child misbehavior to the development of conduct problems at home and school. *Developmental Psychology, 41*, 30–41.

Snyder, J., Schrepferman, L., McEachern, A., Barner, S., Johnson, K., & Provines, J. (2008). Peer deviancy training and peer coercion: Dual processes associated with early-onset conduct problems. *Child Development, 79*, 252–268.

Soby, J. M. (2006). Prenatal exposure to drugs/alcohol: Characteristics and education: Implications of fetal alcohol syndrome and cocaine/polydrug effects. Springfield, IL: Charles C. Thomas.

Solomon, J., & George, C. (Eds.). (1999). *Attachment disorganization.* N.Y.: Guilford Press.

Solomon, J., & George, C. (2008). The measurement of attachment security and related constructs in infancy and early childhood. In J. Cassidy & P. R. Shaver (Eds.), *Handbook of attachment research, theory, and clinical research* (2nd ed., pp. 383–416). New York: Guilford Press.

Sonders, S. A. (2003). *Giggle time: Establishing the social connection.* London, UK: Jessica Kingsley Publishers.

Southwick, S., & Charney, D. (1999). The neurobiology of posttraumatic stress disorder: An integration of animal and human research. In P. Saigh & D. Bremner (Eds.), *Posttraumatic stress disorder: A comprehensive text* (pp. 103–143). Needham Heights, Massachusetts: Allyn and Bacon.

Sowell, E., Thompson, P., Tessner, K., & Toga, A. (2001). Mapping continued brain growth and gray matter density reduction in dorsal frontal cortex: Inverse relationships during postadolescent brain maturation. *Journal of Neuroscience, 21*, 8819–8829.

Spackman, M. P., Fujiki, M., & Brinton, B. (2006). Understanding emotions in context: The effects of language impairment on children's ability to infer emotional reactions. *International Journal of Language and Communication Disorders, 41*, 173–88.

Spangler, G., & Zimmerman, P. (2007, March). *Genetic contribution to attachment disorganization and temperament.* Paper presented at the biennial meeting of the Society for Research in Child Development, Boston, MA.

Sparks, S. N. (1993). *Children of prenatal substance abuse.* Singular Publishing Group, San Diego, CA.

Sparrow, S. S., Cicchetti, D. V., & Balla, D. A. (2005). *Vineland adaptive behavior scales* (2nd ed.) (Vineland-II*)*. San Antonio, TX: Pearson.

Spear, L. P. (2009). Heightened stress responsivity and emotional reactivity during pubertal maturation: Implications for psychopathology. Special section commentary. *Development and Psychopathology, 21*(1), 87–98.

Speltz, M. L. (1990). The treatment of preschool conduct problems: An integration of behavioral and attachment constructs. In M. Greenberg, D. Cicchetti, & M. Cummings (Eds.), *Attachment in the preschool years: Theory, research, and treatment* (pp. 399–426). Chicago: University of Chicago Press.

Spence, S. H. (2003). Social skills training with children and young people: theory, evidence, and practice. *Child & Adolescent Mental Health, 8*, 84–96.

Spencer, N., Devereux, E., Wallace, A., Sundrum, R., Shenoy, M., Bacchis, C., & Logan, S. (2005). Disabling conditions and registration for child abuse and neglect. *Pediatrics, 116*, 609–613,

Spinazola, J., Blaustein, M., & van der Kolk, B. A. (2005). Posttraumatic stress disorder treatment outcome research: The study of unrepresentative samples? *Journal of Traumatic Stress, 8*, 425–436.

Spinrad, T. L., Eisenberg, N., Guertner, B., Popp, T., Smith, C. L., Kupfer, H., ... Hofer, C. (2007). Relations of maternal socialization and toddlers' effortful control to children's adjustment and social competence. *Developmental Psychology, 43*, 1170–1186.

Spinrad, T. L., Stifter, C. A., Donelan, K., McCall, N., & Turner, L. (2004). Mothers' regulation strategies in response to toddlers' affect: Links to later emotion self-regulation. *Social Development, 13*, 40–55.

Sprich, S., Biederman, J., & Crawford, M. H. (2000). Adoptive and biological families of children and adolescents with ADHD. *Journal of the American Academy of Child and Adolescent Psychiatry, 39*, 1432–1437.

Squires, J., & Bricker, D. (2009*). Ages and stages questionnaires,* 3rd ed. (ASQ-3). Baltimore, MD: Paul H. Brookes Publishers.

Sroufe, A. L. (1983). Infant caregiver attachment and patterns of adaptation in preschool: The roots of maladaptation and competence. In M. Perimutter (Ed.), *Minnesota symposium on child psychology* (Vol. 16, pp. 41–79). Hillsdale, NJ: Erlbaum.

Sroufe, L. (2007). The place of development in developmental psychopathology. In A. Marten (Ed.), *Multilevel dynamics in developmental psychopathology: Pathways to the future. The minnesota symposia on child psychology* (pp. 285–299). Mahwah, NJ: Lawrence Erlbaum Associates.

Sroufe, L. A., Egeland, B., Carlson, E., & Collins, W. A. (2005). Placing early development in developmental context: The Minnesota Longitudinal study. In K. E. Grossman, K. Grossman, & E. Waters (Eds.), *Attachment from infancy to adulthood: The major longitudinal studies* (pp. 48–70). New York: Guilford Press.

St. Pierre, R. G., & Layzer, J. I. (1998). Using home visits for multiple purposes: The Comprehensive Child Development Program. *The Future of Children, 8*, 134–151.

Stach, B. (2003). *Comprehensive dictionary of audiology illustrated*. Delmar, NY: Thomson Learning.

Stallard, P. (2005). *A clinician's guide to think good and feel good: Using CBT with children and young people.* West Sussex, UK: John Wiley and Sons.

Steege, M. W., & Brown-Chidsey, R. (2005). Functional behavioral assessment: The cornerstone of effective problem solving. In Brown-Chidsey (Ed.), *Assessment for intervention: A problem-solving approach* (pp. 131–154). New York: Guilford Press.

Steele, H., & Steele, M. (2005a). Understanding and resolving emotional conflict: The London Parent-Child Project. In K. E. Grossman, K. Grossman, & E. Waters, E. (Eds.), *Attachment from infancy to adulthood: The major longitudinal studies* (pp. 137–164). New York: Guilford Press.

Steele, H., & Steele, M. (2005b). The construct of coherence in childhood: The friends and family interview. In K. A. Kerns & R. A. Richardson (Eds.), *Attachment in middle childhood* (pp. 137–160). New York: Guilford Press.

Steele, H., Steele, M., Croft, C., & Fonagy, P. (1999). Infant-mother attachment at one year predicts children's understanding of mixed emotions at six years. *Social Development, 8*, 161–177.

Stein, M., Loverola, C., Hanna, C., Torchia, M., & McLarty, B. (1997). Hippocampal volume in women victimised by childhood sexual abuse. *Psychological Medicine, 27*, 951–959.

Stein, S. M., & Chowdbury, U. (2006). *The disorganized child: A guide for parents and professionals.* London, UK: Jessica Kingsley Publishers.

Steinhausen, H., & Juzi, C. (1996). Elective mutism: Analysis of 100 cases. *Journal of the American Academy of Child and Adolescent Psychiatry, 35*, 606–614.

Steinhoff, K. W., Lerner, M., Kapilinsky, A., Kotking, R., Wigal, S., & Swanson, J. M. (2006). Attention-deficit/hyperactivity disorder. In J. L. Luby (Ed.), *Handbook of preschool mental health: Development, disorders, and treatment* (pp. 63–79). New York: Guilford Press.

Sterber, S., Egger, H. L., & Angold, A. (2007). Diagnostic specificity and non-specificity in the dimensions of preschool psychopathology. *Journal of Child Psychology and Psychiatry and Allied Disciplines, 48*, 1005–1013.

Stern, D. N. (1995). *The motherhood constellation: A unified view of parent-infant psychotherapy.* New York: Basic Books.

Stern, D. N. (2004). *The present moment in psychotherapy and everyday life.* New York: W.W. Norton & Co. Inc.

Sterzer, A., Stadler, B., Krebs, A., Kleinschmidt, A., & Poustka, F. (2005). Abnormal neural responses to emotional visual stimuli in adolescents with conduct disorder. *Biological Psychiatry, 57*, 7–15.

Stevens, C., Fanning, J., Coch, D., Sanders, L, & Nevile, H. (2008). Neural mechanisms of selective auditory attention are enhanced by computerized training: Electrophysiological evidence from language-impaired and typically developing children. *Brain Research, 1205*, 55–69.

Stevens, D., Charman, T., & Blair, R. J. R. (2001). Recognition of emotion in facial expressions and vocal tones in children with psychopathic tendencies. *Journal of Genetic Psychology, 16*, 201–211.

Stewart, M. A. (1970). Hyperactive children. *Scientific American, 222*, 94–98.

Stickgold, R. (2002). EMDR: A putative neurobiological mechanism of action. *Journal of Clinical Psychology, 58*, 61–75.

Stifter, C. A., Putnam, S., & Jahromi, L. (2008). Exuberant and inhibited toddlers: Stability of temperament and risk for problem behavior. *Development and Psychopathology, 20*, 401–421.

Still, G. F. (1902). Some abnormal psychological conditions in children. *Lancet, 1*, 1008–1012, 1077–1082, 1163–1168.

Stipek, D., & Miles, S. (2008). Effects of aggression on achievement: Does conflict with the teacher make it worse? *Child Development, 79*, 1721–1735.

Stock, C. D., & Fisher, P. A. (2006). Language delays among foster children: Implications for policy and practice. *Child Welfare, 85*, 445–461.

Stormshak, E. A., Bierman, K. L., McMahon, R. J., & Lengua, L. J. (2000). Parenting practices and child disruptive behavior problems in early elementary school. *Journal of Clinical Child Psychology, 29*, 17–29.

Stratton, K., Howe, C., & Battaglia, E. (Eds.). (1996). *Fetal alcohol syndrome: Diagnosis, epidemiology, prevention and treatment*. Washington, DC: National Academy Press.

Stratton, K., Howe, C., & Battaglia, K. (2005). *Fetal alcohol syndrome: Diagnosis and epidemiology*. Washington, DC: Academic Press.

Straus, M. A., & Gelles, R. J. (1990). *Physical violence in American families*. New Brunswick, NJ: Transaction.

Strelau, J. (1995). Temperament risk factor: The contribution of temperament to the consequences of the state of stress. In S. S. Hobfoll & M. W. de Vries (Eds.), *Extreme stress and communities: Impact and intervention* (pp. 63–81). Dordrecht, Netherlands: Kluwer Academic Publishers.

Stuber, M. L., & Shermasch, E. (2006). Post-traumatic stress response to life-threatening illnesses in children and their parents. *Child and Adolescent Clinics of North America, 15*, 597–609.

Stucke, T. S. & Sporer, S. L. (2002). When a grandiose self-image is threatened: Narcissism and self-concept clarity as predictors of negative emotions and aggression following ego-threat. *Journal of Personality, 20*, 509–532.

Stuhlman, M. W., & Pianta, R. C. (2009). Profiles of educational quality in first grade. *The Elementary School Journal, 109*, 323–342.

Sturge-Apple, M., Davies, P., & Cummings, E. (2006). Impact of hostility and withdrawal in interparental conflict on parental emotional unavailability and children's adjustment difficulties. *Child Development, 77*, 1623–1641.

Stuss, T., & Knight, R. T. (Eds.). (2002). *Principals of frontal lobe function*. New York: Oxford University Press.

Substance Abuse and Mental Health Services Administration, Office of Applied Studies. (2008). *Results from the 2007 National Survey on Drug Use and Health: National Findings* (NSDUH Series H-34, DHHS Publication No. SMA 08-4343). Rockville, MD: Author.

Sullivan, P. M., & Knutson, J. F. (2000). Maltreatment and disabilities: A population-based epidemiological study. *Child Abuse and Neglect, 24*, 1257–1274.

Summers, J. (2000). Joint Laxity in the index finger and thumb and its relationship to pencil grasp used by children. *Australian Occupational Therapy Journal, 48*, 132–141.

Supplee, L. H., Skuban., E. M., Shaw, D. S., & Prout, J. (2009). Emotion regulation strategies and later externalizing behavior among European American and African American children. *Development and Psychopathology, 21*, 393–416.

Swain, J. E., Lorberbaum, J. P., Kose, S., & Strathearn, L. (2007). Brain basis of early parent-infant interactions: Psychology, physiology, and in vivo functional neuroimaging studies. *Journal of Child Psychology and Psychiatry, 48*, 262–287.

Sweet, M. A., & Applebaum, M. I. (2004). Is home visiting an effective strategy: A meta-analytic review of home visiting programs for families with young children. *Child Development, 75*, 1435–1456.

Szatmari, P., Boyle, M., & Offord, D. R. (1993). Familial aggregation of emotional and behavioral problems of childhood in the general population. *American Journal of Psychiatry, 150*, 1398–1403.

Szyf, M. (2009). Early life, the epigenome and human health. *Acta Paediatrica, 98*, 1082–1084.

Tallal, P., Jernigan, T., & Trauner, D. (1994). Developmental bilateral damage to the caudate nuclei: Implication for speech-language pathology. *Journal of Medical Speech Language Pathology, 2*, 23–28

Tallal, P., Miller, S. L., Bedi, G., Byma, G., Wang, X., Nagarajan, S. S., … Jenkins, W. (1996). Language comprehension in language learning impaired children improved with acoustically modified speech. *Science, 271*, 81–84.

Tamis-LeMonda, C., Shannon, J., Cabrera, N., & Lamb, M. (2004). Fathers and mothers at play with their 2- and 3-year olds: Contributions to language and cognitive development. *Child Development, 75*, 1806–1820.

Tannock, R. (1998). Attention deficit hyperactivity disorder: Advances in cognitive neurobiology and genetics. *Research Journal of Child Psychology and Psychiatry, 39*, 65–100.

Tannock, R., & Brown, T. E. (2009). ADHD with language and/or learning disorders in children and adolescents. In T. E. Brown (Ed.), *ADHD comorbidities: ADHD complicationsin children and adolescents.* Washington, DC: American Psychiatric Publishing.

Tansey, M. A., & Bruner, R. I. (1983). EMG and EEG biofeedback training in the treatment of a 10-year-old hyperactive boy with developmental reading disorder. *Biofeedback and Self-Regulation, 8,* 25–37.

Tarabulsy, G. M., Pascuzzo, K., Moss, E., St-Laurent, D., Bernier, A., Cyr, C., & Dubois-Comtois, K. (2008). Attachment-based intervention for maltreating families. *American Journal of Orthopsychiatry, 78,* 322–332.

Tarshis, N., Rodriguez, B. G., & Seijo, M. D. (2007). Therapeutic approaches to speech and language disorders in early childhood. *Paediatric Annals, 36,* 8.

Task Force on Research Diagnostic Criteria: Infancy and Preschool Age. (2003). Research diagnostic criteria for infants and pre-school children: The process and empirical support. *Journal of the American Academy of Child and Adolescent Psychiatry, 42,* 1504–1512.

Taylor, H. G. (2004). Research on outcomes of pediatric traumatic brain injury: current advances and future directions. *Developmental Neuropsychology, 25,* 199–225.

Taylor, H. G., Klein, N., Drotar, D., Schluchter, M., & Hack, M. (2006). Consequences and risks of < 1000-g birth weight for neuropsychological skills, achievement, and adaptive functioning. *Journal of Developmental and Behavioral Pediatrics, 27,* 459–469.

Taylor, T. K., Eddy, J. M., & Biglan, A. (1999). Interpersonal skills training to reduce aggressive and delinquent behavior: Limited evidence and the need for an evidence-based system of care. *Clinical Child and Family Psychology Review, 2,* 169–182.

Teicher, M. H. (2000). Wounds that won't heal: The neurobiology of child abuse. *Cerebrum: The Dana Forum on Brain Sciences, 2,* 50–68.

Teicher, M. H., Anderson, S. L., Polcari, A., Anderson, C. M., Navalta, C. P., & Kim D. M. (2003). The neurobiological consequences of early stress and childhood maltreatment. *Neuroscience & Biobehavioral Reviews, 27,* 33–44.

Teicher, M. H., Ito, Y., Glod, C. A., Anderson, S. L., Dumont, N., & Ackerman, E. (1997). Preliminary evidence for abnormal cortical development in physically and sexually abused children using EEG coherence and MRI. In R. Yeguda & A. McFarlane (Eds.), *Psychobiology of posttraumatic stress disorder* (pp. 160–176). New York: New York Academy of Sciences.

Teicher, T. (2000). Scars that won't heal: The neurobiology of child abuse. *Scientific American, 286,* 68–75.

Teicher, T., Andersen, S., Polcari, A., Andersen, C., & Navalta, C. (2002). Developmental neurobiology of childhood stress and trauma. *Psychiatric Clinics of North America, 25,* 397–426.

Teisl, M., & Cicchetti, D. (2008). Physical abuse, cognitive and emotional processes and aggressive/disruptive behavior problems. *Social Development, 17,* 1–23.

Temple, E., Deutsch, G. K., Poldrack, R. A., Miller, S. L., Tallal, P. Merzenick, M. M. (2003). Neural deficits in children with dyslexia ameliorated by behavioral remediation: Evidence from functional MRI. *Proceedings of the National Academy of Sciences, USA, 100,* 2860–2865.

Terr, L. (2008). *Magical moments of change: How psychotherapy turns kids around.* New York: W.W. Norton & Company.

Thalhuber, K., Jacobvitz, D., & Hazen, C. (1998, March). *Effects of mothers' past traumatic experiences on mother-infant interactions.* Paper presented at the biennial meeting of the Southwestern Society for Research in Human Development, Galveston, TX.

Theall-Honey, I. A., & Schmidt, L. A. (2006). Do temperamentally shy children process emotion differently from nonshy children? Behavioral psychophysiological and gender differences in reticent preschoolers. *Developmental Psychobiology, 48,* 187–196.

Thiemann, K., & Goldstein, H. (2001). Social stories, written test cues, and video feedback: Effects on social communication of children with autism. *Journal of Applied Behavior Analysis, 24,* 425–446.

Thienemann, M., Moore, P., & Tompkins, K. (2006). A parent-only group intervention for children with anxiety disorders: Pilot study. *Journal of the American Academy of Child and Adolescent Psychiatry, 45,* 37–46.

Thomaes, S., Bushman, B. J., Stegge, H., & Olthof, T. (2008). Trumping shame by blasts of noise: Narcissism, self-esteem, shame, and aggression in young adolescents. *Child Development, 79,* 1792–1801.

Thomas, A., Chess, S., & Birch, H. G. (1968). *Temperament and behavior disorders in children*. New York: New York University Press.

Thomas, R., & Zimmer-Gembeck, M. J. (2011). Accumulating evidence for parent-child interaction therapy in the prevention of child maltreatment. *Child Development, 82*, 177–192.

Thompson, E., & Trevathan, C. (2008). The musical art of infant conversation: Narrating in the time of sympathetic infant experience without rational interpretation before words. *Musicae Scientiae, 12*, 15–46.

Thompson, R. A. (2008). Early attachment and later development: Familiar questions and new answers. In J. Cassidy & P. R. Shaver (Eds.), *Handbook of attachment research, theory, and clinical research* (2nd ed., pp. 348–365). New York: Guilford Press.

Thorell, L. B., Lindqvist, S., Bergman, S., Bohlin, G., & Klingberg, T. (2008). Training and transfer effects of executive functions in preschool children. *Developmental Science, 11*, 969–976.

Thornton, T. N., Craft, C. A., Dahlberg, L. L., Lynch, B. S., & Baer, K. (2002). *Best practices of youth violence prevention: A sourcebook for community action* (rev. ed.). Atlanta, GA: Centers for Disease Control and Prevention, National Center for Injury Prevention and Control.

Tierney, C. D., Brown, P. J., & Serwint, J. R. (2008). In brief: Development of children who have hearing impairment. *Pediatrics in Review, 29*, 71–73.

Tillfors, M., Furmark, T., Marteinsdottir, I., & Fredrikson, M. (2002). Cerebral blood flow during anticipation of public speaking in social phobia: A PET study. *Biological Psychiatry, 52*, 1113–1119.

Timler, G. R. (2008). Social knowledge in children with language impairments: Examination of strategies predicted consequences and goals in peer conflicts. *Clinical Linguistics & Phonetics, 22*, 741–763.

Timler, G. R., Vogler-Elias, D., & McGill, K. F. (2007). Strategies for promoting generalization of social communication skills in pre-school and school age children. *Topics in Language Disorders, 27*, 167–181.

Tisak, M. S., & Jankowski, A. M. (1996). Societal rule evaluations: Adolescent offenders' reasoning about moral, conventional, and personal rules. *Aggressive Behavior, 24*, 347–365.

Tizard, B., & Hodges, J. (1978). The effect of early institutionalised rearing on the development of eight-year-old children. *Journal of Child Psychology and Psychiatry, 19*, 99–118.

Tizard, B., & Rees, J. (1975). The effect of early institutionalised rearing on the behavior problems and affectional relationships of four-year-old children. *Journal of Child Psychology and Psychiatry, 16*, 61–73.

Tomblin, J. B. (1989). Familial concentration of developmental language impairment. *Journal of Speech and Hearing Research, 41*, 287–295.

Tomblin, J. B., Hareman, L. L., & O'Brien, M. (2003). Autism and autism risk in siblings of children with specific language impairments. *International Journal of Language and Communication Disorders, 38*, 235–250.

Tommerdahl, J. (2009). What teachers of students with Social, Emotional, and Behavioral Difficulties (SEBD) need to know about speech and language difficulties. *Emotional and Behavioral Difficulties, 14*, 19–31.

Toplis, F., & Hadwin, J. A. (2006). Using social stories to change problematic lunchtime behavior in school. *Educational Psychology in Practice, 22*, 53–67.

Toth, K., & King, B. H. (2008). Asperger's syndrome: diagnosis and treatment. *American Journal of Psychiatry, 165*, 958–963.

Toth, S. L., Maughan, A., Manly, J. T., Spagnola, M., & Cicchetti, D. (2002). The relative efficacy of two interventions in altering maltreated preschool children's representational models: Implications for attachment theory. *Development and Psychopathology, 14*, 877–908.

Trauma Affect Regulation Guide to Education and Therapy (TARGET) at www.advancedtrauma.com

Tredgold, A. F. (1908). *Mental deficiency (amentia)*. New York: W. Wood.

Tremblay, R. E., Masse, B., Perron, D., LeBlanc, M., Schwartzman, A. E., & Ledingham, J. E. (1992). Early disruptive behavior, poor school achievement, delinquent behavior, and delinquent personality: Longitudinal analysis. *Journal of Consulting and Clinical Psychology, 60*, 64–72.

Trentacosta, C. J., Izard, C. E., Mostow, A. J., & Fine, S. E. (2006). Children's emotional competence and attentional competence in early elementary school. *School Psychology Quarterly, 21*(2), 148–170.

Tronick, E. Z., & Weinberg, M. K. (1997). Depressed mothers and infants: Failure to form dyadic states of consciousness. In L. Murray, & P. J. Cooper (Eds), *Postpartum depression and child development* (pp. 54–81). New York: Guilford.

Trzesniewski, K. H., Donnellan, M. B., Moffitt, T. E., Robins, R. W., Poulton, K., & Caspi, A. (2006). Low self-esteem during adolescence predicts poor health, criminal behavior, and limited economic prospects during adulthood. *Developmental Psychology, 42,* 381–390,

Tucker, D. M., & Luu, P. (2007). Neurophysiology of motivated learning: Adaptive mechanisms underlying cognitive bias in depression. *Cognitive Therapy Research, 3,* 189–209.

Turner, L. M., & Stone, W. L. (2007). Variability in outcome for children with ASD diagnosis at age 2. *Journal of Child Psychology and Psychiatry, 48,* 793–802.

Ukrainetz, T. A. (1998). Stickwriting stories: A quick and easy narrative representation strategy. *Language, Speech and Hearing Services in Schools, 29,* 197–206.

Ulman, A., & Straus, M. A. (2003). Violence by children against mothers in relation to violence between parents and corporal punishment by parents. *Journal of Comparative Family Studies, 34,* 41–60.

Urwin, R., & Ballinger, C. (2005). The effectiveness of sensory integration therapy to improve functional behaviour in adults with learning disabilities: Five single-case experimental designs. *British Journal of Occupational Therapy, 68,* 56–66.

U.S. Department of Health & Human Services. (1999). *Mental health: A report of the surgeon general.* Rockville, MD: Author.

U.S. Department of Health and Human Services, Administration of Children, Youth, and Families (2008). *Child maltreatment 2006.* Washington, DC: US Government Printing Office.

U.S. Surgeon General. (2000). *Advisory on alcohol use in pregnancy.* Washington, D. C.: Author

Valera, E. M., & Seidman, L. J. (2006). Neurobiology of attention-deficit/hyperactivity disorder in preschoolers. *Infants and Young Children, 19,* 94–108.

Vallance, D. D., Im, N., & Cohen, N. J. (1999). Discourse deficits associated with psychiatric disorders and with language impairments in children. *Journal of Child Psychology and Psychiatry, 40,* 693–704.

Van Acker, R., & Mayer, M. J. (2009). Cognitive-behavioral interventions and the social context of the school: A stranger in a strange land. In M. J. Mayer, R. Van Acker, J. E. Lochman, & F. M. Gresham (Eds.), *Cognitive–behavioral interventions for emotional and behavioral disorders: School-based practice* (pp. 82–108). New York: Guilford.

van Baardewijk, Y., Stegge, H., Bushman, B. J., & Vermeiren, R. (2009). Psychopathic traits, victim distress, and aggression in children. *The Journal of Child Psychology and Psychiatry, 50,* 718–725.

van Bakel, H., & Riksen-Walraven, J. (2004). Stress reactivity in 15-month old infants: Links with infant temperament, cognitive competence and attachment security. *Developmental Psychobiology, 44,* 157–167.

Van Daal, J., Verhoeven, L., & van Balkom, H. (2007). Behavior problems in children with language impairment. *Journal of Child Psychology and Psychiatry, 48,* 1139–1147.

Van den Bergh, B. R. H., & Marcoen, A. (2004). High prenatal anxiety is related to ADHD symptoms, externalizing problems, and anxiety in 8- and 9-year olds. *Child Development, 75,* 1085–1097.

van den Boom, D. C. (1994). The influence of temperament and mothering on attachment and exploration: An experimental manipulation of sensitive responsiveness among lower-class mothers with irritable infants. *Child Development, 65,* 1457–1477.

van den Boom, D. C. (1995). Do first-year intervention effects endure? Follow-up during toddlerhood of a sample of Dutch irritable infants. *Child Development, 66,* 1798–1816.

Van der Helm, E., & Walker, M. P. (2007). The role of sleep in emotional brain regulation. In A. M. Kring & D. M. Sloan (Eds.), *Emotion regulation and psychopathology: A transdiagnostic approach to etiology and treatment* (pp. 253–279). New York: Guilford Press.

van der Kolk, B. A. (1987). *Psychological trauma.* Washington, DC: American Psychological Association.

van der Kolk, B. A. (1994). The body keeps the score: Memory and evolving psychobiology of post traumatic stress. *Harvard Review of Psychiatry, 1,* 253–265.

van der Kolk, B. A. (2001). The assessment and treatment of complex PTSD. In R. Yehuda (Ed.), *Traumatic stress.* Washington, DC: American Psychiatric Press.

van der Kolk, B. A. (2003). The neurobiology of childhood trauma and abuse. *Child and Adolescent Clinics of North America, 12,* 293–317.

van der Kolk, B. A. (2005). Developmental trauma disorder. *Psychiatric Annals, 35,* 401–408.

van der Kolk, B. A. (2006). Clinical implications of neuroscience research in PTSD. *Annual New York Academy of Sciences, 40*, 1–17.

van der Kolk, B. A., & Fisler, R. (1995). Dissociation and the fragmentary nature of traumatic memories: Overview and exploratory study. *Journal of Traumatic Stress, 8*, 505–525.

van der Kolk, B. A., Hopper, J. W., & Osterman, J. E. (2001). Exploring the nature of traumatic memory: Combining clinical knowledge with laboratory methods. *Journal of Aggression, Maltreatment & Trauma, 4*, 9–13.

van der Kolk, B. A., McFarlane, A. C., & Weisaeth, L. (Eds.). (1996). *Traumatic stress: The effects of overwhelming experience on mind, body, and society.* New York: Guilford Press.

van der Kolk, B. A., Pelcovitz, D., Roth, S., Mandel, F. S., McFarlane, A., & Herman, J. L. (1996). Dissociation, somatisation, and affect regulation: The complexity of adaptation to trauma. *American Journal of Psychiatry, 153*(Suppl.), 83–93.

van der Kolk, B. A., Roth, S., Pelcovitz, D., & Mandel, F. S. (1992). *Disorders of Extreme Stress: Results from the DSM-IV field trials for PTSD.* Unpublished manuscript.

van der Kolk, B. A., Roth, S., Pelcovitz, D., Sunday, S., & Spinazzola, J. (2005). Disorders of extreme stress: The empirical foundation for a complex adaptation to trauma. *Journal of Traumatic Stress, 18*, 389–399.

Van Goozen, S. H. M., Matthys, W., Cohen-Kettenis, P. T., Buitelaar, J. K., & van Engeland, H. (2000). Hypothalamic-pituitary-adrenal axis and autonomic nervous system activity in disruptive children and matched controls. *Journal of the American Academy of Child and Adolescent Psychiatry, 39*, 1438–1445.

Van Goozen, S. H. M., Matthys, W., Cohen-Kettenis, P. T., Gispen-de Wied, C., Wiegant, V. M., & van Engeland, H. (1998). Salivary cortisol and cardiovascular activity during stress in oppositional-defiant boys and normal controls. *Biological Psychiatry, 43*, 531–539.

Van Horn, P., & Lieberman, A. F. (2009). Using dyadic therapies to treat traumatized young children. In D. Brom, R. Pat-Horenczyk, & J. D. Ford (Eds.), *Treating traumatized children: Risk, resilience and recovery* (pp. 210–224). New York: Routledge.

van IJzendoorn, M., & Bakermans-Kranenburg, M. (2003). Attachment disorders and disorganised attachment: Similar and different. *Attachment and Human Development, 5*, 313–320.

van IJzendoorn, M. H., & Juffer, F. (2006). The Emanuel Miller Memorial Lecture 2006: Adoption as intervention: Meta-analytic evidence for massive catch-up and plasticity in physical, socioemotional, and cognitive development. *Journal of Child Psychology and Psychiatry, 47*, 1228–1245.

van IJzendoorn, M. H., Dijkstra, J., & Bus, A. G. (1995). Attachment, intelligence, and language: A meta-analysis. *Social Development, 4*, 115–128.

van IJzendoorn, M. H., Kranenburg, M. J., Zwart-Woudstra, H. A., Van Bussenbach, A. M., & Lamberman, W. E. (1991). Parental attachment and children's socio-emotional development: Some findings on the validity of the Adult Attachment Interview in the Netherlands. *International Journal of Behavioral Development, 14*, 375–394.

van IJzendoorn, M. H., Schuengel, C., & Bakermans-Kranenburg, M. J. (1999). Disorganized attachment in early childhood: Meta-analysis of precursors, concomitants, and sequelae. *Development and Psychopathology, 11*, 225–249.

van IJzendoorn, M. H., Vereijken, C. M. T. L., Bakermans-Kranenburg, M. J., & Riksen-Walraven, J. M. (2004). Assessing attachment security with the Attachment Q-sort: Meta-analytic evidence for the validity of the observer AQS. *Child Development, 75*, 1188–1213.

Vandenberg, N. L. (2001). The use of weighted vest to increase on-task behavior in children with attention difficulties. *The American Journal of Occupational Therapy, 5*, 621–828.

Vasilev, C. A., Crowell, S. E., Beauchaine, T. P., Mead, H. K., Gatzke-Kopp, L. M. (2009). Correspondence between physiological and self-report measures of emotion dysregulation: A longitudinal investigation of youth with and without psychopathology. *Journal of Child Psychology and Psychiatry, 50*(11), 1357–1364.

Vaughn, B. E., Bost, K. K., & van IJzendoorn, M. H. (2008). Attachment and temperament: Additive and interactive influences on behavior, affect, and cognition during infancy and childhood. In J. Cassidy & P. R. Shaver (Eds.), *Handbook of attachment: Theory, research, and clinical applications* (pp. 192–2160). New York: Guilford Press.

Vaughn, S., & Fuchs, L. S. (2003). Redefining learning disabilities as inadequate response to instruction: The promise and potential problems. *Learning Disabilities Research and Practice, 18,* 137–146.

Veenstra, R., Lindenberg, J., Zijlstra, B. J. H., De Winter, A. F., Verhulst, F. C., & Ormel, J. (2007). The dyadic nature of bullying and victimization: Testing a dual-perspective theory. *Child Development, 78,* 1843–1854.

Verschueren, & Marcoen. (2005). Perceived security of attachment to mother and father: Developmental differences and relations to self-worth and peer relationships at school. In K. A. Kerns & R. A. Richardson (Eds.), *Attachment in middle childhood* (pp. 212–230). New York: Guilford Press.

Vervoort, L., Wolters, L. H., Hoogendoorn, S. M., Prins, P. J., de Haan, E., Nauta, M. H., & Boer, F. (2010). Automatic evaluations in clinically anxious and non-anxious children and adolescents. *Journal of Clinical Child and Adolescent Psychology, 39,* 481–491.

Vesga-Lopez, O., Blanco, C., Keyes, K., Olfson, M., Grant, B., & Hasin, D. (2008). Psychiatric disorders in pregnant and postpartum women in the United States. *Archives of General Psychiatry, 65,* 805–815.

Viana, A. G., Beidel, D. C., & Rabian, B. (2009). Selective mutism: A review and integration of the last 15 years. *Clinical Psychology Review, 29,* 57–67.

Vidal, C., Nicolson, R., DeVito, T., Hayashi, C., Geaga, J., Drost, D., … Thompson, P. (2006). Mapping corpus callosum deficits in autism: An index of aberrant cortical connectivity. *Biological Psychiatry, 60,* 218–225.

Viding, E. (2004). Annotation: Understanding the development of psychopathy. *Journal of Child Psychology and Psychiatry, 45,* 1329–1337.

Viding, E., Blair, R. J. R., Moffitt, T. E., & Plomin, R. (2005). Evidence for substantial genetic risk for psychopathy in 7-year-olds. *Journal of Child Psychology and Psychiatry, 46,* 592–597.

Vitaro, F., Gendreau, P. L., Tremblay, R. E., & Oligny, P. (1998). Reactive and proactive aggression differentially predict later conduct problems. *Journal of Child Psychology and Psychiatry, 39,* 377–385.

Volker, A. N., & Lopata, C. (2008) Autism: A review of biological bases, assessment and intervention. *School Psychology Quarterly, 23*(2), 258–270

Vygotsky, L. S. (1978). In M. Cole, V. John-Steiner, S. Scribner, & E. Souberman (Eds.), *Mind in society: The development of higher psychological processes.* Cambridge, MA: Harvard University Press.

Wachs, T. D. (2000). *Necessary but not sufficient: The respective roles of single and multiple influences on individual development.* Washington, DC: American Psychological Association.

Waddell, C., Offord, D. R., Shepherd, C. A., Hua, J. M., & McEwan, K. (2002). Child psychiatric epidemiology and Canadian public policy-making: The state of the science and the art of the possible. *Canadian Journal of Psychiatry, 47,* 825–832.

Wagner, M., Kutash, K., Duchnowski, A. J., Epstein, M. H., & Sumi, W. C. (2005). The children and youth we serve: A national picture of the characteristics of students with emotional disturbances receiving special education. *Journal of Emotional and Behavioral Disorders, 13,* 79–96.

Wahler, & Bellamy. (1997). Direct and indirect reinforcement processes in parent training. *Journal of Early and Intensive Behavioral Intervention, 1, 120–128.*

Wake, M., Morton-Allen,E., Poulakis, Z., Hiscock, H., Gallagher, S., & Oberklaid, F. (2006). Prevalence, stability, and outcomes of cry-fuss and sleep problems in the fi rst 2 years of life: Prospective community-based study. *Pediatrics,* 117, 836–842.

Wakschlag, L. S., Briggs-Gowen, M., Carter, A., Hill, C., Danis, B., Keenan, K., ... Leventhal, B. L. (2007). A developmental framework for distinguishing disruptive behavior from normative misbehavior in preschool children. *Journal of Child Psychology and Psychiatry and Allied Disciplines, 48,* 976–987.

Wakschlag, L. S., & Danis, B. (2004). Assessment of disruptive behavior in young children: A clinical-developmental framework. In R. Delcarmen-Wiggins & A. S. Carter (Eds.), *Handbook of infant, toddler, and preschool mental health assessment* (pp. 421–440). New York: Oxford University Press.

Wakschlag, L. S., & Danis, B. (2009). Characterizing early childhood disruptive behavior: Enhancing developmental sensitivity. In C. H. Zeanah, Jr. (Ed.), *Handbook of infant mental health* (3rd ed., pp. 392–408). New York: Guilford Press.

Wakschlag, L. S., Lahey, B. B., Loeber, R., Green, S. M., & Leventhal, B. L. (1997). Maternal smoking during pregnancy and the risk of conduct disorder in boys. *Archives of General Psychiatry, 54,* 670–676.

Wakschlag, L. S., Pickett, K., Kasza, K., & Loeber, R. (2006). Is prenatal smoking associated with a developmental pattern of conduct problems in young boys. *Journal of the American Academy of Child and Adolescent Psychiatry, 45*, 461–467.

Wakschlag, L. S., Tolan, P. H., & Leventhal, B. L. (2010). Research review: 'Ain't misbehaving': Towards a developmentally-specific nosology for preschool disruptive behavior. *Journal of Child Psychology and Psychiatry, 51*, 3–22.

Waldfogel, J., Han, W., & Brooks-Gunn, J. (2002). The effects of early maternal employment on child cognitive development. *Demography, 39*, 369–392.

Walker, D., Gugenheim, S., Downs, M. P., Northern, J. L. (1989). Early Language Milestone Scale and language screening of young children. *Pediatrics, 83*, 284–288.

Walker, H. M., Stiller, B., Severson, H. H., Feil, E. G., & Gally, A. (1998). First step to success: Intervening at the point of school entry to prevent antisocial behavior patterns. *Psychology in the Schools, 35*, 259–269.

Wallen, M, Bonney, M & Lennox, L (1996). *The handwriting speed test*. NSW, Australia: Australian Association of Occupational Therapists.

Walter, J. L., & LaFreniere, P. J. (2000). A naturalistic study of effective expression, social competence, and sociometric status in preschoolers. *Early Education and Development, 11*, 109–111.

Wang, T., Tseng, M., Wilson, B. N., & Hu, F. (2009). Functional performance of children with developmental coordination disorder at home and at school. *Developmental Medicine and Child Neurology, 51*, 817–826.

Ward, A., & Rodger, S. (2004). The application of cognitive orientation to daily occupational performance (CO-OP) with children 5–7 years with developmental coordination disorder. *British Journal of Occupational Therapy, 67(6)*, 256–264.

Warner, L. A., & Pottick, K. J. (2006). Functional impairment among preschoolers using mental health services. *Children and Youth Services Review, 28*, 473–486.

Warren, S. L., Huston, L., Egeland, B., & Sroufe, L. A. (1997). Child and adolescent anxiety disorders and early attachment. *Journal of the American Academy of Child and Adolescent Psychiatry, 36*, 637–644.

Waters, E., & Cummings, E. M. (2000). A secure-base from which to explore close relationships. *Child Development, 71*, 164–172.

Waters, E., Kondo-Ikemura, K., Posada, O., & Richters, J. E. (1991). Learning to love: Mechanisms and milestones. In M. Gunnar & L. A. Sroufe (Eds.), *Minnesota symposium on child psychology: Vol. 23, Self processes in early development* (pp. 217–255). Hillsdale, NJ: Erlbaum.

Watkins, K. E., Vargha-Khadem, F., Ashburner, J., Passingham, R. E., Connelly, A., Friston, K. J., … Gadian, D. G. (2002). MRI analysis of an inherited speech and language disorder: Structural brain abnormalities. *Brain, 125*, 465–478.

Watling, R. L., Dietz, J., & White, O. (2001). Comparison of sensory profile scores of young children with and without spectrum disorders. *American Journal of Occupational Therapy, 55*, 416–423.

Watson, A. C., Painter, K. M., & Bornstein, M. H. (2001). Longitudinal relationship between 2-year olds' language and 4-year olds' theory of mind. *Journal of Cognition and Development, 2*, 449–457.

Weaver, I. C. G., D'Alessio, A. C., Brown, S. E., Hellstrom, I. C., Dymov, S., Sharma, S., … Meaney, M. J. (2007). The transcription factor nerve growth factor-inducible protein A mediates epigenetic programming: Altering epigenetic marks by immediate-early genes. *The Journal of Neuroscience, 27*, 1756–1768.

Webb, N. B. (1991). Play therapy crisis intervention with children. In N. B. Webb (Ed.), *Play therapy with children in crisis* (pp. 26–42). New York: Guilford Press.

Weber, C., Hahne, A., Friedrich, M., & Friederici, A. D. (2004). Discrimination of word stress in infant perception: Electrophysiological evidence. *Cognitive Brain Research, 18*, 149–161.

Webster-Stratton, C. (1987). *The parents and children series*. Eugene, OR: Castalia.

Webster-Stratton, C. (1990). Long-term follow-up of families with young conduct problem children: From preschool to grade school. *Journal of Clinical Child Psychology, 19*, 144–149.

Webster-Stratton, C., & Hammond, M. (1997). Treating children with early onset conduct problems: A comparison of child and parent interventions. *Journal of Consulting and Clinical Psychology, 65*, 93–109.

Webster-Stratton, C., & Herbert, M. (1994) *Troubled families – problem children*. New York: Wiley.

Webster-Stratton, C., Kolpacoff, M., & Hollinsworth, T. (1988). Self-administered videotape therapy for families with conduct problem children: Comparison with two cost-effective treatments and a control group. *Journal of Consulting and Clinical Psychology, 56*, 558–566.

Webster-Stratton, C., Mihelic, C., Fagan, A., Arnold, D., Taylor, T., & Tingley, C. (2001). *Blueprints for violence prevention, Book 11: The incredible years: parent, teacher, and child training series.* Golder, CO: Venture Publishing.

Webster-Stratton, C., & Reid, M. (2003). The incredible years, parents, teachers, and children training series: A multifaceted treatment approach for young children with conduct problems. In A. E. Kazdin & R. Weisz (Eds.), *Evidence-based psychotherapy for children and adolescents* (pp. 224–240). New York: Guilford Press.

Webster-Stratton, C., & Taylor. (2001). Nipping early risk factors in the bud: Preventing substance abuse, delinquency, and violence in adolescence through intervention targeted at young children (0–8 years). *Prevention Science, 2*, 165–192.

Wechsler, D. (2002). *Wechsler preschool and primary scale of intelligence* (3rd ed.) (WPPSI-III), Minneapolis, MN: Pearson Assessment.

Wechsler, D. (2004). *Wechsler Intelligence Scale for Children (4th ed.) (WISC-IV). Administration and scoring manual.* San Antonio, TX: Pearson.

Weinberg, L. A., Zetlin, A., & Shea, N. M. (2009). Removing barriers to educating children in foster care through interagency collaboration: A seven county multiple-case study. *Child Welfare, 88*, 77–111.

Weinfeld, N. S., Sroufe, A., Egeland, B., & Carlson, E. (2008). Individual differences in infant-caregiver attachment: Conceptual and empirical aspects of security. In J. Cassidy & P. R. Shaver (Eds.), *Handbook of attachment research, theory, and clinical research* (2nd ed., pp. 78–101). New York: Guilford.

Weinfeld, N. S., Whaley, G. J. L., & Egeland, B. (2004). Continuity, discontinuity, and coherence in attachment from infancy to late adolescence. *Attachment and Human Development, 6*, 73–97.

Weiss, G., & Hechtman, L. T. (1993). *Hyperactive children grown up* (2nd ed.). New York: Guilford Press.

Weiss, M., Hechtman, L., & Weiss, G. (2000). ADHD in parents: Clinical perspectives. *Journal of the American Academy of Child and Adolescent Psychiatry, 39*, 1059–1061.

Weissbourd, B. (1993). Family resource and support programs: Changes and challenges in human services. In D. G. Unger & D. R. Powell (Eds.), *Families as nurturing systems: Supports across the life span* (pp. 69–85). NY: The Haworth Press.

Weisz, J. R., Sandler, I. N., Durlak, J. A., & Anton, B. S. (2005). Promoting and protecting youth mental health through evidence-based prevention and treatment. *American Psychologist, 60*, 628–648.

Weitzman, M., Gortmaker, S., & Sobol, A. (1992). Maternal smoking and behavior problems of children. *Pediatrics, 90*, 342–349.

Wellman, H. M., Cross, D., & Watson, J. (2001). A meta-analysis of theory of mind development: The truth about false belief. *Child Development, 72*, 655–684.

Wells, K. C., Lochman, J. E., & Lenhart, L. A. (2008). *Coping Power parent group program: Facilitator guide.* Oxford: Oxford University Press.

Werner, H., & Strauss, A. A. (1941). Pathology of figure-ground relation in the child. *Journal of Abnormal and Social Psychology, 142*, 547–552.

Wesner, D. O., Dowling, J., & Johnson, F. K. (1982). What is maternal-infant intervention? The role of infant psychotherapy. *Psychiatry: Journal for the Study of Interpersonal Processes, 45*, 307–315.

Westby, C. E., & Cutler, S. K. (1994). Language and ADHD: Understanding the basis and treatment of self-regulatory deficits. *Topics in Language Disorders 14*, 58–76.

Westhues, Nelson, & McLeod. (2003). A meta-analysis of longitudinal research on preschool prevention programs for children. *Prevention and Treatment, 6*, 1–35.

Wetherby, A., Warren, S., & Reichle, J. (Eds.). (1988). *Transitions in prelinguistic communication.* Baltimore, MD: Paul Brookes Publishers.

Wetherby, A. M., Goldstein, H., Cleary, J., Allen, L., & Kublin, K. (2003). Early identification of children with communication disorders: Concurrent and predictive validity of the CSBS developmental profile. *Infants and Young Children, 16*, 161–174.

Wetherby, A. M., & Prizant, B. (1993). *Communication and symbolic behavior scales.* Baltimore, MD: Paul H. Brookes.

Wetherby, A. M., & Prizant, B. M. (2001). *Communication and symbolic behavior scales* (CSBS). Baltimore, MD: Paul H. Brookes Publishers.

Wetherby, A. M., Woods, J., Allen, L., Cleary, J., Dickinson, H., & Lord, C. (2004). Early indicators of autism spectrum disorders in the second year of life. *Journal of Autism and Developmental Disorders, 35*, 473–493.

Whitestead, S. P., & Jacobsen, A. B. (2010). An uncontrolled examination of a 5-day intensive *treatment for pediatric OCD. Behavior Therapy, 41*, 414–422.

Whittle, S., Allen, N., Lubman, D., & Yücel, M. (2006). The neurobiological basis of temperament: Towards a better understanding of psychopathology. *Neuroscience and Biobehavioural Reviews, 30*, 511–525.

Widam, C. S. (2000). Understanding the consequences of childhood victimization. In R. M. Reese (Ed.), *Treatment of child abuse* (pp. 339–361). Baltimore, MD: John Hopkins University Press.

Widiger, T. A., & Samuel, D. B. (2005). Diagnostic categories or dimensions: A question for DSM-V. *Journal of Abnormal Psychology, 114*, 494–504.

Widom, C. (1998). Motivation and mechanisms in the "cycle of violence." In D. J. Hansen (Ed.), *Nebraska symposium on motivation: Vol. 46, Motivation and maltreatment* (pp. 1–37). Lincoln, NE: University of Nebraska Press.

Wiener, A. S., Long, T., DeGangi, G., & Battaile, B. (1996). Sensory processing of infants born prematurely or with regulatory disorders. *Physical & Occupational Therapy in Pediatrics, 16*, 1–17.

Wierzbicki, M., & Pekarik, G. (1993). A meta-analysis of psychotherapy dropout. *Professional Psychology: Research and Practice, 24*, 190–195.

Wiig, E. H., & Secord, W. (1989). *Test of Language Competence—Expanded Edition*. Harcourt Assessment.

Wilbarger, J., Gunnar, M., Schneider, M., & Pollack, N. (2010). Sensory processing in internationally adopted, post-institutionalized children. *Journal of Child Psychology and Psychiatry, 51*, 1105–1114.

Wilbarger, P. (1994). Planning an adequate "sensory diet"—Application of sensory processing theory during the first year of life. *Zero to Three, 5*, 7–12.

Wilbarger, P. (1995). Sensory integration. Special interest section newsletter. *American Occupational Therapy Association, 18*, 1–4.

Wilbarger, P., & Wilbarger, J. (2007). *Sensory defensiveness: A comprehensive treatment approach*. Sensory Tools: Workshop. Australia: Avanti Educational Program.

Wilens, T., & Spencer, T. (1998). Pharmacology of amphetamines. In T. R. Ammerman, & R. Ott (Eds.), *Handbook of substance abuse: Neurobehavioral pharmacology* (pp. 501–513). New York: Plenum Press.

Wilens, T., & Spencer, T. (2000). The stimulants revisited. In C. Stubbe (Eds.), *Child and adolescent clinics of North America* (pp. 573–603). Philadephia, PA: WB Saunders.

Willcutt, E. G., Doyle, A. E., Nigg, J. T., Faraone, S. V., & Pennington, B. F. (2005). A meta-analytic review of executive function theory of ADHD. *Biological Psychiatry, 57*, 1336–1346.

Willcutt, E. G., Pennington, B. F., & DeFries, J. (2000). A twin study of the etiology of co-morbidity between reading disability and attention deficit–hyperactivity disorder. *American Journal of Medical Genetics, 96*, 293–230.

Williams, E., Thomas, K., & Sidebotham, H. (2008). Prevalence and characteristics of autism spectrum disorders in the ALSPAC cohort. *Developmental Medicine Child Neurology, 50*, 672–677.

Williams, J. H., Whiten, A., Suddendorf, T., & Perrott, D. I. (2001). Imitation, mirror neurons, and autism. *Neuroscience and Biobehavioral Review, 25*, 287–295.

Williams, M. S., & Shellenberger, S. (1996). *How does your engine run? A leader's guide to the Alert Program for self regulation*. Albuquerque, NM: Therapy Works Inc.

Williams, W. M., & Sternberg, R. J. (2002). How parents can maximise children's cognitive abilities. In M. H. Bornstein (Ed.), *Handbook of parenting, Vol. 5: Practical issues of parenting* (pp. 169–194). Mahwah, NJ: Lawrence Erlbaum Associates.

Williams, Z. R., Degnan, K. A., Perez-Edgar, K. E., Henderson, H. A., Rubin, K. H., Pine, D. S., … Fox, N. A. (2009). Impact of behavioral inhibition and parenting style on internalizing and externalizing problems from early childhood through adolescence. *Journal of Abnormal Child Psychology, 30*, 1063–1075.

Wilson, H. K., Pianta, R. C., & Stuhlman, M. (2007). Typical classroom experiences in first grade: The role of classroom climate and functional risk in the development of social competencies. *The Elementary School Journal, 108*, 81–96.

Wilson, H. W., Stover, C. S., & Berkowitz, S. J. (2009). Research review: The relationship between childhood violence exposure and juvenile antisocial behavior: A meta-analytic review. *The Journal of Child Psychology and Psychiatry, 50,* 769–779.

Wimmer, H., & Perner, J. (1983). Beliefs about beliefs: Representation and constraining function of wrong beliefs in young children's understanding of deception. *Cognition, 13,* 103–128.

Witelson, S. F., & Pallie, W. (1973). Left hemisphere specialization for language in the newborn: Neuroanatomical evidence in asymmetry. *Brain, 96,* 641–646.

Wolfe, C. D., & Bell, M. A. (2004). Working memory and inhibitory control in early childhood: Contributions from physiology, temperament, and language. *Developmental Psychobiology, 44,* 68–83.

Wolfe, D. L., & Heilmann, J. (2010). Simplified and expanded input in a focused stimulation program for a child with expressive language delay (ELD). *Child Language Teaching and Therapy, 26,* 335–346.

Wood, S. (2000). Treating a sexually abused child in the context of sibling theraplay. In E. Munns (Ed.), *Theraplay: Innovations in attachment-enhancing play therapy* (pp. 139–150). Northvale, NJ: Jason Aronson Inc.

World Health Organization. (1992). *The ICD-10 classification of mental and behavioural disorders: Clinical descriptions and diagnostic guidelines.* Geneva, Switzerland: Author.

World Health Organization. (1993). *ICD-10. International Statistical Classification of Diseases and Related Health Problems.* Geneva, Switzerland: Author.

World Health Organization. (2001). *Prevention of child abuse and neglect: Making the links between human rights and public health.* Geneva, Switzerland: World Health Organization.

World Health Organization. (2001). *The world health report: Mental health, new understanding, new hope.* Geneva: World Health Organization.

World Health Organization. (2002). *Reducing risks, promoting healthy life.* Geneva: World Health Organization.

World Health Organization. (2002). *World report on violence and health.* Geneva, Switzerland: World Health Organization.

World Health Organization. (2004). *International statistical classification of mental and behavioural disorders,* 10th ed. (ICD-10). Washington, DC: American Psychiatric Press, Inc.

World Health Organization. (2006). *World report on violence and health.* Geneva, Switzerland: World Health Organization.

Xu, C., Reid, R., & Steckelberg, A. (2002). Technology applications for children with ADHD: Assessing the empirical support. *Education and Treatment of Children, 25,* 224–248.

Yack, E., Aquilla, P., Sutton, S. (2006). *Building bridges: Through sensory integration.* Las Vegas, NV: Sensory Resources.

Yap, M. B. H., Allen, N. B., & Ladouceur, C. D. (2008). Maternal socialization of positive affect: The impact of invalidation on adolescent emotion regulation and depressive symptomatology. *Child Development, 79*(5), 1415–1431.

Yap, M. B. H., Allen, N. B., O'Shea, M., Di Parsia, P., Simmons, J. G., & Sheeber, L. (2011). Early adolescents' temperament, emotion regulation during mother-child interactions, and depressive symptomatology. *Development and Psychopathology, 23,* 267–282.

Yates, T. M., Egeland, B., & Sroufe, A. (2003). Rethinking resilience: A developmental process perspective. In S. S. Luthar (Ed.), *Resilience and vulnerability: Adaptation in the context of childhood adversities* (pp. 243–266). New York: Guilford Press.

Yates, T. M., Obradovic, J., & Egeland, B. (2010). Transactional relations across contextual strain, parenting quality, and early childhood regulation and adaptation in a high-risk sample. *Development and Psychopathology, 22,* 539–555.

Ybarra, M. L., Mitchell, K. J., Wolak, J., & Finkelhor, D. (2006). Examining characteristics and associated distress related to internet harassment: Findings from the second Youth Internet Safety Survey. *Pediatrics, 118,* 1169–1177.

Yochman, A., Parush, S., & Ornoy, A. (2004). Responses of preschool children with and without ADHD to sensory events in everyday life. *American Journal of Occupational Therapy, 58,* 294–302.

Yoder, P. J., & Warren, S. (1998). Maternal responsivity predicts the prelinguistic communication intervention that facilitates generalized intentional communication. *Journal of Speech, Language, and Hearing Research, 41,* 1207–1219.

Yule, W., Bolton, D., & Udwin, O. (2000). The long-term psychological effects of a disaster experienced in adolescence: The incidence and effects of PTSD. *Journal of Child Psychology and Psychiatry, 41,* 503–511.

Yule, W., Bolton, D., Udwin, O., Boyle, S., O'Ryan, D., & Nurish, J. (2000). The long-term psychological effects of a disaster experienced in adolescence: I: The incidence and course of PTSD. *Journal of Child Psychology & Psychiatry & Allied Disciplines, 41,* 503–511.

Yunger, J. L., Corby, B. C., & Perry, D. G. (2005). Dimensions of attachment in middle childhood. In K. A. Kerns & R. A. Richardson (Eds.), *Attachment in middle childhood* (pp. 137–160). New York: Guilford Press.

Zadeh,Y., Im-Bolter, N., & Cohen, N. J. (2007). Social cognition and externalizing behavior: An investigation of the mediating role of language. *Journal of Abnormal Paychology, 35,* 141–152.

Zahn-Waxler, C., Duggal, S., & Gruber, R. (2002). Parental psychopathology. In M. H. Bornstein (Ed.), *Handbook of parenting: Vol. 4. Social conditions and applied parenting* (2nd ed., pp. 295–327). Mahwah, NJ: Lawrence Erlbaum Associates.

Zametkin, A. J., & Rapoport, J. L. (1987). Neurobiology of attention deficit disorder with hyperactivity: Where have we come in 50 years? *Journal of the American Academy of Child and Adolescent Psychiatry, 26,* 676–686.

Zeanah, C.H., Benoit, D., & Barton, M. (1993). *Working model of the child interview.* Unpublished document, Brown University, RI.

Zeanah, C. H., Benoit, D., & Barton, M. (1995). *Working model of the child interview: Scoring and coding manual.* Unpublished manuscript, Brown University, Providence, R. I.

Zeanah, C. H., Benoit, D., Barton, M., Regan, C., Hirshberg, L. M., & Lipsitt, L. P. (1993). Representations of attachment in mothers and their one-year-old infants. *Journal of the American Academy of Child and Adolescent Psychiatry, 32,* 278–286.

Zeanah, C. H., Smyke, A. T., Koga, S., Carlson, E., & BEIP Core Group. (2005). Attachment in institutionalized and community children in Romania. *Child Development, 76,* 1015–1028.

Zeanah, C. H. Jr., & Boris, N. W. (2000). Disturbances and disorders of attachment in early childhood. In C. H. Zeanah, Jr. (Ed.), *Handbook of infant mental health* (2nd ed., pp. 353–368). New York: Guilford Press.

Zeanah, C. H., Jr., & Smyke, A. T. (2009). Attachment disorders. In C. H. Zeanah, Jr. (Ed.), *Handbook of infant mental health* (3rd ed., pp. 421–434). New York: Guilford Press.

Zeanah , C. H., Jr., Smyke, A., & Settles, L. (2006). Orphanages as a developmental context for early childhood. In K. McCartney & D. Phillips (Eds.), *The Blackwell handbook of early childhood development* (pp. 424–454). Malden, Massachusetts: Blackwell Publishing.

Zelazo, P. D., Craik, F. L., & Booth, I. (2004). Executive function across the life span. *Acta Psychologica, 115,* 167–183.

Zeman, J., Shipman, K., & Penza-Clyve, S. (2001). Development and initial validation of the Children's Emotion Management Scale (EMS). *Journal of Nonverbal Behavior, 25,* 540–547.

Zeman, J., Shipman, K., & Suveg, C. (2002). Anger and sadness regulation: Predictions to internalizing and externalizing symptoms in children. *Journal of Clinical Child and Adolescent Psychology, 31,* 393–398.

Zentalli, S. S. (1988). Production deficiencies in elicited language but not in the spontaneous verbalizations of hyperactive children. *Journal of Abnormal Child Psychology, 16,* 657–673.

Zero to Three. (2005). *Diagnostic classification of mental health and developmental disorders of infancy and early childhood* (revised edition). Washington, DC: Zero To Three Press.

Zhou, Q., Eisenberg, N., Losoya, S. H., Fabes, R. A., Reiser, M., Guthrie, I. K., … Shepard, S. A. (2002). The relations of parental warmth and positive expressiveness in children's empathy-related responding and social functioning: A longitudinal study. *Child Development, 73,* 893–915.

Zhou, Q., Hofer, C., Eisenberg, N., Reiser, M., Spinrad, T. L., & Fabers, R. A. (2007). The developmental trajectories of attention focusing, attentional and behavioral persistence, and externalizing problems during school-age years. *Developmental Psychology, 43,* 369–385.

Ziegler, D. (2005). *Achieving success with impossible children: How to win the battles of wills.* Jasper, OR: Acacia Publishing.

Zigler, E. F., Singer, D. G., & Bishop-Josef, S. J. (2004). *Children's play: The roots of reading.* Washington, DC: ZERO TO THREE PRESS.

Zimmerman, I. L., Steiner, V., & Pond, R. (2005). *Preschool language scale* (4th ed.), San Antonio, TX: Psychological Corporation.

Zimmerman, I.L., Violette, G., Steiner, B.S., & Pond, R.E. (2007). *Preschool Language Scale,* 4th edition, *(PLS-4) Measure of Progress.* PsychCorp, San Antonio, TX. Age 3.0–6.11

Zimmermann, P., Mohr, C., & Spangler, G. (2009). Genetic and attachment influences on adolescents' regulation of autonomy and aggressiveness. *Journal of Child Psychology and Psychiatry, 50*(11), 1339–1347.

Zins, J. E., Bloodworth, M. R., Weissberg, R. P., & Walberg, H. J. (2004). The scientific base linking social and emotional learning to school success. In J. E. Zins (Ed.), *Building academic success on social and emotional learning: What does research say?* (pp. 3–22). New York: Teacheıs College Press, Colombia University.

Zionts, L. T. (2005). Examining relationships between students and teachers: A potential extension of attachment theory? In K. A. Kerns & R.A Richardson (Eds.), *Attachment in middle childhood* (pp. 231–254). New York: Guilford Press.

Zisser, A., & Eyberg, S. M. (2010). Treating oppositional behavior in children using parent-child interaction therapy, In A. E. Kazdin & J. R. Weisz (Eds.), *Evidence-based psychotherapies for children and adolescents* (2nd ed.). New York: Guilford.

Zoccolillo, M. (1992). Co-occurrence of conduct disorder and its adult outcomes with depressive and anxiety disorders: A review. *Journal of the American Academy of Child and Adolescent Psychiatry, 31,* 547–556.

Zubrick, S. R., Taylor, C. L., Rice. M. L., & Slegers, D. (2007). Late language emergence at 24 months: An epidemiological study of prevalence and covariates. *Journal of Speech, Language and Hearing Research, 50,* 1562–1592.

Zwicker, J. G., Missiuna, C. & Boyd, L. A. (2009). Neural correlates of developmental coordination disorder: A review of hypotheses. *Journal of Child Neurology, 24,* 1273–1281.

Index